Contents

A Longman Cultural Edition

Mary Wollstonecraft's

A VINDICATION OF THE RIGHTS OF WOMAN
AND
THE WRONGS OF WOMAN, OR MARIA

Edited by

Anne Mellor and Noelle Chao

University of California, Los Angeles

PEARSON
Longman

New York   Boston   San Francisco
London   Toronto   Sydney   Tokyo   Singapore   Madrid
Mexico City   Munich   Paris   Cape Town   Hong Kong   Montreal

Editor-in-Chief: Joseph P. Terry
Development Editor: Christine Halsey
Executive Marketing Manager: Ann Stypuloski
Production Coordinator: Virginia Riker
Project Coordination, Text Design, and Electronic Page Makeup: Grapevine
    Publishing Services, Inc.
Cover Designer/Manager: John Callahan
Manufacturing Buyer: Lucy Hebard
Printer and Binder: Courier Corporation / Westford
Cover Printer: Phoenix Color Corporation

Cover Image: Bildarchiv Preussischer Kulturbesitz / Art Resource, NY

Library of Congress Cataloging-in-Publication Data

Wollstonecraft, Mary, 1759–1797.
    [Vindication of the rights of woman]
    Mary Wollstonecraft's A vindication of the rights of woman; and, The wrongs of
woman, or, Maria / edited by Anne Mellor; Noelle Chao.
        p. cm. — (A Longman cultural edition)
    Includes bibliographical references.
    ISBN 0-321-18273-1
        1. Women—Fiction. 2. Feminist fiction. 3. Women's rights—Great Britain. 4.
Women—Education—Great Britain. I. Mellor, Anne Kostelanetz. II. Chao, Noelle.
III. Wollstonecraft, Mary, 1759–1797. Wrongs of woman. IV. Title. V. Title:
Wrongs of woman, or, Maria. VI. Series.

PR5841.W8W76 2006
823'.6—dc22

                                                                    2006004032
Copyright © 2007 by Pearson Education, Inc.

Please visit our Web site at www.ablongman.com

ISBN: 0-321-18273-1

1 2 3 4 5 6 7 8 9 10—CRW—09 08 07 06

List of Illustrations

About Longman Cultural Editions

Reading always seems to vibrate with the transformation of the day—now, yesterday, and centuries ago, when the presses first put printed language into wide circulation. Correspondingly, literary culture has always been a matter of change: of new practices confronting established traditions; of texts transforming under the pressure of new techniques of reading and new perspectives of understanding; of canons shifting and expanding; of informing traditions getting reviewed and renewed, recast and reformed by emerging cultural interests and concerns; of culture, too, as a variable "text"—a reading. Inspired by the innovative *Longman Anthology of British Literature,* Longman Cultural Editions respond creatively to the changes, past and recent, by presenting key texts in contexts that illuminate the lively intersections of literature, tradition, and culture. A principal work is made more interesting by materials that place it in relation to its past, present, and future, enabling us to see how it may be reworking traditional debates and practices, how it appears amid the conversations and controversies of its own historical moment, how it gains new significances in subsequent eras of reading and reaction. Readers new to the work will discover attractive paths for exploration, while those more experienced will encounter fresh perspectives and provocative juxtapositions.

Longman Cultural Editions serve not only several kinds of readers but also (appropriately) their several contexts, from various courses of study to independent adventure. Handsomely produced and affordably priced, our volumes offer appealing companions to *The Longman Anthology of British Literature,* in some cases enriching and expanding units originally developed for the *Anthology*, and in other cases presenting this wealth for the first time. The logic and composition of the contexts vary across the series. The constants are the complete text of an important literary work, reliably edited, headed by an inviting introduction, and supplemented by helpful annotation; a table of dates to track its composition, publication, and public reception in relation to biographical, cultural, and historical events; and a guide for further inquiry and study. With these common measures and uncommon assets, Longman Cultural Editions encourage your literary pleasures with resources for lively reflection and adventurous inquiry.

Susan J. Wolfson
General Editor
Professor of English
Princeton University

About This Edition

This is the first edition to combine Mary Wollstonecraft's *Vindication of the Rights of Woman* with her posthumous novel *The Wrongs of Woman, or Maria.* Not only is *The Wrongs of Woman* an obvious sequel to Wollstonecraft's famous feminist tract, it is also an attempt on Wollstonecraft's part to exploit the resources of fiction to promote her political agenda. Despite Wollstonecraft's denunciation of novel-reading in *Vindication of the Rights of Woman* as leading women into dangerous fantasies and diverting them from useful social activities, she had by 1797 come to see that the novel could function as a powerful rhetorical tool to advance social reform. In this respect she was heavily influenced by Clara Reeve's argument in *The Progress of Romance* (1785): Realistic novels that combine accurate descriptions of probable events with sound moral judgments can provide an excellent education for women.

We use the second, corrected edition of *A Vindication of the Rights of Woman,* the one most widely circulated in Wollstonecraft's lifetime and now the standard for scholarship and teaching. The only text of her unfinished *Wrongs of Woman, or Maria* appeared as the first two volumes of the four-volume *Posthumous Works of the Author of A Vindication of the Rights of Woman* (1798), edited by William Godwin. Our notes elucidate terms and concerns current during Wollstonecraft's time. In cases where these items or terms recur, we supplied information for the first instance only.

Our Contexts selections place Wollstonecraft's works within their historical and political milieus. We first document the actual condition of women in her day, drawing on the official report on the use of madhouses to confine unruly women, the legal judgment that constructed married women as "villains" or feudal serfs (The Mansfield Judgment), a contemporary description of prostitution in London by

Johann Wilhelm von Archenholz, and the early feminist historian Catharine Macaulay's searing denunciation of the inferior education of women in her day. Our sample from the published responses to Wollstonecraft's *A Vindication of the Rights of Woman*, which was widely read, reviewed, and criticized, range from the enthusiastically supportive (Mary Hays, Mary Anne Radcliffe, and William Thompson and Anna Wheeler) through a moderated and more cautious feminism (Priscilla Wakefield, Hannah More, and Anna Barbauld) to the aggressively hostile (Richard Polwhele).

For the Contexts material for *The Wrongs of Woman, or Maria*, we turn specifically to literary influences. Hannah More's poem *Sensibility: A Poetical Epistle to the Hon. Mrs. Boscawen* provides a contemporary account of the differences between a negative sensibility and a positive sensibility, a distinction Wollstonecraft endorses in her novel. We illustrate Wollstonecraft's use of Jean-Jacques Rousseau's figure of St. Preux, from his novel *Julie, ou la Nouvelle Héloïse* (1761), for the character of Darnford. Wollstonecraft's invocations of gothic elements depends heavily on the acknowledged mistress of gothic romance, Ann Radcliffe, whose *Sicilian Romance* we excerpt in the Contexts section. Both William Godwin (Wollstonecraft's husband) and Frances Burney provide telling parallels to Maria's fate, the first by offering in *Caleb Williams* a wrongly persecuted protagonist, the second by portraying in her novel *Camilla* a young woman who escapes an unfortunate marriage and decides to write her memoirs as a didactic manual for young women.

For both *A Vindication of the Rights of Woman* and *The Wrongs of Woman, or Maria* we provide a representative sampling of the contemporary reviews published in the leading journals of the day.

For help with our headnotes and footnotes, we are deeply indebted to Marilyn Butler, Noah Comet, Gary Kelly, Peter Manning, Richard Matlak, Carol Poston, Janet Todd, and Susan Wolfson. For material included in our Contexts section for *A Vindication of the Rights of Woman*, we are indebted to *British Literature 1780–1830*, eds. Anne K. Mellor and Richard Matlak (Harcourt Brace, 1996), and to *The Longman Anthology of British Literature*, 2d ed., volume 2A, eds. Peter Manning and Susan Wolfson, general ed. David Damrosch (Longman, 2003).

Anne Mellor
Noelle Chao
University of California, Los Angeles

Table of Dates

[MW: Mary Wollstonecraft]

1759   MW born on April 27 in Spitalfields, London, the second of seven children: Edward (Ned), b. 1757; Henry, b. 1761; Elizabeth (Eliza), b. 1763; Everina, b. 1765; James, b. 1768; and Charles, b. 1770.

George III begins a 60-year reign.

1761   Jean-Jacques Rousseau, *Julie, ou la Nouvelle Héloïse.*

1763–68   Determined to set up as a gentleman farmer, MW's father moves his family successively from London to Epping, Barking (both outside London), and Beverley (in Yorkshire). Failing at these (and later) efforts, he grows violent at home. MW is intensely unhappy and driven to seek affection and nurture elsewhere. While in Beverley, MW develops a close friendship with Jane Arden.

Parliamentary *Report on Private Madhouses* (1763); Lawrence Sterne, *A Sentimental Journey* (1768).

1772   The Mansfield Judgment, declaring that English law offers no justification for slavery in England itself.

1774   Family moves to Hoxton, on the outskirts of London. MW is befriended by Rev. and Mrs. Clare, who assist her education and become a second family.

Louis XVI succeeds to the throne at France.

1775   Through the Clares, MW first meets and develops an intense friendship with Fanny Blood, later the model for Ann in *Mary* and the namesake of MW's first daughter.

1776   Family moves to Laugharne, Wales.

U.S. Declaration of Independence.

Richard Price, *On Civil Liberty*; Adam Smith, *Wealth of Nations*.

1777   Family returns to Walworth, a suburb of London.

1778   As her father's finances deteriorate, MW takes a job as companion to Mrs. Dawson of Bath; visits Bath, Windsor, and Southampton.

1780   Gordon Riots in London.

1781   MW goes to London to nurse her mother.

1782   MW's mother dies; father remarries and moves to Wales. Angry with the familial indifference of Ned, now a London attorney, MW takes responsibility for her siblings, whom she helps support after she moves in with Fanny Blood's family in Walham Green, west of London. October: Eliza marries Meredith Bishop.

U.S. Revolution concludes.

Frances Burney, *Cecilia*; Rousseau, *Confessions*; Hannah More, *Sensibility: A Poetical Epistle*. Henri Fuseli's "The Nightmare" exhibited at the Royal Academy.

1783   Eliza gives birth to a daughter in August and suffers acute postpartum depression. MW attributes this to Eliza's husband's cruelty.

William Pitt's first ministry.

Catharine Macaulay, vol. 8 of her magisterial, anti-monarchical *History of England*.

1784   MW convinces Eliza to run away in secret from her husband and baby, who dies later in the year. After a failed attempt to start a school in Islington, MW opens one at Newington Green, a dissenting community north of London, with Fanny Blood and Eliza. MW begins a friendship with preacher Richard Price and becomes a member of his circle. MW is introduced to Dr. Samuel Johnson. Everina joins her sisters at Newington Green.

1785   Fanny Blood sails for Lisbon to marry Hugh Skeys. MW journeys to Lisbon to assist Fanny during her pregnancy; she dies in childbirth in late November. December: MW returns to London.

1786   MW closes her school because of financial problems. To raise money and improve her spirits, MW begins *Thoughts on the Education of Daughters*, helps her sisters find positions as teachers, and becomes governess for the Viscount Kingsborough family of Mitchelstown (Country Cork) in Ireland. On her way, MW visits Eton; passes the winter with the Kingsboroughs in Dublin.

1787   *Thoughts on the Education of Daughters* is published by Joseph Johnson, earning MW 10 guineas, which she gives to the Blood family. Travels with the Kingsboroughs to Bristol, and writes *Mary* and "Cave of Fancy." In August Lady Kingsborough dismisses MW, disapproving of her daughter's attachment. Returning to London to work as a reader and translator for J. Johnson, MW joins his circle of progressive writers and artists, eventually meeting Thomas Holcroft, Henri Fuseli, Joel Barlow, Horne Tooke, and Anna Letitia Barbauld.

       U.S. Constitution ratified.

1788   *Mary, A Fiction, Original Stories from Real Life*, and *Of the Importance of Religious Opinions* (trans. from Necker) published by Joseph Johnson. MW begins reviewing for *Analytical Review*, a progressive monthly started by J. Johnson and Thomas Christie.

       First mental breakdown of George III.

1789   MW's *Female Reader* published, compiled by "Mr. Cresswick."

       July 14: the Bastille falls, and the French Revolution begins. August: *Declaration of the Rights of Man*. Price's sermon "Discourse on the Love of Our Country" is delivered and focuses the alarmed attention of Edmund Burke.

       Johann Wilhelm von Archenholz, *A Picture of England*.

1790   Published: MW's translation of *Young Grandison*, Maria van de Werken de Cambon's adaptation of Richardson's novel, and her translation of Christian Salzmann's *Elements of Morality*, illustrated by William Blake. November 29: MW's *A Vindication of the Rights of Men* published anonymously, a response to Burke's *Reflections on the Revolution in France*

(November 1). December 18: MW's second edition is published, bearing her name and establishing her reputation.

Helen Maria Williams, *Letters Written in France*; Catharine Macaulay, *Letters on Education*; Ann Radcliffe, *A Sicilian Romance*.

1791   Second edition of *Original Stories*, illustrated by Blake. MW begins writing *A Vindication of the Rights of Woman*, meets William Godwin in November.

William Wilberforce's motion to abolish the slave trade fails in Parliament.

1792   MW's portrait is painted by an unknown artist. January: *A Vindication of the Rights of Woman* published to several favorable reviews. MW meets Talleyrand, whose proposals regarding women's education in France had disappointed her. A second somewhat revised edition of *Rights of Woman* is published later that year. MW plans to write a "Second Part" but never does so. MW becomes passionately attached to the painter Henri Fuseli. After her proposal to join his household is refused, MW departs for France in December. In Paris, she meets leading Girondins and English friends of the Revolution, including Helen Maria Williams and Tom Paine.

Louis XVI and his family are imprisoned; the monarchy is abolished; wide-scale massacres of suspected royalists in September.

Paine, *Rights of Man*, Part II.

1793   January 21: Louis XVI is guillotined. February 1: France declares war on England, and English nationals come under suspicion. MW begins an affair with radical Gilbert Imlay. Girondists fall from power in late May. The Reign of Terror begins, dampening MW's enthusiasm for the Revolution. June: MW moves to Neuilly to escape increasing violence. MW is pregnant and returns to Paris in September. Imlay registers MW at the American Embassy as his "wife" so she can claim the protection of U.S. citizenship (the U.S. was an ally of France). October 16: Marie Antoinette is guillotined. Published: William Godwin, *Political Justice*;

Charlotte Smith, *The Emigrants*; Hannah More, *Village Politics*; Mary Hays, *Letters and Essays*. Anna Barbauld composes "The Rights of Woman."

1794 January: MW moves to Le Havre and starts *An Historical and Moral View of the Origin and Progress of the French Revolution*. Fanny Imlay born in May. July: Robespierre falls and the Terror ends. Imlay returns to England, abandoning MW and Fanny. December: *An Historical and Moral View of the French Revolution* published in London. Habeas corpus suspended; Godwin successfully defends leaders of the London Corresponding Society in a state trial. Published: Godwin, *Caleb Williams*; Ann Radcliffe, *The Mysteries of Udolpho*.

1795 April: MW returns to London to join Imlay and learns of his infidelity; she attempts suicide but is prevented by Imlay. June: MW travels to Scandinavia with her infant daughter and their maid, in connection with Imlay's business concerns. September: MW returns to England. October: Depressed over the loss of Imlay, MW attempts suicide.

Anti-sedition legislation is passed in England.

1796 January: MW publishes *Letters Written during a Short Residence in Sweden, Norway, and Denmark*. March: She meets Imlay for the final time. April: MW meets Godwin again and starts to write *Wrongs of Woman*. By mid-summer, MW begins her relationship with Godwin.

England fears French invasion; France invades Italy.

Mary Hays, *Memoirs of Emma Courtney*; Burney, *Camilla*.

1797 John Opie paints MW's portrait. March 29: MW marries Godwin at Old St. Pancras Church. Although they retain separate households, the marriage is something of a scandal, in part because Godwin had denounced marriage as a monopolistic institution, and in part because it was now evident that MW had not been married to Imlay. Daughter Mary born on August 30. MW dies on September 10 of complications resulting from childbirth and is buried at St. Pancras Churchyard.

Thomas Spence: *The Rights of Infants* (satire).

1798   Godwin publishes *Memoirs of the Author of A Vindication of the Rights of Woman*, MW's first biography, and edits the *Posthumous Works of the Author of A Vindication of the Rights of Woman* (4 volumes), which includes *The Wrongs of Woman, or Maria*, "The Cave of Fancy," "Hints [Chiefly designed to have been incorporated in the Second Part of the *Vindication of the Rights of Woman*]," and her *Letters to Imlay*.

Richard Polwhele, *The Unsex'd Females*, sharpened with information from Godwin's *Memoirs*; Priscilla Bell Wakefield, *Reflections on the Present Condition of the Female Sex*.

1799   Mary Anne Radcliffe, *The Female Advocate*; Hannah More, *Strictures on the Modern System of Female Education*.

1825   "The Rights of Woman" appears in the posthumous *Works of Anna Letitia Barbauld*. Also published: William Thompson and Anna Wheeler, *Appeal of One Half the Human Race, Women, Against the Pretensions of the Other Half, Men, to Retain Them in Political, and Thence in Civil and Domestic Slavery*.

The Rights of Woman

by Mary Wollstonecraft

Frontispiece, *Memoirs of the Author of a Vindication of the Rights of Woman,* by William Godwin (London: J. Johnson, 1798). This idealized image of Wollstonecraft was engraved by James Heath, after a portrait in oil by John Opie painted in 1797 and now in the National Portrait Gallery, London.

Introduction

A Revolutionary Life

The most influential feminist thinker in the Romantic period, and the leading theorist of what we now call liberal or "equality" feminism, Mary Wollstonecraft learned firsthand the ways in which patriarchal society oppressed women. She was born on April 27, 1759, the eldest daughter of Edward John Wollstonecraft, the son of a lower-middle-class Yorkshire weaver who had prospered in Spitalfields, London, and his Irish wife, Elizabeth Dixon. However, her father's failed efforts to become a gentleman farmer first in Epping Forest, then in Barking, and finally in Beverley (Yorkshire), aggravated by his laziness and his increasing alcoholism, caused a precipitous decline in the family's status. Wollstonecraft thus grew up with what biographer Claire Tomalin has called "a powerful sense of grievance." Her parents favored their oldest son, Edward, who received an excellent education, became a lawyer, inherited all of his grandfather's money, and refused any meaningful help to his three younger sisters. The extremely intelligent Mary received only a standard middle-class girl's education: reading, writing, a little math and French, and plain sewing. When she was sixteen, she met a more refined girl, Fanny Blood, whom she passionately loved, emulated, and helped to support with her sewing. At nineteen, Mary was forced to assist her own family's failing finances by becoming a "paid companion" (personal assistant) to the wealthy Mrs. Dawson. At twenty-two, she was summoned home to nurse her dying mother. When her increasingly sullen, brutal father decided to marry their servant girl after her mother's death, Mary determined to leave home forever and earn her own way in the world.

In 1784, with the help of her two sisters and Fanny Blood, Wollstonecraft set up a school for girls, first in Islington and then in Newington Green—an undertaking typical for respectable but "impoverished gentlewomen." Here, Wollstonecraft's own education truly began. At Newington, she met the dynamic Unitarian minister, Dr. Richard Price, who introduced her to the writings of such radical Enlightenment thinkers as Benjamin Franklin, Thomas Jefferson, Condorcet, Voltaire, Jean-Jacques Rousseau, and Joseph Priestley. These philosophers reinforced her belief that one could best serve God by exercising one's rational capacity to know and achieve virtue in one's daily life. The "natural religion" (the Christian Protestant Dissent urged by Price) viewed life on earth as a probationary period in which men and women can perfect themselves through the use of right reason and individual will; viewed God as the First Cause and presiding Wisdom and Virtue of a universe now governed by Natural Law; and viewed the virtuous soul as sufficient to attain heavenly bliss.

To advertise her school, Wollstonecraft wrote her first book, *Thoughts on the Education of Daughters* (1786), arguing for rational female education and preparation for economic independence. This book was too radical for the parents of her pupils, who wished only that their daughters gain the "accomplishments" (to read, write, sing, dance, sketch, and sew) and so withdrew their daughters from the school.

A year after Fanny Blood left in 1785 to marry Hugh Skeys, Wollstonecraft gave up her school and became a governess to the aristocratic Irish family of Robert, Viscount Kingsborough, and Lady Caroline. Dismissed by Lady Caroline both because Sir Robert made an unwanted sexual overture to her and because their daughter had grown too attached to her governess, Wollstonecraft described the follies of this aristocratic world, as well as her passionate relationship with Fanny Blood, in her first, largely autobiographical novel, *Mary, A Fiction* (1788)—one that also contains an acid portrait of a lady who loves her lapdogs more than her children.

Penniless, alienated from her family (even her sisters resented her inability to care for them), lonely (Fanny Blood had died in childbirth), Wollstonecraft turned in 1787 for support to an old friend of Richard Price: the homosexual radical bookseller and publisher, Joseph Johnson. To his lasting credit, Johnson recognized her talents, hired her as a staff writer for his *Analytical Review*, provided lodgings, and urged her to write. In 1788 he published both *Mary* and her *Original Stories from Real Life* for children, with illustrations by William Blake. *The Female Reader*, a compilation of literary and moral texts designed to educate young girls in public benevolence and Christian forbearance, appeared in 1789 under the pseudonym "Mr. Cresswick."

At Johnson's bookshop, Wollstonecraft met leading radical thinkers: Thomas Paine, William Godwin, Thomas Holcroft, Thomas Christie, William Blake, and painter Henri Fuseli, with whom she fell in love. In November 1790, angered at Edmund Burke's surprising attack on the French Revolution, *Reflections on the Revolution in France* (published November 1, 1790), she rushed *A Vindication of the Rights of Men* into print in three weeks. Insisting that all political authority should rest on reason and justice, she argued that everyone is entitled to enjoy and dispense the fruits of his or her own labors, that inequality of rank should be eliminated, and that adulation of "our canonized forefathers" needs to be replaced by independent understanding and sound judgment. For Burke's metaphor of the English nation as a princess in need of chivalrous manly protection, Wollstonecraft substituted the image of the nation as a benevolent family educating its children for mature independence and motivated by "natural affections" to ensure the welfare of all members.

Convinced that the Revolution would quickly establish a republic respecting the rights of all, Wollstonecraft was appalled when in 1791 its minister of education, Charles Maurice de Talleyrand-Perigord (former Bishop of Autun), proposed a system of public education in which boys would be taught the entire range of the sciences, social sciences, and humanities, while girls would get only home economics and sewing. In 1792, Wollstonecraft published her passionate defense of the rights of women to equal education, equal employment, and parliamentary representation, *A Vindication of the Rights of Woman.* Widely read and cited, it saw a second edition the same year. Following the lead of Catharine Macaulay's *Letters on Education* (1790), which she had praised in *Analytical Review*, Wollstonecraft called for "a REVOLUTION in female manners" (p. 230) to change the prevailing opinion of woman as innately emotional, intuitive, illogical, capable of moral sentiment but no rational understanding.

In December 1792, when Fuseli rejected her love, Wollstonecraft sailed to Paris to witness the French Revolution firsthand. From her hotel room, she saw Louis XVI en route to his trial for treason, and she witnessed the onset of the Reign of Terror. She soon fell in love again, this time with American entrepreneur and gambler Gilbert Imlay. Their daughter, christened Fanny Imlay, was born May 14, 1794. Joining Imlay in Le Havre, she worked on *An Historical and Moral View of the Origin and Progress of the French Revolution* (published 1794). Imlay returned to England, and when she followed him in April 1795, she found him in London living with another woman. An attempted suicide was prevented by Imlay, who sent her on a dangerous business trip to Norway to collect insurance on a lost "treasure-ship" he had financed to run the British blockade against France. She was accompanied only by her infant daughter and her French maid, Marguerite. Her correspondence with Imlay, *Letters Written during a Short Residence in Sweden, Norway, and Denmark*, was published by Johnson in 1796. Though meant to sustain Imlay's affection for her, these letters also render an extremely perceptive commentary on the differing political and cultural customs of the Scandinavians.

Wollstonecraft returned to England in September 1795 to find Imlay living openly with an actress. She jumped in rain-soaked clothes off the Putney Bridge into the Thames River and was pulled, unconscious, from the river by some watermen. This scandal—a pregnancy out of wedlock, a bastard daughter abandoned, a lover now flaunting another mistress, two suicide attempts—was widely reported in the press, making it difficult for any respectable British woman to admit support for the author of *A Vindication of the Rights of Woman*. One person who did visit her was William Godwin, leading radical philosopher and anarchist in England. She returned the visit in April 1796, and within three months, they became lovers. Opposed to the institution of marriage, they agreed to keep separate residences. When Wollstonecraft became pregnant, they decided to marry to give their child legitimacy; on August 30, 1797, daughter Mary Wollstonecraft Godwin (later Mary Shelley, author of *Frankenstein*) was born. When Wollstonecraft failed to expel the placenta, her physician, Dr. Poignand, pulled it out with his bare hands, introducing the infection that caused the puerperal fever that killed her on September 10, 1797.

Overwhelmed by grief, Godwin in an act of homage published the *Memoirs of the Author of A Vindication of the Rights of Woman* and the *Posthumous Works of the Author of A Vindication of the*

William Godwin, engraved by James Heath, from a portrait by William Nicholson done in 1816, and published in George Gilfillan's *A First Gallery of Literary Portraits* (Edinburgh: J. Hogg, 1845).

Rights of Woman, including all the love letters to him and Imlay. And despite Wollstonecraft's deeply held Christian beliefs, Godwin—himself an atheist—insisted that she had died a disbeliever. Godwin's well-meant but entirely misjudged act of homage not only allowed the public to brand her a whore and atheist but also destroyed her reputation for the next fifty years, and along with it the credit of her feminism. Nonetheless, Wollstonecraft's radical vision of the mental equality of the sexes survived throughout the nineteenth century both covertly, in the positive allusions in the fiction of such authors as Jane Austen, Charlotte Smith, Elizabeth Inchbald, and Maria Edgeworth, and openly, in the writings of M. J. Jewsbury and the tracts of Mary Hays, Frances Wright, Barbara Leigh-Smith Bodichon, and suffragettes Sylvia Pankhurst, Elizabeth Cady Stanton, and Susan B. Anthony. More than any other eighteenth- or nineteenth-century feminist thinker, Wollstonecraft directly inspired the suffrage movements in both England and America.

A Vindication of the Rights of Woman (1792)

Inspired by the French Revolutionary call for "liberty, equality and fraternity," Wollstonecraft understood that the gender inequality at the core of both the new French republic and old Britain threatened the development of a genuine democracy. To deny education to women was tantamount to denying their personhood, even their divine soul, as well as participation in the natural and the civil rights of mankind. Wollstonecraft therefore initiated her own revolution, "a REVOLUTION in female manners." She grounded this revolution on rigorous logic, arguing that if women are to be held morally and legally responsible, then they must have both a spiritual and mental capacity to distinguish between right and wrong. And if they have this rational faculty, then it must be developed and exercised to its greatest capacity. From this philosophical argument for the equality of women, Wollstonecraft launched a passionate plea for appropriate education, for only if women were educated as fully as men would they be able to realize their capacities for reason and moral virtue. Calculating an appeal to male self-interest, Wollstonecraft argued that better-educated women would not only be more virtuous but would also become better mothers, more interesting wives and "companions," and more responsible citizens.

Wollstonecraft insisted that she was speaking on behalf of all women, not just the most talented: "I do not wish to leave the line of mediocrity" (p. 70). Assuming that most men and women would marry, she argued that women would better serve the needs of society, of children, and of their husbands, as well as of themselves, if they were educated to act more sensibly and virtuously. Thus she devoted a large portion of her *Vindication* to describing the ideal marriage, based on mutual respect, self-esteem, affection, and compatibility. It is, above all, a marriage of *rational love*, rather than erotic passion. Insisting that sexual passion does not last, she contended that the "one grand truth women have yet to learn, though most it imports them to act accordingly" is that "in the choice of a husband, they should not be led astray by the qualities of a lover—for a lover the husband, even supposing him to be wise and virtuous, cannot long remain" (p. 148). As her own life suggests, Wollstonecraft did not mean that women should give up sexual passion, but that they should channel it toward a person rationally deemed to be a suitable life-partner, one of shared interests and values. "Women as well as men ought to have the common appetites and passions of their nature, they are only brutal when unchecked by reason" (p. 161).

In tandem with this ideal of rational, egalitarian marriage, Wollstonecraft contended for even more rights. British women lived under the legal condition of *coverture* (being "covered" by the body of another), which meant they could not own or distribute their own property or possess custody of their own children. Legal reformer Barbara Leigh-Smith Bodichon summarized the laws still in force in 1854:

> A man and wife are one person in law; the wife loses all her rights as a single woman, and her existence is entirely absorbed in that of her husband. He is civilly responsible for her acts. . . .
>
> A woman's body belongs to her husband; she is in his custody, and he can enforce his right by a writ of *habeas corpus*.
>
> What was her personal property before marriage, such as money in hand, money at the bank, jewels, household goods, clothes, etc., becomes absolutely her husband's, and he may assign or dispose of them at his pleasure whether he and his wife live together or not. . . .
>
> The legal custody of children belongs to the father. During the life-time of a sane father, the mother has no rights over her children, except a limited power over infants [while breast-feeding them], and the father may take them from her and dispose of them as he thinks fit.[1]

To Wollstonecraft, *coverture* was tantamount to slavery. Women, she argued, possessed the same souls and natural rights as men and should hold the same civil and legal rights. They should have access to the most prestigious professions, including business, law, medi-

---

[1] *A Brief Summary in Plain Language of the Most Important Laws Concerning Women; Together with a Few Observations Thereon.* London: 1854.

cine, education, and politics. She also urged that they be able to vote for representatives for their particular interests in Parliament: "I really think that women ought to have representatives, instead of being arbitrarily governed without having any direct share allowed them in the deliberations of government" (p. 179). Above all, she demanded for all children between the ages of five and nine a state-supported, coeducational school system that would teach reading, writing, mathematics, history, botany, mechanics, astronomy, and general science. After age nine, gifted children would receive additional education at state expense. If Wollstonecraft's demands now seem self-evidently practical and just (if a bit demanding for nine-year-olds), it is only because the revolution in education, law, and parliamentary representation that she demanded actually did happen, a century or so later.

To defend her utopian vision, Wollstonecraft described in detail the errors and evils of her society's present definition of the female as the subordinate helpmate of the male. Referring to the widely credited views of Milton and Rousseau, she sardonically attacked their portrayals. When Milton tells us, she wrote with heavy sarcasm,

> that women are formed for softness and sweet attractive grace [*Paradise Lost*, 4.297–99], I cannot comprehend his meaning, unless, in the true Mahometan strain, he meant to deprive us of souls, and insinuate that we were beings only designed by sweet attractive grace, and docile blind obedience, to gratify the senses of man when he can no longer soar on the wing of contemplation. (p. 36)

She saved her bitterest attacks for Rousseau, whose gender policies contradicted his radical politics of individual choice and social contract. She was particularly disappointed by the ideal woman Rousseau drew in his novel *Émile*. Portraying Sophy ("female wisdom") as submissive, loving, and ever faithful, Rousseau had asserted,

> The first and most important qualification in a woman is good-nature or sweetness of temper: formed to obey a being so imperfect as man, often full of vices, and always full of faults, she ought to learn betimes even to suffer injustice, and to bear the insults of a husband without complaint. (p. 108)

Rousseau thus gave this curriculum for female education:

> the education of the women should be always relative to the men.
> To please, to be useful to us, to make us love and esteem them, to
> educate us when young, and take care of us when grown up, to
> advise, to console us, to render our lives easy and agreeable: these
> are the duties of women at all times, and what they should be
> taught in their infancy. (p. 104)

Much of *A Vindication* is devoted to illustrating the damage
wrought by this definition of women's nature and social role. Up-
per- and middle-class girls in Wollstonecraft's day were taught to
become adept at arousing and sustaining (but never fully satisfying) male sexual desire in order to capture husbands upon whom
their financial welfare depended. (It was not "respectable" for a
woman to work for money.) They were thus obsessed with personal appearance, with beauty and fashion. Encouraged to be "delicate" and refined, many were what we would now recognize as
anorexic or bulimic.

The disease was fashionable and pernicious:

> I once knew a weak woman of fashion who was more than
> commonly proud of her delicacy and sensibility. She thought a
> distinguishing taste and puny appetite the height of all human
> perfection, and acted accordingly.—I have seen this weak so-
> phisticated being neglect all the duties of life, yet recline with
> self-complacency on a sofa, and boast of her want of appetite as
> a proof of delicacy. (p. 63)

Worse, this model encouraged hypocrisy and insincerity. Trained to
be flirts and sexual teases, women were taught to arouse male sexual
desire by allowing their suitors to take "innocent freedoms" or "lib-
erties" with their person but were forbidden to experience or mani-
fest sexual desire themselves. Since they received no rational education but trained only in "female accomplishments," women were
kept "in a state of perpetual childhood" (p. 25), "created rather to
feel than reason" (p. 84). They were, Wollstonecraft insisted,
"slaves" to their fathers and husbands, and, in revenge, cruel and
petty tyrants to their children and servants.

Taught to be manipulative and sycophantic to their masters, women wound up being "cunning, mean, and selfish" to everyone else (p. 172). They became indolent wives and bad mothers, either overindulgent (to their sons) or hostile (to their infants, often refusing to nurse them), and responsible for the high incidence of childhood disease and infant mortality. Wollstonecraft concluded her *Vindication* with a list of common female follies: a belief in fortune-tellers and superstitions, an excessive fondness for romantic love stories, an obsessive concern with fashion and appearance, the selfish promotion of the members of her own family at the expense of worthy others, mismanaged households, and mistreated servants. While some feminists today have been dismayed by Wollstonecraft's satire of the women of her day, we must keep in mind that she blamed these female follies *on the failure of men* to provide education, respect, and opportunity to become anything other than fools.

Thus men, too, are corrupted, the system of male mastery rendering them demanding, self-indulgent, arrogant, tyrannic, unable to understand the needs of others, to act justly or compassionately, to be rational leaders. While Wollstonecraft's criticism was muted (after all, men comprise the audience she hopes to persuade), she made it clear that a master-slave relationship between husband and wife is evil on both sides: "how can women be just or generous, when they are the slaves of injustice?" (p. 226).

A "REVOLUTION in female manners" would produce women who were sincerely modest, virtuous, and Christian, who acted with prudence as well as an ardent generosity, and men who were kind, responsible, sensible, and just. It would produce egalitarian marriages based on compatibility, mutual affection, sexual desire, and respect:

> we shall not see women affectionate till more equality be established in society, till ranks are confounded and women freed, neither shall we see that dignified domestic happiness, the simple grandeur of which cannot be relished by ignorant or vitiated minds; nor will the important task of education ever be properly begun till the person of a woman is no longer preferred to her mind. (p. 228)

The rational woman; rational love; egalitarian marriage; the preservation of the domestic affections; responsibility for the mental, moral, and physical well-being and growth of all the members of the family; and above all, the acquisition of divine virtue—these are the cornerstones of Wollstonecraft's feminism.

Today, we would call this "liberal" feminism, based on the equality or even "sameness" of men and women, as opposed to a model based on "essential" sexual difference and needs. In this way, Wollstonecraft's moral vision diverges profoundly from the ideology of both the British Enlightenment and the originating leaders of the French Revolution. Where these progressive movements still insisted on the sexual division of labor, Wollstonecraft insisted on the rationality and equality of the female and on the primary importance of the domestic affections and the family. By setting the egalitarian family as the prototype of a genuine democracy, a family in which husband and wife not only regard each other as equals in intelligence, sensitivity, and power but also participate equally in childcare and decision making, Wollstonecraft introduced a truly revolutionary society. We might call this her "family politics." Wollstonecraft clearly shared the French Enlightenment *philosophes*' affirmation of reason and wit, of sound moral principles, and of good taste grounded on wide learning. But she contested the traditional affirmation of the father as the ultimate social, political, and religious authority—as he was, even in the new French Republic. Where Enlightenment thinkers and nonconformist writers such as Voltaire, Thomas Paine, and Thomas Jefferson challenged the authority of the father in the name of the younger son, or challenged the authority of the King in the name of the self-made man, Wollstonecraft categorically challenged the rights of males in the name of all females. She even believed that rational women might possess a greater capacity for divine virtue and thus for political leadership.

Anne K. Mellor

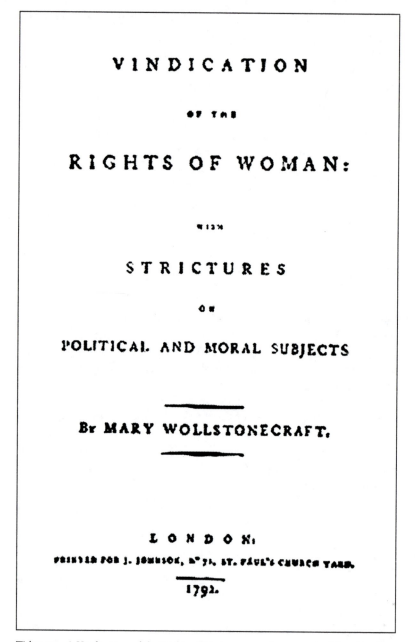

VINDICATION

OF THE

RIGHTS OF WOMAN:

WITH

STRICTURES

ON

POLITICAL AND MORAL SUBJECTS

By MARY WOLLSTONECRAFT.

LONDON:
PRINTED FOR J. JOHNSON, N° 72, ST. PAUL'S CHURCH YARD.
1792.

Title page, *A Vindication of the Rights of Woman*, second corrected edition (London: J. Johnson, 1792).

A Vindication of the
Rights of Woman
(1792)

TO
M. TALLEYRAND-PÉRIGORD
Late Bishop of Autun[1]

Sir,

Having read with great pleasure a pamphlet[2] which you have lately published, I dedicate this volume to you; to induce you to reconsider the subject, and maturely weigh what I have advanced respecting the rights of woman and national education: and I call with the firm tone of humanity; for my arguments, Sir, are dictated by a disinterested spirit—I plead for my sex—not for myself. Independence I have long considered as the grand blessing of life, the basis of every virtue—and independence I will ever secure by contracting my wants, though I were to live on a barren heath. It is then an affection for the whole human race that makes my pen dart rapidly along to support what I believe to be the cause of virtue: and the same motive leads me earnestly to wish to see woman placed in a station in which she would advance, instead of retarding, the progress of those glorious

---

[1]Charles Maurice de Talleyrand-Périgord, prince de Benevent (1754–1838), Bishop of Autun, France, 1788–91. He resigned to support the revolutionary Republic, serving on the Estates General, the Constituent Assembly, and the National Assembly, and as a foreign minister and envoy. He advocated the confiscation of Church property to raise revenue and developed a new system of state-supported education.

[2]In *Rapport sur l'instruction publique, fait au nom de Comité de constitution* (1791), Talleyrand called for a free public education for both sexes of all ages, but followed Rousseau's *Émile, ou Traité de l'Éducation* (1762) in requiring that the education of females should prepare them for a life of subservience to men. France's current system of compulsory free education owes a great deal to Talleyrand's model.

principles that give a substance to morality. My opinion, indeed, respecting the rights and duties of woman, seems to flow so naturally from these simple principles, that I think it scarcely possible, but that some of the enlarged minds who formed your admirable constitution, will coincide with me.[3]

In France there is undoubtedly a more general diffusion of knowledge than in any part of the European world, and I attribute it, in a great measure, to the social intercourse which has long subsisted between the sexes.[4] It is true, I utter my sentiments with freedom, that in France the very essence of sensuality has been extracted to regale the voluptuary, and a kind of sentimental lust has prevailed, which, together with the system of duplicity that the whole tenour of their political and civil government taught, have given a sinister sort of sagacity to the French character, properly termed finesse; from which naturally flow a polish of manners that injures the substance, by hunting sincerity out of society.—And, modesty, the fairest garb of virtue! has been more grossly insulted in France than even in England, till their women have treated as *prudish* that attention to decency, which brutes instinctively observe.

Manners and morals are so nearly allied that they have often been confounded; but, though the former should only be the natural reflection of the latter, yet, when various causes have produced factitious and corrupt manners, which are very early caught, morality becomes an empty name. The personal reserve, and sacred respect for cleanliness and delicacy in domestic life, which French women almost despise, are the graceful pillars of modesty; but, far from despising them, if the pure flame of patriotism have reached their bosoms, they should labour to improve the morals of their fellow-citizens, by teaching men, not only to respect modesty in women, but to acquire it themselves, as the only way to merit their esteem.

Contending for the rights of woman, my main argument is built on this simple principle, that if she be not prepared by education to become the companion of man, she will stop the progress of knowledge and virtue; for truth must be common to all, or it will be ineffi-

---

[3] The 1791 Constitution of the new French Republic conferred citizenship only upon men over the age of 25, and excluded women from political life. Women did not gain the vote in France until 1944.

[4] Editor Carol Poston suggests a reference to the salons of Paris, prominent during the eighteenth century for fostering brilliant conversations about art and literature. Although attended by both sexes, they were hosted and presided over by women of social distinction.

cacious with respect to its influence on general practice. And how can woman be expected to co-operate unless she know why she ought to be virtuous? unless freedom strengthens her reason till she comprehend her duty, and see in what manner it is connected with her real good. If children are to be educated to understand the true principle of patriotism, their mother must be a patriot; and the love of mankind, from which an orderly train of virtues spring, can only be produced by considering the moral and civil interest of mankind; but the education and situation of woman, at present, shuts her out from such investigations.

In this work I have produced many arguments, which to me were conclusive, to prove that the prevailing notion respecting a sexual character was subversive of morality, and I have contended, that to render the human body and mind more perfect, chastity[5] must more universally prevail, and that chastity will never be respected in the male world till the person of a woman is not, as it were, idolized, when little virtue or sense embellish it with the grand traces of mental beauty, or the interesting simplicity of affection.

Consider, Sir, dispassionately, these observations—for a glimpse of this truth seemed to open before you when you observed, "that to see one half of the human race excluded by the other from all participation of government, was a political phaenomenon that, according to abstract principles, it was impossible to explain."[6] If so, on what does your constitution rest? If the abstract rights of man will bear discussion and explanation, those of woman, by a parity of reasoning, will not shrink from the same test: though a different opinion prevails in this country, built on the very arguments which you use to justify the oppression of woman—prescription.

Consider, I address you as a legislator, whether, when men contend for their freedom, and to be allowed to judge for themselves respecting their own happiness, it be not inconsistent and unjust to subjugate women, even though you firmly believe that you are acting in the manner best calculated to promote their happiness? Who made man the exclusive judge, if woman partake with him the gift of reason?

In this style, argue tyrants of every denomination, from the weak king to the weak father of a family; they are all eager to crush reason; yet always assert that they usurp its throne only to be useful. Do you

[5]Sexual self-control (abstinence before marriage, fidelity in marriage) for both sexes.
[6]In *Rapport sur l'instruction publique*, 116.

not act a similar part, when you *force* all women, by denying them civil and political rights, to remain immured in their families groping in the dark? for surely, Sir, you will not assert, that a duty can be binding which is not founded on reason? If indeed this be their destination, arguments may be drawn from reason: and thus augustly supported, the more understanding women acquire, the more they will be attached to their duty—comprehending it—for unless they comprehend it, unless their morals be fixed on the same immutable principle as those of man, no authority can make them discharge it in a virtuous manner. They may be convenient slaves, but slavery will have its constant effect, degrading the master and the abject dependent.

But, if women are to be excluded, without having a voice, from a participation of the natural rights of mankind, prove first, to ward off the charge of injustice and inconsistency, that they want reason—else this flaw in your NEW CONSTITUTION will ever show that man must, in some shape, act like a tyrant, and tyranny, in whatever part of society it rears its brazen front, will ever undermine morality.

I have repeatedly asserted, and produced what appeared to me irrefragable arguments drawn from matters of fact, to prove my assertion, that women cannot, by force, be confined to domestic concerns; for they will, however ignorant, intermeddle with more weighty affairs, neglecting private duties only to disturb, by cunning tricks, the orderly plans of reason which rise above their comprehension.

Besides, whilst they are only made to acquire personal accomplishments,[7] men will seek for pleasure in variety, and faithless husbands will make faithless wives; such ignorant beings, indeed, will be very excusable when, not taught to respect public good, nor allowed any civil rights, they attempt to do themselves justice by retaliation.

The box of mischief[8] thus opened in society, what is to preserve private virtue, the only security of public freedom and universal happiness?

Let there be then no coercion *established* in society, and the common law of gravity prevailing, the sexes will fall into their proper places. And, now that more equitable laws are forming your citizens, marriage may become more sacred: your young men may choose

---

[7]The skills that a well-brought-up young woman of the upper classes acquired to make her attractive for courtship: reading, penmanship, drawing, a smattering of French and Italian, the ability to sing, dance, do fine needlework, and play the piano.

[8]In Greek mythology, the first woman, Pandora, overcome by curiosity, opens a forbidden box, letting loose all the evils of humankind. Only "hope" remained when she closed it. MW makes the box-openers male politicians, not women.

wives from motives of affection, and your maidens allow love to root out vanity.

The father of a family will not then weaken his constitution and debase his sentiments, by visiting the harlot, nor forget, in obeying the call of appetite, the purpose for which it was implanted. And, the mother will not neglect her children to practise the arts of coquetry, when sense and modesty secure her the friendship of her husband.

But, till men become attentive to the duty of a father, it is vain to expect women to spend that time in their nursery which they, "wise in their generation,"[9] choose to spend at their glass[10]; for this exertion of cunning is only an instinct of nature to enable them to obtain indirectly a little of that power of which they are unjustly denied a share: for, if women are not permitted to enjoy legitimate rights, they will render both men and themselves vicious, to obtain illicit privileges.

I wish, Sir, to set some investigations of this kind afloat in France; and should they lead to a confirmation of my principles, when your constitution is revised, the Rights of Woman may be respected, if it be fully proved that reason calls for this respect, and loudly demands JUSTICE for one half of the human race.

I am, SIR,
Your's respectfully,
M. W.

---

[9]"The children of this world are in their generation wiser than the children of light" (Luke 16:8).

[10]Mirror.

ADVERTISEMENT

When I began to write this work, I divided it into three parts, supposing that one volume would contain a full discussion of the arguments which seemed to me to rise naturally from a few simple principles; but fresh illustrations occurring as I advanced, I now present only the first part to the public.

Many subjects, however, which I have cursorily alluded to, call for particular investigation, especially the laws relative to women, and the consideration of their peculiar duties. These will furnish ample matter for a second volume, which in due time will be published, to elucidate some of the sentiments, and complete many of the sketches begun in the first.[1]

---

[1]MW published only one volume. "Hints" for a second volume were published in 1798, in the *Posthumous Works of the Author of A Vindication of the Rights of Woman* (ed. William Godwin).

CONTENTS

INTRODUCTION

After considering the historic page, and viewing the living world with anxious solicitude, the most melancholy emotions of sorrowful indignation have depressed my spirits, and I have sighed when obliged to confess, that either nature has made a great difference between man and man, or that the civilization which has hitherto taken place in the world has been very partial. I have turned over various books written on the subject of education, and patiently observed the conduct of parents and the management of schools; but what has been the result?—a profound conviction that the neglected education of my fellow-creatures is the grand source of the misery I deplore; and that women, in particular, are rendered weak and wretched by a variety of concurring causes, originating from one hasty conclusion. The conduct and manners of women, in fact, evidently prove that their minds are not in a healthy state; for, like the flowers which are planted in too rich a soil, strength and usefulness are sacrificed to beauty; and the flaunting leaves, after having pleased a fastidious eye, fade, disregarded on the stalk, long before the season when they ought to have arrived at maturity.—One cause of this barren blooming I attribute to a false system of education, gathered from the books written on this subject by men who, considering females rather as women than human creatures, have been more anxious to make them alluring mistresses than affectionate wives and rational mothers[1]; and the understanding of the sex has been so bubbled[2] by this specious homage, that the civilized women of the present century, with a few exceptions, are only anxious to inspire love, when they ought to cherish a nobler ambition, and by their abilities and virtues exact respect.

In a treatise, therefore, on female rights and manners, the works which have been particularly written for their improvement must not be overlooked; especially when it is asserted, in direct terms, that the minds of women are enfeebled by false refinement; that the books of instruction, written by men of genius, have had the same tendency as more frivolous productions; and that, in the true style of Mahometanism,[3] they are treated as a kind of subordinate beings, and

---

[1] 1st edition: rational wives.

[2] Deluded.

[3] The widespread Christian misconception that in the religion of Islam women lack souls, and therefore have no afterlife.

not as a part of the human species, when improveable reason is allowed to be the dignified distinction which raises men above the brute creation, and puts a natural sceptre in a feeble hand.

Yet, because I am a woman, I would not lead my readers to suppose that I mean violently to agitate the contested question respecting the equality or inferiority of the sex; but as the subject lies in my way, and I cannot pass it over without subjecting the main tendency of my reasoning to misconstruction, I shall stop a moment to deliver, in a few words, my opinion.—In the government of the physical world it is observable that the female in point of strength is, in general, inferior to the male. This is the law of nature; and it does not appear to be suspended or abrogated in favour of woman. A degree of physical superiority cannot, therefore, be denied—and it is a noble prerogative![4] But not content with this natural pre-eminence, men endeavour to sink us still lower, merely to render us alluring objects for a moment; and women, intoxicated by the adoration which men, under the influence of their senses, pay them, do not seek to obtain a durable interest in their hearts, or to become the friends of the fellow creatures who find amusement in their society.

I am aware of an obvious inference:—from every quarter have I heard exclamations against masculine women; but where are they to be found? If by this appellation men mean to inveigh against their ardour in hunting, shooting, and gaming, I shall most cordially join in the cry; but if it be against the imitation of manly virtues, or, more properly speaking, the attainment of those talents and virtues, the exercise of which ennobles the human character, and which raises females in the scale of animal being, when they are comprehensively termed mankind;—all those who view them with a philosophic eye must, I should think, wish with me, that they may every day grow more and more masculine.

This discussion naturally divides the subject. I shall first consider women in the grand light of human creatures, who in common with men, are placed on this earth to unfold their faculties; and afterwards I shall more particularly point out their peculiar designation.

I wish also to steer clear of an error which many respectable writers have fallen into; for the instruction which has hitherto been addressed to women, has rather been applicable to *ladies,* if the little in-

---

[4]1st edition: the female, in general, is inferior to the male. The male pursues, the female yields—this is the law of nature; and it does not appear to be suspended or abrogated in favour of woman. This physical superiority cannot be denied—and it is a noble prerogative!

direct advice, that is scattered through Sandford and Merton[5] be excepted; but, addressing my sex in a firmer tone, I pay particular attention to those in the middle class, because they appear to be in the most natural state.[6] Perhaps the seeds of false-refinement, immorality, and vanity, have ever been shed by the great. Weak, artificial beings, raised above the common wants and affections of their race, in a premature unnatural manner, undermine the very foundation of virtue, and spread corruption through the whole mass of society! As a class of mankind they have the strongest claim to pity; the education of the rich tends to render them vain and helpless, and the unfolding mind is not strengthened by the practice of those duties which dignify the human character. They only live to amuse themselves, and by the same law which in nature invariably produces certain effects, they soon only afford barren amusement.

But as I purpose taking a separate view of the different ranks of society, and of the moral character of women, in each, this hint is, for the present, sufficient; and I have only alluded to the subject because it appears to me to be the very essence of an introduction to give a cursory account of the contents of the work it introduces.

My own sex, I hope, will excuse me, if I treat them like rational creatures, instead of flattering their *fascinating* graces, and viewing them as if they were in a state of perpetual childhood, unable to stand alone. I earnestly wish to point out in what true dignity and human happiness consists—I wish to persuade women to endeavour to acquire strength, both of mind and body, and to convince them that the soft phrases, susceptibility of heart, delicacy of sentiment, and refinement of taste, are almost synonymous with epithets of weakness, and that those beings who are only the objects of pity and that kind of love, which has been termed its sister, will soon become objects of contempt.

Dismissing then those pretty feminine phrases, which the men condescendingly use to soften our slavish dependence, and despising that weak elegancy of mind, exquisite sensibility, and sweet docility of manners, supposed to be the sexual characteristics of the weaker vessel, I wish to show that elegance is inferior to virtue, that the first object of laudable ambition is to obtain a character as a human be-

[5]Thomas Day's popular children's book, *The History of Sandford and Merton* (3 vols., 1786–89), influenced by Rousseau's *Émile*, contrasts the wealthy spoilt Merton to the poor honest Sandford. The boys are often instructed by the moral tales of their tutor, Mr. Barlow.

[6]"Natural," because the middle classes were uncorrupted by property, wealth, and titles, on the one hand, and not deformed by poverty, on the other.

ing, regardless of the distinction of sex; and that secondary views should be brought to this simple touchstone.

This is a rough sketch of my plan; and should I express my conviction with the energetic emotions that I feel whenever I think of the subject, the dictates of experience and reflection will be felt by some of my readers. Animated by this important object, I shall disdain to cull my phrases or polish my style;—I aim at being useful, and sincerity will render me unaffected; for, wishing rather to persuade by the force of my arguments, than dazzle by the elegance of my language, I shall not waste my time in rounding periods,[7] or in fabricating the turgid bombast of artificial feelings, which, coming from the head, never reach the heart.—I shall be employed about things, not words!—and, anxious to render my sex more respectable members of society, I shall try to avoid that flowery diction which has slided from essays into novels, and from novels into familiar letters and conversation.

These pretty superlatives, dropping glibly from the tongue, vitiate the taste, and create a kind of sickly delicacy that turns away from simple unadorned truth; and a deluge of false sentiments and overstretched feelings, stifling the natural emotions of the heart, render the domestic pleasures insipid, that ought to sweeten the exercise of those severe duties, which educate a rational and immortal being for a nobler field of action.

The education of women has of late been more attended to than formerly; yet they are still reckoned a frivolous sex, and ridiculed or pitied by the writers who endeavour by satire or instruction to improve them. It is acknowledged that they spend many of the first years of their lives in acquiring a smattering of accomplishments; meanwhile strength of body and mind are sacrificed to libertine notions of beauty, to the desire of establishing themselves,[8]—the only way women can rise in the world,—by marriage. And this desire making mere animals of them, when they marry they act as such children may be expected to act:—they dress; they paint, and nickname God's creatures.[9]—Surely these weak beings are only fit for a

---

[7] Formulating elaborately balanced sentences. Although critic Samuel Johnson was celebrated for this style, it is likely that MW has Edmund Burke's *Reflections on the French Revolution* in mind.

[8] Libertine (adj. or noun): unrestrained by moral law; a woman "establishes" herself with a marriage guaranteeing material comfort.

[9] "You jig and amble, and you lisp, you nickname God's creatures and make wantonness your ignorance," Hamlet berates Ophelia (Shakespeare, *Hamlet*, 2.1.146–48).

seraglio![10] Can they be expected to govern a family with judgment, or take care of the poor babes whom they bring into the world?

If then it can be fairly deduced from the present conduct of the sex, from the prevalent fondness for pleasure which takes place of ambition and those nobler passions that open and enlarge the soul; that the instruction which women have hitherto received has only tended, with the constituion of civil society, to render them insignificant objects of desire—mere propagators of fools!—if it can be proved that in aiming to accomplish them, without cultivating their understandings, they are taken out of their sphere of duties, and made ridiculous and useless when the short-lived bloom of beauty is over,[11] I presume that *rational* men will excuse me for endeavouring to persuade them to become more masculine and respectable.

Indeed the word masculine is only a bugbear: there is little reason to fear that women will acquire too much courage or fortitude; for their apparent inferiority with respect to bodily strength, must render them, in some degree, dependent on men in the various relations of life; but why should it be increased by prejudices that give a sex to virtue,[12] and confound simple truths with sensual reveries?

Women are, in fact, so much degraded by mistaken notions of female excellence, that I do not mean to add a paradox when I assert, that this artificial weakness produces a propensity to tyrannize, and gives birth to cunning, the natural opponent of strength, which leads them to play off those contemptible infantine airs that undermine esteem even whilst they excite desire. Let men become more chaste and modest, and if women do not grow wiser in the same ratio, it will be clear that they have weaker understandings. It seems scarcely necessary to say, that I now speak of the sex in general. Many individuals have more sense than their male relatives; and, as nothing preponderates where there is a constant struggle for an equilibrium, without it has naturally more gravity, some women govern their husbands without degrading themselves, because intellect will always govern.

[10]Turkish harem.

[11]A lively writer, I cannot recollect his name, asks what business women turned of forty have to do in the world? [MW]. "I don't know what the devil a woman lives for after thirty; she is only in other folk's way," exclaims libertine Lord Merton, in Frances Burney's *Evelina* (1778).

[12]That only men have the moral capacity for virtue.

CHAPTER I

THE RIGHTS AND INVOLVED DUTIES
OF MANKIND CONSIDERED

In the present state of society it appears necessary to go back to first principles in search of the most simple truths, and to dispute with some prevailing prejudice every inch of ground. To clear my way, I must be allowed to ask some plain questions, and the answers will probably appear as unequivocal as the axioms on which reasoning is built; though, when entangled with various motives of action, they are formally contradicted, either by the words or conduct of men.

In what does man's pre-eminence over the brute creation consist? The answer is as clear as that a half is less than the whole; in Reason.

What acquirement exalts one being above another? Virtue; we spontaneously reply.

For what purpose were the passions implanted? That man by struggling with them might attain a degree of knowledge denied to the brutes; whispers Experience.

Consequently the perfection of our nature and capability of happiness, must be estimated by the degree of reason, virtue, and knowledge, that distinguish the individual, and direct the laws which bind society: and that from the exercise of reason, knowledge and virtue naturally flow, is equally undeniable, if mankind be viewed collectively.

The rights and duties of man thus simplified, it seems almost impertinent to attempt to illustrate truths that appear so incontrovertible; yet such deeply rooted prejudices have clouded reason, and such spurious qualities have assumed the name of virtues, that it is necessary to pursue the course of reason as it has been perplexed and involved in error, by various adventitious circumstances, comparing the simple axiom with casual deviations.

Men, in general, seem to employ their reason to justify prejudices, which they have imbibed, they can scarcely trace how, rather than to root them out. The mind must be strong that resolutely forms its own principles; for a kind of intellectual cowardice prevails which makes many men shrink from the task, or only do it by halves. Yet the imperfect conclusions thus drawn, are frequently very plausible, because they are built on partial experience, on just, though narrow, views.

Going back to first principles, vice skulks, with all its native deformity, from close investigation; but a set of shallow reasoners are always exclaiming that these arguments prove too much, and that a measure rotten at the core may be expedient. Thus expediency is continually contrasted with simple principles, till truth is lost in a mist of words; virtue, in forms, and knowledge rendered a sounding nothing, by the specious prejudices that assume its name.

That the society is formed in the wisest manner, whose constitution is founded on the nature of man, strikes, in the abstract, every thinking being so forcibly, that it looks like presumption to endeavour to bring forward proofs; though proof must be brought, or the strong hold of prescription will never be forced by reason; yet to urge prescription as an argument to justify the depriving men (or women) of their natural rights, is one of the absurd sophisms which daily insult common sense.

The civilization of the bulk of the people of Europe is very partial; nay, it may be made a question, whether they have acquired any virtues in exchange for innocence, equivalent to the misery produced by the vices that have been plastered over unsightly ignorance, and the freedom which has been bartered for splendid slavery. The desire of dazzling by riches, the most certain pre-eminence that man can obtain, the pleasure of commanding flattering sycophants, and many other complicated low calculations of doting self-love, have all contributed to overwhelm the mass of mankind, and make liberty a convenient handle for mock patriotism. For whilst rank and titles are held of the utmost importance, before which Genius "must hide its diminished head,"[1] it is, with a few exceptions, very unfortunate for a nation when a man of abilities, without rank or property, pushes himself forward to notice.—Alas! what unheard of misery have thousands suffered to purchase a cardinal's hat for an intriguing obscure adventurer, who longed to be ranked with princes, or lord it over them by seizing the triple crown![2]

Such, indeed, has been the wretchedness that has flowed from hereditary honours, riches, and monarchy, that men of lively sensibility have almost uttered blasphemy in order to justify the dispensations of providence. Man has been held out as independent of his power who made him, or as a lawless planet darting from its orbit to steal the celestial fire of reason; and the vengeance of heaven, lurking in the subtile flame, like Pandora's pent-up mischiefs,[3] sufficiently punished his temerity, by introducing evil into the world.

---

[1]At the sight of the sun, "all the stars / Hide their diminished heads," says a resentful Satan (Milton, *Paradise Lost*, 4.34–35).

[2]Crown of the Roman Catholic Pope.

[3]See p. 18, n. 8. Zeus sent Pandora to man as a punishment for Prometheus's theft of fire from the gods.

Impressed by this view of the misery and disorder which pervaded society, and fatigued with jostling against artificial fools, Rousseau became enamoured of solitude, and, being at the same time an optimist, he labours with uncommon eloquence to prove that man was naturally a solitary animal.[4] Misled by his respect for the goodness of God, who certainly—for what man of sense and feeling can doubt it!—gave life only to communicate happiness, he considers evil as positive, and the work of man; not aware that he was exalting one attribute at the expense of another, equally necessary to divine perfection.

Reared on a false hypothesis, his arguments in favour of a state of nature are plausible, but unsound. I say unsound; for to assert that a state of nature is preferable to civilization, in all its possible perfection, is, in other words, to arraign supreme wisdom; and the paradoxical exclamation, that God has made all things right, and that error has been introduced by the creature, whom he formed, knowing what he formed, is as unphilosophical as impious.[5]

When that wise Being who created us and placed us here, saw the fair idea, he willed, by allowing it to be so, that the passions should unfold our reason, because he could see that present evil would produce future good. Could the helpless creature whom he called from nothing break loose from his providence, and boldly learn to know good by practising evil, without his permission? No.—How could that energetic advocate for immortality argue so inconsistently? Had mankind remained for ever in the brutal state of nature, which even his magic pen cannot paint as a state in which a single virtue took root, it would have been clear, though not to the sensitive unreflecting wanderer, that man was born to run the circle of life and death, and adorn God's garden for some purpose which could not easily be reconciled with his attributes.

But if, to crown the whole, there were to be rational creatures produced, allowed to rise in excellence by the exercise of powers im-

---

[4]Swiss-French philosopher, novelist, radical political theorist, and composer Jean-Jacques Rosseau (1712–78) was best known for the assertion in *Social Contract* (1762) that mankind is born free but is everywhere in chains. MW refers to his *Discourse on the Origin and Foundation of Human Inequality* (1755), where he describes the original state of human nature as necessarily solitary, celebrates the "noble savage," and argues that human beings grow more wicked as they grow more sociable. In *Confessions* (1782), Rousseau describes his love of solitude.

[5]Rousseau's *Émile* (1762) begins: "All things are good as their Creator made them, but everything degenerates in the hands of man." From William Kenrick's translation, *Emilius and Sophia: Or, A New System of Education* (1763), used by MW. Quotations and references hereafter will refer to this edition.

planted for that purpose; if benignity itself thought fit to call into existence a creature above the brutes,[6] who could think and improve himself, why should that inestimable gift, for a gift it was, if man was so created as to have a capacity to rise above the state in which sensation produced brutal ease, be called, in direct terms, a curse? A curse it might be reckoned, if the whole of our existence were bounded by our continuance in this world; for why should the gracious fountain of life give us passions, and the power of reflecting, only to imbitter our days and inspire us with mistaken notions of dignity? Why should he lead us from love of ourselves to the sublime emotions which the discovery of his wisdom and goodness excites, if these feelings were not set in motion to improve our nature, of which they make a part,[7] and render us capable of enjoying a more godlike portion of happiness? Firmly persuaded that no evil exists in the world that God did not design to take place, I build my belief on the perfection of God.

Rousseau exerts himself to prove that all *was* right originally: a crowd of authors that all *is* now right: and I, that all will *be* right.

But, true to his first position, next to a state of nature, Rousseau celebrates barbarism, and apostrophizing the shade of Fabricius,[8] he forgets that, in conquering the world, the Romans never dreamed of establishing their own liberty on a firm basis, or of extending the reign of virtue. Eager to support his system, he stigmatizes, as vicious, every effort of genius; and, uttering the apotheosis of savage virtues, he exalts those to demi-gods, who were scarcely human—the brutal Spartans,

---

[6]Contrary to the opinion of the anatomists, who argue by analogy from the formation of the teeth, stomach, and intestines, Rousseau will not allow a man to be a carniverous animal. And, carried away from nature by a love of system, he disputes whether man be a gregarious animal, though the long and helpless state of infancy seems to point him out as particularly impelled to pair, the first step towards herding [MW]. Cf. *Emilius*, 1.2.286; 2.4.133–64.

[7]What would you say to a mechanic whom you had desired to make a watch to point out the hour of the day, if, to show his ingenuity, he added wheels to make it a repeater, etc., that perplexed the simple mechanism; should he urge—to excuse himself—had you not touched a certain spring, you would have known nothing of the matter, and that he should have amused himself by making an experiment without doing you any harm, would you not retort fairly upon him, by insisting that if he had not added those needless wheels and springs, the accident could not have happened? [MW]. A repeater: strikes the hour. The watch-maker was a common analogy in 18th-c. discussions of natural religion, and appears in *Émile*.

[8]Roman General Gaius Fabricius Luscinus (d. after 275 BCE), a paragon of incorruptibility, criticized the effeminacy of the later Roman emperors and urged them to return to the business of world conquest. Rousseau invokes his ghost in his first work, *A Discourse on the Sciences and the Arts* (1750), to condemn the arts.

who, in defiance of justice and gratitude, sacrificed, in cold blood, the slaves who had shown themselves heroes to rescue their oppressors.[9]

Disgusted with artificial manners and virtues, the citizen of Geneva,[10] instead of properly sifting the subject, threw away the wheat with the chaff,[11] without waiting to inquire whether the evils which his ardent soul turned from indignantly, were the consequence of civilization or the vestiges of barbarism. He saw vice trampling on virtue, and the semblance of goodness taking place of the reality; he saw talents bent by power to sinister purposes, and never thought of tracing the gigantic mischief up to arbitrary power, up to the hereditary distinctions that clash with the mental superiority that naturally raises a man above his fellows. He did not perceive that regal power, in a few generations, introduces idiotism into the noble stem, and holds out baits to render thousands idle and vicious.

Nothing can set the regal character in a more contemptible point of view, than the various crimes that have elevated men to the supreme dignity. Vile intrigues, unnatural crimes, and every vice that degrades our nature, have been the steps to this distinguished eminence; yet millions of men have supinely allowed the nerveless limbs of the posterity of such rapacious prowlers to rest quietly on their ensanguined thrones.[12]

What but a pestilential vapour can hover over society when its chief director is only instructed in the invention of crimes, or the stupid routine of childish ceremonies? Will men never be wise?—will they never cease to expect corn from tares, and figs from thistles?[13]

It is impossible for any man, when the most favourable circumstances concur, to acquire sufficient knowledge and strength of mind to

[9]In *History of the Peloponnesian War*, Thucydides (5th c. BCE) describes Spartans' betrayal of their warrior slaves (4.80.3–4). Having promised freedom to the bravest, the generals massacred the 2,000 men who claimed this reward, on the grounds that they would be the ones most likely to lead a slave revolt.

[10]Although Rousseau spent little time in his birthplace, Geneva, Switzerland, after the age of 16, he referred to himself as "citoyen de Genève."

[11]An allusion to Matthew 3:12.

[12]Could there be a greater insult offered to the rights of man than the beds of justice in France, when an infant was made the organ of the detestable Dubois! [MW]. A *lit de justice* is a merely ceremonial session held by the king and parliament. When Louis XV became king at age 5, the regent's advisor Guillaume Cardinal Dubois (1656–1723) wielded considerable power.

[13]Jesus warns of false prophets, "Ye shall know them by their fruits. Do men gather grapes of thorns, or figs of thistles?" (Matthew 7:16); "For every tree is known by his own fruit. For of thorns men do not gather figs, nor of a bramble bush gather they grapes" (Luke 6:44).

discharge the duties of a king, entrusted with uncontrouled power; how then must they be violated when his very elevation is an insuperable bar to the attainment of either wisdom or virtue; when all the feelings of a man are stifled by flattery, and reflection shut out by pleasure! Surely it is madness to make the fate of thousands depend on the caprice of a weak fellow creature, whose very station sinks him *necessarily* below the meanest of his subjects! But one power should not be thrown down to exalt another—for all power inebriates weak man; and its abuse proves that the more equality there is established among men, the more virtue and happiness will reign in society. But this and any similar maxim deduced from simple reason, raises an outcry—the church or the state is in danger, if faith in the wisdom of antiquity is not implicit; and they who, roused by the sight of human calamity, dare to attack human authority, are reviled as despisers of God, and enemies of man. These are bitter calumnies, yet they reached one of the best of men,[14] whose ashes still preach peace, and whose memory demands a respectful pause, when subjects are discussed that lay so near his heart.—

After attacking the sacred majesty of Kings, I shall scarcely excite surprise by adding my firm persuasion that every profession, in which great subordination of rank constitutes its power, is highly injurious to morality.

A standing army, for instance, is incompatible with freedom; because subordination and rigour are the very sinews of military discipline; and despotism is necessary to give vigour to enterprizes that one will directs. A spirit inspired by romantic notions of honour, a kind of morality founded on the fashion of the age, can only be felt by a few officers, whilst the main body must be moved by command, like the waves of the sea; for the strong wind of authority pushes the crowd of subalterns forward, they scarcely know or care why, with headlong fury.

Besides, nothing can be so prejudicial to the morals of the inhabitants of country towns as the occasional residence of a set of idle superficial young men, whose only occupation is gallantry, and whose polished manners render vice more dangerous, by concealing its deformity under gay ornamental drapery. An air of fashion, which is but a badge of slavery, and proves that the soul has not a strong individual character, awes simple country people into an imitation of the

---

[14]Dr. Price [MW]. MW's friend, Unitarian minister and radical political philosopher Dr. Richard Price (1723–91) condemned the War with the American Colonies and supported the rights of man. His lecture to the Revolution Society, *Discourse on the Love of Our Country* (1789) was attacked by Burke in *Reflections on the Revolution in France* (1790) and defended by MW in *Vindication of the Rights of Men* (1790).

vices, when they cannot catch the slippery graces, of politeness. Every corps is a chain of despots, who, submitting and tyrannizing without exercising their reason, become dead weights of vice and folly on the community. A man of rank or fortune, sure of rising by interest, has nothing to do but to pursue some extravagant freak[15]; whilst the needy *gentleman*, who is to rise, as the phrase turns, by his merit, becomes a servile parasite or vile pander.

Sailors, the naval gentlemen, come under the same description, only their vices assume a different and a grosser cast. They are more positively indolent, when not discharging the ceremonials of their station; whilst the insignificant fluttering of soldiers may be termed active idleness. More confined to the society of men, the former acquire a fondness for humour and mischievous tricks; whilst the latter, mixing frequently with well-bred women, catch a sentimental cant.—But mind is equally out of the question, whether they indulge the horse-laugh, or polite simper.

May I be allowed to extend the comparison to a profession where more mind is certainly to be found; for the clergy have superior opportunities of improvement, though subordination almost equally cramps their faculties? The blind submission imposed at college to forms of belief serves as a novitiate to the curate, who must obsequiously respect the opinion of his rector or patron, if he mean to rise in his profession. Perhaps there cannot be a more forcible contrast than between the servile dependent gait of a poor curate and the courtly mien of a bishop. And the respect and contempt they inspire, render the discharge of their separate functions equally useless.

It is of great importance to observe that the character of every man is, in some degree, formed by his profession. A man of sense may only have a cast of countenance that wears off as you trace his individuality, whilst the weak, common man has scarcely ever any character,[16] but what belongs to the body; at least, all his opinions have been so steeped in the vat consecrated by authority, that the faint spirit which the grape of his own vine yields cannot be distinguished.

---

[15]Whim, caprice.

[16]In their Broadview Press edition of *Vindication*, Lorne Macdonald and Kathleen Scherf hear an ironic allusion to the opening lines of Alexander Pope's *Epistle II. To a Lady: Of the Characters of Women* (1735): "Nothing so true as what you once let fall, / 'Most women have no characters at all'" (1–2), addressed to his friend Martha Blount.

Society, therefore, as it becomes more enlightened, should be very careful not to establish bodies of men who must necessarily be made foolish or vicious by the very constitution of their profession.

In the infancy of society, when men were just emerging out of barbarism, chiefs and priests, touching the most powerful springs of savage conduct, hope and fear, must have had unbounded sway. An aristocracy, of course, is naturally the first form of government. But, clashing interests soon losing their equipoise, a monarchy and hierarchy break out of the confusion of ambitious struggles, and the foundation of both is secured by feudal tenures. This appears to be the origin of monarchical and priestly power, and the dawn of civilization. But such combustible materials cannot long be pent up; and, getting vent in foreign wars and intestine[17] insurrections, the people acquire some power in the tumult, which obliges their rulers to gloss over their oppression with a shew of right. Thus, as wars, agriculture, commerce, and literature, expand the mind, despots are compelled to make covert corruption hold fast the power which was formerly snatched by open force.[18] And this baneful lurking gangrene is most quickly spread by luxury and superstition, the sure dregs of ambition. The indolent puppet of a court first becomes a luxurious monster, or fastidious sensualist, and then makes the contagion which his unnatural state spread, the instrument of tyranny.

It is the pestiferous purple[19] which renders the progress of civilization a curse, and warps the understanding, till men of sensibility doubt whether the expansion of intellect produces a greater portion of happiness or misery. But the nature of the poison points out the antidote; and had Rousseau mounted one step higher in his investigation, or could his eye have pierced through the foggy atmosphere, which he almost disdained to breathe, his active mind would have darted forward to contemplate the perfection of man in the establishment of true civilization, instead of taking his ferocious flight back to the night of sensual ignorance.

[17]Internal to a country or people.

[18]Men of abilities scatter seeds that grow up and have a great influence on the forming opinion; and when once the public opinion preponderates, through the exertion of reason, the overthrow of arbitrary power is not very distant [MW].

[19]A term for royalty, from the purple togas of the Roman Emperors.

CHAPTER II

THE PREVAILING OPINION OF
A SEXUAL CHARACTER DISCUSSED

To account for, and excuse the tyranny of man, many ingenious arguments have been brought forward to prove, that the two sexes, in the acquirement of virtue, ought to aim at attaining a very different character: or, to speak explicitly, women are not allowed to have sufficient strength of mind to acquire what really deserves the name of virtue. Yet it should seem, allowing them to have souls, that there is but one way appointed by Providence to lead *mankind* to either virtue or happiness.

If then women are not a swarm of ephemeron[1] triflers, why should they be kept in ignorance under the specious name of innocence? Men complain, and with reason, of the follies and caprices of our sex, when they do not keenly satirize our headstrong passions and groveling vices.—Behold, I should answer, the natural effect of ignorance! The mind will ever be unstable that has only prejudices to rest on, and the current will run with destructive fury when there are no barriers to break its force. Women are told from their infancy, and taught by the example of their mothers, that a little knowledge of human weakness, justly termed cunning, softness of temper, *outward* obedience, and a scrupulous attention to a puerile kind of propriety, will obtain for them the protection of man; and should they be beautiful, every thing else is needless, for, at least, twenty years of their lives.

Thus Milton describes our first frail mother; though when he tells us that women are formed for softness and sweet attractive grace, I cannot comprehend his meaning, unless, in the true Mahometan strain, he meant to deprive us of souls, and insinuate that we were beings only designed by sweet attractive grace, and docile blind obedience, to gratify the senses of man when he can no longer soar on the wing of contemplation.[2]

How grossly do they insult us who thus advise us only to render ourselves gentle, domestic brutes! For instance, the winning softness so warmly, and frequently, recommended, that governs by obeying. What childish expressions, and how insignificant is the being—can it be an immortal one?—who will condescend to govern by such sinister methods! "Certainly," says Lord Bacon, "man is of kin to the beasts by his body; and if he be not of kin to God by his spirit, he is a base

---

[1]A winged insect that lives only for a day.

[2]Milton, *Paradise Lost*, 4: "For contemplation he and valour formed, / For softness she and sweet attractive grace" (4.297–98).

and ignoble creature!"[3] Men, indeed, appear to me to act in a very un-philosophical manner when they try to secure the good conduct of women by attempting to keep them always in a state of childhood. Rousseau was more consistent when he wished to stop the progress of reason in both sexes, for if men eat of the tree of knowledge, women will come in for a taste; but, from the imperfect cultivation which their understandings now receive, they only attain a knowledge of evil.[4]

Children, I grant, should be innocent; but when the epithet is applied to men, or women, it is but a civil term for weakness. For if it be allowed that women were destined by Providence to acquire human virtues, and by the exercise of their understandings, that stability of character which is the firmest ground to rest our future hopes upon, they must be permitted to turn to the fountain of light, and not forced to shape their course by the twinkling of a mere satellite. Milton, I grant, was of a very different opinion; for he only bends to the indefeasible right of beauty, though it would be difficult to render two passages which I now mean to contrast, consistent. But into similar inconsistencies are great men often led by their senses.

> "To whom thus Eve with *perfect beauty* adorn'd.
> My Author and Disposer, what thou bidst
> *Unargued* I obey; So God ordains;
> God is *thy law, thou mine*: to know no more
> Is Woman's *happiest* knowledge and her *praise*."[5]

These are exactly the arguments that I have used to children; but I have added, your reason is now gaining strength, and, till it arrives at some degree of maturity, you must look up to me for advice—then you ought to *think*, and only rely on God.

Yet in the following lines Milton seems to coincide with me; when he makes Adam thus expostulate with his Maker.

> "Hast thou not made me here thy substitute,
> And these inferior far beneath me set?
> Among *unequals* what society

[3]Francis Bacon, "Of Atheism," *Essays* (1606).

[4]See Genesis 2–3. MW inverts its sequence of events: "when the woman saw that the tree was good for food, and that it was pleasant to the eyes, and a tree to be desired to make one wise, she took of the fruit thereof, and did eat, and gave also unto her husband with her; and he did eat" (3:6).

[5]Speaking to Adam, *Paradise Lost*, 4.634–38; MW's emphases.

Can sort, what harmony or true delight?
Which must be mutual, in proportion due
Giv'n and receiv'd; but in *disparity*
The one intense, the other still remiss
Cannot well suit with either, but soon prove
Tedious alike: of *fellowship* I speak
Such as I seek, fit to participate
All rational delight—"[6]

In treating, therefore, of the manners of women, let us, disregarding sensual arguments, trace what we should endeavour to make them in order to co-operate, if the expression be not too bold, with the supreme Being.

By individual education, I mean, for the sense of the word is not precisely defined, such an attention to a child as will slowly sharpen the senses, form the temper, regulate the passions as they begin to ferment, and set the understanding to work before the body arrives at maturity; so that the man may only have to proceed, not to begin, the important task of learning to think and reason.

To prevent any misconstruction, I must add, that I do not believe that a private education can work the wonders which some sanguine[7] writers have attributed to it. Men and women must be educated, in a great degree, by the opinions and manners of the society they live in. In every age there has been a stream of popular opinion that has carried all before it, and given a family character, as it were, to the century. It may then fairly be inferred, that, till society be differently constituted, much cannot be expected from education. It is, however, sufficient for my present purpose to assert, that, whatever effect circumstances have on the abilities, every being may become virtuous by the exercise of its own reason; for if but one being was created with vicious inclinations, that is positively bad, what can save us from atheism? or if we worship a God, is not that God a devil?

Consequently, the most perfect education, in my opinion, is such an exercise of the understanding as is best calculated to strengthen the body and form the heart. Or, in other words, to enable the individual to attain such habits of virtue as will render it independent. In fact, it is a farce to call any being virtuous whose virtues do not result from the exercise of its own reason. This was Rousseau's opinion respecting

[6]*Paradise Lost*, 8.381–92; MW's emphases.
[7]Hopeful, optimistic.

men[8]: I extend it to women, and confidently assert that they have been drawn out of their sphere by false refinement, and not by an endeavour to acquire masculine qualities. Still the regal homage which they receive is so intoxicating, that till the manners of the times are changed, and formed on more reasonable principles, it may be impossible to convince them that the illegitimate power, which they obtain, by degrading themselves, is a curse, and that they must return to nature and equality, if they wish to secure the placid satisfaction that unsophisticated affections impart. But for this epoch we must wait—wait, perhaps, till kings and nobles, enlightened by reason, and, preferring the real dignity of man to childish state, throw off their gaudy hereditary trappings: and if then women do not resign the arbitrary power of beauty—they will prove that they have *less* mind than man.

I may be accused of arrogance; still I must declare what I firmly believe, that all the writers who have written on the subject of female education and manners from Rousseau to Dr. Gregory,[9] have contributed to render women more artificial, weak characters, than they would otherwise have been; and, consequently, more useless members of society. I might have expressed this conviction in a lower key; but I am afraid it would have been the whine of affectation, and not the faithful expression of my feelings, of the clear result, which experience and reflection have led me to draw. When I come to that division of the subject, I shall advert to the passages that I more particularly disapprove of, in the works of the authors I have just alluded to; but it is first necessary to observe, that my objection extends to the whole purport of those books, which tend, in my opinion, to degrade one half of the human species, and render women pleasing at the expense of every solid virtue.

Though, to reason on Rousseau's ground, if man did attain a degree of perfection of mind when his body arrived at maturity, it might be proper, in order to make a man and his wife *one*, that she should rely entirely on his understanding; and the graceful ivy, clasping the oak that supported it, would form a whole in which strength and beauty would be equally conspicuous. But, alas! husbands, as well as their helpmates, are often only overgrown children; nay, thanks to early debauchery,

---

[8]"Only reason teaches us good from evil," *Emilius*, 1.1.76; and the confession of faith of the Savoyard curate, 2.4.16–154.

[9]*Emilius*, Book 5; Dr. John Gregory (1724–73), author of the influential conduct book, *A Father's Legacy to His Daughters* (1774); MW excerpted several passages in *The Female Reader*.

scarcely men in their outward form—and if the blind lead the blind, one need not come from heaven to tell us the consequence.[10]

Many are the causes that, in the present corrupt state of society, contribute to enslave women by cramping their understandings and sharpening their senses. One, perhaps, that silently does more mischief than all the rest, is their disregard of order.

To do every thing in an orderly manner, is a most important precept, which women, who, generally speaking, receive only a disorderly kind of education, seldom attend to with that degree of exactness that men, who from their infancy are broken into method, observe. This negligent kind of guess-work, for what other epithet can be used to point out the random exertions of a sort of instinctive common sense, never brought to the test of reason? prevents their generalizing matters of fact—so they do to-day, what they did yesterday, merely because they did it yesterday.

This contempt of the understanding in early life has more baneful consequences than is commonly supposed; for the little knowledge which women of strong minds attain, is, from various circumstances, of a more desultory kind than the knowledge of men, and it is acquired more by sheer observations on real life, than from comparing what has been individually observed with the results of experience generalized by speculation. Led by their dependent situation and domestic employments more into society, what they learn is rather by snatches; and as learning is with them, in general, only a secondary thing, they do not pursue any one branch with that persevering ardour necessary to give vigour to the faculties, and clearness to the judgment. In the present state of society, a little learning is required to support the character of a gentleman; and boys are obliged to submit to a few years of discipline. But in the education of women, the cultivation of the understanding is always subordinate to the acquirement of some corporeal accomplishment; even while enervated by confinement and false notions of modesty, the body is prevented from attaining that grace and beauty which relaxed half-formed limbs never exhibit. Besides, in youth their faculties are not brought forward by emulation; and having no serious scientific study, if they have natural sagacity it is turned too soon on life and manners. They dwell on effects and modifications, without tracing them back to causes; and complicated rules to adjust behaviour are a weak substitute for simple principles.

---

[10]Jesus, the emissary from heaven, cautions, "if the blind lead the blind, both shall fall into the ditch" (Matthew 15:14).

As a proof that education gives this appearance of weakness to females, we may instance the example of military men, who are, like them, sent into the world before their minds have been stored with knowledge or fortified by principles. The consequences are similar; soldiers acquire a little superficial knowledge, snatched from the muddy current of conversation, and, from continually mixing with society, they gain, what is termed a knowledge of the world; and this acquaintance with manners and customs has frequently been confounded with a knowledge of the human heart. But can the crude fruit of casual observation, never brought to the test of judgment, formed by comparing speculation and experience, deserve such a distinction? Soldiers, as well as women, practise the minor virtues with punctilious politeness. Where is then the sexual difference, when the education has been the same? All the difference that I can discern, arises from the superior advantage of liberty, which enables the former to see more of life.

It is wandering from my present subject, perhaps, to make a political remark; but as it was produced naturally by the train of my reflections, I shall not pass it silently over.

Standing armies can never consist of resolute, robust men; they may be well disciplined machines, but they will seldom contain men under the influence of strong passions, or with very vigorous faculties. And as for any depth of understanding, I will venture to affirm, that it is as rarely to be found in the army as amongst women; and the cause, I maintain, is the same. It may be further observed, that officers are also particularly attentive to their persons, fond of dancing, crowded rooms, adventures, and ridicule.[11] Like the *fair* sex, the business of their lives is gallantry.—They were taught to please, and they only live to please. Yet they do not lose their rank in the distinction of sexes, for they are still reckoned superior to women, though in what their superiority consists, beyond what I have just mentioned, it is difficult to discover.

The great misfortune is this, that they both acquire manners before morals, and a knowledge of life before they have, from reflection, any acquaintance with the grand ideal outline of human nature. The consequence is natural; satisfied with common nature, they become a prey to prejudices, and taking all their opinions on credit, they blindly submit to authority. So that if they have any sense, it is a

[11]Why should women be censured with petulant acrimony, because they seem to have a passion for a scarlet coat? Has not an education placed them more on a level with soldiers than any other class of men? [MW]. See the opening of Jonathan Swift's satire, "The Furniture of a Woman's Mind" (1727), a mockery of the vulgar, studied manners of young women.

kind of instinctive glance, that catches proportions, and decides with respect to manners; but fails when arguments are to be pursued below the surface, or opinions analyzed.

May not the same remark be applied to women? Nay, the argument may be carried still further, for they are both thrown out of a useful station by the unnatural distinctions established in civilized life. Riches and hereditary honours have made cyphers of women to give consequence to the numerical figure; and idleness has produced a mixture of gallantry and despotism into society, which leads the very men who are the slaves of their mistresses to tyrannize over their sisters, wives, and daughters. This is only keeping them in rank and file, it is true. Strengthen the female mind by enlarging it, and there will be an end to blind obedience; but, as blind obedience is ever sought for by power, tyrants and sensualists are in the right when they endeavour to keep women in the dark, because the former only want slaves, and the latter a play-thing. The sensualist, indeed, has been the most dangerous of tyrants, and women have been duped by their lovers, as princes by their ministers, whilst dreaming that they reigned over them.

I now principally allude to Rousseau, for his character of Sophia is, undoubtedly, a captivating one, though it appears to me grossly unnatural[12]; however it is not the superstructure, but the foundation of her character, the principles on which her education was built, that I mean to attack; nay, warmly as I admire the genius of that able writer, whose opinions I shall often have occasion to cite, indignation always takes place of admiration, and the rigid frown of insulted virtue effaces the smile of complacency, which his eloquent periods are wont to raise, when I read his voluptuous reveries. Is this the man, who, in his ardour for virtue, would banish all the soft arts of peace, and almost carry us back to Spartan discipline? Is this the man who delights to paint the useful struggles of passion, the triumphs of good dispositions, and the heroic flights which carry the glowing soul out of itself?—How are these mighty sentiments lowered when he describes the pretty foot and enticing airs of his little favourite! But, for the present, I wave[13] the subject, and, instead of severely reprehending the transient effusions of overweening sensibility, I shall only observe, that whoever has cast a benevolent eye on society, must often have been gratified by the sight of humble mutual love, not dignified by sentiment, or strengthened by a

---

[12]In *Émile*, Book 5, Sophia is the ideal soft, obedient woman, who is raised to become the companion for the hero. Her name is the Greek word for "wisdom."

[13]A common spelling for "waive."

union in intellectual pursuits. The domestic trifles of the day have afforded matters for cheerful converse, and innocent caresses have softened toils which did not require great exercise of mind or stretch of thought: yet, has not the sight of this moderate felicity excited more tenderness than respect? An emotion similar to what we feel when children are playing, or animals sporting,[14] whilst the contemplation of the noble struggles of suffering merit has raised admiration, and carried our thoughts to that world where sensation will give place to reason.

Women are, therefore, to be considered either as moral beings, or so weak that they must be entirely subjected to the superior faculties of men.

Let us examine this question. Rousseau declares that a woman should never, for a moment, feel herself independent, that she should be governed by fear to exercise her *natural* cunning, and made a coquetish slave in order to render her a more alluring object of desire, a *sweeter* companion to man, whenever he chooses to relax himself. He carries the arguments, which he pretends to draw from the indications of nature, still further, and insinuates that truth and fortitude, the corner stones of all human virtue, should be cultivated with certain restrictions, because, with respect to the female character, obedience is the grand lesson which ought to be impressed with unrelenting rigour.[15]

What nonsense! When will a great man arise with sufficient strength of mind to puff away the fumes which pride and sensuality have thus spread over the subject! If women are by nature inferior to men, their virtues must be the same in quality, if not in degree, or virtue is a relative idea; consequently their conduct should be founded on the same principles, and have the same aim.

Connected with man as daughters, wives, and mothers, their moral character may be estimated by their manner of fulfilling those simple duties; but the end, the grand end of their exertions should be to unfold their own faculties and acquire the dignity of conscious

[14]Similar feelings has Milton's pleasing picture of paradisiacal happiness ever raised in my mind; yet, instead of envying the lovely pair, I have, with conscious dignity, or satanic pride, turned to hell for sublimer objects. In the same style, when viewing some noble monument of human art, I have traced the emanation of the Deity in the order I admired, till, descending from that giddy height, I have caught myself contemplating the grandest of all human sights;—for fancy quickly placed, in some solitary recess, an outcast of fortune, rising superior to passion and discontent [MW]. Like many of her contemporaries, MW found Satan far more compelling.

[15]"What is most wanted in a woman is gentleness; formed to obey a creature so imperfect as man, a creature often vicious and always faulty, she should early learn to submit to injustice and to suffer the wrongs inflicted on her by her husband without complaint" (*Emilius*, 4.5.31–33).

virtue. They may try to render their road pleasant; but ought never to forget, in common with man, that life yields not the felicity which can satisfy an immortal soul. I do not mean to insinuate, that either sex should be so lost in abstract reflections or distant views, as to forget the affections and duties that lie before them, and are, in truth, the means appointed to produce the fruit of life; on the contrary, I would warmly recommend them, even while I assert, that they afford most satisfaction when they are considered in their true, sober light.

Probably the prevailing opinion, that woman was created for man, may have taken its rise from Moses's poetical story[16]; yet as very few, it is presumed, who have bestowed any serious thought on the subject, ever supposed that Eve was, literally speaking, one of Adam's ribs, the deduction must be allowed to fall to the ground; or, only be so far admitted as it proves that man, from the remotest antiquity, found it convenient to exert his strength to subjugate his companion, and his invention to shew that she ought to have her neck bent under the yoke, because the whole creation was only created for his convenience or pleasure.

Let it not be concluded that I wish to invert the order of things; I have already granted, that, from the constitution of their bodies, men seem to be designed by Providence to attain a greater degree of virtue. I speak collectively of the whole sex; but I see not the shadow of a reason to conclude that their virtues should differ in respect to their nature. In fact, how can they, if virtue has only one eternal standard? I must therefore, if I reason consequentially, as strenuously maintain that they have the same simple direction, as that there is a God.

It follows then that cunning should not be opposed to wisdom, little cares to great exertions, or insipid softness, varnished over with the name of gentleness, to that fortitude which grand views alone can inspire.

I shall be told that woman would then lose many of her peculiar graces, and the opinion of a well known poet might be quoted to refute my unqualified assertion. For Pope has said, in the name of the whole male sex,

> "Yet ne'er so sure our passion to create,
> As when she touch'd the brink of all we hate."[17]

In what light this sally places men and women, I shall leave to the judicious to determine; meanwhile I shall content myself with observ-

---

[16]Genesis 2:18–23; Moses was thought to be its author.
[17]*Of the Characters of Women*, 51–52.

ing, that I cannot discover why, unless they are mortal, females should always be degraded by being made subservient to love or lust.

To speak disrespectfully of love is, I know, high treason against sentiment and fine feelings; but I wish to speak the simple language of truth, and rather to address the head than the heart. To endeavour to reason love out of the world, would be to out Quixote Cervantes,[18] and equally offend against common sense; but an endeavour to restrain this tumultuous passion, and to prove that it should not be allowed to dethrone superior powers, or to usurp the sceptre which the understanding should very coolly wield, appears less wild.

Youth is the season for love in both sexes; but in those days of thoughtless enjoyment provision should be made for the more important years of life, when reflection takes place of sensation. But Rousseau, and most of the male writers who have followed his steps, have warmly inculcated that the whole tendency of female education ought to be directed to one point:—to render them pleasing.[19]

Let me reason with the supporters of this opinion who have any knowledge of human nature, do they imagine that marriage can eradicate the habitude of life? The woman who has only been taught to please will soon find that her charms are oblique sunbeams, and that they cannot have much effect on her husband's heart when they are seen every day, when the summer is passed and gone. Will she then have sufficient native energy to look into herself for comfort, and cultivate her dormant faculties? or, is it not more rational to expect that she will try to please other men; and, in the emotions raised by the expectation of new conquests, endeavour to forget the mortification her love or pride has received? When the husband ceases to be a lover— and the time will inevitably come, her desire of pleasing will then grow languid, or become a spring of bitterness; and love, perhaps, the most evanescent of all passions, gives place to jealousy or vanity.

I now speak of women who are restrained by principle or prejudice; such women, though they would shrink from an intrigue with real abhorrence, yet, nevertheless, wish to be convinced by the homage of gallantry that they are cruelly neglected by their husbands; or, days and weeks are spent in dreaming of the happiness enjoyed by congenial souls till their health is undermined and their spirits broken by discontent. How then can the great art of pleasing be such a neces-

---

[18]In *Don Quixote de la Mancha* (1605), Cervantes mocked the rhetoric and rituals of courtly love; Quixote attempts to rid the world of evil.

[19]*Emilius*, 4.5.19–20.

sary study? it is only useful to a mistress; the chaste wife, and serious mother, should only consider her power to please as the polish of her virtues, and the affection of her husband as one of the comforts that render her task less difficult and her life happier.—But, whether she be loved or neglected, her first wish should be to make herself respectable, and not to rely for all her happiness on a being subject to like infirmities with herself.

The worthy Dr. Gregory fell into a similar error. I respect his heart; but entirely disapprove of his celebrated Legacy to his Daughters.

He advises them to cultivate a fondness for dress, because a fondness for dress, he asserts, is natural to them.[20] I am unable to comprehend what either he or Rousseau mean, when they frequently use this indefinite term. If they told us that in a pre-existent state the soul was fond of dress, and brought this inclination with it into a new body, I should listen to them with a half smile, as I often do when I hear a rant about innate elegance.—But if he only meant to say that the exercise of the faculties will produce this fondness—I deny it. It is not natural; but arises, like false ambition in men, from a love of power.

Dr. Gregory goes much further; he actually recommends dissimulation, and advises an innocent girl to give the lie to her feelings, and not dance with spirit, when gaiety of heart would make her feet eloquent without making her gestures immodest. In the name of truth and common sense, why should not one woman acknowledge that she can take more exercise than another? or, in other words, that she has a sound constitution; and why, to damp innocent vivacity, is she darkly to be told that men will draw conclusions which she little thinks of?[21]—Let the libertine draw what inference he pleases; but, I hope, that no sensible mother will restrain the natural frankness of youth by instilling such indecent cautions. Out of the abundance of the heart the mouth speaketh[22]; and a wiser than Solomon hath said, that the heart should be made clean,[23] and not trivial ceremonies ob-

---

[20] *A Father's Legacy:* "The love of dress is natural to you, and therefore it is proper and reasonable" (55).

[21] *A Father's Legacy:* "I would have you to dance with spirit; but never allow yourselves to be so far transported with mirth, as to forget the delicacy of your sex.—Many a girl dancing in the gaiety and innocence of her heart, is thought to discover a spirit she little dreams of" (57–58).

[22] Jesus admonishes the Pharisees, "for out of the abundance of the heart the mouth speaketh" (Matthew 12:34); see also Luke 6:45.

[23] Jesus distinguishes between purifying the inner self and observing religious customs (Mark 7:18–23; Matthew 23:25–28). See also Luke 11:31–41. The epithet "wiser far / Than Solomon" is given by Milton to Jesus (*Paradise Regained*, 2.205–6).

served, which it is not very difficult to fulfil with scrupulous exactness when vice reigns in the heart.

Women ought to endeavour to purify their heart; but can they do so when their uncultivated understandings make them entirely dependent on their senses for employment and amusement, when no noble pursuit sets them above the little vanities of the day, or enables them to curb the wild emotions that agitate a reed over which every passing breeze has power? To gain the affections of a virtuous man is affectation necessary? Nature has given woman a weaker frame than man; but, to ensure her husband's affections, must a wife, who by the exercise of her mind and body whilst she was discharging the duties of a daughter, wife, and mother, has allowed her constitution to retain its natural strength, and her nerves a healthy tone, is she, I say, to condescend to use art and feign a sickly delicacy in order to secure her husband's affection? Weakness may excite tenderness, and gratify the arrogant pride of man; but the lordly caresses of a protector will not gratify a noble mind that pants for, and deserves to be respected. Fondness is a poor substitute for friendship!

In a seraglio, I grant, that all these arts are necessary; the epicure[24] must have his palate tickled, or he will sink into apathy; but have women so little ambition as to be satisfied with such a condition? Can they supinely dream life away in the lap of pleasure, or the languor of weariness, rather than assert their claim to pursue reasonable pleasures and render themselves conspicuous by practising the virtues which dignify mankind? Surely she has not an immortal soul who can loiter life away merely employed to adorn her person, that she may amuse the languid hours, and soften the cares of a fellow-creature who is willing to be enlivened by her smiles and tricks, when the serious business of life is over.

Besides, the woman who strengthens her body and exercises her mind will, by managing her family and practising various virtues, become the friend, and not the humble dependent of her husband; and if she, by possessing such substantial qualities, merit his regard, she will not find it necessary to conceal her affection, nor to pretend to an unnatural coldness of constitution to excite her husband's passions. In fact, if we revert to history, we shall find that the women who have distinguished themselves have neither been the most beautiful nor the most gentle of their sex.

Nature, or, to speak with strict propriety, God, has made all things right; but man has sought him out many inventions to mar the work. I now allude to that part of Dr. Gregory's treatise, where he ad-

[24]Gourmand.

vises a wife never to let her husband know the extent of her sensibility or affection.[25] Voluptuous precaution, and as ineffectual as absurd.—Love, from its very nature, must be transitory. To seek for a secret that would render it constant, would be as wild a search as for the philosopher's stone,[26] or the grand panacea: and the discovery would be equally useless, or rather pernicious, to mankind. The most holy band of society is friendship. It has been well said, by a shrewd satirist,[27] "that rare as true love is, true friendship is still rarer."

This is an obvious truth, and the cause not lying deep, will not elude a slight glance of inquiry.

Love, the common passion, in which chance and sensation take place of choice and reason, is, in some degree, felt by the mass of mankind; for it is not necessary to speak, at present, of the emotions that rise above or sink below love. This passion, naturally increased by suspense and difficulties, draws the mind out of its accustomed state, and exalts the affections; but the security of marriage, allowing the fever of love to subside, a healthy temperature is thought insipid, only by those who have not sufficient intellect to substitute the calm tenderness of friendship, the confidence of respect, instead of blind admiration, and the sensual emotions of fondness.

This is, must be, the course of nature—friendship or indifference inevitably succeeds love.—And this constitution seems perfectly to harmonize with the system of government which prevails in the moral world. Passions are spurs to action, and open the mind; but they sink into mere appetites, become a personal and momentary gratification, when the object is gained, and the satisfied mind rests in enjoyment. The man who had some virtue whilst he was struggling for a crown, often becomes a voluptuous tyrant when it graces his brow; and, when the lover is not lost in the husband, the dotard, a prey to childish caprices, and fond jealousies, neglects the serious duties of life, and the caresses which should excite confidence in his children are lavished on the overgrown child, his wife.

In order to fulfil the duties of life, and to be able to pursue with vigour the various employments which form the moral character, a

---

[25] *A Father's Legacy:* "If you love him, let me advise you never to discover to him the full extent of your love, no, not although you marry him" (87–88).

[26] An obsession of medieval alchemy, fabled to change base metals into gold and to confer immortality.

[27] Translating La Rouchefoucauld, nobleman renowned for his epigrams. See *Réflexions ou sentences et maximes morales* (1678), No. 473: "Quelque rare que soit que la véritable amour, il l'est encore moins que la véritable amitié."

master and mistress of a family ought not to continue to love each other with passion. I mean to say, that they ought not to indulge those emotions which disturb the order of society, and engross the thoughts that should be otherwise employed. The mind that has never been engrossed by one object wants vigour—if it can long be so, it is weak.

A mistaken education, a narrow, uncultivated mind, and many sexual prejudices, tend to make women more constant than men; but, for the present, I shall not touch on this branch of the subject. I will go still further, and advance, without dreaming of a paradox, that an unhappy marriage is often very advantageous to a family, and that the neglected wife is, in general, the best mother. And this would almost always be the consequence if the female mind were more enlarged: for, it seems to be the common dispensation of Providence, that what we gain in present enjoyment should be deducted from the treasure of life, experience; and that when we are gathering the flowers of the day and revelling in pleasure, the solid fruit of toil and wisdom should not be caught at the same time. The way lies before us, we must turn to the right or left; and he who will pass life away in bounding from one pleasure to another, must not complain if he acquire neither wisdom nor respectability of character.

Supposing, for a moment, that the soul is not immortal, and that man was only created for the present scene,—I think we should have reason to complain that love, infantine fondness, ever grew insipid and palled upon the sense. Let us eat, drink, and love, for to-morrow we die,[28] would be, in fact, the language of reason, the morality of life; and who but a fool would part with a reality for a fleeting shadow? But, if awed by observing the improbable[29] powers of the mind, we disdain to confine our wishes or thoughts to such a comparatively mean field of action; that only appears grand and important, as it is connected with a boundless prospect and sublime hopes, what necessity is there for falsehood in conduct, and why must the sacred majesty of truth be violated to detain a deceitful good that saps the very foundation of virtue? Why must the female mind be tainted by coquetish arts to gratify the sensualist, and prevent love from subsiding into friendship, or compassionate tenderness, when there are not qualities on which friendship can be built? Let the honest heart show itself, and *reason* teach passion to submit to necessity; or, let the dig-

[28]Isaiah 22:13: "let us eat and drink; for to morrow we shall die," one site of the old "carpe diem" (seize the day) trope.

[29]1st edition: improvable.

nified pursuit of virtue and knowledge raise the mind above those emotions which rather imbitter than sweeten the cup of life, when they are not restrained within due bounds.

I do not mean to allude to the romantic passion, which is the concomitant of genius.—Who can clip its wing? But that grand passion not proportioned to the puny enjoyments of life, is only true to the sentiment, and feeds on itself. The passions which have been celebrated for their durability have always been unfortunate. They have acquired strength by absence and constitutional melancholy.—The fancy has hovered round a form of beauty dimly seen—but familiarity might have turned admiration into disgust; or, at least, into indifference, and allowed the imagination leisure to start fresh game. With perfect propriety, according to this view of things, does Rousseau make the mistress of his soul, Eloisa, love St. Preux, when life was fading before her; but this is no proof of the immortality of the passion.[30]

Of the same complexion is Dr. Gregory's advice respecting delicacy of sentiment, which he advises a woman not to acquire, if she have determined to marry.[31] This determination, however, perfectly consistent with his former advice, he calls *indelicate*, and earnestly persuades his daughters to conceal it, though it may govern their conduct:—as if it were indelicate to have the common appetites of human nature.

Noble morality! and consistent with the cautious prudence of a little soul that cannot extend its views beyond the present minute division of existence. If all the faculties of woman's mind are only to be cultivated as they respect her dependence on man; if, when a husband be obtained, she have arrived at her goal, and meanly proud rests satisfied with such a paltry crown, let her grovel contentedly, scarcely raised by her employments above the animal kingdom; but, if, struggling for the prize of her high calling, she look beyond the present scene, let her cultivate her understanding without stopping to consider what character the husband may have whom she is destined to marry. Let her only determine, without being too anxious about present happiness, to acquire the qualities that ennoble a rational being, and a rough inelegant husband may shock her taste without destroying her peace of mind. She will not model her soul to suit the frailties

---

[30]The heroine of *Julie, ou la Nouvelle Héloïse* (1761), a faithful wife to Wolmar, on her deathbed confesses her lifelong passion for her former tutor and lover, St. Preux.

[31]*A Father's Legacy*: "But if you find that marriage is absolutely essential to your happiness . . . shun . . . reading and conversation that warms the imagination, which engages and softens the heart, and raises the taste above the level of common life . . . [otherwise] you may be tired with insipidity and dullness; shocked with indelicacy, or mortified by indifference" (116–18).

of her companion, but to bear with them: his character may be a trial, but not an impediment to virtue.

If Dr. Gregory confined his remark to romantic expectations of constant love and congenial feelings, he should have recollected that experience will banish what advice can never make us cease to wish for, when the imagination is kept alive at the expense of reason.

I own it frequently happens that women who have fostered a romantic unnatural delicacy of feeling, waste their[32] lives in *imagining* how happy they should have been with a husband who could love them with a fervid increasing affection every day, and all day. But they might as well pine married as single—and would not be a jot more unhappy with a bad husband than longing for a good one. That a proper education; or, to speak with more precision, a well stored mind, would enable a woman to support a single life with dignity, I grant; but that she should avoid cultivating her taste, lest her husband should occasionally shock it, is quitting a substance for a shadow. To say the truth, I do not know of what use is an improved taste, if the individual be not rendered more independent of the casualties of life; if new sources of enjoyment, only dependent on the solitary operations of the mind, are not opened. People of taste, married or single, without distinction, will ever be disgusted by various things that touch not less observing minds. On this conclusion the argument must not be allowed to hinge; but in the whole sum of enjoyment is taste to be denominated a blessing?

The question is, whether it procures most pain or pleasure? The answer will decide the propriety of Dr. Gregory's advice, and shew how absurd and tyrannic it is thus to lay down a system of slavery; or to attempt to educate moral beings by any other rules than those deduced from pure reason, which apply to the whole species.

Gentleness of manners, forbearance and long-suffering, are such amiable Godlike qualities,[33] that in sublime poetic strains the Deity has been invested with them; and, perhaps, no representation of his goodness so strongly fastens on the human affections as those that represent him abundant in mercy and willing to pardon.[34] Gentleness, considered in this point of view, bears on its front all the charac-

---

[32]For example, the herd of Novelists [MW]. She is deriding popular fictional romances (similar to today's Harlequin romances).

[33]See St. Paul: "But the fruit of the Spirit is love, joy, peace, longsuffering, gentleness, goodness, faith" (Galatians 5:22), and "With all lowliness and meekness, with longsuffering, forbearing one another in love" (Ephesians 4:2).

[34]The Lord will "have mercy" on the repenting sinner, and he "will abundantly pardon" (Isaiah 55:7).

teristics of grandeur, combined with the winning graces of condescension; but what a different aspect it assumes when it is the submissive demeanour of dependence, the support of weakness that loves, because it wants protection; and is forbearing, because it must silently endure injuries; smiling under the lash at which it dare not snarl. Abject as this picture appears, it is the portrait of an accomplished woman, according to the received opinion of female excellence, separated by specious reasoners from human excellence. Or, they[35] kindly restore the rib, and make one moral being of a man and woman; not forgetting to give her all the "submissive charms."[36]

How women are to exist in that state where there is neither to be marrying nor giving in marriage,[37] we are not told. For though moralists have agreed that the tenor of life seems to prove that *man* is prepared by various circumstances for a future state, they constantly concur in advising *woman* only to provide for the present. Gentleness, docility, and a spaniel-like affection are, on this ground, consistently recommended as the cardinal virtues of the sex; and, disregarding the arbitrary economy of nature, one writer has declared that it is masculine for a woman to be melancholy. She was created to be the toy of man, his rattle, and it must jingle in his ears whenever, dismissing reason, he chooses to be amused.

To recommend gentleness, indeed, on a broad basis is strictly philosophical. A frail being should labour to be gentle. But when forbearance confounds right and wrong, it ceases to be a virtue; and, however convenient it may be found in a companion—that companion will ever be considered as an inferior, and only inspire a vapid tenderness, which easily degenerates into contempt. Still, if advice could really make a being gentle, whose natural disposition admitted not of such a fine polish, something towards the advancement of order would be attained; but if, as might quickly be demonstrated, only affectation be produced by this indiscriminate counsel, which throws a stumbling-block in the way of gradual improvement, and true me-

[35]Vide Rousseau and Swedenborg [MW]. Rousseau argued that because man and wife comprised one moral unit, a wife could not act with moral certainty by herself. Swedish scientist and mystic Emanuel Swedenborg (1688–1772) believed that in heaven, man and wife became one angel, of which the husband was the mind and the wife the desire or will.

[36]Adam "in delight / Both of her beauty and submissive charms / Smiled with superior love" (*Paradise Lost*, 4.497–99).

[37]Asked about the heavenly life of a woman who has remarried, Jesus replies that "in the resurrection they neither marry, nor are given in marriage, but are as the angels of God in heaven" (Matthew 23:20, Mark 12:25, and Luke 20:35).

lioration of temper, the sex is not much benefited by sacrificing solid virtues to the attainment of superficial graces, though for a few years they may procure the individuals regal sway.

As a philosopher, I read with indignation the plausible epithets which men use to soften their insults; and, as a moralist, I ask what is meant by such heterogeneous associations, as fair defects, amiable weaknesses, etc.?[38] If there be but one criterion of morals, but one architype for man, women appear to be suspended by destiny, according to the vulgar tale of Mahomet's coffin[39]; they have neither the unerring instinct of brutes, nor are allowed to fix the eye of reason on a perfect model. They were made to be loved, and must not aim at respect, lest they should be hunted out of society as masculine.

But to view the subject in another point of view. Do passive indolent women make the best wives? Confining our discussion to the present moment of existence, let us see how such weak creatures perform their part? Do the women who, by the attainment of a few superficial accomplishments, have strengthened the prevailing prejudice, merely contribute to the happiness of their husbands? Do they display their charms merely to amuse them? And have women, who have early imbibed notions of passive obedience, sufficient character to manage a family or educate children? So far from it, that, after surveying the history of woman, I cannot help agreeing with the severest satirist, considering the sex as the weakest as well as the most oppressed half of the species. What does history disclose but marks of inferiority, and how few women have emancipated themselves from the galling yoke of sovereign man?—So few, that the exceptions remind me of an ingenious conjecture respecting Newton: that he was probably a being of a superior order, accidentally caged in a human body.[40] Following the same train of thinking, I have been led to imagine that the few extraordinary women who have rushed in eccentrical directions out of the orbit prescribed to their sex, were *male* spirits,

---

[38]After the Fall, Adam complains of Eve as "This fair defect / Of nature" (*Paradise Lost*, 10.891–92), echoed by Pope in *Of the Characters of Women*: "Fine by defect, and delicately weak" (44).

[39]Mohammed's coffin was fabled to be magically suspended in the center of his tomb.

[40]Eminent physicist and mathematician Sir Isaac Newton (1642–1727). In *A Poem, sacred to the memory of Sir Isaac Newton* (1727), James Thomson wondered, "can a soul / Of such extensive, deep, tremendous powers, / Enlarging still, be but a finer breath / Of spirits dancing thro' their tubes awhile, / And then for ever lost in vacant air?" (161–65). MW may also be recalling Pope's *Essay on Man* (1733–34): "Superior beings, when of late they saw / A mortal Man unfold all Nature's law, / Admir'd such wisdom in an earthly shape, / And shew'd a NEWTON as we shew an Ape" (2.31–34).

confined by mistake in female frames. But if it be not philosophical to think of sex when the soul is mentioned, the inferiority must depend on the organs; or the heavenly fire, which is to ferment the clay,[41] is not given in equal portions.

But avoiding, as I have hitherto done, any direct comparison of the two sexes collectively, or frankly acknowledging the inferiority of woman, according to the present appearance of things, I shall only insist that men have increased that inferiority till women are almost sunk below the standard of rational creatures. Let their faculties have room to unfold, and their virtues to gain strength, and then determine where the whole sex must stand in the intellectual scale. Yet let it be remembered, that for a small number of distinguished women I do not ask a place.

It is difficult for us purblind mortals to say to what height human discoveries and improvements may arrive when the gloom of despotism subsides, which makes us stumble at every step; but, when morality shall be settled on a more solid basis, then, without being gifted with a prophetic spirit, I will venture to predict that woman will be either the friend or slave of man. We shall not, as at present, doubt whether she is a moral agent, or the link which unites man with brutes. But, should it then appear, that like the brutes they were principally created for the use of man, he will let them patiently bite the bridle, and not mock them with empty praise; or, should their rationality be proved, he will not impede their improvement merely to gratify his sensual appetites. He will not, with all the graces of rhetoric, advise them to submit implicitly their understanding to the guidance of man. He will not, when he treats of the education of women, assert that they ought never to have the free use of reason, nor would he recommend cunning and dissimulation to beings who are acquiring, in like manner as himself, the virtues of humanity.

Surely there can be but one rule of right, if morality has an eternal foundation, and whoever sacrifices virtue, strictly so called, to present convenience, or whose *duty* it is to act in such a manner, lives only for the passing day, and cannot be an accountable creature.

The poet then should have dropped his sneer when he says,

> "If weak women go astray,
> The stars are more in fault than they."[42]

---

[41]A common term for flesh, or the body.

[42]Matthew Prior (1664–1721), "Hans Carvell," 11–12, the protest of an errant woman, inverting Cassius's remark in Shakespeare's *Julius Caesar*: "The fault, dear Brutus, lies not in the stars, / But in ourselves" (1.2.140–41).

For that they are bound by the adamantine chain of destiny is most certain, if it be proved that they are never to exercise their own reason, never to be independent, never to rise above opinion, or to feel the dignity of a rational will that only bows to God, and often forgets that the universe contains any being but itself and the model of perfection to which its ardent gaze is turned, to adore attributes that, softened into virtues, may be imitated in kind, though the degree overwhelms the enraptured mind.

If, I say, for I would not impress by declamation when Reason offers her sober light, if they be really capable of acting like rational creatures, let them not be treated like slaves; or, like the brutes who are dependent on the reason of man, when they associate with him; but cultivate their minds, give them the salutary, sublime curb of principle, and let them attain conscious dignity by feeling themselves only dependent on God. Teach them, in common with man, to submit to necessity, instead of giving, to render them more pleasing, a sex to morals.

Further, should experience prove that they cannot attain the same degree of strength of mind, perseverance, and fortitude, let their virtues be the same in kind, though they may vainly struggle for the same degree; and the superiority of man will be equally clear, if not clearer; and truth, as it is a simple principle, which admits of no modification, would be common to both. Nay, the order of society as it is at present regulated would not be inverted, for woman would then only have the rank that reason assigned her, and arts could not be practised to bring the balance even, much less to turn it.

These may be termed Utopian[43] dreams.—Thanks to that Being who impressed them on my soul, and gave me sufficient strength of mind to dare to exert my own reason, till, becoming dependent only on him for the support of my virtue, I view, with indignation, the mistaken notions that enslave my sex.

I love man as my fellow; but his scepter, real, or usurped, extends not to me, unless the reason of an individual demands my homage; and even then the submission is to reason, and not to man. In fact, the conduct of an accountable being must be regulated by the operations of its own reason; or on what foundation rests the throne of God?

It appears to me necessary to dwell on these obvious truths, because females have been insulated, as it were; and, while they have been stripped of the virtues that should clothe humanity, they have been decked with artificial graces that enable them to exercise a

---

[43]Impossible, from Sir Thomas More's 16th-c. social treatise, *Utopia*.

short-lived tyranny. Love, in their bosoms, taking place of every nobler passion, their sole ambition is to be fair, to raise emotion instead of inspiring respect; and this ignoble desire, like the servility in absolute monarchies, destroys all strength of character. Liberty is the mother of virtue, and if women be, by their very constitution, slaves, and not allowed to breathe the sharp invigorating air of freedom, they must ever languish like exotics, and be reckoned beautiful flaws in nature.

As to the argument respecting the subjection in which the sex has ever been held, it retorts on man. The many have always been enthralled by the few; and monsters, who scarcely have shewn any discernment of human excellence, have tyrannized over thousands of their fellow-creatures. Why have men of superior endowments submitted to such degradation? For, is it not universally acknowledged that kings, viewed collectively, have ever been inferior, in abilities and virtue, to the same number of men taken from the common mass of mankind—yet, have they not, and are they not still treated with a degree of reverence that is an insult to reason? China is not the only country where a living man has been made a God.[44] *Men* have submitted to superior strength to enjoy with impunity the pleasure of the moment—*women* have only done the same, and therefore till it is proved that the courtier, who servilely resigns the birthright of a man, is not a moral agent, it cannot be demonstrated that woman is essentially inferior to man because she has always been subjugated.

Brutal force has hitherto governed the world, and that the science of politics is in its infancy, is evident from philosophers scrupling to give the knowledge most useful to man that determinate distinction.

I shall not pursue this argument any further than to establish an obvious inference, that as sound politics diffuse liberty, mankind, including woman, will become more wise and virtuous.

---

[44]Chinese emperors were considered divine; Roman Emperor Nero also proclaimed his divinity.

CHAPTER III

THE SAME SUBJECT CONTINUED

Bodily strength from being the distinction of heroes is now sunk into such unmerited contempt that men, as well as women, seem to think it unnecessary: the latter, as it takes from their feminine graces, and from that lovely weakness the source of their undue power; and the former, because it appears inimical to the character of a gentleman.

That they have both by departing from one extreme run into another, may easily be proved; but first it may be proper to observe, that a vulgar error has obtained a degree of credit, which has given force to a false conclusion, in which an effect has been mistaken for a cause.

People of genius have, very frequently, impaired their constitutions by study or careless inattention to their health, and the violence of their passions bearing a proportion to the vigour of their intellects, the sword's destroying the scabbard has become almost proverbial,[1] and superficial observers have inferred from thence, that men of genius have commonly weak, or, to use a more fashionable phrase, delicate constitutions. Yet the contrary, I believe, will appear to be the fact; for, on diligent inquiry, I find that strength of mind has, in most cases, been accompanied by superior strength of body,—natural soundness of constitution,—not that robust tone of nerves and vigour of muscles, which arise from bodily labour, when the mind is quiescent, or only directs the hands.

Dr. Priestley has remarked, in the preface to his biographical chart,[2] that the majority of great men have lived beyond forty-five. And, considering the thoughtless manner in which they have lavished their strength, when investigating a favourite science they have wasted the lamp of life, forgetful of the midnight hour; or, when, lost in poetic dreams, fancy has peopled the scene, and the soul has been disturbed, till it shook the constitution, by the passions that meditation had raised; whose objects, the baseless fabric of a vision,[3] faded before the exhausted eye, they must have had iron frames. Shakespeare never grasped the airy dagger with a nerveless hand,[4] nor did Milton trem-

[1] See Rousseau, *Confessions*: "L'epeé use le fourreau, dit-on quelquefois" (2.5.86). [It is sometimes said that the sword wears out the scabbard. That is my history.]

[2] *A Description of a Chart of Biography* (1765), 25–26, by Joseph Priestley, dissenting theologian, prominent scientist who identified oxygen, and leading radical critic.

[3] An allusion to Prospero, "Like the baseless fabric of this vision" (Shakespeare, *The Tempest*, 4.1.151).

[4] Before embarking on the murder of King Duncan, Macbeth imagines that he sees a dagger (Shakespeare, *Macbeth*, 2.1.33–49). See also 3.4.62–63, Lady Macbeth to Macbeth: "This is the air-drawn dagger which, you said, led you to Duncan."

ble when he led Satan far from the confines of his dreary prison.[5]—
These were not the ravings of imbecility, the sickly effusions of distempered brains; but the exuberance of fancy, that "in a fine phrenzy"[6] wandering, was not continually reminded of its material shackles.

I am aware that this argument would carry me further than it may be supposed I wish to go; but I follow truth, and, still adhering to my first position, I will allow that bodily strength seems to give man a natural superiority over woman; and this is the only solid basis on which the superiority of the sex can be built. But I still insist, that not only the virtue, but the *knowledge* of the two sexes should be the same in nature, if not in degree, and that women, considered not only as moral, but rational creatures, ought to endeavour to acquire human virtues (or perfections) by the *same* means as men, instead of being educated like a fanciful kind of *half* being—one of Rousseau's wild chimeras.[7]

---

[5]In *Paradise Lost*, Book 2.

[6]Shakespeare, *A Midsummer Night's Dream*: "The poet's eye, in a fine frenzy rolling" (5.1.12).

[7]"Researches into abstract and speculative truths, the principles and axioms of sciences, in short, everything which tends to generalise our ideas, is not the proper province of women; their studies should be relative to points of practice; it belongs to them to apply those principles which men have discovered; and it is their part to make observations, which direct men to the establishment of general principles. All the ideas of women, which have not the immediate tendency to points of duty, should be directed to the study of men, and to the attainment of those agreeable accomplishments which have taste for their object; for as to works of genius, they are beyond their capacity; neither have they sufficient precision or power of attention to succeed in sciences which require accuracy; and as to physical knowledge, it belongs to those only who are most active, most inquisitive; who comprehend the greatest variety of objects: in short, it belongs to those who have the strongest powers, and who exercise them most, to judge of the relations between sensible beings and the laws of nature. A woman who is naturally weak, and does not carry her ideas to any great extent, knows how to judge and make a proper estimate of those movements which she sets to work, in order to aid her weakness; and these movements are the passions of men. The mechanism she employs is much more powerful than ours; for all her levers move the human heart. She must have the skill to incline us to do everything which her sex will not enable her to do herself, and which is necessary or agreeable to her; therefore she ought to study the mind of man thoroughly, not the mind of man in general, abstractedly, but the dispositions of those men to whom she is subject, either by the laws of her country or by the force of opinion. She should learn to penetrate into their real sentiments from their conversation, their actions, their looks, and gestures. She should also have the art, by her own conversation, actions, looks, and gestures, to communicate those sentiments which are agreeable to them, without seeming to intend it. Men will argue more philosophically about the human heart; but women will read the heart of man better than they. It belongs to women, if I may be allowed the expression, to form an experimental morality, and to reduce the study of man to a system. Women have most wit, men have most genius; women observe, men reason: from the concurrence of both we

But, if strength of body be, with some show of reason, the boast of men, why are women so infatuated as to be proud of a defect? Rousseau has furnished them with a plausible excuse, which could only have occurred to a man, whose imagination had been allowed to run wild, and refine on the impressions made by exquisite senses;—that they might, forsooth, have a pretext for yielding to a natural appetite without violating a romantic species of modesty, which gratifies the pride and libertinism of man.

Women, deluded by these sentiments, sometimes boast of their weakness, cunningly obtaining power by playing on the *weakness* of men; and they may well glory in their illicit sway, for, like Turkish bashaws,[8] they have more real power than their masters: but virtue is sacrificed to temporary gratifications, and the respectability of life to the triumph of an hour.

Women, as well as despots, have now, perhaps, more power than they would have if the world, divided and subdivided into kingdoms and families, were governed by laws deduced from the exercise of reason; but in obtaining it, to carry on the comparison, their character is degraded, and licentiousness spread through the whole aggregate of society. The many become pedestal to the few. I, therefore, will venture to assert, that till women are more rationally educated, the progress of human virtue and improvement in knowledge must receive continual checks. And if it be granted that woman was not created merely to gratify the appetite of man, or to be the upper servant, who provides his meals and takes care of his linen,[9] it must follow, that the first care of those mothers or fathers, who really attend to the education of females, should be, if not to strengthen the body, at least not to destroy the constitution by mistaken notions of beauty and female excellence; nor should girls ever be allowed to imbibe the pernicious notion that a defect can, by any chemical process of reasoning, become an excellence. In this respect, I am happy to find, that the author of one of the most instructive books, that our country has produced for

---

derive the clearest light and the most perfect knowledge, which the human mind is, of itself, capable of attaining. In one word, from hence we acquire the most intimate acquaintance, both with ourselves and others, of which our nature is capable; and it is thus that art has a constant tendency to perfect those endowments which nature has bestowed.—The world is the book of women." —Rousseau's *Emilius*. I hope my readers still remember the comparison, which I have brought forward, between women and officers [MW, quoting 4.5.74–75].

[8]Military officers or provincial governors, famed for imperiousness.

[9]Undergarments, shirts, bed linen, sheets.

children, coincides with me in opinion; I shall quote his pertinent remarks to give the force of his respectable authority to reason.[10]

But should it be proved that woman is naturally weaker than man, whence does it follow that it is natural for her to labour to become still weaker than nature intended her to be? Arguments of this cast are an insult to common sense, and savour of passion. The *divine right* of husbands, like the divine right of kings, may, it is to be hoped, in this enlightened age, be contested without danger, and, though conviction may not silence many boisterous disputants, yet, when any prevailing prejudice is attacked, the wise will consider, and leave the narrow-minded to rail with thoughtless vehemence at innovation.

The mother, who wishes to give true dignity of character to her daughter, must, regardless of the sneers of ignorance, proceed on a plan diametrically opposite to that which Rousseau has recommended with all the deluding charms of eloquence and philosophical sophistry: for his eloquence renders absurdities plausible, and his dogmatic conclusions puzzle, without convincing, those who have not ability to refute them.

Throughout the whole animal kingdom every young creature requires almost continual exercise, and the infancy of children, com-

[10]A respectable old man gives the following sensible account of the method he pursued when educating his daughter. "I endeavoured to give both to her mind and body a degree of vigour, which is seldom found in the female sex. As soon as she was sufficiently advanced in strength to be capable of the lighter labours of husbandry and gardening, I employed her as my constant companion. Selene, for that was her name, soon acquired a dexterity in all these rustic employments, which I considered with equal pleasure and admiration. If women are in general feeble both in body and mind, it arises less from nature than from education. We encourage a vicious indolence and inactivity, which we falsely call delicacy; instead of hardening their minds by the severer principles of reason and philosophy, we breed them to useless arts, which terminate in vanity and sensuality. In most of the countries which I had visited, they are taught nothing of an higher nature than a few modulations of the voice, or useless postures of the body; their time is consumed in sloth or trifles, and trifles become the only pursuits capable of interesting them. We seem to forget, that it is upon the qualities of the female sex that our own domestic comforts and the education of our children must depend. And what are the comforts or the education which a race of beings, corrupted from their infancy, and unacquainted with all the duties of life, are fitted to bestow? To touch a musical instrument with useless skills, to exhibit their natural or affected graces to the eyes of indolent and debauched young men, to dissipate their husband's patrimony in riotous and unnecessary expenses, these are the only arts cultivated by women in most of the polished nations I had seen. And the consequences are uniformly such as may be expected to proceed from such polluted sources, private misery and public servitude.

But Selene's education was regulated by different views, and conducted upon severer principles, if that can be called severity which opens the mind to a sense of moral and religious duties, and most effectually arms it against the inevitable evils of life." Mr. Day's *Sandford and Merton*, vol. III [MW quoting from "The Conclusion of the Story of Sophron and Tigranes," one of several didactic narratives].

formable to this intimation, should be passed in harmless gambols, that exercise the feet and hands, without requiring very minute direction from the head, or the constant attention of a nurse. In fact, the care necessary for self-preservation is the first natural exercise of the understanding, as little inventions to amuse the present moment unfold the imagination. But these wise designs of nature are counteracted by mistaken fondness or blind zeal. The child is not left a moment to its own direction, particularly a girl, and thus rendered dependent—dependence is called natural.

To preserve personal beauty, woman's glory! the limbs and faculties are cramped with worse than Chinese bands,[11] and the sedentary life which they are condemned to live, whilst boys frolic in the open air, weakens the muscles and relaxes the nerves.—As for Rousseau's remarks, which have since been echoed by several writers, that they have naturally, that is from their birth, independent of education, a fondness for dolls, dressing, and talking[12]—they are so puerile as not to merit a serious refutation. That a girl, condemned to sit for hours together listening to the idle chat of weak nurses, or to attend at her mother's toilet, will endeavour to join the conversation, is, indeed, very natural; and that she will imitate her mother or aunts, and amuse herself by adorning her lifeless doll, as they do in dressing her, poor innocent babe! is undoubtedly a most natural consequence. For men of the greatest abilities have seldom had sufficient strength to rise above the surrounding atmosphere; and, if the page of genius have always been blurred by the prejudices of the age, some allowance should be made for a sex, who, like kings, always see things through a false medium.

Pursuing these reflections, the fondness for dress, conspicuous in woman, may be easily accounted for, without supposing it the result of a desire to please the sex on which they are dependent. The absurdity, in short, of supposing that a girl is naturally a coquette, and that a desire connected with the impulse of nature to propagate the species, should appear even before an improper education has, by

[11]The practice of foot-binding in China began in the 10th c. and lasted until 1911, when it was banned by the government. Binding rendered their feet practically useless, making it extremely difficult for women to work or leave the home. Women with unbound feet were considered unsuitable for marriage. Originally a sign of wealthy status, foot-binding became common in families of all classes. MW may have read of the practice in John Locke's *Some Thoughts Concerning Education* (1693), Article 12.

[12]For these remarks, see ch. V (pp. 104–5).

heating the imagination, called it forth prematurely, is so unphilo-sophical, that such a sagacious observer as Rousseau would not have adopted it, if he had not been accustomed to make reason give way to his desire of singularity, and truth to a favourite paradox.[13]

Yet thus to give a sex to mind was not very consistent with the prin-ciples of a man who argued so warmly, and so well, for the immortality of the soul.[14]—But what a weak barrier is truth when it stands in the way of an hypothesis! Rousseau respected—almost adored virtue—and yet he allowed himself to love with sensual fondness.[15] His imagination constantly prepared inflammable fewel[16] for his inflammable senses; but, in order to reconcile his respect for self-denial, fortitude, and those heroic virtues, which a mind like his could not coolly admire, he labours to invert the law of nature, and broaches a doctrine pregnant with mis-chief and derogatory to the character of supreme wisdom.

His ridiculous stories, which tend to prove that girls are *naturally* attentive to their persons, without laying any stress on daily example, are below contempt.—And that a little miss should have such a cor-rect taste as to neglect the pleasing amusement of making O's, merely because she perceived that it was an ungraceful attitude, should be se-lected with the anecdotes of the learned pig.[17]

I have, probably, had an opportunity of observing more girls in their infancy than J. J. Rousseau[18]—I can recollect my own feelings, and I have looked steadily around me; yet, so far from coinciding with him in opinion respecting the first dawn of the female character,

[13]*Emilius*, 4.5.21.

[14]*Emilius*, 3.4.16–98.

[15]Although Rousseau eventually married his lifelong mistress, Thérèse Le Vasseur, in a self-designed civil ceremony, there were no signed legal documents.

[16]A common spelling for "fuel."

[17]"I once knew a young person who learned to write before she learned to read, and began to write with her needle before she could use a pen. At first, indeed she took it into her head to make no other letter than the O: this letter she was constantly making of all sizes, and always the wrong way. Unluckily, one day, as she was intent on this employment, she happened to see herself in the looking-glass; when, taking a dislike to the constrained attitude in which she sat while writing, she threw away her pen, like another Pallas, and determined against making the O any more. Her brother was also equally averse to writing: it was the confinement, however, and not the constrained at-titude, that most disgusted him." Rousseau's *Emilius* [MW, quoting from 4.5.29].

Sarah Trimmer refers to the "learned pig" in *Fabulous Histories*, Chapter 10 (1784); this pig is able to spell a word suggested by an audience by picking out letters, and uses its snout to tell time. James Boswell's *Life of Johnson* (1791) reports Anna Seward's seeing a learned swine at Nottingham (2.552).

[18]No idle boast: MW was the eldest sister in a family with three girls. She was also a governess and headmistress of a girls' school.

I will venture to affirm, that a girl, whose spirits have not been damped by inactivity, or innocence tainted by false shame, will always be a romp, and the doll will never excite attention unless confinement allows her no alternative. Girls and boys, in short, would play harmlessly together, if the distinction of sex was not inculcated long before nature makes any difference.—I will go further, and affirm, as an indisputable fact, that most of the women, in the circle of my observation, who have acted like rational creatures, or shewn any vigour of intellect, have accidentally been allowed to run wild—as some of the elegant formers of the fair sex would insinuate.

The baneful consequences which flow from inattention to health during infancy, and youth, extend further than is supposed—dependence of body naturally produces dependence of mind; and how can she be a good wife or mother, the greater part of whose time is employed to guard against or endure sickness? Nor can it be expected that a woman will resolutely endeavour to strengthen her constitution and abstain from enervating indulgencies, if artificial notions of beauty, and false descriptions of sensibility, have been early entangled with her motives of action. Most men are sometimes obliged to bear with bodily inconveniencies, and to endure, occasionally, the inclemency of the elements; but genteel women are, literally speaking, slaves to their bodies, and glory in their subjection.

I once knew a weak woman of fashion, who was more than commonly proud of her delicacy and sensibility. She thought a distinguishing taste and puny appetite the height of all human perfection, and acted accordingly.—I have seen this weak sophisticated being neglect all the duties of life, yet recline with self-complacency on a sofa, and boast of her want of appetite as a proof of delicacy that extended to, or, perhaps, arose from, her exquisite sensibility: for it is difficult to render intelligible such ridiculous jargon.—Yet, at the moment, I have seen her insult a worthy old gentlewoman, whom unexpected misfortunes had made dependent on her ostentatious bounty, and who, in better days, had claims on her gratitude. Is it possible that a human creature could have become such a weak and depraved being, if, like the Sybarites,[19] dissolved in luxury, every thing like virtue had not been worn away, or never impressed by precept, a poor substitute, it is true, for cultivation of mind, though it serves as a fence against vice?

[19]Natives of Sybaris, an ancient Greek colony in southern Italy, notorious for decadence.

Such a woman is not a more irrational monster than some of the Roman emperors, who were depraved by lawless power. Yet, since kings have been more under the restraint of law, and the curb, however weak, of honour, the records of history are not filled with such unnatural instances of folly and cruelty, nor does the despotism that kills virtue and genius in the bud, hover over Europe with that destructive blast which desolates Turkey,[20] and renders the men, as well as the soil, unfruitful.

Women are every where in this deplorable state; for, in order to preserve their innocence, as ignorance is courteously termed, truth is hidden from them, and they are made to assume an artificial character before their faculties have acquired any strength. Taught from their infancy that beauty is woman's sceptre, the mind shapes itself to the body, and roaming round its gilt cage, only seeks to adorn its prison. Men have various employments and pursuits which engage their attention, and give a character to the opening mind; but women, confined to one, and having their thoughts constantly directed to the most insignificant part of themselves, seldom extend their views beyond the triumph of the hour. But were their understanding once emancipated from the slavery to which the pride and sensuality of man and their short-sighted desire, like that of dominion in tyrants, of present sway, has subjected them, we should probably read of their weaknesses with surprise. I must be allowed to pursue the argument a little farther.

Perhaps, if the existence of an evil being were allowed, who, in the allegorical language of scripture, went about seeking whom he should devour,[21] he could not more effectually degrade the human character than by giving a man absolute power.

This argument branches into various ramifications.—Birth, riches, and every extrinsic advantage that exalt a man above his fellows, without any mental exertion, sink him in reality below them. In proportion to his weakness, he is played upon by designing men, till the bloated monster has lost all traces of humanity. And that tribes of men, like flocks of sheep, should quietly follow such a leader, is a solecism that only a desire of present enjoyment and narrowness of understanding can solve. Educated in slavish dependence, and enervated by luxury and sloth, where shall we find men who will stand forth to assert the rights of man;—or claim the privilege of moral beings, who should

---

[20]An allusion to the fierce, dry, dust-laden southern wind, and metaphorically to the notorious despotism of the Ottoman Empire.

[21]"Be sober, be vigilant; because your adversary the devil, as a roaring lion, walketh about, seeking whom he may devour" (1 Peter 5:8).

have but one road to excellence? Slavery to monarchs and ministers, which the world will be long in freeing itself from, and whose deadly grasp stops the progress of the human mind, is not yet abolished.

Let not men then in the pride of power, use the same arguments that tyrannic kings and venal ministers have used, and fallaciously assert that woman ought to be subjected because she has always been so.—But, when man, governed by reasonable laws, enjoys his natural freedom, let him despise woman, if she do not share it with him; and, till that glorious period arrives, in descanting on the folly of the sex, let him not overlook his own.

Women, it is true, obtaining power by unjust means, by practising or fostering vice, evidently lose the rank which reason would assign them, and they become either abject slaves or capricious tyrants. They lose all simplicity, all dignity of mind, in acquiring power, and act as men are observed to act when they have been exalted by the same means.

It is time to effect a revolution in female manners—time to restore to them their lost dignity—and make them, as a part of the human species, labour by reforming themselves to reform the world. It is time to separate unchangeable morals from local manners.—If men be demi-gods—why let us serve them! And if the dignity of the female soul be as disputable as that of animals—if their reason does not afford sufficient light to direct their conduct whilst unerring instinct is denied—they are surely of all creatures the most miserable! and, bent beneath the iron hand of destiny, must submit to be a *fair defect* in creation. But to justify the ways of Providence respecting them, by pointing out some irrefragable reason for thus making such a large portion of mankind accountable and not accountable, would puzzle the subtilest casuist.[22]

The only solid foundation for morality appears to be the character of the supreme Being; the harmony of which arises from a balance of attributes;—and, to speak with reverence, one attribute seems to imply the *necessity* of another. He must be just, because he is wise, he must be good, because he is omnipotent. For to exalt one attribute at the expense of another equally noble and necessary, bears the stamp of the warped reason of man—the homage of passion. Man, accustomed to bow down to power in his savage state, can seldom divest

---

[22]*Paradise Lost*, 10.891–92; cf. p. 53, n. 38. Milton's design in *Paradise Lost* is to "assert Eternal Providence, / And justify the ways of God to men" (1.25–26). A casuist is a subtle, slippery reasoner.

himself of this barbarous prejudice, even when civilization determines how much superior mental is to bodily strength; and his reason is clouded by these crude opinions, even when he thinks of the Deity.—His omnipotence is made to swallow up, or preside over his other attributes, and those morals are supposed to limit his power irreverently, who think that it must be regulated by his wisdom.

I disclaim that specious humility which, after investigating nature, stops at the author.—The High and Lofty one, who inhabiteth eternity, doubtless possesses many attributes of which we can form no conception; but reason tells me that they cannot clash with those I adore—and I am compelled to listen to her voice.

It seems natural for man to search for excellence, and either to trace it in the object that he worships, or blindly to invest it with perfection, as a garment. But what good effect can the latter mode of worship have on the moral conduct of a rational being? He bends to power; he adores a dark cloud, which may open a bright prospect to him, to burst in angry, lawless fury, on his devoted head—he knows not why. And, supposing that the Deity acts from the vague impulse of an undirected will, man must also follow his own, or act according to rules, deduced from principles which he disclaims as irreverent. Into this dilemma have both enthusiasts and cooler thinkers fallen, when they laboured to free men from the wholesome restraints which a just conception of the character of God imposes.

It is not impious thus to scan the attributes of the Almighty: in fact, who can avoid it that exercises his faculties? For to love God as the fountain of wisdom, goodness, and power, appears to be the only worship useful to a being who wishes to acquire either virtue or knowledge. A blind unsettled affection may, like human passions, occupy the mind and warm the heart, whilst, to do justice, love mercy, and walk humbly with our God, is forgotten.[23] I shall pursue this subject still further, when I consider religion in a light opposite to that recommended by Dr. Gregory, who treats it as a matter of sentiment or taste.[24]

To return from this apparent digression. It were to be wished that women would cherish an affection for their husbands, founded on the same principle that devotion ought to rest upon. No other firm base is there under heaven—for let them beware of the fallacious light of sentiment; too often used as a softer phrase for sensuality. It

---

[23]"What doth the Lord require of thee, but to do justly, and to love mercy, and to walk humbly with thy God?" (Micah 6:8).

[24]*A Father's Legacy*: "Religion is rather a matter of sentiment than reasoning" (13).

follows then, I think, that from their infancy women should either be shut up like Eastern princes, or educated in such a manner as to be able to think and act for themselves.

Why do men halt between two opinions, and expect impossibilities? Why do they expect virtue from a slave, from a being whom the constitution of civil society has rendered weak, if not vicious?

Still I know that it will require a considerable length of time to eradicate the firmly rooted prejudices which sensualists have planted; it will also require some time to convince women that they act contrary to their real interest on an enlarged scale, when they cherish or affect weakness under the name of delicacy, and to convince the world that the poisoned source of female vices and follies, if it be necessary, in compliance with custom, to use synonymous terms in a lax sense, has been the sensual homage paid to beauty:—to beauty of features; for it has been shrewdly observed by a German writer, that a pretty woman, as an object of desire, is generally allowed to be so by men of all descriptions; whilst a fine woman, who inspires more sublime emotions by displaying intellectual beauty, may be overlooked or observed with indifference, by those men who find their happiness in the gratification of their appetites. I foresee an obvious retort—whilst man remains such an imperfect being as he appears hitherto to have been, he will, more or less, be the slave of his appetites; and those women obtaining most power who gratify a predominant one, the sex is degraded by a physical, if not by a moral necessity.

This objection has, I grant, some force; but while such a sublime precept exists, as, "be pure as your heavenly Father is pure"[25]; it would seem that the virtues of man are not limited by the Being who alone could limit them; and that he may press forward without considering whether he steps out of his sphere by indulging such a noble ambition. To the wild billows it has been said, "thus far shalt thou go, and no further; and here shall thy proud waves be stayed."[26] Vainly then do they beat and foam, restrained by the power that confines the struggling planets in their orbits, matter yields to the great governing Spirit.—But an immortal soul, not restrained by mechanical laws and struggling to free itself from the shackles of matter, contributes to, instead of disturbing, the order of creation, when, co-operating with the

---

[25]Jesus preaches, "Be ye therefore perfect, even as your Father which is in heaven is perfect" (Matthew 5:48); also 1 John 3:3: "And every man that hath this hope in him purifieth himself, even as he is pure."

[26]The Lord speaking to Job out of the whirlwind: "Hitherto shalt thou come, but no further: and here shall thy proud waves be stayed?" (Job 38:11).

Father of spirits, it tries to govern itself by the invariable rule that, in a degree, before which our imagination faints, regulates the universe.

Besides, if women be educated for dependence; that is, to act according to the will of another fallible being, and submit, right or wrong, to power, where are we to stop? Are they to be considered as vicegerents allowed to reign over a small domain, and answerable for their conduct to a higher tribunal, liable to error?

It will not be difficult to prove that such delegates will act like men subjected by fear, and make their children and servants endure their tyrannical oppression. As they submit without reason, they will, having no fixed rules to square their conduct by, be kind, or cruel, just as the whim of the moment directs; and we ought not to wonder if sometimes, galled by their heavy yoke, they take a malignant pleasure in resting it on weaker shoulders.

But, supposing a woman, trained up to obedience, be married to a sensible man, who directs her judgment without making her feel the servility of her subjection, to act with as much propriety by this reflected light as can be expected when reason is taken at second hand, yet she cannot ensure the life of her protector; he may die and leave her with a large family.

A double duty devolves on her; to educate them in the character of both father and mother; to form their principles and secure their property. But, alas! she has never thought, much less acted for herself. She has only learned to please[27] men, to depend gracefully on them;

---

[27]"In the union of the sexes, both pursue one common object, but none in the same manner. From their diversity in this particular, arises the first determinate difference between the moral relations of each. The one should be active and strong, the other passive and weak: it is necessary the one should have both the power and the will, and that the other should make little resistance.

"This principle being established, it follows that woman is expressly formed to please the man: if the obligation be reciprocal also, and the man ought to please in his turn, it is not so immediately necessary: his great merit is in his power, and he pleases merely because he is strong. This, I must confess, is not one of the refined maxims of love; it is, however, one of the laws of nature, prior to love itself.

"If woman be formed to please and be subjected to man, it is her place, doubtless, to render herself agreeable to him, instead of challenging his passion. The violence of his desires depends on her charms; it is by means of these she should urge him to the exertion of those powers which nature hath given him. The most successful method of exciting them, is, to render such exertion necessary by resistance; as in that case, self-love is added to desire, and the one triumphs in the victory which the other obliged to acquire. Hence arise the various modes of attack and defence between the sexes; the boldness of one sex and the timidity of the other; and, in a word, that bashfulness and modesty with which nature hath armed the weak, in order to subdue the strong." Rousseau's *Emilius*. I shall make no other comment on this ingenious passage, than just to observe, that it is the philosophy of lasciviousness [MW; see *Emilius*, 4.5.3–4].

yet, encumbered with children, how is she to obtain another protector—a husband to supply the place of reason? A rational man, for we are not treading on romantic ground, though he may think her a pleasing docile creature, will not choose to marry a *family* for love, when the world contains many more pretty creatures. What is then to become of her? She either falls an easy prey to some mean fortune-hunter, who defrauds her children of their parental inheritance, and renders her miserable; or becomes the victim of discontent and blind indulgence. Unable to educate her sons, or impress them with respect; for it is not a play on words to assert, that people are never respected, though filling an important station, who are not respectable; she pines under the anguish of unavailing impotent regret. The serpent's tooth enters into her very soul, and the vices of licentious youth bring her with sorrow, if not with poverty also, to the grave.[28]

This is not an overcharged picture; on the contrary, it is a very possible case, and something similar must have fallen under every attentive eye.

I have, however, taken it for granted, that she was well-disposed, though experience shews, that the blind may as easily be led into a ditch as along the beaten road. But supposing, no very improbable conjecture, that a being only taught to please must still find her happiness in pleasing;—what an example of folly, not to say vice, will she be to her innocent daughters! The mother will be lost in the coquette, and, instead of making friends of her daughters, view them with eyes askance, for they are rivals—rivals more cruel than any other, because they invite a comparison, and drive her from the throne of beauty, who has never thought of a seat on the bench of reason.

It does not require a lively pencil, or the discriminating outline of a caricature, to sketch the domestic miseries and petty vices which such a mistress of a family diffuses. Still she only acts as a woman ought to act, brought up according to Rousseau's system. She can never be reproached for being masculine, or turning out of her sphere; nay, she may observe another of his grand rules, and, cautiously preserving her reputation free from spot, be reckoned a good kind of woman. Yet in what respect can she be termed good? She abstains, it is true, without any great struggle, from committing gross crimes; but how does she fulfil her duties? Duties!—in truth she has enough to think of to adorn her body and nurse a weak constitution.

---

[28]King Lear laments, "How sharper than a serpent's tooth it is / To have a thankless child!" (Shakespeare, *King Lear*, 1.4.297–98).

With respect to religion, she never presumed to judge for herself; but conformed, as a dependent creature should, to the ceremonies of the church which she was brought up in, piously believing that wiser heads than her own have settled that business:—and not to doubt is her point of perfection. She therefore pays her tythe of mint and cummin—and thanks her God that she is not as other women are.[29] These are the blessed effects of a good education! These the virtues of man's help mate![30]

I must relieve myself by drawing a different picture.

Let fancy now present a woman with a tolerable understanding, for I do not wish to leave the line of mediocrity, whose constitution, strengthened by exercise, has allowed her body to acquire its full vigour; her mind, at the same time, gradually expanding itself to comprehend the moral duties of life, and in what human virtue and dignity consist.

Formed thus by the discharge of the relative duties of her station, she marries from affection, without losing sight of prudence, and looking beyond matrimonial felicity, she secures her husband's respect before it is necessary to exert mean arts to please him and feed a dying flame, which nature doomed to expire when the object became familiar, when friendship and forbearance take place of a more ardent affection.—This is the natural death of love, and domestic peace is not destroyed by struggles to prevent its extinction. I also suppose the husband to be virtuous; or she is still more in want of independent principles.

Fate, however, breaks this tie.—She is left a widow, perhaps, without a sufficient provision; but she is not desolate! The pang of nature is felt; but after time has softened sorrow into melancholy resignation, her heart turns to her children with redoubled fondness, and anxious to provide for them, affection gives a sacred heroic cast to her maternal duties. She thinks that not only the eye

---

[29]Jesus warns, "Woe unto you, scribes and Pharisees, hypocrites! for ye pay tithe of mint and anise and cummin, and have omitted the weightier matters of the law, judgment, mercy, and faith" (Matthew 23:23) and "The Pharisee stood and prayed thus with himself, God, I thank thee, that I am not as other men are" (Luke 18:11). A tithe is one-tenth, the standard payment or tribute.

[30]"O how lovely," exclaims Rousseau, speaking of Sophia, "is her ignorance! Happy is he who is destined to instruct her! She will never pretend to be the tutor of her husband, but will be content to be his pupil. Far from attempting to subject him to her taste, she will accommodate herself to his. She will be more estimable to him, than if she was learned: he will have a pleasure in instructing her." Rousseau's *Emilius*. I shall content myself with simply asking, how friendship can subsist when love expires, between the master and his pupil [MW, from *Emilius*, 4.5.128].

sees her virtuous efforts from whom all her comfort now must flow, and whose approbation is life; but her imagination, a little abstracted and exalted by grief, dwells on the fond hope that the eyes which her trembling hand closed, may still see how she subdues every wayward passion to fulfil the double duty of being the father as well as the mother of her children. Raised to heroism by misfortunes, she represses the first faint dawning of a natural inclination, before it ripens into love, and in the bloom of life forgets her sex—forgets the pleasure of an awakening passion, which might again have been inspired and returned. She no longer thinks of pleasing, and conscious dignity prevents her from priding herself on account of the praise which her conduct demands. Her children have her love, and her brightest hopes are beyond the grave, where her imagination often strays.

I think I see her surrounded by her children, reaping the reward of her care. The intelligent eye meets hers, whilst health and innocence smile on their chubby cheeks, and as they grow up the cares of life are lessened by their grateful attention. She lives to see the virtues which she endeavoured to plant on principles, fixed into habits, to see her children attain a strength of character sufficient to enable them to endure adversity without forgetting their mother's example.

The task of life thus fulfilled, she calmly waits for the sleep of death, and rising from the grave, may say—"Behold, thou gavest me a talent—and here are five talents."[31]

I wish to sum up what I have said in a few words, for I here throw down my gauntlet, and deny the existence of sexual virtues, not excepting modesty. For man and woman, truth, if I understand the meaning of the word, must be the same; yet the fanciful female character, so prettily drawn by poets and novelists, demanding the sacrifice of truth and sincerity, virtue becomes a relative idea, having no other foundation than utility, and of that utility men pretend arbitrarily to judge, shaping it to their own convenience.

Women, I allow, may have different duties to fulfil; but they are *human* duties, and the principles that should regulate the discharge of them, I sturdily maintain, must be the same.

---

[31]In Jesus's parable of the talents (Matthew 25:14–30), a master distributes talents (a coin) among his servants, according to skill. The servant who has received the greatest sum invests and doubles the value of his share; while he who receives only one talent buries it. When the master returns, he praises the former for industry and faithfulness, and scolds the latter for wickedness and sloth. This parable is supposed to demonstrate the proper use of God's gifts.

To become respectable, the exercise of their understanding is necessary, there is no other foundation for independence of character; I mean explicitly to say that they must only bow to the authority, of reason, instead of being the *modest* slaves of opinion.

In the superior ranks of life how seldom do we meet with a man of superior abilities, or even common acquirements? The reason appears to me clear, the state they are born in was an unnatural one. The human character has ever been formed by the employments the individual, or class, pursues; and if the faculties are not sharpened by necessity, they must remain obtuse. The argument may fairly be extended to women; for, seldom occupied by serious business, the pursuit of pleasure gives that insignificancy to their character which renders the society of the *great* so insipid. The same want of firmness, produced by a similar cause, forces them both to fly from themselves to noisy pleasures, and artificial passions, till vanity takes place of every social affection, and the characteristics of humanity can scarcely be discerned. Such are the blessings of civil governments, as they are at present organized, that wealth and female softness equally tend to debase mankind, and are produced by the same cause; but allowing women to be rational creatures, they should be incited to acquire virtues which they may call their own, for how can a rational being be ennobled by any thing that is not obtained by its *own* exertions?

CHAPTER IV

OBSERVATIONS ON THE STATE OF DEGRADATION TO WHICH WOMAN IS REDUCED BY VARIOUS CAUSES

That woman is naturally weak, or degraded by a concurrence of circumstances, is, I think, clear. But this position I shall simply contrast with a conclusion, which I have frequently heard fall from sensible men in favour of an aristocracy: that the mass of mankind cannot be any thing, or the obsequious slaves, who patiently allow themselves to be driven forward, would feel their own consequence, and spurn their chains. Men, they further observe, submit every where to oppression, when they have only to lift up their heads to throw off the yoke; yet, instead of asserting their birthright, they quietly lick the dust, and say, let us eat and drink, for to-morrow we die. Women, I argue from analogy, are degraded by the same propensity to enjoy the present moment; and, at last, despise the freedom which they have not sufficient virtue to struggle to attain. But I must be more explicit.

With respect to the culture of the heart, it is unanimously allowed that sex is out of the question; but the line of subordination in the mental powers is never to be passed over.[1] Only "absolute in loveliness,"[2] the portion of rationality granted to woman, is, indeed, very scanty; for, denying her genius and judgment, it is scarcely possible to divine what remains to characterize intellect.

The stamen[3] of immortality, if I may be allowed the phrase, is the perfectibility of human reason; for, were men created perfect, or did a flood of knowledge break in upon him, when he arrived at maturity, that precluded error, I should doubt whether his existence would be continued after the dissolution of the body. But, in the present state of things, every difficulty in morals that escapes from human discussion, and equally baffles the investigation of profound thinking, and the lightning glance of genius, is an argument on which I build my belief

[1] Into what inconsistencies do men fall when they argue without the compass of principles. Women, weak women, are compared with angels; yet, a superior order of beings should be supposed to possess more intellect than man; or, in what does their superiority consist? In the same strain, to drop the sneer, they are allowed to possess more goodness of heart, piety, and benevolence.—I doubt the fact, though it be courteously brought forward, unless ignorance be allowed to be the mother of devotion; for I am firmly persuaded that, on an average, the proportion between virtue and knowledge, is more upon a par than is commonly granted [MW].

[2] Adam describing Eve to the angel Raphael: "So absolute she seems / And in herself complete" (*Paradise Lost*, 8.547–48).

[3] Fundamental element.

of the immortality of the soul. Reason is, consequentially, the simple power of improvement; or, more properly speaking, of discerning truth. Every individual is in this respect a world in itself. More or less may be conspicuous in one being than another; but the nature of reason must be the same in all, if it be an emanation of divinity, the tie that connects the creature with the Creator; for, can that soul be stamped with the heavenly image, that is not perfected by the exercise of its own reason?[4] Yet outwardly ornamented with elaborate care, and so adorned to delight man, "that with honour he may love,"[5] the soul of woman is not allowed to have this distinction, and man, ever placed between her and reason, she is always represented as only created to see through a gross medium, and to take things on trust. But dismissing these fanciful theories, and considering woman as a whole, let it be what it will, instead of a part of man, the inquiry is whether she have reason or not. If she have, which, for a moment, I will take for granted, she was not created merely to be the solace of man, and the sexual should not destroy the human character.

Into this error men have, probably, been led by viewing education in a false light; not considering it as the first step to form a being advancing gradually towards perfection[6]; but only as a preparation for life. On this sensual error, for I must call it so, has the false system of female manners been reared, which robs the whole sex of its dignity, and classes the brown and fair with the smiling flowers that only adorn the land. This has ever been the language of men, and the fear of departing from a supposed sexual character, has made even women of superior sense adopt the same sentiments.[7] Thus understanding, strictly speak-

---

[4]"The brutes," says Lord Monboddo, "remain in the state in which nature has placed them, except in so far as their natural instinct is improved by the culture *we* bestow upon them" [MW, her emphasis]. MW is quoting James Burnett, Lord Monboddo (1714–99), *Of the Origin and Progress of Language* (Edinburgh, 1774), 1.10.137. This Scottish judge and man of letters actually harbored an uncommon respect for brutes; MW's quotation belies this context.

[5]Vide Milton [MW]. On Adam and Eve: "O when meet now / Such pairs, in love and mutual Honour join'd?" (*Paradise Lost*, 8.57–58).

[6]This word is not strictly just, but I cannot find a better [MW].

[7]"Pleasure's the portion of th' *inferior* kind;
  But glory, virtue, Heaven for *man* designed."

After writing these lines, how could Mrs. Barbauld write the following ignoble comparison?

  "*To a Lady, with some painted flowers.*"
  Flowers to the fair: to you these flowers I bring,
  And strive to greet you with an earlier spring.
  Flowers, SWEET, *and gay, and* DELICATE LIKE YOU;

ing, has been denied to woman; and instinct, sublimated into wit and cunning, for the purposes of life, has been substituted in its stead.

The power of generalizing ideas, of drawing comprehensive conclusions from individual observations, is the only acquirement, for an immortal being, that really deserves the name of knowledge. Merely to observe, without endeavouring to account for any thing, may (in a very incomplete manner) serve as the common sense of life; but where is the store laid up that is to clothe the soul when it leaves the body?

This power has not only been denied to women; but writers have insisted that it is inconsistent, with a few exceptions, with their sexual character. Let men prove this, and I shall grant that woman only exists for man. I must, however, previously remark, that the power of generalizing ideas, to any great extent, is not very common amongst men or women.[8] But this exercise is the true cultivation of the understanding; and every thing conspires to render the cultivation of the understanding more difficult in the female than the male world.

I am naturally led by this assertion to the main subject of the present chapter, and shall now attempt to point out some of the causes that degrade the sex, and prevent women from generalizing their observations.

I shall not go back to the remote annals of antiquity to trace the history of woman; it is sufficient to allow that she has always been either a slave, or a despot, and to remark that each of these situations equally re-

Emblems of innocence, and beauty too.
With flowers the Graces bind their yellow hair,
And flowery wreaths consenting lovers wear.
Flowers, the sole luxury which Nature knew,
In Eden's pure and guiltless garden grew.
To loftier forms are rougher tasks assign'd;
The sheltering oak resists the stormy wind,
The tougher yew repels invading foes,
And the tall pine for future navies grows;
But this soft family, to cares unknown,
Were born for pleasure and delights ALONE.
Gay without toil, and lovely without art,
They spring to CHEER *the sense, and* GLAD *the heart.*
Nor blush, my fair, to own you copy these;
Your BEST, *your* SWEETEST *empire* is—TO PLEASE.

So the men tell us; but virtue, says reason, must be acquired by *rough* toils, and useful struggles with worldly *cares* [MW, her emphases]. Anna Letitia Barbauld (1743–1825), poet, essayist, critic. The first couplet is from "To Mrs. P⁎⁎⁎⁎⁎⁎⁎," with some Drawings of Birds and Insects." In this poem, "th' inferior kind" refers to feathered creatures, and "man" is generic. The second poem, quoted in its entirety, is not addressed to women categorically, but to the class MW also satirizes, "Lady."

[8]Contesting John Locke's thesis in *An Essay on Human Understanding* (1689): "the having of general Ideas, is that which puts a perfect distinction betwixt Man and Brutes" (2.11.9–10).

tards the progress of reason. The grand source of female folly and vice has ever appeared to me to arise from narrowness of mind; and the very constitution of civil governments has put almost insuperable obstacles in the way to prevent the cultivation of the female understanding:—yet virtue can be built on no other foundation! The same obstacles are thrown in the way of the rich, and the same consequences ensue.

Necessity has been proverbially termed the mother of invention—the aphorism may be extended to virtue. It is an acquirement, and an acquirement to which pleasure must be sacrificed—and who sacrifices pleasure when it is within the grasp, whose mind has not been opened and strengthened by adversity, or the pursuit of knowledge goaded on by necessity?—Happy is it when people have the cares of life to struggle with; for these struggles prevent their becoming a prey to enervating vices, merely from idleness! But, if from their birth men and women be placed in a torrid zone, with the meridian sun of pleasure darting directly upon them, how can they sufficiently brace their minds to discharge the duties of life, or even to relish the affections that carry them out of themselves?

Pleasure is the business of woman's life, according to the present modification of society, and while it continues to be so, little can be expected from such weak beings. Inheriting, in a lineal descent from the first fair defect in nature,[9] the sovereignty of beauty, they have, to maintain their power, resigned the natural rights, which the exercise of reason might have procured them, and chosen rather to be short-lived queens than labour to obtain the sober pleasures that arise from equality. Exalted by their inferiority (this sounds like a contradiction), they constantly demand homage as women, though experience should teach them that the men who pride themselves upon paying this arbitrary insolent respect to the sex, with the most scrupulous exactness, are most inclined to tyrannize over, and despise, the very weakness they cherish. Often do they repeat Mr. Hume's sentiments; when, comparing the French and Athenian character, he alludes to women. "But what is more singular in this whimsical nation, say I to the Athenians, is, that a frolick of yours during the Saturnalia,[10] when the slaves are served by their masters, is seriously continued by them through the whole year, and through the whole course of their lives; accompanied too with some circumstances, which still further

---

[9]Another reference to Adam's epithet, *Paradise Lost*, 10.891–92.

[10]The ancient Roman festival of Saturn, god of agriculture, during the week of the winter solstice. Distinctions of rank were suspended, moral restrictions were relaxed, and gifts were exchanged.

augment the absurdity and ridicule. Your sport only elevates for a few days those whom fortune has thrown down, and whom she too, in sport, may really elevate for ever above you. But this nation gravely exalts those, whom nature has subjected to them, and whose inferiority and infirmities are absolutely incurable. The women, though without virtue, are their masters and sovereigns."[11]

Ah! why do women, I write with affectionate solicitude, condescend to receive a degree of attention and respect from strangers, different from that reciprocation of civility which the dictates of humanity and the politeness of civilization authorise between man and man? And, why do they not discover, when "in the noon of beauty's power,"[12] that they are treated like queens only to be deluded by hollow respect, till they are led to resign, or not assume, their natural prerogatives? Confined then in cages like the feathered race, they have nothing to do but to plume themselves, and stalk with mock majesty from perch to perch. It is true they are provided with food and raiment, for which they neither toil nor spin[13]; but health, liberty, and virtue, are given in exchange. But, where, amongst mankind, has been found sufficient strength of mind to enable a being to resign these adventitious prerogatives; one who, rising with the calm dignity of reason above opinion, dared to be proud of the privileges inherent in man? And it is vain to expect it whilst hereditary power chokes the affections and nips reason in the bud.

The passions of men have thus placed women on thrones, and, till mankind become more reasonable, it is to be feared that women will avail themselves of the power which they attain with the least exertion, and which is the most indisputable. They will smile,—yes, they will smile, though told that—

> "In beauty's empire is no mean,
> And woman, either slave or queen,
> Is quickly scorned when not ador'd."[14]

But the adoration comes first, and the scorn is not anticipated.

[11]Scottish Enlightenment philosopher, historian, and religious skeptic David Hume (1711–76). MW quotes "A Dialogue," first published in a posthumous edition of *An Enquiry Concerning the Principles of Morals* (1777; 2.386).

[12]MW uses this phrase to describe the heroine of *Henrietta of Gerstenfeld* (*Analytical Review* I, June 1788); its preface names Christoph Martin Weiland as the author, but it was actually Adam Beuvius.

[13]Matthew 6:28: "And why take you thought for raiment? Consider the lilies of the field, how they grow; they toil not neither do they spin."; also Luke 12:27.

[14]Barbauld, "Song V," 16–18; this first appeared in *Essays on Song-Writing* (1772), published by Barbauld's brother John Aikin.

Louis the XIVth, in particular, spread factitious manners, and caught, in a specious way, the whole nation in his toils; for, establishing an artful chain of despotism, he made it the interest of the people at large, individually to respect his station and support his power. And women, whom he flattered by a puerile attention to the whole sex, obtained in his reign that prince-like distinction so fatal to reason and virtue.[15]

A king is always a king—and a woman always a woman[16]: his authority and her sex, ever stand between them and rational converse. With a lover, I grant, she should be so, and her sensibility will naturally lead her to endeavour to excite emotion, not to gratify her vanity, but her heart. This I do not allow to be coquetry, it is the artless impulse of nature, I only exclaim against the sexual desire of conquest when the heart is out of the question.

This desire is not confined to women: "I have endeavoured," says Lord Chesterfield, "to gain the hearts of twenty women, whose persons I would not have given a fig for."[17] The libertine, who, in a gust of passion, takes advantage of unsuspecting tenderness, is a saint when compared with this cold-hearted rascal; for I like to use significant words. Yet only taught to please, women are always on the watch to please, and with true heroic ardour endeavour to gain hearts merely to resign or spurn them, when the victory is decided, and conspicuous.

I must descend to the minutiae of the subject.

I lament that women are systematically degraded by receiving the trivial attentions, which men think it manly to pay to the sex, when, in fact, they are insultingly supporting their own superiority. It is not condescension to bow to an inferior. So ludicrous, in fact, do these ceremonies appear to me, that I scarcely am able to govern my muscles, when I see a man with eager, and serious solicitude, to lift a handkerchief, or shut a door, when the *lady* could have done it herself, had she only moved a pace or two.

---

[15]*Le Roi Solei* (the sun king) ruled France 1643–1715 and built Versailles, the center of power. He reportedly boasted, "L' état, c'est moi" ("the state, it is me").

[16]And a wit, always a wit, might be added; for the vain fooleries of wits and beauties to obtain attention, and make conquests, are much upon a par [MW].

[17]Misremembering or paraphrasing *Letters to His Son* (1774), Letter CCXCIV (Nov. 16, 1752): "my vanity has very often made me take pains to make a woman in love with me, if I could, for whose person I would not have given a pinch of snuff." The *Letters* of Philip Dormer Stanhope, 4th Earl of Chesterfield (1694–1773), advising his illegitimate son about social decorum and worldly matters, gained wide popularity.

A wild wish has just flown from my heart to my head, and I will not stifle it, though it may excite a horse-laugh.—I do earnestly wish to see the distinction of sex confounded in society, unless where love animates the behaviour. For this distinction is, I am firmly persuaded, the foundation of the weakness of character ascribed to woman; is the cause why the understanding is neglected, whilst accomplishments are acquired with sedulous care: and the same cause accounts for their preferring the graceful before the heroic virtues.

Mankind, including every description, wish to be loved and respected by *something*; and the common herd will always take the nearest road to the completion of their wishes. The respect paid to wealth and beauty is the most certain, and unequivocal; and, of course, will always attract the vulgar eye of common minds. Abilities and virtues are absolutely necessary to raise men from the middle rank of life into notice; and the natural consequence is notorious, the middle rank contains most virtue and abilities. Men have thus, in one station, at least an opportunity of exerting themselves with dignity, and of rising by the exertions which really improve a rational creature; but the whole female sex are, till their character is formed, in the same condition as the rich: for they are born, I now speak of a state of civilization, with certain sexual privileges, and whilst they are gratuitously granted them, few will ever think of works of supererogation, to obtain the esteem of a small number of superior people.

When do we hear of women who, starting out of obscurity, boldly claim respect on account of their great abilities or daring virtues? Where are they to be found?—"To be observed, to be attended to, to be taken notice of with sympathy, complacency, and approbation, are all the advantages which they seek."[18]—True! my male readers will probably exclaim; but let them, before they draw any conclusion, recollect that this was not written originally as descriptive of women, but of the rich. In Dr. Smith's Theory of Moral Sentiments, I have found a general character of people of rank and fortune, that, in my opinion, might with the greatest propriety be applied to the female sex. I refer the sagacious reader to the whole comparison; but must be allowed to quote a passage to enforce an argument that I mean to insist on, as the one most conclusive against a sexual character. For if, excepting warriors, no great men, of any de-

[18]Adam Smith, *The Theory of Moral Sentiments* (1759), 1.3.2: "Of the origin of Ambition, and of the distinction of Ranks." Smith's sentence ends, ". . . are all the advantages which we can propose to derive from it." Political economist Smith (1723–90) is best known today for *Wealth of Nations* (1776).

nomination, have ever appeared amongst the nobility, may it not be fairly inferred that their local situation swallowed up the man, and produced a character similar to that of women, who are *localized*—if I may be allowed the word, by the rank they are placed in, by *courtesy?* Women, commonly called Ladies, are not to be contradicted in company, are not allowed to exert any manual strength; and from them the negative virtues only are expected, when any virtues are expected—patience, docility, good-humour, and flexibility; virtues incompatible with any vigorous exertion of intellect. Besides, by living more with each other, and being seldom absolutely alone, they are more under the influence of sentiments than passions. Solitude and reflection are necessary to give to wishes the force of passions, and to enable the imagination to enlarge the object, and make it the most desirable. The same may be said of the rich; they do not sufficiently deal in general ideas, collected by impassioned thinking, or calm investigation, to acquire that strength of character on which great resolves are built. But hear what an acute observer says of the great.

"Do the great seem insensible of the easy price at which they may acquire the publick admiration; or do they seem to imagine that to them, as to other men, it must be the purchase either of sweat or of blood? By what important accomplishments is the young nobleman instructed to support the dignity of his rank, and to render himself worthy of that superiority over his fellow-citizens, to which the virtue of his ancestors had raised them? Is it by knowledge, by industry, by patience, by self-denial, or by virtue of any kind? As all his words, as all his motions are attended to, he learns an habitual regard to every circumstance of ordinary behaviour, and studies to perform all those small duties with the most exact propriety. As he is conscious how much he is observed, and how much mankind are disposed to favour all his inclinations, he acts, upon the most indifferent occasions, with that freedom and elevation which the thought of this naturally inspires. His air, his manner, his deportment, all mark that elegant and graceful sense of his own superiority, which those who are born to inferior station can hardly ever arrive at. These are the arts by which he proposes to make mankind more easily submit to his authority, and to govern their inclinations according to his own pleasure: and in this he is seldom disappointed. These arts, supported by rank and pre-eminence, are, upon ordinary occasions, sufficient to govern the world. Lewis XIV during the greater part of his reign, was regarded, not only in France, but over all Europe, as the most perfect model of a great prince. But what were the talents and virtues by which he acquired this great reputation? Was it by the scrupulous and inflexible justice of all his undertakings, by the immense dangers and difficulties with which they were attended, or by the unwearied and unrelenting application with which he pursued them? Was it by his extensive knowledge, by his exquisite judgment, or by his heroic valour? It was by none of these qualities. But he was, first of all, the most powerful prince in Europe, and consequently held the highest rank among kings; and then, says his historian,[19] 'he surpassed all his courtiers in the gracefulness of his shape, and the majestic beauty of his features. The sound of his voice, noble and affecting, gained those hearts which his presence intimidated. He had a step and a deportment which could suit only him and his rank, and which would have been ridiculous in any other person. The embarrassment which he occasioned to those who spoke to him, flattered that secret satisfaction with which he felt his own superiority.' These frivolous accomplishments, supported by his rank, and, no doubt too, by a degree of other talents and virtues, which seems, however, not to have been much above mediocrity, established this prince in the esteem of his own age, and have drawn, even from posterity, a good deal of respect for his memory. Compared with these, in his own times, and in his own presence, no other virtue, it seems, appeared to have any merit. Knowledge, industry, valour, and beneficence, trembled, were abashed, and lost all dignity before them."[20]

Woman also thus "in herself complete,"[21] by possessing all these *frivolous* accomplishments, so changes the nature of things

> ———"That what she wills to do or say
> Seems wisest, virtuousest, discreetest, best;
> All higher knowledge in *her presence* falls
> Degraded. Wisdom in discourse with her
> Loses discountenanc'd, and, like Folly, shows;
> Authority and Reason on her wait."[22]

And all this is built on her loveliness!

In the middle rank of life, to continue the comparison, men, in their youth, are prepared for professions, and marriage is not consid-

---

[19]Voltaire; the quotation is Adam Smith's translation (slightly abridged) of a passage from Voltaire's *Siècle de Louis XIV* (Berlin, 1751), 2.24.22–23. Voltaire (1694–1778), a leading figure of the French Enlightenment.

[20]Smith, *Moral Sentiments*, 1.3.2.

[21]Adam on Eve, *Paradise Lost*, 8.548.

[22]The same, 549–54; MW's italics.

ered as the grand feature in their lives, whilst women, on the contrary, have no other scheme to sharpen their faculties. It is not business, extensive plans, or any of the excursive flights of ambition, that engross their attention; no, their thoughts are now employed in rearing such noble structures. To rise in the world, and have the liberty of running from pleasure to pleasure, they must marry advantageously, and to this object their time is sacrificed, and their persons often legally prostituted.[23] A man when he enters any profession has his eye steadily fixed on some future advantage (and the mind gains great strength by having all its efforts directed to one point), and, full of his business, pleasure is considered as mere relaxation; whilst women seek for pleasure as the main purpose of existence. In fact, from the education, which they receive from society, the love of pleasure may be said to govern them all; but does this prove that there is a sex in souls? It would be just as rational to declare that the courtiers in France, when a destructive system of despotism had formed their character, were not men, because liberty, virtue, and humanity, were sacrificed to pleasure and vanity.—Fatal passions, which have ever domineered over the *whole* race!

The same love of pleasure, fostered by the whole tendency of their education, gives a trifling turn to the conduct of women in most circumstances: for instance, they are ever anxious about secondary things; and on the watch for adventures, instead of being occupied by duties.

A man, when he undertakes a journey, has, in general, the end in view; a woman thinks more of the incidental occurrences, the strange things that may possibly occur on the road; the impression that she may make on her fellow-travellers; and, above all, she is anxiously intent on the care of the finery that she carries with her, which is more than ever a part of herself, when going to figure on a new scene; when, to use an apt French turn of expression, she is going to produce a sensation.—Can dignity of mind exist with such trivial cares?

In short, women, in general, as well as the rich of both sexes, have acquired all the follies and vices of civilization, and missed the useful fruit. It is not necessary for me always to premise, that I speak of the condition of the whole sex, leaving exceptions out of the question. Their senses are inflamed, and their understandings neglected, consequently they become the prey of their senses, delicately termed sensi-

---

[23]A description given by Daniel Defoe, *Conjugal Lewdness; or Matrimonial Whore-dom* (1727).

bility, and are blown about by every momentary gust of feeling. Civilized women are, therefore, so weakened by false refinement, that, respecting morals, their condition is much below what it would be were they left in a state nearer to nature. Ever restless and anxious, their over exercised sensibility not only renders them uncomfortable themselves, but troublesome, to use a soft phrase, to others. All their thoughts turn on things calculated to excite emotion; and feeling, when they should reason, their conduct is unstable, and their opinions are wavering—not the wavering produced by deliberation or progressive views, but by contradictory emotions. By fits and starts they are warm in many pursuits; yet this warmth, never concentrated into perseverance, soon exhausts itself; exhaled by its own heat, or meeting with some other fleeting passion, to which reason has never given any specific gravity, neutrality ensues. Miserable indeed, must be that being whose cultivation of mind has only tended to inflame its passions! A distinction should be made between inflaming and strengthening them. The passions thus pampered, whilst the judgment is left unformed, what can be expected to ensue?—Undoubtedly, a mixture of madness and folly!

This observation should not be confined to the *fair* sex; however, at present, I only mean to apply it to them.

Novels, music, poetry, and gallantry, all tend to make women the creatures of sensation, and their character is thus formed in the mould of folly during the time they are acquiring accomplishments, the only improvement they are excited, by their station in society, to acquire. This overstretched sensibility naturally relaxes the other powers of the mind, and prevents intellect from attaining that sovereignty which it ought to attain to render a rational creature useful to others, and content with its own station: for the exercise of the understanding, as life advances, is the only method pointed out by nature to calm the passions.

Satiety has a very different effect, and I have often been forcibly struck by an emphatical description of damnation:—when the spirit is represented as continually hovering with abortive eagerness round the defiled body, unable to enjoy any thing without the organs of sense. Yet, to their senses, are women made slaves, because it is by their sensibility that they obtain present power.

And will moralists pretend to assert, that this is the condition in which one half of the human race should be encouraged to remain with listless inactivity and stupid acquiescence? Kind instructors! what were we created for? To remain, it may be said, innocent; they mean in a state of childhood.—We might as well never have been born, unless it were necessary that we should be created to enable man to acquire the noble privilege of reason, the power of discerning good from evil, whilst we lie down in the dust from whence we were taken, never to rise again.—

It would be an endless task to trace the variety of meannesses, cares, and sorrows, into which women are plunged by the prevailing opinion, that they were created rather to feel than reason, and that all the power they obtain, must be obtained by their charms and weakness:

"Fine by defect, and amiably weak!"[24]

And, made by this amiable weakness entirely dependent, excepting what they gain by illicit sway, on man, not only for protection, but advice, is it surprising that, neglecting the duties that reason alone points out, and shrinking from trials calculated to strengthen their minds, they only exert themselves to give their defects a graceful covering, which may serve to heighten their charms in the eye of the voluptuary, though it sink them below the scale of moral excellence?

Fragile in every sense of the word, they are obliged to look up to man for every comfort. In the most trifling dangers they cling to their support, with parasitical tenacity, piteously demanding succour; and their *natural* protector extends his arm, or lifts up his voice, to guard the lovely trembler—from what? Perhaps the frown of an old cow, or the jump of a mouse; a rat, would be a serious danger. In the name of reason, and even common sense, what can save such beings from contempt; even though they be soft and fair?

These fears, when not affected, may produce some pretty attitudes; but they shew a degree of imbecility which degrades a rational creature in a way women are not aware of—for love and esteem are very distinct things.

I am fully persuaded that we should hear of none of these infantine airs, if girls were allowed to take sufficient exercise, and not confined in close rooms till their muscles are relaxed, and their powers of digestion destroyed. To carry the remark still further, if fear in girls, instead of being cherished, perhaps, created, were treated in the same manner as cowardice in boys, we should quickly see women with more dignified aspects. It is true, they could not then with equal propriety be termed the sweet flowers that smile in the walk of man; but they would be

[24]See Pope's *Of the Characters of Women*, 44: "Fine by defect, and delicately weak."

more respectable members of society, and discharge the important duties of life by the light of their own reason. "Educate women like men," says Rousseau, "and the more they resemble our sex the less power will they have over us."[25] This is the very point I aim at. I do not wish them to have power over men; but over themselves.

In the same strain have I heard men argue against instructing the poor; for many are the forms that aristocracy assumes. "Teach them to read and write," say they, "and you take them out of the station assigned them by nature." An eloquent Frenchman has answered them, I will borrow his sentiments. But they know not, when they make man a brute, that they may expect every instant to see him transformed into a ferocious beast.[26] Without knowledge there can be no morality!

Ignorance is a frail base for virtue! Yet, that it is the condition for which woman was organized, has been insisted upon by the writers who have most vehemently argued in favour of the superiority of man; a superiority not in degree, but essence; though, to soften the argument, they have laboured to prove, with chivalrous generosity, that the sexes ought not to be compared; man was made to reason, woman to feel: and that together, flesh and spirit, they make the most perfect whole, by blending happily reason and sensibility into one character.

And what is sensibility? "Quickness of sensation; quickness of perception; delicacy." Thus is it defined by Dr. Johnson[27]; and the definition gives me no other idea than of the most exquisitely polished instinct. I discern not a trace of the image of God in either sensation or matter. Refined seventy times seven,[28] they are still material; intellect dwells not there; nor will fire ever make lead gold!

I come round to my old argument; if woman be allowed to have an immortal soul, she must have, as the employment of life, an understanding to improve. And when, to render the present state more complete, though every thing proves it to be but a fraction of a

---

[25]*Emilius*, 4.5.17: Rosseau adds, "and when they once become like ourselves, we shall then be truly their masters."

[26]Perhaps Honoré Riqueti, Comte de Mirabeau (1749–91), who warned the Constituent Assembly in 1790 "You have loosed the bull: do you expect he will not use of his horns?"

[27]See *Dictionary* (1755), a publication that earned Johnson fame and the moniker "Dictionary Johnson."

[28]When Peter asks Jesus if he should forgive one who has sinned against him "till seven times," Jesus replies, "I say not unto thee, Until seven times: but, Until seventy times seven" (Matthew 18:21–22).

mighty sum, she is incited by present gratification to forget her grand destination, nature is counteracted, or she was born only to procreate and rot. Or, granting brutes, of every description, a soul, though not a reasonable one, the exercise of instinct and sensibility may be the step, which they are to take, in this life, towards the attainment of reason in the next; so that through all eternity they will lag behind man, who, why we cannot tell, had the power given him of attaining reason in his first mode of existence.

When I treat of the peculiar duties of women, as I should treat of the peculiar duties of a citizen or father, it will be found that I do not mean to insinuate that they should be taken out of their families, speaking of the majority. "He that hath wife and children," says Lord Bacon, "hath given hostages to fortune; for they are impediments to great enterprises, either of virtue or mischief. Certainly the best works, and of greatest merit for the public, have proceeded from the unmarried or childless men."[29] I say the same of women. But, the welfare of society is not built on extraordinary exertions; and were it more reasonably organized, there would be still less need of great abilities, or heroic virtues.

In the regulation of a family, in the education of children, understanding, in an unsophisticated sense, is particularly required: strength both of body and mind; yet the men who, by their writings, have most earnestly laboured to domesticate women, have endeavoured, by arguments dictated by a gross appetite, which satiety had rendered fastidious, to weaken their bodies and cramp their minds. But, if even by these sinister methods they really *persuaded* women, by working on their feelings, to stay at home, and fulfil the duties of a mother and mistress of a family, I should cautiously oppose opinions that led women to right conduct, by prevailing on them to make the discharge of such important duties the main business of life, though reason were insulted. Yet, and I appeal to experience, if by neglecting the understanding they be as much, nay, more detached from these domestic employments, than they could be by the most serious intellectual pursuit, though it may be observed, that the mass of mankind will never vigorously pursue an intellectual object,[30] I may be allowed to infer that reason is absolutely necessary to enable a woman to perform any duty properly, and I must again repeat, that sensibility is not reason.

[29]The first line of "Of Marriage and Single Life," in *Essays* (1625).

[30]The mass of mankind are rather the slaves of their appetites than of their passions [MW].

The comparison with the rich still occurs to me; for, when men neglect the duties of humanity, women will follow their example; a common stream hurries them both along with thoughtless celerity. Riches and honours prevent a man from enlarging his understanding, and enervate all his powers by reversing the order of nature, which has ever made true pleasure the reward of labour. Pleasure—enervating pleasure is, likewise, within women's reach without earning it. But, till hereditary possessions are spread abroad, how can we expect men to be proud of virtue? And, till they are, women will govern them by the most direct means, neglecting their dull domestic duties to catch the pleasure that sits lightly on the wing of time.

"The power of the woman," says some author, "is her sensibility"; and men, not aware of the consequence, do all they can to make this power swallow up every other. Those who constantly employ their sensibility will have most: for example; poets, painters, and composers.[31] Yet, when the sensibility is thus increased at the expense of reason, and even the imagination, why do philosophical men complain of their fickleness? The sexual attention of man particularly acts on female sensibility, and this sympathy has been exercised from their youth up. A husband cannot long pay those attentions with the passion necessary to excite lively emotions, and the heart, accustomed to lively emotions, turns to a new lover, or pines in secret, the prey of virtue or prudence. I mean when the heart has really been rendered susceptible, and the taste formed; for I am apt to conclude, from what I have seen in fashionable life, that vanity is oftener fostered than sensibility by the mode of education, and the intercourse between the sexes, which I have reprobated; and that coquetry more frequently proceeds from vanity than from that inconstancy, which overstrained sensibility naturally produces.

Another argument that has had great weight with me, must, I think, have some force with every considerate benevolent heart. Girls who have been thus weakly educated, are often cruelly left by their parents without any provision; and, of course, are dependent on, not only the reason, but the bounty of their brothers. These brothers are, to view the fairest side of the question, good sort of men, and give as a favour, what children of the same parents had an equal right to. In this equivocal humiliating situation, a docile female may remain

---

[31]Men of these descriptions pour sensibility into their compositions, to amalgamate the gross materials; and, moulding them with passion, give to the inert body a soul; but in woman's imagination, love alone concentrates these ethereal beams [MW].

some time, with a tolerable degree of comfort. But, when the brother marries, a probable circumstance, from being considered as the mistress of the family, she is viewed with averted looks as an intruder, an unnecessary burden on the benevolence of the master of the house and his new partner.

Who can recount the misery, which many unfortunate beings, whose minds and bodies are equally weak, suffer in such situations—unable to work, and ashamed to beg? The wife, a cold-hearted, narrow-minded, woman, and this is not an unfair supposition; for the present mode of education does not tend to enlarge the heart any more than the understanding, is jealous of the little kindness which her husband shews to his relations; and her sensibility not rising to humanity, she is displeased at seeing the property of *her* children lavished on an helpless sister.

These are matters of fact, which have come under my eye again and again. The consequence is obvious, the wife has recourse to cunning to undermine the habitual affection, which she is afraid openly to oppose; and neither tears nor caresses are spared till the spy is worked out of her home, and thrown on the world, unprepared for its difficulties; or sent, as a great effort of generosity, or from some regard to propriety, with a small stipend, and an uncultivated mind, into joyless solitude.

These two women may be much upon a par, with respect to reason and humanity; and changing situations, might have acted just the same selfish part; but had they been differently educated, the case would also have been very different. The wife would not have had that sensibility, of which self is the centre, and reason might have taught her not to expect, and not even to be flattered by, the affection of her husband, if it led him to violate prior duties. She would wish not to him merely because he loved her, but on account of his virtues; and the sister might have been able to struggle for herself instead of eating the bitter bread of dependence.

I am, indeed, persuaded that the heart, as well as the understanding, is opened by cultivation; and by, which may not appear so clear, strengthening the organs; I am not now talking of momentary flashes of sensibility, but of affections. And, perhaps, in the education of both sexes, the most difficult task is so to adjust instruction as not to narrow the understanding, whilst the heart is warmed by the generous juices of spring, just raised by the electric fermentation of the season; nor to dry up the feelings by employing the mind in investigations remote from life.

With respect to women, when they receive a careful education, they are either made fine ladies, brimful of sensibility, and teeming with capricious fancies; or merely notable women. The latter are often friendly, honest creatures, and have a shrewd kind of good sense joined with worldly prudence, that often render them more useful members of society than the fine sentimental lady, though they possess neither greatness of mind nor taste. The intellectual world is shut against them; take them out of their family or neighbourhood, and they stand still; the mind finding no employment, for literature affords a fund of amusement which they have never sought to relish, but frequently to despise. The sentiments and taste of more cultivated minds appear ridiculous, even in those whom chance and family connections have led them to love; but in mere acquaintance they think it all affectation.

A man of sense can only love such a woman on account of her sex, and respect her, because she is a trusty servant. He lets her, to preserve his own peace, scold the servants, and go to church in clothes made of the very best materials. A man of her own size of understanding would, probably, not agree so well with her; for he might wish to encroach on her prerogative, and manage some domestic concerns himself. Yet women, whose minds are not enlarged by cultivation, or the natural selfishness of sensibility expanded by reflection, are very unfit to manage a family; for, by an undue stretch of power, they are always tyrannizing to support a superiority that only rests on the arbitrary distinction of fortune. The evil is sometimes more serious, and domestics are deprived of innocent indulgences, and made to work beyond their strength, in order to enable the notable woman to keep a better table, and outshine her neighbours in finery and parade. If she attend to her children, it is, in general, to dress them in a costly manner—and, whether this attention arise from vanity or fondness, it is equally pernicious.

Besides, how many women of this description pass their days; or, at least, their evenings, discontentedly. Their husbands acknowledge that they are good managers, and chaste wives; but leave home to seek for more agreeable, may I be allowed to use a significant French word, *piquant* society; and the patient drudge, who fulfils her task, like a blind horse in a mill, is defrauded of her just reward; for the wages due to her are the caresses of her husband; and women who have so few resources in themselves, do not very patiently bear this privation of a natural right.

A fine lady, on the contrary, has been taught to look down with contempt on the vulgar employments of life; though she has only been incited to acquire accomplishments that rise a degree above sense; for even corporeal accomplishments cannot be acquired with any degree of precision unless the understanding has been strengthened by exercise. Without a foundation of principles taste is superficial, grace must arise from something deeper than imitation. The imagination, however, is heated, and the feelings rendered fastidious, if not sophisticated; or, a counterpoise of judgment is not acquired, when the heart still remains artless, though it becomes too tender.

These women are often amiable; and their hearts are really more sensible to general benevolence, more alive to the sentiments that civilize life, than the square-elbowed family drudge; but, wanting a due proportion of reflection and self-government, they only inspire love; and are the mistresses of their husbands, whilst they have any hold on their affections; and the platonic friends of his male acquaintance. These are the fair defects[32] in nature; the women who appear to be created not to enjoy the fellowship of man, but to save him from sinking into absolute brutality, by rubbing off the rough angles of his character; and by playful dalliance to give some dignity to the appetite that draws him to them.—Gracious Creator of the whole human race! hast thou created such a being as woman, who can trace thy wisdom in thy works, and feel that thou alone art by thy nature exalted above her,—for no better purpose?—Can she believe that she was only made to submit to man, her equal, a being, who, like her, was sent into the world to acquire virtue?—Can she consent to be occupied merely to please him; merely to adorn the earth, when her soul is capable of rising to thee?—And can she rest supinely dependent on man for reason, when she ought to mount with him the arduous steeps of knowledge?—

Yet, if love be the supreme good, let women be only educated to inspire it, and let every charm be polished to intoxicate the senses; but, if they be moral beings, let them have a chance to become intelligent; and let love to man be only a part of that glowing flame of universal love, which, after encircling humanity, mounts in grateful incense to God.

To fulfil domestic duties much resolution is necessary, and a serious kind of perseverance that requires a more firm support than emotions, however lively and true to nature. To give an example of order, the soul of virtue, some austerity of behaviour must be adopted, scarcely to be expected from a being who, from its infancy, has been

---

[32]Another reference to Adam's epithet for Eve (*Paradise Lost*, 10.891–92).

made the weathercock of its own sensations. Whoever rationally means to be useful must have a plan of conduct; and, in the discharge of the simplest duty, we are often obliged to act contrary to the present impulse of tenderness or compassion. Severity is frequently the most certain, as well as the most sublime proof of affection; and the want of this power over the feelings, and of that lofty, dignified affection, which makes a person prefer the future good of the beloved object to a present gratification, is the reason why so many fond mothers spoil their children, and has made it questionable whether negligence or indulgence be most hurtful: but I am inclined to think, that the latter has done most harm.

Mankind seem to agree that children should be left under the management of women during their childhood. Now, from all the observation that I have been able to make, women of sensibility are the most unfit for this task, because they will infallibly, carried away by their feelings, spoil a child's temper. The management of the temper, the first, and most important branch of education, requires the sober steady eye of reason; a plan of conduct equally distant from tyranny and indulgence: yet these are the extremes that people of sensibility alternately fall into; always shooting beyond the mark. I have followed this train of reasoning much further, till I have concluded, that a person of genius is the most improper person to be employed in education, public or private. Minds of this rare species see things too much in masses, and seldom, if ever, have a good temper. That habitual cheerfulness, termed good-humour, is, perhaps, as seldom united with great mental powers, as with strong feelings. And those people who follow, with interest and admiration, the flights of genius; or, with cooler approbation suck in the instruction which has been elaborately prepared for them by the profound thinker, ought not to be disgusted, if they find the former choleric, and the latter morose; because liveliness of fancy, and a tenacious comprehension of mind, are scarcely compatible with that pliant urbanity which leads a man, at least, to bend to the opinions and prejudices of others, instead of roughly confronting them.

But, treating of education or manners, minds of a superior class are not to be considered, they may be left to chance; it is the multitude, with moderate abilities, who call for instruction, and catch the colour of the atmosphere they breathe. This respectable concourse, I contend, men and women, should not have their sensations heightened in the hot-bed of luxurious indolence, at the expense of their understanding; for, unless there be a ballast of understanding, they will never become either virtuous or free: an aristocracy, founded on property or sterling talents, will ever sweep before it, the alternately timid, and ferocious, slaves of feeling.

Numberless are the arguments, to take another view of the subject, brought forward with a shew of reason, because supposed to be deduced from nature, that men have used morally and physically, to degrade the sex. I must notice a few.

The female understanding has often been spoken of with contempt, as arriving sooner at maturity than the male. I shall not answer this argument by alluding to the early proofs of reason, as well as genius, in Cowley, Milton, and Pope,[33] but only appeal to experience to decide whether young men, who are early introduced into company (and examples now abound), do not acquire the same precocity. So notorious is this fact, that the bare mentioning of it must bring before people, who at all mix in the world, the idea of a number of swaggering apes of men, whose understandings are narrowed by being brought into the society of men when they ought to have been spinning a top or twirling a hoop.

It has also been asserted, by some naturalists, that men do not attain their full growth and strength till thirty; but that women arrive at maturity by twenty.[34] I apprehend that they reason on false ground, led astray by the male prejudice, which deems beauty the perfection of woman—mere beauty of features and complexion, the vulgar acceptation of the word, whilst male beauty is allowed to have some connection with the mind. Strength of body, and that character of countenance which the French term a *physionomie*,[35] women do not acquire before thirty, any more than men. The little artless tricks of children, it is true, are particularly pleasing and attractive; yet, when the pretty freshness of youth is worn off, these artless graces become studied airs, and disgust every person of taste. In the countenance of girls we only look for vivacity and bashful modesty; but, the spring-

---

[33]Many other names might be added [MW]. Abraham Cowley (1618–67) began writing verses at age ten, and published *Poetical Blossoms* when he was fifteen; John Milton (1608–74) wrote verses in both English and Latin when he was young, and was extremely studious at an early age; and Alexander Pope (1688–1744) completed the epic "Alexander" by age fifteen.

[34]Georges, Comte de Buffon, *Natural History* (1780, trans. William Smellie), 2.436: "As their size is smaller, and their muscles, and other parts, less strong, compact, and solid, than those of men, they arrive more early at a state of maturity. A woman at twenty years is as perfectly formed as a man at thirty."

[35]The 18th-c. science of physiognomy used facial features and countenance as an index of mind and character.

tide of life over, we look for soberer sense in the face, and for traces of passion, instead of the dimples of animal spirits; expecting to see individuality of character, the only fastener of the affections.[36] We then wish to converse, not to fondle; to give scope to our imaginations as well as to the sensations of our hearts.

At twenty the beauty of both sexes is equal; but the libertinism of man leads him to make the distinction, and superannuated coquettes are commonly of the same opinion; for, when they can no longer inspire love, they pay for the vigour and vivacity of youth. The French, who admit more of mind into their notions of beauty, give the preference to women of thirty. I mean to say that they allow women to be in their most perfect state, when vivacity gives place to reason, and to that majestic seriousness of character, which marks maturity;—or, the resting point. In youth, till twenty, the body shoots out, till thirty the solids are attaining a degree of density; and the flexible muscles, growing daily more rigid, give character to the countenance; that is, they trace the operations of the mind with the iron pen of fate, and tell us not only what powers are within, but how they have been employed.

It is proper to observe, that animals who arrive slowly at maturity, are the longest lived, and of the noblest species. Men cannot, however, claim any natural superiority from the grandeur of longevity; for in this respect nature has not distinguished the male.

Polygamy is another physical degradation; and a plausible argument for a custom, that blasts every domestic virtue, is drawn from the well-attested fact, that in the countries where it is established, more females are born than males. This appears to be an indication of nature, and to nature, apparently reasonable speculations must yield. A further conclusion obviously presented itself; if polygamy be necessary, woman must be inferior to man, and made for him.

With respect to the formation of the fetus in the womb, we are very ignorant; but it appears to me probable, that an accidental physical cause may account for this phenomenon, and prove it not to be a law of nature. I have met with some pertinent observations on the subject in Foster's Account of the Isles of the South-Sea, that will explain my meaning. After observing that of the two sexes amongst animals, the most vigorous and hottest constitution always prevails, and produces its kind; he adds,—"If this be applied to the inhabitants

---

[36]The strength of an affection is, generally, in the same proportion as the character of the species in the object beloved, lost in that of the individual [MW].

of Africa, it is evident that the men there, accustomed to polygamy, are enervated by the use of so many women, and therefore less vigorous; the women, on the contrary, are of a hotter constitution, not only on account of their more irritable nerves, more sensible organization, and more lively fancy; but likewise because they are deprived in their matrimony of that share of physical love which, in a monogamous condition, would all be theirs; and thus, for the above reasons, the generality of the children are born females.

"In the greater part of Europe it has been proved by the most accurate lists of mortality, that the proportion of men to women is nearly equal, or, if any difference takes place, the males born are more numerous, in the proportion of 105 to 100."[37]

The necessity of polygamy, therefore, does not appear; yet when a man seduces a woman, it should, I think, be termed a *left-handed*[38] marriage, and the man should be *legally* obliged to maintain the woman and her children, unless adultery, a natural divorcement, abrogated the law. And this law should remain in force as long as the weakness of women caused the word seduction to be used as an excuse for their frailty and want of principle; nay, while they depend on man for a subsistence, instead of earning it by the exertion of their own hands or heads. But these women should not, in the full meaning of the relationship, be termed wives, or the very purpose of marriage would be subverted, and all those endearing charities that flow from personal fidelity, and give a sanctity to the tie, when neither love nor friendship unites the hearts, would melt into selfishness. The woman who is faithful to the father of her children demands respect, and should not be treated like a prostitute; though I readily grant that if it be necessary for a man and woman to live together in order to bring up their offspring, nature never intended that a man should have more than one wife.

Still, highly as I respect marriage, as the foundation of almost every social virtue, I cannot avoid feeling the most lively compassion for those unfortunate females who are broken off from society, and

[37]John Reinhold Forster, *Observations Made During a Voyage Round the World* (London, 1778), 425–26. Between 1772 and 1775, Forster (1729–98) circumnavigated the globe with Captain Cook. The second paragraph is not from Forster; it has not been identified.

[38]"Morganatic" or illegal marriage, in which the groom gives his left hand, rather than his right. While the children of such unions (usually the man was of a much higher social rank) were supported, they were denied legal rights, inheritance, and succession to any title.

by one error torn from all those affections and relationships that improve the heart and mind. It does not frequently even deserve the name of error; for many innocent girls become the dupes of a sincere, affectionate heart, and still more are, as it may emphatically be termed, *ruined* before they know the difference between virtue and vice:—and thus prepared by their education for infamy, they become infamous. Asylums and Magdalens[39] are not the proper remedies for these abuses. It is justice, not charity, that is wanting in the world!

A woman who has lost her honour, imagines that she cannot fall lower, and as for recovering her former station, it is impossible; no exertion can wash this stain away. Losing thus every spur, and having no other means of support, prostitution becomes her only refuge, and the character is quickly depraved by circumstances over which the poor wretch has little power, unless she possesses an uncommon portion of sense and loftiness of spirit. Necessity never makes prostitution the business of men's lives; though numberless are the women who are thus rendered systematically vicious. This, however, arises in a great degree, from the state of idleness in which women are educated, who are always taught to look up to man for a maintenance, and to consider their persons as the proper return for his exertions to support them. Meretricious airs, and the whole science of wantonness, have then a more powerful stimulus than either appetite or vanity; and this remark gives force to the prevailing opinion, that with chastity all is lost that is respectable in woman. Her character depends on the observance of one virtue, though the only passion fostered in her heart—is love. Nay, the honour of a woman is not made even to depend on her will.

When Richardson[40] makes Clarissa tell Lovelace that he had robbed her of her honour, he must have had strange notions of honour and virtue. For, miserable beyond all names of misery is the condition of a being, who could be degraded without its own consent! This excess of strictness I have heard vindicated as a salutary error. I

[39]Institutions for the reformation of prostitutes. London's Magdalen Hospital, founded in 1758, was named for St. Mary Magdalene, the archetypal redeemed harlot (see Luke 7:37–50, 8:2).

[40]Dr. Young supports the same opinion, in his plays, when he talks of the misfortune that shunned the light of day [MW]. Samuel Richardson (1689–1761). In his celebrated novel *Clarissa* (1747–48), villain Lovelace rapes the virtuous Clarissa. Edward Young (1683–1765), best known for his extended blank verse meditation *Night Thoughts on Life, Death, and Immortality* (1742–46). In his tragedy *Busiris, King of Egypt* (1719), "So black a story well might shun the day" (1.1) refers to Busiris's usurpation of the throne at the instigation of the King's sister, who then marries the regicide.

shall answer in the words of Leibnitz—"Errors are often useful; but it is commonly to remedy other errors."[41]

Most of the evils of life arise from a desire of present enjoyment that outruns itself. The obedience required of women in the marriage state comes under this description; the mind, naturally weakened by depending on authority, never exerts its own powers, and the obedient wife is thus rendered a weak indolent mother. Or, supposing that this is not always the consequence, a future state of existence is scarcely taken into the reckoning when only negative virtues are cultivated. For, in treating of morals, particularly when women are alluded to, writers have too often considered virtue in a very limited sense, and made the foundation of it *solely* worldly utility; nay, a still more fragile base has been given to this stupendous fabric, and the wayward fluctuating feelings of men have been made the standard of virtue. Yes, virtue as well as religion, has been subjected to the decisions of taste.

It would almost provoke a smile of contempt, if the vain absurdities of man did not strike us on all sides, to observe, how eager men are to degrade the sex from whom they pretend to receive the chief pleasure of life; and I have frequently with full conviction retorted Pope's sarcasm on them[42]; or, to speak explicitly, it has appeared to me applicable to the whole human race. A love of pleasure or sway seems to divide mankind, and the husband who lords it in his little haram thinks only of his pleasure or his convenience. To such lengths, indeed, does an intemperate love of pleasure carry some prudent men, or worn out libertines, who marry to have a safe bed-fellow, that they seduce their own wives.—Hymen[43] banishes modesty, and chaste love takes its flight.

Love, considered as an animal appetite, cannot long feed on itself without expiring. And this extinction in its own flame, may be termed the violent death of love. But the wife who has thus been rendered licentious, will probably endeavour to fill the void left by the loss of her husband's attentions; for she cannot contentedly become merely an upper servant after having been treated like a goddess. She is still handsome, and, instead of transferring her fondness to her children, she only dreams of enjoying the sunshine of life. Besides there are many husbands so devoid of sense and parental affection,

[41]The preface to *Theodicy* (1710) by Gottfried Wilhelm von Leibniz (1646–1716).

[42]*Of the Characters of Women:* "In Men we various Ruling Passions find, / In Women, two almost divide the Kind, / Those only fix'd, they first or last obey, / The Love of Pleasure, and the Love of Sway" (207–10).

[43]God of marriage and the marriage feast.

that during the first effervescence of voluptuous fondness they refuse to let their wives suckle their children.[44] They are only to dress and live to please them: and love—even innocent love, soon sinks into lasciviousness when the exercise of a duty is sacrificed to its indulgence.

Personal attachment is a very happy foundation for friendship; yet, when even two virtuous young people marry, it would, perhaps, be happy if some circumstances checked their passion; if the recollection of some prior attachment, or disappointed affection, made it on one side, at least, rather a match founded on esteem. In that case they would look beyond the present moment, and try to render the whole of life respectable, by forming a plan to regulate a friendship which only death ought to dissolve.

Friendship is a serious affection; the most sublime of all affections, because it is founded on principle, and cemented by time. The very reverse may be said of love. In a great degree, love and friendship cannot subsist in the same bosom; even when inspired by different objects they weaken or destroy each other, and for the same object can only be felt in succession. The vain fears and fond jealousies, the winds which fan the flame of love, when judiciously or artfully tempered, are both incompatible with the tender confidence and sincere respect of friendship.

Love, such as the glowing pen of genius has traced, exists not on earth, or only resides in those exalted, fervid imaginations that have sketched such dangerous pictures. Dangerous, because they not only afford a plausible excuse, to the voluptuary who disguises sheer sensuality under a sentimental veil; but as they spread affectation, and take from the dignity of virtue. Virtue, as the very word imports, should have an appearance of seriousness, if not of austerity; and to endeavour to trick her out in the garb of pleasure, because the epithet has been used as another name for beauty, is to exalt her on a quicksand; a most insidious attempt to hasten her fall by apparent respect. Virtue and pleasure are not, in fact, so nearly allied in this life as some eloquent writers have laboured to prove. Pleasure prepares the fading wreath, and mixes the intoxicating cup; but the fruit which virtue gives, is the recompense of toil: and, gradually seen as it ripens, only affords calm satisfaction; nay, appearing to be the result of the natural tendency of things, it is scarcely observed. Bread, the common food of life, seldom thought of as a blessing, supports the constitution and preserves health; still feasts delight the heart of man,

---

[44]It was common for upper-class women to use wet-nurses.

though disease and even death lurk in the cup or dainty that elevates the spirits or tickles the palate. The lively heated imagination likewise, to apply the comparison, draws the picture of love, as it draws every other picture, with those glowing colours, which the daring hand will steal from the rainbow, that is directed by a mind, condemned in a world like this, to prove its noble origin by panting after unattainable perfection; ever pursuing what it acknowledges to be a fleeting dream. An imagination of this vigorous cast can give existence to insubstantial forms, and stability to the shadowy reveries which the mind naturally falls into when realities are found vapid. It can then depict love with celestial charms, and dote on the grand ideal object—it can imagine a degree of mutual affection that shall refine the soul, and not expire when it has served as a "scale to heavenly"[45]; and, like devotion, make it absorb every meaner affection and desire. In each others arms, as in a temple, with its summit lost in the clouds, the world is to be shut out, and every thought and wish, that do not nurture pure affection and permanent virtue.—Permanent virtue! alas! Rousseau, respectable visionary! thy paradise would soon be violated by the entrance of some unexpected guest. Like Milton's it would only contain angels, or men sunk below the dignity of rational creatures. Happiness is not material, it cannot be seen or felt! Yet the eager pursuit of the good, which every one shapes to his own fancy, proclaims man the lord of this lower world, and to be an intelligential creature, who is not to receive, but acquire happiness. They, therefore, who complain of the delusions of passion, do not recollect that they are exclaiming against a strong proof of the immortality of the soul.

But leaving superior minds to correct themselves, and pay dearly for their experience, it is necessary to observe, that it is not against strong, persevering passions; but romantic wavering feelings that I wish to guard the female heart by exercising the understanding: for these paradisiacal reveries are oftener the effect of idleness than of a lively fancy.

Women have seldom sufficient serious employment to silence their feelings; a round of little cares, or vain pursuits frittering away all strength of mind and organs, they become naturally only objects of sense.—In short, the whole tenour of female education (the education of society) tends to render the best disposed romantic and incon-

---

[45]Milton, *Paradise Lost*: "Love refines / The thoughts, and heart enlarges, hath his seat / In Reason, and is judicious, is the scale / By which to heav'nly Love thou maist ascend" (8.589–92).

stant; and the remainder vain and mean. In the present state of society this evil can scarcely be remedied, I am afraid, in the slightest degree; should a more laudable ambition ever gain ground they may be brought nearer to nature and reason, and become more virtuous and useful as they grow more respectable.

But, I will venture to assert that their reason will never acquire sufficient strength to enable it to regulate their conduct, whilst the making an appearance in the world is the first wish of the majority of mankind. To this weak wish the natural affections, and the most useful virtues are sacrificed. Girls marry merely to *better themselves*, to borrow a significant vulgar phrase, and have such perfect power over their hearts as not to permit themselves to *fall in love* till a man with a superior fortune offers. On this subject I mean to enlarge in a future chapter; it is only necessary to drop a hint at present, because women are so often degraded by suffering the selfish prudence of age to chill the ardour of youth.

From the same source flows an opinion that young girls ought to dedicate great part of their time to needle-work; yet, this employment contracts their faculties more than any other that could have been chosen for them, by confining their thoughts to their persons. Men order their clothes to be made, and have done with the subject; women make their own clothes, necessary or ornamental, and are continually talking about them; and their thoughts follow their hands. It is not indeed the making of necessaries that weakens the mind; but the frippery of dress. For when a woman in the lower rank of life makes her husband's and children's clothes, she does her duty, this is her part of the family business; but when women work only to dress better than they could otherwise afford, it is worse than sheer loss of time. To render the poor virtuous they must be employed, and women in the middle rank of life, did they not ape the fashions of the nobility, without catching their ease, might employ them, whilst they themselves managed their families, instructed their children, and exercised their own minds. Gardening, experimental philosophy,[46] and literature, would afford them subjects to think of and matter for conversation, that in some degree would exercise their understandings. The conversation of French women, who are not so rigidly nailed to their chairs to twist lappets,[47] and knot ribands, is frequently superficial; but, I contend, that it is not half so insipid as that of those Eng-

---

[46]Natural science.

[47]Hanging ribbons, on a head-dress.

lish women whose time is spent in making caps, bonnets, and the whole mischief of trimmings, not to mention shopping, bargain-hunting, etc. etc.; and it is the decent, prudent women, who are most degraded by these practices; for their motive is simply vanity. The wanton who exercises her taste to render her passion alluring, has something more in view.

These observations all branch out of a general one, which I have before made, and which cannot be too often insisted upon, for, speaking of men, women, or professions, it will be found that the employment of the thoughts shapes the character both generally and individually. The thoughts of women ever hover round their persons, and is it surprising that their persons are reckoned most valuable? Yet some degree of liberty of mind is necessary even to form the person; and this may be one reason why some gentle wives have so few attractions beside that of sex. Add to this, sedentary employments render the majority of women sickly—and false notions of female excellence make them proud of this delicacy, though it be another fetter, that by calling the attention continually to the body, cramps the activity of the mind.

Women of quality seldom do any of the manual part of their dress, consequently only their taste is exercised, and they acquire, by thinking less of the finery, when the business of their toilet is over, that ease, which seldom appears in the deportment of women, who dress merely for the sake of dressing. In fact, the observation with respect to the middle rank, the one in which talents thrive best, extends not to women; for those of the superior class, by catching, at least, a smattering of literature, and conversing more with men, on general topics, acquire more knowledge than the women who ape their fashions and faults without sharing their advantages. With respect to virtue, to use the word in a comprehensive sense, I have seen most in low life. Many poor women maintain their children by the sweat of their brow,[48] and keep together families that the vices of the fathers would have scattered abroad; but gentlewomen are too indolent to be actively virtuous, and are softened rather than refined by civilization. Indeed, the good sense which I have met with, among the poor women who have had few advantages of education, and yet have acted heroically, strongly confirmed me in the opinion that trifling employments have rendered woman a trifler. Man, tak-

---

[48]God's curse upon Adam: "In the sweat of thy face shalt thou eat bread" (Genesis 3:19).

ing her[49] body, the mind is left to rust; so that while physical love enervates man, as being his favourite recreation, he will endeavour to enslave woman:—and, who can tell, how many generations may be necessary to give vigour to the virtue and talents of the freed posterity of abject slaves?[50]

In tracing the causes that, in my opinion, have degraded woman, I have confined my observations to such as universally act upon the morals and manners of the whole sex, and to me it appears clear that they all spring from want of understanding. Whether this arise from a physical or accidental weakness of faculties, time alone can determine; for I shall not lay any great stress on the example of a few women[51] who, from having received a masculine education, have acquired courage and resolution; I only contend that the men who have been placed in similar situations, have acquired a similar character—I speak of bodies of men, and that men of genius and talents have started out of a class, in which women have never yet been placed.

[49]"I take her body," says Ranger [MW]. A remark by a debauched character in Benjamin Hoadly's comedy *The Suspicious Husband* (1747). He is reading William Congreve's "Song": "You think she's false. I'm sure she's kind, / I take her body, you her mind; / Which has the better bargain?" (1.1).

[50]"Supposing that women are voluntary slaves—slavery of any kind is unfavourable to human happiness and improvement." *Knox's Essays* [MW]. Vicesimus Knox (1752–1821) was a minister, writer, and reformer of education. In "On the Fear of Appearing Singular," *Essays, Moral and Literary* (1778), the "voluntary slaves" are conformists in general.

[51]Sappho, Eloisa, Mrs. Macaulay, the Empress of Russia, Madame d'Eon, etc. These, and many more, may be reckoned exceptions; and are not all heroes, as well as heroines, exceptions to general rules? I wish to see women neither heroines nor brutes; but reasonable creatures [MW]. **Sappho** (c. 600 BCE) was a celebrated Greek lyric poet. A French noblewoman and intellectual, **Héloïse** (c. 1101–64), secretly married theologian Peter Abelard. When her guardian discovered the match, he had Abelard castrated, and the lovers were separated. Their correspondence inspired Pope's "Eloisa to Abelard" (1717) and Rousseau's *Julie; ou, La Nouvelle Héloïse* (1761). **Catharine Macaulay** (1731–91) was a progressive historian and polemicist. Her eight-volume *History of England* appeared between 1763 and 1783. Reviewing Macaulay's *Letters on Education* (1790), MW described her as a "masculine" writer (*Analytical Review* 8, November 1790). **"Catherine the Great"** (1729–96) became Empress of Russia in 1762 after deposing and probably murdering her husband. As an "enlightened" despot, she promoted social reform and the education of women. **Chevalier d'Eon**, Charles de Beaumont (1728–1810), was a French diplomat and secret agent who often passed for a woman, and was legally declared a woman in 1777 by an edict of the king, and ordered to wear female attire; an autopsy revealed that he was a man.

CHAPTER V

ANIMADVERSIONS ON SOME OF THE WRITERS WHO HAVE RENDERED WOMEN OBJECTS OF PITY, BORDERING ON CONTEMPT

The opinions speciously supported, in some modern publications on the female character and education, which have given the tone to most of the observations made, in a more cursory manner, on the sex, remain now to be examined.

SECTION I

I shall begin with Rousseau, and give a sketch of his character of woman, in his own words, interspersing comments and reflections. My comments, it is true, will all spring from a few simple principles, and might have been deduced from what I have already said; but the artificial structure has been raised with so much ingenuity, that it seems necessary to attack it in a more circumstantial manner, and make the application myself.

Sophia, says Rousseau, should be as perfect a woman as Emilius is a man, and to render her so, it is necessary to examine the character which nature has given to the sex.[1]

He then proceeds to prove that woman ought to be weak and passive, because she has less bodily strength than man; and hence infers, that she was formed to please and to be subject to him; and that it is her duty to render herself *agreeable* to her master—this being the grand end of her existence.[2] Still, however, to give a little mock dignity to lust, he insists that man should not exert his strength, but depend on the will of the woman, when he seeks for pleasure with her.

"Hence we deduce a third consequence from the different constitutions of the sexes; which is, that the strongest should be master in appearance, and be dependent in fact on the weakest; and that not from any frivolous practice of gallantry or vanity of protectorship, but from an invariable law of nature, which, furnishing woman with a greater facility to excite desires than she has given man to satisfy them, makes the latter dependent on the good pleasure of the former, and compels him to endeavour to please in his turn, *in order to obtain her consent that he should be strongest*.[3] On these occasions the most delightful

---

[1]*Emilius*, 4.5.2.

[2]I have already inserted the passage, page 99 [MW]. See p. 58, n. 7.

[3]What nonsense! [MW, her italics].

circumstance a man finds in his victory is, to doubt whether it was the woman's weakness that yielded to his superior strength, or whether her inclinations spoke in his favour: the females are also generally artful enough to leave this matter in doubt. The understanding of women answers in this respect perfectly to their constitution: so far from being ashamed of their weakness, they glory in it; their tender muscles make no resistance; they affect to be incapable of lifting the smallest burthens, and would blush to be thought robust and strong. To what purpose is all this? Not merely for the sake of appearing delicate, but through an artful precaution: it is thus they provide an excuse beforehand, and a right to be feeble when they think it expedient."[4]

I have quoted this passage, lest my readers should suspect that I warped the author's reasoning to support my own arguments. I have already asserted that in educating women these fundamental principles lead to a system of cunning and lasciviousness.

Supposing woman to have been formed only to please, and be subject to man, the conclusion is just, she ought to sacrifice every other consideration to render herself agreeable to him: and let this brutal desire of self-preservation be the grand spring of all her actions, when it is proved to be the iron bed of fate,[5] to fit which her character should be stretched or contracted, regardless of all moral or physical distinctions. But, if, as I think, may be demonstrated, the purposes, of even this life, viewing the whole, be subverted by practical rules built upon this ignoble base, I may be allowed to doubt whether woman were created for man: and, though the cry of irreligion, or even atheism, be raised against me, I will simply declare, that were an angel from heaven to tell me that Moses's beautiful, poetical cosmogony, and the account of the fall of man,[6] were literally true, I could not believe what my reason told me was derogatory to the character of the Supreme Being: and, having no fear of the devil before mine eyes, I venture to call this a suggestion of reason, instead of resting my weakness on the broad shoulders of the first seducer of my frail sex.

"It being once demonstrated," continues Rousseau, "that man and woman are not, nor ought to be, constituted alike in temperament and character, it follows of course that they should not be educated in the same manner. In pursuing the directions of nature, they ought indeed to act in concert, but they should not be engaged in the

---

[4]*Emilius*, 4.5.7–8.

[5]The mythological figure Procrustes offers this to guests under the guise of hospitality. Those too short were stretched on the rack; those too long had their feet cut off.

[6]Moses was thought to be the author of Genesis.

same employments: the end of their pursuits should be the same, but the means they should take to accomplish them, and of consequence their tastes and inclinations, should be different."[7]

* * *

"Whether I consider the peculiar destination of the sex, observe their inclinations, or remark their duties, all things equally concur to point out the peculiar method of education best adapted to them. Woman and man were made for each other; but their mutual dependence is not the same. The men depend on the women only on account of their desires; the women on the men both on account of their desires and their necessities: we could subsist better without them than they without us."[8]

* * *

"For this reason, the education of the women should be always relative to the men. To please, to be useful to us, to make us love and esteem them, to educate us when young, and take care of us when grown up, to advise, to console us, to render our lives easy and agreeable: these are the duties of women at all times, and what they should be taught in their infancy. So long as we fail to recur to this principle, we run wide of the mark, and all the precepts which are given them contribute neither to their happiness nor our own."[9]

* * *

"Girls are from their earliest infancy fond of dress. Not content with being pretty, they are desirous of being thought so; we see, by all their little airs, that this thought engages their attention; and they are hardly capable of understanding what is said to them, before they are to be governed by talking to them of what people will think of their behaviour. The same motive, however, indiscreetly made use of with boys, has not the same effect: provided they are let pursue their amusements at pleasure, they care very little what people think of them. Time and pains are necessary to subject boys to this motive.

"Whencesoever girls derive this first lesson, it is a very good one. As the body is born, in a manner, before the soul, our first concern should be to cultivate the former; this order is common to both sexes,

---

[7]*Emilius*, 4.5.15.

[8]*Emilius*, 4.5.18–19.

[9]*Emilius*, 4.5.19–20.

but the object of that cultivation is different. In the one sex it is the development of corporeal powers; in the other, that of personal charms: not that either the quality of strength or beauty ought to be confined exclusively to one sex; but only that the order of the cultivation of both is in that respect reversed. Women certainly require as much strength as to enable them to move and act gracefully, and men as much address as to qualify them to act with ease."[10]

∗   ∗   ∗

"Children of both sexes have a great many amusements in common; and so they ought; have they not also many such when they are grown up? Each sex has also its peculiar taste to distinguish in this particular. Boys love sports of noise and activity; to beat the drum, to whip the top, and to drag about their little carts: girls, on the other hand, are fonder of things of show and ornament; such as mirrours, trinkets, and dolls: the doll is the peculiar amusement of the females; from whence we see their taste plainly adapted to their destination. The physical part of the art of pleasing lies in dress; and this is all which children are capacitated to cultivate of that art."[11]

∗   ∗   ∗

"Here then we see a primary propensity firmly established, which you need only to pursue and regulate. The little creature will doubtless be very desirous to know how to dress up her doll, to make its sleeve-knots, its flounces, its head-dress, etc. she is obliged to have so much recourse to the people about her, for their assistance in these articles, that it would be much more agreeable to her to owe them all to her own industry. Hence we have a good reason for the first lessons that are usually taught these young females: in which we do not appear to be setting them a task, but obliging them, by instructing them in what is immediately useful to themselves. And, in fact, almost all of them learn with reluctance to read and write; but very readily apply themselves to the use of their needles. They imagine themselves already grown up, and think with pleasure that such qualifications will enable them to decorate themselves."[12]

This is certainly only an education of the body; but Rousseau is not the only man who has indirectly said that merely the person of a

---

[10]*Emilius*, 4.5.21–22.

[11]*Emilius*, 4.5.25.

[12]*Emilius*, 4.5.26–27.

young woman, without any mind, unless animal spirits come under that description, is very pleasing. To render it weak, and what some may call beautiful, the understanding is neglected, and girls forced to sit still, play with dolls and listen to foolish conversations;—the effect of habit is insisted upon as an undoubted indication of nature. I know it was Rousseau's opinion that the first years of youth should be employed to form the body,[13] though in educating Emilius he deviates from this plan; yet, the difference between strengthening the body, on which strength of mind in a great measure depends, and only giving it an easy motion, is very wide.

Rousseau's observations, it is proper to remark, were made in a country where the art of pleasing was refined only to extract the grossness of vice.[14] He did not go back to nature, or his ruling appetite disturbed the operations of reason, else he would not have drawn these crude inferences.

In France boys and girls, particularly the latter, are only educated to please, to manage their persons, and regulate their exterior behaviour; and their minds are corrupted, at a very early age, by the worldly and pious cautions they receive to guard them against immodesty. I speak of past times. The very confessions which mere children were obliged to make, and the questions asked by the holy men, I assert these facts on good authority, were sufficient to impress a sexual character[15]; and the education of society was a school of coquetry and art. At the age of ten or eleven; nay, often much sooner, girls began to coquet, and talked, unreproved, of establishing themselves in the world by marriage.

In short, they were treated like women, almost from their very birth, and compliments were listened to instead of instruction. These, weakening the mind, Nature was supposed to have acted like a stepmother, when she formed this after-thought of creation.

Not allowing them understanding, however, it was but consistent to subject them to authority independent of reason; and to prepare them for this subjection, he gives the following advice:

"Girls ought to be active and diligent; nor is that all; they should also be early subjected to restraint. This misfortune, if it really be

---

[13]Janet Todd notes that, "Rousseau wants [Émile's] early years to be devoted to the education of the senses [1.2.234]; the child should be encouraged to draw, to sing and to articulate" (Todd, 151).

[14]Rousseau spent most of his life in France, and published *Émile* in Paris.

[15]Priests could require confession of sexual transgressions.

one, is inseparable from their sex; nor do they ever throw it off but to suffer more cruel evils. They must be subject, all their lives, to the most constant and severe restraint, which is that of decorum: it is, therefore, necessary to accustom them early to such confinement, that it may not afterwards cost them too dear; and to the suppression of their caprices, that they may the more readily submit to the will of others. If, indeed, they be fond of being always at work, they should be sometimes compelled to lay it aside. Dissipation, levity, and inconstancy, are faults that readily spring up from their first propensities, when corrupted or perverted by too much indulgence. To prevent this abuse, we should teach them, above all things, to lay a due restraint on themselves. The life of a modest woman is reduced, by our absurd institutions, to a perpetual conflict with herself: not but it is just that this sex should partake of the sufferings which arise from those evils it hath caused us."[16]

And why is the life of a modest woman a perpetual conflict? I should answer, that this very system of education makes it so. Modesty, temperance, and self-denial, are the sober offspring of reason; but when sensibility is nurtured at the expense of the understanding, such weak beings must be restrained by arbitrary means, and be subjected to continual conflicts; but give their activity of mind a wider range, and nobler passions and motives will govern their appetites and sentiments.

"The common attachment and regard of a mother, nay, mere habit, will make her beloved by her children, if she do nothing to incur their hate. Even the constraint she lays them under, if well directed, will increase their affection, instead of lessening it; because a state of dependence being natural to the sex, they perceive themselves formed for obedience."[17]

This is begging the question; for servitude not only debases the individual, but its effects seem to be transmitted to posterity. Considering the length of time that women have been dependent, is it surprising that some of them hug their chains, and fawn like the spaniel? "These dogs," observes a naturalist, "at first kept their ears erect; but custom has superseded nature, and a token of fear is become a beauty."[18]

---

[16]*Emilius*, 4.5.30.

[17]*Emilius*, 4.5.31.

[18]In Chapter 4 of "The Natural History of the Dog" (1762), Buffon argues a dog in its natural state has erect ears, but those domesticated—docile spaniels and lap dogs—have been so degenerated that their very ears have drooped. MW may also have in mind William Smellie's *The Philosophy of Natural History* (1790), 1.462, which she had reviewed (*Analytical Review* 8, October 1790).

"For the same reason," adds Rousseau, "women have, or ought to have, but little liberty; they are apt to indulge themselves excessively in what is allowed them. Addicted in every thing to extremes, they are even more transported at their diversions than boys."[19]

The answer to this is very simple. Slaves and mobs have always indulged themselves in the same excesses, when once they broke loose from authority.—The bent bow recoils with violence, when the hand is suddenly relaxed that forcibly held it; and sensibility, the play-thing of outward circumstances, must be subjected to authority, or moderated by reason.

"There results," he continues, "from this habitual restraint a tractableness which women have occasion for during their whole lives, as they constantly remain either under subjection to the men, or to the opinions of mankind; and are never permitted to set themselves above those opinions. The first and most important qualification in a woman is good-nature or sweetness of temper: formed to obey a being so imperfect as man, often full of vices, and always full of faults, she ought to learn betimes even to suffer injustice, and to bear the insults of a husband without complaint; it is not for his sake, but her own, that she should be of a mild disposition. The perverseness and ill-nature of the women only serve to aggravate their own misfortunes, and the misconduct of their husbands; they might plainly perceive that such are not the arms by which they gain the superiority."[20]

Formed to live with such an imperfect being as man, they ought to learn from the exercise of their faculties the necessity of forbearance; but all the sacred rights of humanity are violated by insisting on blind obedience; or, the most sacred rights belong *only* to man.

The being who patiently endures injustice, and silently bears insults, will soon become unjust, or unable to discern right from wrong. Besides, I deny the fact, this is not the true way to form or meliorate the temper; for, as a sex, men have better tempers than women, because they are occupied by pursuits that interest the head as well as the heart; and the steadiness of the head gives a healthy temperature to the heart. People of sensibility have seldom good tempers. The formation of the temper is the cool work of reason, when, as life advances, she mixes with happy art, jarring elements. I never knew a weak or ignorant person who had a good temper, though that constitutional good humour, and that docility, which fear stamps on

[19]*Emilius*, 4.5.31.

[20]*Emilius*, 4.5.32–33.

the behaviour, often obtains the name. I say behaviour, for genuine meekness never reached the heart or mind, unless as the effect of reflection; and that simple restraint produces a number of peccant humours in domestic life, many sensible men will allow, who find some of these gentle irritable creatures, very troublesome companions.

"Each sex," he further argues, "should preserve its peculiar tone and manner; a meek husband may make a wife impertinent; but mildness of disposition on the woman's side will always bring a man back to reason, at least if he be not absolutely a brute, and will sooner or later triumph over him."[21] Perhaps the mildness of reason might sometimes have this effect; but abject fear always inspires contempt; and tears are only eloquent when they flow down fair cheeks.

Of what materials can that heart be composed, which can melt when insulted, and instead of revolting at injustice, kiss the rod? Is it unfair to infer that her virtue is built on narrow views and selfishness, who can caress a man, with true feminine softness, the very moment when he treats her tyrannically? Nature never dictated such insincerity;—and, though prudence of this sort be termed a virtue, morality becomes vague when any part is supposed to rest on falsehood. These are mere expedients, and expedients are only useful for the moment.

Let the husband beware of trusting too implicitly to this servile obedience; for if his wife can with winning sweetness caress him when angry, and when she ought to be angry, unless contempt has stifled a natural effervescence, she may do the same after parting with a lover. These are all preparations for adultery; or, should the fear of the world, or of hell, restrain her desire of pleasing other men, when she can no longer please her husband, what substitute can be found by a being who was only formed, by nature and art, to please man? what can make her amends for this privation, or where is she to seek for a fresh employment? where find sufficient strength of mind to determine to begin the search, when her habits are fixed, and vanity has long ruled her chaotic mind?

But this partial moralist recommends cunning systematically and plausibly.

"Daughters should be always submissive; their mothers, however, should not be inexorable. To make a young person tractable, she ought not to be made unhappy, to make her modest she ought not to be rendered stupid. On the contrary, I should not be displeased at her being permitted to use some art, not to elude punishment in case of disobedience, but to exempt herself from the necessity of obeying. It

[21]*Emilius*, 4.5.33.

is not necessary to make her dependence burdensome, but only to let her feel it. Subtilty is a talent natural to the sex; and, as I am persuaded, all our natural inclinations are right and good in themselves, I am of opinion this should be cultivated as well as the others: it is requisite for us only to prevent its abuse."[22]

"Whatever is, is right,"[23] he then proceeds triumphantly to infer. Granted;—yet, perhaps, no aphorism ever contained a more paradoxical assertion. It is a solemn truth with respect to God. He, reverentially I speak, sees the whole at once, and saw its just proportions in the womb of time; but man, who can only inspect disjointed parts, finds many things wrong; and it is a part of the system, and therefore right, that he should endeavour to alter what appears to him to be so, even while he bows to the Wisdom of his Creator, and respects the darkness he labours to disperse.

The inference that follows is just, supposing the principle to be sound. "The superiority of address, peculiar to the female sex, is a very equitable indemnification for their inferiority in point of strength: without this, woman would not be the companion of man, but his slave: it is by her superiour art and ingenuity that she preserves her equality, and governs him while she affects to obey. Woman has every thing against her, as well our faults, as her own timidity and weakness; she has nothing in her favour, but her subtility and her beauty. Is it not very reasonable, therefore, she should cultivate both?"[24] Greatness of mind can never dwell with cunning, or address; for I shall not boggle about words, when their direct signification is insincerity and falsehood, but content myself with observing, that if any class of mankind be so created that it must necessarily be educated by rules not strictly deducible from truth, virtue is an affair of convention. How could Rousseau dare to assert, after giving this advice, that in the grand end of existence the object of both sexes should be the same, when he well knew that the mind, formed by its pursuits, is expanded by great views swallowing up little ones, or that it becomes itself little?

Men have superiour strength of body; but were it not for mistaken notions of beauty, women would acquire sufficient to enable them to earn their own subsistence, the true definition of independence; and to bear those bodily inconveniences and exertions that are requisite to strengthen the mind.

[22]*Emilius*, 4.5.33.

[23]*Emilius*, 4.5.35. To translate Rousseau's "Ce qui est, est bien" (That which is, is well), William Kenrick supplies Pope's *Essay on Man*, 1.294.

[24]*Emilius*, 4.5.35–36.

Let us then, by being allowed to take the same exercise as boys, not only during infancy, but youth, arrive at perfection of body, that we may know how far the natural superiority of man extends. For what reason or virtue can be expected from a creature when the seed-time of life is neglected? None—did not the winds of heaven casually scatter many useful seeds in fallow ground.

"Beauty cannot be acquired by dress, and coquetry is an art not so early and speedily attained. While girls are yet young, however, they are in a capacity to study agreeable gesture, a pleasing modulation of voice, an easy carriage and behaviour; as well as to take the advantage of gracefully adapting their looks and attitudes to time, place, and occasion. Their application, therefore, should not be solely confined to the arts of industry and the needle, when they come to display other talents, whose utility is already apparent."[25]

"For my part, I would have a young Englishwoman cultivate her agreeable talents, in order to please her future husband, with as much care and assiduity as a young Circassian cultivates her's, to fit her for the Haram of an Eastern bashaw."[26]

To render women completely insignificant, he adds—"The tongues of women are very voluble; they speak earlier, more readily, and more agreeably, than the men; they are accused also of speaking much more; but so it ought to be, and I should be very ready to convert this reproach into a compliment; their lips and eyes have the same activity, and for the same reason. A man speaks of what he knows, a woman of what pleases her; the one requires knowledge, the other taste; the principal object of a man's discourse should be what is useful, that of a woman's what is agreeable. There ought to be nothing in common between their different conversation but truth."[27]

"We ought not, therefore, to restrain the prattle of girls, in the same manner as we should that of boys, with that severe question; *To what purpose are you talking?* but by another, which is no less difficult to answer, *How will your discourse be received?* In infancy, while they are as yet incapable to discern good from evil, they ought to observe it, as a law never to say any thing disagreeable to those whom they are speaking to: what will render the practice of this rule also the more difficult, is, that it must ever be subordinate to the former, of never speak-

[25]*Emilius*, 4.5.40.

[26]*Emilius*, 4.5.42. Rosseau writes *jeune française*; the young women of Circassia, renowned for beauty, were often sold into the harems of Turkish rulers.

[27]*Emilius*, 4.5.45–46.

ing falsely or telling an untruth."[28] To govern the tongue in this manner must require great address indeed; and it is too much practised both by men and women.—Out of the abundance of the heart how few speak![29] So few, that I, who love simplicity, would gladly give up politeness for a quarter of the virtue that has been sacrificed to an equivocal quality which at best should only be the polish of virtue.

But, to complete the sketch. "It is easy to be conceived, that if male children be not in a capacity to form any true notions of religion, those ideas must be greatly above the conception of the females: it is for this very reason, I would begin to speak to them the earlier on this subject; for if we were to wait till they were in a capacity to discuss methodically such profound questions, we should run a risk of never speaking to them on this subject as long as they lived. Reason in women is a practical reason, capacitating them artfully to discover the means of attaining a known end, but which would never enable them to discover that end itself. The social relations of the sexes are indeed truly admirable: from their union there results a moral person, of which woman may be termed the eyes, and man the hand, with this dependence on each other, that it is from the man that the woman is to learn what she is to see, and it is of the woman that man is to learn what he ought to do. If woman could recur to the first principles of things as well as man, and man was capacitated to enter into their *minutiae* as well as woman, always independent of each other, they would live in perpetual discord, and their union could not subsist. But in the present harmony which naturally subsists between them, their different faculties tend to one common end; it is difficult to say which of them conduces the most to it: each follows the impulse of the other; each is obedient, and both are masters."

"As the conduct of a woman is subservient to the public opinion, her faith in matters of religion should, for that very reason, be subject to authority. *Every daughter ought to be of the same religion as her mother, and every wife to be of the same religion as her husband: for, though such religion should be false, that docility which induces the mother and daughter to submit to the order of nature, takes away, in the sight of God, the criminality of their error.*[30] As they are not in a

---

[28]*Emilius*, 4.5.46.

[29]MW inserts "few" into Matthew 12:34: "For out of the abundance of the heart the mouth speaketh."

[30]What is to the consequence, if the mother's and husband's opinion should *chance* not to agree? An ignorant person cannot be reasoned out of an error—and when *persuaded* to give up one prejudice for another the mind is unsettled. Indeed, the husband may not have any religion to teach her, though in such a situation she will be in great want of a support to her virtue, independent of worldly considerations [MW].

capacity to judge for themselves, they ought to abide by the decision of their fathers and husbands as confidently as by that of the Church."[31]

"As authority ought to regulate the religion of the women, it is not so needful to explain to them the reasons for their belief, as to lay down precisely the tenets they are to believe: for the creed, which presents only obscure ideas to the mind, is the source of fanaticism; and that which presents absurdities, leads to infidelity."[32]

Absolute, uncontroverted authority, it seems, must subsist somewhere: but is not this a direct and exclusive appropriation of reason? The *rights* of humanity have been thus confined to the male line from Adam downwards. Rousseau would carry his male aristocracy still further, for he insinuates, that he should not blame those, who contend for leaving woman in a state of the most profound ignorance, if it were not necessary in order to preserve her chastity and justify the man's choice, in the eyes of the world, to give her a little knowledge of men, and the customs produced by human passions; else she might propagate at home without being rendered less voluptuous and innocent by the exercise of her understanding: excepting, indeed, during the first year of marriage, when she might employ it to dress like Sophia. "Her dress is extremely modest in appearance, and yet very coquettish in fact: she does not make a display of her charms, she conceals them; but in concealing them, she knows how to affect your imagination. Every one who sees her will say, There is a modest and discreet girl; but while you are near her, your eyes and affections wander all over her person, so that you cannot withdraw them; and you would conclude, that every part of her dress, simple as it seems, was only put in its proper order to be taken to pieces by the imagination."[33] Is this modesty? Is this a preparation for immortality? Again.—What opinion are we to form of a system of education, when the author says of his heroine, "that with her, doing things well, is but a *secondary* concern; her principal concern is to do them *neatly*."[34]

Secondary, in fact, are all her virtues and qualities, for, respecting religion, he makes her parents thus address her, accustomed to submission—"Your husband will instruct you in *good time*."[35]

After thus cramping a woman's mind, if, in order to keep it fair, he have not made it quite a blank, he advises her to reflect, that a reflect-

---

[31]*Emilius,* 4.5.48–49; MW's emphases.

[32]*Emilius,* 4.5.50.

[33]*Emilius,* 4.5.91.

[34]*Emilius,* 4.5.94; MW's emphases.

[35]*Emilius,* 4.5.97; MW's emphases.

ing man may not yawn in her company, when he is tired of caressing her.—What has she to reflect about who must obey? and would it not be a refinement on cruelty only to open her mind to make the darkness and misery of her fate *visible?*[36] Yet, these are his sensible remarks; how consistent with what I have already been obliged to quote, to give a fair view of the subject, the reader may determine.

"They who pass their whole lives in working for their daily bread, have no ideas beyond their business or their interest, and all their understanding seems to lie in their fingers' ends. This ignorance is neither prejudicial to their integrity nor their morals; it is often of service to them. Sometimes, by means of reflection, we are led to compound with our duty, and we conclude by substituting a jargon of words, in the room of things. Our own conscience is the most enlightened philosopher. There is no need to be acquainted with Tully's offices,[37] to make a man of probity: and perhaps the most virtuous woman in the world, is the least acquainted with the definition of virtue. But it is no less true, that an improved understanding only can render society agreeable; and it is a melancholy thing for a father of a family, who is fond of home, to be obliged to be always wrapped up in himself, and to have nobody about him to whom he can impart his sentiments.

"Besides, how should a woman void of reflection be capable of educating her children? How should she discern what is proper for them? How should she incline them to those virtues she is unacquainted with, or to that merit of which she has no idea? She can only sooth or chide them; render them insolent or timid; she will make them formal coxcombs, or ignorant blockheads; but will never make these sensible or amiable."[38] How indeed should she, when her husband is not always at hand to lend her his reason?—when they both together make but one moral being. A blind will, "eyes without hands," would go a very little way; and perchance his abstract reason, that should concentrate the scattered beams of her practical reason, may be employed in judging of the flavour of wine, descanting on the sauces most proper for turtle; or, more profoundly intent at a card-table, he may be generalizing his ideas as he bets away his fortune, leaving all the *minutiae* of education to his helpmate, or to chance.

[36]Surveying the confines of hell Satan sees: "No light, but rather darkness visible" (*Paradise Lost*, 1.63).

[37]Famous Roman orator and statesman Marcus Tullius Cicero (106–43 BCE) considers virtue in his treatise *De officiis.*

[38]*Emilius,* 4.5.124–25.

But, granting that woman ought to be beautiful, innocent, and silly, to render her a more alluring and indulgent companion;—what is her understanding sacrificed for? And why is all this preparation necessary only, according to Rousseau's own account, to make her the mistress of her husband, a very short time? For no man ever insisted more on the transient nature of love. Thus speaks the philosopher. "Sensual pleasures are transient. The habitual state of the affections always loses by their gratification. The imagination, which decks the object of our desires, is lost in fruition. Excepting the Supreme Being, who is self-existent, there is nothing beautiful but what is ideal."[39]

But he returns to his unintelligible paradoxes again, when he thus addresses Sophia. "Emilius, in becoming your husband, is become your master; and claims your obedience. Such is the order of nature. When a man is married, however, to such a wife as Sophia, it is proper he should be directed by her: this is also agreeable to the order of nature: it is, therefore, to give you as much authority over his heart as his sex gives him over your person, that I have made you the arbiter of his pleasures. It may cost you, perhaps, some disagreeable self-denial; but you will be certain of maintaining your empire over him, if you can preserve it over yourself—what I have already observed, also, shows me that this difficult attempt does not surpass your courage.

"Would you have your husband constantly at your feet? keep him at some distance from your person. You will long maintain the authority in love, if you know but how to render your favours rare and valuable. It is thus you may employ even the arts of coquetry in the service of virtue, and those of love in that of reason."[40]

I shall close my extracts with a just description of a comfortable couple: "And yet you must not imagine, that even such management will always suffice. Whatever precaution be taken, enjoyment will, by degrees, take off the edge of passion. But when love hath lasted as long as possible, a pleasing habitude supplies its place, and the attachment of a mutual confidence succeeds to the transports of passion. Children often form a more agreeable and permanent connection between married people than even love itself. When you cease to be the mistress of Emilius, you will continue to be his wife and friend, you will be the mother of his children."[41]

[39]*Emilius*, 4.5.214.
[40]*Emilius*, 4.5.288–89.
[41]Rousseau's Emilius [MW]; 4.5.289–90.

Children, he truly observes, form a much more permanent connection between married people than love. Beauty, he declares, will not be valued, or even seen after a couple have lived six months together; artificial graces and coquetry will likewise pall on the senses: why then does he say that a girl should be educated for her husband with the same care as for an Eastern haram?

I now appeal from the reveries of fancy and refined licentiousness to the good sense of mankind, whether, if the object of education be to prepare women to become chaste wives and sensible mothers, the method so plausibly recommended in the foregoing sketch, be the one best calculated to produce those ends? Will it be allowed that the surest way to make a wife chaste, is to teach her to practise the wanton arts of a mistress, termed virtuous coquetry, by the sensualist who can no longer relish the artless charms of sincerity, or taste the pleasure arising from a tender intimacy, when confidence is unchecked by suspicion, and rendered interesting by sense?

The man who can be contented to live with a pretty, useful companion, without a mind, has lost in voluptuous gratifications a taste for more refined enjoyments; he has never felt the calm satisfaction, that refreshes the parched heart, like the silent dew of heaven,—of being beloved by one who could understand him.—In the society of his wife he is still alone, unless when the man is sunk in the brute. "The charm of life," says a grave philosophical reasoner, is "sympathy; nothing pleases us more than to observe in other men a fellow-feeling with all the emotions of our own breast."[42]

But, according to the tenour of reasoning, by which women are kept from the tree of knowledge, the important years of youth, the usefulness of age, and the rational hopes of futurity, are all to be sacrificed to render women an object of desire for a *short* time. Besides, how could Rousseau expect them to be virtuous and constant when reason is neither allowed to be the foundation of their virtue, nor truth the object of their inquiries?

But all Rousseau's errors in reasoning arose from sensibility, and sensibility to their charms women are very ready to forgive! When he should have reasoned he became impassioned, and reflection inflamed his imagination instead of enlightening his understanding. Even his virtues also led him farther astray; for, born with a warm constitution and lively fancy, nature carried him toward the other sex with such eager fond-

---

[42]Adam Smith, "Of the Pleasure of Mutual Sympathy," *Theory of Moral Sentiments* (1.1.2).

ness, that he soon became lascivious. Had he given way to these desires, the fire would have extinguished itself in a natural manner; but virtue, and a romantic kind of delicacy, made him practise self-denial; yet when fear, delicacy, or virtue, restrained him, he debauched his imagination, and reflecting on the sensations to which fancy gave force, he traced them in the most glowing colours, and sunk them deep into his soul.

He then sought for solitude, not to sleep with the man of nature; or calmly investigate the causes of things under the shade where Sir Isaac Newton indulged contemplation,[43] but merely to indulge his feelings. And so warmly has he painted what he forcibly felt, that, interesting the heart and inflaming the imagination of his readers; in proportion to the strength of their fancy, they imagine that their understanding is convinced when they only sympathize with a poetic writer, who skilfully exhibits the objects of sense, most voluptuously shadowed or gracefully veiled—And thus making us feel whilst dreaming that we reason, erroneous conclusions are left in the mind.

Why was Rousseau's life divided between ecstasy and misery? Can any other answer be given than this, that the effervescence of his imagination produced both; but had his fancy been allowed to cool, it is possible that he might have acquired more strength of mind. Still, if the purpose of life be to educate the intellectual part of man, all with respect to him was right; yet, had not death led to a nobler scene of action, it is probable that he would have enjoyed more equal happiness on earth, and have felt the calm sensations of the man of nature instead of being prepared for another stage of existence by nourishing the passions which agitate the civilized man.

But peace to his manes![44] I war not with his ashes, but his opinions. I war only with the sensibility that led him to degrade woman by making her the slave of love.

> "—Cursed vassalage,
> First idoliz'd till love's hot fire be o'er,
> Then slaves to those who courted us before."
>
> *Dryden*[45]

---

[43]Sir Isaac Newton (1642–1727) was said to have derived his theory of gravity in 1665 when he saw an apple fall as he was sitting under the shade of a tree in a garden.

[44]The spirit or "shade" of the departed.

[45]Eve speaks these lines in John Dryden's *The State of Innocence: and Fall of Man* (1677), 5.1.58–60; the first line is actually "Curs'd vasalage of all my future kind." Although never set to music or performed, this work was intended as an operatic version of *Paradise Lost*.

The pernicious tendency of those books, in which the writers insidiously degrade the sex whilst they are prostrate before their personal charms, cannot be too often or too severely exposed.

Let us, my dear contemporaries, arise above such narrow prejudices! If wisdom be desirable on its own account, if virtue, to deserve the name, must be founded on knowledge; let us endeavour to strengthen our minds by reflection, till our heads become a balance for our hearts; let us not confine all our thoughts to the petty occurrences of the day, or our knowledge to an acquaintance with our lovers' or husbands' hearts; but let the practice of every duty be subordinate to the grand one of improving our minds, and preparing our affections for a more exalted state!

Beware, then, my friends, of suffering the heart to be moved by every trivial incident: the reed is shaken by a breeze, and annually dies, but the oak stands firm, and for ages braves the storm!

Were we, indeed, only created to flutter our hour out and die— why let us then indulge sensibility, and laugh at the severity of reason.—Yet, alas! even then we should want strength of body and mind, and life would be lost in feverish pleasures or wearisome languor.

But the system of education, which I earnestly wish to see exploded, seems to pre-suppose what ought never to be taken for granted, that virtue shields us from the casualties of life; and that fortune, slipping off her bandage, will smile on a well-educated female, and bring in her hand an Emilius or a Telemachus.[46] Whilst, on the contrary, the reward which virtue promises to her votaries is confined, it seems clear, to their own bosoms; and often must they contend with the most vexatious worldly cares, and bear with the vices and humours of relations for whom they can never feel a friendship.

There have been many women in the world who, instead of being supported by the reason and virtue of their fathers and brothers, have strengthened their own minds by struggling with their vices and follies; yet have never met with a hero, in the shape of a husband; who, paying the debt that mankind owed them, might chance to bring back their reason to its natural dependent state, and restore the usurped prerogative, of rising above opinion, to man.

---

[46]When Sophia reads *Les Aventures de Télémaque fils d'Ulysse* (*The Adventures of Telemachus, Son of Ulysses*) (1699), by François de Salignac de la Mothe-Fénelon, she falls madly in love with the hero (*Emilius*, Book 5). Bandage: blindfold.

SECTION II

Dr. Fordyce's sermons have long made a part of a young woman's library; nay, girls at school are allowed to read them; but I should instantly dismiss them from my pupil's if I wished to strengthen her understanding, by leading her to form sound principles on a broad basis; or, were I only anxious to cultivate her taste; though they must be allowed to contain many sensible observations.[47]

Dr. Fordyce may have had a very laudable end in view; but these discourses are written in such an affected style, that were it only on that account, and had I nothing to object against his *mellifluous* precepts, I should not allow girls to peruse them, unless I designed to hunt every spark of nature out of their composition, melting every human quality into female meekness and artificial grace. I say artificial, for true grace arises from some kind of independence of mind.

Children, careless of pleasing, and only anxious to amuse themselves, are often very graceful; and the nobility who have mostly lived with inferiors, and always had the command of money, acquire a graceful ease of deportment, which should rather be termed habitual grace of body, than that superiour gracefulness which is truly the expression of the mind. This mental grace, not noticed by vulgar eyes, often flashes across a rough countenance, and irradiating every feature, shows simplicity and independence of mind.—It is then we read characters of immortality in the eye, and see the soul in every gesture, though when at rest, neither the face nor limbs may have much beauty to recommend them; or the behaviour, any thing peculiar to attract universal attention. The mass of mankind, however, look for more *tangible* beauty; yet simplicity is, in general, admired, when people do not consider what they admire; and can there be simplicity without sincerity? But, to have done with remarks that are in some measure desultory, though naturally excited by the subject—

In declamatory periods Dr. Fordyce spins out Rousseau's eloquence; and in most sentimental rant, details his opinions respecting the female character, and the behaviour which woman ought to assume to render her lovely.

He shall speak for himself, for thus he makes Nature address man. "Behold these smiling innocents, whom I have graced with my fairest gifts, and committed to your protection; behold them with love and respect; treat them with tenderness and honour. They are timid and want

[47]James Fordyce (1720–96), *Sermons to Young Women* (1765), a popular conduct book.

to be defended. They are frail; O do not take advantage of their weakness! Let their fears and blushes endear them. Let their confidence in you never be abused.—But is it possible, that any of you can be such barbarians, so supremely wicked, as to abuse it? Can you find in your hearts[48] to despoil the gentle, trusting creatures of their treasure, or do any thing to strip them of their native robe of virtue? Curst be the impious hand that would dare to violate the unblemished form of Chastity! Thou wretch! thou ruffian! forbear; nor venture to provoke heaven's fiercest vengeance."[49] I know not any comment that can be made seriously on this curious passage, and I could produce many similar ones; and some, so very sentimental, that I have heard rational men use the word indecent, when they mentioned them with disgust.

Throughout there is a display of cold artificial feelings, and that parade of sensibility which boys and girls should be taught to despise as the sure mark of a little vain mind. Florid appeals are made to heaven, and to the *beauteous innocents*, the fairest images of heaven here below, whilst sober sense is left far behind.—This is not the language of the heart, nor will it ever reach it, though the ear may be tickled.

I shall be told, perhaps, that the public have been pleased with these volumes.—True—and Hervey's Meditations[50] are still read, though he equally sinned against sense and taste.

I particularly object to the lover-like phrases of pumped up passion, which are every where interspersed. If women be ever allowed to walk without leading-strings,[51] why must they be cajoled into virtue by artful flattery and sexual compliments?—Speak to them the language of truth and soberness, and away with the lullaby strains of condescending endearment! Let them be taught to respect themselves as rational creatures, and not led to have a passion for their own insipid persons. It moves my gall to hear a preacher descanting on dress and needle-work[52]; and still more, to hear him address the *British fair, the fairest of the fair*,[53] as if they had only feelings.

Even recommending piety he uses the following argument. "Never, perhaps, does a fine woman strike more deeply, than when,

---

[48]Can you?—Can you? would be the most emphatical comment, were it drawled out in a whining voice [MW].

[49]*Sermons*, 1.3.99–100.

[50]By 1792, James Hervey's immensely popular inspirational volume *Meditations and Contemplations* (1745–47) was in its 26th edition.

[51]Used to support children learning to walk.

[52]See *Sermons*, 1.2.69, 1.6.249–53.

[53]Fordyce is actually aiming the phrase satirically at fashionable ladies.

composed into pious recollection, and possessed with the noblest considerations, she assumes, without knowing it, superior dignity and new graces; so that the beauties of holiness seem to radiate about her, and the by-standers are almost reduced to fancy her already worshipping amongst her kindred angels!"[54] Why are women to be thus bred up with a desire of conquest? the very word, used in this sense, gives me a sickly qualm! Do religion and virtue offer no stronger motives, no brighter reward? Must they always be debased by being made to consider the sex of their companions? Must they be taught always to be pleasing? And when levelling their small artillery at the heart of man, is it necessary to tell them that a little sense is sufficient to render their attention *incredibly soothing*? "As a small degree of knowledge entertains in a woman, so from a woman, though for a different reason, a small expression of kindness delights, particularly if she have beauty!"[55] I should have supposed for the same reason.

Why are girls to be told that they resemble angels; but to sink them below women? Or, that a gentle innocent female is an object that comes nearer to the idea which we have formed of angels than any other. Yet they are told, at the same time, that they are only like angels when they are young and beautiful; consequently, it is their persons, not their virtues, that procure them this homage.

Idle empty words! What can such delusive flattery lead to, but vanity and folly? The lover, it is true, has a poetical licence to exalt his mistress; his reason is the bubble of his passion, and he does not utter a falsehood when he borrows the language of adoration. His imagination may raise the idol of his heart, unblamed, above humanity; and happy would it be for women, if they were only flattered by the men who loved them; I mean, who love the individual, not the sex; but should a grave preacher interlard his discourses with such fooleries?

In sermons or novels, however, voluptuousness is always true to its text. Men are allowed by moralists to cultivate, as Nature directs, different qualities, and assume the different characters, that the same passions, modified almost to infinity, give to each individual. A virtuous man may have a choleric or a sanguine constitution, be gay or grave, unreproved; be firm till he is almost overbearing, or, weakly submissive, have no will or opinion of his own; but all women are to be levelled, by meekness and docility, into one character of yielding softness and gentle compliance.

[54]*Sermons*, 2.11.163.
[55]*Sermons*, 2.13.248.

I will use the preacher's own words. "Let it be observed, that in your sex manly exercises are never graceful; that in them a tone and figure, as well as an air and deportment, of the masculine kind, are always forbidding; and that men of sensibility desire in every woman soft features, and a flowing voice, a form, not robust, and demeanour delicate and gentle."[56]

Is not the following portrait—the portrait of a house slave? "I am astonished at the folly of many women, who are still reproaching their husbands for leaving them alone, for preferring this or that company to theirs, for treating them with this and the other mark of disregard or indifference; when, to speak the truth, they have themselves in a great measure to blame. Not that I would justify the men in any thing wrong on their part. But had you behaved to them with more *respectful observance*, and a more *equal tenderness; studying their humours, overlooking their mistakes, submitting to their opinions* in matters indifferent, passing by little instances of unevenness, caprice, or passion, giving *soft* answers to hasty words, complaining as seldom as possible, and making it your daily care to relieve their anxieties and prevent their wishes, to enliven the hour of dulness, and call up the ideas of felicity: had you pursued this conduct, I doubt not but you would have maintained and even increased their esteem, so far as to have secured every degree of influence that could conduce to their virtue, or your mutual satisfaction; and your house might at this day have been the abode of domestic bliss."[57] Such a woman ought to be an angel—or she is an ass—for I discern not a trace of the human character, neither reason nor passion in this domestic drudge, whose being is absorbed in that of a tyrant's.

Still Dr. Fordyce must have very little acquaintance with the human heart, if he really supposed that such conduct would bring back wandering love, instead of exciting contempt. No, beauty, gentleness, etc. etc. may gain a heart; but esteem, the only lasting affection, can alone be obtained by virtue supported by reason. It is respect for the understanding that keeps alive tenderness for the person.

As these volumes are so frequently put into the hands of young people, I have taken more notice of them than, strictly speaking, they deserve; but as they have contributed to vitiate the taste, and enervate the understanding of many of my fellow-creatures, I could not pass them silently over.

[56]*Sermons*, 2.13.224–25.
[57]*Sermons*, 2.14.264–65; MW's italics.

SECTION III

Such paternal solicitude pervades Dr. Gregory's Legacy to his Daughters,[58] that I enter on the task of criticism with affectionate respect; but as this little volume has many attractions to recommend it to the notice of the most respectable part of my sex, I cannot silently pass over arguments that so speciously support opinions which, I think, have had the most baneful effect on the morals and manners of the female world.

His easy familiar style is particularly suited to the tenor of his advice, and the melancholy tenderness which his respect for the memory of a beloved wife, diffuses through the whole work, renders it very interesting; yet there is a degree of concise elegance conspicuous in many passages that disturbs this sympathy; and we pop on[59] the author, when we only expected to meet the—father.

Besides, having two objects in view, he seldom adhered steadily to either; for wishing to make his daughters amiable, and fearing lest unhappiness should only be the consequence, of instilling sentiments that might draw them out of the track of common life without enabling them to act with consonant independence and dignity, he checks the natural flow of his thoughts, and neither advises one thing nor the other.

In the preface he tells them a mournful truth, "that they will hear, at least once in their lives, the genuine sentiments of a man who has no interest in deceiving them."[60]

Hapless woman! what can be expected from thee when the beings on whom thou art said naturally to depend for reason and support, have all an interest in deceiving thee! This is the root of the evil that has shed a corroding mildew on all thy virtues; and blighting in the bud thy opening faculties, has rendered thee the weak thing thou art! It is this separate interest—this insidious state of warfare, that undermines morality, and divides mankind!

If love have made some women wretched—how many more has the cold unmeaning intercourse of gallantry rendered vain and useless! yet this heartless attention to the sex is reckoned so manly, so polite that, till society is very differently organized, I fear, this vestige of gothic[61] manners will not be done away by a more reasonable and affectionate mode of conduct. Besides, to strip it of its imaginary dignity, I must observe,

[58]Dr. John Gregory's purpose in his *Legacy* (1774), composed after their mother's death and in his declining health, was to bequeath useful instruction to his daughters.

[59]Encounter.

[60]*Legacy*, 6.

[61]Barbarous.

that in the most uncivilized European states this lip-service prevails in a very great degree, accompanied with extreme dissoluteness of morals. In Portugal, the country that I particularly allude to, it takes place of the most serious moral obligations; for a man is seldom assassinated when in the company of a woman. The savage hand of rapine is unnerved by this chivalrous spirit; and, if the stroke of vengeance cannot be stayed—the lady is entreated to pardon the rudeness and depart in peace, though sprinkled, perhaps, with her husband's or brother's blood.[62]

I shall pass over his strictures on religion, because I mean to discuss that subject in a separate chapter.

The remarks relative to behaviour, though many of them very sensible, I entirely disapprove of, because it appears to me to be beginning, as it were, at the wrong end. A cultivated understanding, and an affectionate heart, will never want starched rules of decorum—something more substantial than seemliness will be the result; and, without understanding the behaviour here recommended, would be rank affectation. Decorum, indeed, is the one thing needful![63]—decorum is to supplant nature, and banish all simplicity and variety of character out of the female world. Yet what good end can all this superficial counsel produce? It is, however, much easier to point out this or that mode of behaviour, than to set the reason to work; but, when the mind has been stored with useful knowledge, and strengthened by being employed, the regulation of the behaviour may safely be left to its guidance.

Why, for instance, should the following caution be given when art of every kind must contaminate the mind; and why entangle the grand motives of action, which reason and religion equally combine to enforce, with pitiful worldly shifts and slight of hand tricks to gain the applause of gaping tasteless fools? "Be even cautious in displaying your good sense.[64] It will be thought you assume a superiority over the rest of the company—But if you happen to have any learning, keep it a profound secret, especially from the men who generally look with a jealous and malignant eye on a woman of great parts, and a cultivated understanding."[65] If men of real merit, as he afterwards observes, be superior to this meanness, where is the necessity that the behaviour of the whole sex should be modulated to please fools, or men,

---

[62]An anecdote from *Sketches of Society and Manners in Portugal* (1787), by Arthur William Costigan (James Ferrier), reviewed by MW (*Analytical Review* 1, August 1788).

[63]Echoing Jesus's instruction (Luke 10:42).

[64]Let women once acquire good sense—and if it deserve the name, it will teach them; or, of what use will it be? how to employ it [MW].

[65]*Legacy*, 31–32.

who having little claim to respect as individuals, choose to keep close in their phalanx. Men, indeed, who insist on their common superiority, having only this sexual superiority, are certainly very excusable.

There would be no end to rules for behaviour, if it be proper always to adopt the tone of the company; for thus, for ever varying the key, a *flat* would often pass for a *natural* note.

Surely it would have been wiser to have advised women to improve themselves till they rose above the fumes of vanity; and then to let the public opinion come round—for where are rules of accommodation to stop? The narrow path of truth and virtue inclines neither to the right nor left—it is a straightforward business, and they who are earnestly pursuing their road, may bound over many decorous prejudices, without leaving modesty behind. Make the heart clean,[66] and give the head employment, and I will venture to predict that there will be nothing offensive in the behaviour.

The air of fashion, which many young people are so eager to attain, always strikes me like the studied attitudes of some modern pictures, copied with tasteless servility after the antiques;—the soul is left out, and none of the parts are tied together by what may properly be termed character. This varnish of fashion, which seldom sticks very close to sense, may dazzle the weak; but leave nature to itself, and it will seldom disgust the wise. Besides, when a woman has sufficient sense not to pretend to any thing which she does not understand in some degree, there is no need of determining to hide her talents under a bushel.[67] Let things take their natural course, and all will be well.

It is this system of dissimulation, throughout the volume, that I despise. Women are always to *seem* to be this and that—yet virtue might apostrophize them, in the words of Hamlet—Seems! I know not seems!—Have that within that passeth show!—[68]

Still the same tone occurs; for in another place, after recommending, without sufficiently discriminating delicacy, he adds, "The men will complain of your reserve. They will assure you that a franker behaviour would make you more amiable. But, trust me, they are not sincere when they tell you so.—I acknowledge that on some occasions it might render you more agreeable as companions, but it

[66]Echoing David's cry to God, Psalms 51:10.

[67]MW combines the parable of the candle, Matthew 5:15: "Neither do men light a candle, and put it under a bushel, but on a candlestick" (also Luke 11:33 and Mark 4:21); and the talents, Matthew 25:25: "And I was afraid, and went and hid thy talent in the earth."

[68]Echoing Hamlet's rebuke to his mother's too-brief mourning for his father (1.2.76–85).

would make you less amiable as women: an important distinction, which many of your sex are not aware of."[69]—

This desire of being always women, is the very consciousness that degrades the sex. Excepting with a lover, I must repeat with emphasis, a former observation,—it would be well if they were only agreeable or rational companions.—But in this respect his advice is even inconsistent with a passage which I mean to quote with the most marked approbation.

"The sentiment, that a woman may allow all innocent freedoms, provided her virtue is secure, is both grossly indelicate and dangerous, and has proved fatal to many of your sex."[70] With this opinion I perfectly coincide. A man, or a woman, of any feeling, must always wish to convince a beloved object that it is the caresses of the individual, not the sex, that are received and returned with pleasure; and, that the heart, rather than the senses, is moved. Without this natural delicacy, love becomes a selfish personal gratification that soon degrades the character.

I carry this sentiment still further. Affection, when love is out of the question, authorises many personal endearments, that naturally flowing from an innocent heart, give life to the behaviour; but the personal intercourse of appetite, gallantry, or vanity, is despicable. When a man squeezes the hand of a pretty woman, handing her to a carriage, whom he has never seen before, she will consider such an impertinent freedom in the light of an insult, if she have any true delicacy, instead of being flattered by this unmeaning homage to beauty. These are the privileges of friendship, or the momentary homage which the heart pays to virtue, when it flashes suddenly on the notice—mere animal spirits have no claim to the kindnesses of affection!

Wishing to feed the affections with what is now the food of vanity, I would fain persuade my sex to act from simpler principles. Let them merit love, and they will obtain it, though they may never be told that—"The power of a fine woman over the hearts of men, of men of the finest parts, is even beyond what she conceives."[71]

I have already noticed the narrow cautions with respect to duplicity, female softness, delicacy of constitution[72]; for these are the

---

[69]*Legacy*, 36–37.

[70]*Legacy*, 44.

[71]*Legacy*, 42.

[72]*Legacy*, 50–51: "We so naturally associate the idea of female softness and delicacy, with a corresponding delicacy of constitution, that when a woman speaks of her great strength, her extraordinary appetite, her ability to bear excessive fatigue, we recoil at the description in a way she is little aware of."

changes which he rings round without ceasing—in a more decorous manner, it is true, than Rousseau; but it all comes home to the same point, and whoever is at the trouble to analyze these sentiments, will find the first principles not quite so delicate as the superstructure.

The subject of amusements is treated in too cursory a manner; but with the same spirit.

When I treat of friendship, love, and marriage, it will be found that we materially differ in opinion; I shall not then forestall what I have to observe on these important subjects; but confine my remarks to the general tenor of them, to that cautious family prudence, to those confined views of partial unenlightened affection, which exclude pleasure and improvement, by vainly wishing to ward off sorrow and error—and by thus guarding the heart and mind, destroy also all their energy.—It is far better to be often deceived than never to trust; to be disappointed in love than never to love; to lose a husband's fondness than forfeit his esteem.

Happy would it be for the world, and for individuals, of course, if all this unavailing solicitude to attain worldly happiness, on a confined plan, were turned into an anxious desire to improve the understanding.—"Wisdom is the principal thing: *therefore* get wisdom; and with all thy gettings get understanding."—"How long, ye simple ones, will ye love simplicity, and hate knowledge?"[73] Saith Wisdom to the daughters of men!

SECTION IV

I do not mean to allude to all the writers who have written on the subject of female manners—it would, in fact, be only beating over the old ground, for they have, in general, written in the same strain; but attacking the boasted prerogative of man—the prerogative that may emphatically be called the iron sceptre of tyranny, the original sin of tyrants, I declare against all power built on prejudices, however hoary.

If the submission demanded be founded on justice—there is no appealing to a higher power—for God is Justice itself. Let us then, as children of the same parent, if not bastardized by being the younger born, reason together, and learn to submit to the authority of reason—when her voice is distinctly heard. But, if it be proved, that this throne of prerogative only rests on a chaotic mass of prejudices, that have no inherent principle of order to keep them together, or on an

[73]Proverbs 4:7 and 1:22.

elephant, tortoise, or even the mighty shoulders of a son of the earth,[74] they may escape, who dare to brave the consequence, without any breach of duty, without sinning against the order of things.

Whilst reason raises man above the brutal herd, and death is big with promises, they alone are subject to blind authority who have no reliance on their own strength. "They are free—who will be free!"[75]—

The being who can govern itself has nothing to fear in life; but if any thing be dearer than its own respect, the price must be paid to the last farthing. Virtue, like every thing valuable, must be loved for herself alone; or she will not take up her abode with us. She will not impart that peace, "which passeth understanding,"[76] when she is merely made the stilts of reputation; and respected, with pharisaical exactness, because "honesty is the best policy."

That the plan of life which enables us to carry some knowledge and virtue into another world, is the one best calculated to ensure content in this, cannot be denied; yet few people act according to this principle, though it be universally allowed that it admits not of dispute. Present pleasure, or present power, carry before it these sober convictions; and it is for the day, not for life, that man bargains with happiness. How few!—how very few! have sufficient foresight, or resolution, to endure a small evil at the moment, to avoid a greater hereafter.

Woman in particular, whose virtue[77] is built on mutable prejudices, seldom attains to this greatness of mind; so that, becoming the slave of her own feelings, she is easily subjugated by those of others. Thus degraded, her reason, her misty reason! is employed rather to burnish than to snap her chains.

Indignantly have I heard women argue in the same track as men, and adopt the sentiments that brutalize them, with all the pertinacity of ignorance.

I must illustrate my assertion by a few examples. Mrs. Piozzi, who often repeated by rote, what she did not understand, comes forward with Johnsonian periods.

[74]Ancient Indian cosmology imagined earth as a huge disc supported by three elephants standing on an enormous tortoise. In Greek mythology, Atlas supported the earth on his shoulders.

[75]"He is the free man, whom the *truth* makes free!" *Cowper* [MW, her emphasis]. William Cowper, *The Task* (1785), "The Winter Morning Walk" (5.733), alluding to John 8:32: "And ye shall know the truth, and the truth shall make you free." MW put several excerpts from *The Task* in *The Female Reader*.

[76]St. Paul, to the Philippians: "And the peace of God, which passeth all understanding, shall keep your hearts and minds through Christ Jesus" (4:7).

[77]I mean to use a word that comprehends more than chastity the sexual virtue [MW].

"Seek not for happiness in singularity; and dread a refinement of wisdom as a deviation into folly." Thus she dogmatically addresses a new married man; and to elucidate this pompous exordium, she adds, "I said that the person of your lady would not grow more pleasing to you, but pray let her never suspect that it grows less so: that a woman will pardon an affront to her understanding much sooner than one to her person, is well known; nor will any of us contradict the assertion. All our attainments, all our arts, are employed to gain and keep the heart of man; and what mortification can exceed the disappointment, if the end be not obtained? There is no reproof however pointed, no punishment however severe, that a woman of spirit will not prefer to neglect; and if she can endure it without complaint, it only proves that she means to make herself amends by the attention of others for the slights of her husband!" [78]

These are truly masculine sentiments.—"All our *arts* are employed to gain and keep the heart of man:"—and what is the inference?—if her person, and was there ever a person, though formed with Medicean [79] symmetry, that was not slighted? be neglected, she will make herself amends by endeavouring to please other men. Noble morality! But thus is the understanding of the whole sex affronted, and their virtue deprived of the common basis of virtue. A woman must know, that her person cannot be as pleasing to her husband as it was to her lover, and if she be offended with him for being a human creature, she may as well whine about the loss of his heart as about any other foolish thing.—And this very want of discernment or unreasonable anger, proves that he could not change his fondness for her person into affection for her virtues or respect for her understanding.

Whilst women avow, and act up to such opinions, their understandings, at least, deserve the contempt and obloquy that men, *who never* insult their persons, have pointedly levelled at the female mind. And it is the sentiments of these polite men, who do not wish to be

[78]Hester Lynch Thrale Piozzi (1741–1821), *Letters to and from the Late Samuel Johnson, LL.D.* (1788), letter 72:98–100. From 1763 to 1781, Hester and Henry Thrale (a successful brewer) hosted a circle of artists and writers at their home, including Edmund Burke, Joshua Reynolds, Frances Burney, and (most prominently) Samuel Johnson. After her husband's death, she scandalized her family, friends, and London society, with her engagement to Italian musician Gabriel Piozzi; the marriage in 1784 estranged her from Johnson, her daughter Queeney, and many friends. In addition to the *Letters*, she also published *Anecdotes of the Late Samuel Johnson* (1786).

[79]The Venus de Medici, a famous Greek statue held at the Uffizzi gallery in Florence, was regarded as a standard of female beauty.

encumbered with mind, that vain women thoughtlessly adopt. Yet they should know, that insulted reason alone can spread that *sacred* reserve about the person, which renders human affections, for human affections have always some base alloy, as permanent as is consistent with the grand end of existence—the attainment of virtue.

The Baroness de Stael[80] speaks the same language as the lady just cited, with more enthusiasm. Her eulogium on Rousseau was accidentally put into my hands and her sentiments, the sentiments of too many of my sex, may serve as the text for a few comments. "Though Rousseau," she observes, "has endeavoured to prevent women from interfering in public affairs, and acting a brilliant part in the theatre of politics; yet in speaking of them, how much has he done it to their satisfaction! If he wished to deprive them of some rights foreign to their sex, how has he for ever restored to them all those to which it has a claim! And in attempting to diminish their influence over the deliberations of men, how sacredly has he established the empire they have over their happiness! In aiding them to descend from an usurped throne, he has firmly seated them upon that to which they were destined by nature; and though he be full of indignation against them when they endeavour to resemble men, yet when they come before him with all the *charms, weaknesses, virtues,* and *errors,* of their sex, his respect for their *persons* amounts almost to adoration."[81] True!—For never was there a sensualist who paid more fervent adoration at the shrine of beauty. So devout, indeed, was his respect for the person, that excepting the virtue of chastity, for obvious reasons, he only wished to see it embellished by charms, weaknesses, and errors. He was afraid lest the austerity of reason should disturb the soft playfulness of love. The master wished to have a meretricious slave to fondle, entirely dependent on his reason and bounty; he did not want a companion, whom he should be compelled to esteem, or a friend to whom he could confide the care of his children's education, should death deprive them of their father, before he had fulfilled the sacred task. He denies woman reason, shuts her out from knowledge, and turns her aside from truth; yet his pardon is granted, because "he admits the passion of love." It

[80]Anne-Louise-Germaine Necker, Baronne de Staël (1766–1817). Mme de Staël was one of the foremost female intellectuals of her day; her *Treatise on the Influence of the Passions on the Happiness of Individuals and of Nations* (1796) shaped her generation's response to the works of Rousseau and Kant; *On Germany* introduced continental works, and her famous novel, *Corrine* (1807), became the archetypal story of unhappy female genius.

[81]All quotations are from de Staël, *Letters on the Works and Characters of J. J. Rousseau* (1788; trans. 1789), 15–16.

would require some ingenuity to shew why women were to be under such an obligation to him for thus admitting love; when it is clear that he admits it only for the relaxation of men, and to perpetuate the species; but he talked with passion, and that powerful spell worked on the sensibility of a young encomiast. "What signifies it," pursues this rhapsodist, "to women, that his reason disputes with them the empire, when his heart is devotedly theirs." It is not empire,—but equality, that they should contend for. Yet, if they only wished to lengthen out their sway, they should not entirely trust to their persons, for though beauty may gain a heart, it cannot keep it, even while the beauty is in full bloom, unless the mind lend, at least, some graces.

When women are once sufficiently enlightened to discover their real interest, on a grand scale, they will, I am persuaded, be very ready to resign all the prerogatives of love, that are not mutual, speaking of them as lasting prerogatives, for the calm satisfaction of friendship, and the tender confidence of habitual esteem. Before marriage they will not assume any insolent airs, or afterwards abjectly submit; but endeavouring to act like reasonable creatures, in both situations, they will not be tumbled from a throne to a stool.

Madame Genlis[82] has written several entertaining books for children; and her Letters on Education afford many useful hints, that sensible parents will certainly avail themselves of; but her views are narrow, and her prejudices as unreasonable as strong.

I shall pass over her vehement argument in favour of the eternity of future punishments,[83] because I blush to think that a human being should ever argue vehemently in such a cause, and only make a few remarks on her absurd manner of making the parental authority supplant reason. For every where does she inculcate not only *blind* submission to parents; but to the opinion of the world.[84]

---

[82]Stéphanie-Félicité Ducrest de St. Aubin, Comtesse de Genlis (1746–1830). This celebrated and prolific French woman of letters wrote stories, treatises on education, four volumes of plays for children, and nearly 100 historical romances.

[83]In the story of Cecilia, in *Adelaide and Theodore* (1782; London, 1783), the heroine obeys her father's commands to enter a convent despite her love for Chevalier de Murville. When she falls into a suicidal despair, her father worries that he has acted as the potential "cause of her eternal condemnation" (1.183).

[84]A person is not to act in this or that way, though convinced they are right in so doing, because some equivocal circumstances may lead the world to *suspect* that they acted from different motives.—This is sacrificing the substance for a shadow. Let people but watch their own hearts, and act rightly, as far as they can judge, and they may patiently wait till the opinion of the world comes round. It is best to be directed by a simple motive—for justice has too often been sacrificed to propriety;—another word for convenience [MW].

She tells a story of a young man engaged by his father's express desire to a girl of fortune. Before the marriage could take place she is deprived of her fortune, and thrown friendless on the world. The father practises the most infamous arts to separate his son from her, and when the son detects his villany, and following the dictates of honour marries the girl, nothing but misery ensues, because, forsooth he married *without* his father's consent.[85] On what ground can religion or morality rest when justice is thus set at defiance? With the same view she represents an accomplished young woman, as ready to marry any body that her *mamma* pleased to recommend; and, as actually marrying the young man of her own choice, without feeling any emotions of passion, because that a well educated girl had not time to be in love.[86] Is it possible to have much respect for a system of education that thus insults reason and nature?

Many similar opinions occur in her writings, mixed with sentiments that do honour to her head and heart. Yet so much superstition is mixed with her religion, and so much worldly wisdom with her morality, that I should not let a young person read her works, unless I could afterwards converse on the subjects, and point out the contradictions.

Mrs. Chapone's Letters are written with such good sense, and unaffected humility, and contain so many useful observations, that I only mention them to pay the worthy writer this tribute of respect.[87] I cannot, it is true, always coincide in opinion with her; but I always respect her.

The very word respect brings Mrs. Macaulay[88] to my remembrance. The woman of the greatest abilities, undoubtedly, that this country has ever produced.—And yet this woman has been suffered to die without sufficient respect being paid to her memory.

Posterity, however, will be more just, and remember that Catharine Macaulay was an example of intellectual acquirements supposed to be incompatible with the weakness of her sex. In her style of writing, indeed, no sex appears, for it is like the sense it conveys, strong and clear.

[85]*Tales of the Castle*, trans. Thomas Holcroft (1785), chapter 3, "Theophilus and Olympia."

[86]*Adelaide and Theodore*, 3:237–38.

[87]Hester Chapone (1727–1801), woman of letters, author of the popular *Letters on the Improvement of the Mind: Addressed to a Lady* (1773).

[88]Catharine Sawbridge Macaulay, later Graham (1731–91). See p. 101, n. 51. MW gave *Letters on Education* (1790) enthusiastic notice (*Analytical Review* 8, November 1790). Macaulay's reputation suffered when at age 47, she married 21-year-old William Graham.

I will not call hers a masculine understanding, because I admit not of such an arrogant assumption of reason; but I contend that it was a sound one, and that her judgment, the matured fruit of profound thinking, was a proof that a woman can acquire judgment, in the full extent of the word. Possessing more penetration than sagacity, more understanding than fancy, she writes with sober energy and argumentative closeness; yet sympathy and benevolence give an interest to her sentiments, and that vital heat to arguments, which forces the reader to weigh them.[89]

When I first thought of writing these strictures I anticipated Mrs. Macaulay's approbation, with a little of that sanguine ardour, which it has been the business of my life to depress; but soon heard with the sickly qualm of disappointed hope; and the still seriousness of regret—that she was no more![90]

SECTION V

Taking a view of the different works which have been written on education, Lord Chesterfield's Letters must not be silently passed over. Not that I mean to analyze his unmanly, immoral system, or even to cull any of the useful, shrewd remarks which occur in his epistles— No, I only mean to make a few reflections on the avowed tendency of them—the art of acquiring an early knowledge of the world.—An art, I will venture to assert, that preys secretly, like the worm in the bud,[91] on the expanding powers, and turns to poison the generous juices which should mount with vigour in the youthful frame, inspiring warm affections and great resolves.[92]

For every thing, saith the wise man, there is a season[93];—and who would look for the fruits of autumn during the genial months of spring? But this is mere declamation, and I mean to reason with those

[89]Coinciding in opinion with Mrs. Macaulay relative to many branches of education, I refer to her valuable work, instead of quoting her sentiments to support my own [MW].

[90]Macaulay died on June 22, 1791; the same month, Wollstonecraft planned *A Vindication of the Rights of Woman*, and began in the autumn.

[91]Echoing an adage in Shakespeare's *Twelfth Night*: "She never told her love / But let concealment, like a worm I' the bud / Feed on her damask cheek" (2.4.111–13).

[92]That children ought to be constantly guarded against the vices and follies of the world, appears, to me, a very mistaken opinion; for in the course of my experience, and my eyes have looked abroad, I never knew a youth educated in this manner, who had early imbibed these chilling suspicions, and repeated by rote the hesitating *if* of age, that did not prove a selfish character [MW].

[93]Citing Ecclesiastes 3:1: "To every thing there is a season, and a time to every purpose under the heaven."

worldly-wise instructors, who, instead of cultivating the judgment, instill prejudices, and render hard the heart that gradual experience would only have cooled. An early acquaintance with human infirmities; or, what is termed knowledge of the world, is the surest way, in my opinion, to contract the heart and damp the natural youthful ardour which produces not only great talents, but great virtues. For the vain attempt to bring forth the fruit of experience, before the sapling has thrown out its leaves, only exhausts its strength, and prevents its assuming a natural form; just as the form and strength of subsiding metals are injured when the attraction of cohesion is disturbed.

Tell me, ye who have studied the human mind, is it not a strange way to fix principles by showing young people that they are seldom stable? And how can they be fortified by habits when they are proved to be fallacious by example? Why is the ardour of youth thus to be damped, and the luxuriancy of fancy cut to the quick? This dry caution may, it is true, guard a character from worldly mischances; but will infallibly preclude excellence in either virtue or knowledge.[94] The stumbling-block thrown across every path by suspicion, will prevent any vigorous exertions of genius or benevolence, and life will be stripped of its most alluring charm long before its calm evening, when man should retire to contemplation for comfort and support.

A young man who has been bred up with domestic friends, and led to store his mind with as much speculative knowledge as can be acquired by reading and the natural reflections which youthful ebullitions of animal spirits and instinctive feelings inspire, will enter the world with warm and erroneous expectations. But this appears to be the course of nature; and in morals, as well as in works of taste, we should be observant of her sacred indications, and not presume to lead when we ought obsequiously to follow.

In the world few people act from principle; present feelings, and early habits, are the grand springs; but how would the former be deadened, and the latter rendered iron corroding fetters, if the world were shewn to young people just as it is; when no knowledge of mankind or their own hearts, slowly obtained by experience, rendered them forbearing? Their fellow creatures would not then be viewed as frail beings; like themselves, condemned to struggle with human infirmities, and sometimes displaying the light, and sometimes the dark side of their character; extorting alternate feelings of love

---

[94]I have already observed that an early knowledge of the world, obtained in a natural way, by mixing in the world, has the same effect: instancing officers and women [MW].

and disgust; but guarded against as beasts of prey, till every enlarged social feeling, in a word,—humanity, was eradicated.

In life, on the contrary, as we gradually discover the imperfections of our nature, we discover virtues, and various circumstances attach us to our fellow creatures, when we mix with them, and view the same objects, that are never thought of in acquiring a hasty unnatural knowledge of the world. We see a folly swell into a vice, by almost imperceptible degrees, and pity while we blame; but, if the hideous monster burst suddenly on our sight, fear and disgust rendering us more severe than man ought to be, might lead us with blind zeal to usurp the character of omnipotence, and denounce damnation on our fellow mortals, forgetting that we cannot read the heart, and that we have seeds of the same vices lurking in our own.

I have already remarked that we expect more from instruction, than mere instruction can produce: for, instead of preparing young people to encounter the evils of life with dignity, and to acquire wisdom and virtue by the exercise of their own faculties, precepts are heaped upon precepts, and blind obedience required, when conviction should be brought home to reason.

Suppose, for instance, that a young person in the first ardour of friendship deifies the beloved object—what harm can arise from this mistaken enthusiastic attachment? Perhaps it is necessary for virtue first to appear in a human form to impress youthful hearts; the ideal model, which a more matured and exalted mind looks up to, and shapes for itself, would elude their sight. He who loves not his brother whom he hath seen, how can he love God? asked the wisest of men.[95]

It is natural for youth to adorn the first object of its affection with every good quality, and the emulation produced by ignorance, or, to speak with more propriety, by inexperience, brings forward the mind capable of forming such an affection, and when, in the lapse of time, perfection is found not to be within the reach of mortals, virtue, abstractedly, is thought beautiful, and wisdom sublime. Admiration then gives place to friendship, properly so called, because it is cemented by esteem; and the being walks alone only dependent on heaven for that emulous panting after perfection which ever glows in a noble mind. But this knowledge a man must gain by the exertion of his own faculties; and this is surely the blessed fruit of disappointed hope! for He who delighteth to diffuse happiness and shew mercy to

[95] "If a man say, I love God, and hateth his brother, he is a liar: for he that loveth not his brother whom he hath seen, how can he love God whom he hath not seen?" (1 John 4:20).

the weak creatures, who are learning to know him, never implanted a good propensity to be a tormenting ignis fatuus.[96]

Our trees are now allowed to spread with wild luxuriance, nor do we expect by force to combine the majestic marks of time with youthful graces; but wait patiently till they have struck deep their root, and braved many a storm.—Is the mind then, which, in proportion to its dignity, advances more slowly towards perfection, to be treated with less respect? To argue from analogy, every thing around us is in a progressive state; and when an unwelcome knowledge of life produces almost a satiety of life, and we discover by the natural course of things that all that is done under the sun is vanity,[97] we are drawing near the awful close of the drama. The days of activity and hope are over, and the opportunities which the first stage of existence has afforded of advancing in the scale of intelligence, must soon be summed up.—A knowledge at this period of the futility of life, or earlier, if obtained by experience, is very useful, because it is natural; but when a frail being is shewn the follies and vices of man, that he may be taught prudently to guard against the common casualties of life by sacrificing his heart—surely it is not speaking harshly to call it the wisdom of this world, contrasted with the nobler fruit of piety and experience.

I will venture a paradox, and deliver my opinion without reserve; if men were only born to form a circle of life and death, it would be wise to take every step that foresight could suggest to render life happy. Moderation in every pursuit would then be supreme wisdom; and the prudent voluptuary might enjoy a degree of content, though he neither cultivated his understanding nor kept his heart pure. Prudence, supposing we were mortal, would be true wisdom, or, to be more explicit, would procure the greatest portion of happiness, considering the whole of life, but knowledge beyond the conveniences of life would be a curse.

Why should we injure our health by close study? The exalted pleasure which intellectual pursuits afford would scarcely be equivalent to the hours of languor that follow; especially, if it be necessary to take into the reckoning the doubts and disappointments that cloud our researches. Vanity and vexation close every inquiry: for the cause which we particularly wished to discover flies like the horizon before us as we advance. The ignorant, on the contrary, resemble children, and suppose, that if they could walk straight forward they should at

---

[96]"False fire," a delusion or deception.

[97]Echoing Ecclesiastes 1:14: "I have seen all the works that are done under the sun; and, behold, all is vanity and vexation of spirit."

last arrive where the earth and clouds meet. Yet, disappointed as we are in our researches, the mind gains strength by the exercise, sufficient, perhaps, to comprehend the answers which, in another step of existence, it may receive to the anxious questions it asked, when the understanding with feeble wing was fluttering round the visible effects to dive into the hidden cause.

The passions also, the winds of life, would be useless, if not injurious, did the substance which composes our thinking being, after we have thought in vain, only become the support of vegetable life, and invigorate a cabbage, or blush in a rose. The appetites would answer every earthly purpose, and produce more moderate and permanent happiness. But the powers of the soul that are of little use here, and, probably, disturb our animal enjoyments, even while conscious dignity makes us glory in possessing them, prove that life is merely an education, a state of infancy, to which the only hopes worth cherishing should not be sacrificed. I mean, therefore, to infer, that we ought to have a precise idea of what we wish to attain by education, for the immortality of the soul is contradicted by the actions of many people who firmly profess the belief.

If you mean to secure ease and prosperity on earth as the first consideration, and leave futurity to provide for itself; you act prudently in giving your child an early insight into the weaknesses of his nature. You may not, it is true, make an Inkle[98] of him; but do not imagine that he will stick to more than the letter of the law, who has very early imbibed a mean opinion of human nature; nor will he think it necessary to rise much above the common standard. He may avoid gross vices, because honesty is the best policy; but he will never aim at attaining great virtues. The example of writers and artists will illustrate this remark.

I must therefore venture to doubt whether what has been thought an axiom in morals may not have been a dogmatical assertion made by men who have coolly seen mankind through the medium of books, and say, in direct contradiction to them, that the regulation of

[98]The story of Inkle and Yarico appeared to wide notice in Richard Steele's *The Spectator*, No. 11 (March 13, 1711); MW included this in *The Female Reader* (1789). Adapting a short anecdote in Richard Ligon's *A True and Exact History of the Island of Barbados* (1657), Steele chronicles the love affair. Shipwrecked and attacked by Indians, English merchant Inkle is rescued and nurtured by Indian maid Yarico. They become lovers, and he promises to marry her. But when they are rescued by a British ship, Inkle decides to sell Yarico into slavery; her hopes of altering his resolution by revealing her pregnancy only raised her price. A comic opera based on Steele's account, *Inkle and Yarico* (1787) by George Colman the Younger and Samuel Arnold, remained a stage favorite into the 19th c.

the passions is not, always, wisdom.—On the contrary, it should seem, that one reason why men have superior judgment, and more fortitude than women, is undoubtedly this, that they give a freer scope to the grand passions, and by more frequently going astray enlarge their minds. If then by the exercise of their own[99] reason they fix on some stable principle, they have probably to thank the force of their passions, nourished by *false* views of life, and permitted to overleap the boundary that secures content. But if, in the dawn of life, we could soberly survey the scenes before as in perspective, and see every thing in its true colours, how could the passions gain sufficient strength to unfold the faculties?

Let me now as from an eminence survey the world stripped of all its false delusive charms. The clear atmosphere enables me to see each object in its true point of view, while my heart is still. I am calm as the prospect in a morning when the mists, slowly dispersing, silently unveil the beauties of nature, refreshed by rest.

In what light will the world now appear?—I rub my eyes and think, perchance, that I am just awakening from a lively dream.

I see the sons and daughters of men pursuing shadows, and anxiously wasting their powers to feed passions which have no adequate object—if the very excess of these blind impulses, pampered by that lying, yet constantly trusted guide, the imagination, did not, by preparing them for some other state, render short-sighted mortals wiser without their own concurrence; or, what comes to the same thing, when pursuing some imaginary present good.

After viewing objects in this light, it would not be very fanciful to imagine that this world was a stage on which a pantomime is daily performed for the amusement of superior beings.[100] How would they be diverted to see the ambitious man consuming himself by running after a phantom, and, "pursuing the bubble fame in the cannon's mouth"[101] that was to blow him to nothing: for when consciousness is lost, it matters not whether we mount in a whirlwind or descend in

---

[99]"I find that all is but lip-wisdom which wants experience," says Sidney [MW]. Sir Phillip Sidney (1554–86), Renaissance poet and courtier. *The Countess of Pembroke's Arcadia* (1590), 1.18.

[100]Shakespeare, *As You Like It*, "All the world's a stage / And all the men and women merely players" (2.7.139–40). The pantomimes of the 18th c., a popular genre of entertainment derived from Italian *commedia dell'arte* and harlequinades, were far from silent: they incorporated singing, music, and dialogue, along with dancing, physical comedy, and elaborate sets.

[101]A soldier's pursuit, in the view of cynic Jaques (*As You Like It*, 2.7.152–53).

rain. And should they compassionately invigorate his sight and shew him the thorny path which led to eminence, that like a quicksand sinks as he ascends, disappointing his hopes when almost within his grasp, would he not leave to others the honour of amusing them, and labour to secure the present moment, though from the constitution of his nature he would not find it very easy to catch the flying stream? Such slaves are we to hope and fear!

But, vain as the ambitious man's pursuits would be, he is often striving for something more substantial than fame—that indeed would be the veriest meteor, the wildest fire that could lure a man to ruin.—What! renounce the most trifling gratification to be applauded when he should be no more! Wherefore this struggle, whether man be mortal or immortal, if that noble passion did not really raise the being above his fellows?—

And love! What diverting scenes would it produce—Pantaloon's tricks[102] must yield to more egregious folly. To see a mortal adorn an object with imaginary charms, and then fall down and worship the idol which he had himself set up—how ridiculous! But what serious consequences ensue to rob man of that portion of happiness, which the Deity by calling him into existence has (or, on what can his attributes rest!) indubitably promised: would not all the purposes of life have been much better fulfilled if he had only felt what has been termed physical love? And, would not the sight of the object, not seen through the medium of the imagination, soon reduce the passion to an appetite, if reflection, the noble distinction of man, did not give it force, and make it an instrument to raise him above this earthly dross, by teaching him to love the centre of all perfection; whose wisdom appears clearer and clearer in the works of nature, in proportion as reason is illuminated and exalted by contemplation, and by acquiring that love of order which the struggles of passion produce?

The habit of reflection, and the knowledge attained by fostering any passion, might be shewn to be equally useful, though the object be proved equally fallacious; for they would all appear in the same light, if they were not magnified by the governing passion implanted in us by the Author of all good, to call forth and strengthen the faculties of each individual, and enable it to attain all the experience that an infant can obtain, who does certain things, it cannot tell why.

---

[102]Pantaloon, a stock character of *commedia dell'arte*, is typically an enfeebled older man, whose amorous yearnings and avaricious designs are the subject of much ridicule, consistently foiled by the rest of the players. Shakespeare's Jaques satirizes the old man as a "lean and slippered pantaloon" (*AYLI*, 2.7.157–58).

I descend from my height, and mixing with my fellow-creatures, feel myself hurried along the common stream; ambition, love, hope, and fear, exert their wonted power, though we be convinced by reason that their present and most attractive promises are only lying dreams; but had the cold hand of circumspection damped each generous feeling before it had left any permanent character, or fixed some habit, what could be expected, but selfish prudence and reason just rising above instinct? Who that has read Dean Swift's disgusting description of the Yahoos, and insipid one of Houyhnhnm[103] with a philosophical eye, can avoid seeing the futility of degrading the passions, or making man rest in contentment?

The youth should *act*, for had he the experience of a grey head he would be fitter for death than life, though his virtues, rather residing in his head than his heart, could produce nothing great, and his understanding, prepared for this world, would not, by its noble flights, prove that it had a title to a better.

Besides, it is not possible to give a young person a just view of life; he must have struggled with his own passions before he can estimate the force of the temptation which betrayed his brother into vice. Those who are entering life, and those who are departing, see the world from such very different points of view, that they can seldom think alike, unless the unfledged reason of the former never attempted a solitary flight.

When we hear of some daring crime—it comes full on us in the deepest shade of turpitude, and raises indignation; but the eye that gradually saw the darkness thicken, must observe it with more compassionate forbearance. The world cannot be seen by an unmoved spectator, we must mix in the throng, and feel as men feel before we can judge of their feelings. If we mean, in short, to live in the world to grow wiser and better, and not merely to enjoy the good things of life, we must attain a knowledge of others at the same time that we become acquainted with ourselves—knowledge acquired any other way only hardens the heart and perplexes the understanding.

I may be told, that the knowledge thus acquired, is sometimes purchased at too dear a rate. I can only answer that I very much doubt whether any knowledge can be attained without labour and sorrow; and those who wish to spare their children both, should not

---

[103]In Book 4 of Jonathan Swift's *Gulliver's Travels* (1726), Gulliver meets the Houyhnhnms, passionless equines whose "reason" borders on inhumanity, and the Yahoos, bestial human beings dominated by passion.

complain, if they are neither wise nor virtuous. They only aimed at making them prudent; and prudence, early in life, is but the cautious craft of ignorant self-love.

I have observed that young people, to whose education particular attention has been paid, have, in general, been very superficial and conceited, and far from pleasing in any respect, because they had neither the unsuspecting warmth of youth, nor the cool depth of age. I cannot help imputing this unnatural appearance principally to that hasty premature instruction, which leads them presumptuously to repeat all the crude notions they have taken upon trust, so that the careful education which they received, makes them all their lives the slaves of prejudices.

Mental as well as bodily exertion is, at first, irksome, so much so, that the many would fain let others both work and think for them. An observation which I have often made will illustrate my meaning. When in a circle of strangers, or acquaintances, a person of moderate abilities asserts an opinion with heat, I will venture to affirm, for I have traced this fact home, very often, that it is a prejudice. These echoes have a high respect for the understanding of some relation or friend, and without fully comprehending the opinions, which they are so eager to retail, they maintain them with a degree of obstinacy, that would surprise even the person who concocted them.

I know that a kind of fashion now prevails of respecting prejudices; and when any one dares to face them, though actuated by humanity and armed by reason, he is superciliously asked whether his ancestors were fools. No, I should reply; opinions, at first, of every description, were all, probably, considered, and therefore were founded on some reason; yet not unfrequently, of course, it was rather a local expedient than a fundamental principle, that would be reasonable at all times. But, moss-covered opinions assume the disproportioned form of prejudices, when they are indolently adopted only because age has given them a venerable aspect, though the reason on which they were built ceases to be a reason, or cannot be traced. Why are we to love prejudices, merely because they are prejudices?[104] A prejudice is a fond obstinate persuasion for which we can give no reason; for the moment a reason can be given for an opinion, it ceases to be a prejudice, though it may be an error in judgment: and are we then advised to cherish opinions only to set reason at defi-

---

[104]Vide Mr. Burke [MW]. In *Reflections on the Revolution in France* (1790), Burke contends that predispositions ("prejudice") should be cherished as distilled cultural wisdom.

ance? This mode of arguing, if arguing it may be called, reminds me of what is vulgarly termed a woman's reason. For women sometimes declare that they love, or believe, certain things, *because* they love, or believe them.

It is impossible to converse with people to any purpose, who only use affirmatives and negatives. Before you can bring them to a point, to start fairly from, you must go back to the simple principles that were antecedent to the prejudices broached by power; and it is ten to one but you are stopped by the philosophical assertion, that certain principles are as practically false as they are abstractly true.[105] Nay, it may be inferred, that reason has whispered some doubts, for it generally happens that people assert their opinions with the greatest heat when they begin to waver; striving to drive out their own doubts by convincing their opponent, they grow angry when those gnawing doubts are thrown back to prey on themselves.

The fact is, that men expect from education, what education cannot give. A sagacious parent or tutor may strengthen the body and sharpen the instruments by which the child is to gather knowledge; but the honey must be the reward of the individual's own industry. It is almost as absurd to attempt to make a youth wise by the experience of another, as to expect the body to grow strong by the exercise which is only talked of, or seen.[106] Many of those children whose conduct has been most narrowly watched, become the weakest men, because their instructors only instill certain notions into their minds, that have no other foundation than their authority; and if they be loved or respected, the mind is cramped in its exertions and wavering in its advances. The business of education in this case, is only to conduct the shooting tendrils to a proper pole; yet after laying precept upon precept, without allowing a child to acquire judgment itself, parents expect them to act in the same manner by this borrowed fallacious light, as if they had illuminated it themselves; and be, when they enter life, what their parents are at the close. They do not consider that the tree, and even the human body, does not strengthen its fibres till it has reached its full growth.

[105]Convince a man against his will, / He's of the same opinion still [MW]. See Samuel Butler's satire, *Hudibras* (1662–63): "He that complies against his will, / Is of his own opinion still" (3.3.547–48).

[106]"One sees nothing when one is content to contemplate only: it is necessary to act oneself to be able to see how others act." *Rousseau* [MW]. In *Julie, ou, La Nouvelle Héloïse*, 2.17.

There appears to be something analogous in the mind. The senses and the imagination give a form to the character, during childhood and youth; and the understanding, as life advances, gives firmness to the first fair purposes of sensibility—till virtue, arising rather from the clear conviction of reason than the impulse of the heart, morality is made to rest on a rock against which the storms of passion vainly beat.

I hope I shall not be misunderstood when I say, that religion will not have this condensing energy, unless it be founded on reason. If it be merely the refuge of weakness or wild fanaticism, and not a governing principle of conduct, drawn from self-knowledge, and a rational opinion respecting the attributes of God, what can it be expected to produce? The religion which consists in warming the affections, and exalting the imagination, is only the poetical part, and may afford the individual pleasure without rendering it a more moral being. It may be a substitute for worldly pursuits; yet narrow, instead of enlarging the heart: but virtue must be loved as in itself sublime and excellent, and not for the advantages it procures or the evils it averts, if any great degree of excellence be expected. Men will not become moral when they only build airy castles in a future world to compensate for the disappointments which they meet with in this; if they turn their thoughts from relative duties to religious reveries.

Most prospects in life are marred by the shuffling worldly wisdom of men, who, forgetting that they cannot serve God and mammon,[107] endeavour to blend contradictory things.—If you wish to make your son rich, pursue one course—if you are only anxious to make him virtuous, you must take another; but do not imagine that you can bound from one road to the other without losing your way.[108]

[107]See Matthew 6:24 and Luke 16:13.

[108]See an excellent essay on this subject by Mrs. Barbauld, in Miscellaneous Pieces in Prose [MW]. Referring to "Against Inconsistency in Our Expectations" (1773).

CHAPTER VI

THE EFFECT WHICH AN EARLY ASSOCIATION OF IDEAS HAS UPON THE CHARACTER

Educated in the enervating style recommended by the writers on whom I have been animadverting; and not having a chance, from their subordinate state in society, to recover their lost ground, is it surprising that women every where appear a defect in nature? Is it surprising, when we consider what a determinate effect an early association of ideas has on the character, that they neglect their understandings, and turn all their attention to their persons?

The great advantages which naturally result from storing the mind with knowledge, are obvious from the following considerations. The association of our ideas is either habitual or instantaneous; and the latter mode seems rather to depend on the original temperature of the mind than on the will. When the ideas, and matters of fact, are once taken in, they lie by for use, till some fortuitous circumstance makes the information dart into the mind with illustrative force, that has been received at very different periods of our lives.[1] Like the lightning's flash are many recollections; one idea assimilating and explaining another, with astonishing rapidity. I do not now allude to that quick perception of truth, which is so intuitive that it baffles research, and makes us at a loss to determine whether it is reminiscence or ratiocination, lost sight of in its celerity, that opens the dark cloud. Over those instantaneous associations we have little power; for when the mind is once enlarged by excursive flights, or profound reflection, the raw materials will, in some degree, arrange themselves. The understanding, it is true, may keep us from going out of drawing[2] when we group our thoughts, or transcribe from the imagination the warm sketches of fancy; but the animal spirits, the individual character, give the colouring. Over this subtile electric fluid,[3] how little power do we possess, and over it how little power can reason obtain! These

---

[1] A theory of knowledge known as "associationism," developed by David Hartley (1705–57) and David Hume (1711–76).

[2] Perspective.

[3] I have sometimes, when inclined to laugh at materialists, asked whether, as the most powerful effects in nature are apparently produced by fluids, the magnetic, etc. the passions might not be fine volatile fluids that embraced humanity, keeping the more refractory elementary parts together—or whether they were simply a liquid fire that pervaded the more sluggish materials, giving them life and heat? [MW]. MW is jesting at the form of science that would locate life and passion in something like a measurable fluid or electric current.

fine intractable spirits appear to be the essence of genius, and beaming in its eagle eye, produce in the most eminent degree the happy energy of associating thoughts that surprise, delight, and instruct. These are the glowing minds that concentrate pictures for their fellow-creatures; forcing them to view with interest the objects reflected from the impassioned imagination, which they passed over in nature.

I must be allowed to explain myself. The generality of people cannot see or feel poetically, they want fancy, and therefore fly from solitude in search of sensible objects; but when an author lends them his eyes they can see as he saw, and be amused by images they could not select, though lying before them.

Education thus only supplies the man of genius with knowledge to give variety and contrast to his associations; but there is an habitual association of ideas, that grows "with our growth,"[4] which has a great effect on the moral character of mankind; and by which a turn is given to the mind that commonly remains throughout life. So ductile is the understanding, and yet so stubborn, that the associations which depend on adventitious circumstances, during the period that the body takes to arrive at maturity, can seldom be disentangled by reason. One idea calls up another, its old associate, and memory, faithful to the first impressions, particularly when the intellectual powers are not employed to cool our sensations, retraces them with mechanical exactness.

This habitual slavery, to first impressions, has a more baneful effect on the female than the male character, because business and other dry employments of the understanding, tend to deaden the feelings and break associations that do violence to reason. But females, who are made women of when they are mere children, and brought back to childhood when they ought to leave the go-cart for ever, have not sufficient strength of mind to efface the superinductions of art that have smothered nature.

Every thing that they see or hear serves to fix impressions, call forth emotions, and associate ideas, that give a sexual character to the mind. False notions of beauty and delicacy stop the growth of their limbs and produce a sickly soreness, rather than delicacy of organs; and thus weakened by being employed in unfolding instead of examining the first associations, forced on them by every surrounding object, how can they attain the vigour necessary to enable them to throw off that factitious character?—where find strength to recur to

[4]Pope, *An Essay on Man* (1733–34), 2.136: "Grows with his growth, and strengthens with his strength"—referring to the adverse effect of passion on the human frame. MW puts this in a positive syntax.

reason and rise superior to a system of oppression, that blasts the fair promises of spring? This cruel association of ideas, which every thing conspires to twist into all their habits of thinking, or, to speak with more precision, of feeling, receives new force when they begin to act a little for themselves; for they then perceive that it is only through their address to excite emotions in men, that pleasure and power are to be obtained. Besides, the books professedly written for their instruction, which make the first impression on their minds, all inculcate the same opinions. Educated then in worse than Egyptian bondage,[5] it is unreasonable, as well as cruel, to upbraid them with faults that can scarcely be avoided, unless a degree of native vigour be supposed, that falls to the lot of very few amongst mankind.

For instance, the severest sarcasms have been levelled against the sex, and they have been ridiculed for repeating "a set of phrases learnt by rote,"[6] when nothing could be more natural, considering the education they receive, and that their "highest praise is to obey, unargued"[7]—the will of man. If they be not allowed to have reason sufficient to govern their own conduct—why, all they learn—must be learned by rote! And when all their ingenuity is called forth to adjust their dress, "a passion for a scarlet coat,"[8] is so natural, that it never surprised me; and, allowing Pope's summary of their character to be just, "that every woman is at heart a rake,"[9] why should they be bitterly censured for seeking a congenial mind, and preferring a rake to a man of sense?

Rakes know how to work on their sensibility, whilst the modest merit of reasonable men has, of course, less effect on their feelings, and they cannot reach the heart by the way of the understanding, because they have few sentiments in common.

It seems a little absurd to expect women to be more reasonable than men in their *likings*, and still to deny them the uncontrouled use of reason. When do men *fall-in-love* with sense? When do they, with their superior powers and advantages, turn from the person to the mind? And

[5]The enslavement of the Jewish tribes (Exodus 1:1–22).

[6]The opening line of Swift's "The Furniture of a Woman's Mind."

[7]Milton, *Paradise Lost*, 4.635–38: Milton's Eve says to Adam, "what thou bidst / Unargu'd I obey; so God ordains, / God is thy law, thou mine: to know no more / Is woman's happiest knowledge and her praise." See ch. II, p. 37.

[8]Swift, "The Furniture of a Woman's Mind," 2. See ch. II, p. 41.

[9]Pope, *Of the Characters of Women*: "Men, some to Bus'ness, some to Pleasure take; / But ev'ry Woman is at heart a Rake" (215–16); a "rake" usually refers to a man of immoral character.

how can they then expect women, who are only taught to observe behaviour, and acquire manners rather than morals, to despise what they have been all their lives labouring to attain? Where are they suddenly to find judgment enough to weigh patiently the sense of an awkward virtuous man, when his manners, of which they are made critical judges, are rebuffing, and his conversation cold and dull, because it does not consist of pretty repartees, or well turned compliments? In order to admire or esteem any thing for a continuance, we must, at least, have our curiosity excited by knowing, in some degree, what we admire; for we are unable to estimate the value of qualities and virtues, above our comprehension. Such a respect, when it is felt, may be very sublime; and the confused consciousness of humility may render the dependent creature an interesting object, in some points of view; but human love must have grosser ingredients; and the person very naturally will come in for its share—and, an ample share it mostly has!

Love is, in a great degree, an arbitrary passion, and will reign, like some other stalking mischiefs, by its own authority, without deigning to reason; and it may also be easily distinguished from esteem, the foundation of friendship, because it is often excited by evanescent beauties and graces, though, to give an energy to the sentiment, something more solid must deepen their impression and set the imagination to work, to make the most fair—the first good.

Common passions are excited by common qualities.—Men look for beauty and the simper of good-humoured docility: women are captivated by easy manners; a gentleman-like man seldom fails to please them, and their thirsty ears eagerly drink the insinuating nothings of politeness, whilst they turn from the unintelligible sounds of the charmer—reason, charm he never so wisely. With respect to superficial accomplishments, the rake certainly has the advantage; and of these females can form an opinion, for it is their own ground. Rendered gay and giddy by the whole tenor of their lives, the very aspect of wisdom, or the severe graces of virtue, must have a lugubrious appearance to them; and produce a kind of restraint from which they and love, sportive child, naturally revolt. Without taste, excepting of the lighter kind, for taste is the offspring of judgment, how can they discover that true beauty and grace must arise from the play of the mind? and how can they be expected to relish in a lover what they do not, or very imperfectly, possess themselves? The sympathy that unites hearts, and invites to confidence, in them is so very faint, that it cannot take fire, and thus mount to passion. No, I repeat it, the love cherished by such minds, must have grosser fewel!

The inference is obvious; till women are led to exercise their understandings, they should not be satirized for their attachment to rakes; or even for being rakes at heart, when it appears to be the inevitable consequence of their education. They who live to please—must find their enjoyments, their happiness, in pleasure! It is a trite, yet true remark, that we never do any thing well, unless we love it for its own sake.

Supposing, however, for a moment, that women were, in some future revolution of time, to become, what I sincerely wish them to be, even love would acquire more serious dignity, and be purified in its own fires; and virtue giving true delicacy to their affections, they would turn with disgust from a rake. Reasoning then, as well as feeling, the only province of woman, at present, they might easily guard against exteriour graces, and quickly learn to despise the sensibility that had been excited and hackneyed in the ways of women, whose trade was vice; and allurements, wanton airs. They would recollect that the flame, one must use appropriated expressions, which they wished to light up, had been exhausted by lust, and that the sated appetite, losing all relish for pure and simple pleasures, could only be roused by licentious arts or variety. What satisfaction could a woman of delicacy promise herself in a union with such a man, when the very artlessness of her affection might appear insipid? Thus does Dryden describe the situation,

> ——————"Where love is duty, on the female side,
> On theirs mere sensual gust, and sought with surly pride."[10]

But one grand truth women have yet to learn, though much it imports them to act accordingly. In the choice of a husband, they should not be led astray by the qualities of a lover—for a lover the husband, even supposing him to be wise and virtuous, cannot long remain.

Were women more rationally educated, could they take a more comprehensive view of things, they would be contented to love but once in their lives; and after marriage calmly let passion subside into friendship—into that tender intimacy, which is the best refuge from care; yet is built on such pure, still affections, that idle jealousies would not be allowed to disturb the discharge of the sober duties of

---

[10]*Fables Ancient and Modern; Translated into Verse* (1700), "Palamon and Arcite," 3.230–31. In this adaptation of Chaucer's "Knight's Tale" (*Canterbury Tales*), heroine Emily prays to Diana, goddess of chastity, to save her from the degradations of "the nuptial state" (227).

life, or to engross the thoughts that ought to be otherwise employed. This is a state in which many men live; but few, very few women. And the difference may easily be accounted for, without recurring to a sexual character. Men, for whom we are told women were made, have too much occupied the thoughts of women; and this association has so entangled love with all their motives of action; and, to harp a little on an old string, having been solely employed either to prepare themselves to excite love, or actually putting their lessons in practice, they cannot live without love. But, when a sense of duty, or fear of shame, obliges them to restrain this pampered desire of pleasing beyond certain lengths, too far for delicacy, it is true, though far from criminality, they obstinately determine to love, I speak of the passion, their husbands to the end of the chapter—and then acting the part which they foolishly exacted from their lovers, they become abject wooers, and fond slaves.

Men of wit and fancy are often rakes; and fancy is the food of love.[11] Such men will inspire passion. Half the sex, in its present infantine state, would pine for a Lovelace[12]; a man so witty, so graceful, and so valiant: and can they *deserve* blame for acting according to principles so constantly inculcated? They want a lover, and protector; and behold him kneeling before them—bravery prostrate to beauty! The virtues of a husband are thus thrown by love into the back ground, and gay hopes, or lively emotions, banish reflection till the day of reckoning come; and come it surely will, to turn the sprightly lover into a surly suspicious tyrant, who contemptuously insults the very weakness he fostered. Or, supposing the rake reformed, he cannot quickly get rid of old habits. When a man of abilities is first carried away by his passions, it is necessary that sentiment and taste varnish the enormities of vice, and give a zest to brutal indulgences; but when the gloss of novelty is worn off, and pleasure palls upon the sense, lasciviousness becomes barefaced, and enjoyment only the desperate effort of weakness flying from reflection as from a legion of devils. Oh! virtue, thou art not an empty name! All that life can give—thou givest!

If much comfort cannot be expected from the friendship of a reformed rake of superiour abilities, what is the consequence when he

[11]Echoing the lovesick young man in Shakespeare's *Twelfth Night*: "If music be the food of love, play on" (1.1.1).

[12]The rake who rapes the virtuous heroine in Samuel Richardson's novel *Clarissa* (1748–49). In his preface, Richardson says the novel is meant "To warn the inconsiderate and Thoughtless of the one sex . . . upon that dangerous but too commonly received notion, *that a reformed Rake makes the best Husband.*"

lacketh sense, as well as principles? Verily misery, in its most hideous shape. When the habits of weak people are consolidated by time, a reformation is barely possible; and actually makes the beings miserable who have not sufficient mind to be amused by innocent pleasure; like the tradesman who retires from the hurry of business, nature presents to them only a universal blank; and the restless thoughts prey on the damped spirits.[13] Their reformation, as well as his retirement, actually makes them wretched because it deprives them of all employment, by quenching the hopes and fears that set in motion their sluggish minds.

If such be the force of habit; if such be the bondage of folly, how carefully ought we to guard the mind from storing up vicious associations; and equally careful should we be to cultivate the understanding, to save the poor wight[14] from the weak dependent state of even harmless ignorance. For it is the right use of reason alone which makes us independent of every thing—excepting the unclouded Reason—"Whose service is perfect freedom."[15]

[13]I have frequently seen this exemplified in women whose beauty could no longer be repaired. They have retired from the noisy scenes of dissipation; but, unless they became methodists, the solitude of the select society of their family connections or acquaintance, has presented only a fearful void; consequently, nervous complaints, and all the vapourish train of idleness, rendered them quite as useless, and far more unhappy, than when they joined the giddy throng [MW]. Milton describes "Nature's works" as a "Universal blank" (*Paradise Lost*, 3.48–49).

[14]Person.

[15]Adapting *The Book of Common Prayer* (1549), "Morning Prayer, Second Collect, for Peace": "O God . . . whose service is perfect freedom" (17). Editor Carol Poston notes that in her *Letters on Education* Catharine Macaulay summons the same text to contend that "the empire of religious sentiment, and the empire of reason, is the same" (422–23).

CHAPTER VII

MODESTY.—COMPREHENSIVELY CONSIDERED, AND NOT AS A SEXUAL VIRTUE

Modesty! Sacred offspring of sensibility and reason!—true delicacy of mind!—may I unblamed presume to investigate thy nature, and trace to its covert the mild charm, that mellowing each harsh feature of a character, renders what would otherwise only inspire cold admiration—lovely!—Thou that smoothest the wrinkles of wisdom, and softenest the tone of the sublimest virtues till they all melt into humanity;—thou that spreadest the ethereal cloud that, surrounding love, heightens every beauty, it half shades, breathing those coy sweets that steal into the heart, and charm the senses—modulate for me the language of persuasive reason, till I rouse my sex from the flowery bed, on which they supinely sleep life away![1]

In speaking of the association of our ideas, I have noticed two distinct modes[2]; and in defining modesty, it appears to me equally proper to discriminate that purity of mind, which is the effect of chastity, from a simplicity of character that leads us to form a just opinion of ourselves, equally distant from vanity or presumption, though by no means incompatible with a lofty consciousness of our own dignity. Modesty, in the latter signification of the term, is, that soberness of mind which teaches a man not to think more highly of himself than he ought to think, and should be distinguished from humility, because humility is a kind of self-abasement.

A modest man often conceives a great plan, and tenaciously adheres to it, conscious of his own strength, till success gives it a sanction that determines its character. Milton was not arrogant when he suffered a suggestion of judgment to escape him that proved a prophecy[3]; nor was General Washington when he accepted the command of the American forces.[4] The latter has always been characterized as a modest man; but had he been merely humble, he would

---

[1]A stylistic allusion to Milton's invocation to "holy Light" at the opening of *Paradise Lost*, 3.1–55.

[2]See ch. VI, p. 144: "the association of our ideas is either habitual or instantaneous."

[3]Milton assumed his future fame in a youthful poem from the 1630s, "Ad Patrem" [To Father], 2.115–20.

[4]George Washington became Commander in Chief of the American Revolutionary Army on June 15, 1775.

probably have shrunk back irresolute, afraid of trusting to himself the direction of an enterprise, on which so much depended.

A modest man is steady, an humble man timid, and a vain one presumptuous:—this is the judgment, which the observation of many characters, has led me to form. Jesus Christ was modest, Moses was humble, and Peter vain.

Thus, discriminating modesty from humility in one case, I do not mean to confound it with bashfulness in the other. Bashfulness, in fact, is so distinct from modesty, that the most bashful lass, or raw country lout, often become the most impudent; for their bashfulness being merely the instinctive timidity of ignorance, custom soon changes it into assurance.[5]

The shameless behaviour of the prostitutes, who infest the streets of this metropolis, raising alternate emotions of pity and disgust, may serve to illustrate this remark. They trample on virgin bashfulness with a sort of bravado, and glorying in their shame, become more audaciously lewd than men, however depraved, to whom this sexual quality has not been gratuitously granted, ever appear to be. But these poor ignorant wretches never had any modesty to lose, when they consigned themselves to infamy; for modesty is a virtue, not a quality. No, they were only bashful, shame-faced innocents; and losing their innocence, their shame-facedness was rudely brushed off; a virtue would have left some vestiges in the mind, had it been sacrificed to passion, to make us respect the grand ruin.

Purity of mind, or that genuine delicacy, which is the only virtuous support of chastity, is near akin to that refinement of humanity, which never resides in any but cultivated minds. It is something nobler than innocence, it is the delicacy of reflection, and not the coyness of ignorance. The reserve of reason, which, like habitual cleanliness, is seldom seen in any great degree, unless the soul is active, may

---

[5] "Such is the country-maiden's fright,
   When first a red-coat is in sight;
   Behind the door she hides her face;
   Next time at distance eyes the lace:
   She now can all his terrors stand,
   Nor from his squeeze withdraws her hand,
   She plays familiar in his arms,
   And ev'ry soldier hath his charms;
   From tent to tent she spreads her flame;
   For custom conquers fear and shame."—GAY [MW]
"The Tame Stag" in *Fables* (1727), 27–36; by John Gay (1685–1732), best known for *The Beggar's Opera*.

easily be distinguished from rustic shyness or wanton skittishness; and, so far from being incompatible with knowledge, it is its fairest fruit. What a gross idea of modesty had the writer of the following remark! "The lady who asked the question whether women may be instructed in the modern system of botany, consistently with female delicacy?—was accused of ridiculous prudery: nevertheless, if she had proposed the question to me, I should certainly have answered— They cannot."[6] Thus is the fair book of knowledge to be shut with an everlasting seal! On reading similar passages I have reverentially lifted up my eyes and heart to Him who liveth for ever and ever, and said, O my Father, hast Thou by the very constitution of her nature forbid Thy child to seek Thee in the fair forms of truth? And, can her soul be sullied by the knowledge that awfully calls her to Thee?

I have then philosophically pursued these reflections till I inferred that those women who have most improved their reason must have the most modesty—though a dignified sedateness of deportment may have succeeded the playful, bewitching bashfulness of youth.[7]

And thus have I argued. To render chastity the virtue from which unsophisticated modesty will naturally flow, the attention should be called away from employments which only exercise the sensibility; and the heart made to beat time to humanity, rather than to throb with love. The woman who has dedicated a considerable portion of her time to pursuits purely intellectual, and whose affections have been exercised by humane plans of usefulness, must have more purity of mind, as a natural consequence, than the ignorant beings whose time and thoughts have been occupied by gay pleasures or schemes to conquer hearts.[8] The regulation of the behaviour is not modesty,

[6]In *A Volume of Letters to His Son at the University* (Cambridge, 1790), 32.307, physician and naturalist John Berkenhout (1730?–1801) argues that the Linnean system— which classified plants by sexual organs—would be inappropriate study for women.

[7]Modesty, is the graceful calm virtue of maturity; bashfulness, the charm of vivacious youth [MW].

[8]I have conversed, as man with man, with medical men, on anatomical subjects; and compared the proportions of the human body with artists—yet such modesty did I meet with, that I was never reminded by word or look of my sex, of the absurd rules which make modesty a pharisaical cloak of weakness. And I am persuaded that in the pursuit of knowledge women would never be insulted by sensible men, and rarely by men of any description, if they did not by mock modesty remind them that they were women: actuated by the same spirit as the Portugueze ladies, who would think their charms insulted, if, when left alone with a man, he did not, at least, attempt to be grossly familiar with their persons. Men are not always men in the company of women, nor would women always remember that they are women, if they were allowed to acquire more understanding [MW]. *Pharisaical*: in the manner of the ancient Pharisees, followers of the letter of the law and exhibitors of such "virtue."

though those who study rules of decorum are, in general, termed modest women. Make the heart clean, let it expand and feel for all that is human, instead of being narrowed by selfish passions; and let the mind frequently contemplate subjects that exercise the understanding, without heating the imagination, and artless modesty will give the finishing touches to the picture.

She who can discern the dawn of immortality, in the streaks that shoot athwart the misty night of ignorance, promising a clearer day, will respect, as a sacred temple, the body that enshrines such an improvable soul. True love, likewise, spreads this kind of mysterious sanctity round the beloved object, making the lover most modest when in her presence.[9] So reserved is affection that, receiving or returning personal endearments, it wishes, not only to shun the human eye, as a kind of profanation; but to diffuse an encircling cloudy obscurity to shut out even the saucy sparkling sunbeams. Yet, that affection does not deserve the epithet of chaste, which does not receive a sublime gloom of tender melancholy, that allows the mind for a moment to stand still and enjoy the present satisfaction, when a consciousness of the Divine presence is felt—for this must ever be the food of joy!

As I have always been fond of tracing to its source in nature any prevailing custom, I have frequently thought that it was a sentiment of affection for whatever had touched the person of an absent or lost friend, which gave birth to that respect for relicks, so much abused by selfish priests. Devotion, or love, may be allowed to hallow the garments as well as the person; for the lover must want fancy who has not a sort of sacred respect for the glove or slipper of his mistress. He could not confound them with vulgar things of the same kind. This fine sentiment, perhaps, would not bear to be analyzed by the experimental philosopher—but of such stuff is human rapture made up!—A shadowy phantom glides before us, obscuring every other object; yet when the soft cloud is grasped, the form melts into common air, leaving a solitary void, or sweet perfume, stolen from the violet, that memory long holds dear. But, I have tripped unawares on fairy ground, feeling the balmy gale of spring stealing on me, though november frowns.

As a sex, women are more chaste than men, and as modesty is the effect of chastity, they may deserve to have this virtue ascribed to them in rather an appropriated sense; yet, I must be allowed to add an hesitating if:—for I doubt whether chastity will produce modesty, though it may propriety of conduct, when it is merely a respect for

[9]Male or female; for the world contains many modest men [MW].

the opinion of the world,[10] and when coquetry and the love-lorn tales of novelists employ the thoughts. Nay, from experience, and reason, I should be led to expect to meet with more modesty amongst men than women, simply because men exercise their understandings more than women.

But, with respect to propriety of behaviour, excepting one class of females, women have evidently the advantage. What can be more disgusting than that impudent dross of gallantry, thought so manly, which makes many men stare insultingly at every female they meet? Can it be termed respect for the sex? No, this loose behaviour shews such habitual depravity, such weakness of mind, that it is vain to expect much public or private virtue, till both men and women grow more modest—till men, curbing a sensual fondness for the sex, or an affectation of manly assurance, more properly speaking, impudence, treat each other with respect—unless appetite or passion give the tone, peculiar to it, to their behaviour. I mean even personal respect—the modest respect of humanity, and fellow-feeling—not the libidinous mockery of gallantry, nor the insolent condescension of protectorship.

To carry the observation still further, modesty must heartily disclaim, and refuse to dwell with that debauchery of mind, which leads a man coolly to bring forward, without a blush, indecent allusions, or obscene witticisms, in the presence of a fellow creature; women are now out of the question, for then it is brutality. Respect for man, as man, is the foundation of every noble sentiment. How much more modest is the libertine who obeys the call of appetite or fancy, than the lewd joker who sets the table in a roar!

This is one of the many instances in which the sexual distinction respecting modesty has proved fatal to virtue and happiness. It is, however, carried still further, and woman, weak woman! made by her education the slave of sensibility, is required, on the most trying occasions, to resist that sensibility. "Can any thing," says Knox, "be more absurd than keeping women in a state of ignorance, and yet so vehemently to insist on their resisting temptation?"[11]—Thus when virtue or honour make it proper to check a passion, the burden is thrown on the weaker shoulders, contrary to reason and true modesty, which, at least, should render the self-denial mutual, to say nothing of the generosity of bravery, supposed to be a manly virtue.

---

[10]The immodest behaviour of many married women, who are nevertheless faithful to their husbands' beds, will illustrate this remark [MW].

[11]*Essays, Moral and Literary* (1782), 154.

In the same strain runs Rousseau's and Dr. Gregory's advice respecting modesty, strangely miscalled! for they both desire a wife to leave it in doubt whether sensibility or weakness led her to her husband's arms.—The woman is immodest who can let the shadow of such a doubt remain in her husband's mind a moment.

But to state the subject in a different light.—The want of modesty, which I principally deplore as subversive of morality, arises from the state of warfare so strenuously supported by voluptuous men as the very essence of modesty, though, in fact, its bane; because it is a refinement on lust, that men fall into who have not sufficient virtue to relish the innocent pleasures of love. A man of delicacy carries his notions of modesty still further, for neither weakness nor sensibility will gratify him—he looks for affection.

Again; men boast of their triumphs over women, what do they boast of? Truly the creature of sensibility was surprised by her sensibility into folly—into vice[12]; and the dreadful reckoning falls heavily on her own weak head, when reason wakes. For where art thou to find comfort, forlorn and disconsolate one? He who ought to have directed thy reason, and supported thy weakness, has betrayed thee! In a dream of passion thou consented to wander through flowery lawns, and heedlessly stepping over the precipice to which thy guide, instead of guarding, lured thee, thou startest from thy dream only to face a sneering, frowning world, and to find thyself alone in a waste, for he that triumphed in thy weakness is now pursuing new conquests; but for thee—there is no redemption on this side the grave!—And what resource hast thou in an enervated mind to raise a sinking heart?

But, if the sexes be really to live in a state of warfare, if nature have pointed it out, let them act nobly, or let pride whisper to them, that the victory is mean when they merely vanquish sensibility. The real conquest is that over affection not taken by surprise—when, like Heloisa,[13] a woman gives up all the world, deliberately, for love. I do not now consider the wisdom or virtue of such a sacrifice, I only contend that it was a sacrifice to affection, and not merely to sensibility, though she had her share.—And I must be allowed to call her a modest woman, before I dismiss this part of the subject, by saying, that till men are more chaste women will be immodest. Where, indeed, could modest women find husbands from whom they would not continually turn with disgust? Modesty must be equally cultivated by both

[12]The poor moth fluttering round a candle, burns its wings [MW].
[13]See ch. IV, p. 101, n. 51.

sexes, or it will ever remain a sickly hot-house plant, whilst the affectation of it, the fig leaf borrowed by wantonness, may give a zest to voluptuous enjoyments.

Men will probably still insist that woman ought to have more modesty than man; but it is not dispassionate reasoners who will most earnestly oppose my opinion. No, they are the men of fancy, the favourites of the sex, who outwardly respect and inwardly despise the weak creatures whom they thus sport with. They cannot submit to resign the highest sensual gratification, nor even to relish the epicurism of virtue—self-denial.

To take another view of the subject, confining my remarks to women.

The ridiculous falsities[14] which are told to children, from mistaken notions of modesty, tend very early to inflame their imaginations and set their little minds to work, respecting subjects, which nature never intended they should think of till the body arrived at some degree of maturity; then the passions naturally begin to take place of the senses, as instruments to unfold the understanding, and form the moral character.

In nurseries, and boarding-schools, I fear, girls are first spoiled; particularly in the latter. A number of girls sleep in the same room, and wash together. And, though I should be sorry to contaminate an innocent creature's mind by instilling false delicacy, or those indecent prudish notions, which early cautions respecting the other sex naturally engender, I should be very anxious to prevent their acquiring nasty, or immodest habits; and as many girls have learned very nasty tricks, from ignorant servants, the mixing them thus indiscriminately together, is very improper.

To say the truth women are, in general, too familiar with each other, which leads to that gross degree of familiarity that so frequently renders the marriage state unhappy. Why in the name of decency are sisters, female intimates, or ladies and their waiting-women, to be so grossly familiar as to forget the respect which one

[14]Children very early see cats with their kittens, birds with their young ones, etc. Why then are they not to be told that their mothers carry and nourish them in the same way? As there would then be no appearance of mystery they would never think of the subject more. Truth may always be told to children, if it be told gravely; but it is the immodesty of affected modesty, that does all the mischief; and this smoke heats the imagination by vainly endeavouring to obscure certain objects. If, indeed, children could be kept entirely from improper company, we should never allude to any such subjects; but as this is impossible, it is best to tell them the truth, especially as such information, not interesting them, will make no impression on their imagination [MW].

human creature owes to another? That squeamish delicacy which shrinks from the most disgusting offices when affection[15] or humanity lead us to watch at a sick pillow, is despicable. But, why women in health should be more familiar with each other than men are, when they boast of their superior delicacy, is a solecism in manners which I could never solve.

In order to preserve health and beauty, I should earnestly recommend frequent ablutions, to dignify my advice that it may not offend the fastidious ear; and, by example, girls ought to be taught to wash and dress alone, without any distinction of rank; and if custom should make them require some little assistance, let them not require it till that part of the business is over which ought never to be done before a fellow-creature; because it is an insult to the majesty of human nature. Not on the score of modesty, but decency; for the care which some modest women take, making at the same time a display of that care, not to let their legs be seen, is as childish as immodest.[16]

I could proceed still further, till I animadverted on some still more nasty customs, which men never fall into. Secrets are told—where silence ought to reign; and that regard to cleanliness, which some religious sects have, perhaps, carried too far, especially the Essenes,[17] amongst the Jews, by making that an insult to God which is only an insult to humanity, is violated in a beastly manner. How can *delicate* women obtrude on notice that part of the animal œconomy, which is so very disgusting? And is it not very rational to conclude, that the women who have not been taught to respect the human nature of their own sex, in these particulars, will not long respect the mere difference of sex in their husbands? After their maidenish bashfulness is once lost, I, in fact, have generally observed, that women fall into old habits; and treat their husbands as they did their sisters or female acquaintance.

Besides, women from necessity, because their minds are not cultivated, have recourse very often to what I familiarly term bodily wit; and their intimacies are of the same kind. In short, with respect to both mind and body, they are too intimate. That decent personal reserve which is

---

[15]Affection would rather make one choose to perform these offices, to spare the delicacy of a friend, by still keeping a veil over them, for the personal helplessness, produced by sickness, is of an humbling nature [MW].

[16]I remember to have met with a sentence, in a book of education, that made me smile. "It would be needless to caution you against putting your hand, by chance, under your neck-handkerchief; for a modest woman never did so!" [MW].

[17]A Jewish sect in ancient Palestine that practiced ritual washings and other laws of purity.

the foundation of dignity of character, must be kept up between woman and woman, or their minds will never gain strength or modesty.

On this account also, I object to many females being shut up together in nurseries, schools, or convents. I cannot recollect without indignation, the jokes and hoiden tricks, which knots of young women indulge themselves in, when in my youth accident threw me, an awkward rustic, in their way. They were almost on a par with the double meanings, which shake the convivial table when the glass has circulated freely. But, it is vain to attempt to keep the heart pure, unless the head is furnished with ideas, and set to work to compare them, in order to acquire judgment, by generalizing simple ones; and modesty, by making the understanding damp the sensibility.

It may be thought that I lay too great a stress on personal reserve; but it is ever the handmaid of modesty. So that were I to name the graces that ought to adorn beauty, I should instantly exclaim, cleanliness, neatness, and personal reserve. It is obvious, I suppose, that the reserve I mean, has nothing sexual in it, and that I think it *equally* necessary in both sexes. So necessary, indeed, is that reserve and cleanliness which indolent women too often neglect, that I will venture to affirm that when two or three women live in the same house, the one will be most respected by the male part of the family, who reside with them, leaving love entirely out of the question, who pays this kind of habitual respect to her person.

When domestic friends meet in a morning, there will naturally prevail an affectionate seriousness, especially, if each look forward to the discharge of daily duties; and it may be reckoned fanciful, but this sentiment has frequently risen spontaneously in my mind, I have been pleased after breathing the sweet-bracing morning air, to see the same kind of freshness in the countenances I particularly loved; I was glad to see them braced, as it were, for the day, and ready to run their course with the sun. The greetings of affection in the morning are by these means more respectful than the familiar tenderness which frequently prolongs the evening talk. Nay, I have often felt hurt, not to say disgusted, when a friend has appeared, whom I parted with full dressed the evening before, with her clothes huddled on, because she chose to indulge herself in bed till the last moment.

Domestic affection can only be kept alive by these neglected attentions; yet if men and women took half as much pains to dress habitually neat, as they do to ornament, or rather to disfigure, their persons, much would be done towards the attainment of purity of mind. But women only dress to gratify men of gallantry; for the lover is always best pleased with the simple garb that fits close to the shape. There is an impertinence in ornaments that rebuffs affection; because love always clings round the idea of home.

As a sex, women are habitually indolent; and every thing tends to make them so. I do not forget the spurts of activity which sensibility produces; but as these flights of feelings only increase the evil, they are not to be confounded with the slow, orderly walk of reason. So great in reality is their mental and bodily indolence, that till their body be strengthened and their understanding enlarged by active exertions, there is little reason to expect that modesty will take place of bashfulness. They may find it prudent to assume its semblance; but the fair veil will only be worn on gala days.

Perhaps, there is not a virtue that mixes so kindly with every other as modesty.—It is the pale moon-beam that renders more interesting every virtue it softens, giving mild grandeur to the contracted horizon. Nothing can be more beautiful than the poetical fiction, which makes Diana with her silver crescent, the goddess of chastity.[18] I have sometimes thought, that wandering with sedate step in some lonely recess, a modest dame of antiquity must have felt a glow of conscious dignity when, after contemplating the soft shadowy landscape, she has invited with placid fervour the mild reflection of her sister's beams to turn to her chaste bosom.

A Christian has still nobler motives to incite her to preserve her chastity and acquire modesty, for her body has been called the Temple of the living God[19]; of that God who requires more than modesty of mien. His eye searcheth the heart; and let her remember, that if she hope to find favour in the sight of purity itself, her chastity must be founded on modesty, and not on worldly prudence; or verily a good reputation will be her only reward; for that awful intercourse, that sacred communication, which virtue establishes between man and his Maker, must give rise to the wish of being pure as he is pure![20]

After the foregoing remarks, it is almost superfluous to add, that I consider all those feminine airs of maturity, which succeed bashfulness, to which truth is sacrificed, to secure the heart of a husband, or rather to force him to be still a lover when nature would, had she not

---

[18]The Roman goddess of the moon, virgin, huntress, and the helper of women in childbirth.

[19]"Know ye not that ye are the temple of God, and that the Spirit of God dwelleth in you?" (1 Corinthians 3:16).

[20]"Be ye therefore perfect, even as your Father which is in heaven is perfect" (Matthew 5:48, also 1 John 3:3).

been interrupted in her operations, have made love give place to friendship, as immodest. The tenderness which a man will feel for the mother of his children is an excellent substitute for the ardour of unsatisfied passion; but to prolong that ardour it is indelicate, not to say immodest, for women to feign an unnatural coldness of constitution. Women as well as men ought to have the common appetites and passions of their nature, they are only brutal when unchecked by reason: but the obligation to check them is the duty of mankind, not a sexual duty. Nature, in these respects, may safely be left to herself; let women only acquire knowledge and humanity, and love will teach them modesty.[21] There is no need of falsehoods, disgusting as futile, for studied rules of behaviour only impose on shallow observers; a man of sense soon sees through, and despises the affectation.

The behaviour of young people, to each other, as men and women, is the last thing that should be thought of in education. In fact, behaviour in most circumstances is now so much thought of, that simplicity of character is rarely to be seen: yet, if men were only anxious to cultivate each virtue, and let it take root firmly in the mind, the grace resulting from it, its natural exterior mark, would soon strip affectation of its flaunting plumes; because, fallacious as unstable, is the conduct that is not founded upon truth!

Would ye, O my sisters, really possess modesty, ye must remember that the possession of virtue, of any denomination, is incompatible with ignorance and vanity! ye must acquire that soberness of mind, which the exercise of duties, and the pursuit of knowledge, alone inspire, or ye will still remain in a doubtful dependent situation, and only be loved whilst ye are fair! The downcast eye, the rosy blush, the retiring grace, are all proper in their season; but modesty, being the child of reason, cannot long exist with the sensibility that is not tempered by reflection. Besides, when love, even innocent love, is the whole employ of your lives, your hearts will be too soft to afford modesty that tranquil retreat, where she delights to dwell, in close union with humanity.

---

[21]The behaviour of many newly married women has often disgusted me. They seem anxious never to let their husbands forget the privilege of marriage; and to find no pleasure in his society unless he is acting the lover. Short, indeed, must be the reign of love, when the flame is thus constantly blown up, without its receiving any solid fewel! [MW].

CHAPTER VIII

MORALITY UNDERMINED BY SEXUAL NOTIONS OF THE IMPORTANCE OF A GOOD REPUTATION

It has long since occurred to me that advice respecting behaviour, and all the various modes of preserving a good reputation, which have been so strenuously inculcated on the female world, were specious poisons, that incrusting morality eat away the substance. And, that this measuring of shadows produced a false calculation, because their length depends so much on the height of the sun, and other adventitious circumstances.

Whence arises the easy fallacious behaviour of a courtier? From his situation, undoubtedly: for standing in need of dependents, he is obliged to learn the art of denying without giving offence, and, of evasively feeding hope with the chameleon's food[1]: thus does politeness sport with truth, and eating away the sincerity and humanity natural to man, produce the fine gentleman.

Women likewise acquire, from a supposed necessity, an equally artificial mode of behaviour. Yet truth is not with impunity to be sported with, for the practised dissembler, at last, become the dupe of his own arts, loses that sagacity, which has been justly termed common sense; namely, a quick perception of common truths: which are constantly received as such by the unsophisticated mind, though it might not have had sufficient energy to discover them itself, when obscured by local prejudices. The greater number of people take their opinions on trust to avoid the trouble of exercising their own minds, and these indolent beings naturally adhere to the letter, rather than the spirit of a law, divine or human.[2] "Women," says some author, I cannot recollect who, "mind not what only heaven sees." Why, indeed, should they? it is the eye of man that they have been taught to dread—and if they can lull their Argus[3] to sleep, they seldom think of heaven or themselves, because their reputation is safe; and it is reputation, not chastity and all its fair train, that they are employed to keep free from spot, not as a virtue, but to preserve their station in the world.

To prove the truth of this remark, I need only advert to the intrigues of married women, particularly in high life, and in countries

---

[1]Thought to be air.

[2]Referring to Paul's instruction to the Corinthians that "the letter killeth, but the spirit giveth life" (2 Cor. 3:6).

[3]The hundred-eyed monster of mythology, sent by jealous Hera as watchguard over Zeus's lover Io. Zeus's messenger Hermes lulled Argus to sleep and killed him.

where women are suitably married, according to their respective ranks, by their parents. If an innocent girl become a prey to love, she is degraded for ever, though her mind was not polluted by the arts which married women, under the convenient cloke of marriage, practise; nor has she violated any duty—but the duty of respecting herself. The married woman, on the contrary, breaks a most sacred engagement, and becomes a cruel mother when she is a false and faithless wife. If her husband have still an affection for her, the arts which she must practise to deceive him, will render her the most contemptible of human beings; and, at any rate, the contrivances necessary to preserve appearances, will keep her mind in that childish, or vicious, tumult, which destroys all its energy. Besides, in time, like those people who habitually take cordials to raise their spirits, she will want an intrigue to give life to her thoughts, having lost all relish for pleasures that are not highly seasoned by hope or fear.

Sometimes married women act still more audaciously; I will mention an instance.

A woman of quality, notorious for her gallantries, though as she still lived with her husband, nobody chose to place her in the class where she ought to have been placed, made a point of treating with the most insulting contempt a poor timid creature, abashed by a sense of her former weakness, whom a neighbouring gentleman had seduced and afterwards married. This woman had actually confounded virtue with reputation; and, I do believe, valued herself on the propriety of her behaviour before marriage, though when once settled to the satisfaction of her family, she and her lord were equally faithless,—so that the half alive heir to an immense estate came from heaven knows where!

To view this subject in another light.

I have known a number of women who, if they did not love their husbands, loved nobody else, give themselves entirely up to vanity and dissipation, neglecting every domestic duty; nay, even squandering away all the money which should have been saved for their helpless younger children, yet have plumed themselves on their unsullied reputation, as if the whole compass of their duty as wives and mothers was only to preserve it. Whilst other indolent women, neglecting every personal duty, have thought that they deserved their husbands' affection, because, forsooth, they acted in this respect with propriety.

Weak minds are always fond of resting in the ceremonials of duty, but morality offers much simpler motives; and it were to be wished that superficial moralists had said less respecting behaviour, and outward observances, for unless virtue, of any kind, be built on knowledge, it will only produce a kind of insipid decency. Respect for the opinion of the world, has, however, been termed the principal duty of woman in the most express words, for Rousseau declares, "that reputation is no less indispensable than chastity."[4] "A man," adds he, "secure in his own good conduct, depends only on himself, and may brave the public opinion: but a woman, in behaving well, performs but half her duty; as what is thought of her, is as important to her as what she really is. It follows hence, that the system of a woman's education should, in this respect, be directly contrary to that of ours. Opinion is the grave of virtue among the men; but its throne among women." It is strictly logical to infer that the virtue that rests on opinion is merely worldly, and that it is the virtue of a being to whom reason has been denied. But, even with respect to the opinion of the world, I am convinced that this class of reasoners are mistaken.

This regard for reputation, independent of its being one of the natural rewards of virtue, however, took its rise from a cause that I have already deplored as the grand source of female depravity, the impossibility of regaining respectability by a return to virtue, though men preserve theirs during the indulgence of vice. It was natural for women then to endeavour to preserve what once lost—was lost for ever, till this care swallowing up every other care, reputation for chastity, became the one thing needful to the sex. But vain is the scrupulosity of ignorance, for neither religion nor virtue, when they reside in the heart, require such a puerile attention to mere ceremonies, because the behaviour must, upon the whole, be proper, when the motive is pure.

To support my opinion I can produce very respectable authority; and the authority of a cool reasoner ought to have weight to enforce consideration, though not to establish a sentiment. Speaking of the general laws of morality, Dr. Smith observes,—"That by some very extraordinary and unlucky circumstance, a good man may come to be suspected of a crime of which he was altogether incapable, and upon that account be most unjustly exposed for the remaining part of his life to the horror and aversion of mankind. By an accident of this kind he may be said to lose his all, notwithstanding his integrity and justice, in the same manner as a cautious man, notwithstanding his utmost circumspection, may be ruined by an earthquake or an inundation. Accidents of the first kind, however, are perhaps still more

---

[4]*Emilius*, 4.5.19; Rosseau is adamant that women's "glory lies not only in their conduct, but in their reputation; and it is impossible for any, who consents to be accounted infamous, to be ever virtuous."

rare, and still more contrary to the common course of things than those of the second; and it still remains true, that the practice of truth, justice, and humanity, is a certain and almost infallible method of acquiring what those virtues chiefly aim at, the confidence and love of those we live with. A person may be easily misrepresented with regard to a particular action; but it is scarce possible that he should be so with regard to the general tenor of his conduct. An innocent man may be believed to have done wrong: this, however, will rarely happen. On the contrary, the established opinion of the innocence of his manners will often lead us to absolve him where he has really been in the fault, notwithstanding very strong presumptions." [5]

I perfectly coincide in opinion with this writer, for I verily believe that few of either sex were ever despised for certain vices without deserving to be despised. I speak not of the calumny of the moment, which hovers over a character, like one of the dense morning fogs of November, over this metropolis, till it gradually subsides before the common light of day, I only contend that the daily conduct of the majority prevails to stamp their character with the impression of truth. Quietly does the clear light, shining day after day, refute the ignorant surmise, or malicious tale, which has thrown dirt on a pure character. A false light distorted, for a short time, its shadow—reputation; but it seldom fails to become just when the cloud is dispersed that produced the mistake in vision.

Many people, undoubtedly, in several respects obtain a better reputation than, strictly speaking, they deserve; for unremitting industry will mostly reach its goal in all races. They who only strive for this paltry prize, like the Pharisees, who prayed at the corners of streets, to be seen of men, [6] verily obtain the reward they seek; for the heart of man cannot be read by man! Still the fair fame that is naturally reflected by good actions, when the man is only employed to direct his steps aright, regardless of the lookers-on, is, in general, not only more true, but more sure.

There are, it is true, trials when the good man must appeal to God from the injustice of man; and amidst the whining candour or hissings of envy, erect a pavilion in his own mind to retire to till the rumour be overpast; nay, the darts of undeserved censure may pierce an innocent tender bosom through with many sorrows; but these are all exceptions

---

[5] Smith, *Theory of Moral Sentiments*, 3.5.

[6] "And when thou prayest, thou shalt not be as the hypocrites are: for they love to pray standing in the synagogues and in the corners of the streets, that they may be seen of men" (Matthew 6:5).

to general rules. And it is according to common laws that human behaviour ought to be regulated. The eccentric orbit of the comet never influences astronomical calculations respecting the invariable order established in the motion of the principal bodies of the solar system.

I will then venture to affirm, that after a man is arrived at maturity, the general outline of his character in the world is just, allowing for the before-mentioned exceptions to the rule. I do not say that a prudent, worldly-wise man, with only negative virtues and qualities, may not sometimes obtain a smoother reputation than a wiser or a better man. So far from it, that I am apt to conclude from experience, that where the virtue of two people is nearly equal, the most negative character will be liked best by the world at large, whilst the other may have more friends in private life. But the hills and dales, clouds and sunshine, conspicuous in the virtues of great men, set off each other; and though they afford envious weakness a fairer mark to shoot at, the real character will still work its way to light, though bespattered by weak affection, or ingenious malice.[7]

With respect to that anxiety to preserve a reputation hardly earned, which leads sagacious people to analyze it, I shall not make the obvious comment; but I am afraid that morality is very insidiously undermined, in the female world, by the attention being turned to the shew instead of the substance. A simple thing is thus made strangely complicated; nay, sometimes virtue and its shadow are set at variance. We should never, perhaps, have heard of Lucretia,[8] had she died to preserve her chastity instead of her reputation. If we really deserve our own good opinion we shall commonly be respected in the world; but if we pant after higher improvement and higher attainments, it is not sufficient to view ourselves as we suppose that we are viewed by others, though this has been ingeniously argued, as the foundation of our moral sentiments.[9] Because each by-stander may have his own prejudices, beside the prejudices of his age or country. We should rather endeavour to view ourselves as we suppose that Being views us who seeth each thought ripen into action, and whose

---

[7]I allude to various biographical writings, but particularly to Boswell's Life of Johnson [MW]. James Boswell's celebrated *Life of Samuel Johnson* (1791), though meticulously documenting Johnson's petty dislikes, moral weaknesses, and behavioral peculiarities, casts an exemplary, heroic figure.

[8]This wife of Lucius Tarquinius Collatinus was raped by the king's son Tarquinius Sextus (5th c. BCE). After exacting an oath of vengeance from her father and husband, she stabbed herself—events that led to the collapse of the Tarquins' rule, and the birth of the Roman republic.

[9]Smith [MW]. She is referring to *Theory of Moral Sentiments*, 3.2.

judgment never swerves from the eternal rule of right. Righteous are all his judgments—just as merciful![10]

The humble mind that seeketh to find favour in His sight, and calmly examines its conduct when only His presence is felt, will seldom form a very erroneous opinion of its own virtues. During the still hour of self-collection the angry brow of offended justice will be fearfully deprecated, or the tie which draws man to the Deity will be recognized in the pure sentiment of reverential adoration, that swells the heart without exciting any tumultuous emotions. In these solemn moments man discovers the germ of those vices, which like the Java tree shed a pestiferous vapour around—death is in the shade![11] and he perceives them without abhorrence, because he feels himself drawn by some cord of love to all his fellow-creatures, for whose follies he is anxious to find every extenuation in their nature—in himself. If I, he may thus argue, who exercise my own mind, and have been refined by tribulation, find the serpent's egg[12] in some fold of my heart, and crush it with difficulty, shall not I pity those who have stamped with less vigour, or who have heedlessly nurtured the insidious reptile till it poisoned the vital stream it sucked? Can I, conscious of my secret sins, throw off my fellow-creatures, and calmly see them drop into the chasm of perdition, that yawns to receive them.—No! no! The agonized heart will cry with suffocating impatience—I too am a man! and have vices, hid, perhaps, from human eye, that bend me to the dust before God, and loudly tell me, when all is mute, that we are formed of the same earth, and breathe the same element. Humanity thus rises naturally out of humility, and twists the cords of love that in various convolutions entangle the heart.

This sympathy extends still further, till a man well pleased observes force in arguments that do not carry conviction to his own bosom, and he gladly places in the fairest light, to himself, the shews of reason that have led others astray, rejoiced to find some reason in all the errors of man; though before convinced that he who rules the day makes his sun to shine on all. Yet, shaking hands thus as it were with corruption, one foot on earth, the other with bold stride mounts to heaven, and claims kindred with superiour natures. Virtues, unobserved by man, drop

---

[10]Echoing Psalms 19:9: "the judgments of the Lord are true and righteous altogether."

[11]As an afterword to *Loves of the Plants* (1788), Erasmus Darwin wryly retells the legend of the Java tree, thought (incorrectly) to be poisonous: its vapor left the surrounding land littered with skeletons; condemned criminals were sent to the Java tree.

[12]To justify the assassination of Julius Caesar, Shakespeare's Brutus reasons, "think him as a serpent's egg / Which, hatch'd, would, as his kind, grow mischievous" (*Julius Caesar*, 2.1.32–33).

their balmy fragrance at this cool hour, and the thirsty land, refreshed by the pure streams of comfort that suddenly gush out, is crowned with smiling verdure; this is the living green on which that eye may look with complacency that is too pure to behold iniquity!

But my spirits flag; and I must silently indulge the reverie these reflections lead to, unable to describe the sentiments, that have calmed my soul, when watching the rising sun, a soft shower drizzling through the leaves of neighbouring trees, seemed to fall on my languid, yet tranquil spirits, to cool the heart that had been heated by the passions which reason laboured to tame.

The leading principles which run through all my disquisitions, would render it unnecessary to enlarge on this subject, if a constant attention to keep the varnish of the character fresh, and in good condition, were not often inculcated as the sum total of female duty; if rules to regulate the behaviour, and to preserve the reputation, did not too frequently supersede moral obligations. But, with respect to reputation, the attention is confined to a single virtue—chastity. If the honour of a woman, as it is absurdly called, be safe, she may neglect every social duty; nay, ruin her family by gaming and extravagance; yet still present a shameless front—for truly she is an honourable woman!

Mrs. Macaulay has justly observed, that "there is but one fault which a woman of honour may not commit with impunity." She then justly and humanely adds—"This has given rise to the trite and foolish observation, that the first fault against chastity in woman has a radical power to deprave the character. But no such frail beings come out of the hands of nature. The human mind is built of nobler materials than to be easily corrupted; and with all their disadvantages of situation and education, women seldom become entirely abandoned till they are thrown into a state of desperation, by the venomous rancour of their own sex."[13]

But, in proportion as this regard for the reputation of chastity is prized by women, it is despised by men: and the two extremes are equally destructive to morality.

Men are certainly more under the influence of their appetites than women; and their appetites are more depraved by unbridled indulgence and the fastidious contrivances of satiety. Luxury has introduced a refinement in eating, that destroys the constitution; and, a degree of gluttony which is so beastly, that a perception of seemliness

[13]*Letters on Education*, 210–12; Macaulay elaborates the "one fault": "let her only take care that she is not caught in a love intrigue, and she may lie, she may deceive, she may defame, she may ruin her family with gaming, and the peace of twenty others with her coquettry, and yet preserve both her reputation and her peace."

of behaviour must be worn out before one being could eat immoderately in the presence of another, and afterwards complain of the oppression that his intemperance naturally produced. Some women, particularly French women, have also lost a sense of decency in this respect; for they will talk very calmly of an indigestion. It were to be wished that idleness was not allowed to generate, on the rank soil of wealth, those swarms of summer insects that feed on putrefaction, we should not then be disgusted by the sight of such brutal excesses.

There is one rule relative to behaviour that, I think, ought to regulate every other; and it is simply to cherish such an habitual respect for mankind as may prevent us from disgusting a fellow-creature for the sake of a present indulgence. The shameful indolence of many married women, and others a little advanced in life, frequently leads them to sin against delicacy. For, though convinced that the person is the band of union between the sexes, yet, how often do they from sheer indolence, or, to enjoy some trifling indulgence, disgust?

The depravity of the appetite which brings the sexes together, has had a still more fatal effect. Nature must ever be the standard of taste, the gauge of appetite—yet how grossly is nature insulted by the voluptuary. Leaving the refinements of love out of the question; nature, by making the gratification of an appetite, in this respect, as well as every other, a natural and imperious law to preserve the species, exalts the appetite, and mixes a little mind and affection with a sensual gust.[14] The feelings of a parent mingling with an instinct merely animal, give it dignity; and the man and woman often meeting on account of the child, a mutual interest and affection is excited by the exercise of a common sympathy. Women then having necessarily some duty to fulfil, more noble than to adorn their persons, would not contentedly be the slaves of casual lust; which is now the situation of a very considerable number who are, literally speaking, standing dishes to which every glutton may have access.

I may be told that great as this enormity is, it only affects a devoted part of the sex—devoted for the salvation of the rest. But, false as every assertion might easily be proved, that recommends the sanctioning a small evil to produce a greater good; the mischief does not stop here, for the moral character, and peace of mind, of the chaster part of the sex, is undermined by the conduct of the very women to whom they allow no refuge from guilt: whom they inexorably consign to the exercise of arts that lure their husbands from them, de-

---

[14] Appetite; see the use by Dryden, p. 148.

bauch their sons, and force them, let not modest women start, to assume, in some degree, the same character themselves. For I will venture to assert, that all the causes of female weakness, as well as depravity, which I have already enlarged on, branch out of one grand cause—want of chastity in men.

This intemperance, so prevalent, depraves the appetite to such a degree, that a wanton stimulus is necessary to rouse it; but the parental design of nature is forgotten, and the mere person, and that for a moment, alone engrosses the thoughts. So voluptuous, indeed, often grows the lustful prowler, that he refines on female softness. Something more soft than woman is then sought for; till, in Italy and Portugal, men attend the levees of equivocal beings, to sigh for more than female languor.[15]

To satisfy this genus of men, women are made systematically voluptuous, and though they may not all carry their libertinism to the same height, yet this heartless intercourse with the sex, which they allow themselves, depraves both sexes, because the taste of men is vitiated; and women, of all classes, naturally square their behaviour to gratify the taste by which they obtain pleasure and power. Women becoming, consequently, weaker, in mind and body, than they ought to be, were one of the grand ends of their being taken into the account, that of bearing and nursing children, have not sufficient strength to discharge the first duty of a mother; and sacrificing to lasciviousness the parental affection, that ennobles instinct, either destroy the embryo in the womb, or cast it off when born. Nature in every thing demands respect, and those who violate her laws seldom violate them with impunity. The weak enervated women who particularly catch the attention of libertines, are unfit to be mothers, though they may conceive; so that the rich sensualist, who has rioted among women, spreading depravity and misery, when he wishes to perpetuate his name, receives from his wife only an half-formed being that inherits both its father's and mother's weakness.

Contrasting the humanity of the present age with the barbarism of antiquity, great stress has been laid on the savage custom of exposing the children whom their parents could not maintain[16]; whilst the man of sensibility, who thus, perhaps, complains, by his promiscuous

[15]Levee: a formal reception of visitors, usually male. London also had homosexual or "molly" clubs in the 18th c.; see Ned Ward, *A Compleat and Humourous Account of all the Remarkable Clubs and Societies in the Cities of London and Westminster* (1749); "equivocal beings" are men who look like women.

[16]In ancient Greece, unwanted infants were left outside in the country, to die.

amours produces a most destructive barrenness and contagious flagitiousness[17] of manners. Surely nature never intended that women, by satisfying an appetite, should frustrate the very purpose for which it was implanted?

I have before observed, that men ought to maintain the women whom they have seduced; this would be one means of reforming female manners, and stopping an abuse that has an equally fatal effect on population and morals. Another, no less obvious, would be to turn the attention of woman to the real virtue of chastity; for to little respect has that woman a claim, on the score of modesty, though her reputation may be white as the driven snow, who smiles on the libertine whilst she spurns the victims of his lawless appetites and their own folly.

Besides, she has a taint of the same folly, pure as she esteems herself, when she studiously adorns her person only to be seen by men, to excite respectful sighs, and all the idle homage of what is called innocent gallantry. Did women really respect virtue for its own sake, they would not seek for a compensation in vanity, for the self-denial which they are obliged to practise to preserve their reputation, nor would they associate with men who set reputation at defiance.

The two sexes mutually corrupt and improve each other. This I believe to be an indisputable truth, extending it to every virtue. Chastity, modesty, public spirit, and all the noble train of virtues, on which social virtue and happiness are built, should be understood and cultivated by all mankind, or they will be cultivated to little effect. And, instead of furnishing the vicious or idle with a pretext for violating some sacred duty, by terming it a sexual one, it would be wiser to shew that nature has not made any difference, for that the unchaste man doubly defeats the purpose of nature, by rendering women barren, and destroying his own constitution, though he avoids the shame that pursues the crime in the other sex. These are the physical consequences, the moral are still more alarming; for virtue is only a nominal distinction when the duties of citizens, husbands, wives, fathers, mothers, and directors of families, become merely the selfish ties of convenience.

Why then do philosophers look for public spirit? Public spirit must be nurtured by private virtue, or it will resemble the factitious sentiment which makes women careful to preserve their reputation, and men their honour. A sentiment that often exists unsupported by virtue, unsupported by that sublime morality which makes the habitual breach of one duty a breach of the whole moral law.

[17]Villainy, corruption.

CHAPTER IX

OF THE PERNICIOUS EFFECTS WHICH ARISE FROM THE UNNATURAL DISTINCTIONS ESTABLISHED IN SOCIETY

From the respect paid to property flow, as from a poisoned fountain, most of the evils and vices which render this world such a dreary scene to the contemplative mind. For it is in the most polished society that noisome reptiles and venomous serpents lurk under the rank herbage; and there is voluptuousness pampered by the still sultry air, which relaxes every good disposition before it ripens into virtue.

One class presses on another, for all are aiming to procure respect on account of their property: and property, once gained, will procure the respect due only to talents and virtue. Men neglect the duties incumbent on man, yet are treated like demi-gods; religion is also separated from morality by a ceremonial veil, yet men wonder that the world is almost literally speaking, a den of sharpers or oppressors.

There is a homely proverb, which speaks a shrewd truth, that whoever the devil finds idle he will employ. And what but habitual idleness can hereditary wealth and titles produce? For man is so constituted that he can only attain a proper use of his faculties by exercising them, and will not exercise them unless necessity, of some kind, first set the wheels in motion. Virtue likewise can only be acquired by the discharge of relative duties; but the importance of these sacred duties will scarcely be felt by the being who is cajoled out of his humanity by the flattery of sycophants. There must be more equality established in society, or morality will never gain ground, and this virtuous equality will not rest firmly even when founded on a rock,[1] if one half of mankind be chained to its bottom by fate, for they will be continually undermining it through ignorance or pride.

It is vain to expect virtue from women till they are, in some degree, independent of men; nay, it is vain to expect that strength of natural affection, which would make them good wives and mothers. Whilst they are absolutely dependent on their husbands they will be cunning, mean, and selfish, and the men who can be gratified by the fawning fondness of spaniel-like affection, have not much delicacy, for love is not to be bought, in any sense of the words, its silken

---

[1]Jesus advises that the one who follows his preaching is like "a wise man, which built his house upon a rock: And the rain descended, and the floods came, and the winds blew, and beat upon that house; and it fell not: for it was founded upon a rock" (Matthew 7:24–25).

wings are instantly shrivelled up when any thing beside a return in kind is sought. Yet whilst wealth enervates men; and women live, as it were, by their personal charms, how can we expect them to discharge those ennobling duties which equally require exertion and self-denial. Hereditary property sophisticates[2] the mind, and the unfortunate victims to it, if I may so express myself, swathed from their birth,[3] seldom exert the locomotive faculty of body or mind; and, thus viewing every thing through one medium, and that a false one, they are unable to discern in what true merit and happiness consist. False, indeed, must be the light when the drapery of situation hides the man, and makes him stalk in masquerade,[4] dragging from one scene of dissipation to another the nerveless limbs that hang with stupid listlessness, and rolling round the vacant eye which plainly tells us that there is no mind at home.

I mean, therefore, to infer that the society is not properly organized which does not compel men and women to discharge their respective duties, by making it the only way to acquire that countenance from their fellow-creatures, which every human being wishes some way to attain. The respect, consequently, which is paid to wealth and mere personal charms, is a true north-east blast, that blights the tender blossoms of affection and virtue. Nature has wisely attached affections to duties, to sweeten toil, and to give that vigour to the exertions of reason which only the heart can give. But, the affection which is put on merely because it is the appropriated insignia[5] of a certain character, when its duties are not fulfilled, is one of the empty compliments which vice and folly are obliged to pay to virtue and the real nature of things.

To illustrate my opinion, I need only observe, that when a woman is admired for her beauty, and suffers herself to be so far intoxicated by the admiration she receives, as to neglect to discharge the indispensable duty of a mother, she sins against herself by neglecting to cultivate an affection that would equally tend to make her useful and happy. True happiness, I mean all the contentment, and virtuous satisfaction, that can be snatched in this imperfect state, must arise from well regulated affections; and an affection includes a duty. Men are

[2]Corrupts.

[3]"Swaddled," preventing all movement; by the 1790s, this practice was dying out in England.

[4]Masked ball, a popular form of public entertainment.

[5]Borrowed badges.

not aware of the misery they cause, and the vicious weakness they cherish, by only inciting women to render themselves pleasing; they do not consider that they thus make natural and artificial duties clash, by sacrificing the comfort and respectability of a woman's life to voluptuous notions of beauty, when in nature they all harmonize.

Cold would be the heart of a husband, were he not rendered unnatural by early debauchery, who did not feel more delight at seeing his child suckled by its mother, than the most artful wanton tricks could ever raise; yet this natural way of cementing the matrimonial tie, and twisting esteem with fonder recollections, wealth leads women to spurn.[6] To preserve their beauty, and wear the flowery crown of the day, which gives them a kind of right to reign for a short time over the sex, they neglect to stamp impressions on their husbands' hearts, that would be remembered with more tenderness when the snow on the head began to chill the bosom, than even their virgin charms. The maternal solicitude of a reasonable affectionate woman is very interesting, and the chastened dignity with which a mother returns the caresses that she and her child receive from a father who has been fulfilling the serious duties of his station, is not only a respectable, but a beautiful sight. So singular, indeed, are my feelings, and I have endeavoured not to catch factitious[7] ones, that after having been fatigued with the sight of insipid grandeur and the slavish ceremonies that with cumberous pomp supplied the place of domestic affections, I have turned to some other scene to relieve my eye by resting it on the refreshing green every where scattered by nature. I have then viewed with pleasure a woman nursing her children, and discharging the duties of her station with, perhaps, merely a servant maid to take off her hands the servile part of the household business. I have seen her prepare herself and children, with only the luxury of cleanliness, to receive her husband, who returning weary home in the evening, found smiling babes and a clean hearth. My heart has loitered in the midst of the group, and has even throbbed with sympathetic emotion, when the scraping of the well known foot has raised a pleasing tumult.

Whilst my benevolence has been gratified by contemplating this artless picture, I have thought that a couple of this description, equally necessary and independent of each other, because each fulfilled the respective duties of their station, possessed all that life could give.—Raised sufficiently above abject poverty not to be obliged to

---

[6]Hired breast-feeding was common upper-class practice.

[7]Artificial; insincere.

weigh the consequence of every farthing they spend, and having sufficient to prevent their attending to a frigid system of œconomy which
narrows both heart and mind. I declare, so vulgar are my concep-
tions, that I know not what is wanted to render this the happiest as
well as the most respectable situation in the world, but a taste for literature, to throw a little variety and interest into social converse, and
some superfluous money to give to the needy and to buy books. For it
is not pleasant when the heart is opened by compassion and the head
active in arranging plans of usefulness, to have a prim urchin continually twitching back the elbow to prevent the hand from drawing out
an almost empty purse, whispering at the same time some prudential
maxim about the priority of justice.

Destructive, however, as riches and inherited honours are to the
human character, women are more debased and cramped, if possible,
by them, than men, because men may still, in some degree, unfold
their faculties by becoming soldiers and statesmen.

As soldiers, I grant, they can now only gather, for the most part, vain
glorious laurels, whilst they adjust to a hair the European balance, taking
especial care that no bleak northern nook or sound incline the beam.[8]
But the days of true heroism are over, when a citizen fought for his
country like a Fabricius or a Washington, and then returned to his farm
to let his virtuous fervour run in a more placid, but not a less salutary,
stream. No, our British heroes are oftener sent from the gaming table
than from the plow[9]; and their passions have been rather inflamed by
hanging with dumb suspense on the turn of a die, than sublimated by
panting after the adventurous march of virtue in the historic page.

The statesman, it is true, might with more propriety quit the Faro
Bank,[10] or card-table, to guide the helm, for he has still but to shuffle
and trick. The whole system of British politics, if system it may courteously be called, consisting in multiplying dependents and contriving

[8]Rival British and Spanish claims to Nootka Sound, a natural harbor on the west coast
of Vancouver Island (SW British Columbia, Canada), led to Spain's seizure of four
British merchant ships in 1789. The Nootka Conventions of 1790–92 gave both coun-
tries trading rights, ending Spain's monopoly on trade and settlement in the Pacific
Northwest. MW also refers to Nootka Sound in her *Letters Written during a Short
Residence in Sweden, Norway, and Denmark* (1796).

[9]In 485 BCE, former consul Cincinnatus was called from his farm to defend Rome as
commander-in-chief against the Aequi. Defeating the Aequi in 16 days, he returned to
his farm—an emblem of the virtuous man who eschews fame and power, preferring
humble agrarian life. "American Cincinnatus" George Washington returned to his
plantation after the war, and again after his presidency. Famously incorruptible Roman general Fabricius (3rd c. BCE) ended his life in quiet poverty.

[10]The kitty (or stake-pot) for players' bets in the card game Faro.

taxes which grind the poor to pamper the rich; thus a war, or any wild goose chase, is, as the vulgar use the phrase, a lucky turn-up of patronage for the minister, whose chief merit is the art of keeping himself in place. It is not necessary then that he should have bowels[11] for the poor, so he can secure for his family the odd trick. Or should some shew of respect, for what is termed with ignorant ostentation an Englishman's birth-right, be expedient to bubble[12] the gruff mastiff that he has to lead by the nose, he can make an empty shew, very safely, by giving his single voice, and suffering his light squadron to file off to the other side. And when a question of humanity is agitated he may dip a sop in the milk of human kindness, to silence Cerberus,[13] and talk of the interest which his heart takes in an attempt to make the earth no longer cry for vengeance as it sucks in its children's blood, though his cold hand may at the very moment rivet their chains, by sanctioning the abominable traffick.[14] A minister is no longer a minister, than while he can carry a point, which he is determined to carry.—Yet it is not necessary that a minister should feel like a man, when a bold push might shake his seat.

But, to have done with these episodical observations, let me return to the more specious slavery which chains the very soul of woman, keeping her for ever under the bondage of ignorance.

The preposterous distinctions of rank, which render civilization a curse, by dividing the world between voluptuous tyrants, and cunning envious dependents, corrupt, almost equally, every class of people, because respectability is not attached to the discharge of the relative duties of life, but to the station, and when the duties are not fulfilled the affections cannot gain sufficient strength to fortify the virtue of which they are the natural reward. Still there are some loop-holes out of which a man may creep, and dare to think and act for himself; but for a woman it is an herculean task, because she has difficulties peculiar to her sex to overcome, which require almost superhuman powers.

A truly benevolent legislator always endeavours to make it the interest of each individual to be virtuous; and thus private virtue becoming the cement of public happiness, an orderly whole is consolidated by the tendency of all the parts towards a common centre. But, the private or public virtue of woman is very problematical; for Rousseau, and a

---

[11]Compassion.

[12]Delude.

[13]Lady Macbeth fears her husband "is too full o' the milk of human kindness" (*Macbeth*, 1.5.17). Cerberus is the three-headed dog who guards the gates of the underworld.

[14]The slave trade; the abolition movement was very active in the early 1790s, but did not succeed in ending the British trade until 1807.

numerous list of male writers, insist that she should all her life be subjected to a severe restraint, that of propriety. Why subject her to propriety—blind propriety, if she be capable of acting from a nobler spring, if
she be an heir of immortality? Is sugar always to be produced by vital
blood? Is one half of the human species, like the poor African slaves, to
be subject to prejudices that brutalize them, when principles would be
a surer guard, only to sweeten the cup of man?[15] Is not this indirectly
to deny woman reason? for a gift is a mockery, if it be unfit for use.

Women are, in common with men, rendered weak and luxurious
by the relaxing pleasures which wealth procures; but added to this
they are made slaves to their persons, and must render them alluring
that man may lend them his reason to guide their tottering steps
aright. Or should they be ambitious, they must govern their tyrants
by sinister tricks, for without rights there cannot be any incumbent
duties. The laws respecting woman, which I mean to discuss in a future part, make an absurd unit of a man and his wife; and then, by
the easy transition of only considering him as responsible, she is reduced to a mere cypher.[16]

The being who discharges the duties of its station is independent;
and, speaking of women at large, their first duty is to themselves as
rational creatures, and the next, in point of importance, as citizens, is
that, which includes so many, of a mother. The rank in life which dis-
penses with their fulfilling this duty, necessarily degrades them by
making them mere dolls. Or, should they turn to something more important than merely fitting drapery upon a smooth block, their minds
are only occupied by some soft platonic attachment; or, the actual
management of an intrigue may keep their thoughts in motion; for
when they neglect domestic duties, they have it not in their power to
take the field and march and counter-march like soldiers, or wrangle
in the senate to keep their faculties from rusting.

I know that, as a proof of the inferiority of the sex, Rousseau has
exultingly exclaimed, How can they leave the nursery for the
camp![17]—And the camp has by some moralists been termed the
school of the most heroic virtues; though, I think, it would puzzle a

---

[15]The boycott of slave-produced sugar and sugar products such as rum and molasses
was a highly successful initiative of the abolitionist movement, especially among women.

[16]See William Blackstone, *Commentaries on the Laws of England* (1765): "By marriage, the husband and wife are one person in law: that is, the very being or legal existence of the woman is suspended during the marriage, or at least is incorporated and
consolidated into that of the husband: under whose wing, protection and *cover*, she
performs everything" (1.15.430).

[17]"Can a woman be one day a nurse, and the next a soldier?" (*Emilius*, 4.5.13).

keen casuist to prove the reasonableness of the greater number of wars that have dubbed heroes. I do not mean to consider this question critically; because, having frequently viewed these freaks[18] of ambition as the first natural mode of civilization, when the ground must be torn up, and the woods cleared by fire and sword, I do not choose to call them pests; but surely the present system of war has little connection with virtue of any denomination, being rather the school of *finesse*[19] and effeminacy, than of fortitude.

Yet, if defensive war, the only justifiable war, in the present advanced state of society, where virtue can shew its face and ripen amidst the rigours which purify the air on the mountain's top, were alone to be adopted as just and glorious, the true heroism of antiquity might again animate female bosoms.—But fair and softly, gentle reader, male or female, do not alarm thyself, for though I have compared the character of a modern soldier with that of a civilized woman, I am not going to advise them to turn their distaff into a musket, though I sincerely wish to see the bayonet converted into a pruning-hook.[20] I only recreated an imagination, fatigued by contemplating the vices and follies which all proceed from a feculent[21] stream of wealth that has muddied the pure rills of natural affection, by supposing that society will some time or other be so constituted, that man must necessarily fulfil the duties of a citizen, or be despised, and that while he was employed in any of the departments of civil life, his wife, also an active citizen, should be equally intent to manage her family, educate her children, and assist her neighbours.

But, to render her really virtuous and useful, she must not, if she discharge her civil duties, want, individually, the protection of civil laws; she must not be dependent on her husband's bounty for her subsistence during his life, or support after his death—for how can a being be generous who has nothing of its own? or virtuous, who is not free? The wife, in the present state of things, who is faithful to her husband, and neither suckles nor educates her children, scarcely deserves the name of a wife, and has no right to that of a citizen. But take away natural rights, and duties become null.

Women then must be considered as only the wanton solace of men, when they become so weak in mind and body, that they cannot exert

---

[18]Whims.

[19]Artfulness, stratagem.

[20]The prophecy of Isaiah: "And they shall beat their swords into plowshares, and their spears into pruning hooks" (2:4).

[21]Foul, fetid.

themselves, unless to pursue some frothy pleasure, or to invent some frivolous fashion. What can be a more melancholy sight to a thinking mind, than to look into the numerous carriages that drive helter-skelter about this metropolis in a morning full of pale-faced creatures who are flying from themselves. I have often wished, with Dr. Johnson, to place some of them in a little shop with half a dozen children looking up to their languid countenances for support.[22] I am much mistaken, if some latent vigour would not soon give health and spirit to their eyes, and some lines drawn by the exercise of reason on the blank cheeks, which before were only undulated by dimples, might restore lost dignity to the character, or rather enable it to attain the true dignity of its nature. Virtue is not to be acquired even by speculation, much less by the negative supineness that wealth naturally generates.

Besides, when poverty is more disgraceful than even vice, is not morality cut to the quick? Still to avoid misconstruction, though I consider that women in the common walks of life are called to fulfil the duties of wives and mothers, by religion and reason, I cannot help lamenting that women of a superiour cast have not a road open by which they can pursue more extensive plans of usefulness and independence. I may excite laughter, by dropping an hint, which I mean to pursue, some future time, for I really think that women ought to have representatives, instead of being arbitrarily governed without having any direct share allowed them in the deliberations of government.[23]

But, as the whole system of representation is now, in this country, only a convenient handle for despotism, they need not complain, for they are as well represented as a numerous class of hard working mechanics,[24] who pay for the support of royalty when they can scarcely stop their children's mouths with bread. How are they represented whose very sweat supports the splendid stud of an heir apparent, or varnishes the chariot of some female favourite who looks down on shame? Taxes on the very necessaries of life, enable an endless tribe of idle princes and princesses to pass with stupid pomp before a gaping crowd, who almost worship the very parade which costs them so dear. This is mere gothic grandeur, something like the barbarous useless parade of having sentinels on horseback at Whitehall,[25] which I could never view without a mixture of contempt and indignation.

[22]"The Mischiefs of Total Idleness," *The Rambler No. 85* (January 8, 1751).

[23]British women could not vote until 1928.

[24]Manual laborers.

[25]The center of the British government offices.

How strangely must the mind be sophisticated when this sort of state impresses it! But, till these monuments of folly are levelled by virtue, similar follies will leaven the whole mass. For the same character, in some degree, will prevail in the aggregate of society: and the refinements of luxury, or the vicious repinings of envious poverty, will equally banish virtue from society, considered as the characteristic of that society, or only allow it to appear as one of the stripes of the harlequin coat,[26] worn by the civilized man.

In the superiour ranks of life, every duty is done by deputies, as if duties could ever be waved, and the vain pleasures which consequent idleness forces the rich to pursue, appear so enticing to the next rank, that the numerous scramblers for wealth sacrifice every thing to tread on their heels. The most sacred trusts are then considered as sinecures, because they were procured by interest, and only sought to enable a man to keep *good company*. Women, in particular, all want to be ladies. Which is simply to have nothing to do, but listlessly to go they scarcely care where, for they cannot tell what.

But what have women to do in society? I may be asked, but to loiter with easy grace; surely you would not condemn them all to suckle fools and chronicle small beer![27] No. Women might certainly study the art of healing, and be physicians as well as nurses. And midwifery, decency seems to allot to them, though I am afraid the word midwife, in our dictionaries, will soon give place to *accoucheur*,[28] and one proof of the former delicacy of the sex be effaced from the language.

They might, also, study politics, and settle their benevolence on the broadest basis; for the reading of history will scarcely be more useful than the perusal of romances, if read as mere biography; if the character of the times, the political improvements, arts, etc. be not observed. In short, if it be not considered as the history of man; and not of particular men, who filled a niche in the temple of fame, and dropped into the black rolling stream of time, that silently sweeps all before it, into the shapeless void called—eternity.—For shape, can it be called, "that shape hath none?"[29]

Business of various kinds, they might likewise pursue, if they were educated in a more orderly manner, which might save many from common and legal prostitution. Women would not then marry for a sup-

---

[26]Multicolored garb of the comic trickster.

[27]Villain Iago's view of what women are good for, nursing babies and keeping track of petty household business (Shakespeare, *Othello*, 2.1.160).

[28]Male childbirth physician.

[29]Milton's famous description of death in *Paradise Lost*, 2.666–67.

port, as men accept of places under government, and neglect the implied duties; nor would an attempt to earn their own subsistence, a most laudable one! sink them almost to the level of those poor abandoned creatures who live by prostitution. For are not milliners and mantua-makers[30] reckoned the next class? The few employments open to women, so far from being liberal, are menial; and when a superiour education enables them to take charge of the education of children as governesses, they are not treated like the tutors of sons, though even clerical tutors are not always treated in a manner calculated to render them respectable in the eyes of their pupils, to say nothing of the private comfort of the individual. But as women educated like gentlewomen, are never designed for the humiliating situation which necessity sometimes forces them to fill; these situations are considered in the light of a degradation; and they know little of the human heart, who need to be told, that nothing so painfully sharpens sensibility as such a fall in life.[31]

Some of these women might be restrained from marrying by a proper spirit or delicacy, and others may not have had it in their power to escape in this pitiful way from servitude; is not that government then very defective, and very unmindful of the happiness of one half of its members, that does not provide for honest, independent women, by encouraging them to fill respectable stations? But in order to render their private virtue a public benefit, they must have a civil existence in the state, married or single; else we shall continually see some worthy woman, whose sensibility has been rendered painfully acute by undeserved contempt, droop like "the lily broken down by a plow-share."[32]

It is a melancholy truth; yet such is the blessed effect of civilization! the most respectable women are the most oppressed; and, unless they have understandings far superiour to the common run of understandings, taking in both sexes, they must, from being treated like contemptible beings, become contemptible. How many women thus waste life away the prey of discontent, who might have practised as physicians, regulated a farm, managed a shop, and stood erect, supported by their own industry, instead of hanging their heads surcharged with the dew of sensibility, that consumes the beauty to

---

[30]Dressmakers and needleworkers, so low paid that prostitution was often more lucrative.

[31]In the mid 1780s, MW worked as a governess to the older daughters of an aristocratic Irish family. See p. 4.

[32]In Fénelon's *Télémaque*, Ideomeneus obeys the gods' decree to kill his son, who dies "as a beautiful Lilly in the midst of the Field, cut up from the Root by the Plowshare, lies down and languishes on the Ground" (*The Adventures of Telemachus*, trans. Isaac Littlebury, 1699). See also Robert Burns's "To a Mountain Daisy, On turning one down, with the Plough," 49–54.

which it at first gave lustre; nay, I doubt whether pity and love are so near akin as poets feign, for I have seldom seen much compassion excited by the helplessness of females, unless they were fair; then, perhaps, pity was the soft handmaid of love, or the harbinger of lust.

How much more respectable is the woman who earns her own bread by fulfilling any duty, than the most accomplished beauty!—beauty did I say?—so sensible am I of the beauty of moral loveliness, or the harmonious propriety that attunes the passions of a well-regulated mind, that I blush at making the comparison; yet I sigh to think how few women aim at attaining this respectability by withdrawing from the giddy whirl of pleasure, or the indolent calm that stupifies the good sort of women it sucks in.

Proud of their weakness, however, they must always be protected, guarded from care, and all the rough toils that dignify the mind.—If this be the fiat of fate, if they will make themselves insignificant and contemptible, sweetly to waste "life away," let them not expect to be valued when their beauty fades, for it is the fate of the fairest flowers to be admired and pulled to pieces by the careless hand that plucked them. In how many ways do I wish, from the purest benevolence, to impress this truth on my sex; yet I fear that they will not listen to a truth that dear bought experience has brought home to many an agitated bosom, nor willingly resign the privileges of rank and sex for the privileges of humanity, to which those have no claim who do not discharge its duties.

Those writers are particularly useful, in my opinion, who make man feel for man, independent of the station he fills, or the drapery of factitious sentiments. I then would fain convince reasonable men of the importance of some of my remarks; and prevail on them to weigh dispassionately the whole tenor of my observations.—I appeal to their understandings; and, as a fellow-creature, claim, in the name of my sex, some interest in their hearts. I entreat them to assist to emancipate their companion, to make her a *help meet* for them!

Would men but generously snap our chains, and be content with rational fellowship instead of slavish obedience, they would find us more observant daughters, more affectionate sisters, more faithful wives, more reasonable mothers—in a word, better citizens. We should then love them with true affection, because we should learn to respect ourselves; and the peace of mind of a worthy man would not be interrupted by the idle vanity of his wife, nor the babes sent to nestle in a strange bosom,[33] having never found a home in their mother's.

---

[33]Hired wet-nursing.

CHAPTER X

PARENTAL AFFECTION

Parental affection is, perhaps, the blindest modification of perverse self-love; for we have not, like the French,[1] two terms to distinguish the pursuit of a natural and reasonable desire, from the ignorant calculations of weakness. Parents often love their children in the most brutal manner, and sacrifice every relative duty to promote their advancement in the world.—To promote, such is the perversity of unprincipled prejudices, the future welfare of the very beings whose present existence they embitter by the most despotic stretch of power. Power, in fact, is ever true to its vital principle, for in every shape it would reign without controul or inquiry. Its throne is built across a dark abyss, which no eye must dare to explore, lest the baseless fabric[2] should totter under investigation. Obedience, unconditional obedience, is the catch-word of tyrants of every description, and to render "assurance doubly sure,"[3] one kind of despotism supports another. Tyrants would have cause to tremble if reason were to become the rule of duty in any of the relations of life, for the light might spread till perfect day appeared. And when it did appear, how would men smile at the sight of the bugbears at which they started during the night of ignorance, or the twilight of timid inquiry.

Parental affection, indeed, in many minds, is but a pretext to tyrannize where it can be done with impunity, for only good and wise men are content with the respect that will bear discussion. Convinced that they have a right to what they insist on, they do not fear reason, or dread the sifting of subjects that recur to natural justice: because they firmly believe that the more enlightened the human mind becomes the deeper root will just and simple principles take. They do not rest in expedients, or grant that what is metaphysically true can be practically false; but disdaining the shifts of the moment they calmly wait till time, sanctioning innovation, silences the hiss of selfishness or envy.

If the power of reflecting on the past, and darting the keen eye of contemplation into futurity, be the grand privilege of man, it must be

---

[1] *L'amour propre. L'amour de soi meme* [MW]. In "A Dissertation on the Origin of Inequality" (1754), Rousseau distinguishes between a natural *amour de soi meme* moderated by compassion, and the *amour propre* of the social being who preserves self-esteem by manipulating others.

[2] Prospero's term for his illusions (*The Tempest*, 4.1.151). Fabric: structure. See also ch. III, p. 57, n. 3.

[3] The policy that drives Macbeth to murder Macduff (*Macbeth*, 4.1.80–83).

granted that some people enjoy this prerogative in a very limited degree. Every thing new appears to them wrong; and not able to distinguish the possible from the monstrous, they fear where no fear should find a place, running from the light of reason, as if it were a firebrand; yet the limits of the possible have never been defined to stop the sturdy innovator's hand.

Woman, however, a slave in every situation to prejudice, seldom exerts enlightened maternal affection; for she either neglects her children, or spoils them by improper indulgence. Besides, the affection of some women for their children is, as I have before termed it, frequently very brutish; for it eradicates every spark of humanity. Justice, truth, every thing is sacrificed by these Rebekah's,[4] and for the sake of their *own* children they violate the most sacred duties, forgetting the common relationship that binds the whole family on earth together. Yet, reason seems to say, that they who suffer one duty, or affection, to swallow up the rest, have not sufficient heart or mind to fulfil that one conscientiously. It then loses the venerable aspect of a duty, and assumes the fantastic form of a whim.

As the care of children in their infancy is one of the grand duties annexed to the female character by nature, this duty would afford many forcible arguments for strengthening the female understanding, if it were properly considered.

The formation of the mind must be begun very early, and the temper, in particular, requires the most judicious attention—an attention which women cannot pay who only love their children because they are their children, and seek no further for the foundation of their duty, than in the feelings of the moment. It is this want of reason in their affections which makes women so often run into extremes, and either be the most fond or most careless and unnatural mothers.

To be a good mother—a woman must have sense, and that independence of mind which few women possess who are taught to depend entirely on their husbands. Meek wives are, in general, foolish mothers; wanting their children to love them best, and take their part, in secret, against the father, who is held up as a scarecrow. When chastisement is necessary, though they have offended the mother, the father must inflict the punishment; he must be the judge in all disputes: but I shall more fully discuss this subject when I treat

---

[4]Rebekah assisted her favorite son Jacob in deceiving his dying father so that he would receive the inheritance intended for his elder twin Esau (Genesis 27).

of private education,[5] I now only mean to insist, that unless the understanding of woman be enlarged, and her character rendered more firm, by being allowed to govern her own conduct, she will never have sufficient sense or command of temper to manage her children properly. Her parental affection, indeed, scarcely deserves the name, when it does not lead her to suckle her children, because the discharge of this duty is equally calculated to inspire maternal and filial affection: and it is the indispensable duty of men and women to fulfil the duties which give birth to affections that are the surest preservatives against vice. Natural affection, as it is termed, I believe to be a very faint tie, affections must grow out of the habitual exercise of a mutual sympathy; and what sympathy does a mother exercise who sends her babe to a nurse, and only takes it from a nurse to send it to a school?

In the exercise of their maternal feelings providence has furnished women with a natural substitute for love, when the lover becomes only a friend, and mutual confidence takes place of overstrained admiration—a child then gently twists the relaxing cord, and a mutual care produces a new mutual sympathy.—But a child, though a pledge of affection, will not enliven it, if both father and mother be content to transfer the charge to hirelings; for they who do their duty by proxy should not murmur if they miss the reward of duty—parental affection produces filial duty.

[5]See ch. XII, p. 191.

CHAPTER XI

DUTY TO PARENTS

There seems to be an indolent propensity in man to make prescription always take place of reason, and to place every duty on an arbitrary foundation. The rights of kings are deduced in a direct line from the King of kings; and that of parents from our first parent.

Why do we thus go back for principles that should always rest on the same base, and have the same weight to-day that they had a thousand years ago—and not a jot more? If parents discharge their duty they have a strong hold and sacred claim on the gratitude of their children; but few parents are willing to receive the respectful affection of their offspring on such terms. They demand blind obedience, because they do not merit a reasonable service: and to render these demands of weakness and ignorance more binding, a mysterious sanctity is spread round the most arbitrary principle; for what other name can be given to the blind duty of obeying vicious or weak beings merely because they obeyed a powerful instinct?

The simple definition of the reciprocal duty, which naturally subsists between parent and child, may be given in a few words: The parent who pays proper attention to helpless infancy has a right to require the same attention when the feebleness of age comes upon him. But to subjugate a rational being to the mere will of another, after he is of age to answer to society for his own conduct, is a most cruel and undue stretch of power; and, perhaps, as injurious to morality as those religious systems which do not allow right and wrong to have any existence, but in the Divine will.

I never knew a parent who had paid more than common attention to his children, disregarded[1]; on the contrary, the early habit of relying almost implicitly on the opinion of a respected parent is not easily shook, even when matured reason convinces the child that his father is not the wisest man in the world. This weakness, for a weakness it is, though the epithet amiable may be tacked to it, a reasonable man must steel himself against; for the absurd duty, too often inculcated, of obeying a parent only on account of his being a parent, shackles the mind, and prepares it for a slavish submission to any power but reason.

---

[1]Dr. Johnson makes the same observation [MW]. See "On the Tyranny of Parents," *The Rambler* 148 (August 17, 1751): "tenderness once excited will be hourly increased by the natural contagion of felicity, by the repercussion of communicated pleasure."

I distinguish between the natural and accidental duty due to parents.

The parent who sedulously endeavours to form the heart and enlarge the understanding of his child, has given that dignity to the discharge of a duty, common to the whole animal world, that only reason can give. This is the parental affection of humanity, and leaves instinctive natural affection far behind. Such a parent acquires all the rights of the most sacred friendship, and his advice, even when his child is advanced in life, demands serious consideration.

With respect to marriage, though after one and twenty a parent seems to have no right to withhold his consent on any account; yet twenty years of solicitude call for a return, and the son ought, at least, to promise not to marry for two or three years, should the object of his choice not entirely meet with the approbation of his first friend.

But, respect for parents is, generally speaking, a much more debasing principle; it is only a selfish respect for property. The father who is blindly obeyed, is obeyed from sheer weakness, or from motives that degrade the human character.

A great proportion of the misery that wanders, in hideous forms, around the world, is allowed to rise from the negligence of parents; and still these are the people who are most tenacious of what they term a natural right, though it be subversive of the birth-right of man, the right of acting according to the direction of his own reason.

I have already very frequently had occasion to observe, that vicious or indolent people are always eager to profit by enforcing arbitrary privileges; and, generally, in the same proportion as they neglect the discharge of the duties which alone render the privileges reasonable. This is at the bottom a dictate of common sense, or the instinct of self-defence, peculiar to ignorant weakness; resembling that instinct, which makes a fish muddy the water it swims in to elude its enemy, instead of boldly facing it in the clear stream.

From the clear stream of argument, indeed, the supporters of prescription, of every denomination, fly; and, taking refuge in the darkness, which, in the language of sublime poetry, has been supposed to surround the throne of Omnipotence, they dare to demand that implicit respect which is only due to His unsearchable ways.[2] But, let me not be thought presumptuous, the darkness which hides our God from us, only respects speculative truths—it never obscures moral

---

[2]See Paul's epistle to the Romans: "how unsearchable are his judgments, and his ways past finding out!" (11:33).

ones, they shine clearly, for God is light,[3] and never, by the constitution of our nature, requires the discharge of a duty, the reasonableness of which does not beam on us when we open our eyes.

The indolent parent of high rank may, it is true, extort a shew of
respect from his child, and females on the continent are particularly
subject to the views of their families, who never think of consulting
their inclination, or providing for the comfort of the poor victims of
their pride. The consequence is notorious; these dutiful daughters become adulteresses, and neglect the education of their children, from
whom they, in their turn, exact the same kind of obedience.

Females, it is true, in all countries, are too much under the dominion of their parents; and few parents think of addressing their children in the following manner, though it is in this reasonable way that
Heaven seems to command the whole human race. It is your interest
to obey me till you can judge for yourself; and the Almighty Father of
all has implanted an affection in me to serve as a guard to you whilst
your reason is unfolding; but when your mind arrives at maturity,
you must only obey me, or rather respect my opinions, so far as they
coincide with the light that is breaking in on your own mind.

A slavish bondage to parents cramps every faculty of the mind;
and Mr. Locke very judiciously observes, that "if the mind be curbed
and humbled too much in children; if their spirits be abased and broken much by too strict an hand over them; they lose all their vigour
and industry."[4] This strict hand may in some degree account for the
weakness of women; for girls, from various causes, are more kept
down by their parents, in every sense of the word, than boys. The
duty expected from them is, like all the duties arbitrarily imposed on
women, more from a sense of propriety, more out of respect for decorum, than reason; and thus taught slavishly to submit to their parents, they are prepared for the slavery of marriage. I may be told that
a number of women are not slaves in the marriage state. True, but
they then become tyrants; for it is not rational freedom, but a lawless
kind of power resembling the authority exercised by the favourites of
absolute monarchs, which they obtain by debasing means. I do not,
likewise, dream of insinuating that either boys or girls are always
slaves, I only insist that when they are obliged to submit to authority
blindly, their faculties are weakened, and their tempers rendered im-

---

[3] 1 John 1:5, echoed by Milton, in the invocation to "Holy Light" at the opening of *Paradise Lost*, Book 3.

[4] *Some Thoughts Concerning Education* (1693), article 46.2.

perious or abject. I also lament that parents, indolently availing themselves of a supposed privilege, damp the first faint glimmering of reason, rendering at the same time the duty, which they are so anxious to enforce, an empty name; because they will not let it rest on the only basis on which a duty can rest securely: for unless it be founded on knowledge, it cannot gain sufficient strength to resist the squalls of passion, or the silent sapping of self-love. But it is not the parents who have given the surest proof of their affection for their children, or, to speak more properly, who, by fulfilling their duty, have allowed a natural parental affection to take root in their hearts, the child of exercised sympathy and reason, and not the over-weening offspring of selfish pride, who most vehemently insist on their children submitting to their will merely because it is their will. On the contrary, the parent, who sets a good example, patiently lets that example work; and it seldom fails to produce its natural effect—filial reverence.

Children cannot be taught too early to submit to reason, the true definition of that necessity, which Rousseau insisted on, without defining it; for to submit to reason is to submit to the nature of things, and to that God, who formed them so, to promote our real interest.

Why should the minds of children be warped as they just begin to expand, only to favour the indolence of parents who insist on a privilege without being willing to pay the price fixed by nature? I have before had occasion to observe, that a right always includes a duty, and I think it may, likewise, fairly be inferred, that they forfeit the right, who do not fulfil the duty.

It is easier, I grant, to command than reason; but it does not follow from hence that children cannot comprehend the reason why they are made to do certain things habitually: for, from a steady adherence to a few simple principles of conduct flows that salutary power which a judicious parent gradually gains over a child's mind. And this power becomes strong indeed, if tempered by an even display of affection brought home to the child's heart. For, I believe, as a general rule, it must be allowed that the affection which we inspire always resembles that we cultivate; so that natural affections, which have been supposed almost distinct from reason, may be found more nearly connected with judgment than is commonly allowed. Nay, as another proof of the necessity of cultivating the female understanding, it is but just to observe, that the affections seem to have a kind of animal capriciousness when they merely reside in the heart.

It is the irregular exercise of parental authority that first injures the mind, and to these irregularities girls are more subject than boys.

The will of those who never allow their will to be disputed, unless they happen to be in a good humour, when they relax proportionally, is almost always unreasonable. To elude this arbitrary authority girls very early learn the lessons which they afterwards practise on their husbands; for I have frequently seen a little sharp-faced miss rule a whole family, excepting that now and then mamma's anger will burst out of some accidental cloud;—either her hair was ill-dressed,[5] or she had lost more money at cards, the night before, than she was willing to own to her husband; or some such moral cause of anger.

After observing sallies of this kind, I have been led into a melancholy train of reflection respecting females, concluding that when their first affection must lead them astray, or make their duties clash till they rest on mere whims and customs, little can be expected from them as they advance in life. How indeed can an instructor remedy this evil? for to teach them virtue on any solid principle is to teach them to despise their parents. Children cannot, ought not, to be taught to make allowance for the faults of their parents, because every such allowance weakens the force of reason in their minds, and makes them still more indulgent to their own. It is one of the most sublime virtues of maturity that leads us to be severe with respect to ourselves, and forbearing to others; but children should only be taught the simple virtues, for if they begin too early to make allowance for human passions and manners, they wear off the fine edge of the criterion by which they should regulate their own, and become unjust in the same proportion as they grow indulgent.

The affections of children, and weak people, are always selfish; they love their relatives, because they are beloved by them, and not on account of their virtues. Yet, till esteem and love are blended together in the first affection, and reason made the foundation of the first duty, morality will stumble at the threshold. But, till society is very differently constituted, parents, I fear, will still insist on being obeyed, because they will be obeyed, and constantly endeavour to settle that power on a Divine right which will not bear the investigation of reason.

---

[5] I myself heard a little girl once say to a servant, "My mamma has been scolding me finely this morning, because her hair was not dressed to please her." Though this remark was pert, it was just. And what respect could a girl acquire for such a parent without doing violence to reason? [MW].

CHAPTER XII

ON NATIONAL EDUCATION[1]

The good effects resulting from attention to private education will ever be very confined, and the parent who really puts his own hand to the plow, will always, in some degree, be disappointed, till education becomes a grand national concern. A man cannot retire into a desert with his child, and if he did he could not bring himself back to childhood, and become the proper friend and play-fellow of an infant or youth. And when children are confined to the society of men and women, they very soon acquire that kind of premature manhood which stops the growth of every vigorous power of mind or body. In order to open their faculties they should be excited to think for themselves; and this can only be done by mixing a number of children together, and making them jointly pursue the same objects.

A child very soon contracts a benumbing indolence of mind, which he has seldom sufficient vigour afterwards to shake off, when he only asks a question instead of seeking for information, and then relies implicitly on the answer he receives. With his equals in age this could never be the case, and the subjects of inquiry, though they might be influenced, would not be entirely under the direction of men, who frequently damp, if not destroy, abilities, by bringing them forward too hastily: and too hastily they will infallibly be brought forward, if the child be confined to the society of a man, however sagacious that man may be.

Besides, in youth the seeds of every affection should be sown, and the respectful regard, which is felt for a parent, is very different from the social affections that are to constitute the happiness of life as it advances. Of these equality is the basis, and an intercourse of sentiments unclogged by that observant seriousness which prevents disputation, though it may not inforce submission. Let a child have ever such an affection for his parent, he will always languish to play and prattle with children; and the very respect he feels, for filial esteem always has a dash of fear mixed with it, will, if it do not teach him cunning, at least prevent him from pouring out the little secrets which first open the heart to friendship and confidence, gradually leading to more expansive benevolence. Added to this, he will never acquire that frank ingenuousness of behaviour, which young people can only attain by being frequently in society where they dare to speak what

[1] Also the title of Talleyrand's pamphlet, to which MW's dedication refers.

they think; neither afraid of being reproved for their presumption, nor laughed at for their folly.

Forcibly impressed by the reflections which the sight of schools, as they are at present conducted, naturally suggested, I have formerly delivered my opinion rather warmly in favour of a private education[2]; but further experience has led me to view the subject in a different light. I still, however, think schools, as they are now regulated, the hot-beds of vice and folly, and the knowledge of human nature, supposed to be attained there, merely cunning selfishness.

At school boys become gluttons and slovens, and, instead of cultivating domestic affections, very early rush into the libertinism which destroys the constitution before it is formed; hardening the heart as it weakens the understanding.

I should, in fact, be averse to boarding-schools, if it were for no other reason than the unsettled state of mind which the expectation of the vacations produces. On these the children's thoughts are fixed with eager anticipating hopes, for, at least, to speak with moderation, half of the time, and when they arrive they are spent in total dissipation and beastly indulgence.

But, on the contrary, when they are brought up at home, though they may pursue a plan of study in a more orderly manner than can be adopted when near a fourth part of the year is actually spent in idleness, and as much more in regret and anticipation; yet they there acquire too high an opinion of their own importance, from being allowed to tyrannize over servants, and from the anxiety expressed by most mothers, on the score of manners, who, eager to teach the accomplishments of a gentleman, stifle, in their birth, the virtues of a man. Thus brought into company when they ought to be seriously employed, and treated like men when they are still boys, they become vain and effeminate.

The only way to avoid two extremes equally injurious to morality, would be to contrive some way of combining a public and private education. Thus to make men citizens two natural steps might be taken, which seem directly to lead to the desired point; for the domestic affections, that first open the heart to the various modifications of humanity, would be cultivated, whilst the children were nevertheless allowed to spend great part of their time, on terms of equality, with other children.

---

[2]In the review of Macaulay's *Letters on Education* for *Analytical Review* 8 (November 1790).

I still recollect, with pleasure, the country day school; where a boy trudged in the morning, wet or dry, carrying his books, and his dinner, if it were at a considerable distance; a servant did not then lead master by the hand, for, when he had once put on coat and breeches, he was allowed to shift for himself, and return alone in the evening to recount the feats of the day close at the parental knee. His father's house was his home, and was ever after fondly remembered; nay, I appeal to many superiour men, who were educated in this manner, whether the recollection of some shady lane where they conned[3] their lesson; or, of some stile, where they sat making a kite, or mending a bat, has not endeared their country to them?

But, what boy ever recollected with pleasure the years he spent in close confinement, at an academy near London? unless, indeed, he should, by chance, remember the poor scare-crow of an usher,[4] whom he tormented; or, the tartman, from whom he caught a cake, to devour it with a cattish appetite of selfishness. At boarding-schools of every description, the relaxation of the junior boys is mischief; and of the senior, vice. Besides, in great schools, what can be more prejudicial to the moral character than the system of tyranny and abject slavery which is established amongst the boys, to say nothing of the slavery to forms, which makes religion worse than a farce? For what good can be expected from the youth who receives the sacrament of the Lord's supper, to avoid forfeiting half a guinea, which he probably afterwards spends in some sensual manner? Half the employment of the youths is to elude the necessity of attending public worship; and well they may, for such a constant repetition of the same thing must be a very irksome restraint on their natural vivacity. As these ceremonies have the most fatal effect on their morals, and as a ritual performed by the lips, when the heart and mind are far away, is not now stored up by our church as a bank to draw on for the fees of the poor souls in purgatory, why should they not be abolished?

But the fear of innovation, in this country, extends to every thing.—This is only a covert fear, the apprehensive timidity of indolent slugs, who guard, by sliming it over, the snug place, which they consider in the light of an hereditary estate; and eat, drink, and enjoy themselves, instead of fulfilling the duties, excepting a few empty forms, for which it was endowed. These are the people who most strenuously insist on the will of the founder being observed, crying

---

[3]Learned.
[4]Schoolmaster's assistant, responsible for discipline.

out against all reformation, as if it were a violation of justice. I am now alluding particularly to the relics of popery[5] retained in our colleges, when the protestant members seem to be such sticklers for the established church; but their zeal never makes them lose sight of the spoil of ignorance, which rapacious priests of superstitious memory have scraped together. No, wise in their generation,[6] they venerate the prescriptive right of possession, as a strong hold, and still let the sluggish bell tinkle to prayers, as during the days when the elevation of the host was supposed to atone for the sins of the people, lest one reformation should lead to another, and the spirit kill the letter.[7] These Romish customs have the most baneful effect on the morals of our clergy; for the idle vermin who two or three times a day perform in the most slovenly manner a service which they think useless, but call their duty, soon lose a sense of duty. At college, forced to attend or evade public worship, they acquire an habitual contempt for the very service, the performance of which is to enable them to live in idleness. It is mumbled over as an affair of business, as a stupid boy repeats his task, and frequently the college cant escapes from the preacher the moment after he has left the pulpit, and even whilst he is eating the dinner which he earned in such a dishonest manner.

Nothing, indeed, can be more irreverent than the cathedral service as it is now performed in this country, neither does it contain a set of weaker men than those who are the slaves of this childish routine. A disgusting skeleton of the former state is still exhibited; but all the solemnity that interested the imagination, if it did not purify the heart, is stripped off. The performance of high mass on the continent must impress every mind, where a spark of fancy glows, with that awful melancholy, that sublime tenderness, so near akin to devotion. I do not say that these devotional feelings are of more use, in a moral sense, than any other emotion of taste; but I contend that the theatrical pomp which gratifies our senses, is to be preferred to the cold parade that insults the understanding without reaching the heart.

Amongst remarks on national education, such observations cannot be misplaced, especially as the supporters of these establishments, degenerated into puerilities, affect to be the champions of religion.—

---

[5]The doctrines and customs of the Roman Catholic Church.

[6]"The children of this world are in their generation wiser than the children of light" (Luke 16:8).

[7]Another reference to Paul's teaching that "the letter killeth, but the spirit giveth life" (2 Corinthians 3:6).

Religion, pure source of comfort in this vale of tears! how has thy clear stream been muddied by the dabblers, who have presumptuously endeavoured to confine in one narrow channel, the living waters that ever flow towards God—the sublime ocean of existence! What would life be without that peace which the love of God, when built on humanity, alone can impart? Every earthly affection turns back, at intervals, to prey upon the heart that feeds it; and the purest effusions of benevolence, often rudely damped by man, must mount as a free-will offering to Him who gave them birth, whose bright image they faintly reflect.

In public schools, however, religion, confounded with irksome ceremonies and unreasonable restraints, assumes the most ungracious aspect: not the sober austere one that commands respect whilst it inspires fear; but a ludicrous cast, that serves to point a pun. For, in fact, most of the good stories and smart things will enliven the spirits that have been concentrated at whist, are manufactured out of the incidents to which the very men labour to give a droll turn who countenance the abuse to live on the spoil.

There is not, perhaps, in the kingdom, a more dogmatical, or luxurious set of men, than the pedantic tyrants who reside in colleges and preside at public schools. The vacations are equally injurious to the morals of the masters and pupils, and the intercourse, which the former keep up with the nobility, introduces the same vanity and extravagance into their families, which banish domestic duties and comforts from the lordly mansion, whose state is awkwardly aped. The boys, who live at a great expense with the masters and assistants, are never domesticated, though placed there for that purpose; for, after a silent dinner, they swallow a hasty glass of wine, and retire to plan some mischievous trick, or to ridicule the person or manners of the very people they have just been cringing to, and whom they ought to consider as the representatives of their parents.

Can it then be a matter of surprise that boys become selfish and vicious who are thus shut out from social converse? or that a mitre[8] often graces the brow of one of these diligent pastors?

The desire of living in the same style, as the rank just above them, infects each individual and every class of people, and meanness is the concomitant of this ignoble ambition; but those professions are most debasing whose ladder is patronage; yet, out of one of these professions the tutors of youth are, in general, chosen. But, can they be expected to

[8]The bishop's headdress.

inspire independent sentiments, whose conduct must be regulated by the cautious prudence that is ever on the watch for preferment?

So far, however, from thinking of the morals of boys, I have heard several masters of schools argue, that they only undertook to teach Latin and Greek; and that they had fulfilled their duty, by sending some good scholars to college.

A few good scholars, I grant, may have been formed by emulation and discipline; but, to bring forward these clever boys, the health and morals of a number have been sacrificed. The sons of our gentry and wealthy commoners are mostly educated at these seminaries, and will any one pretend to assert that the majority, making every allowance, come under the description of tolerable scholars?

It is not for the benefit of society that a few brilliant men should be brought forward at the expense of the multitude. It is true, that great men seem to start up, as great revolutions occur, at proper intervals, to restore order, and to blow aside the clouds that thicken over the face of truth; but let more reason and virtue prevail in society, and these strong winds would not be necessary. Public education, of every denomination, should be directed to form citizens; but if you wish to make good citizens, you must first exercise the affections of a son and a brother. This is the only way to expand the heart; for public affections, as well as public virtues, must ever grow out of the private character, or they are merely meteors that shoot athwart a dark sky, and disappear as they are gazed at and admired.

Few, I believe, have had much affection for mankind, who did not first love their parents, their brothers, sisters, and even the domestic brutes, whom they first played with. The exercise of youthful sympathies forms the moral temperature; and it is the recollection of these first affections and pursuits that gives life to those that are afterwards more under the direction of reason. In youth, the fondest friendships are formed, the genial juices mounting at the same time, kindly mix; or, rather the heart, tempered for the reception of friendship, is accustomed to seek for pleasure in something more noble than the churlish gratification of appetite.

In order then to inspire a love of home and domestic pleasures, children ought to be educated at home, for riotous holidays only make them fond of home for their own sakes. Yet, the vacations, which do not foster domestic affections, continually disturb the course of study, and render any plan of improvement abortive which includes temperance; still, were they abolished, children would be entirely separated from their parents, and I question whether they would become better citizens by sacrificing the preparatory affections, by destroying the force of relationships that render the marriage state as necessary as respectable. But, if a private education produce self-importance, or insulate a man in his family, the evil is only shifted, not remedied.

This train of reasoning brings me back to a subject, on which I mean to dwell, the necessity of establishing proper day-schools.

But, these should be national establishments, for whilst schoolmasters are dependent on the caprice of parents, little exertion can be expected from them, more than is necessary to please ignorant people. Indeed, the necessity of a master's giving the parents some sample of the boys abilities, which during the vacation is shewn to every visitor,[9] is productive of more mischief than would at first be supposed. For it is seldom done entirely, to speak with moderation, by the child itself; thus the master countenances falsehood, or winds the poor machine up to some extraordinary exertion, that injures the wheels, and stops the progress of gradual improvement. The memory is loaded with unintelligible words, to make a shew of, without the understanding's acquiring any distinct ideas: but only that education deserves emphatically to be termed cultivation of mind, which teaches young people how to begin to think. The imagination should not be allowed to debauch the understanding before it gained strength, or vanity will become the forerunner of vice: for every way of exhibiting the acquirements of a child is injurious to its moral character.

How much time is lost in teaching them to recite what they do not understand? whilst, seated on benches, all in their best array, the mammas listen with astonishment to the parrot-like prattle, uttered in solemn cadences, with all the pomp of ignorance and folly. Such exhibitions only serve to strike the spreading fibres of vanity through the whole mind; for they neither teach children to speak fluently, nor behave gracefully. So far from it, that these frivolous pursuits might comprehensively be termed the study of affectation; for we now rarely see a simple, bashful boy, though few people of taste were ever disgusted by that awkward sheepishness so natural to the age, which schools and an early introduction into society, have changed into impudence and apish grimace.

Yet, how can these things be remedied whilst school-masters depend entirely on parents for a subsistence; and, when so many rival

---

[9]I now particularly allude to the numerous academies in and about London, and to the behaviour of the trading part of this great city [MW].

schools hang out their lures, to catch the attention of vain fathers and mothers, whose parental affection only leads them to wish that their children should outshine those of their neighbours?

Without great good luck, a sensible, conscientious man, would starve before he could raise a school, if he disdained to bubble weak parents by practising the secret tricks of the craft.

In the best regulated schools, however, where swarms are not crammed together, many bad habits must be acquired; but, at common schools, the body, heart, and understanding, are equally stunted, for parents are often only in quest of the cheapest school, and the master could not live, if he did not take a much greater number than he could manage himself; nor will the scanty pittance, allowed for each child, permit him to hire ushers sufficient to assist in the discharge of the mechanical part of the business. Besides, whatever appearance the house and garden may make, the children do not enjoy the comfort of either, for they are continually reminded by irksome restrictions that they are not at home, and the state-rooms, garden, etc., must be kept in order for the recreation of the parents; who, of a Sunday, visit the school, and are impressed by the very parade that renders the situation of their children uncomfortable.

With what disgust have I heard sensible women, for girls are more restrained and cowed than boys, speak of the wearisome confinement, which they endured at school. Not allowed, perhaps, to step out of one broad walk in a superb garden, and obliged to pace with steady deportment stupidly backwards and forwards, holding up their heads and turning out their toes, with shoulders braced back, instead of bounding, as nature directs to complete her own design, in the various attitudes so conducive to health.[10] The pure animal spirits, which make both mind and body shoot out, and unfold the tender blossoms of hope, are turned sour, and vented in vain wishes or pert repinings, that contract the faculties and spoil the temper; else they

---

[10]I remember a circumstance that once came under my own observation, and raised my indignation. I went to visit a little boy at a school where young children were prepared for a large one. The master took me into the school-room, etc. but whilst I walked down a broad gravel walk, I could not help observing that the grass grew very luxuriantly on each side of me. I immediately asked the child some questions, and found that the poor boys were not allowed to stir off the walk, and that the master sometimes permitted sheep to be turned in to crop the untrodden grass. The tyrant of this domain used to sit by a window that overlooked the prison yard, and one nook turning from it, where the unfortunate babes could sport freely, he enclosed, and planted it with potatoes. The wife likewise was equally anxious to keep the children in order, lest they should dirty or tear their clothes [MW].

mount to the brain, and sharpening the understanding before it gains proportionable strength, produce that pitiful cunning which disgracefully characterizes the female mind—and I fear will ever characterize it whilst women remain the slaves of power!

The little respect paid to chastity in the male world is, I am persuaded, the grand source of many of the physical and moral evils that torment mankind, as well as of the vices and follies that degrade and destroy women; yet at school, boys infallibly lose that decent bashfulness, which might have ripened into modesty, at home.

And what nasty indecent tricks do they not also learn from each other, when a number of them pig together in the same bedchamber, not to speak of the vices, which render the body weak, whilst they effectually prevent the acquisition of any delicacy of mind.[11] The little attention paid to the cultivation of modesty, amongst men, produces great depravity in all the relationships of society; for, not only love—love that ought to purify the heart, and first call forth all the youthful powers, to prepare the man to discharge the benevolent duties of life, is sacrificed to premature lust; but, all the social affections are deadened by the selfish gratifications, which very early pollute the mind, and dry up the generous juices of the heart. In what an unnatural manner is innocence often violated; and what serious consequences ensue to render private vices a public pest. Besides, an habit of personal order, which has more effect on the moral character, than is, in general, supposed, can only be acquired at home, where that respectable reserve is kept up which checks the familiarity, that sinking into beastliness, undermines the affection it insults.

I have already animadverted on the bad habits which females acquire when they are shut up together; and, I think, that the observation may fairly be extended to the other sex, till the natural inference is drawn which I have had in view throughout—that to improve both sexes they ought, not only in private families, but in public schools, to be educated together. If marriage be the cement of society, mankind should all be educated after the same model, or the intercourse of the sexes will never deserve the name of fellowship, nor will women ever fulfil the peculiar duties of their sex, till they become enlightened citizens, till they become free by being enabled to earn their own subsistence, independent of men; in the same manner, I mean, to prevent misconstruction, as one man is independent of another. Nay, marriage will never be held sacred till women, by being brought up

[11]Masturbation was considered physically and morally corrupting.

with men, are prepared to be their companions rather than their mistresses; for the mean doublings of cunning will ever render them contemptible, whilst oppression renders them timid. So convinced am I of this truth, that I will venture to predict that virtue will never prevail in society till the virtues of both sexes are founded on reason; and, till the affections common to both are allowed to gain their due strength by the discharge of mutual duties.

Were boys and girls permitted to pursue the same studies together, those graceful decencies might early be inculcated which produce modesty without those sexual distinctions that taint the mind. Lessons of politeness, and that formulary of decorum, which treads on the heels of falsehood, would be rendered useless by habitual propriety of behaviour. Not, indeed, put on for visitors like the courtly robe of politeness, but the sober effect of cleanliness of mind. Would not this simple elegance of sincerity be a chaste homage paid to domestic affections, far surpassing the meretricious compliments that shine with false lustre in the heartless intercourse of fashionable life? But, till more understanding preponderates in society, there will ever be a want of heart and taste, and the harlot's *rouge* will supply the place of that celestial suffusion which only virtuous affections can give to the face. Gallantry, and what is called love, may subsist without simplicity of character; but the main pillars of friendship, are respect and confidence—esteem is never founded on it cannot tell what!

A taste for the fine arts requires great cultivation; but not more than a taste for the virtuous affections; and both suppose that enlargement of mind which opens so many sources of mental pleasure. Why do people hurry to noisy scenes, and crowded circles? I should answer, because they want activity of mind, because they have not cherished the virtues of the heart. They only, therefore, see and feel in the gross, and continually pine after variety, finding every thing that is simple insipid.

This argument may be carried further than philosophers are aware of, for if nature destined woman, in particular, for the discharge of domestic duties, she made her susceptible of the attached affections in a great degree. Now women are notoriously fond of pleasure; and, naturally must be so according to my definition, because they cannot enter into the minutiae of domestic taste; lacking judgment, the foundation of all taste. For the understanding, in spite of sensual cavillers, reserves to itself the privilege of conveying pure joy to the heart.

With what a languid yawn have I seen an admirable poem thrown down, that a man of true taste returns to, again and again with rapture; and, whilst melody has almost suspended respiration, a lady has asked me where I bought my gown. I have seen also an eye glanced coldly over a most exquisite picture, rest, sparkling with pleasure, on a caricature rudely sketched; and whilst some terrific feature in nature has spread a sublime stillness through my soul, I have been desired to observe the pretty tricks of a lap-dog, that my perverse fate forced me to travel with. Is it surprising that such a tasteless being should rather caress this dog than her children? Or, that she should prefer the rant of flattery to the simple accents of sincerity?

To illustrate this remark I must be allowed to observe, that men of the first genius, and most cultivated minds, have appeared to have the highest relish for the simple beauties of nature; and they must have forcibly felt, what they have so well described, the charm which natural affections, and unsophisticated feelings spread round the human character. It is this power of looking into the heart, and responsively vibrating with each emotion, that enables the poet to personify each passion, and the painter to sketch with a pencil of fire.

True taste is ever the work of the understanding employed in observing natural effects; and till women have more understanding, it is vain to expect them to possess domestic taste. Their lively senses will ever be at work to harden their hearts, and the emotions struck out of them will continue to be vivid and transitory, unless a proper education store their mind with knowledge.

It is the want of domestic taste, and not the acquirement of knowledge, that takes women out of their families, and tears the smiling babe from the breast that ought to afford it nourishment. Women have been allowed to remain in ignorance, and slavish dependence, many, very many years, and still we hear of nothing but their fondness of pleasure and sway, their preference of rakes and soldiers, their childish attachment to toys, and the vanity that makes them value accomplishments more than virtues.

History brings forward a fearful catalogue of the crimes which their cunning has produced, when the weak slaves have had sufficient address to over-reach their masters. In France, and in how many other countries, have men been the luxurious despots, and women the crafty ministers?—Does this prove that ignorance and dependence domesticate them? Is not their folly the by-word of the libertines, who relax in their society; and do not men of sense continually lament that an immoderate fondness for dress and dissipation carries the mother of a family for ever from home? Their hearts have not been debauched by knowledge, or their minds led astray by scientific pursuits; yet, they do not fulfil the peculiar duties which as women they are called upon by nature to fulfil. On the contrary, the state of warfare which subsists between the sexes, makes them employ those wiles, that often frustrate the more open designs of force.

When, therefore, I call women slaves, I mean in a political and civil sense; for, indirectly they obtain too much power, and are debased by their exertions to obtain illicit sway.

Let an enlightened nation[12] then try what effect reason would have to bring them back to nature, and their duty; and allowing them to share the advantages of education and government with man, see whether they will become better, as they grow wiser and become free. They cannot be injured by the experiment; for it is not in the power of man to render them more insignificant than they are at present.

To render this practicable, day-schools, for particular ages, should be established by government, in which boys and girls might be educated together. The school for the younger children, from five to nine years of age, ought to be absolutely free and open to all classes.[13] A sufficient number of masters should also be chosen by a select committee, in each parish, to whom any complaint of negligence, etc. might be made, if signed by six of the children's parents.

Ushers would then be unnecessary; for I believe experience will ever prove that this kind of subordinate authority is particularly injurious to the morals of youth. What, indeed, can tend to deprave the character more than outward submission and inward contempt? Yet how can boys be expected to treat an usher with respect, when the master seems to consider him in the light of a servant, and almost to countenance the ridicule which becomes the chief amusement of the boys during the play hours?

But nothing of this kind could occur in an elementary day-school, where boys and girls, the rich and poor, should meet together. And to prevent any of the distinctions of vanity, they should be dressed alike, and all obliged to submit to the same discipline, or leave the school. The school-room ought to be surrounded by a large piece of ground, in which the children might be usefully exercised, for at this age they should not be confined to any sedentary employment for more than an hour at a time. But these relaxations might all be rendered a part of el-

---

[12]France [MW].

[13]Treating this part of the subject, I have borrowed some hints from a very sensible pamphlet, written by the late Bishop of Autun on Public Education [MW], i.e., Talleyrand's *Rapport sur l'Instruction Publique* (Paris, 1791).

ementary education, for many things improve and amuse the senses, when introduced as a kind of show, to the principles of which, dryly laid down, children would turn a deaf ear. For instance, botany, mechanics, and astronomy. Reading, writing, arithmetic, natural history, and some simple experiments in natural philosophy, might fill up the day; but these pursuits should never encroach on gymnastic plays in the open air. The elements of religion, history, the history of man, and politics, might also be taught by conversations, in the socratic form.[14]

After the age of nine, girls and boys, intended for domestic employments, or mechanical trades, ought to be removed to other schools, and receive instruction, in some measure appropriated to the destination of each individual, the two sexes being still together in the morning; but in the afternoon, the girls should attend a school, where plainwork, mantua-making, millinery, etc. would be their employment.

The young people of superior abilities, or fortune, might now be taught, in another school, the dead and living languages, the elements of science, and continue the study of history and politics, on a more extensive scale, which would not exclude polite literature.

Girls and boys still together? I hear some readers ask: yes. And I should not fear any other consequence than that some early attachment might take place; which, whilst it had the best effect on the moral character of the young people, might not perfectly agree with the views of the parents, for it will be a long time, I fear, before the world will be so far enlightened that parents, only anxious to render their children virtuous, shall allow them to choose companions for life themselves.

Besides, this would be a sure way to promote early marriages, and from early marriages the most salutary physical and moral effects naturally flow. What a different character does a married citizen assume from the selfish coxcomb, who lives, but for himself, and who is often afraid to marry lest he should not be able to live in a certain style. Great emergencies excepted, which would rarely occur in a society of which equality was the basis, a man can only be prepared to discharge the duties of public life, by the habitual practice of those inferiour ones which form the man.

In this plan of education the constitution of boys would not be ruined by the early debaucheries, which now make men so selfish, or girls rendered weak and vain, by indolence, and frivolous pursuits. But, I presuppose, that such a degree of equality should be established between

---

[14]Instruction by question and answer, modeled on the Greek philosopher Socrates in Plato's *Dialogues*.

the sexes as would shut out gallantry and coquetry, yet allow friendship and love to temper the heart for the discharge of higher duties.

These would be schools of morality—and the happiness of man, allowed to flow from the pure springs of duty and affection, what advances might not the human mind make? Society can only be happy and free in proportion as it is virtuous; but the present distinctions, established in society, corrode all private, and blast all public virtue.

I have already inveighed against the custom of confining girls to their needle, and shutting them out from all political and civil employments; for by thus narrowing their minds they are rendered unfit to fulfil the peculiar duties which nature has assigned them.

Only employed about the little incidents of the day, they necessarily grow up cunning. My very soul has often sickened at observing the sly tricks practised by women to gain some foolish thing on which their silly hearts were set. Not allowed to dispose of money, or call any thing their own, they learn to turn the market penny[15]; or, should a husband offend, by staying from home, or give rise to some emotions of jealousy—a new gown, or any pretty bawble, smooths Juno's angry brow.[16]

But these *littlenesses* would not degrade their character, if women were led to respect themselves, if political and moral subjects were opened to them; and, I will venture to affirm, that this is the only way to make them properly attentive to their domestic duties.—An active mind embraces the whole circle of its duties, and finds time enough for all. It is not, I assert, a bold attempt to emulate masculine virtues; it is not the enchantment of literary pursuits, or the steady investigation of scientific subjects, that leads women astray from duty. No, it is indolence and vanity—the love of pleasure and the love of sway,[17] that will reign paramount in an empty mind. I say empty emphatically, because the education which women now receive scarcely deserves the name. For the little knowledge that they are led to acquire, during the important years of youth, is merely relative to accomplishments; and accomplishments without a bottom, for unless the understanding be cultivated, superficial and monotonous is every grace. Like the charms of a made up face, they only strike the senses in a crowd; but at home, wanting mind, they want variety. The conse-

---

[15]Skim from the money entrusted to them for marketing.

[16]The legendary jealous wife of Jupiter harassed his mistresses and persecuted his illegitimate offspring.

[17]Pope, *Of the Characters of Women*, 210.

quence is obvious; in gay scenes of dissipation we meet the artificial mind and face, for those who fly from solitude dread, next to solitude, the domestic circle; not having it in their power to amuse or interest, they feel their own insignificance, or find nothing to amuse or interest themselves.

Besides, what can be more indelicate than a girl's *coming out*[18] in the fashionable world? Which, in other words, is to bring to market a marriageable miss, whose person is taken from one public place to another, richly caparisoned. Yet, mixing in the giddy circle under restraint, these butterflies long to flutter at large, for the first affection of their souls is their own persons, to which their attention has been called with the most sedulous care whilst they were preparing for the period that decides their fate for life. Instead of pursuing this idle routine, sighing for tasteless shew, and heartless state, with what dignity would the youths of both sexes form attachments in the schools that I have cursorily pointed out; in which, as life advanced, dancing, music, and drawing, might be admitted as relaxations, for at these schools young people of fortune ought to remain, more or less, till they were of age. Those, who were designed for particular professions, might attend, three or four mornings in the week, the schools appropriated for their immediate instruction.

I only drop these observations at present, as hints; rather, indeed, as an outline of the plan I mean, than a digested one; but I must add, that I highly approve of one regulation mentioned in the pamphlet[19] already alluded to, that of making the children and youths independent of the masters respecting punishments. They should be tried by their peers, which would be an admirable method of fixing sound principles of justice in the mind, and might have the happiest effect on the temper, which is very early soured or irritated by tyranny, till it becomes peevishly cunning, or ferociously overbearing.

My imagination darts forward with benevolent fervour to greet these amiable and respectable groups, in spite of the sneering of cold hearts, who are at liberty to utter, with frigid self-importance, the damning epithet—romantic; the force of which I shall endeavour to blunt by repeating the words of an eloquent moralist.[20]—"I know not whether the allusions of a truly humane heart, whose zeal renders every thing easy, be not preferable to that rough and repulsing rea-

---

[18]Formal entrance into society, and in particular the marriage-market.

[19]The Bishop of Autun's [MW]. Talleyrand's *Rapport*.

[20]Not identified.

son, which always finds an indifference for the public good, the first obstacle to whatever would promote it."

I know that libertines will also exclaim, that woman would be unsexed by acquiring strength of body and mind, and that beauty, soft bewitching beauty! would no longer adorn the daughters of men. I am of a very different opinion, for I think that, on the contrary, we should then see dignified beauty, and true grace; to produce which, many powerful physical and moral causes would concur.—Not relaxed beauty, it is true, or the graces of helplessness; but such as appears to make us respect the human body as a majestic pile fit to receive a noble inhabitant, in the relics of antiquity.

I do not forget the popular opinion that the Grecian statues were not modelled after nature. I mean, not according to the proportions of a particular man; but that beautiful limbs and features were selected from various bodies to form an harmonious whole. This might, in some degree, be true. The fine ideal picture of an exalted imagination might be superiour to the materials which the statuary found in nature, and thus it might with propriety be termed rather the model of mankind than of a man. It was not, however, the mechanical selection of limbs and features; but the ebullition of an heated fancy that burst forth, and the fine senses and enlarged understanding of the artist selected the solid matter, which he drew into this glowing focus.

I observed that it was not mechanical, because a whole was produced—a model of that grand simplicity, of those concurring energies, which arrest our attention and command our reverence. For only insipid lifeless beauty is produced by a servile copy of even beautiful nature. Yet, independent of these observations, I believe that the human form must have been far more beautiful than it is at present, because extreme indolence, barbarous ligatures, and many causes, which forcibly act on it, in our luxurious state of society, did not retard its expansion, or render it deformed. Exercise and cleanliness appear to be not only the surest means of preserving health, but of promoting beauty, the physical causes only considered; yet, this is not sufficient, moral ones must concur, or beauty will be merely of that rustic kind which blooms on the innocent, wholesome, countenances of some country people, whose minds have not been exercised. To render the person perfect, physical and moral beauty ought to be attained at the same time; each lending and receiving force by the combination. Judgment must reside on the brow, affection and fancy beam in the eye, and humanity curve the cheek, or vain is the sparkling of the finest eye or the elegantly turned finish of the fairest features: whilst in every motion that displays the active limbs and well-knit joints, grace and modesty should appear. But this fair assemblage is not to be brought together by chance; it is the reward of exertions calculated to support each other; for judgment can only be acquired by reflection, affection by the discharge of duties, and humanity by the exercise of compassion to every living creature.

Humanity to animals should be particularly inculcated as a part of national education, for it is not at present one of our national virtues. Tenderness for their humble dumb domestics, amongst the lower class, is oftener to be found in a savage than a civilized state. For civilization prevents that intercourse which creates affection in the rude hut, or mud hovel, and leads uncultivated minds who are only depraved by the refinements which prevail in the society, where they are trodden under foot by the rich, to domineer over them to revenge the insults that they are obliged to bear from their superiours.

This habitual cruelty is first caught at school, where it is one of the rare sports of the boys to torment the miserable brutes that fall in their way. The transition, as they grow up, from barbarity to brutes to domestic tyranny over wives, children, and servants, is very easy. Justice, or even benevolence, will not be a powerful spring of action unless it extend to the whole creation; nay, I believe that it may be delivered as an axiom, that those who can see pain, unmoved, will soon learn to inflict it.

The vulgar are swayed by present feelings, and the habits which they have accidentally acquired; but on partial feelings much dependence cannot be placed, though they be just; for, when they are not invigorated by reflection, custom weakens them, till they are scarcely perceptible. The sympathies of our nature are strengthened by pondering cogitations, and deadened by thoughtless use. Macbeth's heart smote him more for one murder, the first,[21] than for a hundred subsequent ones, which were necessary to back it. But, when I used the epithet vulgar, I did not mean to confine my remark to the poor, for partial humanity, founded on present sensations, or whim, is quite as conspicuous, if not more so, amongst the rich.

The lady who sheds tears for the bird starved in a snare, and execrates the devils in the shape of men, who goad to madness the poor ox, or whip the patient ass, tottering under a burden above its strength, will, nevertheless, keep her coachman and horses whole hours waiting for her, when the sharp frost bites, or the rain beats against the well-

[21]Of king Duncan.

closed windows which do not admit a breath of air to tell her how roughly the wind blows without. And she who takes her dogs to bed, and nurses them with a parade of sensibility, when sick, will suffer her babes to grow up crooked in a nursery. This illustration of my argument is drawn from a matter of fact. The woman whom I allude to was handsome, reckoned very handsome, by those who do not miss the mind when the face is plump and fair; but her understanding had not been led from female duties by literature, nor her innocence debauched by knowledge. No, she was quite feminine, according to the masculine acceptation of the word; and, so far from loving these spoiled brutes that filled the place which her children ought to have occupied, she only lisped out a pretty mixture of French and English nonsense, to please the men who flocked round her.[22] The wife, mother, and human creature, were all swallowed up by the factitious character which an improper education and the selfish vanity of beauty had produced.

I do not like to make a distinction without a difference, and I own that I have been as much disgusted by the fine lady who took her lap-dog to her bosom instead of her child; as by the ferocity of a man, who, beating his horse, declared, that he knew as well when he did wrong, as a Christian.

This brood of folly shews how mistaken they are who, if they allow women to leave their harams, do not cultivate their understandings, in order to plant virtues in their hearts. For had they sense, they might acquire that domestic taste which would lead them to love with reasonable subordination their whole family, from their husband to the house-dog; nor would they ever insult humanity in the person of the most menial servant by paying more attention to the comfort of a brute, than to that of a fellow-creature.

My observations on national education are obviously hints; but I principally wish to enforce the necessity of educating the sexes together to perfect both, and of making children sleep at home that they may learn to love home; yet to make private support, instead of smothering, public affections, they should be sent to school to mix with a number of equals, for only by the jostlings of equality can we form a just opinion of ourselves.

To render mankind more virtuous, and happier of course, both sexes must act from the same principle; but how can that be expected when only one is allowed to see the reasonableness of it? To render

---

[22]Perhaps a memory of Lady Kingsborough, the model for satiric portrait in *Mary, A Fiction.*

also the social compact truly equitable, and in order to spread those enlightening principles, which alone can meliorate the fate of man, women must be allowed to found their virtue on knowledge, which is scarcely possible unless they be educated by the same pursuits as men. For they are now made so inferiour by ignorance and low desires, as not to deserve to be ranked with them; or, by the serpentine wrigglings of cunning they mount the tree of knowledge, and only acquire sufficient to lead men astray.

It is plain from the history of all nations, that women cannot be confined to merely domestic pursuits, for they will not fulfil family duties, unless their minds take a wider range, and whilst they are kept in ignorance they become in the same proportion the slaves of pleasure as they are the slaves of man. Nor can they be shut out of great enterprises, though the narrowness of their minds often make them mar, what they are unable to comprehend.

The libertinism, and even the virtues of superiour men, will always give women, of some description, great power over them; and these weak women, under the influence of childish passions and selfish vanity, will throw a false light over the objects which the very men view with their eyes, who ought to enlighten their judgment. Men of fancy, and those sanguine characters who mostly hold the helm of human affairs, in general, relax in the society of women; and surely I need not cite to the most superficial reader of history the numerous examples of vice and oppression which the private intrigues of female favourites have produced; not to dwell on the mischief that naturally arises from the blundering interposition of well-meaning folly. For in the transactions of business it is much better to have to deal with a knave than a fool, because a knave adheres to some plan; and any plan of reason may be seen through much sooner than a sudden flight of folly. The power which vile and foolish women have had over wise men, who possessed sensibility, is notorious; I shall only mention one instance.

Who ever drew a more exalted female character than Rousseau? though in the lump he constantly endeavoured to degrade the sex. And why was he thus anxious? Truly to justify to himself the affection which weakness and virtue had made him cherish for that fool Theresa. He could not raise her to the common level of her sex; and therefore he laboured to bring woman down to her's. He found her a convenient humble companion, and pride made him determine to find some superior virtues in the being whom he chose to live with; but did not her conduct during his life, and after his death, clearly shew how grossly he was mistaken who called her a celestial innocent.[23] Nay, in the bitterness of his heart, he himself laments, that when his bodily infirmities made him no longer treat her like a woman, she ceased to have an affection for him.[24] And it was very natural that she should, for having so few sentiments in common, when the sexual tie was broken, what was to hold her? To hold her affection whose sensibility was confined to one sex, nay, to one man, it requires sense to turn sensibility into the broad channel of humanity; many women have not mind enough to have an affection for a woman, or a friendship for a man. But the sexual weakness that makes woman depend on man for a subsistence, produces a kind of cattish affection which leads a wife to purr about her husband as she would about any man who fed and caressed her.

Men are, however, often gratified by this kind of fondness, which is confined in a beastly manner to themselves; but should they ever become more virtuous, they will wish to converse at their fire-side with a friend, after they cease to play with a mistress.

Besides, understanding is necessary to give variety and interest to sensual enjoyments, for low, indeed, in the intellectual scale, is the mind that can continue to love when neither virtue nor sense give a human appearance to an animal appetite. But sense will always preponderate; and if women be not, in general, brought more on a level with men, some superiour women like the Greek courtezans,[25] will assemble the men of abilities around them, and draw from their families many citizens, who would have stayed at home had their wives had more sense, or the graces which result from the exercise of the understanding and fancy, the legitimate parents of taste. A woman of talents, if she be not absolutely ugly, will always obtain great power, raised by the weakness of her sex; and in proportion as men acquire virtue and delicacy, by the exertion of reason, they will look for both in women, but they can only acquire them in the same way that men do.

In France or Italy, have the women confined themselves to domestic life? though they have not hitherto had a political existence, yet,

[23]See *Les Confessions*, part II (1790), 4.8.190: "Le coeur de ma Thérèse était celui d'un ange" (The heart of my Thérèse was that of an angel.) Uneducated seamstress Thérèse Le Vasseur was Rousseau's lifelong mistress.

[24]Rousseau suffered from a congenital defect of the urinary tract, and in 1762 elected to abstain from sexual intercourse. This decision may have been influenced by guilt over abandoning his children to a foundling hospital, and a desire for no further offspring.

[25]These well-educated, highly intelligent women often wielded considerable indirect influence.

have they not illicitly had great sway? corrupting themselves and the men with whose passions they played. In short, in whatever light I view the subject, reason and experience convince me that the only method of leading women to fulfil their peculiar duties, is to free them from all restraint by allowing them to participate in the inherent rights of mankind.

Make them free, and they will quickly become wise and virtuous, as men become more so; for the improvement must be mutual, or the injustice which one half of the human race are obliged to submit to, retorting on their oppressors, the virtue of man will be worm-eaten by the insect whom he keeps under his feet.

Let men take their choice, man and woman were made for each other, though not to become one being; and if they will not improve women, they will deprave them!

I speak of the improvement and emancipation of the whole sex, for I know that the behaviour of a few women, who, by accident, or following a strong bent of nature, have acquired a portion of knowledge superiour to that of the rest of their sex, has often been overbearing; but there have been instances of women who, attaining knowledge, have not discarded modesty, nor have they always pedantically appeared to despise the ignorance which they laboured to disperse in their own minds. The exclamations then which any advice respecting female learning, commonly produces, especially from pretty women, often arise from envy. When they chance to see that even the lustre of their eyes, and the flippant sportiveness of refined coquetry will not always secure them attention, during a whole evening, should a woman of a more cultivated understanding endeavour to give a rational turn to the conversation, the common source of consolation is, that such women seldom get husbands. What arts have I not seen silly women use to interrupt by *flirtation*, a very significant word to describe such a manoeuvre, a rational conversation which made the men forget that they were pretty women.

But, allowing what is very natural to man, that the possession of rare abilities is really calculated to excite over-weening pride, disgusting in both men and women—in what a state of inferiority must the female faculties have rusted when such a small portion of knowledge as those women attained, who have sneeringly been termed learned women, could be singular?—Sufficiently so to puff up the possessor, and excite envy in her contemporaries, and some of the other sex. Nay, has not a little rationality exposed many women to the severest censure? I advert to well known facts, for I have frequently heard women ridiculed, and every little weakness exposed, only because they adopted the advice of some medical men, and deviated from the beaten track in their mode of treating their infants.[26] I have actually heard this barbarous aversion to innovation carried still further, and a sensible woman stigmatized as an unnatural mother, who has thus been wisely solicitous to preserve the health of her children, when in the midst of her care she has lost one by some of the casualties of infancy, which no prudence can ward off. Her acquaintance have observed that this was the consequence of new-fangled notions—the new-fangled notions of ease and cleanliness. And those who pretending to experience, though they have long adhered to prejudices that have, according to the opinion of the most sagacious physicians, thinned the human race, almost rejoiced at the disaster after that gave a kind of sanction to prescription.

Indeed, if it were only on this account, the national education of women is of the utmost consequence, for what a number of human sacrifices are made to that moloch[27] prejudice! And in how many ways are children destroyed by the lasciviousness of man? The want of natural affection, in many women, who are drawn from their duty by the admiration of men, and the ignorance of others, render the infancy of man a much more perilous state than that of brutes; yet men are unwilling to place women in situations proper to enable them to acquire sufficient understanding to know how even to nurse their babes.

So forcibly does this truth strike me, that I would rest the whole tendency of my reasoning upon it, for whatever tends to incapacitate the maternal character, takes woman out of her sphere.

But it is vain to expect the present race of weak mothers either to take that reasonable care of a child's body, which is necessary to lay the foundation of a good constitution, supposing that it do not suffer for the sins of its fathers[28]; or, to manage its temper so judiciously that the child will not have, as it grows up, to throw off all that its mother, its first instructor, directly or indirectly taught; and unless the mind have uncommon vigour, womanish follies will stick to the character throughout life. The weakness of the mother will be

[26]That is, insisting on nursing. One advocate, notes Janet Todd, was Ben Lara, whose "Essay on the Injurious Customs of Mothers not Suckling their own Children" (1791) MW reviewed for the *Analytical Review*, July 1791.

[27]Canaanite idol to whom children were sacrificed.

[28]That is, infection by venereal disease, with reference to God's "visiting the iniquity of the fathers upon the children unto the third and fourth generation" (Exodus 20:5, cf. Exodus 34:7, Numbers 14:18, and Deuteronomy 5:9).

visited on the children! And whilst women are educated to rely on their husbands for judgment, this must ever be the consequence, for there is no improving an understanding by halves, nor can any being act wisely from imitation, because in every circumstance of life there is a kind of individuality, which requires an exertion of judgment to modify general rules. The being who can think justly in one track, will soon extend its intellectual empire; and she who has sufficient judgment to manage her children, will not submit, right or wrong, to her husband, or patiently to the social laws which make a nonentity of a wife.

In public schools women, to guard against the errors of ignorance, should be taught the elements of anatomy and medicine, not only to enable them to take proper care of their own health, but to make them rational nurses of their infants, parents, and husbands; for the bills of mortality are swelled by the blunders of self-willed old women, who give nostrums[29] of their own without knowing any thing of the human frame. It is likewise proper only in a domestic view, to make women acquainted with the anatomy of the mind, by allowing the sexes to associate together in every pursuit; and by leading them to observe the progress of the human understanding in the improvement of the sciences and arts; never forgetting the science of morality, or the study of the political history of mankind.

A man has been termed a microcosm; and every family might also be called a state. States, it is true, have mostly been governed by arts that disgrace the character of man; and the want of a just constitution, and equal laws, have so perplexed the notions of the worldly wise, that they more than question the reasonableness of contending for the rights of humanity. Thus morality, polluted in the national reservoir, sends off streams of vice to corrupt the constituent parts of the body politic; but should more noble, or rather, more just principles regulate the laws, which ought to be the government of society, and not those who execute them, duty might become the rule of private conduct.

Besides, by the exercise of their bodies and minds women would acquire that mental activity so necessary in the maternal character, united with the fortitude that distinguishes steadiness of conduct from the obstinate perverseness of weakness. For it is dangerous to advise the indolent to be steady, because they instantly become rigor-

---

[29]The bills are weekly records of burials kept since the Great Plague of 1603. Nostrums are quack remedies.

ous, and to save themselves trouble, punish with severity faults that the patient fortitude of reason might have prevented.

But fortitude presupposes strength of mind; and is strength of mind to be acquired by indolent acquiescence? by asking advice instead of exerting the judgment? by obeying through fear, instead of practising the forbearance, which we all stand in need of ourselves?—The conclusion which I wish to draw, is obvious; make women rational creatures, and free citizens, and they will quickly become good wives, and mothers; that is—if men do not neglect the duties of husbands and fathers.

Discussing the advantages which a public and private education combined, as I have sketched, might rationally be expected to produce, I have dwelt most on such as are particularly relative to the female world, because I think the female world oppressed; yet the gangrene, which the vices engendered by oppression have produced, is not confined to the morbid[30] part, but pervades society at large: so that when I wish to see my sex become more like moral agents, my heart bounds with the anticipation of the general diffusion of that sublime contentment which only morality can diffuse.

---

[30]Diseased or dying.

CHAPTER XIII

SOME INSTANCES OF THE FOLLY WHICH THE IGNORANCE OF WOMEN GENERATES; WITH CONCLUDING REFLECTIONS ON THE MORAL IMPROVEMENT THAT A REVOLUTION IN FEMALE MANNERS MIGHT NATURALLY BE EXPECTED TO PRODUCE

There are many follies, in some degree, peculiar to women: sins against reason of commission as well as of omission; but all flowing from ignorance or prejudice, I shall only point out such as appear to be particularly injurious to their moral character. And in animadverting on them, I wish especially to prove, that the weakness of mind and body, which men have endeavoured, impelled by various motives, to perpetuate, prevents their discharging the peculiar duty of their sex: for when weakness of body will not permit them to suckle their children, and weakness of mind makes them spoil their tempers—is woman in a natural state?

SECTION I

One glaring instance of the weakness which proceeds from ignorance, first claims attention, and calls for severe reproof.

In this metropolis a number of lurking leeches infamously gain a subsistence by practising on the credulity of women, pretending to cast nativities,[1] to use the technical phrase; and many females who, proud of their rank and fortune, look down on the vulgar with sovereign contempt, shew by this credulity, that the distinction is arbitrary, and that they have not sufficiently cultivated their minds to rise above vulgar prejudices. Women, because they have not been led to consider the knowledge of their duty as the one thing necessary to know, or, to live in the present moment by the discharge of it, are very anxious to peep into futurity, to learn what they have to expect to render life interesting, and to break the vacuum of ignorance.

I must be allowed to expostulate seriously with the ladies who follow these idle inventions; for ladies, mistresses of families, are not ashamed to drive in their own carriages to the door of the cunning man.[2] And if any of them should peruse this work, I entreat them to

[1]Horoscopes.

[2]I once lived in the neighbourhood of one of these men, a *handsome* man, and saw with surprise and indignation, women, whose appearance and attendance bespoke that rank in which females are supposed to receive a superiour education, flock to his door [MW].

answer to their own hearts the following questions, not forgetting that they are in the presence of God.

Do you believe that there is but one God, and that he is powerful, wise, and good?

Do you believe that all things were created by him, and that all beings are dependent on him?

Do you rely on his wisdom, so conspicuous in his works, and in your own frame, and are you convinced that he has ordered things which do not come under the cognizance of your senses, in the same perfect harmony, to fulfil his designs?

Do you acknowledge that the power of looking into futurity, and seeing things that are not, as if they were, is an attribute of the Creator? And should he, by an impression on the minds of his creatures, think fit to impart to them some event hid the shades of time yet unborn, to whom would the secret be revealed by immediate inspiration? The opinion of ages will answer this question—to reverend old men, to people distinguished for eminent piety.

The oracles of old were thus delivered by priests dedicated to the service of the God who was supposed to inspire them. The glare of worldly pomp which surrounded these impostors, and the respect paid to them by artful politicians, who knew how to avail themselves of this useful engine to bend the necks of the strong under the dominion of the cunning, spread a sacred mysterious veil of sanctity over their lies and abominations. Impressed by such solemn devotional parade, a Greek, or Roman lady might be excused, if she inquired of the oracle, when she was anxious to pry into futurity, or inquire about some dubious event: and her inquiries, however contrary to reason, could not be reckoned impious.—But, can the professors of Christianity ward off that imputation? Can a Christian suppose that the favourites of the most High, the highly favoured, would be obliged to lurk in disguise, and practise the most dishonest tricks to cheat silly women out of the money—which the poor cry for in vain?

Say not that such questions are an insult to common sense—for it is your own conduct, O ye foolish women! which throws an odium on your sex! And these reflections should make you shudder at your thoughtlessness, and irrational devotion.—For I do not suppose that all of you laid aside your religion, such as it is, when you entered those mysterious dwellings. Yet, as I have throughout supposed myself talking to ignorant women, for ignorant ye are in the most emphatical sense of the word, it would be absurd to reason with you on the egregious folly of desiring to know what the Supreme Wisdom has concealed.

Probably you would not understand me, were I to attempt to shew you that it would be absolutely inconsistent with the grand purpose of life, that of rendering human creatures wise and virtuous: and that, were it sanctioned by God, it would disturb the order established in creation; and if it be not sanctioned by God, do you expect to hear truth? Can events be foretold, events which have not yet assumed a body to become subject to mortal inspection, can they be foreseen by a vicious worldling, who pampers his appetites by preying on the foolish ones?

Perhaps, however, you devoutly believe in the devil, and imagine, to shift the question, that he may assist his votaries; but, if really respecting the power of such a being, an enemy to goodness and to God, can you go to church after having been under such an obligation to him?

From these delusions to those still more fashionable deceptions, practised by the whole tribe of magnetisers,[3] the transition is very natural. With respect to them, it is equally proper to ask women a few questions.

Do you know anything of the construction of the human frame? If not, it is proper that you should be told what every child ought to know, that when its admirable œconomy has been disturbed by intemperance or indolence, I speak not of violent disorders, but of chronical diseases, it must be brought into a healthy state again, by slow degrees, and if the functions of life have not been materially injured, regimen, another word for temperance, air, exercise, and a few medicines, prescribed by persons who have studied the human body, are the only human means, yet discovered, of recovering that inestimable blessing health, that will bear investigation.

Do you then believe that these magnetisers, who, by hocus pocus tricks, pretend to work a miracle, are delegated by God, or assisted by the solver of all these kind of difficulties—the devil?

Do they, when they put to flight, as it is said, disorders that have baffled the powers of medicine, work in conformity to the light of reason? or, do they effect these wonderful cures by supernatural aid?

By a communication, an adept may answer, with the world of spirits. A noble privilege, it must be allowed. Some of the ancients mention familiar daemons, who guarded them from danger by kindly intimating, we cannot guess in what manner, when any danger was

---

[3]Healers using hypnosis, or "mesmerism," after its influential practitioner Friedrich Mesmer (1733–1815), who believed that magnets could cure disease by "animal magnetism."

nigh; or, pointed out what they ought to undertake. Yet the men who laid claim to this privilege, out of the order of nature, insisted that it was the reward, or consequence, of superiour temperance and piety. But the present workers of wonders are not raised above their fellows by superiour temperance or sanctity. They do not cure for the love of God, but money. These are the priests of quackery, though it is true they have not the convenient expedient of selling masses for souls in purgatory,[4] or churches where they can display crutches, and models of limbs made sound by a touch or a word.

I am not conversant with the technical terms, or initiated into the arcana, therefore, I may speak improperly; but it is clear that men who will not conform to the law of reason, and earn a subsistence in an honest way, by degrees, are very fortunate in becoming acquainted with such obliging spirits. We cannot, indeed, give them credit for either great sagacity or goodness, else they would have chosen more noble instruments, when they wished to shew themselves the benevolent friends of man.

It is, however, little short of blasphemy to pretend to such powers!

From the whole tenour of the dispensations of Providence, it appears evident to sober reason, that certain vices produce certain effects; and can any one so grossly insult the wisdom of God, as to suppose that a miracle will be allowed to disturb his general laws, to restore to health the intemperate and vicious, merely to enable them to pursue the same course with impunity? Be whole, and sin no more, said Jesus.[5] And, are greater miracles to be performed by those who do not follow his footsteps, who healed the body to reach the mind?

The mentioning of the name of Christ, after such vile impostors, may displease some of my readers—I respect their warmth; but let them not forget that the followers of these delusions bear his name, and profess to be the disciples of him, who said, by their works we should know who were the children of God or the servants of sin. I allow that it is easier to touch the body of a saint, or to be magnetised, than to restrain our appetites or govern our passions; but health of body or mind can only be recovered by these means, or we make the Supreme Judge partial and revengeful.

Is he a man that he should change, or punish out of resentment? He—the common father, wounds but to heal, say reason, and our

---

[4]Roman Catholic masses to release a soul from purgatory could be purchased, sometimes at exorbitant fees.

[5]See John 5:14.

irregularities producing certain consequences, we are forcibly shewn the nature of vice; that thus learning to know good from evil, by experience, we may hate one and love the other, in proportion to the wisdom which we attain. The poison contains the antidote; and we either reform our evil habits and cease to sin against our own bodies, to use the forcible language of scripture, or a premature death, the punishment of sin, snaps the thread of life.

Here an awful stop is put to our inquiries.—But, why should I conceal my sentiments? Considering the attributes of God, I believe that whatever punishment may follow, will tend, like the anguish of disease, to shew the malignity of vice, for the purpose of reformation. Positive punishment appears so contrary to the nature of God, discoverable in all his works, and in our own reason, that I could sooner believe that the Deity paid no attention to the conduct of men, than that he punished without the benevolent design of reforming.

To suppose only that an all-wise and powerful Being, as good as he is great, should create a being foreseeing, that after fifty or sixty years of feverish existence, it would be plunged into never ending woe—is blasphemy. On what will the worm feed that is never to die?[6] On folly, on ignorance, say ye—I should blush indignantly at drawing the natural conclusion could I insert it, and wish to withdraw myself from the wing of my God! On such a supposition, I speak with reverence, he would be a consuming fire. We should wish, though vainly, to fly from his presence when fear absorbed love, and darkness involved all his counsels!

I know that many devout people boast of submitting to the Will of God blindly, as to an arbitrary sceptre or rod, on the same principle as the Indians worship the devil. In other words, like people in the common concerns of life, they do homage to power, and cringe under the foot that can crush them. Rational religion, on the contrary, is a submission to the will of a being so perfectly wise, that all he wills must be directed by the proper motive—must be reasonable.

And, if thus we respect God, can we give credit to mysterious insinuations, which insult his laws? can we believe, though it should stare us in the face, that he would work a miracle to authorize confusion by sanctioning an error? Yet we must either allow these impious conclusions, or treat with contempt every promise to restore health to a diseased body by supernatural means, or to foretell the incidents that can only be foreseen by God.

[6]Echoing Isaiah 66:24.

SECTION II

Another instance of that feminine weakness of character, often produced by a confined education, is a romantic twist of the mind, which has been very properly termed *sentimental.*

Women subjected by ignorance to their sensations, and only taught to look for happiness in love, refine on sensual feelings, and adopt metaphysical notions respecting that passion, which lead them shamefully to neglect the duties of life, and frequently in the midst of these sublime refinements they plump into actual vice.

These are the women who are amused by the reveries of the stupid novelists, who, knowing little of human nature, work up stale tales, and describe meretricious scenes, all retailed in a sentimental jargon, which equally tend to corrupt the taste, and draw the heart aside from its daily duties. I do not mention the understanding, because never having been exercised, its slumbering energies rest inactive, like the lurking particles of fire which are supposed universally to pervade matter.[7]

Females, in fact, denied all political privileges, and not allowed, as married women, excepting in criminal cases, a civil existence, have their attention naturally drawn from the interest of the whole community to that of the minute parts, though the private duty of any member of society must be very imperfectly performed when not connected with the general good. The mighty business of female life is to please, and restrained from entering into more important concerns by political and civil oppression, sentiments become events, and reflection deepens what it should, and would have effaced, if the understanding had been allowed to take a wider range.

But, confined to trifling employments, they naturally imbibe opinions which the only kind of reading calculated to interest an innocent frivolous mind, inspires. Unable to grasp any thing great, is it surprising that they find the reading of history a very dry task, and disquisitions addressed to the understanding intolerably tedious, and almost unintelligible? Thus are they necessarily dependent on the novelist for amusement. Yet, when I exclaim against novels, I mean when contrasted with those works which exercise the understanding and regulate the imagination.—For any kind of reading I think better than leaving a blank still a blank, because the mind must receive a degree of enlargement and obtain a little strength by a slight exertion of its think-

---

[7]Although French chemist Lavoisier had discredited their existence by 1790, English scientist Joseph Priestley continued to credit their existence.

ing powers; besides, even the productions that are only addressed to the imagination, raise the reader a little above the gross gratification of appetites, to which the mind has not given a shade of delicacy.

This observation is the result of experience; for I have known several notable women, and one in particular, who was a very good woman—as good as such a narrow mind would allow her to be, who took care that her daughters (three in number) should never see a novel. As she was a woman of fortune and fashion, they had various masters to attend them, and a sort of menial governess to watch their footsteps. From their masters they learned how tables, chairs, etc. were called in French and Italian; but as the few books thrown in their way were far above their capacities, or devotional, they neither acquired ideas nor sentiments, and passed their time, when not compelled to repeat *words*, in dressing, quarrelling with each other, or conversing with their maids by stealth, till they were brought into company as marriageable.

Their mother, a widow, was busy in the mean time in keeping up her connections, as she termed a numerous acquaintance, lest her girls should want a proper introduction into the great world. And these young ladies, with minds vulgar in every sense of the word, and spoiled tempers, entered life puffed up with notions of their own consequence, and looking down with contempt on those who could not vie with them in dress and parade.

With respect to love, nature, or their nurses, had taken care to teach them the physical meaning of the word; and, as they had few topics of conversation, and fewer refinements of sentiment, they expressed their gross wishes not in very delicate phrases, when they spoke freely, talking of matrimony.

Could these girls have been injured by the perusal of novels? I almost forgot a shade in the character of one of them; she affected a simplicity bordering on folly, and with a simper would utter the most immodest remarks and questions, the full meaning of which she had learned whilst secluded from the world, and afraid to speak in her mother's presence, who governed with a hand: they were all educated, as she prided herself, in a most exemplary manner; and read their chapters and psalms before breakfast, never touching a silly novel.

This is only one instance; but I recollect many other women who, not led by degrees to proper studies, and not permitted to choose for themselves, have indeed been overgrown children; or have obtained, by mixing in the world, a little of what is termed common sense: that is, a distinct manner of seeing common occurrences, as they stand detached: but what deserves the name of intellect, the power of gaining general or abstract ideas, or even intermediate ones, was out of the question. Their minds were quiescent, and when they were not roused by sensible objects and employments of that kind, they were low-spirited, would cry, or go to sleep.

When, therefore, I advise my sex not to read such flimsy works, it is to induce them to read something superiour; for I coincide in opinion with a sagacious man, who, having a daughter and niece under his care, pursued a very different plan with each.

The niece, who had considerable abilities, had, before she was left to his guardianship, been indulged in desultory reading. Her he endeavoured to lead, and did lead to history and moral essays; but his daughter, whom a fond weak mother had indulged, and who consequently was averse to every thing like application, he allowed to read novels: and used to justify his conduct by saying, that if she ever attained a relish for reading them, he should have some foundation to work upon; and that erroneous opinions were better than none at all.

In fact the female mind has been so totally neglected, that knowledge was only to be acquired from this muddy source, till from reading novels some women of superiour talents learned to despise them.

The best method, I believe, that can be adopted to correct a fondness for novels is to ridicule them: not indiscriminately, for then it would have little effect; but, if a judicious person, with some turn for humour, would read several to a young girl, and point out both by tones, and apt comparisons with pathetic incidents and heroic characters in history, how foolishly and ridiculously they caricatured human nature, just opinions might be substituted instead of romantic sentiments.

In one respect, however, the majority of both sexes resemble, and equally shew a want of taste and modesty. Ignorant women, forced to be chaste to preserve their reputation, allow their imagination to revel in the unnatural and meretricious scenes sketched by the novel writers of the day, slighting as insipid the sober dignity, and matron graces of history,[8] whilst men carry the same vitiated taste into life, and fly for amusement to the wanton, from the unsophisticated charms of virtue, and the grave respectability of sense.

Besides, the reading of novels makes women, and particularly ladies of fashion, very fond of using strong expressions and superla-

[8]I am not now alluding to that superiority of mind which leads to the creation of ideal beauty, when he, surveyed with a penetrating eye, appears a tragi-comedy, in which little can be seen to satisfy the heart without the help of fancy [MW].

tives in conversation; and, though the dissipated artificial life which they lead prevents their cherishing any strong legitimate passion, the language of passion in affected tones slips for ever from their glib tongues, and every trifle produces those phosphoric bursts which only mimick in the dark the flame of passion.

SECTION III

Ignorance and the mistaken cunning that nature sharpens in weak heads as a principle of self-preservation, render women very fond of dress, and produce all the vanity which such a fondness may naturally be expected to generate, to the exclusion of emulation and magnanimity.

I agree with Rousseau that the physical part of the art of pleasing consists in ornaments, and for that very reason I should guard girls against the contagious fondness for dress so common to weak women, that they may not rest in the physical part. Yet, weak are the women who imagine that they can long please without the aid of the mind, or, in other words, without the moral art of pleasing. But the moral art, if it be not a profanation to use the word art, when alluding to the grace which is an effect of virtue, and not the motive of action, is never to be found with ignorance; the sportiveness of innocence, so pleasing to refined libertines of both sexes, is widely different in its essence from this superiour gracefulness.

A strong inclination for external ornaments ever appears in barbarous states, only the men not the women adorn themselves; for where women are allowed to be so far on a level with men, society has advanced, at least, one step in civilization.

The attention to dress, therefore, which has been thought a sexual propensity, I think natural to mankind. But I ought to express myself with more precision. When the mind is not sufficiently opened to take pleasure in reflection, the body will be adorned with sedulous care; and ambition will appear in tattooing or painting it.

So far is this first inclination carried, that even the hellish yoke of slavery cannot stifle the savage desire of admiration which the black heroes inherit from both their parents, for all the hardly earned savings of a slave are commonly expended in a little tawdry finery. And I have seldom known a good male or female servant that was not particularly fond of dress. Their clothes were their riches; and, I argue from analogy, that the fondness for dress, so extravagant in females, arises from the same cause—want of cultivation of mind. When men meet they converse about business, politics, or literature; but, says

Swift, "how naturally do women apply their hands to each others lappets and ruffles."[9] And very natural is it—for they have not any business to interest them, have not a taste for literature, and they find politics dry, because they have not acquired a love for mankind by turning their thoughts to the grand pursuits that exalt the human race, and promote general happiness.

Besides, various are the paths to power and fame which by accident or choice men pursue, and though they jostle against each other, for men of the same profession are seldom friends, yet there is a much greater number of their fellow-creatures with whom they never clash. But women are very differently situated with respect to each other— for they are all rivals.

Before marriage it is their business to please men; and after, with a few exceptions, they follow the same scent with all the persevering pertinacity of instinct. Even virtuous women never forget their sex in company, for they are for ever trying to make themselves *agreeable*. A female beauty, and a male wit, appear to be equally anxious to draw the attention of the company to themselves; and the animosity of contemporary wits is proverbial.

Is it then surprising that when the sole ambition of woman centres in beauty, and interest gives vanity additional force, perpetual rivalships should ensue? They are all running the same race, and would rise above the virtue of mortals, if they did not view each other with a suspicious and even envious eye.

An immoderate fondness for dress, for pleasure, and for sway,[10] are the passions of savages; the passions that occupy those uncivilized beings who have not yet extended the dominion of the mind, or even learned to think with the energy necessary to concatenate that abstract train of thought which produces principles. And that women from their education and the present state of civilized life, are in the same condition, cannot, I think be controverted. To laugh at them then, or satirize the follies of a being who is never to be allowed to act freely from the light of her own reason, is as absurd as cruel; for, that they who are taught blindly to obey authority, will endeavour cunningly to elude it, is most natural and certain.

[9] "A Letter to a Young Lady on Her Marriage": "And when you are among yourselves, how naturally, after the first Complements, do you apply your hands to each others Lappets and Ruffles and Mantra's, as if the whole business of your Lives, and the publick concern of the World, depended upon the Cut or Colour of your Dresses" (*Miscellanies in Verse and Prose* [1727], 2.330).

[10] Another echo of Pope, *Of the Characters of Women*, 210.

Yet let it be proved that they ought to obey man implicitly, and I shall immediately agree that it is woman's duty to cultivate a fondness for dress, in order to please, and a propensity to cunning for her own preservation.

The virtues, however, which are supported by ignorance must ever be wavering—the house built on sand could not endure a storm.[11] It is almost unnecessary to draw the inference.—If women are to be made virtuous by authority, which is a contradiction in terms, let them be immured in seraglios and watched with a jealous eye.—Fear not that the iron will enter into their souls—for the souls that can bear such treatment are made of yielding materials, just animated enough to give life to the body.

> "Matter too soft a lasting mark to bear
> And best distinguished by black, brown, or fair."[12]

The most cruel wounds will of course soon heal, and they may still people the world, and dress to please man—all the purposes! which certain celebrated writers have allowed that they were created to fulfil.

SECTION IV

Women are supposed to possess more sensibility, and even humanity, than men, and their strong attachments and instantaneous emotions of compassion are given as proofs; but the clinging affection of ignorance has seldom any thing noble in it, and may mostly be resolved into selfishness, as well as the affection of children and brutes. I have known many weak women whose sensibility was entirely engrossed by their husbands; and as for their humanity, it was very faint indeed, or rather it was only a transient emotion of compassion. Humanity does not consist "in a squeamish ear," says an eminent orator.[13] "It belongs to the mind as well as the nerves."

But this kind of exclusive affection, though it degrades the individual, should not be brought forward as a proof of the inferiority of the sex, because it is the natural consequence of confined views: for even women of superior sense, having their attention turned to little

[11]Says Jesus, those who fail to heed his teaching may be "likened unto a foolish man, which built his house upon the sand: And the rain descended, and the floods came, and the winds blew, and beat upon that house; and it fell" (Matthew 7:26–27).

[12]Pope, *Of the Characters of Women*, 3–4.

[13]Not identified.

employments, and private plans, rarely rise to heroism, unless when spurred on by love! and love, as an heroic passion, like genius, appears but once in an age. I therefore agree with the moralist who asserts, "that women have seldom so much generosity as men"[14]; and that their narrow affections, to which justice and humanity are often sacrificed, render the sex apparently inferior, especially, as they are commonly inspired by men; but I contend that the heart would expand as the understanding gained strength, if women were not depressed from their cradles.

I know that a little sensibility, and great weakness, will produce a strong sexual attachment, and that reason must cement friendship; consequently, I allow that more friendship is to be found in the male than the female world, and that men have a higher sense of justice. The exclusive affections of women seem indeed to resemble Cato's most unjust love for his country.[15] He wished to crush Carthage, not to save Rome, but to promote its vain-glory; and, in general, it is to similar principles that humanity is sacrificed, for genuine duties support each other.

Besides, how can women be just or generous, when they are the slaves of injustice?

SECTION V

As the rearing of children, that is, the laying a foundation of sound health both of body and mind in the rising generation, has justly been insisted on as the peculiar destination of woman, the ignorance that incapacitates them must be contrary to the order of things. And I contend that their minds can take in much more, and ought to do so, or they will never become sensible mothers. Many men attend to the breeding of horses, and overlook the management of the stable, who would, strange want of sense and feeling! think themselves degraded by paying attention to the nursery; yet, how many children are absolutely murdered by the ignorance of women! But when they escape, and are destroyed neither by unnatural negligence nor blind fondness, how few are managed properly with respect to the infant mind!

[14]Smith, *Theory of Moral Sentiments*, Part IV, chapter 2: "Humanity is the virtue of a woman, generosity of a man. The fair sex, who have commonly much more tenderness than ours, have seldom so much generosity."

[15]After visiting Carthage in 157 BCE, Roman statesman Cato the Elder was convinced that the supremacy of Rome required the destruction of Carthage. He is said to have concluded every speech of his to the senate with "Delenda est Carthago" (Carthage must be destroyed). In *The Theory of Moral Sentiments*, Adam Smith calls this "the savage patriotism of a strong but coarse mind" (6.3.2).

So that to break the spirit, allowed to become vicious at home, a child is sent to school; and the methods taken there, which must be taken to keep a number of children in order, scatter the seeds of almost every vice in the soil thus forcibly torn up.

I have sometimes compared the struggles of these poor children, who ought never to have felt restraint, nor would, had they been always held in with an even hand, to the despairing plunges of a spirited filly, which I have seen breaking on a strand: its feet sinking deeper and deeper in the sand every time it endeavoured to throw its rider, till at last it sullenly submitted.

I have always found horses, animals I am attached to, very tractable when treated with humanity and steadiness, so that I doubt whether the violent methods taken to break them, do not essentially injure them; I am, however, certain that a child should never be thus forcibly tamed after it had injudiciously been allowed to run wild: for every violation of justice and reason, in the treatment of children, weakens their reason. And, so early do they catch a character, that the base of the moral character, experience leads me to infer, is fixed before their seventh year, the period during which women are allowed the sole management of children. Afterwards it too often happens that half the business of education is to correct, and very imperfectly is it done, if done hastily, the faults, which they would never have acquired if their mothers had had more understanding.

One striking instance of the folly of women must not be omitted.—The manner in which they treat servants in the presence of children, permitting them to suppose that they ought to wait on them, and bear their humours. A child should always be made to receive assistance from a man or woman as a favour; and, as the first lesson of independence, they should practically be taught, by the example of their mother, not to require that personal attendance, which it is an insult to humanity to require, when in health; and instead of being led to assume airs of consequence, a sense of their own weakness should first make them feel the natural equality of man. Yet, how frequently have I indignantly heard servants imperiously called to put children to bed, and sent away again and again, because master or miss hung about mamma, to stay a little longer. Thus made slavishly to attend the little idol, all those most disgusting humours were exhibited which characterize a spoiled child.

In short, speaking of the majority of mothers, they leave their children entirely to the care of servants; or, because they are their children, treat them as if they were little demi-gods, though I have always observed, that the women who thus idolize their children, seldom shew common humanity to servants, or feel the least tenderness for any children but their own.

It is, however, these exclusive affections, and an individual manner of seeing things, produced by ignorance, which keep women for ever at a stand, with respect to improvement, and make many of them dedicate their lives to their children only to weaken their bodies and spoil their tempers, frustrating also any plan of education that a more rational father may adopt; for unless a mother concur, the father who restrains will ever be considered as a tyrant.

But, fulfilling the duties of a mother, a woman with a sound constitution, may still keep her person scrupulously neat, and assist to maintain her family, if necessary, or by reading and conversations with both sexes, indiscriminately, improve her mind. For nature has so wisely ordered things, that did women suckle their children, they would preserve their own health, and there would be such an interval between the birth of each child, that we should seldom see a houseful of babes. And did they pursue a plan of conduct, and not waste their time in following the fashionable vagaries of dress, the management of their household and children need not shut them out from literature, or prevent their attaching themselves to a science, with that steady eye which strengthens the mind, or practising one of the fine arts that cultivate the taste.

But, visiting to display finery, card-playing, and balls, not to mention the idle bustle of morning trifling, draw women from their duty to render them insignificant, to render them pleasing, according to the present acceptation of the word, to every man, but their husband. For a round of pleasures in which the affections are not exercised, cannot be said to improve the understanding, though it be erroneously called seeing the world; yet the heart is rendered cold and averse to duty, by such a senseless intercourse, which becomes necessary from habit even when it has ceased to amuse.

But, we shall not see women affectionate till more equality be established in society, till ranks are confounded and women freed, neither shall we see that dignified domestic happiness, the simple grandeur of which cannot be relished by ignorant or vitiated minds; nor will the important task of education ever be properly begun till the person of a woman is no longer preferred to her mind. For it would be as wise to expect corn from tares, or figs from thistles, as that a foolish ignorant woman should be a good mother.[16]

---

[16]See ch. I, p. 32, n. 13.

SECTION VI

It is not necessary to inform the sagacious reader, now I enter on my concluding reflections, that the discussion of this subject merely consists in opening a few simple principles, and clearing away the rubbish which obscured them. But, as all readers are not sagacious, I must be allowed to add some explanatory remarks to bring the subject home to reason—to that sluggish reason, which supinely takes opinions on trust, and obstinately supports them to spare itself the labour of thinking.

Moralists have unanimously agreed, that unless virtue be nursed by liberty, it will never attain due strength—and what they say of man I extend to mankind, insisting that in all cases morals must be fixed on immutable principles; and, that the being cannot be termed rational or virtuous, who obeys any authority, but that of reason.

To render women truly useful members of society, I argue that they should be led, by having their undertakings cultivated on a large scale, to acquire a rational affection for their country, founded on knowledge, because it is obvious that we are little interested about what we do not understand. And to render this general knowledge of due importance, I have endeavoured to shew that private duties are never properly fulfilled unless the understanding enlarges the heart; and that public virtue is only an aggregate of private. But, the distinctions established in society undermine both, by beating out the solid gold of virtue, till it becomes only the tinsel-covering of vice; for whilst wealth renders a man more respectable than virtue, wealth will be sought before virtue; and, whilst women's persons are caressed, when a childish simper shews an absence of mind—the mind will lie fallow. Yet, true voluptuousness must proceed from the mind—for what can equal the sensations produced by mutual affection, supported by mutual respect? What are the cold, or feverish caresses of appetite, but sin embracing death,[17] compared with the modest overflowings of a pure heart and exalted imagination? Yes, let me tell the libertine of fancy when he despises understanding in woman—that the mind, which he disregards, gives life to the enthusiastic affection from which rapture, short-lived as it is, alone can flow! And, that, without virtue, a sexual attachment must expire, like a tallow candle in the socket, creating intolerable disgust. To prove this, I need only observe, that men who have wasted great part of their lives with women, and with whom

[17]MW rewrites Milton's allegory of Death raped by her incestuous son, Sin (*Paradise Lost*, 2.790–809).

they have sought for pleasure with eager thirst, entertain the meanest opinion of the sex.—Virtue, true refiner of joy!—if foolish men were to fright thee from earth, in order to give loose to all their appetites without a check—some sensual wight of taste would scale the heavens to invite thee back, to give a zest to pleasure!

That women at present are by ignorance rendered foolish or vicious, is, I think, not to be disputed; and, that the salutary effects tending to improve mankind might be expected from a REVOLUTION in female manners, appears, at least, with a face of probability, to rise out of the observation. For as marriage has been termed the parent of those endearing charities which draw man from the brutal herd, the corrupting intercourse that wealth, idleness, and folly, produce between the sexes, is more universally injurious to morality than all the other vices of mankind collectively considered. To adulterous lust the most sacred duties are sacrificed, because before marriage, men, by a promiscuous intimacy with women, learned to consider love as a selfish gratification—learned to separate it not only from esteem, but from the affection merely built on habit, which mixes a little humanity with it. Justice and friendship are also set at defiance, and that purity of taste is vitiated which would naturally lead a man to relish an artless display of affection rather than affected airs. But that noble simplicity of affection, which dares to appear unadorned, has few attractions for the libertine, though it be the charm, which by cementing the matrimonial tie, secures to the pledges of a warmer passion the necessary parental attention; for children will never be properly educated till friendship subsists between parents. Virtue flies from a house divided against itself—and a whole legion of devils take up their residence there.[18]

The affection of husbands and wives cannot be pure when they have so few sentiments in common, and when so little confidence is established at home, as must be the case when their pursuits are so different. That intimacy from which tenderness should flow, will not, cannot subsist between the vicious.

Contending, therefore, that the sexual distinction which men have so warmly insisted upon, is arbitrary, I have dwelt on an observation, that several sensible men, with whom I have conversed on the subject, allowed to be well founded; and it is simply this, that the lit-

---

[18]Jesus warns, "Every kingdom divided against itself is brought to desolation; and every city or house divided against itself shall not stand" (Matthew 12:25); a homeless man tells Jesus his name is "Legion: because many devils were entered into him . . ." (Luke 8:30).

tle chastity to be found amongst men, and consequent disregard of modesty, tend to degrade both sexes; and further, that the modesty of women, characterized as such, will often be only the artful veil of wantonness instead of being the natural reflection of purity, till modesty be universally respected.

From the tyranny of man, I firmly believe, the greater number of female follies proceed; and the cunning, which I allow makes at present a part of their character, I likewise have repeatedly endeavoured to prove, is produced by oppression.

Were not dissenters,[19] for instance, a class of people, with strict truth, characterized as cunning? And may I not lay some stress on this fact to prove, that when any power but reason curbs the free spirit of man, dissimulation is practised, and the various shifts of art are naturally called forth? Great attention to decorum, which was carried to a degree of scrupulosity, and all that puerile bustle about trifles and consequential solemnity, which Butler's caricature of a dissenter, brings before the imagination, shaped their persons as well as their minds in the mould of prim littleness.[20] I speak collectively, for I know how many ornaments to human nature have been enrolled amongst sectaries[21]; yet, I assert, that the same narrow prejudice for their sect, which women have for their families, prevailed in the dissenting part of the community, however worthy in other respects; and also that the same timid prudence, or headstrong efforts, often disgraced the exertions of both. Oppression thus formed many of the features of their character perfectly to coincide with that of the oppressed half of mankind; for is it not notorious that dissenters were, like women, fond of deliberating together, and asking advice of each other, till by a complication of little contrivances, some little end was brought about? A similar attention to preserve their reputation was conspicuous in the dissenting and female world, and was produced by a similar cause.

Asserting the rights which women in common with men ought to contend for, I have not attempted to extenuate their faults; but to prove them to be the natural consequence of their education and sta-

---

[19]Those who dissented from the established Church of England; many of MW's friends and acquaintances were dissenters.

[20]Samuel Butler (1612–80) portrayed a hypocritical dissenter in his "Hypocritical Nonconformist" (in the posthumous *Genuine Remains in Verse and Prose* [1759], 2.35), and in his celebrated satiric romance, *Hudibras* (1662–63), its mock-hero a meddling Puritan knight.

[21]Religious sects.

tion in society. If so, it is reasonable to suppose that they will change their character, and correct their vices and follies, when they are allowed to be free in a physical, moral, and civil sense.[22]

Let woman share the rights, and she will emulate the virtues of man, for she must grow more perfect when emancipated, or justify the authority that chains such a weak being to her duty.—If the latter, it will be expedient to open a fresh trade with Russia for whips[23]; a present which a father should always make to his son-in-law on his wedding day, that a husband may keep his whole family in order by the same means; and without any violation of justice reign, wielding this sceptre, sole master of his house, because he is the only being in it who has reason:—the divine, indefeasible earthly sovereignty breathed into man by the Master of the universe. Allowing this position, women have not any inherent rights to claim; and, by the same rule, their duties vanish, for rights and duties are inseparable.

Be just then, O ye men of understanding! and mark not more severely what women do amiss, than the vicious tricks of the horse or the ass for whom ye provide provender—and allow her the privileges of ignorance, to whom ye deny the rights of reason, or ye will be worse than Egyptian task-masters, expecting virtue where nature has not given understanding!

---

[22]I had further enlarged on the advantages which might reasonably be expected to result from an improvement in female manners, towards the general reformation of society; but it appeared to me that such reflections would more properly close the last volume [MW]. No further volumes were published.

[23]Russians were notorious for wife-beating and for flogging convicts and peasants.

The Wrongs of Woman, or Maria

by Mary Wollstonecraft

Introduction

Five years after publishing *A Vindication of the Rights of Woman*, Wollstonecraft began a sequel, a novel in which she laid bare the social evils and legal injustices perpetrated against women in late eighteenth-century England. She deliberately broadened her scope, focusing as much on lower-class women as on the literate middle classes to whom she addressed *A Vindication*. She further showed how the genre of the novel could be recuperated for political purposes. The corrected and uncorrected portions of the manuscript of this novel, together with Wollstonecraft's contradictory outlines and sketches for its conclusion, were published by William Godwin in *Posthumous Works of the Author of A Vindication of the Rights of Woman* (London: Joseph Johnson, 1798).

The Wrongs of Woman as Autobiography

A far more pessimistic vision than *Vindication*, *The Wrongs of Woman* draws heavily on Wollstonecraft's experiences, especially her unhappy childhood and her love affair with Gilbert Imlay. Maria Venables' account of her family history bears a striking resemblance to Wollstonecraft's own, with one notable exception: Wollstonecraft had no loving, wealthy uncle to alleviate her sufferings. Like Maria, Wollstonecraft faithfully nursed her mother during her long final illness, only to be sent away at the last moment so that her mother could die in her favored son's arms. Wollstonecraft's sister Eliza married a man, Meredith Bishop, who was a working-class version of George Venables: brutish, irrational, and cruel. Wollstonecraft was so dismayed that she persuaded Eliza to abandon both husband and newborn child, a decision that Eliza ever afterward regretted. Gilbert Imlay is clearly the model for Maria's lover Darnford.

What Are the "Wrongs" of Woman?

Wollstonecraft's title contains a deliberate ambiguity: The wrongs "of" woman are both the wrongs done *to* women and the wrongs done *by* women. Wollstonecraft begins her novel by detailing the wrongs committed against women in late eighteenth-century England.

Marriage

"Marriage had bastilled me for life" (pp. 316–17), Maria Venables announces with a metaphor that gives the political argument: The British legal institution of *coverture* reduced wives to the same condition as the prisoners in the notorious French prison, the Bastille, suffering an arbitrary tyranny from which there was no recourse to justice or liberty. Thus constrained, British wives were legal "slaves." In 1772, Lord Mansfield had ruled that the institution of slavery was illegal on English soil, yet by letting stand the claim that marriage was a form of "villeinage" (or indentured servitude), he implicitly upheld the view that slavery within marriage was not illegal. It was this legal construction of the British wife as a slave that Wollstonecraft had in mind when in *Vindication* she referred to "the slavery of marriage" (p. 188): "I call women slaves, I mean in a political and civil sense" (p. 202). She insists on this again in *The Wrongs of Woman*, where Maria protests, "Was not the world a vast prison, and women born slaves?" (p. 253).

Like an African slave, Maria's body is bought and sold without her consent. Her uncle values her body at £5,000 (a nice fortune in the eighteenth century), a dowry given to a man who promptly gambles away this money. George Venables then sexually abuses Maria, legally raping her—enforcing his "conjugal rights"—repeatedly. He then sells her for £500 to his friend, treating her like a prostitute. Attempting to escape this completely legal abuse, Maria recognizes that "A wife being as much a man's property as his horse, or his ass, she has nothing she can call her own" (p. 320). Not even her own body: Here Wollstonecraft uncovered the sexist dimensions of John Locke's argument that the basis of a liberal republic is the concept that "every man has property in his own person." In a critique of Locke titled *The Sexual Contract* (1988), Carol Pateman noted that under British law no woman possessed her own person. Wollstonecraft sharpened this argument with a telling detail: When George Venables impresses Maria by giving her alms for charity, it is with a guinea (p. 302), the coin minted by the Royal African Trading Society specifically to pay for kidnapped and enslaved Africans. The guinea (£1 plus one shilling because a pound of slave flesh was worth "more") was circulated in West Guinea, and so closely associated with the slave trade that slave ships were commonly called "guinea-men." Venables is thus revealed as a "guinea-man," a slave owner and slave trader. His name further identifies him with the state and the church, the two sources of patriarchal power, specifically King George III of England and the historian of the early English church, the "Venerable Bede."

When we first encounter Maria, she is imprisoned in a madhouse. In late eighteenth-century England, men had a legal right to confine wives and female relatives at home or in private madhouses. *A Report from the Committee appointed to Enquire into the State of the Private Madhouses in this Kingdom* documented the extensive use of madhouses to imprison disobedient wives and daughters. In order to prevent Maria's escape from her marriage, her husband has legally drugged her, ripped her newborn nursing daughter from her breast, and confined her to a private madhouse.

In her Author's Preface, Wollstonecraft insists that Maria's case is not unique, but representative. *The Wrongs of Woman* gives numerous examples across *all* classes: Upper-middle-class and sane Maria is imprisoned in a madhouse; lower-middle-class Peggy, wife of a sailor who has been legally kidnapped ("impressed") into the King's Navy, has lost her home, her furniture, and her clothes and is forced into begging and prostitution (p. 298); an upper-working-class landlady and shopkeeper is regularly beaten by a husband who then spends all her earnings on drink (p. 331); a middle-working-class servant girl who has scraped up enough money to run a boarding-house is married to a footman who steals all her money to run off with a "slut," then returns, after six years in the army, to take all her money, reducing her to beggary (p. 336–37). At the lowest rung, the bastard-child Jemima is "born a slave" (p. 278), hired out to do slave labor first for her wet nurse, then her stepmother, and finally for the owner of a slop-shop (a used clothing store). She runs away to become a thief and prostitute, then the mistress of an aging libertine of "vitiated tastes"; when he dies, she attempts honest labor as a washerwoman but is summarily dismissed when she is injured at work. Finally, she becomes the attendant in a woman's madhouse, forced to do the keeper's bidding.

Wollstonecraft designed these comprehensive portrayals of the wrongs done to women to broadcast the necessity for legal reform. Above all, she hoped that women could gain the legal status of "persons" so they could own the "property in their own person," their own bodies and the wages of their own labor. She also mounted a case for liberalizing the laws governing marriage, divorce, and child custody. Maria's revered uncle presents a powerfully cogent argument for a marriage based on rational love and for the legality of divorce when such a marriage does not exist (p. 319–20). Under the double standard of British law, men could commit adultery but women could not. The irrationality is depicted in the legal case Venables brings against Maria's lover Darnford, suing him for having "criminal conversation" with his wife—for "alienating his wife's affections" and thereby stealing his property. When Maria, who has no legal standing in court, writes to the judge that Venables never possessed her "affections" in the first place, the judge rejects her argument as an example of French Revolutionary doctrine and decides in favor of Venables.

Work

The second greatest wrong done to women is society's failure to provide respectable and profitable employment, beyond the poorly paid, demeaning work of governess, companion, and fancy needlework. Sewing by candlelight soon ruins the eyesight, and being a governess or companion is "a dependence next to menial" (p. 311). Working-class women must accept back-breaking physical labor, beggary, thievery, or prostitution. No wonder Maria sighs in her memoir for her lost daughter, "to find employment was then to find variety, the animating principle of nature" (p. 254). Given women's precarious economic situation, women were often forced to turn against each other in order to survive. Jemima can obtain a home for herself only by driving out her libertine lover's former mistress, a pregnant servant girl who then drowns herself (p. 286). But Wollstonecraft balances the account of women's cruelty to other women with examples of sisterhood: Maria cares for her younger sisters, the landladies try to help Maria as much as is in their power, and Jemima finally enables Maria to escape.

Sensibility and the Female Body

Wollstonecraft was even more concerned with showing the subtle but equally devastating wrongs that women do to themselves, unintentionally but voluntarily. The greatest of these is an indulgence in the wrong kind of sensibility. In the eighteenth century, "sensibility" was a charged concept. The most progressive definition produced by the leading philosophers of the Scottish and English Enlightenment (Lord Shaftesbury, David Hume, and Adam Smith) equated it with a benevolent sympathy, the foundation both of individual virtue and refined civilization. In its most radical political implications, sensibility was democratic: The virtuous life of compassionate benevolence to all living things was available to everyone. The society with sensibility would operate on an ethic of care, a moral policy that no one should get hurt. Sensibility thus infused such nineteenth-century reform movements as the campaigns to abolish slavery, to relieve the poor, to reform the prisons, and to provide public hospitals.

In her first novel, *Mary, A Fiction* (1788), Wollstonecraft had invoked sensibility as "the foundation of all our happiness." Heroine Mary enthuses,

> Sensibility is the most exquisite feeling of which the human soul is susceptible: when it pervades us, we feel happy; and could it last unmixed, we might form some conjecture of the bliss of those paradisiacal days, when the obedient passions were under the dominion of reason, and the impulses of the heart did not need correction.
>
> It is this quickness, this delicacy of feeling, which enables us to relish the sublime touches of the poet, and the painter; it is this, which expands the soul, gives an enthusiastic greatness, mixed with tenderness, when we view the magnificent objects of nature; or hear of a good action. . . . Softened by tenderness; the soul is disposed to be virtuous. Is any sensual gratification to be compared to that of feeling the eyes moistened after having comforted the unfortunate?[1]

---

[1] *Mary, A Fiction*, ed. Janet Todd. London: Penguin Books, 1991, 43.

Sensibility is ideally aligned with reason, producing what critic Chris Jones has called the educated heart.[2] As another critic, Ann Jessie Van Sant, proposed, "Sensibility when associated with moral and aesthetic response is sometimes as close in meaning to elevated thought as to feeling."[3]

Sensibility carried a powerful gender implication. Thought to have more delicate nervous systems than men, females were also thought to have a greater capacity for feeling or sensibility. Sensibility was thus closely allied to the female body, to the sensations as well as mental impressions. Many women writers of Wollstonecraft's day, notably and influentially Hannah More, insisted that since women were capable of a more refined sensibility, they were more virtuous than men and thus should command more cultural respect. But this gendering also had negative consequences. As Wollstonecraft lamented, too many women cultivated feeling to excess, eagerly seeking out real or fictional suffering to rouse them to tears, often spending long hours sobbing over a novel while doing nothing to alleviate real misery. In *Rights of Woman*, Wollstonecraft argued fiercely against this culture of emotional intensity for its own sake. Such women, she insisted, were but "creatures of sensation" (p. 83): "Their senses are inflamed, and their understandings neglected, consequently they become the prey of their senses, delicately termed sensibility, and are blown about by every momentary gust of feeling" (pp. 82–83).

In *The Wrongs of Woman*, Wollstonecraft dramatized these dangers. Maria Venables initially appears just such a "creature of sensation." Already in severe pain of being robbed of her baby and confined in a madhouse, she has no capacity for "sober reflection" (p. 250). And here, books feed this "intoxicated sensibility" (p. 255)—they are stories of passionate but frustrated love (Dryden's romance of Guiscard and Sigismunda, Rousseau's *Julie, ou la Nouvelle Héloïse*, based on the historical romance of Eloise and Abelard). Moreover, the "voluptuous" Maria (p. 270) is deeply invested in the sensations of her own body—now racked by the pain of her "burning bosom" (p. 249), she is revolted by her husband's "squalid appearance . . . lolling in an

---

[2] "Mary Wollstonecraft's *Vindications* and Their Political Tradition," in *The Cambridge Companion to Mary Wollstonecraft*, ed. Claudia Johnson. Cambridge: Cambridge University Press, 2002, 45.

[3] *Eighteenth-Century Sensibility and the Novel*, 7.

arm-chair, in a dirty powdering gown, soiled linen, ungartered stockings, and tangled hair, yawning and stretching himself" (p. 310). When she catches a glimpse of Darnford in the prison yard, her sexual desire is aroused by his "steady, bold step, and the whole air of his person" (p. 262).

Maria's confinement in a madhouse thus has double meaning. On the one hand, it demonstrates the power of a patriarchal society to define "madness" and to incarcerate as "insane" those who resist—a discourse tracked by Michel Foucault's *Madness and Civilisation* (1965). On the other hand, her "intoxicated sensibility" suggests a disorder, an "uproar of the passions" that blacks out the "lucid beam of reason" (p. 264). Feeding on romantic novels, she imagines Darnford as Rousseau's St. Preux, her lover and savior, just as she had earlier idealized the wicked George Venables: "I fancied myself in love— in love with the disinterestedness, fortitude, generosity, dignity, and humanity, with which I had invested the hero I dubbed" (p. 298). Despite Darnford's history (we learn that he is an arrogant, snobbish, self-serving libertine and opportunist), Maria sees him as her salvation, dismissing his faults as "the generous luxuriancy of a noble mind" (p. 266).

Maria will learn to read more critically, to see the discrepancy between books and the real world, as Jemima has learned before her. With new capacities for rational understanding, she will recognize that "True sensibility, the sensibility which is the auxiliary of virtue and the soul of genius, is in society so occupied with the feelings of others, as scarcely to regard its own sensations" (p. 336). In so doing, she may open the way to a new mode of sexual desire, one that aligns desires with rational perception.

Genre and Structure

Maria is both a reader and a writer. Her compositions raise a critical question: How can a female writer speak so as to be heard and believed? What is an appropriate genre and style for a convincing voice? Wollstonecraft's opening paragraphs raise the issue of genre:

> Abodes of horror have frequently been described, and castles, filled with spectres and chimeras, conjured up by the magic spell of genius to harrow the soul, and absorb the wondering mind. (p. 249)

This sounds like the bestselling genre of the 1790s, gothic romance, complete with ghosts, ruined castles, and sublime terror. But Wollstonecraft insisted she was writing a true story, a history, a realistic representation of women's sufferings. So, too, Maria abjures romantic "rhapsodies" in favor of autobiography, a memoir designed to "instruct" her daughter. *The Wrongs of Woman, or Maria* is clearly intended to be a realistic novel and not a gothic romance— and yet Maria sits in "a mansion of despair" that threatens to "fire her brain"(p. 249), where she is "haunted by Mr. Venables' image" (p. 338) and pursued by demons. How should we address this apparent contradiction? Wollstonecraft meant to show that these "gothic" horrors are social realities for women: The world of the gothic exists within the average English household, that violence against women is everywhere most monstrous and most ordinary.

Concluding the Novel

The fragmentary notes for ending *The Wrongs of Woman* published by William Godwin suggest two very different conclusions. In both versions, George Venables wins his suit against Darnford, who then leaves England and a pregnant Maria rather than pay his fine. Maria discovers that Darnford, like Gilbert Imlay, has taken another mistress. In despair, she loses her child (either miscarriage or an abortion). The notes then diverge.

In one version, Maria commits suicide, implying that in any realistic novel of the 1790s, the female voice must be silenced, both as author and as subject, since a woman has no legal personhood: The judge in Venable's case insists that it is a "fallacy" to let women "plead their feelings, as an excuse" for their actions (p. 354). A second, longer version is more optimistic. Overdosing on a sleeping draught (laudanum), Maria is saved by Jemima, who has found her first daughter. As Wollstonecraft herself had done after her second suicide attempt, Maria agrees to "live for my child." In an alternative to marriage, a family-of-choice composed of women, Jemima will be a co-mother and fully paid partner in the rearing of Maria's daughter. What both endings have in common is the suggestion (a revolutionary one) that heterosexual marriages and families based on law and blood do not work. If *A Vindication of the Rights of Woman* had proposed that a new, utopian society based on sexual equality and companionate marriage might be possible, *The Wrongs of Woman* erases this possibility with a relentless catalogue of marriages in which wives are beaten, robbed, raped, thrown out, abandoned, incarcerated, in which husbands are tyrants and delinquents. That all marriages contracted under British law may contract into prisons and the legalized enslavement of women is the deepest terror of *The Wrongs of Woman*, and it's no gothic nightmare, but rather, a political insight of the severest sensibility.

Anne K. Mellor

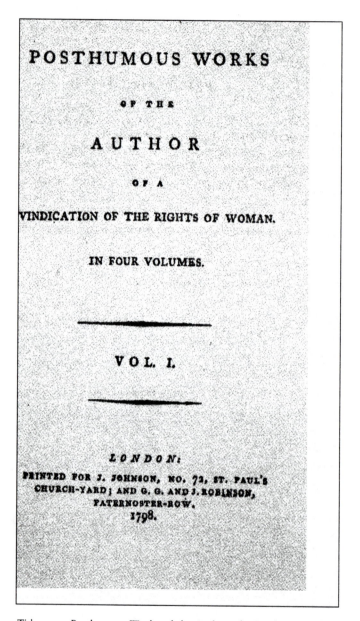

POSTHUMOUS WORKS

OF THE

AUTHOR

OF A

VINDICATION OF THE RIGHTS OF WOMAN.

IN FOUR VOLUMES.

———————

VOL. I.

———————

LONDON:

PRINTED FOR J. JOHNSON, NO, 72, ST. PAUL'S
CHURCH-YARD; AND G. G. AND J. ROBINSON,
PATERNOSTER-ROW.
1798.

Title page, *Posthumous Works of the Author of a Vindication of the Rights of Woman*. In Four Volumes. Ed. William Godwin (London: 1798).

The Wrongs of Woman,
or Maria
(1798)

‿ℰ∿ℒ‿

A FRAGMENT IN TWO VOLUMES

PREFACE

The public are here presented with the last literary attempt of an author, whose fame has been uncommonly extensive, and whose talents
have probably been most admired, by the persons by whom talents
are estimated with the greatest accuracy and discrimination. There
are few, to whom her writings could in any case have given pleasure,
that would have wished that this fragment should have been suppressed, because it is a fragment. There is a sentiment, very dear to
minds of taste and imagination, that finds a melancholy delight in
contemplating these unfinished productions of genius, these sketches
of what, if they had been filled up in a manner adequate to the
writer's conception, would perhaps have given a new impulse to the
manners of a world.

The purpose and structure of the following work, had long
formed a favourite subject of meditation with its author, and she
judged them capable of producing an important effect. The composition had been in progress for a period of twelve months. She was anxious to do justice to her conception, and recommenced and revised
the manuscript several different times. So much of it as is here given
to the public, she was far from considering as finished, and, in a letter
to a friend directly written on this subject, she says, "I am perfectly
aware that some of the incidents ought to be transposed, and heightened by more harmonious shading; and I wished in some degree to

avail myself of criticism, before I began to adjust my events into a story, the outline of which I had sketched in my mind."[1] The only friends to whom the author communicated her manuscript, were Mr. Dyson,[2] the translator of the Sorcerer, and the present editor; and it was impossible for the most inexperienced author to display a stronger desire of profiting by the censures and sentiments that might be suggested.[3]

In revising these sheets for the press, it was necessary for the editor, in some places, to connect the more finished parts with the pages of an older copy, and a line or two in addition sometimes appeared requisite for that purpose. Wherever such a liberty has been taken, the additional phrases will be found inclosed in brackets; it being the editor's most earnest desire, to intrude nothing of himself into the work, but to give to the public the words, as well as ideas, of the real author.

What follows in the ensuing pages, is not a preface regularly drawn out by the author, but merely hints for a preface, which, though never filled up in the manner the writer intended, appeared to be worth preserving.

W. GODWIN.

---

[1] A more copious extract of this letter is subjoined to the author's preface [WG].

[2] Godwin cites London radical George Dyson (d. 1822) as one of "four principal oral instructors" who influenced his intellectual development. The letter in the Author's Preface is addressed for Dyson. Dyson's translation of Veit Weber's *The Sorcerer* was published in 1795.

[3] The part communicated consisted of the first fourteen chapters [WG].

AUTHOR'S PREFACE.

The Wrongs of Woman, like the wrongs of the oppressed part of mankind, may be deemed necessary by their oppressors: but surely there are a few, who will dare to advance before the improvement of the age, and grant that my sketches are not the abortion of a distempered fancy, or the strong delineations of a wounded heart.

In writing this novel, I have rather endeavoured to pourtray passions than manners.

In many instances I could have made the incidents more dramatic, would I have sacrificed my main object, the desire of exhibiting the misery and oppression, peculiar to women, that arise out of the partial laws and customs of society.

In the invention of the story, this view restrained my fancy; and the history ought rather to be considered, as of woman, than of an individual.

The sentiments I have embodied.

In many works of this species, the hero is allowed to be mortal, and to become wise and virtuous as well as happy, by a train of events and circumstances. The heroines, on the contrary, are to be born immaculate; and to act like goddesses of wisdom, just come forth highly finished Minervas from the head of Jove.[1]

[The following is an extract of a letter from the author to a friend, to whom she communicated her manuscript.]

For my part, I cannot suppose any situation more distressing, than for a woman of sensibility, with an improving mind, to be bound to such a man as I have described for life; obliged to renounce all the humanizing affections, and to avoid cultivating her taste, lest her perception of grace and refinement of sentiment, should sharpen to agony the pangs of disappointment. Love, in which the imagination mingles its bewitching colouring, must be fostered by delicacy. I should despise, or rather call her an ordinary woman, who could endure such a husband as I have sketched.

---

[1]Alluding to the myth of Minerva, the Roman goddess of wisdom, who sprang fully formed and in armor, from the forehead of her father Jove (Jupiter), the king of the gods.

These appear to me (matrimonial despotism of heart and conduct) to be the peculiar Wrongs of Woman, because they degrade the mind. What are termed great misfortunes, may more forcibly impress the mind of common readers; they have more of what may justly be termed *stage-effect*; but it is the delineation of finer sensations, which, in my opinion, constitutes the merit of our best novels. This is what I have in view; and to show the wrongs of different classes of women, equally oppressive, though, from the difference of education, necessarily various.

VOLUME I

CHAPTER I

Abodes of horror have frequently been described, and castles, filled with spectres and chimeras, conjured up by the magic spell of genius to harrow the soul, and absorb the wondering mind. But, formed of such stuff as dreams are made of,[1] what were they to the mansion of despair, in one corner of which Maria sat, endeavouring to recall her scattered thoughts!

Surprise, astonishment, that bordered on distraction, seemed to have suspended her faculties, till, waking by degrees to a keen sense of anguish, a whirlwind of rage and indignation roused her torpid pulse. One recollection with frightful velocity following another, threatened to fire her brain, and make her a fit companion for the terrific inhabitants, whose groans and shrieks were no unsubstantial sounds of whistling winds, or startled birds, modulated by a romantic fancy, which amuse while they affright; but such tones of misery as carry a dreadful certainty directly to the heart. What effect must they then have produced on one, true to the touch of sympathy, and tortured by maternal apprehension!

Her infant's image was continually floating on Maria's sight, and the first smile of intelligence remembered, as none but a mother, an unhappy mother, can conceive. She heard her half speaking half cooing, and felt the little twinkling fingers on her burning bosom—a bosom bursting with the nutriment for which this cherished child might now be pining in vain. From a stranger she could indeed receive the maternal aliment, Maria was grieved at the thought—but who would watch her with a mother's tenderness, a mother's self-denial?

The retreating shadows of former sorrows rushed back in a gloomy train, and seemed to be pictured on the walls of her prison, magnified by the state of mind in which they were viewed—Still she mourned for her child, lamented she was a daughter, and anticipated the aggravated ills of life that her sex rendered almost inevitable, even while dreading she was no more. To think that she was blotted out of existence was agony, when the imagination had been long employed to expand her faculties; yet to suppose her turned adrift on an unknown sea, was scarcely less afflicting.

[1]Magician Prospero's description of life: "We are such stuff / As dreams are made on." (*Tempest*, 4.1.156–57); spectres and chimeras populate the regions of hell in Milton's *Paradise Lost*.

After being two days the prey of impetuous, varying emotions, Maria began to reflect more calmly on her present situation, for she had actually been rendered incapable of sober reflection, by the discovery of the act of atrocity of which she was the victim. She could not have imagined, that, in all the fermentation of civilized depravity, a similar plot could have entered a human mind. She had been stunned by an unexpected blow; yet life, however joyless, was not to be indolently resigned, or misery endured without exertion, and proudly termed patience. She had hitherto meditated only to point the dart of anguish, and suppressed the heart heavings of indignant nature merely by the force of contempt. Now she endeavoured to brace her mind to fortitude, and to ask herself what was to be her employment in her dreary cell? Was it not to effect her escape, to fly to the succour of her child, and to baffle the selfish schemes of her tyrant—her husband?

These thoughts roused her sleeping spirit, and the self-possession returned, that seemed to have abandoned her in the infernal solitude into which she had been precipitated. The first emotions of overwhelming impatience began to subside, and resentment gave place to tenderness, and more tranquil meditation; though anger once more stopt the calm current of reflection, when she attempted to move her manacled arms. But this was an outrage that could only excite momentary feelings of scorn, which evaporated in a faint smile; for Maria was far from thinking a personal insult the most difficult to endure with magnanimous indifference.

She approached the small grated window of her chamber, and for a considerable time only regarded the blue expanse; though it commanded a view of a desolate garden, and of part of a huge pile of buildings, that, after having been suffered, for half a century, to fall to decay, had undergone some clumsy repairs, merely to render it habitable. The ivy had been torn off the turrets, and the stones not wanted to patch up the breaches of time, and exclude the warring elements, left in heaps in the disordered court. Maria contemplated this scene she knew not how long; or rather gazed on the walls, and pondered on her situation. To the master of this most horrid of prisons, she had, soon after her entrance, raved of injustice, in accents that would have justified his treatment, had not a malignant smile, when she appealed to his judgment, with a dreadful conviction stifled her remonstrating complaints. By force, or openly, what could be done? But surely some expedient might occur to an active mind, without any other employment, and possessed of sufficient resolution to put the risk of life into the balance with the chance of freedom.

A woman entered in the midst of these reflections, with a firm, deliberate step, strongly marked features, and large black eyes, which she fixed steadily on Maria's, as if she designed to intimidate her, saying at the same time—"You had better sit down and eat your dinner, than look at the clouds."

"I have no appetite," replied Maria, who had previously determined to speak mildly; "why then should I eat?"

"But, in spite of that, you must and shall eat something. I have had many ladies under my care, who have resolved to starve themselves; but, soon or late, they gave up their intent, as they recovered their senses."

"Do you really think me mad?" asked Maria, meeting the searching glance of her eye.

"Not just now. But what does that prove?—only that you must be the more carefully watched, for appearing at times so reasonable. You have not touched a morsel since you entered the house."—Maria sighed intelligibly.—"Could any thing but madness produce such a disgust for food?"

"Yes, grief; you would not ask the question if you knew what it was." The attendant shook her head; and a ghastly smile of desperate fortitude served as a forcible reply, and made Maria pause, before she added—"Yet I will take some refreshment: I mean not to die.—No; I will preserve my senses; and convince even you, sooner than you are aware of, that my intellects have never been disturbed, though the exertion of them may have been suspended by some infernal drug."

Doubt gathered still thicker on the brow of her guard, as she attempted to convict her of mistake.

"Have patience!" exclaimed Maria, with a solemnity that inspired awe. "My God! how have I been schooled into the practice!" A suffocation of voice betrayed the agonizing emotions she was labouring to keep down; and conquering a qualm of disgust, she calmly endeavoured to eat enough to prove her docility, perpetually turning to the suspicious female, whose observation she courted, while she was making the bed and adjusting the room.

"Come to me often," said Maria, with a tone of persuasion, in consequence of a vague plan that she had hastily adopted, when, after surveying this woman's form and features, she felt convinced that she had an understanding above the common standard; "and believe me mad, till you are obliged to acknowledge the contrary." The woman was no fool, that is, she was superior to her class; nor had misery quite petrified the life's-blood of humanity, to which reflections on our own misfortunes only give a more orderly course. The manner, rather than the expostulations, of Maria made a slight suspicion dart into her mind with corresponding sympathy, which various other avocations, and the habit of banishing compunction, prevented her, for the present, from examining more minutely.

But when she was told that no person, excepting the physician appointed by her family, was to be permitted to see the lady at the end of the gallery, she opened her keen eyes still wider, and uttered a—"hem!" before she enquired—"Why?" She was briefly told, in reply, that the malady was hereditary, and the fits not occurring but at very long and irregular intervals, she must be carefully watched; for the length of these lucid periods only rendered her more mischievous, when any vexation or caprice brought on the paroxysm of phrensy.

Had her master trusted her, it is probable that neither pity nor curiosity would have made her swerve from the straight line of her interest; for she had suffered too much in her intercourse with mankind, not to determine to look for support, rather to humouring their passions, than courting their approbation by the integrity of her conduct. A deadly blight had met her at the very threshold of existence; and the wretchedness of her mother seemed a heavy weight fastened on her innocent neck, to drag her down to perdition. She could not heroically determine to succour an unfortunate; but, offended at the bare supposition that she could be deceived with the same ease as a common servant, she no longer curbed her curiosity; and, though she never seriously fathomed her own intentions, she would sit, every moment she could steal from observation, listening to the tale, which Maria was eager to relate with all the persuasive eloquence of grief.

It is so cheering to see a human face, even if little of the divinity of virtue beam in it, that Maria anxiously expected the return of the attendant, as of a gleam of light to break the gloom of idleness. Indulged sorrow, she perceived, must blunt or sharpen the faculties to the two opposite extremes; producing stupidity, the moping melancholy of indolence; or the restless activity of a disturbed imagination. She sunk into one state, after being fatigued by the other: till the want of occupation became even more painful than the actual pressure or apprehension of sorrow; and the confinement that froze her into a nook of existence, with an unvaried prospect before her, the most insupportable of evils. The lamp of life seemed to be spending itself to chase the vapours of a dungeon which no art could dissipate.—And to what purpose did she rally all her energy?—Was not the world a vast prison, and women born slaves?

Though she failed immediately to rouse a lively sense of injustice in the mind of her guard, because it had been sophisticated[2] into misanthropy, she touched her heart. Jemima (she had only a claim to a Christian name, which had not procured her any Christian privileges)[3] could patiently hear of Maria's confinement on false pretences; she had felt the crushing hand of power, hardened by the exercise of injustice, and ceased to wonder at the perversions of the understanding, which systematize oppression; but, when told that her child, only four months old, had been torn from her, even while she was discharging the tenderest maternal office, the woman awoke in a bosom long estranged from feminine emotions, and Jemima determined to alleviate all in her power, without hazarding the loss of her place, the sufferings of a wretched mother, apparently injured, and certainly unhappy. A sense of right seems to result from the simplest act of reason, and to preside over the faculties of the mind, like the master-sense of feeling, to rectify the rest[4]; but (for the comparison may be carried still farther) how often is the exquisite sensibility of both weakened or destroyed by the vulgar occupations, and ignoble pleasures of life?

The preserving her situation was, indeed, an important object to Jemima, who had been hunted from hole to hole, as if she had been a beast of prey, or infected with a moral plague. The wages she received, the greater part of which she hoarded, as her only chance for independence, were much more considerable than she could reckon on obtaining any where else, were it possible that she, an outcast

---

[2]Corrupted.

[3]Jemima, as a bastard with no acknowledged father, has only a first name, usually given at christening. It is a rueful irony that Jemima is the name Job gives to the first of his daughters after his restoration to prosperity; he gives them "inheritance" with their brothers (Job 42:13–14).

[4]The Enlightenment view that reason can perceive right from wrong, and direct behavior accordingly—voiced by Richard Price and Godwin, among others.

from society, could be permitted to earn a subsistence in a reputable family. Hearing Maria perpetually complain of listlessness, and the not being able to beguile grief by resuming her customary pursuits, she was easily prevailed on, by compassion, and that involuntary respect for abilities, which those who possess them can never eradicate, to bring her some books and implements for writing. Maria's conversation had amused and interested her, and the natural consequence was a desire, scarcely observed by herself, of obtaining the esteem of a person she admired. The remembrance of better days was rendered more lively; and the sentiments then acquired appearing less romantic than they had for a long period, a spark of hope roused her mind to new activity.

How grateful was her attention to Maria! Oppressed by a dead weight of existence, or preyed on by the gnawing worm of discontent, with what eagerness did she endeavour to shorten the long days, which left no traces behind! She seemed to be sailing on the vast ocean of life, without seeing any land-mark to indicate the progress of time; to find employment was then to find variety, the animating principle of nature.

CHAPTER II

Earnestly as Maria endeavoured to soothe, by reading, the anguish of her wounded mind, her thoughts would often wander from the subject she was led to discuss, and tears of maternal tenderness obscured the reasoning page. She descanted on "the ills which flesh is heir to,"[1] with bitterness, when the recollection of her babe was revived by a tale of fictitious woe, that bore any resemblance to her own; and her imagination was continually employed, to conjure up and embody the various phantoms of misery, which folly and vice had let loose on the world. The loss of her babe was the tender string; against other cruel remembrances she laboured to steel her bosom; and even a ray of hope, in the midst of her gloomy reveries, would sometimes gleam on the dark horizon of futurity, while persuading herself that she ought to cease to hope, since happiness was no where to be found.—

---

[1] In a famous soliloquy, Hamlet laments, "The heart-ache, and the thousand natural shocks / That flesh is heir to" (3.1.63–64).

But of her child, debilitated by the grief with which its mother had been assailed before it saw the light, she could not think without an impatient struggle.

"I, alone, by my active tenderness, could have saved," she would exclaim, "from an early blight, this sweet blossom; and, cherishing it, I should have had something still to love."

In proportion as other expectations were torn from her, this tender one had been fondly clung to, and knit into her heart.

The books she had obtained, were soon devoured, by one who had no other resource to escape from sorrow, and the feverish dreams of ideal wretchedness or felicity, which equally weaken the intoxicated sensibility. Writing was then the only alternative, and she wrote some rhapsodies descriptive of the state of her mind; but the events of her past life pressing on her, she resolved circumstantially to relate them, with the sentiments that experience, and more matured reason, would naturally suggest. They might perhaps instruct her daughter, and shield her from the misery, the tyranny, her mother knew not how to avoid.

This thought gave life to her diction, her soul flowed into it, and she soon found the task of recollecting almost obliterated impressions very interesting. She lived again in the revived emotions of youth, and forgot her present in the retrospect of sorrows that had assumed an unalterable character.

Though this employment lightened the weight of time, yet, never losing sight of her main object, Maria did not allow any opportunity to slip of winning on the affections of Jemima; for she discovered in her a strength of mind, that excited her esteem, clouded as it was by the misanthropy of despair.

An insulated being, from the misfortune of her birth, she despised and preyed on the society by which she had been oppressed, and loved not her fellow-creatures, because she had never been beloved. No mother had ever fondled her, no father or brother had protected her from outrage; and the man who had plunged her into infamy, and deserted her when she stood in greatest need of support, deigned not to smooth with kindness the road to ruin. Thus degraded, was she let loose on the world; and virtue, never nurtured by affection, assumed the stern aspect of selfish independence.

This general view of her life, Maria gathered from her exclamations and dry remarks. Jemima indeed displayed a strange mixture of interest and suspicion; for she would listen to her with earnestness, and then suddenly interrupt the conversation, as if afraid of resigning, by giving way to her sympathy, her dear-bought knowledge of the world.

Maria alluded to the possibility of an escape, and mentioned a compensation, or reward; but the style in which she was repulsed made her cautious, and determine not to renew the subject, till she knew more of the character she had to work on. Jemima's countenance, and dark hints, seemed to say, "You are an extraordinary woman; but let me consider, this may only be one of your lucid intervals." Nay, the very energy of Maria's character, made her suspect that the extraordinary animation she perceived might be the effect of madness. "Should her husband then substantiate his charge, and get possession of her estate, from whence would come the promised annuity, or more desired protection? Besides, might not a woman, anxious to escape, conceal some of the circumstances which made against her? Was truth to be expected from one who had been entrapped, kidnapped, in the most fraudulent manner?"

In this train Jemima continued to argue, the moment after compassion and respect seemed to make her swerve; and she still resolved not to be wrought on to do more than soften the rigour of confinement, till she could advance on surer ground.

Maria was not permitted to walk in the garden; but sometimes, from her window, she turned her eyes from the gloomy walls, in which she pined life away, on the poor wretches who strayed along the walks, and contemplated the most terrific of ruins—that of a human soul. What is the view of the fallen column, the mouldering arch, of the most exquisite workmanship, when compared with this living memento of the fragility, the instability, of reason, and the wild luxuriancy of noxious passions? Enthusiasm turned adrift, like some rich stream overflowing its banks, rushes forward with destructive velocity, inspiring a sublime concentration of thought. Thus thought Maria—These are the ravages over which humanity must ever mournfully ponder, with a degree of anguish not excited by crumbling marble, or cankering brass, unfaithful to the trust of monumental fame. It is not over the decaying productions of the mind, embodied with the happiest art, we grieve most bitterly. The view of what has been done by man, produces a melancholy, yet aggrandizing, sense of what remains to be achieved by human intellect; but a mental convulsion, which, like the devastation of an earthquake, throws all the elements of thought and imagination into confusion, makes contemplation giddy, and we fearfully ask on what ground we ourselves stand.

Melancholy and imbecility marked the features of the wretches allowed to breathe at large; for the frantic, those who in a strong imagination had lost a sense of woe, were closely confined. The playful tricks and mischievous devices of their disturbed fancy, that suddenly broke out, could not be guarded against, when they were permitted to enjoy any portion of freedom; for, so active was their imagination, that every new object which accidentally struck their senses, awoke to phrenzy their restless passions; as Maria learned from the burden of their incessant ravings.

Sometimes, with a strict injunction of silence, Jemima would allow Maria, at the close of evening, to stray along the narrow avenues that separated the dungeon-like apartments, leaning on her arm. What a change of scene! Maria wished to pass the threshold of her prison, yet, when by chance she met the eye of rage glaring on her, yet unfaithful to its office, she shrunk back with more horror and affright, than if she had stumbled over a mangled corpse. Her busy fancy pictured the misery of a fond heart, watching over a friend thus estranged, absent, though present—over a poor wretch lost to reason and the social joys of existence; and losing all consciousness of misery in its excess. What a task, to watch the light of reason quivering in the eye, or with agonizing expectation to catch the beam of recollection; tantalized by hope, only to feel despair more keenly, at finding a much loved face or voice, suddenly remembered, or pathetically implored, only to be immediately forgotten, or viewed with indifference or abhorrence!

The heart-rending sigh of melancholy sunk into her soul; and when she retired to rest, the petrified figures she had encountered, the only human forms she was doomed to observe, haunting her dreams with tales of mysterious wrongs, made her wish to sleep to dream no more.

Day after day rolled away, and tedious as the present moment appeared, they passed in such an unvaried tenor, Maria was surprised to find that she had already been six weeks buried alive, and yet had such faint hopes of effecting her enlargement. She was, earnestly as she had sought for employment, now angry with herself for having been amused by writing her narrative; and grieved to think that she had for an instant thought of any thing, but contriving to escape.

Jemima had evidently pleasure in her society: still, though she often left her with a glow of kindness, she returned with the same chilling air; and, when her heart appeared for a moment to open, some suggestion of reason forcibly closed it, before she could give utterance to the confidence Maria's conversation inspired.

Discouraged by these changes, Maria relapsed into despondency, when she was cheered by the alacrity with which Jemima brought her a fresh parcel of books; assuring her, that she had taken some pains to obtain them from one of the keepers, who attended a gentleman confined in the opposite corner of the gallery.

Maria took up the books with emotion. "They come," said she, "perhaps, from a wretch condemned, like me, to reason on the nature of madness, by having wrecked minds continually under his eye; and almost to wish himself—as I do—mad, to escape from the contemplation of it." Her heart throbbed with sympathetic alarm; and she turned over the leaves with awe, as if they had become sacred from passing through the hands of an unfortunate being, oppressed by a similar fate.

Dryden's Fables,[2] Milton's Paradise Lost, with several modern productions, composed the collection. It was a mine of treasure. Some marginal notes, in Dryden's Fables, caught her attention: they were written with force and taste; and, in one of the modern pamphlets, there was a fragment left, containing various observations on the present state of society and government, with a comparative view of the politics of Europe and America. These remarks were written with a degree of generous warmth, when alluding to the enslaved state of the labouring majority, perfectly in unison with Maria's mode of thinking.

She read them over and over again; and fancy, treacherous fancy, began to sketch a character, congenial with her own, from these shadowy outlines.—"Was he mad?" She re-perused the marginal notes, and they seemed the production of an animated, but not of a disturbed imagination. Confined to this speculation, every time she reread them, some fresh refinement of sentiment, or accuteness of thought impressed her, which she was astonished at herself for not having before observed.

What a creative power has an affectionate heart! There are beings who cannot live without loving, as poets love; and who feel the electric spark of genius, wherever it awakens sentiment or grace. Maria had often thought, when disciplining her wayward heart, "that to charm, was

---

[2]*Fables Ancient and Modern* (1700). Such a "collection" appears in the pages of MW's *Vindication*.

to be virtuous." "They who make me wish to appear the most amiable and good in their eyes, must possess in a degree," she would exclaim, "the graces and virtues they call into action."

She took up a book on the powers of the human mind; but, her attention strayed from cold arguments on the nature of what she felt, while she was feeling, and she snapt the chain of the theory to read Dryden's Guiscard and Sigismunda.[3]

Maria, in the course of the ensuing day, returned some of the books, with the hope of getting others—and more marginal notes. Thus shut out from human intercourse, and compelled to view nothing but the prison of vexed spirits, to meet a wretch in the same situation, was more surely to find a friend, than to imagine a countryman one, in a strange land, where the human voice conveys no information to the eager ear.

"Did you ever see the unfortunate being to whom these books belong?" asked Maria, when Jemima brought her supper. "Yes. He sometimes walks out, between five and six, before the family is stirring, in the morning, with two keepers; but even then his hands are confined."

"What! is he so unruly?" enquired Maria, with an accent of disappointment.

"No, not that I perceive," replied Jemima; "but he has an untamed look, a vehemence of eye, that excites apprehension. Were his hands free, he looks as if he could soon manage both his guards: yet he appears tranquil."

"If he be so strong, he must be young," observed Maria.

"Three or four and thirty, I suppose; but there is no judging of a person in his situation."

"Are you sure that he is mad?" interrupted Maria with eagerness. Jemima quitted the room, without replying.

"No, no, he certainly is not!" exclaimed Maria, answering herself; "the man who could write those observations was not disordered in his intellects."

She sat musing, gazing at the moon, and watching its motion as it seemed to glide under the clouds. Then, preparing for bed, she thought,

---

[3] A tale from Boccaccio translated in *Fables Ancient and Modern*. Sigismonda, the widowed daughter, defies her tyrant father Tancred in a secret affair with his squire Guiscard. When Tancred discovers the relationship, she offers a spirited defense of female sexual desire and a woman's right to choose her own partner—regardless of class. Critic Gary Kelly comments on the force of romance narrative over abstract treatise in making the case.

"Of what use could I be to him, or he to me, if it be true that he is unjustly confined?—Could he aid me to escape, who is himself more closely watched?—Still I should like to see him." She went to bed, dreamed of her child, yet woke exactly at half after five o'clock, and starting up, only wrapped a gown around her, and ran to the window. The morning was chill, it was the latter end of September; yet she did not retire to warm herself and think in bed, till the sound of the servants, moving about the house, convinced her that the unknown would not walk in the garden that morning. She was ashamed at feeling disappointed; and began to reflect, as an excuse to herself, on the little objects which attract attention when there is nothing to divert the mind; and how difficult it was for women to avoid growing romantic, who have no active duties or pursuits.

At breakfast, Jemima enquired whether she understood French? for, unless she did, the stranger's stock of books was exhausted. Maria replied in the affirmative; but forbore to ask any more questions respecting the person to whom they belonged. And Jemima gave her a new subject for contemplation, by describing the person of a lovely maniac, just brought into an adjoining chamber. She was singing the pathetic ballad of old Robin Gray, with[4] the most heart-melting falls and pauses.[5] Jemima had half-opened the door, when she distinguished her voice, and Maria stood close to it, scarcely daring to respire, lest a modulation should escape her, so exquisitely sweet, so passionately wild. She began with sympathy to pourtray to herself another victim, when the lovely warbler flew, as it were, from the spray, and a torrent of unconnected exclamations and questions burst from her, interrupted by fits of laughter, so horrid, that Maria shut the door, and, turning her eyes up to heaven, exclaimed—"Gracious God!"

Several minutes elapsed before Maria could enquire respecting the rumour of the house (for this poor wretch was obviously not confined without a cause); and then Jemima could only tell her, that it

[4]In the 1798 edition, there is a blank space between "Rob" and "with," but the full title is included in the French translation (1798) and the American edition (Philadelphia, 1799).

[5]Lady Anne Lindsay, "Auld Robin Gray," *Ancient and Modern Scottish Songs*, ed. David Herd (1776). This famous ballad is a tale of marital misery. When Jamie goes to sea in hopes of making his fortune, his sweetheart Jenny is persuaded by her impoverished parents to marry wealthy "auld Robin Gray"; when Jamie returns, the lovers bid farewell.

was said, "she had been married, against her inclination, to a rich old man, extremely jealous (no wonder, for she was a charming creature); and that, in consequence of his treatment, or something which hung on her mind, she had, during her first lying-in, lost her senses."[6]

What a subject of meditation—even to the very confines of madness.

"Woman, fragile flower! why were you suffered to adorn a world exposed to the inroad of such stormy elements?" thought Maria, while the poor maniac's strain was still breathing on her ear, and sinking into her very soul.

Towards the evening, Jemima brought her Rousseau's *Heloïse*[7]; and she sat reading with eyes and heart, till the return of her guard to extinguish the light. One instance of her kindness was, the permitting Maria to have one, till her own hour of retiring to rest. She had read this work long since; but now it seemed to open a new world to her— the only one worth inhabiting. Sleep was not to be wooed; yet, far from being fatigued by the restless rotation of thought, she rose and opened her window, just as the thin watery clouds of twilight made the long silent shadows visible. The air swept across her face with a voluptuous freshness that thrilled[8] to her heart, awakening indefinable emotions; and the sound of a waving branch, or the twittering of a startled bird, alone broke the stillness of reposing nature. Absorbed by the sublime sensibility which renders the consciousness of existence felicity, Maria was happy, till an autumnal scent, wafted by the breeze of morn from the fallen leaves of the adjacent wood, made her recollect that the season had changed since her confinement; yet life afforded no variety to solace an afflicted heart. She returned dispirited to her couch, and thought of her child till the broad glare of day again invited her to the window. She looked not for the unknown, still how great was her vexation at perceiving the back of a man, certainly he, with his two attendants, as he turned into a side-path which

---

[6]The story evokes the brief marriage of MW's sister Eliza, as well as the description of a fair maniac in Frances Burney's *Camilla* (4.4), which MW mentions in her review of the novel (*Analytical Review* 24, August 1796).

[7]The heroine of *Julie, ou la Nouvelle Héloïse* (1761) falls in love with her tutor Saint Preux, but her father prohibits their marriage because of his social position. Their secret affair is finally ended by Julie's father, who arranges her marriage to Baron Wolmar. Although Julie remains faithful, on her deathbed, she declares her lasting love for Saint Preux.

[8]"Pierced, penetrated" (OED).

led to the house! A confused recollection of having seen somebody who resembled him, immediately occurred, to puzzle and torment her with endless conjectures.[9] Five minutes sooner, and she should have seen his face, and been out of suspense—was ever any thing so unlucky! His steady, bold step, and the whole air of his person, bursting as it were from a cloud, pleased her, and gave an outline to the imagination to sketch the individual form she wished to recognize.

Feeling the disappointment more severely than she was willing to believe, she flew to Rousseau, as her only refuge from the idea of him, who might prove a friend, could she but find a way to interest him in her fate; still the personification of Saint Preux, or of an ideal lover far superior, was after this imperfect model, of which merely a glance had been caught, even to the minutiæ of the coat and hat of the stranger. But if she lent St. Preux, or the demi-god of her fancy, his form, she richly repaid him by the donation of all St. Preux's sentiments and feelings, culled to gratify her own, to which he seemed to have an undoubted right, when she read on the margin of an impassioned letter, written in the well-known hand—"Rousseau alone, the true Prometheus of sentiment,[10] possessed the fire of genius necessary to pourtray the passion, the truth of which goes so directly to the heart."

Maria was again true to the hour, yet had finished Rousseau, and begun to transcribe some selected passages; unable to quit either the author or the window, before she had a glimpse of the countenance she daily longed to see; and, when seen, it conveyed no distinct idea to her mind where she had seen it before. He must have been a transient acquaintance; but to discover an acquaintance was fortunate, could she contrive to attract his attention, and excite his sympathy.

Every glance afforded colouring for the picture she was delineating on her heart; and once, when the window was half open, the sound of his voice reached her. Conviction flashed on her; she had certainly, in a moment of distress, heard the same accents. They were manly, and characteristic of a noble mind; nay, even sweet—or sweet they seemed to her attentive ear.

She started back, trembling, alarmed at the emotion a strange coincidence of circumstances inspired, and wondering why she thought

---

[9]See Godwin's second note to ch. III (p. 269, n. 7).

[10]The Greek titan God Prometheus defied Zeus when he stole fire from Mount Olympus and gave it to man, and was tormented for his transgression. MW's daughter Mary subtitled *Frankenstein* "or, The Modern Prometheus."

so much of a stranger, obliged as she had been by his timely interference; [for she recollected, by degrees, all the circumstances of their former meeting.][11] She found however that she could think of nothing else; or, if she thought of her daughter, it was to wish that she had a father whom her mother could respect and love.

CHAPTER III

When perusing the first parcel of books, Maria had, with her pencil, written in one of them a few exclamations, expressive of compassion and sympathy, which she scarcely remembered, till turning over the leaves of one of the volumes, lately brought to her, a slip of paper dropped out, which Jemima hastily snatched up.

"Let me see it," demanded Maria impatiently, "You surely are not afraid of trusting me with the effusions of a madman?" "I must consider," replied Jemima; and withdrew, with the paper in her hand.

In a life of such seclusion, the passions gain undue force[1]; Maria therefore felt a great degree of resentment and vexation, which she had not time to subdue, before Jemima, returning, delivered the paper.

"Whoever you are, who partake of my fate, accept my sincere commiseration—I would have said protection; but the privilege of man is denied me.

"My own situation forces a dreadful suspicion on my mind—I may not always languish in vain for freedom—say are you—I cannot ask the question; yet I will remember you when my remembrance can be of any use. I will enquire, *why* you are so mysteriously detained—and I *will* have an answer.

"HENRY DARNFORD."

By the most pressing intreaties, Maria prevailed on Jemima to permit her to write a reply to this note. Another and another succeeded, in which explanations were not allowed relative to their present situation; but Maria, with sufficient explicitness, alluded to a

---

[11]Godwin's interpretation; see his note to ch. XIII (p. 335, n. 2).

[1]Gary Kelly notes that MW's "detailed observation of the psychological effects of solitude" goes back to her first novel, *Mary*. In a letter to Godwin (August 17, 1796), she refers to herself as a "*Solitary Walker.*"

former obligation[2]; and they insensibly entered on an interchange of sentiments on the most important subjects. To write these letters was the business of the day, and to receive them the moment of sunshine. By some means, Darnford having discovered Maria's window, when she next appeared at it, he made her, behind his keepers, a profound bow of respect and recognition.

Two or three weeks glided away in this kind of intercourse, during which period Jemima, to whom Maria had given the necessary information respecting her family, had evidently gained some intelligence, which increased her desire of pleasing her charge, though she could not yet determine to liberate her. Maria took advantage of this favourable charge, without too minutely enquiring into the cause; and such was her eagerness to hold human converse, and to see her former protector, still a stranger to her, that she incessantly requested her guard to gratify her more than curiosity.

Writing to Darnford, she was led from the sad objects before her, and frequently rendered insensible to the horrid noises around her, which previously had continually employed her feverish fancy. Thinking it selfish to dwell on her own sufferings, when in the midst of wretches, who had not only lost all that endears life, but their very selves, her imagination was occupied with melancholy earnestness to trace the mazes of misery, through which so many wretches must have passed to this gloomy receptacle of disjointed souls, to the grand source of human corruption. Often at midnight was she waked by the dismal shrieks of demoniac rage, or of excruciating despair, uttered in such wild tones of indescribable anguish as proved the total absence of reason, and roused phantoms of horror in her mind, far more terrific than all that dreaming superstition ever drew. Besides, there was frequently something so inconceivably picturesque in the varying gestures of unrestrained passion, so irresistibly comic in their sallies, or so heart-piercingly pathetic in the little airs they would sing, frequently bursting out after an awful silence, as to fascinate the attention, and amuse the fancy, while torturing the soul. It was the uproar of the passions which she was compelled to observe; and to mark the lucid beam of reason, like a light trembling in a socket, or like the flash which divides the threatening clouds of angry heaven only to display the horrors which darkness shrouded.

[2]Her marriage to George Venables.

Jemima would labour to beguile the tedious evenings, by describing the persons and manners of the unfortunate beings, whose figures or voices awoke sympathetic sorrow in Maria's bosom; and the stories she told were the more interesting, for perpetually leaving room to conjecture something extraordinary. Still Maria, accustomed to generalize her observations, was led to conclude from all she heard, that it was a vulgar error to suppose that people of abilities were the most apt to lose the command of reason. On the contrary, from most of the instances she could investigate, she thought it resulted, that the passions only appeared strong and disproportioned, because the judgment was weak and unexercised; and that they gained strength by the decay of reason, as the shadows lengthen during the sun's decline.

Maria impatiently wished to see her fellow-sufferer; but Darnford was still more earnest to obtain an interview. Accustomed to submit to every impulse of passion, and never taught, like women, to restrain the most natural, and acquire, instead of the bewitching frankness of nature, a factitious propriety of behaviour, every desire became a torrent that bore down all opposition.

His travelling trunk, which contained the books lent to Maria, had been sent to him, and with a part of its contents he bribed his principal keeper; who, after receiving the most solemn promise that he would return to his apartment without attempting to explore any part of the house, conducted him, in the dusk of the evening, to Maria's room.

Jemima had apprized her charge of the visit, and she expected with trembling impatience, inspired by a vague hope that he might again prove her deliverer, to see a man who had before rescued her from oppression.[3] He entered with an animation of countenance, formed to captivate an enthusiast; and, hastily turned his eyes from her to the apartment, which he surveyed with apparent emotions of compassionate indignation. Sympathy illuminated his eye, and, taking her hand, he respectfully bowed on it, exclaiming—"This is extraordinary!—again to meet you, and in such circumstances!" Still, impressive as was the coincidence of events which brought them once more together, their full hearts did not overflow.—[4]

---

[3] See Godwin's second note in ch. III (p. 269, n. 7).

[4] The copy which had received the author's last corrections breaks off in this place, and the pages which follow, to the end of Chap. IV, are printed from a copy in a less finished state [WG]. The text in brackets is WG's.

[And though, after this first visit, they were permitted frequently to repeat their interviews, they were for some time employed in] a reserved conversation, to which all the world might have listened; excepting, when discussing some literary subject, flashes of sentiment, inforced by each relaxing feature, seemed to remind them that their minds were already acquainted.

[By degrees, Darnford entered into the particulars of his story.] In a few words, he informed her that he had been a thoughtless, extravagant young man; yet, as he described his faults, they appeared to be the generous luxuriancy of a noble mind. Nothing like meanness tarnished the lustre of his youth, nor had the worm of selfishness lurked in the unfolding bud, even while he had been the dupe of others. Yet he tardily acquired the experience necessary to guard him against future imposition.

"I shall weary you," continued he, "by my egotism; and did not powerful emotions draw me to you,"—his eyes glistened as he spoke, and a trembling seemed to run through his manly frame,—"I would not waste these precious moments in talking of myself.

"My father and mother were people of fashion; married by their parents. He was fond of the turf, she of the card-table. I, and two or three other children since dead, were kept at home till we became intolerable. My father and mother had a visible dislike to each other, continually displayed; the servants were of the depraved kind usually found in the houses of people of fortune. My brothers and parents all dying, I was left to the care of guardians, and sent to Eton.[5] I never knew the sweets of domestic affection, but I felt the want of indulgence and frivolous respect at school. I will not disgust you with a recital of the vices of my youth, which can scarcely be comprehended by female delicacy. I was taught to love by a creature I am ashamed to mention; and the other women with whom I afterwards became intimate, were of a class of which you can have no knowledge. I formed my acquaintance with them at the theatres; and, when vivacity danced in their eyes, I was not easily disgusted by the vulgarity which flowed from their lips. Having spent, a few years after I was of age, [the whole of] a considerable patrimony, excepting a few hundreds, I had no resource but to purchase a commission in a new-raised regiment, destined to subjugate America. The regret I felt to renounce a life of pleasure, was counterbalanced by the curiosity I had to see

[5]Founded by Henry VIII, the oldest, most prestigious boys' school in England, attended by royalty and aristocrats.

America, or rather to travel; [nor had any of those circumstances occurred to my youth, which might have been calculated] to bind my
country to my heart. I shall not trouble you with the details of a military life. My blood was still kept in motion; till, towards the close of
the contest, I was wounded and taken prisoner.

"Confined to my bed, or chair, by a lingering cure, my only refuge
from the preying activity of my mind, was books, which I read with
great avidity, profiting by the conversation of my host, a man of
sound understanding. My political sentiments now underwent a total
change; and, dazzled by the hospitality of the Americans, I determined to take up my abode with freedom. I, therefore, with my usual
impetuosity, sold my commission, and travelled into the interior parts
of the country, to lay out my money to advantage. Added to this, I
did not much like the puritanical manners of the large towns. Inequality of condition was there most disgustingly galling. The only
pleasure wealth afforded, was to make an ostentatious display of it;
for the cultivation of the fine arts, or literature, had not introduced
into the first circles that polish of manners which renders the rich so
essentially superior to the poor in Europe. Added to this, an influx of
vices had been let in by the Revolution, and the most rigid principles
of religion shaken to the centre, before the understanding could be
gradually emancipated from the prejudices which led their ancestors
undauntedly to seek an inhospitable clime and unbroken soil. The
resolution, that led them, in pursuit of independence, to embark on
rivers like seas, to search for unknown shores, and to sleep under the
hovering mists of endless forests, whose baleful damps agued their
limbs, was now turned into commercial speculations, till the national
character exhibited a phenomenon in the history of the human
mind—a head enthusiastically enterprising, with cold selfishness of
heart. And woman, lovely woman!—they charm every where—still
there is a degree of prudery, and a want of taste and ease in the manners of the American women, that renders them, in spite of their roses
and lilies, far inferior to our European charmers. In the country, they
have often a bewitching simplicity of character; but, in the cities, they
have all the airs and ignorance of the ladies who give the tone to the
circles of the large trading towns in England. They are fond of their
ornaments, merely because they are good, and not because they embellish their persons; and are more gratified to inspire the women
with jealousy of these exterior advantages, than the men with love.

All the frivolity which often (excuse me, Madam) renders the society of modest women so stupid in England, here seemed to throw still more leaden fetters on their charms. Not being an adept in gallantry, I found that I could only keep myself awake in their company by making downright love to[6] them.

"But, not to intrude on your patience, I retired to the track of land which I had purchased in the country, and my time passed pleasantly enough while I cut down the trees, built my house, and planted my different crops. But winter and idleness came, and I longed for more elegant society, to hear what was passing in the world, and to do something better than vegetate with the animals that made a very considerable part of my household. Consequently, I determined to travel. Motion was a substitute for variety of objects; and, passing over immense tracks of country, I exhausted my exuberant spirits, without obtaining much experience. I every where saw industry the fore-runner and not the consequence, of luxury; but this country, every thing being on an ample scale, did not afford those picturesque views, which a certain degree of cultivation is necessary gradually to produce. The eye wandered without an object to fix upon over immeasureable plains, and lakes that seemed replenished by the ocean, whilst eternal forests of small clustering trees, obstructed the circulation of air, and embarrassed the path, without gratifying the eye of taste. No cottage smiling in the waste, no travellers hailed us, to give life to silent nature; or, if perchance we saw the print of a footstep in our path, it was a dreadful warning to turn aside; and the head ached as if assailed by the scalping knife. The Indians who hovered on the skirts of the European settlements had only learned of their neighbours to plunder, and they stole their guns from them to do it with more safety.

"From the woods and back settlements, I returned to the towns, and learned to eat and drink most valiantly; but without entering into commerce (and I detested commerce) I found I could not live there; and, growing heartily weary of the land of liberty and vulgar aristocracy, seated on her bags of dollars, I resolved once more to visit Europe. I wrote to a distant relation in England, with whom I had been educated, mentioning the vessel in which I intended to sail. Arriving in London, my senses were intoxicated. I ran from street to street, from theatre to theatre, and the women of the town (again I must beg pardon for my habitual frankness) appeared to me like angels.

[6]Wooing; "gallantry" is gentlemanly flirtation, volleying of compliments.

"A week was spent in this thoughtless manner, when, returning very late to the hotel in which I had lodged ever since my arrival, I was knocked down in a private street, and hurried, in a state of insensibility, into a coach, which brought me hither, and I only recovered my senses to be treated like one who had lost them. My keepers are deaf to my remonstrances and enquiries, yet assure me that my confinement shall not last long. Still I cannot guess, though I weary myself with conjectures, why I am confined, or in what part of England this house is situated. I imagine sometimes that I hear the sea roar, and wished myself again on the Atlantic, till I had a glimpse of you."[7]

A few moments were only allowed to Maria to comment on this narrative, when Darnford left her to her own thoughts, to the "never ending, still beginning,"[8] task of weighing his words, recollecting his tones of voice, and feeling them reverberate on her heart.

CHAPTER IV

Pity, and the forlorn seriousness of adversity, have both been considered as dispositions favourable to love, while satirical writers have attributed the propensity to the relaxing effect of idleness; what chance then had Maria of escaping, when pity, sorrow, and solitude all conspired to soften her mind, and nourish romantic wishes, and, from a natural progress, romantic expectations?

Maria was six-and-twenty. But, such was the native soundness of her constitution, that time had only given to her countenance the character of her mind. Revolving thought, and exercised affections had banished some of the playful graces of innocence, producing insensibly that irregularity of features which the struggles of the understanding to trace or govern the strong emotions of the heart, are wont to imprint on the yielding mass. Grief and care had mellowed, without obscuring, the bright tints of youth, and the thoughtfulness which

[7]The introduction of Darnford as the deliverer of Maria in a former instance, appears to have been an afterthought of the author. This has occasioned the omission of any allusion to that circumstance in the preceding narration. EDITOR [WG]. This neglects both Maria's "confused recollection" (ch. II) and her impatience "to see a man who had before rescued her from oppression" (ch. III).

[8]Dryden, *Alexander's Feast* (1697): after recounting Alexander's defeat of the Persian emperor, Timotheus sings of war as "Never ending, still beginning, / Fighting still, and still destroying: / If the world be worth thy winning, / Think, O think it worth enjoying" (101–4).

resided on her brow did not take from the feminine softness of her features; nay, such was the sensibility which often mantled over it, that she frequently appeared, like a large proportion of her sex, only born to feel; and the activity of her well-proportioned, and even almost voluptuous figure, inspired the idea of strength of mind, rather than of body. There was a simplicity sometimes indeed in her manner, which bordered on infantine ingenuousness, that led people of common discernment to underrate her talents, and smile at the flights of her imagination. But those who could not comprehend the delicacy of her sentiments, were attached by her unfailing sympathy, so that she was very generally beloved by characters of very different descriptions; still, she was too much under the influence of an ardent imagination to adhere to common rules.

There are mistakes of conduct which at five-and-twenty prove the strength of the mind, that, ten or fifteen years after, would demonstrate its weakness, its incapacity to acquire a sane judgment. The youths who are satisfied with the ordinary pleasures of life, and do not sigh after ideal phantoms of love and friendship, will never arrive at great maturity of understanding; but if these reveries are cherished, as is too frequently the case with women, when experience ought to have taught them in what human happiness consists, they become as useless as they are wretched. Besides, their pains and pleasures are so dependent on outward circumstances, on the objects of their affections, that they seldom act from the impulse of a nerved mind, able to choose its own pursuit.

Having had to struggle incessantly with the vices of mankind, Maria's imagination found repose in pourtraying the possible virtues the world might contain. Pygmalion formed an ivory maid, and longed for an informing soul.[1] She, on the contrary, combined all the qualities of a hero's mind, and fate presented a statue in which she might enshrine them.

We mean not to trace the progress of this passion, or recount how often Darnford and Maria were obliged to part in the midst of an interesting conversation. Jemima ever watched on the tip-toe of fear, and frequently separated them on a false alarm, when they would have given worlds to remain a little longer together.

A magic lamp now seemed to be suspended in Maria's prison, and fairy landscapes flitted round the gloomy walls, late so blank. Rush-

---

[1] In the old myth, Greek sculptor Pygmalion fell in love with his statue of a beautiful woman; in pity, Aphrodite, goddess of love, brought it to rapturous life.

Le Premier Baiser de l'Amour [The First Kiss of Passionate Love], illustration from the 1808 Paris edition of Jean-Jacques Rousseau's novel, *Julie, ou la Nouvelle Héloïse*. This image was drawn by Pierre Prud'hon and engraved by Jacques-Louis Copia in 1795. Reproduced from Alexis François, *Le premier baiser de l'amour; ou, Jean-Jacques Rousseau, inspirateur d'estampes* (Geneva: Sonor, 1920), Planche XVI.

ing from the depth of despair, on the seraph wing of hope, she found herself happy.—She was beloved, and every emotion was rapturous.

To Darnford she had not shown a decided affection; the fear of outrunning his, a sure proof of love, made her often assume a coldness and indifference foreign from her character; and, even when giving way to the playful emotions of a heart just loosened from the frozen bond of grief, there was a delicacy in her manner of expressing her sensibility, which made him doubt whether it was the effect of love.

One evening, when Jemima left them, to listen to the sound of a distant footstep, which seemed cautiously to approach, he seized Maria's hand—it was not withdrawn. They conversed with earnestness of their situation; and, during the conversation, he once or twice gently drew her towards him. He felt the fragrance of her breath, and longed, yet feared, to touch the lips from which it issued; spirits of purity seemed to guard them, while all the enchanting graces of love sported on her cheeks, and languished in her eyes.

Jemima entering, he reflected on his diffidence with poignant regret, and, she once more taking alarm, he ventured, as Maria stood near his chair, to approach her lips with a declaration of love. She drew back with solemnity, he hung down his head abashed; but lifting his eyes timidly, they met her's; she had determined, during that instant, and suffered their rays to mingle. He took, with more ardour, reassured, a half-consenting, half-reluctant kiss, reluctant only from modesty; and there was a sacredness in her dignified manner of reclining her glowing face on his shoulder, that powerfully impressed him. Desire was lost in more ineffable emotions, and to protect her from insult and sorrow—to make her happy, seemed not only the first wish of his heart, but the most noble duty of his life. Such angelic confidence demanded the fidelity of honour; but could he, feeling her in every pulsation, could he ever change, could he be a villain? The emotion with which she, for a moment, allowed herself to be pressed to his bosom, the tear of rapturous sympathy, mingled with a soft melancholy sentiment of recollected disappointment, said—more of truth and faithfulness, than the tongue could have given utterance to in hours! They were silent—yet discoursed, how eloquently? till, after a moment's reflection, Maria drew her chair by the side of his, and, with a composed sweetness of voice, and supernatural benignity of countenance, said, "I must open my whole heart to you; you must be told who I am, why I am here, and why, telling you I am a wife, I blush not to"—the blush spoke the rest.

Jemima was again at her elbow, and the restraint of her presence did not prevent an animated conversation, in which love, sly urchin, was ever at bo-peep.[2]

So much of heaven did they enjoy, that paradise bloomed around them; or they, by a powerful spell, had been transported into Armida's garden.[3] Love, the grand enchanter, "lapt them in Elysium,"[4] and every sense was harmonized to joy and social extacy. So animated, indeed, were their accents of tenderness, in discussing what, in other circumstances, would have been common-place subjects, that Jemima felt, with surprise, a tear of pleasure trickling down her rugged cheeks. She wiped it away, half ashamed; and when Maria kindly enquired the cause, with all the eager solicitude of a happy being wishing to impart to all nature its overflowing felicity, Jemima owned that it was the first tear that social enjoyment had ever drawn from her. She seemed indeed to breathe more freely; the cloud of suspicion cleared away from her brow; she felt herself, for once in her life, treated like a fellow-creature.

Imagination! who can paint thy power; or reflect the evanescent tints of hope fostered by thee? A despondent gloom had long obscured Maria's horizon—now the sun broke forth, the rainbow appeared, and every prospect was fair. Horror still reigned in the darkened cells, suspicion lurked in the passages, and whispered along the walls. The yells of men possessed, sometimes made them pause, and wonder that they felt so happy, in a tomb of living death. They even chid themselves for such apparent insensibility; still the world contained not three happier beings. And Jemima, after again patrolling the passage, was so softened by the air of confidence which breathed around her, that she voluntarily began an account of herself.

CHAPTER V

"My father," said Jemima, "seduced my mother, a pretty girl, with whom he lived fellow-servant; and she no sooner perceived the natural, the dreaded consequence, than the terrible conviction flashed on her—

[2]The act of looking out and then drawing back as if frighted, or with the purpose to fright some other (Johnson's *Dictionary*).

[3]In Torquato Tasso's *Gerusalemme Liberata* (1581), sorceress Armida lures Christian knights into her enchanted garden, where they are overcome by indolence (4.5).

[4]Milton's enchanter Comus likens the virtuous Lady's song to the song of Circe and the Sirens, which "would take the prison'd soul, / And lap it in Elysium" (*Comus*, 256–67).

that she was ruined. Honesty, and a regard for her reputation, had been the only principles inculcated by her mother; and they had been so forcibly impressed, that she feared shame, more than the poverty to which it would lead. Her incessant importunities to prevail upon my father to screen her from reproach by marrying her, as he had promised in the fervour of seduction, estranged him from her so completely, that her very person became distasteful to him; and he began to hate, as well as despise me, before I was born.

"My mother, grieved to the soul by his neglect, and unkind treatment, actually resolved to famish herself; and injured her health by the attempt; though she had not sufficient resolution to adhere to her project, or renounce it entirely. Death came not at her call; yet sorrow, and the methods she adopted to conceal her condition, still doing the work of a house-maid, had such an effect on her constitution, that she died in the wretched garret, where her virtuous mistress had forced her to take refuge in the very pangs of labour, though my father, after a slight reproof, was allowed to remain in his place—allowed by the mother of six children, who, scarcely permitting a footstep to be heard, during her month's indulgence, felt no sympathy for the poor wretch, denied every comfort required by her situation.

"The day my mother died, the ninth after my birth, I was consigned to the care of the cheapest nurse my father could find; who suckled her own child at the same time, and lodged as many more as she could get, in two cellar-like apartments.

"Poverty, and the habit of seeing children die off her hands, had so hardened her heart, that the office of a mother did not awaken the tenderness of a woman; nor were the feminine caresses which seem a part of the rearing of a child, ever bestowed on me. The chicken has a wing to shelter under; but I had no bosom to nestle in, no kindred warmth to foster me. Left in dirt, to cry with cold and hunger till I was weary, and sleep without ever being prepared by exercise, or lulled by kindness to rest; could I be expected to become any thing but a weak and rickety babe? Still, in spite of neglect, I continued to exist, to learn to curse existence, [her countenance grew ferocious as she spoke,] and the treatment that rendered me miserable, seemed to sharpen my wits. Confined then in a damp hovel, to rock the cradle of the succeeding tribe, I looked like a little old woman, or a hag shrivelling into nothing. The furrows of reflection and care contracted the youthful cheek, and gave a sort of supernatural wildness to the ever watchful eye. During this period, my father had married another fellow-servant, who loved him less, and knew better how to manage his passion, than my mother. She likewise proving with child, they agreed to keep a shop: my step-mother, if, being an illegitimate offspring, I may venture thus to characterize her, having obtained a sum of a rich relation, for that purpose.

"Soon after her lying-in,[1] she prevailed on my father to take me home, to save the expence of maintaining me, and of hiring a girl to assist her in the care of the child. I was young, it was true, but appeared a knowing little thing, and might be made handy. Accordingly I was brought to her house; but not to a home—for a home I never knew. Of this child, a daughter, she was extravagantly fond; and it was a part of my employment, to assist to spoil her, by humouring all her whims, and bearing all her caprices. Feeling her own consequence, before she could speak, she had learned the art of tormenting me, and if I ever dared to resist, I received blows, laid on with no compunctious hand, or was sent to bed dinnerless, as well as supperless.[2] I said that it was a part of my daily labour to attend this child, with the servility of a slave; still it was but a part. I was sent out in all seasons, and from place to place, to carry burdens far above my strength, without being allowed to draw near the fire, or ever being cheered by encouragement or kindness. No wonder then, treated like a creature of another species, that I began to envy, and at length to hate, the darling of the house. Yet, I perfectly remember, that it was the caresses, and kind expressions of my step-mother, which first excited my jealous discontent. Once, I cannot forget it, when she was calling in vain her wayward child to kiss her, I ran to her, saying, 'I will kiss you, ma'am!' and how did my heart, which was in my mouth, sink, what was my debasement of soul, when pushed away with—'I do not want you, pert thing!' Another day, when a new gown had excited the highest good humour, and she uttered the appropriate *dear*, addressed unexpectedly to me, I thought I could never do enough to please her; I was all alacrity, and rose proportionably in my own estimation.

"As her daughter grew up, she was pampered with cakes and fruit, while I was, literally speaking, fed with the refuse of the table,

---

[1]Final weeks of pregnancy.

[2]Dinner is the midday meal; supper is the evening meal.

with her leavings. A liquorish[3] tooth is, I believe, common to children, and I used to steal any thing sweet, that I could catch up with a chance of concealment. When detected, she was not content to chastize me herself at the moment, but, on my father's return in the evening (he was a shopman), the principal discourse was to recount my faults, and attribute them to the wicked disposition which I had brought into the world with me, inherited from my mother. He did not fail to leave the marks of his resentment on my body, and then solaced himself by playing with my sister.—I could have murdered her at those moments. To save myself from these unmerciful corrections, I resorted to falshood, and the untruths which I sturdily maintained, were brought in judgment against me, to support my tyrant's inhuman charge of my natural propensity to vice. Seeing me treated with contempt, and always being fed and dressed better, my sister conceived a contemptuous opinion of me, that proved an obstacle to all affection; and my father, hearing continually of my faults, began to consider me as a curse entailed on him for his sins: he was therefore easily prevailed on to bind me apprentice to one of my step-mother's friends, who kept a slop-shop in Wapping.[4] I was represented (as it was said) in my true colours; but she, 'warranted,' snapping her fingers, 'that she should break my spirit or heart.'

"My mother replied, with a whine, 'that if any body could make me better, it was such a clever woman as herself; though, for her own part, she had tried in vain; but good-nature was her fault.'

"I shudder with horror, when I recollect the treatment I had now to endure. Not only under the lash of my task-mistress, but the drudge of the maid, apprentices and children, I never had a taste of human kindness to soften the rigour of perpetual labour. I had been introduced as an object of abhorrence into the family; as a creature of whom my step-mother, though she had been kind enough to let me live in the house with her own child, could make nothing. I was described as a wretch, whose nose must be kept to the grinding stone— and it was held there with an iron grasp. It seemed indeed the privilege

---

[3]Sweet.

[4]In the dock area of London a slop-shop sells cheap, ready-made clothes. Lower-class children, usually boys, were apprenticed both to relieve their families of their maintenance and to learn a craft or trade. Typically beginning at age 8, apprenticeships bound the child for 7 years of unpaid labor in exchange for training, shelter, food, and clothing. Apprentices were notoriously vulnerable to abuse, often treated as slaves and sometimes quartered in the barn rather than the home.

of their superior nature to kick me about, like the dog or cat. If I were attentive, I was called fawning, if refractory, an obstinate mule, and like a mule I received their censure on my loaded back. Often has my mistress, for some instance of forgetfulness, thrown me from one side of the kitchen to the other, knocked my head against the wall, spit in my face, with various refinements on barbarity that I forbear to enumerate, though they were all acted over again by the servant, with additional insults, to which the appellation of *bastard*,[5] was commonly added, with taunts or sneers. But I will not attempt to give you an adequate idea of my situation, lest you, who probably have never been drenched with the dregs of human misery, should think I exaggerate.

"I stole now, from absolute necessity,—bread; yet whatever else was taken, which I had it not in my power to take, was ascribed to me. I was the filching cat, the ravenous dog, the dumb brute, who must bear all; for if I endeavoured to exculpate myself, I was silenced, without any enquiries being made, with 'Hold your tongue, you never tell truth.' Even the very air I breathed was tainted with scorn; for I was sent to the neighbouring shops with Glutton, Liar, or Thief, written on my forehead. This was, at first, the most bitter punishment; but sullen pride, or a kind of stupid desperation, made me, at length, almost regardless of the contempt, which had wrung from me so many solitary tears at the only moments when I was allowed to rest.

"Thus was I the mark of cruelty till my sixteenth year; and then I have only to point out a change of misery; for a period[6] I never knew. Allow me first to make one observation. Now I look back, I cannot help attributing the greater part of my misery, to the misfortune of having been thrown into the world without the grand support of life—a mother's affection. I had no one to love me; or to make me respected, to enable me to acquire respect. I was an egg dropped on the sand; a pauper by nature, hunted from family to family, who belonged to nobody—and nobody cared for me. I was despised from my birth, and denied the chance of obtaining a footing for myself in society. Yes; I had not even the chance of being considered as a fellow-creature— yet all the people with whom I lived, brutalized as they were by the

---

[5]The legal term for a child born out of wedlock. English common law denied bastards the rights of inheritance, even of care, and left them to the care of the poor houses. The social and legal contempt is evident in the metaphorical extension of the term to indicate inferiority and falseness.

[6]Termination.

low cunning of trade, and the despicable shifts of poverty, were not without bowels,[7] though they never yearned for me. I was, in fact, born a slave, and chained by infamy to slavery during the whole of existence, without having any companions to alleviate it by sympathy, or teach me how to rise above it by their example. But, to resume the thread of my tale—

"At sixteen, I suddenly grew tall, and something like comeliness appeared on a Sunday, when I had time to wash my face, and put on clean clothes. My master had once or twice caught hold of me in the passage; but I instinctively avoided his disgusting caresses. One day however, when the family were at a methodist meeting,[8] he contrived to be alone in the house with me, and by blows—yes; blows and menaces, compelled me to submit to his ferocious desire; and, to avoid my mistress's fury, I was obliged in future to comply, and skulk to my loft at his command, in spite of increasing loathing.

"The anguish which was now pent up in my bosom, seemed to open a new world to me: I began to extend my thoughts beyond myself, and grieve for human misery, till I discovered, with horror—ah! what horror!—that I was with child. I know not why I felt a mixed sensation of despair and tenderness, excepting that, ever called a bastard, a bastard appeared to me an object of the greatest compassion in creation.

"I communicated this dreadful circumstance to my master, who was almost equally alarmed at the intelligence; for he feared his wife, and public censure at the meeting. After some weeks of deliberation had elapsed, I in continual fear that my altered shape would be noticed, my master gave me a medicine in a phial, which he desired me to take, telling me, without any circumlocution, for what purpose it was designed.[9] I burst into tears, I thought it was killing myself—yet was such a self as I worth preserving? He cursed me for a fool, and left me to my own reflections. I could not resolve to take this infernal potion; but I wrapped it up in an old gown, and hid it in a corner of my box.

"Nobody yet suspected me, because they had been accustomed to view me as a creature of another species. But the threatening storm at last broke over my devoted[10] head—never shall I forget it! One Sunday evening when I was left, as usual, to take care of the house, my

[7]Compassion.

[8]Methodists were popularly thought to be sexual libertines.

[9]Miscarriage.

[10]Doomed.

master came home intoxicated, and I became the prey of his brutal appetite. His extreme intoxication made him forget his customary caution, and my mistress entered and found us in a situation that could not have been more hateful to her than me. Her husband was 'pot-valiant,' he feared her not at the moment, nor had he then much reason, for she instantly turned the whole force of her anger another way. She tore off my cap, scratched, kicked, and buffetted me, till she had exhausted her strength, declaring, as she rested her arm, 'that I had wheedled her husband from her.—But, could any thing better be expected from a wretch, whom she had taken into her house out of pure charity?' What a torrent of abuse rushed out? till, almost breathless, she concluded with saying, 'that I was born a strumpet; it ran in my blood, and nothing good could come to those who harboured me.'

"My situation was, of course, discovered, and she declared that I should not stay another night under the same roof with an honest family. I was therefore pushed out of doors, and my trumpery thrown after me, when it had been contemptuously examined in the passage, lest I should have stolen any thing.

"Behold me then in the street, utterly destitute![11] Whither could I creep for shelter? To my father's roof I had no claim, when not pursued by shame—now I shrunk back as from death, from my mother's cruel reproaches, my father's execrations. I could not endure to hear him curse the day I was born, though life had been a curse to me. Of death I thought, but with a confused emotion of terror, as I stood leaning my head on a post, and starting at every footstep, lest it should be my mistress coming to tear my heart out. One of the boys of the shop passing by, heard my tale, and immediately repaired to his master, to give him a description of my situation; and he touched the right key—the scandal it would give rise to, if I were left to repeat my tale to every enquirer. This plea came home to his reason, who had been sobered by his wife's rage, the fury of which fell on him when I was out of her reach, and he sent the boy to me with half-a-guinea,[12] desiring him to conduct me to a house, where beggars, and other wretches, the refuse of society, nightly lodged.

"This night was spent in a state of stupefaction, or desperation. I detested mankind, and abhorred myself.

[11]See *Vindication*, chs. IV and VIII: "men ought to maintain the women whom they have seduced" (pp. 94 and 171).

[12]Coin worth 10 shillings, 6 pence; the guinea was first minted for the slave trade.

"In the morning I ventured out, to throw myself in my master's way, at his usual hour of going abroad. I approached him, he 'damned me for a b—, declared I had disturbed the peace of the family, and that he had sworn to his wife, never to take any more notice of me.' He left me; but, instantly returning, he told me that he should speak to his friend, a parish-officer,[13] to get a nurse for the brat I laid to him; and advised me, if I wished to keep out of the house of correction, not to make free with his name.

"I hurried back to my hole, and, rage giving place to despair, sought for the potion that was to procure abortion, and swallowed it, with a wish that it might destroy me, at the same time that it stopped the sensations of new-born life, which I felt with indescribable emotion. My head turned round, my heart grew sick, and in the horrors of approaching dissolution, mental anguish was swallowed up. The effect of the medicine was violent, and I was confined to my bed several days; but, youth and a strong constitution prevailing, I once more crawled out, to ask myself the cruel question, 'Whither I should go?' I had but two shillings left in my pocket, the rest had been expended, by a poor woman who slept in the same room, to pay for my lodging, and purchase the necessaries of which she partook.

"With this wretch I went into the neighbouring streets to beg, and my disconsolate appearance drew a few pence from the idle, enabling me still to command a bed; till, recovering from my illness, and taught to put on my rags to the best advantage, I was accosted from different motives, and yielded to the desire of the brutes I met, with the same detestation that I had felt for my still more brutal master. I have since read in novels of the blandishments of seduction, but I had not even the pleasure of being enticed into vice.[14]

"I shall not," interrupted Jemima, "lead your imagination into all the scenes of wretchedness and depravity, which I was condemned to view; or mark the different stages of my debasing misery. Fate dragged me through the very kennels of society; I was still a slave, a bastard, a common property. Become familiar with vice, for I wish to conceal nothing from you, I picked the pockets of the drunkards who abused me; and proved by my conduct, that I deserved the epithets, with which they loaded me at moments when distrust ought to cease.

[13]Responsible for providing bastards and the poor with a minimal level of subsistence.

[14]MW regarded prostitution as a social evil (see *Vindication*, ch. VII), and reviewed *The Evils of Adultery and Prostitution* for *Analytical Review* (September 1792).

"Detesting my nightly occupation, though valuing, if I may so use the word, my independence, which only consisted in choosing the street in which I should wander, or the roof, when I had money, in which I should hide my head, I was some time before I could prevail on myself to accept of a place in a house of ill fame, to which a girl, with whom I had accidentally conversed in the street, had recommended me. I had been hunted almost into a fever, by the watchmen of the quarter of the town I frequented; one, whom I had unwittingly offended, giving the word to the whole pack. You can scarcely conceive the tyranny exercised by these wretches: considering themselves as the instruments of the very laws they violate, the pretext which steels their conscience, hardens their heart. Not content with receiving from us, outlaws of society (let other women talk of favours) a brutal gratification gratuitously as a privilege of office, they extort a tithe of prostitution, and harrass with threats the poor creatures whose occupation affords not the means to silence the growl of avarice. To escape from this persecution, I once more entered into servitude.

"A life of comparative regularity restored my health; and—do not start—my manners were improved, in a situation where vice sought to render itself alluring, and taste was cultivated to fashion the person, if not to refine the mind. Besides, the common civility of speech, contrasted with the gross vulgarity to which I had been accustomed, was something like the polish of civilization. I was not shut out from all intercourse of humanity. Still I was galled by the yoke of service, and my mistress often flying into violent fits of passion, made me dread a sudden dismission, which I understood was always the case. I was therefore prevailed on, though I felt a horror of men, to accept the offer of a gentleman, rather in the decline of years, to keep his house, pleasantly situated in a little village near Hampstead.[15]

"He was a man of great talents, and of brilliant wit; but, a worn-out votary of voluptuousness, his desires became fastidious in proportion as they grew weak, and the native tenderness of his heart was undermined by a vitiated imagination. A thoughtless career of libertinism and social enjoyment, had injured his health to such a degree, that, whatever pleasure his conversation afforded me (and my esteem was ensured by proofs of the generous humanity of his disposition), the being his mistress was purchasing it at a very dear rate. With such a keen perception of the delicacies of sentiment, with an imagination

[15]Suburb north of London.

invigorated by the exercise of genius, how could he sink into the grossness of sensuality!

"But, to pass over a subject which I recollect with pain, I must remark to you, as an answer to your often-repeated question, 'Why my sentiments and language were superior to my station?' that I now began to read, to beguile the tediousness of solitude, and to gratify an inquisitive, active mind. I had often, in my childhood, followed a ballad-singer, to hear the sequel of a dismal story, though sure of being severely punished for delaying to return with whatever I was sent to purchase. I could just spell and put a sentence together, and I listened to the various arguments, though often mingled with obscenity, which occurred at the table where I was allowed to preside: for a literary friend or two frequently came home with my master, to dine and pass the night. Having lost the privileged respect of my sex, my presence, instead of restraining, perhaps gave the reins to their tongues; still I had the advantage of hearing discussions, from which, in the common course of life, women are excluded.

"You may easily imagine, that it was only by degrees that I could comprehend some of the subjects they investigated, or acquire from their reasoning what might be termed a moral sense. But my fondness of reading increasing, and my master occasionally shutting himself up in this retreat, for weeks together, to write, I had many opportunities of improvement. At first, considering money (I was right!" exclaimed Jemima, altering her tone of voice) "as the only means, after my loss of reputation, of obtaining respect, or even the toleration of humanity, I had not the least scruple to secrete a part of the sums intrusted to me, and to screen myself from detection by a system of falshood. But, acquiring new principles, I began to have the ambition of returning to the respectable part of society, and was weak enough to suppose it possible. The attention of my unassuming instructor, who, without being ignorant of his own powers, possessed great simplicity of manners, strengthened the illusion. Having sometimes caught up hints for thought, from my untutored remarks, he often led me to discuss the subjects he was treating, and would read to me his productions, previous to their publication, wishing to profit by the criticism of unsophisticated feeling. The aim of his writings was to touch the simple springs of the heart; for he despised the would-be oracles, the self-elected philosophers, who fright away fancy, while sifting each grain of thought to prove that slowness of comprehension is wisdom.

"I should have distinguished this as a moment of sunshine, a happy period in my life, had not the repugnance the disgusting libertinism of my protector inspired, daily become more painful.—And, indeed, I soon did recollect it as such with agony, when his sudden death (for he had recourse to the most exhilarating cordials to keep up the convivial tone of his spirits) again threw me into the desert of human society. Had he had any time for reflection, I am certain he would have left the little property in his power to me: but, attacked by the fatal apoplexy in town, his heir, a man of rigid morals, brought his wife with him to take possession of the house and effects, before I was even informed of his death,—'to prevent,' as she took care indirectly to tell me, 'such a creature as she supposed me to be, from purloining any of them, had I been apprized of the event in time.'

"The grief I felt at the sudden shock the information gave me, which at first had nothing selfish in it, was treated with contempt, and I was ordered to pack up my clothes; and a few trinkets and books, given me by the generous deceased, were contested, while they piously hoped, with a reprobating shake of the head, 'that God would have mercy on his sinful soul!' With some difficulty, I obtained my arrears of wages; but asking—such is the spirit-grinding consequence of poverty and infamy—for a character[16] for honesty and economy, which God knows I merited, I was told by this—why must I call her woman?—'that it would go against her conscience to recommend a kept mistress.' Tears started in my eyes, burning tears; for there are situations in which a wretch is humbled by the contempt they are conscious they do not deserve.

"I returned to the metropolis; but the solitude of a poor lodging was inconceivably dreary, after the society I had enjoyed. To be cut off from human converse, now I had been taught to relish it, was to wander a ghost among the living. Besides, I foresaw, to aggravate the severity of my fate, that my little pittance would soon melt away. I endeavoured to obtain needle-work; but, not having been taught early, and my hands being rendered clumsy by hard work, I did not sufficiently excel to be employed by the ready-made linen shops,[17] when so many women, better qualified, were suing for it. The want of a character prevented my getting a place; for, irksome as servitude

[16]Letter of reference, necessary for respectable employment.

[17]Shops which made and sold linen wear such as shirts and underclothes.

would have been to me, I should have made another trial, had it been feasible. Not that I disliked employment, but the inequality of condition to which I must have submitted. I had acquired a taste for literature, during the five years I had lived with a literary man, occasionally conversing with men of the first abilities of the age; and now to descend to the lowest vulgarity, was a degree of wretchedness not to be imagined unfelt. I had not, it is true, tasted the charms of affection, but I had been familiar with the graces of humanity.

"One of the gentlemen, whom I had frequently dined in company with, while I was treated like a companion, met me in the street, and enquired after my health. I seized the occasion, and began to describe my situation; but he was in haste to join, at dinner, a select party of choice spirits; therefore, without waiting to hear me, he impatiently put a guinea into my hand, saying, 'It was a pity such a sensible woman should be in distress—he wished me well from his soul.'

"To another I wrote, stating my case, and requesting advice. He was an advocate for unequivocal sincerity; and had often, in my presence, descanted on the evils which arise in society from the despotism of rank and riches.

"In reply, I received a long essay on the energy of the human mind, with continual allusions to his own force of character. He added, 'That the woman who could write such a letter as I had sent him, could never be in want of resources, were she to look into herself, and exert her powers; misery was the consequence of indolence, and, as to my being shut out from society, it was the lot of man to submit to certain privations.'

"How often have I heard," said Jemima, interrupting her narrative, "in conversation, and read in books, that every person willing to work may find employment? It is the vague assertion, I believe, of insensible indolence, when it relates to men; but, with respect to women, I am sure of its fallacy, unless they will submit to the most menial bodily labour; and even to be employed at hard labour is out of the reach of many, whose reputation misfortune or folly has tainted.

"How writers, professing to be friends to freedom, and the improvement of morals, can assert that poverty is no evil, I cannot imagine."[18]

"No more can I," interrupted Maria; "yet they even expatiate on the peculiar happiness of indigence, though in what it can consist, ex-

---

[18]Usually citing scripture, e.g., Jesus's "Blessed be the poor" (Luke 6:20).

cepting in brutal rest, when a man can barely earn a subsistence, I cannot imagine. The mind is necessarily imprisoned in its own little tenement; and, fully occupied by keeping it in repair, has not time to rove abroad for improvement. The book of knowledge is closely clasped, against those who must fulfil their daily task of severe manual labour or die; and curiosity, rarely excited by thought or information, seldom moves on the stagnate lake of ignorance."

"As far as I have been able to observe," replied Jemima, "prejudices, caught up by chance, are obstinately maintained by the poor, to the exclusion of improvement; they have not time to reason or reflect to any extent, or minds sufficiently exercised to adopt the principles of action, which form perhaps the only basis of contentment in every station."[19]

"And independence," said Darnford, "they are necessarily strangers to, even the independence of despising their persecutors. If the poor are happy, or can be happy, *things are very well as they are.* And I cannot conceive on what principle those writers contend for a change of system, who support this opinion. The authors on the other side of the question are much more consistent, who grant the fact; yet, insisting that it is the lot of the majority to be oppressed in this life, kindly turn them over to another, to rectify the false weights and measures of this, as the only way to justify the dispensations of Providence. I have not," continued Darnford, "an opinion more firmly fixed by observation in my mind, than that, though riches may fail to produce proportionate happiness, poverty most commonly excludes it, by shutting up all the avenues to improvement."

"And as for the affections," added Maria, with a sigh, "how gross, and even tormenting do they become, unless regulated by an improving mind! The culture of the heart ever, I believe, keeps pace with that of the mind. But pray go on," addressing Jemima, "though your narrative gives rise to the most painful reflections on the present state of society."

"Not to trouble you," continued she, "with a detailed description of all the painful feelings of unavailing exertion, I have only to tell you, that at last I got recommended to wash in a few families, who did me the favour to admit me into their houses, without the most strict enquiry, to wash from one in the morning till eight at night, for eighteen

---

[19]The copy which appears to have received the author's last corrections, ends at this place [WG].

or twenty-pence a day.[20] On the happiness to be enjoyed over a wash-ing-tub I need not comment; yet you will allow me to observe, that this was a wretchedness of situation peculiar to my sex. A man with half my industry, and, I may say, abilities, could have procured a decent livelihood, and discharged some of the duties which knit mankind to-gether; whilst I, who had acquired a taste for the rational, nay, in hon-est pride let me assert it, the virtuous enjoyments of life, was cast aside as the filth of society. Condemned to labour, like a machine, only to earn bread, and scarcely that, I became melancholy and desperate.

"I have now to mention a circumstance which fills me with re-morse, and fear it will entirely deprive me of your esteem. A trades-man became attached to me, and visited me frequently,—and I at last obtained such a power over him, that he offered to take me home to his house.—Consider, dear madam, I was famishing: wonder not that I became a wolf!—The only reason for not taking me home immedi-ately, was the having a girl in the house, with child by him—and this girl—I advised him—yes, I did! would I could forget it!—to turn out of doors: and one night he determined to follow my advice. Poor wretch! she fell upon her knees, reminded him that he had promised to marry her, that her parents were honest!—What did it avail?—She was turned out.

"She approached her father's door, in the skirts of London,—listened at the shutters,—but could not knock. A watchman had observed her go and return several times—Poor wretch!—[The re-morse Jemima spoke of, seemed to be stinging her to the soul, as she proceeded.]

"She left it, and, approaching a tub where horses were watered, she sat down in it, and, with desperate resolution, remained in that attitude—till resolution was no longer necessary!

"I happened that morning to be going out to wash, anticipating the moment when I should escape from such hard labour. I passed by, just as some men, going to work, drew out the stiff, cold corpse—Let me not recal the horrid moment!—I recognized her pale visage; I lis-tened to the tale told by the spectators, and my heart did not burst. I thought of my own state, and wondered how I could be such a mon-ster!—I worked hard; and, returning home, I was attacked by a fever. I suffered both in body and mind. I determined not to live with the

[20]This report of washerwomen's slightly more than penny-an-hour wage is historically accurate.

wretch. But he did not try me; he left the neighbourhood. I once more returned to the wash-tub.

"Still this state, miserable as it was, admitted of aggravation. Lifting one day a heavy load, a tub fell against my shin, and gave me great pain. I did not pay much attention to the hurt, till it became a serious wound; being obliged to work as usual, or starve. But, finding myself at length unable to stand for any time, I thought of getting into an hospital. Hospitals, it should seem (for they are comfortless abodes for the sick) were expressly endowed for the reception of the friendless; yet I, who had on that plea a right to assistance, wanted the recommendation of the rich and respectable, and was several weeks languishing for admittance; fees were demanded on entering; and, what was still more unreasonable, security for burying me, that expence not coming into the letter of the charity. A guinea was the stipulated sum—I could as soon have raised a million; and I was afraid to apply to the parish for an order, lest they should have passed me, I knew not whither.[21] The poor woman at whose house I lodged, compassionating my state, got me into the hospital; and the family where I received the hurt, sent me five shillings, three and six-pence of which I gave at my admittance—I know not for what.

"My leg grew quickly better; but I was dismissed before my cure was completed, because I could not afford to have my linen washed to appear decently, as the virago of a nurse said, when the gentlemen (the surgeons) came. I cannot give you an adequate idea of the wretchedness of an hospital; every thing is left to the care of people intent on gain. The attendants seem to have lost all feeling of compassion in the bustling discharge of their offices; death is so familiar to them, that they are not anxious to ward it off. Every thing appeared to be conducted for the accommodation of the medical men and their pupils, who came to make experiments on the poor, for the benefit of the rich. One of the physicians, I must not forget to mention, gave me half-a-crown, and ordered me some wine, when I was at the lowest ebb. I thought of making my case known to the lady-like matron; but her forbidding countenance prevented me. She condescended to look on the patients, and make general enquiries, two or three times a week; but the nurses knew the hour when the visit of ceremony would commence, and every thing was as it should be.

[21]Poor relief was only administered to individuals in the parish where they had last been legally settled.

"After my dismission, I was more at a loss than ever for a subsistence, and, not to weary you with a repetition of the same unavailing attempts, unable to stand at the washing-tub, I began to consider the rich and poor as natural enemies, and became a thief from principle.[22] I could not now cease to reason, but I hated mankind. I despised myself, yet I justified my conduct. I was taken, tried, and condemned to six months' imprisonment in a house of correction. My soul recoils with horror from the remembrance of the insults I had to endure, till, branded with shame, I was turned loose in the street, pennyless. I wandered from street to street, till, exhausted by hunger and fatigue, I sunk down senseless at a door, where I had vainly demanded a morsel of bread. I was sent by the inhabitant to the work-house, to which he had surlily bid me go, saying, he 'paid enough in conscience to the poor,' when, with parched tongue, I implored his charity.[23] If those well-meaning people who exclaim against beggars, were acquainted with the treatment the poor receive in many of these wretched asylums, they would not stifle so easily involuntary sympathy, by saying that they have all parishes to go to, or wonder that the poor dread to enter the gloomy walls. What are the common run of work-houses, but prisons, in which many respectable old people, worn out by immoderate labour, sink into the grave in sorrow, to which they are carried like dogs!"

Alarmed by some indistinct noise, Jemima rose hastily to listen, and Maria, turning to Darnford, said, "I have indeed been shocked beyond expression when I have met a pauper's funeral. A coffin carried on the shoulders of three or four ill-looking wretches, whom the imagination might easily convert into a band of assassins, hastening to conceal the corpse, and quarrelling about the prey on their way. I know it is of little consequence how we are consigned to the earth; but I am led by this brutal insensibility, to what even the animal creation appears forcibly to feel, to advert to the wretched, deserted manner in which they died."

"True," rejoined Darnford, "and, till the rich will give more than a part of their wealth, till they will give time and attention to the

---

[22]In Godwin's political novel *Caleb Williams* (1794), the captain of the thieves makes a similar speech (3.3).

[23]The wealthier residents of a parish paid a "Poor tax" to support its dependents. By the late 1790s, on the theory that poverty stemmed from indolence, "poor laws" were being proposed in Parliament to prohibit alms-giving (charity) and to put the poor in workhouses, where the wages were appallingly low and families typically broken up.

wants of the distressed, never let them boast of charity. Let them open their hearts, and not their purses, and employ their minds in the service, if they are really actuated by humanity; or charitable institutions will always be the prey of the lowest order of knaves."

Jemima returning, seemed in haste to finish her tale. "The overseer farmed the poor[24] of different parishes, and out of the bowels of poverty was wrung the money with which he purchased this dwelling, as a private receptacle for madness. He had been a keeper at a house of the same description, and conceived that he could make money much more readily in his old occupation. He is a shrewd—shall I say it?—villain. He observed something resolute in my manner, and offered to take me with him, and instruct me how to treat the disturbed minds he meant to intrust to my care. The offer of forty pounds a year,[25] and to quit a workhouse, was not to be despised, though the condition of shutting my eyes and hardening my heart was annexed to it.

"I agreed to accompany him; and four years have I been attendant on many wretches, and"—she lowered her voice,—"the witness of many enormities. In solitude my mind seemed to recover its force, and many of the sentiments which I imbibed in the only tolerable period of my life, returned with their full force. Still what should induce me to be the champion for suffering humanity?—Who ever risked any thing for me?—Who ever acknowledged me to be a fellow-creature?"—

Maria took her hand, and Jemima, more overcome by kindness than she had ever been by cruelty, hastened out of the room to conceal her emotions.

Darnford soon after heard his summons, and, taking leave of him, Maria promised to gratify his curiosity, with respect to herself, the first opportunity.

CHAPTER VI

Active as love was in the heart of Maria, the story she had just heard made her thoughts take a wider range. The opening buds of hope closed, as if they had put forth too early, and the happiest day of her

---

[24] Made money from them, as if they were a cash crop, by hiring them out as laborers with part of their meager wages taken as commission as allowed by law.

[25] At the end of the 18th c., farm workers on a 6-day week earned £15–20 a year.

life was overcast by the most melancholy reflections. Thinking of Jemima's peculiar fate and her own, she was led to consider the oppressed state of women, and to lament that she had given birth to a daughter. Sleep fled from her eyelids, while she dwelt on the wretchedness of unprotected infancy, till sympathy with Jemima changed to agony, when it seemed probable that her own babe might even now be in the very state she so forcibly described.

Maria thought, and thought again. Jemima's humanity had rather been benumbed than killed, by the keen frost she had to brave at her entrance into life; an appeal then to her feelings, on this tender point, surely would not be fruitless; and Maria began to anticipate the delight it would afford her to gain intelligence of her child. This project was now the only subject of reflection; and she watched impatiently for the dawn of day, with that determinate purpose which generally insures success.

At the usual hour, Jemima brought her breakfast, and a tender note from Darnford. She ran her eye hastily over it, and her heart calmly hoarded up the rapture a fresh assurance of affection, affection such as she wished to inspire, gave her, without diverting her mind a moment from its design. While Jemima waited to take away the breakfast, Maria alluded to the reflections, that had haunted her during the night to the exclusion of sleep. She spoke with energy of Jemima's unmerited sufferings, and of the fate of a number of deserted females, placed within the sweep of a whirlwind, from which it was next to impossible to escape. Perceiving the effect her conversation produced on the countenance of her guard, she grasped the arm of Jemima with that irresistible warmth which defies repulse, exclaiming—"With your heart, and such dreadful experience, can you lend your aid to deprive my babe of a mother's tenderness, a mother's care? In the name of God, assist me to snatch her from destruction! Let me but give her an education—let me but prepare her body and mind to encounter the ills which await her sex, and I will teach her to consider you as her second mother, and herself as the prop of your age. Yes, Jemima, look at me—observe me closely, and read my very soul; you merit a better fate;" she held out her hand with a firm gesture of assurance; "and I will procure it for you, as a testimony of my esteem, as well as of my gratitude."

Jemima had not power to resist this persuasive torrent; and, owning that the house in which she was confined, was situated on the banks of the Thames, only a few miles from London, and not on the sea-coast, as Darnford had supposed, she promised to invent some excuse for her absence, and go herself to trace the situation, and enquire concerning the health, of this abandoned daughter. Her manner implied an intention to do something more, but she seemed unwilling to impart her design; and Maria, glad to have obtained the main point, thought it best to leave her to the workings of her own mind; convinced that she had the power of interesting her still more in favour of herself and child, by a simple recital of facts.

In the evening, Jemima informed the impatient mother, that on the morrow she should hasten to town before the family hour of rising, and received all the information necessary, as a clue to her search. The "Good night!" Maria uttered was peculiarly solemn and affectionate. Glad expectation sparkled in her eye; and, for the first time since her detention, she pronounced the name of her child with pleasureable fondness; and, with all the garrulity of a nurse, described her first smile when she recognized her mother. Recollecting herself, a still kinder "Adieu!" with a "God bless you!"—that seemed to include a maternal benediction, dismissed Jemima.

The dreary solitude of the ensuing day, lengthened by impatiently dwelling on the same idea, was intolerably wearisome. She listened for the sound of a particular clock, which some directions of the wind allowed her to hear distinctly. She marked the shadow gaining on the wall; and, twilight thickening into darkness, her breath seemed oppressed while she anxiously counted nine.—The last sound was a stroke of despair on her heart; for she expected every moment, without seeing Jemima, to have her light extinguished by the savage female who supplied her place. She was even obliged to prepare for bed, restless as she was, not to disoblige her new attendant. She had been cautioned not to speak too freely to her; but the caution was needless, her countenance would still more emphatically have made her shrink back. Such was the ferocity of manner, conspicuous in every word and gesture of this hag, that Maria was afraid to enquire, why Jemima, who had faithfully promised to see her before her door was shut for the night, came not?—and, when the key turned in the lock, to consign her to a night of suspence, she felt a degree of anguish which the circumstances scarcely justified.

Continually on the watch, the shutting of a door, or the sound of a footstep, made her start and tremble with apprehension, something like what she felt, when, at her entrance, dragged along the gallery, she began to doubt whether she were not surrounded by demons?

Fatigued by an endless rotation of thought and wild alarms, she looked like a spectre, when Jemima entered in the morning; especially as her eyes darted out of her head, to read in Jemima's countenance, almost as pallid, the intelligence she dared not trust her tongue to demand. Jemima put down the tea-things, and appeared very busy in arranging the table. Maria took up a cup with trembling hand, then forcibly recovering her fortitude, and restraining the convulsive movement which agitated the muscles of her mouth, she said, "Spare yourself the pain of preparing me for your information, I adjure you!—My child is dead!" Jemima solemnly answered, "Yes;" with a look expressive of compassion and angry emotions. "Leave me," added Maria, making a fresh effort to govern her feelings, and hiding her face in her handkerchief, to conceal her anguish—"It is enough— I know that my babe is no more—I will hear the particulars when I am"—*calmer*, she could not utter; and Jemima, without importuning her by idle attempts to console her, left the room.

Plunged in the deepest melancholy, she would not admit Darnford's visits; and such is the force of early associations even on strong minds, that, for a while, she indulged the superstitious notion that she was justly punished by the death of her child, for having for an instant ceased to regret her loss. Two or three letters from Darnford, full of soothing, manly tenderness, only added poignancy to these accusing emotions; yet the passionate style in which he expressed, what he termed the first and fondest wish of his heart, "that his affection might make her some amends for the cruelty and injustice she had endured," inspired a sentiment of gratitude to heaven; and her eyes filled with delicious tears, when, at the conclusion of his letter, wishing to supply the place of her unworthy relations, whose want of principle he execrated, he assured her, calling her his dearest girl, "that it should henceforth be the business of his life to make her happy."

He begged, in a note sent the following morning, to be permitted to see her, when his presence would be no intrusion on her grief; and so earnestly intreated to be allowed, according to promise, to beguile the tedious moments of absence, by dwelling on the events of her past life, that she sent him the memoirs which had been written for her daughter, promising Jemima the perusal as soon as he returned them.

CHAPTER VII

"Addressing these memoirs to you, my child, uncertain whether I shall ever have an opportunity of instructing you, many observations will probably flow from my heart, which only a mother—a mother schooled in misery, could make.

"The tenderness of a father who knew the world, might be great; but could it equal that of a mother—of a mother, labouring under a portion of the misery, which the constitution of society seems to have entailed on all her kind? It is, my child, my dearest daughter, only such a mother, who will dare to break through all restraint to provide for your happiness—who will voluntarily brave censure herself, to ward off sorrow from your bosom. From my narrative, my dear girl, you may gather the instruction, the counsel, which is meant rather to exercise than influence your mind.—Death may snatch me from you, before you can weigh my advice, or enter into my reasoning[1]: I would then, with fond anxiety, lead you very early in life to form your grand principle of action, to save you from the vain regret of having, through irresolution, let the spring-tide of existence pass away, unimproved, unenjoyed.—Gain experience—ah! gain it—while experience is worth having, and acquire sufficient fortitude to pursue your own happiness; it includes your utility, by a direct path. What is wisdom too often, but the owl of the goddess,[2] who sits moping in a desolated heart; around me she shrieks, but I would invite all the gay warblers of spring to nestle in your blooming bosom.—Had I not wasted years in deliberating, after I ceased to doubt, how I ought to have acted—I might now be useful and happy.—For my sake, warned by my example, always appear what you are, and you will not pass through existence without enjoying its genuine blessings, love and respect.

"Born in one of the most romantic parts of England, an enthusiastic fondness for the varying charms of nature is the first sentiment I recollect; or rather it was the first consciousness of pleasure that employed and formed my imagination.

"My father had been a captain of a man of war; but, disgusted with the service, on account of the preferment of men whose chief

[1] A concern expressed by James Gregory in the introduction to *A Father's Legacy to His Daughters*.

[2] Athena, goddess of wisdom, whose emblem is an owl.

merit was their family connections or borough interest,[3] he retired into the country; and, not knowing what to do with himself—married. In his family, to regain his lost consequence, he determined to keep up the same passive obedience, as in the vessels in which he had commanded. His orders were not to be disputed; and the whole house was expected to fly, at the word of command, as if to man the shrouds, or mount aloft in an elemental strife, big with life or death. He was to be instantaneously obeyed, especially by my mother, whom he very benevolently married for love; but took care to remind her of the obligation, when she dared, in the slightest instance, to question his absolute authority. My eldest brother, it is true, as he grew up, was treated with more respect by my father; and became in due form the deputy-tyrant of the house. The representative of my father, a being privileged by nature—a boy, and the darling of my mother, he did not fail to act like an heir apparent. Such indeed was my mother's extravagant partiality, that, in comparison with her affection for him, she might be said not to love the rest of her children. Yet none of the children seemed to have so little affection for her. Extreme indulgence had rendered him so selfish, that he only thought of himself; and from tormenting insects and animals, he became the despot of his brothers, and still more of his sisters.

"It is perhaps difficult to give you an idea of the petty cares which obscured the morning of my life; continual restraint in the most trivial matters; unconditional submission to orders, which, as a mere child, I soon discovered to be unreasonable, because inconsistent and contradictory. Thus are we destined to experience a mixture of bitterness, with the recollection of our most innocent enjoyments.

"The circumstances which, during my childhood, occurred to fashion my mind, were various; yet, as it would probably afford me more pleasure to revive the fading remembrance of new-born delight, than you, my child, could feel in the perusal, I will not entice you to stray with me into the verdant meadow, to search for the flowers that youthful hopes scatter in every path; though, as I write, I almost scent the fresh green of spring—of that spring which never returns!

"I had two sisters, and one brother, younger than myself; my brother Robert was two years older, and might truly be termed the idol of his parents, and the torment of the rest of the family. Such in-

[3]Lucrative military offices were frequently procured this way.

deed is the force of prejudice, that what was called spirit and wit in him, was cruelly repressed as forwardness in me.

"My mother had an indolence of character, which prevented her from paying much attention to our education. But the healthy breeze of a neighbouring heath, on which we bounded at pleasure, volatilized the humours that improper food might have generated. And to enjoy open air and freedom, was paradise, after the unnatural restraint of our fire-side, where we were often obliged to sit three or four hours together, without daring to utter a word, when my father was out of humour, from want of employment, or of a variety of boisterous amusement. I had however one advantage, an instructor, the brother of my father, who, intended for the church, had of course received a liberal education. But, becoming attached to a young lady of great beauty and large fortune, and acquiring in the world some opinions not consonant with the profession for which he was designed, he accepted, with the most sanguine expectations of success, the offer of a nobleman to accompany him to India, as his confidential secretary.

"A correspondence was regularly kept up with the object of his affection; and the intricacies of business, peculiarly wearisome to a man of a romantic turn of mind, contributed, with a forced absence, to increase his attachment. Every other passion was lost in this master-one, and only served to swell the torrent. Her relations, such were his waking dreams, who had despised him, would court in their turn his alliance, and all the blandishments of taste would grace the triumph of love.—While he basked in the warm sunshine of love, friendship also promised to shed its dewy freshness; for a friend, whom he loved next to his mistress, was the confident, who forwarded the letters from one to the other, to elude the observation of prying relations. A friend false in similar circumstances, is, my dearest girl, an old tale; yet, let not this example, or the frigid caution of cold-blooded moralists, make you endeavour to stifle hopes, which are the buds that naturally unfold themselves during the spring of life! Whilst your own heart is sincere, always expect to meet one glowing with the same sentiments; for to fly from pleasure, is not to avoid pain!

"My uncle realized, by good luck, rather than management, a handsome fortune; and returning on the wings of love, lost in the most enchanting reveries, to England, to share it with his mistress and his friend, he found them—united.

"There were some circumstances, not necessary for me to recite, which aggravated the guilt of the friend beyond measure, and the deception, that had been carried on to the last moment, was so base, it produced the most violent effect on my uncle's health and spirits. His native country, the world! lately a garden of blooming sweets, blasted by treachery, seemed changed into a parched desert, the abode of hissing serpents. Disappointment rankled in his heart; and, brooding over his wrongs, he was attacked by a raging fever, followed by a derangement of mind, which only gave place to habitual melancholy, as he recovered more strength of body.

"Declaring an intention never to marry, his relations were ever clustering about him, paying the grossest adulation to a man, who, disgusted with mankind, received them with scorn, or bitter sarcasms. Something in my countenance pleased him, when I began to prattle. Since his return, he appeared dead to affection; but I soon, by showing him innocent fondness, became a favourite; and endeavouring to enlarge and strengthen my mind, I grew dear to him in proportion as I imbibed his sentiments. He had a forcible manner of speaking, rendered more so by a certain impressive wildness of look and gesture, calculated to engage the attention of a young and ardent mind. It is not then surprising that I quickly adopted his opinions in preference, and reverenced him as one of a superior order of beings. He inculcated, with great warmth, self-respect, and a lofty consciousness of acting right, independent of the censure or applause of the world; nay, he almost taught me to brave, and even despise its censure, when convinced of the rectitude of my own intentions.

"Endeavouring to prove to me that nothing which deserved the name of love or friendship, existed in the world, he drew such animated pictures of his own feelings, rendered permanent by disappointment, as imprinted the sentiments strongly on my heart, and animated my imagination. These remarks are necessary to elucidate some peculiarities in my character, which by the world are indefinitely termed romantic.

"My uncle's increasing affection led him to visit me often. Still, unable to rest in any place, he did not remain long in the country to soften domestic tyranny; but he brought me books, for which I had a passion, and they conspired with his conversation, to make me form an ideal picture of life. I shall pass over the tyranny of my father, much as I suffered from it; but it is necessary to notice, that it undermined my mother's health; and that her temper, continually irritated by domestic bickering, became intolerably peevish.

"My eldest brother was articled to a neighbouring attorney, the shrewdest, and, I may add, the most unprincipled man in that part of the country. As my brother generally came home every Saturday, to astonish my mother by exhibiting his attainments, he gradually assumed a right of directing the whole family, not excepting my father. He seemed to take a peculiar pleasure in tormenting and humbling me; and if I ever ventured to complain of this treatment to either my father or mother, I was rudely rebuffed for presuming to judge of the conduct of my eldest brother.

"About this period a merchant's family came to settle in our neighbourhood. A mansion-house in the village, lately purchased, had been preparing the whole spring, and the sight of the costly furniture, sent from London, had excited my mother's envy, and roused my father's pride. My sensations were very different, and all of a pleasurable kind. I longed to see new characters, to break the tedious monotony of my life; and to find a friend, such as fancy had pourtrayed. I cannot then describe the emotion I felt, the Sunday they made their appearance at church. My eyes were rivetted on the pillar round which I expected first to catch a glimpse of them, and darted forth to meet a servant who hastily preceded a group of ladies, whose white robes and waving plumes, seemed to stream along the gloomy aisle, diffusing the light, by which I contemplated their figures.

"We visited them in form; and I quickly selected the eldest daughter for my friend. The second son, George, paid me particular attention, and finding his attainments and manners superior to those of the young men of the village, I began to imagine him superior to the rest of mankind. Had my home been more comfortable, or my previous acquaintance more numerous, I should not probably have been so eager to open my heart to new affections.

"Mr. Venables, the merchant, had acquired a large fortune by unremitting attention to business; but his health declining rapidly, he was obliged to retire, before his son, George, had acquired sufficient experience, to enable him to conduct their affairs on the same prudential plan, his father had invariably pursued. Indeed, he had laboured to throw off his authority, having despised his narrow plans and cautious speculation. The eldest son could not be prevailed on to enter the firm; and, to oblige his wife, and have peace in the house, Mr. Venables had purchased a commission for him in the guards.

"I am now alluding to circumstances which came to my knowledge long after; but it is necessary, my dearest child, that you should know the character of your father, to prevent your despising your mother; the only parent inclined to discharge a parent's duty. In London, George had acquired habits of libertinism, which he carefully concealed from his father and his commercial connections. The mask he wore, was so complete a covering of his real visage, that the praise his father lavished on his conduct, and, poor mistaken man! on his principles, contrasted with his brother's, rendered the notice he took of me peculiarly flattering. Without any fixed design, as I am now convinced, he continued to single me out at the dance, press my hand at parting, and utter expressions of unmeaning passion, to which I gave a meaning naturally suggested by the romantic turn of my thoughts. His stay in the country was short; his manners did not entirely please me; but, when he left us, the colouring of my picture became more vivid—Whither did not my imagination lead me? In short, I fancied myself in love—in love with the disinterestedness, fortitude, generosity, dignity, and humanity, with which I had invested the hero I dubbed. A circumstance which soon after occurred, rendered all these virtues palpable. [The incident is perhaps worth relating on other accounts, and therefore I shall describe it distinctly.]

"I had a great affection for my nurse, old Mary, for whom I used often to work, to spare her eyes. Mary had a younger sister, married to a sailor, while she was suckling me; for my mother only suckled my eldest brother, which might be the cause of her extraordinary partiality. Peggy, Mary's sister, lived with her, till her husband, becoming a mate in a West-India trader, got a little before-hand in the world. He wrote to his wife from the first port in the Channel, after his most successful voyage, to request her to come to London to meet him; he even wished her to determine on living there for the future, to save him the trouble of coming to her the moment he came on shore; and to turn a penny by keeping a green-stall. It was too much to set out on a journey the moment he had finished a voyage, and fifty miles by land, was worse than a thousand leagues by sea.

"She packed up her alls,[4] and came to London—but did not meet honest Daniel. A common misfortune prevented her, and the poor are bound to suffer for the good of their country—he was pressed in the river—and never came on shore.[5]

[4] Northern dialect for "goods and chattels" (Joseph Wright, *English Dialect Dictionary*).

[5] The Impressment into forced military service was a common practice, preying on drunks and the defenseless poor in particular.

"Peggy was miserable in London, not knowing, as she said, 'the face of any living soul.' Besides, her imagination had been employed, anticipating a month or six weeks' happiness with her husband. Daniel was to have gone with her to Sadler's Wells, and Westminster Abbey, and to many sights, which he knew she never heard of in the country. Peggy too was thrifty, and how could she manage to put his plan in execution alone? He had acquaintance; but she did not know the very name of their places of abode. His letters were made up of—How do you does, and God bless yous,—information was reserved for the hour of meeting.

"She too had her portion of information, near at heart. Molly and Jacky were grown such little darlings, she was almost angry that daddy did not see their tricks. She had not half the pleasure she should have had from their prattle, could she have recounted to him each night the pretty speeches of the day. Some stories, however, were stored up—and Jacky could say papa with such a sweet voice, it must delight his heart. Yet when she came, and found no Daniel to greet her, when Jacky called papa, she wept, bidding 'God bless his innocent soul, that did not know what sorrow was.'—But more sorrow was in store for Peggy, innocent as she was.—Daniel was killed in the first engagement, and then the *papa* was agony, sounding to the heart.

"She had lived sparingly on his wages, while there was any hope of his return; but, that gone, she returned with a breaking heart to the country, to a little market town, nearly three miles from our village. She did not like to go to service, to be snubbed about, after being her own mistress. To put her children out to nurse was impossible: how far would her wages go? and to send them to her husband's parish,[6] a distant one, was to lose her husband twice over.

"I had heard all from Mary, and made my uncle furnish a little cottage for her, to enable her to sell—so sacred was poor Daniel's advice, now he was dead and gone—a little fruit, toys and cakes. The minding of the shop did not require her whole time, nor even the keeping her children clean, and she loved to see them clean; so she took in washing, and altogether made a shift to earn bread for her children, still weeping for Daniel, when Jacky's arch looks made her think of his father.—It was pleasant to work for her children.—'Yes; from morning till night, could she have had a kiss from their father, God rest his soul! Yes; had it pleased Providence to have let him come back without a leg or an arm, it would have been the same thing to her—for she did not love him because he maintained them—no; she had hands of her own.'

[6]See pp. 287–88, n. 21 and 23.

"The country people were honest, and Peggy left her linen out to dry very late. A recruiting party, as she supposed, passing through, made free with a large wash; for it was all swept away, including her own and her children's little stock.

"This was a dreadful blow; two dozen of shirts, stocks and handkerchiefs. She gave the money which she had laid by for half a year's rent, and promised to pay two shillings a week till all was cleared; so she did not lose her employment. This two shillings a week, and the buying a few necessaries for the children, drove her so hard, that she had not a penny to pay her rent with, when a twelvemonth's became due.

"She was now with Mary, and had just told her tale, which Mary instantly repeated—it was intended for my ear. Many houses in this town, producing a borough-interest, were included in the estate purchased by Mr. Venables, and the attorney with whom my brother lived, was appointed his agent, to collect and raise the rents.

"He demanded Peggy's, and, in spite of her intreaties, her poor goods had been seized and sold. So that she had not, and what was worse her children, 'for she had known sorrow enough,' a bed to lie on. She knew that I was good-natured—right charitable, yet not liking to ask for more than needs must, she scorned to petition while people could any how be made to wait. But now, should she be turned out of doors, she must expect nothing less than to lose all her customers, and then she must beg or starve—and what would become of her children?—'had Daniel not been pressed—but God knows best—all this could not have happened.'

"I had two mattrasses on my bed; what did I want with two, when such a worthy creature must lie on the ground? My mother would be angry, but I could conceal it till my uncle came down; and then I would tell him all the whole truth, and if he absolved me, heaven would.

"I begged the house-maid to come up stairs with me (servants always feel for the distresses of poverty, and so would the rich if they knew what it was). She assisted me to tie up the mattrass; I discovering, at the same time, that one blanket would serve me till winter, could I persuade my sister, who slept with me, to keep my secret. She entering in the midst of the package, I gave her some new feathers, to silence her. We got the mattrass down the back stairs, unperceived, and I helped to carry it, taking with me all the money I had, and what I could borrow from my sister.

"When I got to the cottage, Peggy declared that she would not take what I had brought secretly; but, when, with all the eager eloquence inspired by a decided purpose, I grasped her hand with weeping eyes, assuring her that my uncle would screen me from blame, when he was once more in the country, describing, at the same time, what she would suffer in parting with her children, after keeping them so long from being thrown on the parish, she reluctantly consented.

"My project of usefulness ended not here; I determined to speak to the attorney; he frequently paid me compliments. His character did not intimidate me; but, imagining that Peggy must be mistaken, and that no man could turn a deaf ear to such a tale of complicated distress, I determined to walk to the town with Mary the next morning, and request him to wait for the rent, and keep my secret, till my uncle's return.

"My repose was sweet; and, waking with the first dawn of day, I bounded to Mary's cottage. What charms do not a light heart spread over nature! Every bird that twittered in a bush, every flower that enlivened the hedge, seemed placed there to awaken me to rapture—yes; to rapture. The present moment was full fraught with happiness; and on futurity I bestowed not a thought, excepting to anticipate my success with the attorney.

"This man of the world, with rosy face and simpering features, received me politely, nay kindly; listened with complacency to my remonstrances, though he scarcely heeded Mary's tears. I did not then suspect, that my eloquence was in my complexion, the blush of seventeen, or that, in a world where humanity to women is the characteristic of advancing civilization, the beauty of a young girl was so much more interesting than the distress of an old one. Pressing my hand, he promised to let Peggy remain in the house as long as I wished.—I more than returned the pressure—I was so grateful and so happy. Emboldened by my innocent warmth, he then kissed me—and I did not draw back—I took it for a kiss of charity.

"Gay as a lark, I went to dine at Mr. Venables'. I had previously obtained five shillings from my father, towards re-clothing the poor children of my care, and prevailed on my mother to take one of the girls into the house, whom I determined to teach to work[7] and read.

"After dinner, when the younger part of the circle retired to the music room, I recounted with energy my tale; that is, I mentioned Peggy's distress, without hinting at the steps I had taken to relieve her. Miss Venables gave me half-a-crown; the heir five shillings; but

---

[7]Needlework, a common trade for women, extremely oppressive and low paid.

George sat unmoved. I was cruelly distressed by the disappointment—I scarcely could remain on my chair; and, could I have got out of the room unperceived, I should have flown home, as if to run away from myself. After several vain attempts to rise, I leaned my head against the marble chimney-piece, and gazing on the evergreens that filled the fire-place, moralized on the vanity of human expectations; regardless of the company. I was roused by a gentle tap on my shoulder from behind Charlotte's chair. I turned my head, and George slid a guinea[8] into my hand, putting his finger to his mouth, to enjoin me silence.

"What a revolution took place, not only in my train of thoughts, but feelings! I trembled with emotion—now, indeed, I was in love. Such delicacy too, to enhance his benevolence! I felt in my pocket every five minutes, only to feel the guinea; and its magic touch invested my hero with more than mortal beauty. My fancy had found a basis to erect its model of perfection on; and quickly went to work, with all the happy credulity of youth, to consider that heart as devoted to virtue, which had only obeyed a virtuous impulse. The bitter experience was yet to come, that has taught me how very distinct are the principles of virtue, from the casual feelings from which they germinate.

CHAPTER VIII

"I have perhaps dwelt too long on a circumstance, which is only of importance as it marks the progress of a deception that has been so fatal to my peace; and introduces to your notice a poor girl, whom, intending to serve, I led to ruin. Still it is probable that I was not entirely the victim of mistake; and that your father, gradually fashioned by the world, did not quickly become what I hesitate to call him—out of respect to my daughter.

"But, to hasten to the more busy scenes of my life. Mr. Venables and my mother died the same summer; and, wholly engrossed by my attention to her, I thought of little else. The neglect of her darling, my brother Robert, had a violent effect on her weakened mind; for, though boys may be reckoned the pillars of the house without doors, girls are often the only comfort within. They but too frequently waste their health and spirits attending a dying parent, who leaves them in com-

---

[8]A coin worth slightly more than £1, first minted for the slave trade. See the Introduction, pp. 236–37.

parative poverty. After closing, with filial piety, a father's eyes, they are chased from the paternal roof, to make room for the first-born, the son, who is to carry the empty family-name down to posterity; though, occupied with his own pleasures, he scarcely thought of discharging, in the decline of his parent's life, the debt contracted in his childhood. My mother's conduct led me to make these reflections. Great as was the fatigue I endured, and the affection my unceasing solicitude evinced, of which my mother seemed perfectly sensible, still, when my brother, whom I could hardly persuade to remain a quarter of an hour in her chamber, was with her alone, a short time before her death, she gave him a little hoard, which she had been some years accumulating.

"During my mother's illness, I was obliged to manage my father's temper, who, from the lingering nature of her malady, began to imagine that it was merely fancy. At this period, an artful kind of upper servant attracted my father's attention, and the neighbours made many remarks on the finery, not honestly got, exhibited at evening service. But I was too much occupied with my mother to observe any change in her dress or behaviour, or to listen to the whisper of scandal.

"I shall not dwell on the death-bed scene, lively as is the remembrance, or on the emotion produced by the last grasp of my mother's cold hand; when blessing me, she added, 'A little patience, and all will be over!' Ah! my child, how often have those words rung mournfully in my ears—and I have exclaimed—'A little more patience, and I too shall be at rest!'

"My father was violently affected by her death, recollected instances of his unkindness, and wept like a child.

"My mother had solemnly recommended my sisters to my care, and bid me be a mother to them. They, indeed, became more dear to me as they became more forlorn; for, during my mother's illness, I discovered the ruined state of my father's circumstances, and that he had only been able to keep up appearances, by the sums which he borrowed of my uncle.

"My father's grief, and consequent tenderness to his children, quickly abated, the house grew still more gloomy or riotous; and my refuge from care was again at Mr. Venables'; the young 'squire having taken his father's place, and allowing, for the present, his sister to preside at his table. George, though dissatisfied with his portion of the fortune, which had till lately been all in trade, visited the family as usual. He was now full of speculations in trade, and his brow became clouded by care. He seemed to relax in his attention to me, when the presence of my uncle gave a new turn to his behaviour. I was too unsuspecting, too disinterested, to trace these changes to their source.

My home every day became more and more disagreeable to me; my liberty was unnecessarily abridged, and my books, on the pretext that they made me idle, taken from me. My father's mistress was with child, and he, doating on her, allowed or overlooked her vulgar manner of tyrannizing over us. I was indignant, especially when I saw her endeavouring to attract, shall I say seduce? my younger brother. By allowing women but one way of rising in the world, the fostering the libertinism of men, society makes monsters of them, and then their ignoble vices are brought forward as a proof of inferiority of intellect.

The wearisomeness of my situation can scarcely be described. Though my life had not passed in the most even tenour with my mother, it was paradise to that I was destined to endure with my father's mistress, jealous of her illegitimate authority. My father's former occasional tenderness, in spite of his violence of temper, had been soothing to me; but now he only met me with reproofs or portentous frowns. The housekeeper, as she was now termed, was the vulgar despot of the family; and assuming the new character of a fine lady, she could never forgive the contempt which was sometimes visible in my countenance, when she uttered with pomposity her bad English, or affected to be well bred.

To my uncle I ventured to open my heart; and he, with his wonted benevolence, began to consider in what manner he could extricate me out of my present irksome situation. In spite of his own disappointment, or, most probably, actuated by the feelings that had been petrified, not cooled, in all their sanguine fervour, like a boiling torrent of lava suddenly dashing into the sea, he thought a marriage of mutual inclination (would envious stars permit it) the only chance for happiness in this disastrous world. George Venables had the reputation of being attentive to business, and my father's example gave great weight to this circumstance; for habits of order in business would, he conceived, extend to the regulation of the affections in domestic life. George seldom spoke in my uncle's company, except to utter a short, judicious question, or to make a pertinent remark, with all due deference to his superior judgment; so that my uncle seldom left his company without observing, that the young man had more in him than people supposed.

In this opinion he was not singular; yet, believe me, and I am not swayed by resentment, these speeches so justly poized, this silent deference, when the animal spirits of other young people were throwing off youthful ebullitions, were not the effect of thought or humility, but sheer barrenness of mind, and want of imagination. A colt of mettle will curvet and shew his paces. Yes; my dear girl, these prudent young men want all the fire necessary to ferment their faculties, and are characterized as wise, only because they are not foolish. It is true, that George was by no means so great a favourite of mine as during the first year of our acquaintance; still, as he often coincided in opinion with me, and echoed my sentiments; and having myself no other attachment, I heard with pleasure my uncle's proposal; but thought more of obtaining my freedom, than of my lover. But, when George, seemingly anxious for my happiness, pressed me to quit my present painful situation, my heart swelled with gratitude—I knew not that my uncle had promised him five thousand pounds.

Had this truly generous man mentioned his intention to me, I should have insisted on a thousand pounds being settled on each of my sisters; George would have contested; I should have seen his selfish soul; and—gracious God! have been spared the misery of discovering, when too late, that I was united to a heartless, unprincipled wretch. All my schemes of usefulness would not then have been blasted. The tenderness of my heart would not have heated my imagination with visions of the ineffable delight of happy love; nor would the sweet duty of a mother have been so cruelly interrupted.

But I must not suffer the fortitude I have so hardly acquired, to be undermined by unavailing regret. Let me hasten forward to describe the turbid stream in which I had to wade—but let me exultingly declare that it is passed—my soul holds fellowship with him no more. He cut the Gordian knot,[1] which my principles, mistaken ones, respected; he dissolved the tie, the fetters rather, that ate into my very vitals—and I should rejoice, conscious that my mind is freed, though confined in hell itself; the only place that even fancy can imagine more dreadful than my present abode.

These varying emotions will not allow me to proceed. I heave sigh after sigh; yet my heart is still oppressed. For what am I reserved? Why was I not born a man, or why was I born at all?

END OF VOLUME I

[1]A term for extreme difficulty, derived from the old legend that whoever could untie the intricate knot tied by King Gordius should rule Asia. Alexander the Great sliced it with his sword.

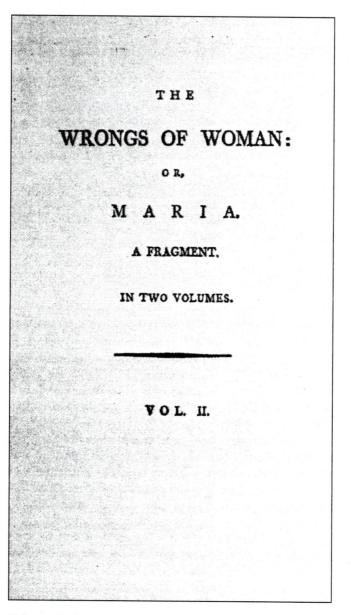

Title page for the second volume of *The Wrongs of Woman*.

VOLUME II

CHAPTER IX

"I resume my pen to fly from thought. I was married; and we hastened to London. I had purposed taking one of my sisters with me; for a strong motive for marrying, was the desire of having a home at which I could receive them, now their own grew so uncomfortable, as not to deserve the cheering appellation. An objection was made to her accompanying me, that appeared plausible; and I reluctantly acquiesced. I was however willingly allowed to take with me Molly, poor Peggy's daughter. London and preferment, are ideas commonly associated in the country; and, as blooming as May, she bade adieu to Peggy with weeping eyes. I did not even feel hurt at the refusal in relation to my sister, till hearing what my uncle had done for me, I had the simplicity to request, speaking with warmth of their situation, that he would give them a thousand pounds a-piece, which seemed to me but justice. He asked me, giving me a kiss, 'If I had lost my senses?' I started back, as if I had found a wasp in a rose-bush. I expostulated. He sneered; and the demon of discord entered our paradise, to poison with his pestiferous breath every opening joy.

"I had sometimes observed defects in my husband's understanding; but, led astray by a prevailing opinion, that goodness of disposition is of the first importance in the relative situations of life, in proportion as I perceived the narrowness of his understanding, fancy enlarged the boundary of his heart. Fatal error! How quickly is the so much vaunted milkiness of nature turned into gall, by an intercourse with the world, if more generous juices do not sustain the vital source of virtue!

"One trait in my character was extreme credulity; but, when my eyes were once opened, I saw but too clearly all I had before over-looked. My husband was sunk in my esteem; still there are youthful emotions, which, for a while, fill up the chasm of love and friendship. Besides, it required some time to enable me to see his whole character in a just light, or rather to allow it to become fixed. While circum-stances were ripening my faculties, and cultivating my taste, com-merce and gross relaxations were shutting his against any possibility of improvement, till, by stifling every spark of virtue in himself, he began to imagine that it no where existed.

"Do not let me lead you astray, my child, I do not mean to assert, that any human being is entirely incapable of feeling the generous emo-tions, which are the foundation of every true principle of virtue; but they are frequently, I fear, so feeble, that, like the inflammable quality which more or less lurks in all bodies, they often lie for ever dormant; the circumstances never occurring, necessary to call them into action.

"I discovered however by chance, that, in consequence of some losses in trade, the natural effect of his gambling desire to start suddenly into riches, the five thousand pounds given me by my uncle, had been paid very opportunely. This discovery, strange as you may think the assertion, gave me pleasure; my husband's embarrassments endeared him to me. I was glad to find an excuse for his conduct to my sisters, and my mind became calmer.

"My uncle introduced me to some literary society; and the theatres were a never-failing source of amusement to me. My delighted eye followed Mrs. Siddons, when, with dignified delicacy, she played Calista; and I involuntarily repeated after her, in the same tone, and with a long-drawn sigh,

'Hearts like our's were pair'd—not match'd.'[1]

"These were, at first, spontaneous emotions, though, becoming acquainted with men of wit and polished manners, I could not sometimes help regretting my early marriage; and that, in my haste to escape from a temporary dependence, and expand my newly fledged wings, in an unknown sky, I had been caught in a trap, and caged for life. Still the novelty of London, and the attentive fondness of my husband, for he had some personal regard for me, made several months glide away. Yet, not forgetting the situation of my sisters, who were still very young, I prevailed on my uncle to settle a thousand pounds on each; and to place them in a school near town, where I could frequently visit, as well as have them at home with me.

"I now tried to improve my husband's taste, but we had few subjects in common; indeed he soon appeared to have little relish for my society, unless he was hinting to me the use he could make of my uncle's wealth. When we had company, I was disgusted by an ostentatious display of riches, and I have often quitted the room, to avoid listening to exaggerated tales of money obtained by lucky hits.

[1]The celebrated tragedian Sarah Siddons (1755–1830), a friend of MW and WG, was famous for the role of Calista, heroine of Nicholas Rowe's popular tragedy *The Fair Penitent* (1703). "Such hearts as ours were never paired above; / Ill suited to each other; joined not matched," she says to Altamount, the virtuous lover chosen by her father whom she scorns in favor of Lothario (2.1.99–100). Seduced and abandoned by Lothario, she commits suicide.

"With all my attention and affectionate interest, I perceived that I could not become the friend or confident of my husband. Every thing I learned relative to his affairs I gathered up by accident; and I vainly endeavoured to establish, at our fire-side, that social converse, which often renders people of different characters dear to each other. Returning from the theatre, or any amusing party, I frequently began to relate what I had seen and highly relished; but with sullen taciturnity he soon silenced me. I seemed therefore gradually to lose, in his society, the soul, the energies of which had just been in action. To such a degree, in fact, did his cold, reserved manner affect me, that, after spending some days with him alone, I have imagined myself the most stupid creature in the world, till the abilities of some casual visitor convinced me that I had some dormant animation, and sentiments above the dust in which I had been groveling. The very countenance of my husband changed; his complexion became sallow, and all the charms of youth were vanishing with its vivacity.

"I give you one view of the subject; but these experiments and alterations took up the space of five years; during which period, I had most reluctantly extorted several sums from my uncle, to save my husband, to use his own words, from destruction. At first it was to prevent bills being noted, to the injury of his credit; then to bail him; and afterwards to prevent an execution from entering the house. I began at last to conclude, that he would have made more exertions of his own to extricate himself, had he not relied on mine, cruel as was the task he imposed on me; and I firmly determined that I would make use of no more pretexts.

"From the moment I pronounced this determination, indifference on his part was changed into rudeness, or something worse.

"He now seldom dined at home, and continually returned at a late hour, drunk, to bed. I retired to another apartment; I was glad, I own, to escape from his; for personal intimacy without affection, seemed, to me the most degrading, as well as the most painful state in which a woman of any taste, not to speak of the peculiar delicacy of fostered sensibility, could be placed. But my husband's fondness for women was of the grossest kind, and imagination was so wholly out of the question, as to render his indulgences of this sort entirely promiscuous, and of the most brutal nature. My health suffered, before my heart was entirely estranged by the loathsome information; could I then have returned to his sullied arms, but as a victim to the prejudices of mankind, who have made women the property of their husbands? I discovered even, by his conversation, when intoxicated, that his favourites were wantons of the lowest class, who could by their vulgar, indecent mirth, which he called nature, rouse his sluggish spirits. Meretricious ornaments and manners were necessary to attract his attention. He seldom looked twice at a modest woman, and sat silent in their company; and the charms of youth and beauty had not the slightest effect on his senses, unless the possessors were initiated in vice. His intimacy with profligate women, and his habits of thinking, gave him a contempt for female endowments; and he would repeat, when wine had loosed his tongue, most of the common-place sarcasms levelled at them, by men who do not allow them to have minds, because mind would be an impediment to gross enjoyment. Men who are inferior to their fellow men, are always most anxious to establish their superiority over women. But where are these reflections leading me?

"Women who have lost their husband's affection, are justly reproved for neglecting their persons, and not taking the same pains to keep, as to gain a heart; but who thinks of giving the same advice to men, though women are continually stigmatized for being attached to fops; and from the nature of their education, are more susceptible of disgust? Yet why a woman should be expected to endure a sloven, with more patience than a man, and magnanimously to govern herself, I cannot conceive; unless it be supposed arrogant in her to look for respect as well as a maintenance. It is not easy to be pleased, because, after promising to love, in different circumstances, we are told that it is our duty. I cannot, I am sure (though, when attending the sick, I never felt disgust) forget my own sensations, when rising with health and spirit, and after scenting the sweet morning, I have met my husband at the breakfast table. The active attention I had been giving to domestic regulations, which were generally settled before he rose, or a walk, gave a glow to my countenance, that contrasted with his squallid appearance. The squeamishness of stomach alone, produced by the last night's intemperance, which he took no pains to conceal, destroyed my appetite. I think I now see him lolling in an arm-chair, in a dirty powdering gown, soiled linen, ungartered stockings, and tangled hair, yawning and stretching himself. The newspaper was immediately called for, if not brought in on the tea-board, from which he would scarcely lift his eyes while I poured out the tea, excepting to ask for some brandy to put into it, or to declare that he could not eat. In answer to any question, in his best humour, it was a drawling 'What do you say, child?' But if I demanded money for the house expences, which I put off till the last moment, his customary reply, often prefaced with an oath, was, 'Do you think me, madam, made of money?'—The butcher, the baker, must wait; and, what was worse, I was often obliged to witness his surly dismission of tradesmen, who were in want of their money, and whom I sometimes paid with the presents my uncle gave me for my own use.

At this juncture my father's mistress, by terrifying his conscience, prevailed on him to marry her; he was already become a methodist; and my brother, who now practised for himself, had discovered a flaw in the settlement made on my mother's children, which set it aside, and he allowed my father, whose distress made him submit to any thing, a tithe of his own, or rather our fortune.

My sisters had left school, but were unable to endure home, which my father's wife rendered as disagreeable as possible, to get rid of girls whom she regarded as spies on her conduct. They were accomplished, yet you can (may you never be reduced to the same destitute state!) scarcely conceive the trouble I had to place them in the situation of governesses, the only one in which even a well-educated woman, with more than ordinary talents, can struggle for a subsistence; and even this is a dependence next to menial. Is it then surprising, that so many forlorn women, with human passions and feelings, take refuge in infamy? Alone in large mansions, I say alone, because they had no companions with whom they could converse on equal terms, or from whom they could expect the endearments of affection, they grew melancholy, and the sound of joy made them sad; and the youngest, having a more delicate frame, fell into a decline. It was with great difficulty that I, who now almost supported the house by loans from my uncle, could prevail on the *master* of it, to allow her a room to die in. I watched her sick bed for some months, and then closed her eyes, gentle spirit! for ever. She was pretty, with very engaging manners; yet had never an opportunity to marry, excepting to a very old man. She had abilities sufficient to have shone in any profession, had there been any professions for women, though she shrunk at the name of milliner or mantua-maker as degrading to a gentlewoman. I would not term this feeling false pride to any one but you, my child, whom I fondly hope to see (yes; I will indulge the hope for a moment!) possessed of that energy of character which gives dignity to any station; and with that clear, firm spirit that will enable you to choose a situation for yourself, or submit to be classed in the lowest, if it be the only one in which you can be the mistress of your own actions.

"Soon after the death of my sister, an incident occurred, to prove to me that the heart of a libertine is dead to natural affection; and to convince me, that the being who has appeared all tenderness, to gratify a selfish passion, is as regardless of the innocent fruit of it, as of the object, when the fit is over. I had casually observed an old, mean-looking woman, who called on my husband every two or three months to receive some money. One day entering the passage of his little counting-house, as she was going out, I heard her say, 'The child is very weak; she cannot live long, she will soon die out of your way, so you need not grudge her a little physic.'

"'So much the better,' he replied, 'and pray mind your own business, good woman.'

"I was struck by his unfeeling, inhuman tone of voice, and drew back, determined when the woman came again, to try to speak to her, not out of curiosity, I had heard enough, but with the hope of being useful to a poor, outcast girl.

"A month or two elapsed before I saw this woman again; and then she had a child in her hand that tottered along, scarcely able to sustain her own weight. They were going away, to return at the hour Mr. Venables was expected; he was now from home. I desired the woman to walk into the parlour. She hesitated, yet obeyed. I assured her that I should not mention to my husband (the word seemed to weigh on my respiration), that I had seen her, or his child. The woman stared at me with astonishment; and I turned my eyes on the squalid object [that accompanied her.] She could hardly support herself, her complexion was sallow, and her eyes inflamed, with an indescribable look of cunning, mixed with the wrinkles produced by the peevishness of pain.

"'Poor child!' I exclaimed. 'Ah! you may well say poor child,' replied the woman. 'I brought her here to see whether he would have the heart to look at her, and not get some advice. I do not know what they deserve who nursed her. Why, her legs bent under her like a bow when she came to me, and she has never been well since; but, if they were no better paid than I am, it is not to be wondered at, sure enough.'

"On further enquiry I was informed, that this miserable spectacle was the daughter of a servant, a country girl, who caught Mr. Venables' eye, and whom he seduced. On his marriage he sent her away, her situation being too visible. After her delivery, she was thrown on the town; and died in an hospital within the year. The babe was sent to a parish-nurse, and afterwards to this woman, who did not seem much better; but what was to be expected from such a close bargain? She was only paid three shillings a week for board and washing.[2]

"The woman begged me to give her some old clothes for the child, assuring me, that she was almost afraid to ask master for money to buy even a pair of shoes.

"I grew sick at heart. And, fearing Mr. Venables might enter, and oblige me to express my abhorrence, I hastily enquired where she lived, promised to pay her two shillings a week more, and to call on her in a day or two; putting a trifle into her hand as a proof of my good intention.

"If the state of this child affected me, what were my feelings at a discovery I made respecting Peggy—?[3]

CHAPTER X

"My father's situation was now so distressing, that I prevailed on my uncle to accompany me to visit him; and to lend me his assistance, to prevent the whole property of the family from becoming the prey of my brother's rapacity; for, to extricate himself out of present difficulties, my father was totally regardless of futurity. I took down with me some presents for my step-mother; it did not require an effort for me to treat her with civility, or to forget the past.

"This was the first time I had visited my native village, since my marriage. But with what different emotions did I return from the busy world, with a heavy weight of experience benumbing my imagination, to scenes, that whispered recollections of joy and hope most eloquently to my heart! The first scent of the wild flowers from the heath, thrilled through my veins, awakening every sense to pleasure. The icy hand of despair seemed to be removed from my bosom; and—forgetting my husband—the nurtured visions of a romantic mind, bursting on me with all their original wildness and gay exuberance, were again

---

[2]An accurate account of this economy.

[3]The manuscript is imperfect here. An episode seems to have been intended, which was never committed to paper. EDITOR [WG].

hailed as sweet realities. I forgot, with equal facility, that I ever felt sorrow, or knew care in the country; while a transient rainbow stole athwart the cloudy sky of despondency. The picturesque form of several favourite trees, and the porches of rude cottages, with their smiling hedges, were recognized with the gladsome playfulness of childish vivacity. I could have kissed the chickens that pecked on the common; and longed to pat the cows, and frolic with the dogs that sported on it. I gazed with delight on the windmill, and thought it lucky that it should be in motion, at the moment I passed by; and entering the dear green-lane, which led directly to the village, the sound of the well-known rookery gave that sentimental tinge to the varying sensations of my active soul, which only served to heighten the lustre of the luxuriant scenery. But, spying, as I advanced, the spire, peeping over the withered tops of the aged elms that composed the rookery, my thoughts flew immediately to the church-yard, and tears of affection, such was the effect of my imagination, bedewed my mother's grave! Sorrow gave place to devotional feelings. I wandered through the church in fancy, as I used sometimes to do on a Saturday evening. I recollected with what fervour I addressed the God of my youth: and once more with rapturous love looked above my sorrows to the Father of nature. I pause—feeling forcibly all the emotions I am describing; and (reminded, as I register my sorrows, of the sublime calm I have felt, when in some tremendous solitude, my soul rested on itself, and seemed to fill the universe) I insensibly breathe soft, hushing every wayward emotion, as if fearing to sully with a sigh, a contentment so extatic.

"Having settled my father's affairs, and, by my exertions in his favour, made my brother my sworn foe, I returned to London. My husband's conduct was now changed; I had during my absence, received several affectionate, penitential letters from him; and he seemed on my arrival, to wish by his behaviour to prove his sincerity. I could not then conceive why he acted thus; and, when the suspicion darted into my head, that it might arise from observing my increasing influence with my uncle, I almost despised myself for imagining that such a degree of debasing selfishness could exist.

"He became, unaccountable as was the change, tender and attentive; and, attacking my weak side, made a confession of his follies, and lamented the embarrassments in which I, who merited a far different fate, might be involved. He besought me to aid him with my counsel, praised my understanding, and appealed to the tenderness of my heart.

"This conduct only inspired me with compassion. I wished to be his friend; but love had spread his rosy pinions, and fled far, far away; and had not (like some exquisite perfumes, the fine spirit of which is continually mingling with the air) left a fragrance behind, to mark where he had shook his wings. My husband's renewed caresses then became hateful to me; his brutality was tolerable, compared to his distasteful fondness. Still, compassion, and the fear of insulting his supposed feelings, by a want of sympathy, made me dissemble, and do violence to my delicacy. What a task!

"Those who support a system of what I term false refinement, and will not allow great part of love in the female, as well as male breast, to spring in some respects involuntarily, may not admit that charms are as necessary to feed the passion, as virtues to convert the mellowing spirit into friendship. To such observers I have nothing to say, any more than to the moralists, who insist that women ought to, and can love their husbands, because it is their duty. To you, my child, I may add, with a heart tremblingly alive to your future conduct, some observations, dictated by my present feelings, on calmly reviewing this period of my life. When novelists or moralists praise as a virtue, a woman's coldness of constitution, and want of passion; and make her yield to the ardour of her lover out of sheer compassion, or to promote a frigid plan of future comfort, I am disgusted. They may be good women, in the ordinary acceptation of the phrase, and do no harm; but they appear to me not to have those 'finely fashioned nerves,' which render the senses exquisite. They may possess tenderness; but they want that fire of the imagination, which produces *active* sensibility, and *positive* virtue. How does the woman deserve to be characterized, who marries one man, with a heart and imagination devoted to another? Is she not an object of pity or contempt, when thus sacrilegiously violating the purity of her own feelings? Nay, it is as indelicate, when she is indifferent, unless she be constitutionally insensible; then indeed it is a mere affair of barter; and I have nothing to do with the secrets of trade. Yes; eagerly as I wish you to possess true rectitude of mind, and purity of affection, I must insist that a heartless conduct is the contrary of virtuous. Truth is the only basis of virtue; and we cannot, without depraving our minds, endeavour to please a lover or husband, but in proportion as he pleases us. Men, more effectually to enslave us, may inculcate this partial morality, and lose sight of virtue in subdividing it into the duties of particular stations; but let us not blush for nature without a cause!

"After these remarks, I am ashamed to own, that I was pregnant. The greatest sacrifice of my principles in my whole life, was the allowing my husband again to be familiar with my person, though to this cruel act of self-denial, when I wished the earth to open and swallow me, you owe your birth; and I the unutterable pleasure of being a mother. There was something of delicacy in my husband's bridal attentions; but now his tainted breath, pimpled face, and blood-shot eyes, were not more repugnant to my senses, than his gross manners, and loveless familiarity to my taste.

"A man would only be expected to maintain; yes, barely grant a subsistence, to a woman rendered odious by habitual intoxication; but who would expect him, or think it possible to love her? And unless 'youth, and genial years were flown,' it would be thought equally unreasonable to insist, [under penalty of] forfeiting almost every thing reckoned valuable in life, that he should not love another: whilst woman, weak in reason, impotent in will, is required to moralize, sentimentalize herself to stone, and pine her life away, labouring to reform her embruted mate. He may even spend in dissipation, and intemperance, the very intemperance which renders him so hateful, her property, and by stinting her expences, not permit her to beguile in society, a wearisome, joyless life; for over their mutual fortune she has no power, it must all pass through his hand. And if she be a mother, and in the present state of women, it is a great misfortune to be prevented from discharging the duties, and cultivating the affections of one, what has she not to endure?—But I have suffered the tenderness of one to lead me into reflections that I did not think of making, to interrupt my narrative—yet the full heart will overflow.

"Mr. Venables' embarrassments did not now endear him to me; still, anxious to befriend him, I endeavoured to prevail on him to retrench his expences; but he had always some plausible excuse to give, to justify his not following my advice. Humanity, compassion, and the interest produced by a habit of living together, made me try to relieve, and sympathize with him; but, when I recollected that I was bound to live with such a being for ever—my heart died within me; my desire of improvement became languid, and baleful, corroding melancholy took possession of my soul. Marriage had bastilled[1] me

---

[1] A verb shaped from the famous prison in Paris, the storming of which inaugurated the French Revolution.

The Bastille, anonymous eighteenth-century French engraving of France's notorious prison in central Paris. The citizens' attack on the Bastille, which freed fourteen prisoners, initiated the French Revolution on July 14, 1789.

for life. I discovered in myself a capacity for the enjoyment of the various pleasures existence affords; yet, fettered by the partial laws of society, this fair globe was to me an universal blank.[2]

"When I exhorted my husband to economy, I referred to himself. I was obliged to practise the most rigid, or contract debts, which I had too much reason to fear would never be paid. I despised this paltry privilege of a wife, which can only be of use to the vicious or inconsiderate, and determined not to increase the torrent that was bearing him down. I was then ignorant of the extent of his fraudulent speculations, whom I was bound to honour and obey.

"A woman neglected by her husband, or whose manners form a striking contrast with his, will always have men on the watch to soothe and flatter her. Besides, the forlorn state of a neglected woman, not destitute of personal charms, is particularly interesting,

[2]How blind Milton describes the world in the famous opening of the third book of *Paradise Lost.*

and rouses that species of pity, which is so near akin, it easily slides into love. A man of feeling thinks not of seducing, he is himself seduced by all the noblest emotions of his soul. He figures to himself all the sacrifices a woman of sensibility must make, and every situation in which his imagination places her, touches his heart, and fires his passions. Longing to take to his bosom the shorn lamb, and bid the drooping buds of hope revive, benevolence changes into passion: and should he then discover that he is beloved, honour binds him fast, though foreseeing that he may afterwards be obliged to pay severe damages to the man, who never appeared to value his wife's society, till he found that there was a chance of his being indemnified for the loss of it.

"Such are the partial laws enacted by men; for, only to lay a stress on the dependent state of a woman in the grand question of the comforts arising from the possession of property, she is [even in this article] much more injured by the loss of the husband's affection, than he by that of his wife; yet where is she, condemned to the solitude of a deserted home, to look for a compensation from the woman, who seduces him from her? She cannot drive an unfaithful husband from his house, nor separate, or tear, his children from him, however culpable he may be; and he, still the master of his own fate, enjoys the smiles of a world, that would brand her with infamy, did she, seeking consolation, venture to retaliate.

"These remarks are not dictated by experience; but merely by the compassion I feel for many amiable women, the *out-laws* of the world. For myself, never encouraging any of the advances that were made to me, my lovers dropped off like the untimely shoots of spring. I did not even coquet with them; because I found, on examining myself, I could not coquet with a man without loving him a little; and I perceived that I should not be able to stop at the line of what are termed *innocent freedoms*, did I suffer any. My reserve was then the consequence of delicacy. Freedom of conduct has emancipated many women's minds; but my conduct has most rigidly been governed by my principles, till the improvement of my understanding has enabled me to discern the fallacy of prejudices at war with nature and reason.

"Shortly after the change I have mentioned in my husband's conduct, my uncle was compelled by his declining health, to seek the succour of a milder climate, and embark for Lisbon. He left his will in the hands of a friend, an eminent solicitor; he had previously questioned me relative to my situation and state of mind, and declared very freely, that he could place no reliance on the stability of my husband's professions. He had been deceived in the unfolding of his character; he now thought it fixed in a train of actions that would inevitably lead to ruin and disgrace.

"The evening before his departure, which we spent alone together, he folded me to his heart, uttering the endearing appellation of 'child.'—My more than father! why was I not permitted to perform the last duties of one, and smooth the pillow of death? He seemed by his manner to be convinced that he should never see me more; yet requested me, most earnestly, to come to him, should I be obliged to leave my husband. He had before expressed his sorrow at hearing of my pregnancy, having determined to prevail on me to accompany him, till I informed him of that circumstance. He expressed himself unfeignedly sorry that any new tie should bind me to a man whom he thought so incapable of estimating my value; such was the kind language of affection.

"I must repeat his own words; they made an indelible impression on my mind:

"'The marriage state is certainly that in which women, generally speaking, can be most useful; but I am far from thinking that a woman, once married, ought to consider the engagement as indissoluble (especially if there be no children to reward her for sacrificing her feelings) in case her husband merits neither her love, nor esteem. Esteem will often supply the place of love; and prevent a woman from being wretched, though it may not make her happy. The magnitude of a sacrifice ought always to bear some proportion to the utility in view; and for a woman to live with a man, for whom she can cherish neither affection nor esteem, or even be of any use to him, excepting in the light of a house-keeper, is an abjectness of condition, the enduring of which no concurrence of circumstances can ever make a duty in the sight of God or just men. If indeed she submits to it merely to be maintained in idleness, she has no right to complain bitterly of her fate; or to act, as a person of independent character might, as if she had a title to disregard general rules.

"But the misfortune is, that many women only submit in appearance, and forfeit their own respect to secure their reputation in the world. The situation of a woman separated from her husband, is undoubtedly very different from that of a man who has left his wife. He, with lordly dignity, has shaken of a clog; and the allowing her food and raiment, is thought sufficient to secure his reputation from taint. And, should she have been inconsiderate, he will be celebrated for his generosity and forbearance. Such is the respect paid to the master-key of property! A woman, on the contrary, resigning what is termed her natural protector (though he never was so, but in name) is despised and shunned, for asserting the independence of mind distinctive of a rational being, and spurning at slavery.'

"During the remainder of the evening, my uncle's tenderness led him frequently to revert to the subject, and utter, with increasing warmth, sentiments to the same purport. At length it was necessary to say 'Farewell!'—and we parted—gracious God! to meet no more.

CHAPTER XI

"A Gentleman of large fortune and of polished manners, had lately visited very frequently at our house, and treated me, if possible, with more respect than Mr. Venables paid him; my pregnancy was not yet visible; his society was a great relief to me, as I had for some time past, to avoid expence, confined myself very much at home. I ever disdained unnecessary, perhaps even prudent concealments; and my husband, with great ease, discovered the amount of my uncle's parting present. A copy of a writ was the stale pretext to extort it from me; and I had soon reason to believe that it was fabricated for the purpose. I acknowledge my folly in thus suffering myself to be continually imposed on. I had adhered to my resolution not to apply to my uncle, on the part of my husband, any more; yet, when I had received a sum sufficient to supply my own wants, and to enable me to pursue a plan I had in view, to settle my younger brother in a respectable employment, I allowed myself to be duped by Mr. Venables' shallow pretences, and hypocritical professions.

"Thus did he pillage me and my family, thus frustrate all my plans of usefulness. Yet this was the man I was bound to respect and esteem: as if respect and esteem depended on an arbitrary will of our own! But a wife being as much a man's property as his horse, or his ass, she has nothing she can call her own. He may use any means to get at what the law considers as his,[1] the moment his wife is in possession of it, even to the forcing of a lock, as Mr. Venables did, to search for notes in my writing-desk—and all this is done with a show of equity, because, forsooth, he is responsible for her maintenance.

"The tender mother cannot *lawfully* snatch from the gripe of the gambling spendthrift, or beastly drunkard, unmindful of his offspring, the fortune which falls to her by chance; or (so flagrant is the injustice) what she earns by her own exertions. No; he can rob her with impunity, even to waste publicly on a courtezan; and the laws of her country—if women have a country—afford her no protection or redress from the oppressor, unless she have the plea of bodily fear; yet how many ways are there of goading the soul almost to madness, equally unmanly, though not so mean? When such laws were framed, should not impartial lawgivers have first decreed, in the style of a great assembly, who recognized the existence of an *être suprême*,[2] to fix the national belief, that the husband should always be wiser and more virtuous than his wife, in order to entitle him, with a show of justice, to keep this idiot, or perpetual minor, for ever in bondage. But I must have done—on this subject, my indignation continually runs away with me.

"The company of the gentleman I have already mentioned, who had a general acquaintance with literature and subjects of taste, was grateful to me; my countenance brightened up as he approached, and I unaffectedly expressed the pleasure I felt. The amusement his conversation afforded me, made it easy to comply with my husband's request, to endeavour to render our house agreeable to him.

"His attentions became more pointed; but, as I was not of the number of women, whose virtue, as it is termed, immediately takes alarm, I endeavoured, rather by raillery than serious expostulation, to give a different turn to his conversation. He assumed a new mode of attack, and I was, for a while, the dupe of his pretended friendship.

"I had, merely in the style of *badinage*,[3] boasted of my conquest, and repeated his lover-like compliments to my husband. But he

---

[1]An accurate account of property laws in marriage. See William Blackstone's *Commentaries on the Laws of England* (1765–69), 1.14.3 and 2.29.6, with a basis in the Old Testament (Exodus 20:17).

[2]On May 7, 1794, Robespierre persuaded the National Convention to acknowledge the existence of a Supreme Being.

[3]Light raillery, humorous banter.

begged me, for God's sake, not to affront his friend, or I should destroy all his projects, and be his ruin. Had I had more affection for my husband, I should have expressed my contempt of this time-serving politeness: now I imagined that I only felt pity; yet it would have puzzled a casuist to point out in what the exact difference consisted.

"This friend began now, in confidence, to discover to me the real state of my husband's affairs. 'Necessity,' said Mr. S——; why should I reveal his name? for he affected to palliate the conduct he could not excuse, 'had led him to take such steps, by accommodation bills,[4] buying goods on credit, to sell them for ready money, and similar transactions, that his character in the commercial world was gone. He was considered,' he added, lowering his voice, 'on 'Change[5] as a swindler.'

"I felt at that moment the first maternal pang. Aware of the evils my sex have to struggle with, I still wished, for my own consolation, to be the mother of a daughter; and I could not bear to think, that the *sins* of her father's entailed disgrace, should be added to the ills to which woman is heir.

"So completely was I deceived by these shows of friendship (nay, I believe, according to his interpretation, Mr. S—— really was my friend) that I began to consult him respecting the best mode of retrieving my husband's character: it is the good name of a woman only that sets to rise no more. I knew not that he had been drawn into a whirlpool, out of which he had not the energy to attempt to escape. He seemed indeed destitute of the power of employing his faculties in any regular pursuit. His principles of action were so loose, and his mind so uncultivated, that every thing like order appeared to him in the shape of restraint; and, like men in the savage state, he required the strong stimulus of hope or fear, produced by wild speculations, in which the interests of others went for nothing, to keep his spirits awake. He one time professed patriotism, but he knew not what it was to feel honest indignation; and pretended to be an advocate for liberty, when, with as little affection for the human race as for individuals, he thought of nothing but his own gratification. He was just such a citizen, as a father. The sums he adroitly obtained by a violation of the laws of his country, as well as those of humanity, he would

---

[4]Loans.

[5]In the financial world, particularly the stock exchange.

allow a mistress to squander; though she was, with the same *sang froid*,[6] consigned, as were his children, to poverty, when another proved more attractive.

"On various pretences, his friend continued to visit me; and, observing my want of money, he tried to induce me to accept of pecuniary aid; but this offer I absolutely rejected, though it was made with such delicacy, I could not be displeased.

"One day he came, as I thought accidentally, to dinner. My husband was very much engaged in business, and quitted the room soon after the cloth was removed. We conversed as usual, till confidential advice led again to love. I was extremely mortified. I had a sincere regard for him, and hoped that he had an equal friendship for me. I therefore began mildly to expostulate with him. This gentleness he mistook for coy encouragement; and he would not be diverted from the subject. Perceiving his mistake, I seriously asked him how, using such language to me, he could profess to be my husband's friend? A significant sneer excited my curiosity, and he, supposing this to be my only scruple, took a letter deliberately out of his pocket, saying, 'Your husband's honour is not inflexible. How could you, with your discernment, think it so? Why, he left the room this very day on purpose to give me an opportunity to explain myself; *he* thought me too timid—too tardy.'

"I snatched the letter with indescribable emotion. The purport of it was to invite him to dinner, and to ridicule his chivalrous respect for me. He assured him, 'that every woman had her price, and, with gross indecency, hinted, that he should be glad to have the duty of a husband taken off his hands. These he termed *liberal sentiments*. He advised him not to shock my romantic notions, but to attack my credulous generosity, and weak pity; and concluded with requesting him to lend him five hundred pounds for a month or six weeks.' I read this letter twice over; and the firm purpose it inspired, calmed the rising tumult of my soul. I rose deliberately, requested Mr. S— to wait a moment, and instantly going into the counting-house, desired Mr. Venables to return with me to the dining-parlour.

"He laid down his pen, and entered with me, without observing any change in my countenance. I shut the door, and, giving him the letter, simply asked, 'whether he wrote it, or was it a forgery?'

[6]Coolness, indifference.

"Nothing could equal his confusion. His friend's eye met his, and he muttered something about a joke—But I interrupted him—'It is sufficient—We part for ever.'

"I continued, with solemnity, 'I have borne with your tyranny and infidelities. I disdain to utter what I have borne with. I thought you unprincipled, but not so decidedly vicious. I formed a tie, in the sight of heaven—I have held it sacred; even when men, more conformable to my taste, have made me feel—I despise all subterfuge!—that I was not dead to love. Neglected by you, I have resolutely stifled the enticing emotions, and respected the plighted faith you outraged. And you dare now to insult me, by selling me to prostitution!—Yes—equally lost to delicacy and principle—you dared sacrilegiously to barter the honour of the mother of your child.'

"Then, turning to Mr. S—, I added, 'I call on you, Sir, to witness,' and I lifted my hands and eyes to heaven, 'that, as solemnly as I took his name, I now abjure it,' I pulled off my ring, and put it on the table; 'and that I mean immediately to quit his house, never to enter it more. I will provide for myself and child. I leave him as free as I am determined to be myself—he shall be answerable for no debts of mine.'

"Astonishment closed their lips, till Mr. Venables, gently pushing his friend, with a forced smile, out of the room, nature for a moment prevailed, and, appearing like himself, he turned round, burning with rage, to me: but there was no terror in the frown, excepting when contrasted with the malignant smile which preceded it. He bade me 'leave the house at my peril; told me he despised my threats; I had no resource; I could not swear the peace against him!—I was not afraid of my life!—he had never struck me!'[7]

"He threw the letter in the fire, which I had incautiously left in his hands; and, quitting the room, locked the door on me.

"When left alone, I was a moment or two before I could recollect myself. One scene had succeeded another with such rapidity, I almost doubted whether I was reflecting on a real event. 'Was it possible? Was I, indeed, free?'—Yes; free I termed myself, when I decidedly perceived the conduct I ought to adopt. How had I panted for liberty—liberty, that I would have purchased at any price, but that of my own esteem! I rose, and shook myself; opened the window, and methought

---

[7] Legal separations were granted only in cases of physical cruelty or female adultery.

the air never smelled so sweet. The face of heaven grew fairer as I viewed it, and the clouds seemed to flit away obedient to my wishes, to give my soul room to expand. I was all soul, and (wild as it may appear) felt as if I could have dissolved in the soft balmy gale that kissed my cheek, or have glided below the horizon on the glowing, descending beams. A seraphic satisfaction animated, without agitating my spirits; and my imagination collected, in visions sublimely terrible, or soothingly beautiful, an immense variety of the endless images, which nature affords, and fancy combines, of the grand and fair. The lustre of these bright picturesque sketches faded with the setting sun; but I was still alive to the calm delight they had diffused through my heart.

"There may be advocates for matrimonial obedience, who, making a distinction between the duty of a wife and of a human being, may blame my conduct.—To them I write not—my feelings are not for them to analyze; and may you, my child, never be able to ascertain, by heart-rending experience, what your mother felt before the present emancipation of her mind!

"I began to write a letter to my father, after closing one to my uncle; not to ask advice, but to signify my determination; when I was interrupted by the entrance of Mr. Venables. His manner was changed. His views on my uncle's fortune made him averse to my quitting his house, or he would, I am convinced, have been glad to have shaken off even the slight restraint my presence imposed on him; the restraint of showing me some respect. So far from having an affection for me, he really hated me, because he was convinced that I must despise him.

"He told me, that, 'As I now had had time to cool and reflect, he did not doubt but that my prudence, and nice sense of propriety, would lead me to overlook what was passed.'

"'Reflection,' I replied, 'had only confirmed my purpose, and no power on earth could divert me from it.'

"Endeavouring to assume a soothing voice and look, when he would willingly have tortured me, to force me to feel his power, his countenance had an infernal expression, when he desired me, 'Not to expose myself to the servants, by obliging him to confine me in my apartment; if then I would give my promise not to quit the house precipitately, I should be free—and—.' I declared, interrupting him, 'that I would promise nothing. I had no measures to keep with him— I was resolved, and would not condescend to subterfuge.'

"He muttered, 'that I should soon repent of these preposterous airs;' and, ordering tea to be carried into my little study, which had a communication with my bed-chamber, he once more locked the door upon me, and left me to my own meditations. I had passively followed him up stairs, not wishing to fatigue myself with unavailing exertion.

"Nothing calms the mind like a fixed purpose. I felt as if I had heaved a thousand weight from my heart; the atmosphere seemed lightened; and, if I execrated the institutions of society, which thus enable men to tyrannize over women, it was almost a disinterested sentiment. I disregarded present inconveniences, when my mind had done struggling with itself,—when reason and inclination had shaken hands and were at peace. I had no longer the cruel task before me, in endless perspective, aye, during the tedious for ever of life, of labour-ing to overcome my repugnance—of labouring to extinguish the hopes, the maybes of a lively imagination. Death I had hailed as my only chance for deliverance; but, while existence had still so many charms, and life promised happiness, I shrunk from the icy arms of an unknown tyrant, though far more inviting than those of the man, to whom I supposed myself bound without any other alternative; and was content to linger a little longer, waiting for I knew not what, rather than leave 'the warm precincts of the cheerful day,'[8] and all the unenjoyed affection of my nature.

"My present situation gave a new turn to my reflection; and I wondered (now the film seemed to be withdrawn, that obscured the piercing sight of reason) how I could, previously to the deciding out-rage, have considered myself as everlastingly united to vice and folly! 'Had an evil genius cast a spell at my birth; or a demon stalked out of chaos, to perplex my understanding, and enchain my will, with delu-sive prejudices?'

"I pursued this train of thinking; it led me out of myself, to expa-tiate on the misery peculiar to my sex. 'Are not,' I thought, 'the despots for ever stigmatized, who, in the wantonness of power, com-manded even the most atrocious criminals to be chained to dead bod-ies? though surely those laws are much more inhuman, which forge adamantine fetters to bind minds together, that never can mingle in social communion! What indeed can equal the wretchedness of that

---

[8]Quoting Thomas Gray's famous *Elegy Written in a Country Church-yard* (1751): "For who to dumb Forgetfulness a prey, / This pleasing anxious being e're resigned, / Left the warm precincts of the cheerful day, / Nor cast one longing ling'ring look be-hind?" (85–88).

state, in which there is no alternative, but to extinguish the affections, or encounter infamy?'

CHAPTER XII

"Towards midnight Mr. Venables entered my chamber; and, with calm audacity preparing to go to bed, he bade me make haste, 'for that was the best place for husbands and wives to end their differences.' He had been drinking plentifully to aid his courage.

"I did not at first deign to reply. But perceiving that he affected to take my silence for consent, I told him that, 'If he would not go to another bed, or allow me, I should sit up in my study all night.' He attempted to pull me into the chamber, half joking. But I resisted; and, as he had determined not to give me any reason for saying that he used violence, after a few more efforts, he retired, cursing my obstinacy, to bed.

"I sat musing some time longer; then, throwing my cloak around me, prepared for sleep on a sopha. And, so fortunate seemed my deliverance, so sacred the pleasure of being thus wrapped up in myself, that I slept profoundly, and woke with a mind composed to encounter the struggles of the day. Mr. Venables did not wake till some hours after; and then he came to me half-dressed, yawning and stretching, with haggard eyes, as if he scarcely recollected what had passed the preceding evening. He fixed his eyes on me for a moment, then, calling me a fool, asked 'How long I intended to continue this pretty farce? For his part, he was devilish sick of it; but this was the plague of marrying women who pretended to know something.'

"I made no other reply to this harangue, than to say, 'That he ought to be glad to get rid of a woman so unfit to be his companion—and that any change in my conduct would be mean dissimulation; for maturer reflection only gave the sacred seal of reason to my first resolution.'

"He looked as if he could have stamped with impatience, at being obliged to stifle his rage; but, conquering his anger (for weak people, whose passions seem the most ungovernable, restrain them with the greatest ease, when they have a sufficient motive), he exclaimed, 'Very pretty, upon my soul! very pretty, theatrical flourishes! Pray, fair Roxana,[1] stoop from your altitudes, and remember that you are acting a part in real life.'

---

[1] The murderess in Nathaniel Lee's tragedy *The Rival Queens, or the Death of Alexander the Great* (1677).

"He uttered this speech with a self-satisfied air, and went down stairs to dress.

"In about an hour he came to me again; and in the same tone said, 'That he came as my gentleman-usher to hand me down to breakfast.'

"'Of the black rod?'[2] asked I.

"This question, and the tone in which I asked it, a little disconcerted him. To say the truth, I now felt no resentment; my firm resolution to free myself from my ignoble thraldom, had absorbed the various emotions which, during six years, had racked my soul. The duty pointed out by my principles seemed clear; and not one tender feeling intruded to make me swerve. The dislike which my husband had inspired was strong; but it only led me to wish to avoid, to wish to let him drop out of my memory; there was no misery, no torture that I would not deliberately have chosen, rather than renew my lease of servitude.

"During the breakfast, he attempted to reason with me on the folly of romantic sentiments; for this was the indiscriminate epithet he gave to every mode of conduct or thinking superior to his own. He asserted, 'that all the world were governed by their own interest; those who pretended to be actuated by different motives, were only deeper knaves, or fools crazed by books, who took for gospel all the rodomantade[3] nonsense written by men who knew nothing of the world. For his part, he thanked God, he was no hypocrite; and, if he stretched a point sometimes, it was always with an intention of paying every man his own.'

"He then artfully insinuated, 'that he daily expected a vessel to arrive, a successful speculation, that would make him easy for the present, and that he had several other schemes actually depending, that could not fail. He had no doubt of becoming rich in a few years, though he had been thrown back by some unlucky adventures at the setting out.'

"I mildly replied, 'That I wished he might not involve himself still deeper.'

"He had no notion that I was governed by a decision of judgment, not to be compared with a mere spurt of resentment. He knew not what it was to feel indignation against vice, and often boasted of his

---

[2]In the House of Lords, officers of the black rod summoned defendants for trial.

[3]Vainglorious brag or boast, derived from Rodomonte, Ariosto's blustering warrior.

placable temper, and readiness to forgive injuries. True; for he only considered the being deceived, as an effort of skill he had not guarded against; and then, with a cant of candour, would observe, 'that he did not know how he might himself have been tempted to act in the same circumstances.' And, as his heart never opened to friendship, it never was wounded by disappointment. Every new acquaintance he protested, it is true, was 'the cleverest fellow in the world;' and he really thought so; till the novelty of his conversation or manners ceased to have any effect on his sluggish spirits. His respect for rank or fortune was more permanent, though he chanced to have no design of availing himself of the influence of either to promote his own views.

"After a prefatory conversation,—my blood (I thought it had been cooler) flushed over my whole countenance as he spoke—he alluded to my situation. He desired me to reflect—'and act like a prudent woman, as the best proof of my superior understanding; for he must own I had sense, did I know how to use it. I was not,' he laid a stress on his words, 'without my passions; and a husband was a convenient cloke.—He was liberal in his way of thinking; and why might not we, like many other married people, who were above vulgar prejudices, tacitly consent to let each other follow their own inclination?—He meant nothing more, in the letter I made the ground of complaint; and the pleasure which I seemed to take in Mr. S.'s company, led him to conclude, that he was not disagreeable to me.'

"A clerk brought in the letters of the day, and I, as I often did, while he was discussing subjects of business, went to the *piano forte*, and began to play a favourite air to restore myself, as it were, to nature, and drive the sophisticated sentiments I had just been obliged to listen to, out of my soul.

"They had excited sensations similar to those I have felt, in viewing the squalid inhabitants of some of the lanes and back streets of the metropolis, mortified at being compelled to consider them as my fellow-creatures, as if an ape had claimed kindred with me. Or, as when surrounded by a mephitical[4] fog, I have wished to have a volley of cannon fired, to clear the incumbered atmosphere, and give me room to breathe and move.

"My spirits were all in arms, and I played a kind of extemporary prelude. The cadence was probably wild and impassioned, while, lost in thought, I made the sounds a kind of echo to my train of thinking.

[4]Mephitis: a pestilential vapour.

"Pausing for a moment, I met Mr. Venables' eyes. He was observing me with an air of conceited satisfaction, as much as to say—'My last insinuation has done the business—she begins to know her own interest.' Then gathering up his letters, he said, 'That he hoped he should hear no more romantic stuff, well enough in a miss just come from boarding school;' and went, as was his custom, to the counting-house. I still continued playing; and, turning to a sprightly lesson, I executed it with uncommon vivacity. I heard footsteps approach the door, and was soon convinced that Mr. Venables was listening; the consciousness only gave more animation to my fingers. He went down into the kitchen, and the cook, probably by his desire, came to me, to know what I would please to order for dinner. Mr. Venables came into the parlour again, with apparent carelessness. I perceived that the cunning man was over-reaching himself; and I gave my directions as usual, and left the room.

"While I was making some alteration in my dress, Mr. Venables peeped in, and, begging my pardon for interrupting me, disappeared. I took up some work (I could not read), and two or three messages were sent to me, probably for no other purpose, but to enable Mr. Venables to ascertain what I was about.

"I listened whenever I heard the street-door open; at last I imagined I could distinguish Mr. Venables' step, going out. I laid aside my work; my heart palpitated; still I was afraid hastily to enquire; and I waited a long half hour, before I ventured to ask the boy whether his master was in the counting-house?

"Being answered in the negative, I bade him call me a coach, and collecting a few necessaries hastily together, with a little parcel of letters and papers which I had collected the preceding evening, I hurried into it, desiring the coachman to drive to a distant part of the town.

"I almost feared that the coach would break down before I got out of the street; and, when I turned the corner, I seemed to breathe a freer air. I was ready to imagine that I was rising above the thick atmosphere of earth; or I felt, as wearied souls might be supposed to feel on entering another state of existence.

"I stopped at one or two stands of coaches to elude pursuit, and then drove round the skirts of the town to seek for an obscure lodging, where I wished to remain concealed, till I could avail myself of my uncle's protection. I had resolved to assume my own name immediately, and openly to avow my determination, without any formal vindication, the moment I had found a home, in which I could rest free from the daily alarm of expecting to see Mr. Venables enter.

"I looked at several lodgings; but finding that I could not, without a reference to some acquaintance, who might inform my tyrant, get admittance into a decent apartment—men have not all this trouble—I thought of a woman whom I had assisted to furnish a little haberdasher's shop,[5] and who I knew had a first floor to let.

"I went to her, and though I could not persuade her, that the quarrel between me and Mr. Venables would never be made up, still she agreed to conceal me for the present; yet assuring me at the same time, shaking her head, that, when a woman was once married, she must bear every thing. Her pale face, on which appeared a thousand haggard lines and delving wrinkles, produced by what is emphatically termed fretting, inforced her remark; and I had afterwards an opportunity of observing the treatment she had to endure, which grizzled[6] her into patience. She toiled from morning till night; yet her husband would rob the till, and take away the money reserved for paying bills; and, returning home drunk, he would beat her if she chanced to offend him, though she had a child at the breast.

"These scenes awoke me at night; and, in the morning, I heard her, as usual, talk to her dear Johnny—he, forsooth, was her master; no slave in the West Indies had one more despotic; but fortunately she was of the true Russian breed of wives.[7]

"My mind, during the few past days, seemed, as it were, disengaged from my body; but, now the struggle was over, I felt very forcibly the effect which perturbation of spirits produces on a woman in my situation.

"The apprehension of a miscarriage, obliged me to confine myself to my apartment near a fortnight; but I wrote to my uncle's friend for money, promising 'to call on him, and explain my situation, when I was well enough to go out; mean time I earnestly intreated him, not to mention my place of abode to any one, lest my husband—such the law considered him—should disturb the mind he could not conquer. I mentioned my intention of setting out for Lisbon, to claim my uncle's protection, the moment my health would permit.'

[5]Selling small articles of dress.
[6]Grey-haired.
[7]See *Vindication*, ch. XIII, p. 232, n. 23.

"The tranquillity however, which I was recovering, was soon interrupted. My landlady came up to me one day, with eyes swollen with weeping, unable to utter what she was commanded to say. She declared, 'That she was never so miserable in her life; that she must appear an ungrateful monster; and that she would readily go down on her knees to me, to intreat me to forgive her, as she had done to her husband to spare her the cruel task.' Sobs prevented her from proceeding, or answering my impatient enquiries, to know what she meant.

"When she became a little more composed, she took a newspaper out of her pocket, declaring, 'that her heart smote her, but what could she do?—she must obey her husband.' I snatched the paper from her. An advertisement quickly met my eye, purporting, that 'Maria Venables had, without any assignable cause, absconded from her husband; and any person harbouring her, was menaced with the utmost severity of the law.'

"Perfectly acquainted with Mr. Venables' meanness of soul, this step did not excite my surprise, and scarcely my contempt. Resentment in my breast, never survived love. I bade the poor woman, in a kind tone, wipe her eyes, and request her husband to come up, and speak to me himself.

"My manner awed him. He respected a lady, though not a woman; and began to mutter out an apology.

"'Mr. Venables was a rich gentleman; he wished to oblige me, but he had suffered enough by the law already, to tremble at the thought; besides, for certain, we should come together again, and then even I should not thank him for being accessary to keeping us asunder.—A husband and wife were, God knows, just as one,—and all would come round at last.' He uttered a drawling 'Hem!' and then with an arch look, added—'Master might have had his little frolics—but—Lord bless your heart!—men would be men while the world stands.'

"To argue with this privileged first-born of reason, I perceived, would be vain. I therefore only requested him to let me remain another day at his house, while I sought for a lodging; and not to inform Mr. Venables that I had ever been sheltered there.

"He consented, because he had not the courage to refuse a person for whom he had an habitual respect; but I heard the pent-up choler burst forth in curses, when he met his wife, who was waiting impatiently at the foot of the stairs, to know what effect my expostulations would have on him.

"Without wasting any time in the fruitless indulgence of vexation, I once more set out in search of an abode in which I could hide myself for a few weeks.

"Agreeing to pay an exorbitant price, I hired an apartment, without any reference being required relative to my character: indeed, a glance at my shape seemed to say, that my motive for concealment was sufficiently obvious. Thus was I obliged to shroud my head in infamy.

"To avoid all danger of detection—I use the appropriate word, my child, for I was hunted out like a felon—I determined to take possession of my new lodgings that very evening.

"I did not inform my landlady where I was going. I knew that she had a sincere affection for me, and would willingly have run any risk to show her gratitude; yet I was fully convinced, that a few kind words from Johnny would have found the woman in her, and her dear benefactress, as she termed me in an agony of tears, would have been sacrificed, to recompense her tyrant for condescending to treat her like an equal. He could be kind-hearted, as she expressed it, when he pleased. And this thawed sternness, contrasted with his habitual brutality, was the more acceptable, and could not be purchased at too dear a rate.

"The sight of the advertisement made me desirous of taking refuge with my uncle, let what would be the consequence; and I repaired in a hackney coach (afraid of meeting some person who might chance to know me, had I walked) to the chambers of my uncle's friend.

"He received me with great politeness (my uncle had already prepossessed him in my favour), and listened, with interest, to my explanation of the motives which had induced me to fly from home, and skulk in obscurity, with all the timidity of fear that ought only to be the companion of guilt. He lamented, with rather more gallantry than, in my situation, I thought delicate, that such a woman should be thrown away on a man insensible to the charms of beauty or grace. He seemed at a loss what to advise me to do, to evade my husband's search, without hastening to my uncle, whom, he hesitating said, I might not find alive. He uttered this intelligence with visible regret; requested me, at least, to wait for the arrival of the next packet[8]; offered me what money I wanted, and promised to visit me.

[8]Packet-boat, inexpensive transportation.

"He kept his word; still no letter arrived to put an end to my painful state of suspense. I procured some books and music, to beguile the tedious solitary days.

> 'Come, ever smiling Liberty,
> And with thee bring thy jocund train:'[9]

I sung—and sung till, saddened by the strain of joy, I bitterly lamented the fate that deprived me of all social pleasure. Comparative liberty indeed I had possessed myself of; but the jocund train lagged far behind!

CHAPTER XIII

"By watching my only visitor, my uncle's friend, or by some other means, Mr. Venables discovered my residence, and came to enquire for me. The maid-servant assured him there was no such person in the house. A bustle ensued—I caught the alarm—listened—distinguished his voice, and immediately locked the door. They suddenly grew still; and I waited near a quarter of an hour, before I heard him open the parlour door, and mount the stairs with the mistress of the house, who obsequiously declared that she knew nothing of me.

"Finding my door locked, she requested me to 'open it, and prepare to go home with my husband, poor gentleman! to whom I had already occasioned sufficient vexation.' I made no reply. Mr. Venables then, in an assumed tone of softness, intreated me, 'to consider what he suffered, and my own reputation, and get the better of childish resentment.' He ran on in the same strain, pretending to address me, but evidently adapting his discourse to the capacity of the landlady; who, at every pause, uttered an exclamation of pity; or 'Yes, to be sure—Very true, sir.'

"Sick of the farce, and perceiving that I could not avoid the hated interview, I opened the door, and he entered. Advancing with easy assurance to take my hand, I shrunk from his touch, with an involuntary start, as I should have done from a noisome reptile, with more disgust than terror. His conductress was retiring, to give us, as she said, an op-

---

[9]From George Frideric Handel's *Judas Maccabaeus*, with lyrics by Thomas Morel (1746).

portunity to accommodate matters. But I bade her come in, or I would go out; and curiosity impelled her to obey me.

"Mr. Venables began to expostulate; and this woman, proud of his confidence, to second him. But I calmly silenced her, in the midst of a vulgar harangue, and turning to him, asked, 'Why he vainly tormented me? declaring that no power on earth should force me back to his house.'

"After a long altercation, the particulars of which, it would be to no purpose to repeat, he left the room. Some time was spent in loud conversation in the parlour below, and I discovered that he had brought his friend, an attorney, with him.[1]

The tumult on the landing place, brought out a gentleman, who had recently taken apartments in the house; he enquired why I was thus assailed?[2] The voluble attorney instantly repeated the trite tale. The stranger turned to me, observing, with the most soothing politeness and manly interest, that 'my countenance told a very different story.' He added, 'that I should not be insulted, or forced out of the house, by any body.'

"'Not by her husband?' asked the attorney.

"'No, sir, not by her husband.' Mr. Venables advanced towards him—But there was a decision in his attitude, that so well seconded that of his voice,[3]

They left the house: at the same time protesting, that any one that should dare to protect me, should be prosecuted with the utmost rigour.

"They were scarcely out of the house, when my landlady came up to me again, and begged my pardon, in a very different tone. For, though Mr. Venables had bid her, at her peril, harbour me, he had not attended, I found, to her broad hints, to discharge the lodging. I instantly promised to pay her, and make her a present to compensate for my abrupt departure, if she would procure me another lodging, at a sufficient distance; and she, in return, repeating Mr. Venables' plausible tale, I raised her indignation, and excited her sympathy, by telling her briefly the truth.

---

[1] 1798 edn.] three lines of asterisks follow.

[2] The introduction of Darnford as the deliverer of Maria, in an early stage of the history, is already stated (Chap. III.) to have been an after-thought of the author. This has probably caused the imperfectness of the manuscript in the above passage; though, at the same time, it must be acknowledged to be somewhat uncertain, whether Darnford is the stranger intended in this place. It appears from Chap. XVII, that an interference of a more decisive nature was designed to be attributed to him. EDITOR [WG].

[3] 1798 edn.] two lines of asterisks follow.

"She expressed her commiseration with such honest warmth, that I felt soothed; for I have none of that fastidious sensitiveness, which a vulgar accent or gesture can alarm to the disregard of real kindness. I was ever glad to perceive in others the humane feelings I delighted to exercise; and the recollection of some ridiculous characteristic circumstances, which have occurred in a moment of emotion, has convulsed me with laughter, though at the instant I should have thought it sacrilegious to have smiled. Your improvement, my dearest girl, being ever present to me while I write, I note these feelings, because women, more accustomed to observe manners than actions, are too much alive to ridicule. So much so, that their boasted sensibility is often stifled by false delicacy. True sensibility, the sensibility which is the auxiliary of virtue, and the soul of genius, is in society so occupied with the feelings of others, as scarcely to regard its own sensations. With what reverence have I looked up at my uncle, the dear parent of my mind! when I have seen the sense of his own sufferings, of mind and body, absorbed in a desire to comfort those, whose misfortunes were comparatively trivial. He would have been ashamed of being as indulgent to himself, as he was to others. 'Genuine fortitude,' he would assert, 'consisted in governing our own emotions, and making allowance for the weaknesses in our friends, that we would not tolerate in ourselves.' But where is my fond regret leading me!

"'Women must be submissive,' said my landlady. 'Indeed what could most women do? Who had they to maintain them, but their husbands? Every woman, and especially a lady, could not go through rough and smooth, as she had done, to earn a little bread.'

"She was in a talking mood, and proceeded to inform me how she had been used in the world. 'She knew what it was to have a bad husband, or she did not know who should.' I perceived that she would be very much mortified, were I not to attend to her tale, and I did not attempt to interrupt her, though I wished her, as soon as possible, to go out in search of a new abode for me, where I could once more hide my head.

"She began by telling me, 'That she had saved a little money in service; and was over-persuaded (we must all be in love once in our lives) to marry a likely man, a footman in the family, not worth a groat. My plan,' she continued, 'was to take a house, and let out lodgings; and all went on well, till my husband got acquainted with an impudent slut, who chose to live on other people's means—and then all went to rack and ruin. He ran in debt to buy her fine clothes, such clothes as I never thought of wearing myself, and—would you believe it?—he signed an execution on my very goods, bought with the money I worked so hard to get; and they came and took my bed from under me, before I heard a word of the matter. Aye, madam, these are misfortunes that you gentlefolks know nothing of;—but sorrow is sorrow, let it come which way it will.

"'I sought for a service again—very hard, after having a house of my own!—but he used to follow me, and kick up such a riot when he was drunk, that I could not keep a place; nay, he even stole my clothes, and pawned them; and when I went to the pawnbroker's, and offered to take my oath that they were not bought with a farthing of his money, they said, 'It was all as one, my husband had a right to whatever I had.'

"'At last he listed for a soldier, and I took a house, making an agreement to pay for the furniture by degrees; and I almost starved myself, till I once more got before-hand in the world.

"'After an absence of six years (God forgive me! I thought he was dead) my husband returned; found me out, and came with such a penitent face, I forgave him, and clothed him from head to foot. But he had not been a week in the house, before some of his creditors arrested him; and, he selling my goods, I found myself once more reduced to beggary; for I was not as well able to work, go to bed late, and rise early, as when I quitted service; and then I thought it hard enough. He was soon tired of me, when there was nothing more to be had, and left me again.

"'I will not tell you how I was buffeted about, till, hearing for certain that he had died in an hospital abroad, I once more returned to my old occupation; but have not yet been able to get my head above water: so, madam, you must not be angry if I am afraid to run any risk, when I know so well, that women have always the worst of it, when law is to decide.'

"After uttering a few more complaints, I prevailed on my landlady to go out in quest of a lodging; and, to be more secure, I condescended to the mean shift of changing my name.

"But why should I dwell on similar incidents!—I was hunted, like an infected beast, from three different apartments, and should not have been allowed to rest in any, had not Mr. Venables, informed of my uncle's dangerous state of health, been inspired with the fear of hurrying me out of the world as I advanced in my pregnancy, by thus tormenting and obliging me to take sudden journeys to avoid him; and then his speculations on my uncle's fortune must prove abortive.

"One day, when he had pursued me to an inn, I fainted, hurrying from him; and, falling down, the sight of my blood alarmed him, and obtained a respite for me. It is strange that he should have retained any hope, after observing my unwavering determination; but, from the mildness of my behaviour, when I found all my endeavours to change his disposition unavailing, he formed an erroneous opinion of my character, imagining that, were we once more together, I should part with the money he could not legally force from me, with the same facility as formerly. My forbearance and occasional sympathy he had mistaken for weakness of character; and, because he perceived that I disliked resistance, he thought my indulgence and compassion mere selfishness, and never discovered that the fear of being unjust, or of unnecessarily wounding the feelings of another, was much more painful to me, than any thing I could have to endure myself. Perhaps it was pride which made me imagine, that I could bear what I dreaded to inflict; and that it was often easier to suffer, than to see the sufferings of others.

"I forgot to mention that, during this persecution, I received a letter from my uncle, informing me, 'that he only found relief from continual change of air; and that he intended to return when the spring was a little more advanced (it was now the middle of February), and then we would plan a journey to Italy, leaving the fogs and cares of England far behind.' He approved of my conduct, promised to adopt my child, and seemed to have no doubt of obliging Mr. Venables to hear reason. He wrote to his friend, by the same post, desiring him to call on Mr. Venables in his name; and, in consequence of the remonstrances he dictated, I was permitted to lie-in tranquilly.

"The two or three weeks previous, I had been allowed to rest in peace; but, so accustomed was I to pursuit and alarm, that I seldom closed my eyes without being haunted by Mr. Venables' image, who seemed to assume terrific or hateful forms to torment me, wherever I turned.—Sometimes a wild cat, a roaring bull, or hideous assassin, whom I vainly attempted to fly; at others he was a demon, hurrying me to the brink of a precipice, plunging me into dark waves, or horrid gulfs; and I woke, in violent fits of trembling anxiety, to assure myself that it was all a dream, and to endeavour to lure my waking thoughts to wander to the delightful Italian vales, I hoped soon to visit; or to picture some august ruins, where I reclined in fancy on a mouldering column, and escaped, in the contemplation of the heart-enlarging virtues of antiquity, from the turmoil of cares that had depressed all the daring purposes of my soul. But I was not long allowed to calm my mind by the exercise of my imagination; for the third day after your birth, my child, I was surprised by a visit from my elder brother; who came in the most abrupt manner, to inform me of the death of my uncle. He had left the greater part of his fortune to my child, appointing me its guardian; in short, every step was taken to enable me to be mistress of his fortune, without putting any part of it in Mr. Venables' power. My brother came to vent his rage on me, for having, as he expressed himself, 'deprived him, my uncle's eldest nephew, of his inheritance;' though my uncle's property, the fruit of his own exertion, being all in the funds, or on landed securities, there was not a shadow of justice in the charge.

"As I sincerely loved my uncle, this intelligence brought on a fever, which I struggled to conquer with all the energy of my mind; for, in my desolate state, I had it very much at heart to suckle you, my poor babe. You seemed my only tie to life, a cherub, to whom I wished to be a father, as well as a mother; and the double duty appeared to me to produce a proportionate increase of affection. But the pleasure I felt, while sustaining you, snatched from the wreck of hope, was cruelly damped by melancholy reflections on my widowed state—widowed by the death of my uncle. Of Mr. Venables I thought not, even when I thought of the felicity of loving your father, and how a mother's pleasure might be exalted, and her care softened by a husband's tenderness.—'Ought to be!' I exclaimed; and I endeavoured to drive away the tenderness that suffocated me; but my spirits were weak, and the unbidden tears would flow. 'Why was I,' I would ask thee, but thou didst not heed me,—'cut off from the participation of the sweetest pleasure of life?' I imagined with what extacy, after the pains of child-bed, I should have presented my little stranger, whom I had so long wished to view, to a respectable father, and with what maternal fondness I should have pressed them both to my heart!—Now I kissed her with less delight, though with the most endearing compassion, poor helpless one! when I perceived a slight resemblance of him, to whom she owed her existence; or, if any gesture reminded me of him, even in his best days, my heart heaved, and I pressed the innocent to my bosom, as if to purify it—yes, I blushed to think that its purity had been sullied, by allowing such a man to be its father.

"After my recovery, I began to think of taking a house in the country, or of making an excursion on the continent, to avoid Mr. Venables; and to open my heart to new pleasures and affection. The spring was melting into summer, and you, my little companion, began to smile—that smile made hope bud out afresh, assuring me the world was not a desert. Your gestures were ever present to my fancy; and I dwelt on the joy I should feel when you would begin to walk and lisp. Watching your wakening mind, and shielding from every rude blast my tender blossom, I recovered my spirits—I dreamed not of the frost—'the killing frost,'[4] to which you were destined to be exposed.—But I lose all patience—and execrate the injustice of the world—folly! ignorance!—I should rather call it; but, shut up from a free circulation of thought, and always pondering on the same griefs, I writhe under the torturing apprehensions, which ought to excite only honest indignation, or active compassion; and would, could I view them as the natural consequence of things. But, born a woman—and born to suffer, in endeavouring to repress my own emotions, I feel more acutely the various ills my sex are fated to bear—I feel that the evils they are subject to endure, degrade them so far below their oppressors, as almost to justify their tyranny; leading at the same time superficial reasoners to term that weakness the cause, which is only the consequence of short-sighted despotism.

CHAPTER XIV

"As my mind grew calmer, the visions of Italy again returned with their former glow of colouring; and I resolved on quitting the kingdom for a time, in search of the cheerfulness, that naturally results from a change of scene, unless we carry the barbed arrow with us, and only see what we feel.

"During the period necessary to prepare for a long absence, I sent a supply to pay my father's debts, and settled my brothers in eligible situations; but my attention was not wholly engrossed by my family,

---

[4]After Cardinal Wolsey's treacheries are discovered, resulting in his resignation and imprisonment, he meditates on the state of man, who puts forth hope today, blossoms tomorrow, and on the third day is blighted by "a killing frost" (Shakespeare, *Henry VIII*, 3.2.352–58).

though I do not think it necessary to enumerate the common exertions of humanity. The manner in which my uncle's property was settled, prevented me from making the addition to the fortune of my surviving sister, that I could have wished; but I had prevailed on him to bequeath her two thousand pounds, and she determined to marry a lover, to whom she had been some time attached. Had it not been for this engagement, I should have invited her to accompany me in my tour; and I might have escaped the pit, so artfully dug in my path, when I was the least aware of danger.

"I had thought of remaining in England, till I weaned my child; but this state of freedom was too peaceful to last, and I had soon reason to wish to hasten my departure. A friend of Mr. Venables, the same attorney who had accompanied him in several excursions to hunt me from my hiding places, waited on me to propose a reconciliation. On my refusal, he indirectly advised me to make over to my husband—for husband he would term him—the greater part of the property I had at command, menacing me with continual persecution unless I complied, and that, as a last resort, he would claim the child. I did not, though intimidated by the last insinuation, scruple to declare, that I would not allow him to squander the money left to me for far different purposes, but offered him five hundred pounds, if he would sign a bond not to torment me any more. My maternal anxiety made me thus appear to waver from my first determination, and probably suggested to him, or his diabolical agent, the infernal plot, which has succeeded but too well.

"The bond was executed; still I was impatient to leave England. Mischief hung in the air when we breathed the same; I wanted seas to divide us, and waters to roll between, till he had forgotten that I had the means of helping him through a new scheme. Disturbed by the late occurrences, I instantly prepared for my departure. My only delay was waiting for a maid-servant, who spoke French fluently, and had been warmly recommended to me. A valet I was advised to hire, when I fixed on my place of residence for any time.

"My God, with what a light heart did I set out for Dover!—It was not my country, but my cares, that I was leaving behind. My heart seemed to bound with the wheels, or rather appeared the centre on which they twirled. I clasped you to my bosom, exclaiming 'And you will be safe—quite safe—when—we are once on board the packet.— Would we were there!' I smiled at my idle fears, as the natural effect of continual alarm; and I scarcely owned to myself that I dreaded Mr. Venables's cunning, or was conscious of the horrid delight he would feel, at forming stratagem after stratagem to circumvent me. I was already in the snare—I never reached the packet—I never saw thee more.—I grow breathless. I have scarcely patience to write down the details. The maid—the plausible woman I had hired—put, doubtless, some stupifying potion in what I ate or drank, the morning I left town. All I know is, that she must have quitted the chaise, shameless wretch! and taken (from my breast) my babe with her. How could a creature in a female form see me caress thee, and steal thee from my arms! I must stop, stop to repress a mother's anguish; lest, in bitterness of soul, I imprecate the wrath of heaven on this tiger, who tore my only comfort from me.

"How long I slept I know not; certainly many hours, for I woke at the close of day, in a strange confusion of thought. I was probably roused to recollection by some one thundering at a huge, unwieldy gate. Attempting to ask where I was, my voice died away, and I tried to raise it in vain, as I have done in a dream. I looked for my babe with affright; feared that it had fallen out of my lap, while I had so strangely forgotten her; and, such was the vague intoxication, I can give it no other name, in which I was plunged, I could not recollect when or where I last saw you; but I sighed, as if my heart wanted room to clear my head.

"The gates opened heavily, and the sullen sound of many locks and bolts drawn back, grated on my very soul, before I was appalled by the creeking of the dismal hinges, as they closed after me. The gloomy pile was before me, half in ruins; some of the aged trees of the avenue were cut down, and left to rot where they fell; and as we approached some mouldering steps, a monstrous dog darted forwards to the length of his chain, and barked and growled infernally.

"The door was opened slowly, and a murderous visage peeped out, with a lantern. 'Hush!' he uttered, in a threatning tone, and the affrighted animal stole back to his kennel. The door of the chaise flew back, the stranger put down the lantern, and clasped his dreadful arms around me. It was certainly the effect of the soporific draught, for, instead of exerting my strength, I sunk without motion, though not without sense, on his shoulder, my limbs refusing to obey my will. I was carried up the steps into a close-shut hall. A candle flaring in the socket, scarcely dispersed the darkness, though it displayed to me the ferocious countenance of the wretch who held me.

"He mounted a wide staircase. Large figures painted on the walls seemed to start on me, and glaring eyes to meet me at every turn. Entering a long gallery, a dismal shriek made me spring out of my conductor's arms, with I know not what mysterious emotion of terror; but I fell on the floor, unable to sustain myself.

"A strange-looking female started out of one of the recesses, and observed me with more curiosity than interest; till, sternly bid retire, she flitted back like a shadow. Other faces, strongly marked, or distorted, peeped through the half-opened doors, and I heard some incoherent sounds. I had no distinct idea where I could be—I looked on all sides, and almost doubted whether I was alive or dead.

"Thrown on a bed, I immediately sunk into insensibility again; and next day, gradually recovering the use of reason, I began, starting affrighted from the conviction, to discover where I was confined—I insisted on seeing the master of the mansion—I saw him—and perceived that I was buried alive.—

"Such, my child, are the events of thy mother's life to this dreadful moment—Should she ever escape from the fangs of her enemies, she will add the secrets of her prison-house—and—"

Some lines were here crossed out, and the memoirs broke off abruptly with the names of Jemima and Darnford.

APPENDIX

[ADVERTISEMENT.[1]

The performance, with a fragment of which the reader has now been presented, was designed to consist of three parts. The preceding sheets were considered as constituting one of those parts. Those persons who in the perusal of the chapters, already written and in some degree finished by the author, have felt their hearts awakened, and their curiosity excited as to the sequel of the story, will, of course, gladly accept even of the broken paragraphs and half-finished sentences, which have been found committed to paper, as materials for the remainder. The fastidious and cold-hearted critic may perhaps feel himself repelled by the incoherent form in which they are presented. But an inquisitive

[1]Presumably written by Godwin.

temper willingly accepts the most imperfect and mutilated information, where better is not to be had: and readers, who in any degree resemble the author in her quick apprehension of sentiment, and of the pleasures and pains of imagination, will, I believe, find gratification, in contemplating sketches, which were designed in a short time to have received the finishing touches of her genius; but which must now for ever remain a mark to record the triumphs of mortality, over schemes of usefulness, and projects of public interest.]

CHAPTER XV

Darnford returned the memoirs to Maria, with a most affectionate letter, in which he reasoned on "the absurdity of the laws respecting matrimony, which, till divorces could be more easily obtained, was," he declared, "the most insufferable bondage. Ties of this nature could not bind minds governed by superior principles; and such beings were privileged to act above the dictates of laws they had no voice in framing, if they had sufficient strength of mind to endure the natural consequence. In her case, to talk of duty, was a farce, excepting what was due to herself. Delicacy, as well as reason, forbade her ever to think of returning to her husband: was she then to restrain her charming sensibility through mere prejudice? These arguments were not absolutely impartial, for he disdained to conceal, that, when he appealed to her reason, he felt that he had some interest in her heart.—The conviction was not more transporting, than sacred—a thousand times a day, he asked himself how he had merited such happiness?—and as often he determined to purify the heart she deigned to inhabit—He intreated to be again admitted to her presence."

He was; and the tear which glistened in his eye, when he respectfully pressed her to his bosom, rendered him peculiarly dear to the unfortunate mother. Grief had stilled the transports of love, only to render their mutual tenderness more touching. In former interviews, Darnford had contrived, by a hundred little pretexts, to sit near her, to take her hand, or to meet her eyes—now it was all soothing affection, and esteem seemed to have rivalled love. He adverted to her narrative, and spoke with warmth of the oppression she had endured.—His eyes, glowing with a lambent flame, told her how much he wished to restore her to liberty and love; but he kissed her hand, as if it had been that of a saint; and spoke of the loss of her child, as if it had been his own.—What could have been more flattering to Maria?—Every instance of self-denial was registered in her heart, and she loved him, for loving her too well to give way to the transports of passion.

They met again and again; and Darnford declared, while passion suffused his cheeks, that he never before knew what it was to love.—

One morning Jemima informed Maria, that her master intended to wait on her, and speak to her without witnesses. He came, and brought a letter with him, pretending that he was ignorant of its contents, though he insisted on having it returned to him. It was from the attorney already mentioned, who informed her of the death of her child, and hinted, "that she could not now have a legitimate heir, and that, would she make over the half of her fortune during life, she should be conveyed to Dover, and permitted to pursue her plan of travelling."

Maria answered with warmth, "That she had no terms to make with the murderer of her babe, nor would she purchase liberty at the price of her own respect."

She began to expostulate with her jailor; but he sternly bade her "Be silent—he had not gone so far, not to go further."

Darnford came in the evening. Jemima was obliged to be absent, and she, as usual, locked the door on them, to prevent interruption or discovery.—The lovers were, at first, embarrassed; but fell insensibly into confidential discourse. Darnford represented, "that they might soon be parted," and wished her "to put it out of the power of fate to separate them."

As her husband she now received him, and he solemnly pledged himself as her protector—and eternal friend.—

There was one peculiarity in Maria's mind: she was more anxious not to deceive, than to guard against deception; and had rather trust without sufficient reason, than be for ever the prey of doubt. Besides, what are we, when the mind has, from reflection, a certain kind of elevation, which exalts the contemplation above the little concerns of prudence! We see what we wish, and make a world of our own—and, though reality may sometimes open a door to misery, yet the moments of happiness procured by the imagination, may, without a paradox, be reckoned among the solid comforts of life. Maria now, imagining that she had found a being of celestial mould—was happy,—nor was she deceived.—He was then plastic in her impassioned hand—and reflected all the sentiments which animated and warmed her.[1]

[1] 1798 edn.] two lines of dashes follow.

CHAPTER XVI

One morning confusion seemed to reign in the house, and Jemima came in terror, to inform Maria, "that her master had left it, with a determination, she was assured (and too many circumstances corroborated the opinion, to leave a doubt of its truth) of never returning. I am prepared then," said Jemima, "to accompany you in your flight."

Maria started up, her eyes darting towards the door, as if afraid that some one should fasten it on her for ever.

Jemima continued, "I have perhaps no right now to expect the performance of your promise; but on you it depends to reconcile me with the human race."

"But Darnford!"—exclaimed Maria, mournfully—sitting down again, and crossing her arms—"I have no child to go to, and liberty has lost its sweets."

"I am much mistaken, if Darnford is not the cause of my master's flight—his keepers assure me, that they have promised to confine him two days longer, and then he will be free—you cannot see him; but they will give a letter to him the moment he is free.—In that inform him where he may find you in London; fix on some hotel. Give me your clothes; I will send them out of the house with mine, and we will slip out at the garden-gate. Write your letter while I make these arrangements, but lose no time!"

In an agitation of spirit, not to be calmed, Maria began to write to Darnford. She called him by the sacred name of "husband," and bade him "hasten to her, to share her fortune, or she would return to him."—An hotel in the Adelphi[1] was the place of rendezvous.

The letter was sealed and given in charge; and with light footsteps, yet terrified at the sound of them, she descended, scarcely breathing, and with an indistinct fear that she should never get out at the garden gate. Jemima went first.

A being, with a visage that would have suited one possessed by a devil, crossed the path, and seized Maria by the arm. Maria had no fear but of being detained—"Who are you? what are you?" for the form was scarcely human. "If you are made of flesh and blood," his ghastly eyes glared on her, "do not stop me!"

"Woman," interrupted a sepulchral voice, "what have I to do with thee?"—Still he grasped her hand, muttering a curse.

[1]Elegant terraced housing between the Thames and Fleet Street built in 1768–72.

"No, no; you have nothing to do with me," she exclaimed, "this is a moment of life and death!"—

With supernatural force she broke from him, and, throwing her arms round Jemima, cried, "Save me!" The being, from whose grasp she had loosed herself, took up a stone as they opened the door, and with a kind of hellish sport threw it after them. They were out of his reach.

When Maria arrived in town, she drove to the hotel already fixed on. But she could not sit still—her child was ever before her; and all that had passed during her confinement, appeared to be a dream. She went to the house in the suburbs, where, as she now discovered, her babe had been sent. The moment she entered, her heart grew sick; but she wondered not that it had proved its grave. She made the necessary enquiries, and the church-yard was pointed out, in which it rested under a turf. A little frock which the nurse's child wore (Maria had made it herself) caught her eye. The nurse was glad to sell it for half-a-guinea, and Maria hastened away with the relic, and, re-entering the hackney-coach which waited for her, gazed on it, till she reached her hotel.

She then waited on the attorney who had made her uncle's will, and explained to him her situation. He readily advanced her some of the money which still remained in his hands, and promised to take the whole of the case into consideration. Maria only wished to be permitted to remain in quiet—She found that several bills, apparently with her signature, had been presented to her agent, nor was she for a moment at a loss to guess by whom they had been forged; yet, equally averse to threaten or intreat, she requested her friend [the solicitor] to call on Mr. Venables. He was not to be found at home; but at length his agent, the attorney, offered a conditional promise to Maria, to leave her in peace, as long as she behaved with propriety, if she would give up the notes. Maria inconsiderately consented—Darnford was arrived, and she wished to be only alive to love; she wished to forget the anguish she felt whenever she thought of her child.

They took a ready-furnished lodging together, for she was above disguise; Jemima insisting on being considered as her house-keeper, and to receive the customary stipend. On no other terms would she remain with her friend.

Darnford was indefatigable in tracing the mysterious circumstances of his confinement. The cause was simply, that a relation, a very distant one, to whom he was heir, had died intestate, leaving a considerable fortune. On the news of Darnford's arrival [in England, a person, intrusted with the management of the property, and who had the writings in his possession, determining, by one bold stroke, to strip Darnford of the succession,] had planned his confinement; and [as soon as he had taken the measures he judged most conducive to his object, this ruffian, together with his instrument,] the keeper of the private mad-house, left the kingdom. Darnford, who still pursued his enquiries, at last discovered that they had fixed their place of refuge at Paris.

Maria and he determined therefore, with the faithful Jemima, to visit that metropolis, and accordingly were preparing for the journey, when they were informed that Mr. Venables had commenced an action against Darnford for seduction and adultery.[2] The indignation Maria felt cannot be explained; she repented of the forbearance she had exercised in giving up the notes. Darnford could not put off his journey, without risking the loss of his property: Maria therefore furnished him with money for his expedition; and determined to remain in London till the termination of this affair.

She visited some ladies with whom she had formerly been intimate, but was refused admittance; and at the opera, or Ranelagh,[3] they could not recollect her. Among these ladies there were some, not her most intimate acquaintance, who were generally supposed to avail themselves of the cloke of marriage, to conceal a mode of conduct, that would for ever have damned their fame, had they been innocent, seduced girls. These particularly stood aloof.—Had she remained with her husband, practising insincerity, and neglecting her child to manage an intrigue, she would still have been visited and respected. If, instead of openly living with her lover, she could have condescended to call into play a thousand arts, which, degrading her own mind, might have allowed the people who were not deceived, to pretend to be so, she would have been caressed and treated like an honourable woman. "And Brutus is an honourable man!" said Mark-Antony with equal sincerity.[4]

With Darnford she did not taste uninterrupted felicity; there was a volatility in his manner which often distressed her; but love gladdened

---

[2]Seeking damages against an alleged seducer is the first step in a civil suit of adultery.

[3]A fashionable public garden in Chelsea.

[4]The name in the manuscript is by mistake written Caesar. EDITOR [WG, on "Brutus"]. "For Brutus is an honorable man," says Mark Antony, with increasing irony, in his funeral oration for Julius Caesar (3.2), a speech that turns the Roman mob against Brutus and the other assassins. An "honorable woman" is one with a reputation for marital fidelity.

the scene; besides, he was the most tender, sympathizing creature in the world. A fondness for the sex often gives an appearance of humanity to the behaviour of men, who have small pretensions to the reality; and they seem to love others, when they are only pursuing their own gratification. Darnford appeared ever willing to avail himself of her taste and acquirements, while she endeavoured to profit by his decision of character, and to eradicate some of the romantic notions, which had taken root in her mind, while in adversity she had brooded over visions of unattainable bliss.

The real affections of life, when they are allowed to burst forth, are buds pregnant with joy and all the sweet emotions of the soul; yet they branch out with wild ease, unlike the artificial forms of felicity, sketched by an imagination painful alive. The substantial happiness, which enlarges and civilizes the mind, may be compared to the pleasure experienced in roving through nature at large, inhaling the sweet gale natural to the clime; while the reveries of a feverish imagination continually sport themselves in gardens full of aromatic shrubs, which cloy while they delight, and weaken the sense of pleasure they gratify. The heaven of fancy, below or beyond the stars, in this life, or in those ever-smiling regions surrounded by the unmarked ocean of futurity, have an insipid uniformity which palls. Poets have imagined scenes of bliss; but, sencing out sorrow, all the extatic emotions of the soul, and even its grandeur, seem to be equally excluded. We dose over the unruffled lake, and long to scale the rocks which fence the happy valley of contentment, though serpents hiss in the pathless desert, and danger lurks in the unexplored wiles.[5] Maria found herself more indulgent as she was happier, and discovered virtues, in characters she had before disregarded, while chasing the phantoms of elegance and excellence, which sported in the meteors that exhale in the marshes of misfortune. The heart is often shut by romance against social pleasure; and, fostering a sickly sensibility, grows callous to the soft touches of humanity.

To part with Darnford was indeed cruel.—It was to feel most painfully alone; but she rejoiced to think, that she should spare him the care and perplexity of the suit, and meet him again, all his own. Marriage, as at present constituted, she considered as leading to im-

---

[5]In Samuel Johnson's *History of Rasselas: Prince of Abyssinia* (1759), Rasselas wearies of the monotonous perfection of life in the happy valley; and with his tutor, his sister, and her maid, he flees this home, only to wander the world, vainly searching for happiness.

morality—yet, as the odium of society impedes usefulness, she wished to avow her affection to Darnford, by becoming his wife according to established rules; not to be confounded with women who act from very different motives, though her conduct would be just the same without the ceremony as with it, and her expectations from him not less firm. The being summoned to defend herself from a charge which she was determined to plead guilty to, was still galling, as it roused bitter reflections on the situation of women in society.

CHAPTER XVII

Such was her state of mind when the dogs of law were let loose on her. Maria took the task of conducting Darnford's defence upon herself. She instructed his counsel to plead guilty to the charge of adultery; but to deny that of seduction.

The counsel for the plaintiff opened the cause, by observing, "that his client had ever been an indulgent husband, and had borne with several defects of temper, while he had nothing criminal to lay to the charge of his wife. But that she left his house without assigning any cause. He could not assert that she was then acquainted with the defendant; yet, when he was once endeavouring to bring her back to her home, this man put the peace-officers to flight, and took her he knew not whither. After the birth of her child, her conduct was so strange, and a melancholy malady having afflicted one of the family, which delicacy forbade the dwelling on, it was necessary to confine her. By some means the defendant enabled her to make her escape, and they had lived together, in despite of all sense of order and decorum. The adultery was allowed, it was not necessary to bring any witnesses to prove it; but the seduction, though highly probable from the circumstances which he had the honour to state, could not be so clearly proved.—It was of the most atrocious kind, as decency was set at defiance, and respect for reputation, which shows internal compunction, utterly disregarded."

A strong sense of injustice had silenced every emotion, which a mixture of true and false delicacy might otherwise have excited in Maria's bosom. She only felt in earnest to insist on the privilege of her nature. The sarcasms of society, and the condemnation of a mistaken world, were nothing to her, compared with acting contrary to those feelings which were the foundation of her principles. [She therefore eagerly put herself forward, instead of desiring to be absent, on this memorable occasion.]

Convinced that the subterfuges of the law were disgraceful, she wrote a paper, which she expressly desired might be read in court:

"Married when scarcely able to distinguish the nature of the engagement, I yet submitted to the rigid laws which enslave women, and obeyed the man whom I could no longer love. Whether the duties of the state are reciprocal, I mean not to discuss; but I can prove repeated infidelities which I overlooked or pardoned.[1] Witnesses are not wanting to establish these facts. I at present maintain the child of a maid servant, sworn to him, and born after our marriage. I am ready to allow, that education and circumstances lead men to think and act with less delicacy, than the preservation of order in society demands from women; but surely I may without assumption declare, that, though I could excuse the birth, I could not the desertion of this unfortunate babe:—and, while I despised the man, it was not easy to venerate the husband. With proper restrictions however, I revere the institution which fraternizes the world. I exclaim against the laws which throw the whole weight of the yoke on the weaker shoulders, and force women, when they claim protectorship as mothers, to sign a contract, which renders them dependent on the caprice of the tyrant, whom choice or necessity has appointed to reign over them. Various are the cases, in which a woman ought to separate herself from her husband; and mine, I may be allowed emphatically to insist, comes under the description of the most aggravated.

"I will not enlarge on those provocations which only the individual can estimate; but will bring forward such charges only, the truth of which is an insult upon humanity. In order to promote certain destructive speculations, Mr. Venables prevailed on me to borrow certain sums of a wealthy relation; and, when I refused further compliance, he thought of bartering my person; and not only allowed opportunities to, but urged, a friend from whom he borrowed money, to seduce me. On the discovery of this act of atrocity, I determined to leave him, and in the most decided manner, for ever. I consider all obligation as made void by his conduct; and hold, that schisms which proceed from want of principles, can never be healed.

---

[1]An irrelevant proof in a legal code that gives only a husband grounds of adultery. A wife could seek a divorce only on grounds of impotence, bigamy, incest, or dire physical cruelty.

"He received a fortune with me to the amount of five thousand pounds. On the death of my uncle, convinced that I could provide for my child, I destroyed the settlement of that fortune. I required none of my property to be returned to me, nor shall enumerate the sums extorted from me during six years that we lived together.

"After leaving, what the law considers as my home, I was hunted like a criminal from place to place, though I contracted no debts, and demanded no maintenance—yet, as the laws sanction such proceeding, and make women the property of their husbands, I forbear to animadvert. After the birth of my daughter, and the death of my uncle, who left a very considerable property to myself and child, I was exposed to new persecution; and, because I had, before arriving at what is termed years of discretion, pledged my faith, I was treated by the world, as bound for ever to a man whose vices were notorious. Yet what are the vices generally known, to the various miseries that a woman may be subject to, which, though deeply felt, eating into the soul, elude description, and may be glossed over! A false morality is even established, which makes all the virtue of women consist in chastity, submission, and the forgiveness of injuries.

"I pardon my oppressor—bitterly as I lament the loss of my child, torn from me in the most violent manner. But nature revolts, and my soul sickens at the bare supposition, that it could ever be a duty to pretend affection, when a separation is necessary to prevent my feeling hourly aversion.

"To force me to give my fortune, I was imprisoned—yes; in a private madhouse.—There, in the heart of misery, I met the man charged with seducing me. We became attached—I deemed, and ever shall deem, myself free. The death of my babe dissolved the only tie which subsisted between me and my, what is termed, lawful husband.

"To this person, thus encountered, I voluntarily gave myself, never considering myself as any more bound to transgress the laws of moral purity, because the will of my husband might be pleaded in my excuse, than to transgress those laws to which [the policy of artificial society has] annexed [positive] punishments.—While no command of a husband can prevent a woman from suffering for certain crimes, she must be allowed to consult her conscience, and regulate her conduct, in some degree, by her own sense of right. The respect I owe to myself, demanded my strict adherence to my determination of never viewing Mr. Venables in the light of a husband, nor could it forbid me from encouraging another. If I am unfortunately united to an unprincipled man, am I for ever to be shut out from fulfilling the duties of a wife and mother?[2]—I wish my country to approve of my conduct; but, if laws exist, made by the strong to oppress the weak, I appeal to my own sense of justice, and declare that I will not live with the individual, who has violated every moral obligation which binds man to man.

"I protest equally against any charge being brought to criminate the man, whom I consider as my husband. I was six-and-twenty when I left Mr. Venables' roof; if ever I am to be supposed to arrive at an age to direct my own actions, I must by that time have arrived at it.—I acted with deliberation.—Mr. Darnford found me a forlorn and oppressed woman, and promised the protection women in the present state of society want.—But the man who now claims me—was he deprived of my society by this conduct? The question is an insult to common sense, considering where Mr. Darnford met me.—Mr. Venables' door was indeed open to me—nay, threats and intreaties were used to induce me to return; but why? Was affection or honour the motive?—I cannot, it is true, dive into the recesses of the human heart—yet I presume to assert, [borne out as I am by a variety of circumstances,] that he was merely influenced by the most rapacious avarice.

"I claim then a divorce, and the liberty of enjoying, free from molestation, the fortune left to me by a relation, who was well aware of the character of the man with whom I had to contend.—I appeal to the justice and humanity of the jury—a body of men, whose private judgment must be allowed to modify laws, that must be unjust, because definite rules can never apply to indefinite circumstances[3]—and I deprecate punishment [upon the man of my choice, freeing him, as I solemnly do, from the charge of seduction.]

"I did not put myself into a situation to justify a charge of adultery, till I had, from conviction, shaken off the fetters which bound me to Mr. Venables.—While I lived with him, I defy the voice of calumny to sully what is termed the fair fame of woman.—Neglected by my husband, I never encouraged a lover; and preserved with scrupulous care, what is termed my honour, at the expence of my peace, till he, who should have been its guardian, laid traps to ensnare me. From

[2]Children were presumptively the possession of their father, a prejudice that kept many mothers in abusive marriages.

[3]In *Political Justice*, Godwin thus distinguishes law from justice.

that moment I believed myself, in the sight of heaven, free—and no power on earth shall force me to renounce my resolution."

The judge, in summing up the evidence, alluded to "the fallacy of letting women plead their feelings, as an excuse for the violation of the marriage-vow. For his part, he had always determined to oppose all innovation, and the new-fangled notions which incroached on the good old rules of conduct. We did not want French principles in public or private life—and, if women were allowed to plead their feelings, as an excuse or palliation of infidelity, it was opening a floodgate for immorality. What virtuous woman thought of her feelings?—It was her duty to love and obey the man chosen by her parents and relations, who were qualified by their experience to judge better for her, than she could for herself. As to the charges brought against the husband, they were vague, supported by no witnesses, excepting that of imprisonment in a private mad-house. The proofs of an insanity in the family, might render that however a prudent measure; and indeed the conduct of the lady did not appear that of a person of sane mind. Still such a mode of proceeding could not be justified, and might perhaps entitle the lady [in another court] to a sentence of separation from bed and board,[4] during the joint lives of the parties; but he hoped that no Englishman would legalize adultery, by enabling the adulteress to enrich her seducer. Too many restrictions could not be thrown in the way of divorces, if we wished to maintain the sanctity of marriage; and, though they might bear a little hard on a few, very few individuals, it was evidently for the good of the whole."

CONCLUSION,
BY THE EDITOR

Very few hints exist respecting the plan of the remainder of the work. I find only two detached sentences, and some scattered heads for the continuation of the story. I transcribe the whole.

I

"Darnford's letters were affectionate; but circumstances occasioned delays, and the miscarriage of some letters rendered the reception of

[4]An ecclesiastical court could grant such a separation, which prohibited remarriage but provided alimony.

wished-for answers doubtful: his return was necessary to calm Maria's mind."

II

"As Darnford had informed her that his business was settled, his delaying to return seemed extraordinary; but love to excess, excludes fear or suspicion."

The scattered heads for the continuation of the story, are as follow.[1]

I

"Trial for adultery—Maria defends herself—A separation from bed and board is the consequence—Her fortune is thrown into chancery[1]—Darnford obtains a part of his property—Maria goes into the country."

II

"A prosecution for adultery commenced—Trial—Darnford sets out for France—Letters—Once more pregnant—He returns—Mysterious behaviour—Visit—Expectation—Discovery—Interview—Consequence."

III

"Sued by her husband—Damages awarded to him—Separation from bed and board—Darnford goes abroad—Maria into the country—Provides for her father—Is shunned—Returns to London—Expects to see her lover—The rack of expectation—Finds herself again with child—Delighted—A discovery—A visit—A miscarriage—Conclusion."

IV

"Divorced by her husband—Her lover unfaithful—Pregnancy—Miscarriage—Suicide."

---

[1]To understand these minutes, it is necessary the reader should consider each of them as setting out from the same point in the story, viz. the point to which it is brought down in the preceding chapter [WG].

[2]The Court of Chancery, established to provide rulings not available in the common-law courts, became increasingly bureaucratic, and litigation was notoriously drawn out and expensive. By the 1790s, most of its cases concerned inheritance and claims for damages.

[The following passage appears in some respects to deviate from the preceding hints. It is superscribed],

"THE END.

"She swallowed the laudanum[1]; her soul was calm—the tempest had subsided—and nothing remained but an eager longing to forget herself—to fly from the anguish she endured to escape from thought—from this hell of disappointment.

"Still her eyes closed not—one remembrance with frightful velocity followed another—All the incidents of her life were in arms, embodied to assail her, and prevent her sinking into the sleep of death.—Her murdered child again appeared to her, mourning for the babe of which she was the tomb.—'And could it have a nobler?—Surely it is better to die with me, than to enter on life without a mother's care!—I cannot live!—but could I have deserted my child the moment it was born?—thrown it on the troubled wave of life, without a hand to support it?'—She looked up: 'What have I not suffered!—may I find a father where I am going!'—Her head turned; a stupor ensued; a faintness—'Have a little patience,' said Maria, holding her swimming head (she thought of her mother), 'this cannot last long; and what is a little bodily pain to the pangs I have endured?'

"A new vision swam before her. Jemima seemed to enter—leading a little creature, that, with tottering footsteps, approached the bed. The voice of Jemima sounding as at a distance, called her—she tried to listen, to speak, to look!

"'Behold your child!' exclaimed Jemima. Maria started off the bed, and fainted.—Violent vomiting followed.

"When she was restored to life, Jemima addressed her with great solemnity: '—led me to suspect, that your husband and brother had deceived you, and secreted the child. I would not torment you with doubtful hopes, and I left you (at a fatal moment) to search for the child!—I snatched her from misery—and (now she is alive again) would you leave her alone in the world, to endure what I have endured?'

"Maria gazed wildly at her, her whole frame was convulsed with emotion; when the child, whom Jemima had been tutoring all the jour-

---

[1] A mixture of opium grains and alcohol, a popular painkiller for a range of ailments, and in overdose, fatal. MW's daughter Fanny probably committed suicide this way in 1814.

ney, uttered the word 'Mamma!' She caught her to her bosom, and burst into a passion of tears—then, resting the child gently on the bed, as if afraid of killing it,—she put her hand to her eyes, to conceal as it were the agonizing struggle of her soul. She remained silent for five minutes, crossing her arms over her bosom, and reclining her head,—then exclaimed: 'The conflict is over!—I will live for my child!'"

A few readers perhaps, in looking over these hints, will wonder how it could have been practicable, without tediousness, or remitting in any degree the interest of the story, to have filled, from these slight sketches, a number of pages, more considerable than those which have been already presented. But, in reality, these hints, simple as they are, are pregnant with passion and distress. It is the refuge of barren authors, only, to crowd their fictions with so great a number of events, as to suffer no one of them to sink into the reader's mind. It is the province of true genius to develop events, to discover their capabilities, to ascertain the different passions and sentiments with which they are fraught, and to diversify them with incidents, that give reality to the picture, and take a hold upon the mind of a reader of taste, from which they can never be loosened. It was particularly the design of the author, in the present instance, to make her story subordinate to a great moral purpose, that "of exhibiting the misery and oppression, peculiar to women, that arise out of the partial laws and customs of society.—This view restrained her fancy."[2] It was necessary for her, to place in a striking point of view, evils that are too frequently overlooked, and to drag into light those details of oppression, of which the grosser and more insensible part of mankind make little account.

[2]See author's preface [WG].

CONTEXTS

The Rights of Women

The Condition of Women

British Committee to Investigate Madhouses (1763)

Answering complaints about the conditions of private madhouses, a committee was appointed on January 27, 1763, to investigate the matter. They delivered their findings to the House of Commons on February 22, 1763. That same day, an order was given to print the findings of the report.

from *A Report from the Committee appointed to Enquire into the State of the Private Madhouses in this Kingdom* (1763)

The Committee appointed to enquire into the State of the Private Madhouses in this Kingdom, and report the same, with their Opinion thereupon, to the House,[1] have resolved upon the following Report:

The Committee being sensible how much a Subject of this Nature is liable to frequent Digression and Irregularity in the Examination of Witnesses, and thinking to keep the Enquiry as much as possible from running unnecessarily into the Stories and Transactions of private Life, they resolved, very early in their Proceedings, to confine themselves to the two Points, which seemed, in their Judgment, to be referred to them by the House: And they now beg Leave to be permitted to follow the same Method in their Report, which they strictly observed in their Examination.

[1]House of Commons.

These two Points were:

1st, The Manner of admitting Persons into Houses now kept for the Reception of Lunatics; and,

2dly, The Treatment of them, during their Confinement.

The first Person, who appeared before your Committee, was Mrs. Hester Williams, complaining of her having been carried, by Stratagem, to a House kept for the Reception of Lunatics, and of the severe Treatment she received during her Confinement; but your Committee having no reason to conclude, either from her own State of her Case, or from the Witnesses, which she brought in support of it, or from other Persons attending to prove her actual Insanity at the Time of her being carried to the Madhouse, that her Case has been such as to be itself any conclusive Proof of Abuse in the Method of Admission to these Houses, or to be a sufficient Ground for the Interposition of the Legislature, they presume to pass cursorily over a Complaint, in itself very general, affecting the Characters of Persons of fair Character in private Life, and materially contradicted in the Facts and Allegations of it, by many Witnesses of Weight and Authority.

The next Complaint, who appeared before your Committee, was Mrs. Hawley, whose Representation of her Case to the Committee, was as follows: That, being, on the 5th of September 1762, invited, in an affectionate Letter, by her Mother and Husband, to go upon a Party of Pleasure to Turnham Green, she was, by them carried to a Madhouse at Chelsea, kept by Turlington.

That, upon her being carried into the House, she knelt down, and exhorted the Keeper to let her go, who refused her, upon the Authority of her Mother directing him to keep her confined. She alleged, that she was shut up Night and Day, in a Chamber locked and baricadoed; refused the Use of Pen and Paper, no Notice permitted to be carried to any Relation or Friend, and treated with Severity; and she added, that, during the whole Time, she was never visited by her Mother, nor ever desired to take any Medicines whatever—that she continued under Confinement in the said House till the 4th of October, when she was, in Pursuance of a Writ of Habeas Corpus[2] granted by Lord Mansfield, carried before his Lordship, who discharged her.

---

[2]Latin for "you have the body." A writ of habeas corpus is a judicial mandate ordering that an inmate be brought to court for the purpose of ascertaining whether or not the individual is imprisoned lawfully and whether or not a release from custody is permissible.

In Support of this Representation, Mrs. Hawley called Mr. La Fortune, who declared, that he had known Mrs. Hawley for above two Years past: That, on the 5th of September, the Day of her Confinement, she had dined at his House, and that she then told him, she had received an affectionate Letter from her Mother, desiring her to go with her, upon a Party, to Turnham Green; that he advised her not to trust too much to sudden Changes of Temper, and to be upon her Guard: That, upon his starting this Objection, she desired him, in case she was absent more than two Days, to enquire after her; and that, upon enquiring for her, and being told she was gone to Sion; and, upon going to Sion, without finding her there, he suspected she was put into a Madhouse; upon which he applied to Lord Mansfield for a Habeas Corpus, who refused the Writ, upon the Suggestion that he was not a Relation, but, at the same Time, ordered Doctor Riddle, a Surgeon in Marlborough Street, to visit Mrs. Hawley.

To pursue the Thread of this Evidence, Mr. Riddle was called before your Committee, who said, that upon being ordered to go to Turlington's Madhouse, at Chelsea, and visit Mrs. Hawley, he was refused Admittance, and assured that no such Person was there.

That, during the Dispute, Mrs. Hawley coming to the Window, he saw her, and spoke to her; and that, on his Return to Lord Mansfield, he informed his Lordship of what had happened, and declared, he believed Mrs. Hawley to be in her Senses.

Mrs. Hawley having been asked, Whether she knew of any other Persons in the same Circumstances with herself, confined in the same House? and she naming Mrs. Smith, the Committee thought it necessary to order her to attend.

Mrs. Smith informed your committee, that she had been carried to Turlington's Madhouse by her Husband, who left her there with an Assurance that he would return very soon.

That Mr. King, the Keeper of the House, told her, that her Husband had taken this Lodging for that Night, that her Husband told her, in a Letter which she received the next Day, that he was glad that he had left her in so pleasant a Situation; to which she returned no Answer.

That she was told, from Time to Time, she must make herself easy; that she should have been happy to have put an End to her Confinement; and that it was now two Years since she had been carried to this House.

She added, that, during her Confinement, she had been attended by no Physician, or Apothecary whatever.

The next Person, who attended the Committee, was Mrs. Durant, who complained that, about eight Years ago, she was carried to Miles's Madhouse, at Hoxton, and that, during her Confinement there, she was ordered no Medicines, nor attended by any body.

That she was refused all Opportunity of sending to her Friends, during the three Weeks of her Confinement; and that she was released by her Mother, attended by Mr. Lediard, a Justice of the Peace, upon whose Arrival, as Mrs. Durant alleges, her Chains were privately knocked off.

Mrs. Gold, the Mother of Mrs. Durant, informed the Committee, that, upon receiving an anonymous Letter, giving her an Account that her Daughter went away about three Weeks before with her Husband, and had not since been heard of, she applied to her Son-in-law, insisting of knowing from him where her Daughter was.

That, upon his Refusal to give her any satisfactory Account of his Wife, she applied to Mr. Lediard, a Justice of the Peace, who drew from Mr. Durant a Confession, that his Wife was gone to Miles's Madhouse at Hoxton.

That, upon the Mother and the Justice going to Miles's, they were refused the Sight of Mrs. Durant, upon the Pretence that Mr. Miles was not at home, until, upon Mr. Lediard being understood by the Person of the House to be a Magistrate, they were admitted. Mrs. Durant was then brought into the Parlour, where Mrs. Miles confessed to Mr. Lediard, that she did not think her mad, and that, on the contrary, she was confined there only by her Husband's Order.

Mr. Morrison, attending, at the Desire of Mrs. Durant, to prove that she was not Insane at the Time of her being forced into Confinement, he declared, that he was at Mrs. Gold's, the Mother of Mrs. Durant, when the anonymous Letter came, informing her of her Daughter's Confinement.

That he had seen Mrs. Durant frequently near the Time of her being carried into Confinement, and never had the least Doubt of her being in her Senses, that he was present when Mrs. Gold received the anonymous Letter, and advised her to look after her Daughter; that he was also present the next Day, when the Conversation passed between Mrs. Gold, Mr. Lediard, and Mr. Durant, in which Mr. Durant acknowledged his Wife was in a Madhouse, and that being present also when Mr. Lediard and Mrs. Gold returned from the Madhouse, he then saw Mrs. Durant, who had no Marks whatever of any Degree of Insanity, and that Mr. Durant, the Husband, and his Wife, did then and there make up all Disagreements at his Interposition.

It having appeared to the Committee, in the Course of the several Complaints, and the consequential Examinations, that the extraordinary Imprisonments, upon the Imputation of Lunacy, have happened in the Houses kept by Turlington and Miles, your Committee thought they should ill discharge their Duty, or answer the Expectations of the House, if they did not summon Mr. Turlington himself, whom they thought, both the Objects of the Enquiry, and the common Principles of Justice, required should be ordered to attend.

Mr. Turlington informed the Committee, that he kept a House at Chelsea for the Reception of Lunatics, but added, that he usually leaves the Management of the House, and the Admission of Patients, to Mr. King, his Agent.

Upon being asked, What Instructions he gave to Mr. King in respect to the Admission of Persons? he avowed, that the Rule was general to admit all Persons, who were brought: and that, in the Administration of the House, he received a Report of the Persons admitted, from Time to Time, but left the Business in general to Mr. King.

He added, that though the House is intended for the Reception of Lunatics, other Persons are admitted as Lodgers.

That no Physicians attend the House; that no Register of the Persons is kept; that he considered Mrs. Smith, mentioned in a former Part of this Report, merely as a Boarder; and that he took her into Confinement merely at the Desire of her Husband, who alleged, that the Neighbours were afraid she would set the House on Fire; that he received six Guineas a Quarter[3] for her Maintenance; and that it was not in her Power to go out of the House if she would. He acknowledged, that he remembered Mrs. Hawley, whom he said he believed to have been a Lunatic, and that she was released by a Habeas Corpus, directed to Mr. King: he denied, in general, the Severities charged upon the House by other Witnesses, and expressly asserted, that Chains were never used.

[3]Compare this amount to Jemima's wages in ch. V of *Wrongs of Woman.*

Mr. Turlington having, in Defence of the Proceedings of his House, referred himself to Mr. King as the Person intrusted and employed by him, the Committee thought it necessary to summon him.

Mr. King said, he had been in the Wool Trade; but, for six Years past, he had been employed by Mr. Turlington to keep his Madhouse.

That he had received no written Directions from Mr. Turlington; that he found several Patients in the House on his being employed, and all Lunatics; that, since his being employed, he had admitted several for Drunkenness and for other Reasons of the same Sort, alledged by their Friends or Relations bringing them, which he had always thought a sufficient Authority.

As the Treatment of the Persons confined, he said that they had the Liberty of walking in the Garden, and passing from one Room to another; and as to their Diet and Apartments, he said it was according to the Allowance they paid, which was from sixty to twenty Pounds a Year.

He admitted, that he knew Mrs. Hawley; that she was confined at the Representation of a Woman, who called herself her Mother; and that the Reason alledged by her, for the Confinement of her Daughter, was Drunkenness. He said, he did not remember that she was refused Pen, Ink, and Paper; but, at the same Time acknowledged it was the established Order of the House, that no Letters should be sent, by any of the Persons confined, to their Friends or Relations.

Being asked, Upon what Authority he admitted People charged only with Drunkenness into a House of Confinement kept for the Reception of Lunatics?

He answered, Upon the Authority of the Persons who brought them; and he frankly confessed, that, out of the whole Number of Persons whom he had confined, he had never admitted one as a Lunatic during the six Years he had been intrusted with the Superintendency of the House.

Upon being then asked, If he ever refused any Persons who were brought upon any Pretence whatsoever provided they could pay for their Board?

He answered, No.

To close this Evidence, and bring it to a clear and final Issue, Mr. King was asked this general Question, Whether if two Strangers should come to his House, one calling herself the Mother of the other, and charging her Daughter with Drunkenness, he would confine the

Daughter upon this Representation of the Woman calling herself the Mother, though she was a Stranger to him, and the Daughter herself was apparently sober at that Time.

He said, He certainly should.

Your Committee being desirous of obtaining every Degree of Assistance and Information which might enable them more perfectly to obey the Orders of the House; they desired the Attendance of Doctor Battie and Doctor Monro[e], two very eminent Physicians distinguished by their Knowledge and their Practice in Cases of Lunacy.

Doctor Battie gave it as his Opinion to your Committee, that the Private Madhouses require some better Regulations; that he hath long been of this Opinion; that the Admission of Persons brought as Lunatics is too loose and too much at large, depending upon Persons not competent Judges; and that frequent Visitation is necessary for the Inspection of the Lodging, Diet, Cleanliness, and Treatment.

Being asked, If he ever had met Persons of sane Mind in Confinement for Lunacy?

He said, it frequently happened. He related the Case of a Woman perfectly in her Senses brought as a Lunatic by her Husband to a House under the Doctor's Direction, whose Husband, upon Dr. Battie insisting he should take home his Wife, and expressing his Surprize at his Conduct, justified himself by frankly saying, He understood the House to be a Sort of Bridewell, or Place of Correction. . . .

Dr. Monroe informed your Committee, that he does not doubt but several Persons have been improperly confined upon the Pretence of Lunacy, and he cited two particular Instances happening in two different Madhouses.

He gave it as his Opinion, that the Method and Grounds of admitting Patients for Lunacy is too loose and too much at large.

That in the Case of Mrs. Durant mentioned in this Report, Miles the Keeper of the Madhouse at Hoxton confessed to the Doctor that he had been imposed upon, and Dr. Monroe said, that, in his Opinion, the present State of the Private Madhouses required Regulation, with Respect to the Persons permitted to keep such Houses, the Admission of Patients, and the Visitation.

Your Committee are sensible, that in their Enquiry they confined themselves to a few Cases and to a few Houses; but to obviate any conclusion from thence, that Cases existing are rare; and the Abuse, the Misconduct only of particular Persons; They beg Leave to assure the House, that a Variety of other Instances arising in other Houses offered themselves for Examination; and that Turlington's House was in no Degree a selected Case, but taken up by the Committee in the Course of the Enquiry, and merely as it presented itself upon the Report of the Witnesses: Your Committee restraining themselves out of a Regard to the Peace and Satisfaction of private Families, from the Examination of more Cases than they judged to be necessary and sufficient to establish the Reality of the two great Abuses complained of in the present State of Private Madhouses, the Force of the Evidence and the Testimony of the Witnesses being, at the same Time so amply confirmed and materially strengthened by the Confessions of Persons keeping Private Madhouses, and by the Authority, Opinions, and Experience of Dr. Battie and Dr. Monroe.

Whereupon your Committee came to the following Resolution: Resolved,

That it is the Opinion of this Committee, that the present State of the Private Madhouses in this Kingdom requires the Interposition of the Legislature. . . .

William Murray, Lord Mansfield (1705–1793)

On May 14, 1772, William Murray, Lord Mansfield, presiding on the King's Bench, ruled in the case of James Somerset, a black slave who had been brought to England, versus his master, Mr. Stewart of Virginia, that slavery was not lawful in England. Lord Mansfield maintained that England was "a soil whose air is deemed too pure for slaves to breathe in." Somerset thereby gained his freedom, making England a mecca for slaves in the British West Indies. Significantly, in that case, Mr. Dunning, the lawyer defending Stewart, argued that slavery, like marriage, was a "municipal" rather than a "natural" relationship, and thus constructed by legal custom, similar to feudal villeinage, rather than subject to "natural" law. The implied parallel between wives and slaves—and Lord Mansfield's refusal to rule against the "municipal" servitude of wives—did not escape the attention of the women writers of the period.

from *The Mansfield Judgment* (1772)[1]

On return to an habeas corpus, requiring Captain Knowles to shew cause for the seizure and detainure of the complainant Somerset, a negro—the case appeared to be this—

That the negro had been a slave to Mr. Stewart, in Virginia, had been purchased from the African coast, in the course of the slave trade, as tolerated in the plantations; that he had been brought to England by his master, who intending his return, by force sent him on board of Captain Knowles's vessel, lying in the river; and was there, by the order of his master, in the custody of Captain Knowles, detained against his consent; until returned in obedience to the writ. . . .

Mr. Hargrave [arguing on behalf of Somerset].—The importance of the question will I hope justify to your Lordships the solicitude with which I rise to defend it; and however unequal I feel myself, will command attention. . . . I shall endeavour to state the grounds from which Mr. Stewart's supposed right arises; and then offer, as appears to me, sufficient confutation to his claim over the negro, as property, after having him brought over to England. . . . The question on that is not whether slavery is lawful in the colonies (where a concurrence of unhappy circumstances has caused it to be established as necessary) but whether in England? Not whether it ever has existed in England; but whether it be not now abolished? Various definitions have been given of slavery; one of the most considerable is the following: a service for life, for bare necessaries. Harsh and terrible to human nature as even such a condition is, slavery is very insufficiently defined by these circumstances—it includes not the power of the master over the slave's person, property, and limbs, life only excepted; it includes not the right over all acquirements of the slave's labour; nor includes the alienation of the unhappy object from his original master, to whatever absolute lord, interest, caprice or malice, may chuse to transfer him; it includes not the descendible property from father to son, and in like manner continually of the slave and all his descendants. Let us reflect on the consequences of servitude in a light still more important. The corruption of manners in the master, from the entire subjection of the slaves he possesses to his sole will; from whence spring forth luxury,

[1]The English Reports 98 (King's Bench Division 27), Easter Term, 12 Geo. 3, 1772, K.B.: SOMERSET against STEWART, May 14, 1772.

pride, cruelty, with the infinite enormities appertaining to their train; the danger to the master, from the revenge of his much injured and unredressed dependant; debasement of the mind of the slave, for want of means and motives of improvement; and peril to the constitution under which the slave cannot but suffer, and which he will naturally endeavour to subvert, as the only means of retrieving comfort and security to himself.—The humanity of modern times has much mitigated this extreme rigour of slavery; shall an attempt to introduce perpetual servitude here to this island hope for countenance? Will not all the other mischiefs of mere utter servitude revive, if once the idea of absolute property, under the immediate sanction of the laws of this country extend itself to those who have been brought over to a soil whose air is deemed too pure for slaves to breathe in it; but the laws, the genius and spirit of the constitution, forbid the approach of slavery, will not suffer its existence here. . . .

Mr. Alleyne [arguing on behalf of Somerset].— . . . But slavery is not a natural, 'tis a municipal relation; an institution therefore confined to certain places, and necessarily dropt by passage into a country where such municipal regulations do not exist.

Mr. Dunning [arguing on behalf of Stewart].— . . . Freedom has been asserted as a natural right, and therefore unalienable and unrestrainable; there is perhaps no branch of this right, but in some places at all times, and in all places at different times, has been restrained: nor could society otherwise be conceived to exist. For the great benefit of the public and individuals, natural liberty, which consists in doing what one likes, is altered to the doing what one ought. . . . A distinction was endeavoured to be established between natural and municipal relations; but the natural relations are not those only which attend the person of the man, political do so too; with which the municipal are most closely connected: municipal laws, strictly, are those confined to a particular place; political, are those in which the municipal laws of many States may and do concur. The relation of husband and wife, I think myself warranted in questions, as a natural relation: does it subsist for life; or to answer the natural purposes which may reasonably be supposed often to terminate sooner? Yet this is one of these relations which follow a man every where. If only natural relations had that property, the effect would be very limited indeed. In fact the municipal laws are principally employed in determining the manner by which relations are created; and which manner varies in various countries, and in the same country at different periods; the political relation itself continuing usually unchanged by the change of place. There is but one form at present with us, by which the relation of husband and wife can be constituted; there was a time when otherwise. . . . Let me take notice, neither the air of England is too pure for a slave to breathe in, nor the laws of England have rejected servitude. Villenage in this country is said to be worn out; the propriety of the expression strikes me a little. Are the laws not existing by which it was created? . . .

Sergeant Davy [on behalf of Somerset].— . . . Mr. Dunning availed himself of a wrong interpretation of the word natural; 'twas used as moral, which no laws can supercede. All contracts, I do not venture to assert are of a moral nature; but I know not any law to confirm an immoral contract, and execute it. The contract of marriage is a moral contract, established for moral purposes, enforcing moral obligations; the right of taking property by descent, the legitimacy of children; . . . these, and many other consequences, flow from the marriage properly solemnised; are governed by the municipal laws of that particular State, under whose institutions the contracting and disposing parties live as subjects . . . it has been asserted, and is now repeated by me, this air is too pure for a slave to breathe in; I trust I shall not quit this Court without certain conviction of the truth of that assertion.

Lord Mansfield [presiding judge].— . . . The new question is, whether any dominion, authority or coercion can be exercised in this country, on a slave according to the American laws? . . .

Trinity Term, June 22, 1772

Lord Mansfield.—On the part of Somerset, the case which we gave notice should be decided this day, the Court now proceeds to give its opinion. . . . . The state of slavery is of such a nature, that it is incapable of being introduced on any reasons, moral or political; but only positive law, which preserves its force long after the reasons, occasion, and time itself from whence it was created, is erased from memory: it is so odious, that nothing can be suffered to support it, but positive law. Whatever inconveniences, therefore, may follow from a decision, I cannot say this case is allowed or approved by the law of England; and therefore the black must be discharged.

Johann Wilhelm von Archenholz (1743–1812)

Born in a suburb of Danzig, Germany, on September 3, 1743, Johann Wilhelm von Archenholz served in the military and traveled extensively throughout Europe. Erudite, tasteful, and stylish, he was an active member of the most fashionable social circles and worked for several well-respected journals. His literary reputation was established by England and Italy *(1785), which went through multiple editions and was translated several times. This success was followed by* Annals of England *(Germany, 1788), a collection of anecdotes on law, custom, and society. Translated the following year from French into English, it was published as* A Picture of England. *The following excerpt offers a detailed male perspective on the condition of English prostitutes, an interesting counterpoint to Wollstonecraft's.*

from *A Picture of England* (1789)

from "Women of the Town"[1]

I am now arrived at a subject unfortunately inexhaustible, I mean the *women of the town*.[2] It is well known how handsome the English ladies are, and I am sorry to add, that the greatest part of this class of women abuse, in the most shameful manner, the charms with which nature has so prodigally endowed them. London is said to contain fifty thousand prostitutes, without reckoning kept mistresses. The most wretched of these live with *matrons*, who lodge, board, and clothe them. The dress worn by the very lowest of them is silk, according to the custom which luxury has generally introduced into England. Sometimes they escape from their prison, with their little wardrobes under their arms, and trade on their *own bottoms*, when, if they are unfortunate, or happen not to be economical, they are soon dragged to gaol by their creditors.

---

[1] "Women of the Town," 2.3.89–96.

[2] As Tony Henderson has argued, the term suggests that "prostitution was understood as an essentially urban phenomenon" (*Disorderly Women in Eighteenth-Century London* [London: Longman, 1999, 175]). Henderson notes that "'Women of the Town' was not the most pejorative title attached to prostitutes, although it moved one writer in 1799 to lament that 'the very title seems to level them with the pavement on which they wander—they are a property equally regarded as common, equally base, equally to be trampled on,'" citing *Thoughts on the Means of Alleviating the Miseries Attendant Upon Common Prostitution* (1799, 2).

The uncertainty of receiving payment makes the house-keepers charge them double the common price for lodgings. They hire by the week a first floor, and pay for it more than the owner gives for the whole premises, taxes included. Without these, thousands of houses would be empty, in the western parts of the town. In the parish of Mary-le-bone only, which is the largest and best peopled in the capital, thirty thousand ladies of pleasure reside, of whom seventeen hundred are reckoned to be house-keepers. These live very well, and without ever being disturbed by the magistrates. They are indeed so much their own mistresses, that if a justice of the peace attempted to trouble them in their apartments, they might turn him out of doors; for as they pay the same taxes as the other parishioners, they are consequently entitled to the same privileges.

Their apartments are elegantly, and sometimes magnificently furnished; they keep several servants, and some have their own carriages. Many of them have annuities paid them by their seducers, and others settlements into which they have surprised their lovers in the moment of intoxication. The testimony of these women, even of the lowest of them, is always received as evidence in the courts of justice. All this generally gives them a certain dignity of conduct, which can scarcely be reconciled with their profession.

The higher classes of these females are uncommonly honest; you may entrust them with a purse crammed with gold, without running any risk whatever. They can never be prevailed upon to grant favours to the lover of one of their companions, even if they are sure that the circumstance will be kept a profound secret. One of my friends made a proposal of this kind, and was refused; he redoubled his presents and his caresses, but in vain: "I am, sir" says she, "an unhappy female, obliged to live by this dishonourable profession; and Heaven is my witness, that I am in want of money; but I will never consent to have any connection with the acquaintance of my friend. If you were an Englishman, I might not be so difficult; but as you are a foreigner, I cannot. What opinion would you have of us, if I were to gratify your wishes?" Not satisfied with her excuse, he ridiculed her delicacy, and tempted her with more money; but, notwithstanding her poverty, she persisted in her refusal, and all this from national pride.

During the elections for members of parliament, it is not unusual to see these ladies refuse to barter their favours for large sums of money, and reserve their charms for the purchase of votes, in favour of certain patriots, whom they esteem. Such virtues greatly lessen the infamy of their profession. I have seen many people of rank walk with them in public, and allow them to take hold of their arms, in the most familiar manner. I have even beheld more than one minister plenipotentiary conversing publicly at Vauxhall, with females of this description. Although their rank requires a decorum, which would be unnecessary among the English nobility; yet these gentlemen easily accede to the customs of a country, when they are in favour of liberty.

One of these ladies, called Kitty Fisher, was very celebrated, about twenty-five years since, on account of the elegance and delicacy with which she sacrificed to Venus. She was indebted to nature for an uncommon portion of beauty, judgment, and wit, joined to a most agreeable and captivating vivacity. The union of so many perfections procured the esteem, and fascinated the desires of those who prefer Cyprian delights[3] to all the other pleasures of life. This lady knew her own merit; she demanded a hundred guineas a night, for the use of her charms, and she was never without votaries, to whom the offering did not seem too exorbitant. Among these was the late Duke of York, brother to the king; who one morning left fifty pounds on her toilet.[4] This present so much offended Miss Fisher, that she declared that her doors should ever be shut against him in future; and to shew, by the most convincing proofs, how much she despised his present, she clapt the bank-note between two slices of bread and butter, and ate it for her breakfast.

The idea of the pleasures to be enjoyed in the capital inspires the girls in the country with the most longing desire to participate in them. Imagination inflames their little heads, and presents every object under an exaggerated appearance. The young people of both sexes, who have been educated at a distance from town, imagine the metropolis to resemble that paradise promised to the Mahometans, by their great prophet. Is it to be then wondered at, that they form so many little projects to abandon their homes, and reside in the center of pleasure? Or that a maiden, without experience, should be easily deceived, when the proposition comes from a lover?

When an amorous couple have no hopes of getting their parents' consent to their union, they foolishly think that they are obliged to run away, and they accordingly make for London. This fatal elope-

---

[3]Licentious, lewd; from the reputation of the cult of Venus, goddess of love, on the eastern Mediterranean isle of Cyprus.

[4]Dresser.

ment raises the indignation of the young woman's relations, who are deaf to her prayers, and the young man becoming more pressing every day, she yields to his desires, in the hope of being more happy. The ungrateful lover, after being satiated with her charms, abandons her: thus left without any help, alone, unknown, she remains in the midst of an immense city, where trick and intrigue every day produce the most atrocious and singular scenes.

Some severe censor may here say, that in this deplorable situation she might take the high road, and beg her way to her father's house, or, having received some education, she might get into service. These two resources are impossible in England. The amiable professor Moritz[5] has already proved, by his own example, that journies on foot are entirely impracticable in that island. But if they were, could a young and beautiful creature venture to travel by herself? In the second place, who would employ a person, whose character could not be ascertained, and who has no one to speak in her behalf? And if she were willing, and fortunate enough to overcome so many disadvantages, would she be permitted? Her hostess, her creditors, the true or sham officers of justice; the most infernal schemes, and most scandalous practices, are employed against the poor wretch, till, yielding to necessity, she is constrained to consent to whatever is required of her.

One need not be astonished, after this, to hear that there are so many unfortunate women, who often possess all the virtues, and all the good qualities, which we admire and cherish in their sex; youth, beauty, mildness, education, principle; and even that delicate coyness, which is the most powerful attraction to love. The ladies of pleasure in London actually give us an idea of the celebrated Grecian courtesans, who charmed the heroes of Athens, and whom the sage Socrates himself often honoured with his visits.

Let it be recollected, however, that I now speak only of a few, for it is very uncommon, not to say impossible, to find such precious qualities, among those vile prostitutes, whose kind of life stifles in their breasts every seed of virtue, if any indeed ever existed therein. At all seasons of the year, they sally out towards the dusk, arrayed in the most gaudy colours, and fill the principal streets. They accost the passengers, and offer to accompany them: they even surround them in crowds, stop and overwhelm them with caresses and entreaties. The

[5]Karl Philipp Moritz (1757–93), professor of aesthetics and archeology at the Berlin Academy of Arts.

better kind, however, content themselves with walking about, till they themselves are addressed. Many married women, who live in the distant parts of the town, prostitute themselves in Westminster, where they are unknown. I have beheld with a surprise, mingled with terror, girls from eight to nine years old make a proffer of their charms; and such is the corruption of the human heart, that even they have their lovers. Towards midnight, when the young women have disappeared, and the streets become deserted, then the old wretches, of fifty or sixty years of age, descend from their garrets, and attack the intoxicated passengers, who are often prevailed upon to satisfy their passions in the open street, with these female monsters.

Catharine Sawbridge Macaulay (1731–1791)

Daughter of a wealthy landowner in Kent and an heiress of a London banker, Catharine Sawbridge grew up in comfort and was left well off at the death of her husband, an eminent London obstetrician, in 1776. Her major work is the controversial eight-volume History of England from the Accession of James I to that of the Brunswick Line *(the current monarchy), published over twenty years (1763–83). Its defense of Oliver Cromwell's regicidal government and its generally antimonarchal perspective endeared Macaulay to Wollstonecraft and earned Edmund Burke's contempt of her as a "republican Virago." Not surprisingly, her political writings were more popular in France and America than in England. As with Wollstonecraft, her politics produced enemies and vicious misogynist attacks on her private life, attacks gleefully sharpened by her marriage in 1778 to the twenty-one-year-old surgeon's mate William Graham.* Letters on Education *deeply influenced Wollstonecraft, who regarded Macaulay as "the woman of the greatest abilities, undoubtedly, that this country has ever produced."*

from *Letters on Education* (1790)

"Letter 22: No Characteristic Difference in Sex"

The great difference that is observable in the characters of the sexes, Hortensia,[1] as they display themselves in the scenes of social life, has given rise to much false speculation on the natural qualities of the

[1]The fictitious recipient of the letter.

female mind.—For though the doctrine of innate ideas, and innate affections, are in a great measure exploded by the learned, yet few persons reason so closely and so accurately on abstract subjects as, through a long chain of deductions, to bring forth a conclusion which in no respect militates with their premises.

It is a long time before the crowd give up opinions they have been taught to look upon with respect. . . . It is from such causes that the notion of a sexual difference in the human character has, with very few exceptions, universally prevailed from the earliest times, and the pride of one sex, and the ignorance and vanity of the other, have helped to support an opinion which a close observation of Nature, and a more accurate way of reasoning, would disprove.

It must be confessed, that the virtues of the males among the human species, though mixed and blended with a variety of vices and errors, have displayed a bolder and a more consistent picture of excellence than female nature has hitherto done. It is on these reasons that, when we compliment the appearance of a more than ordinary energy in the female mind, we call it masculine; and hence it is, that Pope has elegantly said *a perfect woman's but a softer man.*[2] And if we take in the consideration, that there can be but one rule of moral excellence for beings made of the same materials, organized after the same manner, and subjected to similar laws of Nature, we must either agree with Mr. Pope, or we must reverse the proposition, and say, that *a perfect man is a woman formed after a coarser mold.* The difference that actually does subsist between the sexes, is too flattering for men to be willingly imputed to accident; for what accident occasions, wisdom might correct; and it is better, says Pride, to give up the advantages we might derive from the perfection of our fellow associates, than to own that Nature has been just in the equal distribution of her favours. These are the sentiments of the men: but mark how readily they are yielded to by the women; not from humility I assure you, but merely to preserve with character those fond vanities on which they set their hearts. No; suffer them to idolize their persons, to throw away their life in the pursuit of trifles, and to indulge in the gratification of the meaner passions, and they will heartily join in the sentence of their degradation.

---

[2]A slight misquotation of *Epistle II*, "Of the Characters of Women": "Heaven, when it strives to polish all it can / Its last best work, but forms a softer man" (271–72).

Among the most strenuous asserters of a sexual difference in character, Rousseau is the most conspicuous, both on account of that warmth of sentiment which distinguishes all his writings, and the eloquence of his compositions: but never did enthusiasm and the love of paradox, those enemies to philosophical disquisition, appear in more strong opposition to plain sense than in Rousseau's definition of this difference.[3] He sets out with a supposition, that Nature intended the subjection of the one sex to the other; that consequently there must be an inferiority of intellect in the subjected party; but as man is a very imperfect being, and apt to play the capricious tyrant, Nature, to bring things nearer to an equality, bestowed on the woman such attractive graces, and such an insinuating address, as to turn the balance on the other scale. Thus Nature, in a giddy mood, recedes from her purposes, and subjects prerogative to an influence which must produce confusion and disorder in the system of human affairs. Rousseau saw this objection; and in order to obviate it, he has made up a moral person of the union of the two sexes, which, for contradiction and absurdity, outdoes every metaphysical riddle that was ever formed in the schools. In short, it is not reason, it is not wit; it is pride and sensuality that speak in Rousseau, and, in this instance, has lowered the man of genius to the licentious pedant. . . . for so little did a wise and just Providence intend to make the condition of slavery an unalterable law of female nature, that in the same proportion as the male sex have consulted the interest of their own happiness, they have relaxed in their tyranny over women; and such is their use in the system of mundane creation, and such their natural influence over the male mind, that were these advantages properly exerted, they might carry every point of any importance to their honour and happiness. However, till that period arrives in which women will act wisely, we will amuse ourselves in talking of their follies.

The situation and education of women, Hortensia, is precisely that which must necessarily tend to corrupt and debilitate both the powers of mind and body. From a false notion of beauty and delicacy, their system of nerves is depraved before they come out of their nursery; and this kind of depravity has more influence over the mind, and consequently over morals, than is commonly appre-

---

[3]Rousseau's arguments throughout *Émile,* especially Book 5 on the character of Sophia.

hended. But it would be well if such causes only acted towards the debasement of the sex; their moral education is, if possible, more absurd than their physical. The principles and nature of virtue, which is never properly explained to boys, is kept quite a mystery to girls. They are told indeed, that they must abstain from those vices which are contrary to their personal happiness, or they will be regarded as criminals, both by God and man; but all the higher parts of rectitude, every thing that ennobles our being, and that renders us both innoxious and useful, is either not taught, or is taught in such a manner as to leave no proper impression on the mind. This is so obvious a truth, that the defects of female education have ever been a fruitful topic of declamation for the moralist; but not one of this class of writers have laid down any judicious rules for amendment. Whilst we still retain the absurd notion of a sexual excellence, it will mitigate against the perfecting a plan of education for either sex. The judicious Addison animadverts on the absurdity of bringing a young lady up with no higher idea of the end of education than to make her agreeable to a husband, and confining the necessary excellence for this happy acquisition to the mere graces of person.[4]

Every parent and tutor may not express himself in the same manner as is marked out by Addison; yet certain it is, that the admiration of the other sex is held out to women as the highest honour they can attain; and whilst this is considered as their *summum bonum* [highest good] and the beauty of their persons the chief *desideratum* [thing wanted] of men, Vanity, and its companion Envy, must taint, in their characters, every native and every acquired excellence. Nor can you, Hortensia, deny, that these qualities, when united to ignorance, are fully equal to the engendering and rivetting all those vices and foibles which are peculiar to the female sex; vices and foibles which have caused them to be considered, in ancient times, as beneath cultivation, and in modern days have subjected them to the censure and ridicule of writers of all descriptions, from the deep thinking philosopher to the man of ton[5] and gallantry, who, by the bye, sometimes distinguishes himself by qualities which are not greatly superior to

---

[4]Joseph Addison (1672–1719), essayist and poet. Macaulay wrongly attributes to Addison an unsigned essay on this subject in *The Spectator* by his collaborator, Richard Steele. Animadverts: criticizes.

[5]Fashion.

those he despises in women. Nor can I better illustrate the truth of this observation than by the following picture, to be found in the polite and gallant Chesterfield. "Women," says his Lordship, "are only children of a larger growth. They have an entertaining tattle, sometimes wit; but for solid reasoning, and good sense, I never in my life knew one that had it, or who acted or reasoned in consequence of it for four and twenty hours together. A man of sense only trifles with them, plays with them, humours and flatters them, as he does an engaging child; but he neither consults them, nor trusts them in serious matters."[6]

Responses to Wollstonecraft

Anna Letitia Barbauld (1743–1825)

Anna Letitia Aikin was the eldest child of Dr. John Aikin, a theologian and tutor at Warrington Academy, a dissenting Presbyterian public school. She received a superior education, studying French, Italian, Latin, and Greek, science and mathematics, as well as the libertarian political principles of Britain's leading dissenters. She was urged into print by her brother John, publishing Miscellaneous Pieces in Prose *with him in 1773 and in that same year a first volume of poems. In 1774 she married the Rev. Rochemont Barbauld, the son of a French Presbyterian minister. Resisting suggestions that they open a finishing school for girls, the Barbaulds established their own dissenting academy in Palgrove, Suffolk, where Anna took charge of the education of the younger boys. Her* Hymns in Prose for Children *(1781), written for her students, immediately became enormously popular and was translated into several European languages. Although the school was extremely successful both financially and academically, the deterioration of Rochemont's mental health prevented the Barbaulds from continuing this enterprise. They moved to London, where Anna devoted herself to literary labors. She rapidly became the leading female literary and social critic of this period,*

---

[6]*Letters to His Son* no. 294 (November 16, 1752), also cited in *Vindication*, ch. IV. Philip Chesterfield (1694–1773), statesman, author, and wit, wrote letters of advice to his illegitimate son from age five until his own death; published in 1774, these became famous (or infamous) for their comments on sexual behavior and rituals.

publishing influential essays and poems. She played an important role in the public opposition to the slave trade, proclaiming her support of William Wilberforce, the leading parliamentary advocate for the abolition of the slave trade, in a poetic epistle in 1791. Her program for national reform based on the principles of individual and domestic morality, Sins of Government, Sins of the Nation, *appeared in 1793.*

Barbauld composed "The Rights of Woman" in 1793 in angry response to Wollstonecraft's contemptuous dismissal of her poem "To a Lady, with some painted Flowers" (pp. 74–75). The poem was not published until after Barbauld's death in 1825. In the fourth chapter of A Vindication of the Rights of Woman, *Wollstonecraft had cited Barbauld as an example of how a woman of "superior sense" can voice a sentiment that "robs the whole sex of its dignity" (p. 74). However, Barbauld's writings put forward many of the same values that Wollstonecraft herself championed, including a lament on novel-reading and an insistence that the best wives, mothers, and family managers are educated in "the general character of a rational being."*

The Rights of Woman (1825; comp. 1793)

Yes, injured Woman! rise, assert thy right!
Woman! too long degraded, scorned, opprest;
O born to rule in partial[1] Law's despite,
Resume thy native empire o'er the breast!

Go forth arrayed in panoply[2] divine;   5
That angel pureness which admits no stain;
Go, bid proud Man his boasted rule resign,
And kiss the golden sceptre of thy reign.

Go, gird thyself with grace; collect thy store
Of bright artillery glancing from afar;   10
Soft melting tones thy thundering cannon's roar,
Blushes and fears thy magazine[3] of war.

Thy rights are empire: urge no meaner[4] claim,—
Felt, not defined, and if debated, lost;

[1]One-sided.
[2]Armor.
[3]Storehouse.
[4]Lower.

Like sacred mysteries, which withheld from fame,   15
Shunning discussion, are revered the most.

Try all that wit and art suggest to bend
Of thy imperial foe the stubborn knee;
Make treacherous Man thy subject, not thy friend:
Thou mayst command, but never canst be free.   20

Awe the licentious, and restrain the rude;
Soften the sullen, clear the cloudy brow:
Be, more than princes' gifts, thy favours sued;—
She hazards all, who will the least allow.

But hope not, courted idol of mankind,   25
On this proud eminence secure to stay;
Subduing and subdued, thou soon shalt find
Thy coldness soften, and thy pride give way.

Then, then, abandon each ambitious thought,
Conquest or rule thy heart shall feebly move,   30
In Nature's school, by her soft maxims taught,
That separate rights are lost in mutual love.

Mary Hays (1760–1843)

*Self-educated daughter of middle-class Rational Dissenters, Mary Hays
was part of a radical circle that included George Dyer, Joseph Johnson,
Thomas Paine, Anna Barbauld, William Godwin, and Mary Wollstonecraft. She supported herself by her writing; besides producing
numerous religious tracts, pedagogical fiction for children, and political
journalism, she wrote several novels, including* Memoirs of Emma Courtney *(1796) and* The Victim of Prejudice *(1799). Her* Letters and Essays,
Moral, and Miscellaneous *eloquently defends Wollstonecraft's feminist
opinions, supports Jacobin notions of the rights of man, and upholds
Godwin's doctrines of necessity and perfectibility through the agency of
reason.* Appeal to the Men of Great Britain in Behalf of Women *was published anonymously in an increasingly conservative political climate.
Hays assumes the natural equality of the sexes and passionately chal-
lenges both scriptural authority and custom for their unjustified elevation
of the male sex.*

from *Letters and Essays, Moral, and Miscellaneous* (1793)

No. III

Of all bondage, mental bondage is surely the most fatal; the absurd despotism which has hitherto, with more than gothic barbarity, enslaved the female mind, the enervating and degrading system of manners by which the understandings of women have been chained down to frivolity and trifles, have increased the general tide of effeminacy and corruption. To conform to the perpetual fluctuation of fashion (and few have the courage to dare the "slow and moving finger of scorn,"[1] which is pointed at every external singularity) requires almost their whole time and attention, and leaves little leisure for intellectual improvement.

> Say dreamers of gay dreams!
> How will you weather an eternal night,
> Where such expedients fail?[2]

It has been alleged, that this constant variation of mode is serviceable to commerce, and promotes a brisk circulation of money; or with more propriety it might be said a quick succession of bankruptcies: but however this may be, it is I conceive making too expensive an offering at the golden shrine of Plutus[3] to sacrifice all the dignified and rational pursuits of life. A few distinguished individuals, feeling the powers of their own minds (for what can curb the celestial energy of genius?) are endeavouring to dispel the magical illusions of custom, and restore degraded woman to the glory of rationality, and to fitness for immortality. The rights of woman, and the name of Woollstonecraft [*sic*], will go down to posterity with reverence, when the pointless sarcasms of witlings are forgotten. I am aware that some men of real good sense and candor, have supposed that the idea of there being no sexual character, is carried in this most admirable

---

[1] Shakespeare, *Othello*, 4.2.55–56: Believing his wife an adulteress, Othello laments that he has been made "A fixed figure for the time of scorn / To point his slow unmoving finger at!" (printed as "His slow and moving finger" in the Knight and Staunton edition).

[2] Edward Young, "Night II" of *Night Thoughts* (1772), 253–55, satirically addressing all those male fops and "wit's oracles" who "deem / One moment unamused a misery / Not made for feeble man."

[3] Pluto, Greek god of the dead.

work a little too far. Let them reflect for a moment on the extremes which the opposite opinion has produced; and say from whence arises the most formidable danger? Is there any cause to apprehend that we may subject our feelings too much to the guidance of reason? Or that we shall conduct the business of our families with too much order and equity: to the wise and good only, I now appeal! would you not dare to give up any of the allurements of the mistress (if indeed any need be given up worth the preserving) to the refined pleasure of living with a rational and equal companion? In such an intercourse, when enlivened by love, if happiness resides on earth, surely it is to be found! where the advantages are reciprocal, for each reflects back with interest, the light they receive. Similarity of mind and principle is the only true basis of harmony. Great superiority of either side causes a narrow jealousy, or a painful constraint; there is nothing so irksome as to converse with people who cannot understand you.

Others (I mean the vulgar of every rank) terrified at the very idea of our feeling and asserting our rights to rationality, raise innumerable cavils and objections, all originating from the same source, a pertinacious and jealous adherence to a narrow and mistaken self-interest, and the petty word authority. It is this which makes the priest on certain occasions raise an alarm about the safety of the church, the sovereign with paternal solicitude endeavour to guard his people from light and knowledge, by royal proclamations and prohibitions, and the Ephesians to exclaim that their "craft" is "in danger."[4] Must I inform these profound politicians, that every infringement of right weakens duty, every stretch of prerogative gives a mortal wound to monarchy, and every weak fence of proscription prepares the way for their utter demolition, and for laying Hierarchy waste? The love of arbitrary power, with morbid influence, corrupts the human mind; and after the factitious strength of the delirium, exhausted by the unnatural exertion, sinks it into helpless effeminacy and cowardly despondence, the usurper must sooner or later be the victim of his usurpation. . . .

---

[4]The Biblical *Epistle to the Ephesians* (attributed to St. Paul) deals primarily with the moral duties of married persons, parents, and children and strongly urges its readers to submit to the church's authority.

from *Appeal to the Men of Great Britain in Behalf of Women* (1798)

What Men Would Have Women to Be

Of all the systems,—if indeed a bundle of contradictions and absurdities may be called a system,—which human nature in its moments of intoxication has produced; that which men have contrived with a view to forming the minds, and regulating the conduct of women, is perhaps the most completely absurd. And, though the consequences are often very serious to both sexes, yet if one could for a moment forget these, and consider it only as a system, it would rather be found a subject of mirth and ridicule than serious anger.

What a chaos!—What a mixture of strength and weakness,—of greatness and littleness,—of sense and folly,—of exquisite feeling and total insensibility,—have they jumbled together in their imaginations,—and then given to their pretty darling the name of woman!

> ———Reason we resign;
> Against our senses we adopt the plan
> Which reverence, fear, and folly think divine.
> Yearsley[1]

What Women Are

To say what women *really* are, would be a very difficult task indeed; we must therefore endeavour, to describe them by negatives. As, perhaps, the only thing that can be advanced with certainty on the subject, is,—what they are *not*. For it is very clear, that they are not what they ought to be, that they are not what men would have them to be, and to finish the portrait, that they are not what they appear to be. Indeed, indeed, they cannot say with honest Hamlet, that they "know now what seem is."[2] I hope however that these observations will not be considered as a libel upon the sex; for as this inconsistency and uncertainty of character is a matter of necessity and not of choice,

---

[1] Ann Yearsley (1752–1806), working-class poet. Quoted from "To the Honorable H[orace] W[alpole], on Reading *The Castle of Otranto* December 1784." In the poem, Yearsley wrote about the various women in Walpole's famous gothic novel, with varying approval and disapproval. The full stanza begins: "Implicit Faith, all hail! Imperial man / Exacts submission; reason we resign . . ." and "Reverence, Fear, and Folly" have capital letters (53–56).

[2] Hamlet's claim in rebuke of his mother's seeming grief over the death of her husband (1.2.76). Wollstonecraft uses these lines to rebuke women (p. 125).

they are rather objects of pity than of blame. And as their defects are generally speaking, I presume, those of education, rather than of nature, the men have more subject for remorse than triumph. . . .

In the first place then, I hold it as an infallible truth, and a truth that few will attempt to deny; that any race of people, or I should rather say any class of rational beings,—though by no means inferior originally in intellectual endowments,—may be held in a state of subjection and dependence from generation to generation, by another party, who, by a variety of circumstances, none of them depending on actual, original superiority of mind, may have established an authority over them. And it must be acknowledged a truth equally infallible, that any class so held in a state of subjection and dependence, will degenerate both in body and mind. . . .

But it must be confessed, that even those who consider the human species, in a more liberal and extensive point of view,—who do not see sufficient grounds for those claims so haughtily advanced on the part of the men,—yet suppose the necessity of subordination on one side unavoidable. They therefore fear, that women, were their eyes opened to their natural equality and consequence, would not so tamely submit to the cruel injustice with which they are treated, in many of the leading points in life. And they know that nothing would tend so much to this *eclaircissement*,[3] as an education, which by exercising their reason, and unfolding their talents, should point out to themselves, how they might exert them to the utmost. Such a development of mind would undoubtedly enable them to see and reason upon what principles, all the other regulations of society were formed,— which however they may deviate in execution, are evidently founded on justice and humanity,—and would consequently enable them to bring home and apply those principles to the situation of their sex in general. Thus awakened to a sense of their injuries, they would behold with astonishment and indignation, the arts which had been employed, to keep them in a state of perpetual babyism. . . .

And this is precisely a case in point. For, in the first place it cannot be proved, that men are fitter to govern women, than women are to govern themselves, in the unlimited sense that men aspire to; except comparative experiment had been fairly and repeatedly made. Or, except superiority of mind had from the beginning, been so completely, so distinctly, and so uniformly marked; that it could bear no

[3]French: clarification.

more dispute, that men should take the whole command into their own hands, than that mature age, should care for helpless infancy.

Men however, having taken for granted, and endeavoured to establish without proof, that they have some degree of intellectual superiority over women; have the consequences of their government, been equal to their declarations of superior wisdom, or answerable to their wishes, or to their ideas, of the possible perfection of the female sex, even in that secondary view in which they chuse to consider them? I apprehend they will not say so. Or if they do, the sex will by no means join them. For chained and blindfolded as they most certainly are, with respect to their own rights;—they know,—they feel conscious—of capability of greater degrees of perfection, than they are permitted to arrive at. Yes they see—there is not an individual among them, who does not at times see,—and feel too with keenest anguish,—that mind, as has been finely said, is of no sex. . . .

What Women Ought to Be

Women then, I must take it upon me to say, ought to be considered as the companions and equals, not as the inferiors,—much less as they virtually are,—as the slaves of men. In every station they are entitled to esteem, as well as love, when deserving, and virtuous, in the different connections of life,—They were originally intended, to be the helpmates of the other sex, as the Scripture most emphatically and explicitly calls them[4]; and not their drudges in the common ranks, and the tolls of their passions and prejudices in the higher. . . .

Having said as much on the two first charges, as the limited nature of this sketch will admit; I shall now consider the last—That knowledge renders women masculine, and consequently disgusting in their manners.—In doing this I think my argument will prove a two-edged sword. I think it must prove, that neither has learning a direct, and inevitable tendency to render women masculine; nor if it did so, would it render them consequently, and infallibly disagreeable to the men. . . .

If therefore we are to understand by a masculine woman, one who emulates those virtues and accomplishments, which as common to human nature, are common to both sexes; the attempt is natural, amiable, and highly honorable to that woman, under whatever name her conduct may be disguised or censured.

[4]Genesis 2:18.

But if on the other hand we mean by a masculine woman, one who apes the exercises, the attributes, the unrestrained passions, and the numberless improprieties, which men fondly *chuse* to think suitable enough for their own sex—and which excesses to say the truth after all, chiefly distinguish their moral characters from those of women—I must say that knowledge has no tendency whatever to produce such aukward imitations; and I must confess, that such are masculine in the worst sense of the word, and as we should imagine consequently disagreeable. This however as we hinted before would be a hasty and ill-grounded conclusion, though apparently founded in reason, for the fact is otherwise; and the present age furnishes examples enough, that women may be truly masculine in their conduct and demeanor, without wounding the delicacy of the men. . . .

I will own, however, that even if the pretensions of the sexes were finally adjusted, and that equilibrium established, which I have endeavoured to point out as necessary to the peace and satisfaction of both; that perfection, or compleat happiness, is not to be expected. Of this however we are certain, that if universal justice were to prevail among mankind,—in which of course we include womankind,—that we should then be on the high road to happiness; of which we might reasonably hope to taste a competent share in this world, and might safely trust to a good providence for the perfection of it in another. . . .

Richard Polwhele (1760–1838)

Reverend Richard Polwhele was educated at Oxford, first training for the law. He wrote poetry, histories, journalism, theological tracts, and translations of Greek literature and was a frequent contributor to some leading conservative journals of his day, including the Anti-Jacobin. *Among his mother's friends were Hannah More and Catharine Macaulay, whom he met in 1777. By 1798, both Macaulay and Wollstonecraft were dead, and a reactionary political climate as well as Godwin's* Memoirs of the Author of A Vindication of the Rights of Woman *had dealt "rights of woman" a serious setback. The only issue to command popular support was female education in modest, virtuous intelligence, trained to piety, obedience, and domestic duty, in order to form good Christian daughters, wives, and mothers. Fresh from reading Godwin's memoir, Polwhele, with tones tipping from nasty to horrified, had castigated its scandals in a review for the* European Magazine. *His satiric poem casts radicals such as Wollstonecraft as "unnatural," "licentious," anti-Christian revolutionaries, driven by godless "Reason." So as not to seem flatly misogynist, Polwhele ends his poem celebrating the more conservative eighteenth-century Bluestocking women, a "kindred train" who "influence" through "modest virtue." He ventriloquizes his praise through the voice of their disciple Hannah More, whose views on the "natural" differences of the sexes and their separate spheres he warmly endorses. Polwhele's voluminous footnotes are an important part of his polemic. We include some, especially ones on the question of women's rights.*

from *The Unsex'd Females* (1798)

Thou, who with all the poet's genuine rage,
Thy "fine eye rolling" o'er "this aweful age,"[1]
Where polish'd life unfolds its various views,
Hast mark'd the magic influence of the muse;
Sever'd, with nice precision, from her beam   5
Of genial power, her false and feeble gleam;
Expos'd the Sciolist's[2] vain-glorious claim,
And boldly thwarted Innovation's aim,
Where witlings wildly think, or madly dare,[3]
With Honor, Virtue, Truth, announcing war;   10
Survey with me, what ne'er our fathers saw,
A female band despising NATURE's law,[4]

[1]The addressee is another Tory conservative scourge, Thomas James Mathias, whose long satirical poem *The Pursuits of Literature* (1794–97), also encased in footnotes, inspired Polwhele's. In his Preface to the 4th dialogue of this popular poem (16 editions), Mathias lamented that "our *unsexed* female writers now instruct, or confuse, us and themselves, in the labyrinth of politics, or turn us wild with Gallic frenzy"— French-inspired ideas and fashions. He begins representing himself "not unconscious of this awful age" (1.7), echoing Milton's representation of himself and other visionary poets as chastisers of their own age, "fall'n on evil days" (*Paradise Lost*, 7.25). Theseus in *A Midsummer Night's Dream* describes "the poet's eye, in a fine frenzy rolling" (5.1.12).

[2]Displayer of superficial learning.

[3]"Greatly think, or nobly die." Pope [Polwhele's note, slightly misquoting l. 10 of *Elegy to the Memory of an Unfortunate Lady*, about a woman who seems to have committed suicide in despair of love].

[4]Nature is the grand basis of all laws human and divine: and the woman, who has no regard to nature, either in the decoration of her person, or the culture of her mind, will soon "walk after the flesh, in the lust of uncleanness, and despise government" [Polwhele's note, quoting 2 Peter 2.10; Rousseau and other defenders of sexual inequality routinely invoke "Natural" or "Nature's" law].

As "proud defiance"[5] flashes from their arms,
And vengeance smothers all their softer charms.
   I shudder at the new unpictur'd scene,   15
Where unsex'd woman vaunts the imperious mien;
Where girls, affecting to dismiss the heart,
Invoke the Proteus of petrific art;[6]
With equal ease, in body or in mind,
To Gallic freaks or Gallic faith[7] resign'd,   20
The crane-like neck, as Fashion bids, lay bare,
Or frizzle, bold in front, their borrow'd hair;[8]
Scarce by a gossamery film carest,
Sport, in full view, the meretricious breast;[9]
Loose the chaste cincture,[10] where the graces shone,   25
And languish'd all the Loves, the ambrosial zone;
As lordly domes inspire dramatic rage,
Court prurient Fancy to the private stage;
With bliss botanic[11] as their bosoms heave,

[5]"A troop came next, who crowns and armour wore, / And proud defiance in their looks they bore." Pope. The Amazonian band—the female Quixotes of the new philosophy, are, here, too justly characterised [Polwhele's note]. The quotation is from *The Temple of Fame* (1711, ll. 342–43), the troop answering "the direful trump of Slander." The Amazons, legendary race of warrior women from Scythia, near the Black Sea, frequently assailed the Greeks; they were fabled to have burnt off the right breast (*a*, without; *mazos*, breast) to facilitate use of bow or javelin; the term is used, not always disparagingly, for any "masculine" woman, or, disparagingly, as a synonym for virago. Quixotes (from Cervantes' hero) are impractical idealists.

[6]Proteus: god able to change shapes at will; petrific: able to turn to stone, as if a Medusa, an unfeeling woman.

[7]French fashions and the new French (Godless) religion.

[8]Wigs.

[9]To "sport a face," is a cant phrase in one of our Universities, by which is meant an impudent obtrusion of a man's person in company. It is not inapplicable, perhaps, to the open bosom—a fashion which we have never invited or sanctioned. The fashions of France, which have been always imitated by the English, were, heretofore, unexceptionable in a moral point of view; since, however ridiculous or absurd, they were innocent. But they have now their source among prostitutes—among women of the most abandoned character [Polwhele's note]. Meretricious: whorish. An 18th-c. French aristocratic fashion was a fancy-gown neckline plunged below the bosom, displaying it bare.

[10]A wide belt around the waist and sometimes the bosom, as a girdle; it is "chaste" for concealing breasts and hips.

[11]Botany has lately become a fashionable amusement with the ladies. But how the study of the sexual system of plants can accord with female modesty, I am not able to comprehend. I had first written: "More eager for illicit knowlege [*sic*] pant, / With lustful boys anatomize a plant; / The virtues of its dust prolific speak, / Or point its pistill with unblushing cheek." I have, several times, seen boys and girls botanizing together [Pol-

Still pluck forbidden fruit, with mother Eve,   30
For puberty in sighing florets pant,
Or point the prostitution of a plant;
Dissect[12] its organ of unhallow'd lust,
And fondly gaze the titillating[13] dust;
With liberty's sublimer views expand,   35
And o'er the wreck of kingdoms[14] sternly stand;
And, frantic, midst the democratic storm,
Pursue, Philosophy! thy phantom-form.
    Far other is the female shape and mind,
By modest luxury heighten'd and refin'd;   40
Those limbs, that figure, tho' by Fashion grac'd,
By Beauty polish'd, and adorn'd by Taste;
That soul, whose harmony perennial flows,
In Music trembles, and in Color glows;

whele's note]. Such judgment of the immodesty of botanizing was probably fueled by Erasmus Darwin, whose popular poem, *The Botanic Garden*, especially Part II, *The Loves of the Plants* (1789; 1791), is explicit about sexual organs and activity.

[12]Miss Wollstonecraft does not blush to say, in an introduction to a book designed for the use of young ladies, that, "in order to lay the axe at the root of corruption, it would be proper to familiarize the sexes to an unreserved discussion of those topics, which are generally avoided in conversation from a principle of false delicacy; and that it would be right to speak of the organs of generation as freely as we mention our eyes or our hands." To such language our botanizing girls are doubtless familiarized: and, they are in a fair way of becoming worthy disciples of Miss W. If they do not take heed to their ways, they will soon exchange the blush of modesty for the bronze of impudence [Polwhele's note, alluding to Luke 3:9]. He misrepresents Wollstonecraft's statement in "Introductory Address to Parents," *Elements of Morality, For the Use of Children* (1792): concerned with masturbation and other "impure" practices, she contends that "the most efficacious method to root out this dreadful evil, which poisons the source of human happiness, would be to speak to children of the organs of generation as freely as we speak of the other parts of the body, and explain to them the noble use which they were designed for, and how they may be injured." In *Rights of Woman* (ch. VII: "Modesty") she refutes as "absurd" the "gross idea" that botany is inconsistent with female modesty, and lists it among the subjects that boys and girls might study together (ch. XII: "On National Education").

[13]"Each pungent grain of titillating dust." Pope; "The prolific dust"—of the botanist [Polwhele's note, alluding to the "Charge of *Snuff*"—"The pungent Grains of titillating Dust"—Belinda hurls at her adversary in *The Rape of the Lock* (5.84)].

[14]The female advocates of Democracy in this country, though they have had no opportunity of imitating the French ladies, in their atrocious acts of cruelty; have yet assumed a stern serenity in the contemplation of those savage excesses. "To express their abhorrence of royalty, they (the French ladies) threw away the character of their sex, and bit the amputated limbs of their murdered countrymen.—I say this on the authority of a young gentleman who saw it.—I am sorry to add, that the relation, accompanied with looks of horror and disgust, only provoked a contemptuous smile from an illuminated British fair-one." See Robinson [Polwhele's note, quoting *Proofs of a Conspiracy*].

Which bids sweet Poesy reclaim the praise   45
With faery light to gild fastidious days,
From sullen clouds relieve domestic care,
And melt in smiles the withering frown of war.
Ah! once the female Muse, to NATURE true,
The unvalued store from FANCY, FEELING drew;   50
Won, from the grasp of woe, the roseate hours,
Cheer'd life's dim vale, and strew'd the grave with flowers.
    But lo! where, pale amidst the wild,[15] she draws
Each precept cold from sceptic Reason's[16] vase;
Pours with rash arm the turbid stream along,   55
And in the foaming torrent whelms the throng.[17]
    Alas! her pride sophistic[18] flings a gloom,
To chase, sweet Innocence! thy vernal bloom,
Of each light joy to damp the genial glow,
And with new terrors clothe the groupe of woe,   60
Quench the pure daystar[19] in oblivion deep,
And, Death! restore thy "long, unbroken sleep."[20]
    See Wollstonecraft, whom no decorum checks,
Arise, the intrepid champion of her sex;
O'er humbled man assert the sovereign claim,   65
And slight the timid blush[21] of virgin fame.
    "Go, go (she cries) ye tribes of melting maids,
Go, screen your softness in sequester'd shades;
With plaintive whispers woo the unconscious grove,

[15]"A wild, where flowers and weeds promiscuous shoot; / A garden tempting with forbidden fruit." Pope [Polwhele's note, quoting *Essay on Man* (1733): *Epistle I*, 7–8].

[16]A troubled stream only, can proceed from the vase of scepticism [Polwhele's note, alluding to the Revolutionaries' (Godless) ideology of "Reason"].

[17]"Raging waves, foaming out their own shame"—St. Jude. Such were those infamous publications of Paine and others, which, like the torrents of December, threatened to sweep all before them—to overwhelm the multitude [Polwhele's note].

[18]Specious.

[19]Sun.

[20]"We, the great, the valiant and the wise, / When once the seal of death hath clos'd our eyes, / Shut in the hollow tomb obscure and deep, / Slumber, to wake no more, one long unbroken sleep." Moschus [Polwhele's note; Moschus: 2nd-c. BCE Greek pastoral poet, whom he translated in a well-received publication of 1786].

[21]That Miss Wollstonecraft was a sworn enemy to blushes, I need not remark. But many of my readers, perhaps, will be astonished to hear, that at several of our boarding-schools for young ladies, a blush incurs a penalty [Polwhele's note].

And feebly perish, as depis'd ye love.   70
What tho' the fine Romances of Rousseau
Bid the frame flutter, and the bosom glow;
Tho' the rapt Bard, your empire fond to own,
Fall prostrate and adore your living throne,
The living throne his hands presum'd to rear,   75
Its seat a simper, and its base a tear;[22]
Soon shall the sex disdain the illusive sway,
And wield the sceptre in yon blaze of day;
Ere long, each little artifice discard,
No more by weakness[23] winning fond regard;   80
Nor eyes, that sparkle from their blushes, roll,
Nor catch the languors of the sick'ning soul,
Nor the quick flutter, nor the coy reserve,
But nobly boast the firm gymnastic nerve;[24]
Nor more affect with Delicacy's fan   85
To hide the emotion from congenial man;
To the bold heights where glory beams, aspire,
Blend mental energy with Passion's fire,
Surpass their rivals in the powers of mind
And vindicate *the Rights of womankind.*"   90
    She spoke: and veteran BARBAULD[25] caught the strain,

[22]According to Rousseau, the empire of women is the empire of softness—of address: their commands, are caresses; their menaces, are tears [Polwhele's note, referring to Rousseau's views on women in *La Nouvelle Heloise* (1760) and *Émile* (1762), both criticized in *Rights of Woman*].

[23]"Like monarchs, we have been flattered into imbecillity, by those who wish to take advantage of our weakness," says Mary Hays (*Essays and Letters*, 92). But, whether flattered or not, women were always weak: and female weakness hath accomplished, what the force of arms could not effect [Polwhele's note, quoting her passionate endorsement of Wollstonecraft's *Rights of Woman*. Hays's feminist *Appeal to the Men of Great Britain on Behalf of Women* appeared anonymously in 1798.]

[24]Miss Wollstonecraft seriously laments the neglect of all muscular exercises, at our female Boarding-schools [Polwhele's note].

[25]Here . . . I have formed a groupe of female Writers; whose productions have been appreciated by the public as works of learning or genius—though not praised with that extravagance of panegyric, which was once a customary tribute to the literary compositions of women. In this country, a female author was formerly esteemed a Phenomenon in Literature: and she was sure of a favourable reception among the critics, in consideration of her sex. This species of gallantry, however, conveyed no compliment to her understanding. It implied such an inferiority of woman in the scale of intellect as was justly humiliating: and critical forbearance was mortifying to female vanity. At the present day, indeed, our literary women are so numerous, that their judges, wa[i]ving all complimentary civilities, decide upon their merits with the same

And deem'd her songs of Love, her Lyrics vain;
And ROBINSON[26] to Gaul her Fancy gave,
And trac'd the picture of a Deist's grave!
And charming SMITH[27] resign'd her power to please,   95
Poetic feeling and poetic ease;
And HELEN,[28] fir'd by Freedom, bade adieu

rigid impartiality as it seems right to exercise towards the men. The tribunal of criticism is no longer charmed into complacence by the blushes of modest apprehension. It no longer imagines the pleading eye of feminine diffidence that speaks a consciousness of comparative imbecillity, or a fearfulness of having offended by intrusion. Experience hath drawn aside the flimsy veil of affected timidity, that only served to hide the smile of complacency; the glow of self-gratulation. Yet, alas! the crimsoning blush of modesty, will be always more attractive, than the sparkle of confident intelligence.—Mrs. Barbauld stands the most conspicuous figure in the groupe. She is a veteran in Literature . . . Her poetry . . . is certainly, chaste and elegant. . . . I was sorry to find Mrs. B. . . . classed with such females as a Wollstonecraft. . . . But though Mrs. B. has lately published several political tracts, which if not discreditable to her talents and virtues, can by no means add to her reputation, yet, I am sure, she must reprobate, with me, the alarming eccentricities of Miss Wollstonecraft [Polwhele's note].

[26]In Mrs. Robinson's Poetry, there is a peculiar delicacy: but her Novels, as literary compositions, have no great claim to approbation—As containing the doctrines of Philosophism, they merit the severest censure. Would that, for the sake of herself and her beautiful daughter (whose personal charms are only equalled by the elegance of her mind) would, that, for the sake of the public morality, Mrs. Robinson were persuaded to dismiss the gloomy phantom of annihilation; to think seriously of a future retribution; and to communicate to the world, a recantation of errors that originated in levity, and have been nursed by pleasure! I have seen her, "glittering like the morning-star, full of life, and splendor and joy!" Such, and more glorious, may I meet her again, when the just "shall shine forth as the brightness of the firmament, and as the stars for ever and ever!" [Polwhele, quoting Burke's famous description of his first sight of princess Marie Antoinette; *Reflections,* 72]. "Philosophism" refers to the Enlightenment ideology of progress and human perfectibility through reason.

[27]The Sonnets of Charlotte Smith, have a pensiveness peculiarly their own. It is not the monotonous plaintiveness of Shenstone, the gloomy melancholy of Gray, or the meek subdued spirit of Collins. It is a strain of wild, yet softened sorrow, that breathes a romantic air, without losing, for a moment, its mellowness. Her images, often original, are drawn from nature: the most familiar, have a new and charming aspect. Sweetly picturesque, she creates with the pencil of a Gilpin, and infuses her own soul into the landscape. There is so uncommon a variety in her expression, that I could read a thousand of such sonnets without lassitude. In general, a very few Sonnets fatigue attention, partly owing to the sameness of their construction. Petrarch, indeed, I can relish for a considerable time: but Spenser and Milton soon produce somnolence. . . . But why does she suffer her mind to be infected with the Gallic mania? [Polwhele's note]. Other references are to the 18th-c. poets William Shenstone, Thomas Gray, and William Collins, and to William Gilpin (1724–1804), author of illustrated picturesque tours of Britain.

[28]Miss Helen Williams is, doubtless, a true poet. But is it not extraordinary, that such a genius, a female and so young, should have become a politician—that the fair Helen, whose notes of love have charmed the moonlight vallies, should stand forward, an

To all the broken visions of Peru.
And YEARSELEY,[29] who had warbled, Nature's child,
Midst twilight dews, her minstrel ditties wild,   100
(Tho' soon a wanderer from her meads and milk,
She long'd to rustle, like her sex, in silk)
Now stole that modish grin, the sapient sneer,
And flippant HAYS[30] assum'd a cynic leer . . .

Priscilla Bell Wakefield (1751–1832)

Of Quaker background, married to a prosperous London merchant, and devoted to philanthropy, Priscilla Bell Wakefield is best known for the instructional children's books she wrote in the 1790s, with subjects rang-

intemperate advocate for Gallic licentiousness—that such a woman should import with her, a blast more pestilential than that of Avernus, though she has so often delighted us with melodies, soft as the sighs of the Zephyr, delicious as the airs of Paradise? [Polwhele's note]. See Williams's *Letters from France* (1792–96); her long political poem condemning imperial conquest, *Peru*, was published in 1784. Avernus is a lake in Italy thought to be the gate to the underworld; zephyr is the spring breeze.

[29]Mrs. Yearseley's [*sic*] Poems, as the product of an untutored milk-woman, certainly entitled her to patronage: and patronage she received, from Miss H. More, liberal beyond example. Yet, such is the depravity of the human heart, that this milk-woman had no sooner her hut cheered by the warmth of benevolence, than she spurned her benefactor from her door. . . . My business, however, with Mrs. Y. is to recall her, if possible, from her Gallic wanderings—if an appeal to native ingenuousness be not too late; if the fatal example of the Arch-priestess of female Libertinism, have any influence on a mind once stored with the finest moral sentiment [Polwhele's note]. The "fatal example" is Wollstonecraft.

[30]Mary Hays from her "Letters and Essays" . . . is evidently a Wollstonecraftian. "I cannot mention (says she) the admirable advocate for the rights of women, without pausing to pay a tribute of grateful respect, in the name of my sex, to the virtue and talents of a writer, who with equal courage and ability, hath endeavoured to rescue the female mind from those prejudices which have been the canker of genuine virtue. . . . The rights of woman and the name of Wollstonecraft, will go down to posterity with reverence." Mary Hays ridicules "the good lady who studied her Bible, and obliged her children to say their prayers, and go statedly to church." Her expressions respecting the European Governments are, in a high degree, inflammatory [Polwhele's note]. The attacks on Wollstonecraft continue in subsequent notes, recounting her infatuation with the married Fuseli, her affair with Imlay, her suicide attempts despite a young daughter, her premarital affair with Godwin, and her lack of church attendance or death-bed conversion. "I cannot but think, that the Hand of Providence is visible, in her life, her death and in [Godwin's] Memoirs. . . . As she was given up to her 'heart's lusts,' and let 'to follow her own imaginations,' that the fallacy of and the effects of an irreligious conduct, might be manifested to the world; and as she died a death that strongly marked the distinction of the sexes, by pointing out the destiny of women and the diseases to which they are liable."

ing from travel in Europe and the British empire to botany and zoology. Among her philanthropic projects were the promotion of "frugality banks" for the working classes and the establishment of a "lying-in" (childbirth) hospital for poor women. The prison reformer Elizabeth Fry was her niece. Wakefield's one work for adults, Reflections on the Present Condition of the Female Sex, *published in 1798, vigorously argues for better education and more liberal employment opportunities for women at a time when their vocations were limited to domestic situations as servants, nurses, governesses, housekeepers, or slightly more independent enterprises such as schoolmistresses, seamstresses, and shopkeepers.*

from *Reflections on the Present Condition of the Female Sex; with Suggestions for its Improvement* (1798)

In civilized nations it has ever been the misfortune of the sex to be too highly elevated, or too deeply depressed; now raised above the condition of mortals, upon the score of their personal attractions; and now debased below that of reasonable creatures, with respect to their intellectual endowments. The result of this improper treatment has been a neglect of the mental powers, which women really possess, but know not how to exercise; and they have been contented to barter the dignity of reason, for the imaginary privilege of an empire, of the existence of which they can entertain no reasonable hope beyond the duration of youth and beauty. . . .

But notwithstanding these disadvantages, and others of less perceptible influence, the diffusion of christianity, and the progress of civilization, have raised the importance of the female character; and it has become a branch of philosophy, not a little interesting, to ascertain the offices which the different ranks of women are required to fulfil. Their rights and their duties have lately occupied the pens of writers of eminence; the employments which may properly exercise their faculties, and fill up their time in a useful manner, without encroaching upon those professions, which are appropriate to men, remain to be defined. There are many branches of science, as well as useful occupations, in which women may employ their time and their talents, beneficially to themselves and to the community, without destroying the peculiar characteristic of their sex, or exceeding the most exact limits of modesty and decorum. Whatever obliges them to mix in the public haunts of men, or places the young in too familiar a situation with the other sex; whatever is obnoxious to the delicacy and reserve of the female character, or destructive, in the smallest degree, to the strictest moral purity, is inadmissible. The sphere of feminine action is contracted by numberless difficulties, that are no impediments to masculine exertions. Domestic privacy is the only sure asylum for the juvenile part of the sex; nor can the grave matron step far beyond that boundary with propriety. Unfitted, by their relative situation in society, for many honourable and lucrative employments, those only are suitable for them, which can be pursued without endangering their virtue, or corrupting their manners.

But, under these restrictions, there may be found a multitude of objects adapted to the useful exertions of female talents, which it will be the principal design of these Reflections to point out, after making some remarks upon the present state of female education, and suggesting some improvements towards its reformation.

And here the author may perhaps be allowed to express her hope, that among the numbers of the female world, who appear to be satisfied with inferiority, many require only to be awakened to a true sense of their own real consequence, to be induced to support it by a rational improvement of those hours, which they have hitherto wasted in the most frivolous occupations. The promotion of so useful a design, is the only apology for intruding her opinions upon the subject; and it will be esteemed her highest recompence, should her observations contribute to its accomplishment. . . .

The difficulty of meeting with persons properly qualified to be the preceptors and guides of the uncorrupted minds of youth, is allowed to be great, and suggests the advantages which might arise, from the establishment of institutions for the express purpose of educating young women, of small expectations, for the office. These institutions should be sufficiently endowed, to provide masters in every useful science, and to furnish a well-chosen library, consisting of the most approved authors, with globes, and other suitable apparatus for instruction, and after a certain number of years, women only should be nominated to the charge of instruction. The effect of such seminaries would be a constant succession of female teachers properly prepared for their destination, not only by a regular course of study, but also by a thorough initiation into the philosophical principles of education, founded upon the opinions of the most eminent writers upon the subject. Another beneficial consequence would be, the affording a respectable subsistence to great numbers of young women, who are reduced to misery through want of employment, by enabling them to teach those sciences, which are exclusively taught by masters, an evil that calls loudly for redress. Surely it can never be denied, that the instruction of girls in every department of knowledge or art, is a fair field for the exertion of female talents. . . .

There is scarcely a more helpless object in the wide circle of misery which the vicissitudes of civilized society display, than a woman genteelly educated, whether single or married, who is deprived, by any unfortunate accident, of the protection and support of male relations; unaccustomed to struggle with difficulty, unacquainted with any resource to supply an independent maintenance, she is reduced to the depths of wretchedness, and not infrequently, if she be young and handsome, is driven by despair to those paths which lead to infamy. Is it not time to find a remedy for such evils, when the contention of nations has produced the most affecting transitions in private life, and transferred the affluent and the noble to the humiliating extremes of want and obscurity? When our streets teem with multitudes of unhappy women, many of whom might have been rescued from their present degradation, or who would perhaps never have fallen into it, had they been instructed in the exercise of some art or profession, which would have enabled them to procure for themselves a respectable support by their own industry. . . .

That which is moral excellence in one rational being, deserves the same estimation in another; therefore, if it be really honourable in a man, to exert the utmost of his abilities, whether mental or corporal, in the acquisition of a competent support for himself, and for those who have a natural claim upon his protection; it must be equally so in a woman, nay, perhaps still more incumbent, as in many cases, there is nothing so inimical to the preservation of her virtue as a state of poverty, which leaves her dependant upon the generosity of others, to supply those accommodations, which use has rendered necessary to her comfort.

There appears then no moral impediment to prevent women from the application of their talents to purposes of utility; on the contrary, an improvement in public manners must infallibly result from it; as their influence over the other sex is universally acknowledged, it may be boldly asserted, that a conversion of their time from trifling and unproductive employments, to those that are both useful and profitable, would operate as a check upon luxury, dissipation, and prodigality, and retard the progress of that general dissoluteness, the offspring of idleness, which is deprecated by all political writers, as the sure forerunner of national decay. . . .

Men monopolize not only the most advantageous employments, and such as exclude women from the exercise of them, by the publicity of their nature, or the extensive knowledge they require, but even many of those, which are consistent with the female character. Another heavy discouragement to the industry of women, is the inequality of the reward of their labour, compared with that of men, an injustice which pervades every species of employment performed by both sexes.[1]

In employments which depend upon bodily strength the distinction is just; for it cannot be pretended that the generality of women can earn as much as men, where the produce of their labour is the result of corporeal exertion; but it is a subject of great regret, that this inequality should prevail, even where an equal share of skill and application are exerted. Male stay-makers, mantua-makers,[2] and hair-dressers are better paid than female artists of the same professions; but surely it will never be urged as an apology for this disproportion, that women are not as capable of making stays, gowns, dressing hair, and similar arts, as men; if they are not superior to them, it can only be accounted for upon this principle, that the prices they receive for their labour are not sufficient to repay them for the expence of qualifying themselves for their business, and that they sink under the mortification of being regarded as artizans of inferior estimation, whilst the men, who supplant them, receive all the encouragement of large profits and full employment, which is ensured to them by the folly of fashion. The occasion for this remark is a disgrace upon those who patronize such a brood of effeminate beings in the garb of men, when sympathy with their humblest sisters should direct them to act in a manner exactly opposite, by holding out every incitement to the industry of their own sex. This evil indeed

---

[1]This abuse is in no instance more conspicuous, than in the wages of domestic servants. A footman, especially of the higher kind, whose most laborious task is to wait at table, gains, including clothes, vails, and other perquisites, at least £50 per annum, whilst a cook-maid, who is mistress of her profession, does not obtain £20, though her office is laborious, unwholesome, and requires a much greater degree of skill than that of a valet. A similar disproportion is observable among the inferior servants of the establishment [Wakefield's note]. Vails: tips.

[2]Stay-makers: corsetmakers; mantua-makers: dressmakers.

calls loudly upon women of rank and fortune for redress: they should determine to employ women only, wherever they can be employed; they should procure female instructors for their children; they should frequent no shops that are not served by women; they should wear no clothes that are not made by them; they should reward them as liberally as they do the men who have hitherto supplanted them. Let it be considered a common cause to give them every possible advantage. For once let fashion be guided by reason, and let the mode sanction a preference to women in every profession, to which their pretensions are equal with those of the other sex. This is a patronage which the necessitous have a right to expect from the rich and powerful, whether they are poor by birth, or are unfortunately become so by that mutability of fortune to which every rank is liable. . . .

The serving of retail shops, which deal in articles of female consumption, should be exclusively appropriated to women. For were the multitudes of men, who are constantly employed in measuring linen, gauze, ribbons, and lace; selling perfumes and cosmetics; setting a value on feathers and trinkets; and displaying their talents in praising the elegance of bonnets and caps, to withdraw, they might benefit the community, by exchanging such frivolous avocations for something more worthy of the masculine character, and by this measure afford an opportunity of gaining a creditable livelihood to many destitute women, whom a dreadful necessity drives to the business of prostitution. . . . Every undertaker should employ women, for the express purpose of supplying the female dead, with those things which are requisite. How shocking is the idea of our persons being exposed, even after death, to the observation of a parcel of undertaker's men. . . . In the present state of things, if a poor frail unthinking girl yields to the ardent solicitations of the man who has won her affections, and he be so villainous as to abandon her, she is lost without resource, especially if she be qualified for no occupation but service; deprived of character, no person will take her into their family; the wants of nature must be satisfied, even at the price which produces utter destruction; and the forlorn deserted one is compelled to betake herself to that course, which presently terminates all hope of restoration to the esteem of others, or to her own approbation. . . .

There are some professions and trades customarily in the hands of men, which might be conveniently exercised by either sex.—Many parts of the business of a stationer, particularly ruling account books or making pens. The compounding of medicines in an apothecary's shop, requires no other talents than care and exactness; and if opening a vein[3] occasionally be an indispensible requisite, a woman may acquire the capacity of doing it for those of her own sex at least. . . . Pastry and confectionary appear particularly consonant to the habits of women, though generally performed by men: perhaps the heat of the ovens, and the strength requisite to fill and empty them, may render male assistants necessary; but certainly women are most eligible to mix up the ingredients, and prepare the various kinds of cake for baking.—Light turnery[4] and toy-making, depend more upon dexterity and invention than force, and are therefore suitable work for women and children.

There must be public houses for the reception of travellers, and labourers who are single, and have no homes: it were happy indeed for the community, that they were confined to such purposes, instead of being converted into receptacles for intemperance. . . . Without recommending it as an eligible employment for women, reasons may be urged for the widows of publicans, or even other women of a certain age, engaging in it; as houses of this description, which are under female management, are generally the most orderly, and the most successful.

Mary Anne Radcliffe (c. 1746–post 1810)

Born the only child to a mother of thirty and a father of seventy-six anxious for an heir, Mary Anne Radcliffe gained a handsome fortune when he died two years later. In her teens, she eloped with a charming friend of her mother, some twenty years her senior, Joseph Radcliffe. He sired eight children, but liking alcohol and being not particularly good at "economy, method or industry" (Radcliffe wrote in her Memoir *of 1810), what he didn't spend of her fortune on recreation he squandered on a series of ill-advised business ventures. Radcliffe realized that it was up to her to support herself and the children. She tried, variously, and without success, a shoe shop, a school, a coffee house, a cake shop, selling patent medicines, taking lodgers—even as she was wracked with rheumatism. None of*

[3]Bleeding, for medical purposes.
[4]Pottery.

these ventures succeeded. Not knowing what else to do, she sent her sons away to school and her daughters to live with her mother, while she went to work as a lady's companion and housekeeper, then as a governess, a position that sexual harassment forced her to abandon. Bitter at finding men monopolizing respectable trades for women, so that the most desperate turned to beggary and prostitution, she began The Female Advocate; or An Attempt to Recover the Rights of Women from Male Usurpation *in 1792 (its full title announcing a debt to Wollstonecraft) and published it in 1799. Radcliffe's class politics are much more rigid than Wollstonecraft's: While Radcliffe does assail the Vagrant Act's punishment of begging and defends many prostitutes as not morally culpable but economically desperate, she distinguishes these "innocents" from the "guilty" and discriminates in her proposed remedies "between the well-bred female, who is reduced by the unseen hand of fate, and the very poor and abject, whose birth has deprived them of the knowledge of refinement or delicacy."*

from *The Female Advocate* (1799)

from "To the Reader"

The subject of the following pages is an attempt to delineate the situation of those poor, helpless, females whose sufferings, from a variety of causes, are too grievous to be borne; the sources and dire consequences of which the exalted in life cannot form the least conception, unless they condescend to examine for themselves, when, it is to be hoped, their grievances will be sought into and redressed. The munificence of the people of Great Britain, which is ever ready and adequate to the support, aid, and comfort, of the afflicted, when their troubles are fully investigated; and the great number of unfortunate women, who, doubtless, would rejoice to become virtuous and useful members of society, in some lawful employment, have encouraged the author to offer this feeble representation. Nor can she despair of eventual success . . . if she is but so happy as to excite the attention of those whose souls are enlarged with the exalted ideas of Christian charity. . . .

The author, at the same time, wishes it to be understood, that she has not been stimulated, from vain and ambitious views, to appear in print, but rather from the pure philanthropic motive of throwing in her humble mite towards the much-wished-for relief of these most pitiable objects of distress.

from *Introduction*

I contend not with the lords of the creation, for any other privilege than that protection, which they themselves avow to be the *real rights of women*. . . . Advantages, in Britain, being monopolized by the male sex, permit me to ask, if it is not their duty, at least, to afford protection in their stead; for, surely, if they refuse to protect, they have no right whatever to govern. . . .

All women possess not the Amazonian spirit of a Wolstonecraft [*sic*].[1] But, indeed, unremitted oppression is sometimes a sufficient apology for their throwing off the gentle garb of a female, and assuming some more masculine appearance; yet, when the curtain of misrepresentation is once withdrawn, it is to be hoped, (not doubted) that the cause of complaint will quickly be removed.

from *Part First. The Fatal Consequences of Men Traders Engrossing Women's Occupations*

When we look around us, nothing is more conspicuous in the eyes of the world, than the distresses of women. I do not say those whom a kind Providence hath placed under the immediate care of a tender father, or an affectionate and kind husband; or, *by chance,* a friend, or brother. But these, alas! comprise only one part of the community. Notwithstanding all are of the same nature, and were formed by the same Divine Power, yet their comforts differ very widely indeed. Still, as women seem formed by nature to seek protection from man, why, in the name of justice, refuse the boon? Does it not become highly worthy the attention of men in general, to consider in what manner to redress the grievances *already within their notice?*

Perhaps it may be said, and very justly, that, considering human frailty, there is amongst women, as well as men, a vast number of vicious and undeserving. Granted; still, is it not better to pass over a hundred guilty, than let punishment fall upon one innocent person?—Besides, IS THERE NOT A POSSIBILITY OF FORMING A PLAN OF DISCRIMINATION, FOR THE BENEFIT OF THOSE ONLY WHO MERIT SUCH HUMANE AND FRIENDLY INTERFERENCE? . . . Let us proceed to the ground-work of the design; and, before any further steps are taken, ask, What can be said in favour of men-milliners, men-mantua-makers, and men stay-makers? besides all the numerous train of

[1]A positive use, compared to Polwhele; see p. 390, n. 5.

other professions, such as hair-dressers, &c. &c.; all of which occupations are much more calculated for women than men. . . . "Look,"
says an observer, "to the shops of perfumers, toymen, and others of a
similar occupation; and, above all, look to the haberdashery maga-
zines, where from ten to twenty fellows, six feet high, may be counted in each, to the utter exclusion of poor females, who could sell a
tooth-pick, or a few ribbons, just as well." . . . A tax upon these fellows would be very salutary, so say I. . . . Men may be much better
employed than in filling women's occupations. For, in the words of
St. Luke, these poor females may very justly say, "to dig I cannot, to
beg I am ashamed."[2] From this evil precedent, there is no other alternative for these poor women, but beggary or vice!

Let us then, if you please, select one of these distressed females,
out of the prodigious multitude, and pursue her through the humiliating scene of beggary. . . . Certain it must be, that after, perhaps, a
life of ease and affluence, to be compelled to such a mortifying situation, requires more than a common share of fortitude to support.
Still this prevailing passion, with all its train of attendants, must be
subdued, in the dreadful situation of beggary which cannot fail to
bring down the spirits of these unhappy victims, with more oppressive force than it is in the power of words to express, or pen to paint,
and can only be conceived, *in part*, by the silent sensations of those
who can adopt another's woes, and trace the passions of the human
mind. . . . See her trembling limbs, which are scarcely able to support
her load of wretchedness, whilst she asks an alms from the casual
passenger. She who, perhaps, a short time since, charmed her
acquaintance with her sprightly conversation and virtuous example,
by one adverse stroke, is nevertheless so soon become the contempt,
the scorn, and the outcast of mortals! Nor is this wretched doom
confined to youth alone; but, by the cruel hand of fate, the poor,
dejected mother, as well as daughter, is condemned to share the same
direful misfortunes, and be reduced to the same low state of
wretchedness, from which their characters are stigmatized with
infamy, and to which they unavoidably fall a sacrifice. In this miserable state they must for ever remain, until the spirit of oppression
and mistaken prejudice is eradicated, and the heavy cloud of misrepresentation cleared away, through a proper investigation of the

[2]From Jesus's parable of the unjust steward, Luke 16:3.

cause, which, doubtless, will lead to a conviction: that the distress and wretchedness of these poor, abandoned creatures originate chiefly from the avaricious and mercenary views of that set of beings, who are "Eating the bread of the hungry, and drinking the drink of the thirsty." Nor are these poor women allowed "to pick up the crumbs," which will appear in the sequel.

In the mean time, let us, if you please, take another view of this poor mother and her miserable daughter, in this forlorn and distressing state of beggary, and there see what relief they obtain, from their piercing accents and broken sighs—little more, it is to be feared, than contempt or insults. Even the hand of charity, accustomed to bestow on the needy, no sooner observes the appearance of youth, or a capability of industry, than it is instantly withdrawn, and kept in reserve (as it is thought) for some more proper object.

Good heavens, what a scene of woe! when the poor mother and her helpless daughter are turned adrift, to the mercy of an unfeeling world; which neither their genteel education, or delicate constitutions, broken down by poverty and hardships, can prevent. O! what distress, in a situation like this! . . . In vain do they supplicate their former friends, for the voice of censure has pointed them out as infamous! Good God! what grief can equal this? Abandoned by friends, and left to the reproach, contempt, and censure of a cruel world, without a provision, or any probable means of gaining a subsistence, or even the smallest glimpse of a distant hope.

And, though shocking to relate, yet such is the miserable situation of thousands of defenceless women. . . . What says the Vagrant Act?[3]—"Persons who beg in the streets are idle and disorderly; and any person who apprehends and carries such a beggar before a justice, shall receive five shillings, when the said justice may commit them to a house of correction."

However shocking the sentence, what numbers of these poor objects have been dragged away by the ruthless hand of the unfeeling savage, to some loathsome prison, without regard to the more refined or delicate sensations of one or another? Good heavens! there surely needs no Siddonian powers to heighten such a tragic scene.[4]

---

[3]Part of the Poor Laws prohibiting begging, these acts were also used to suppress loitering and prostitution.

[4]Sarah Siddons (1755–1831) was celebrated for her roles in Shakespearean tragedy.

She who, perhaps, was reared with all the gentle softness and maternal care of a fond parent; she, who so lately was looked upon as an ornament to her sex, until the pressure of misfortunes compelled her to seek for bread, to be at once confined in a dark prison, there to be obliged to hear all the opprobrious language of the very lowest set of beings, and that under a storm of oaths and imprecations, which, of itself, must pierce her very soul. There to have her ears grated with the rattling of bolts and bars, and all the adamantine fetters of misery. Good God! is it possible we can see our fellow creatures debased so low! . . .

What numbers of unguarded young men, even with hearts inclined to virtue, have unhappily been drawn on to vice, by the powerful insinuations of these poor abandoned females, who, like Eve in Paradise, is no sooner fallen herself, than, by deceitful artifice, she spreads the net of destruction to catch others. For example: need we go any farther than the theatres, the resort of all, both good and bad, and where abandoned females, of all ages and degrees of profligacy, attend to make their harvest, and gather in their unlawful plunder, to supply the ordinary wants of the ensuing day? And what can better answer the purpose of decoy than the drama? for, should it be comedy, the obscenity which prevails in many of our modern plays, cannot fail to act as poison upon the young mind: or is it tragedy, what can have a greater influence upon the feelings of sensibility, or sooner awaken the tender passions, which these miserable women take special care to translate to their own evil purposes?[5] . . .

Nor does the dreadful calamity end here; for, notwithstanding so many unfortunate females have been obliged to seek bread in the paths of vice, and so many young men have fallen victims to their folly and wickedness, still the same devouring jaws of destruction are open for its future prey; nor can they ever possibly close, until the grievous precedent of men usurping females' occupations is entirely done away, *or some proper substitute provided*, so as to enable women to share the common necessaries along with their fellow-creatures: till then, we need not wonder at the vast number of pick-pockets and housebreakers which, at all times, infest the streets, to the disturbance of civil society. . . .

---

[5]Theaters were widely suspect as places of social mixing, disreputable characters, and prostitutes.

It is said, the city of London alone pays upwards of twenty thousand pounds annually to patrols, beadles,[6] and watchmen; and it may be a much greater sum; yet, that of itself seems a vast sum indeed, to be raised by levy, in which the honest trader must unavoidably contribute a large share. Would not that contribution answer a much better purpose in providing for the necessitous poor, such as we have just been treating of, and who are judged unfit objects to be received into a parish workhouse[7]; being, *as it is termed*, able enough to earn their own bread out of the house?

Yet, so long as there continues a prohibition against women having an employment, it is to be feared, double the sum already raised by the inhabitants will be found inefficacious. . . . That political and private happiness are invariably connected, is beyond a doubt; and that the morals of this nation are very corrupt, is but too visible, from the vast numbers of disgraceful women who infest the face of the country. . . .

That great numbers would be happy in contributing to the aid and relief of those who appear to be objects of distress, is beyond a doubt: but, alas! for helpless, injured females! the heavy clouds of prejudice and misrepresentation have thrown so dark a veil between them and the pity of the world, that they are despised by all. Yet, when the curtain is once withdrawn, and the tragic scene exposed to open view, leading these poor creatures from obscurity into open light, then will be the crisis, when every good Christian may be impowered to soften the affliction of another's woes; and though it may not be in the power of every sympathising breast to contribute towards their temporal wants, they may still be impowered to sooth their sorrows, rather than drive the envenomed arrows of censure still deeper into their afflicted bosoms.

. . . The efficacy of these reflections to a feeling and generous mind, that can participate in another's woes, cannot be doubted; yet what will all that pity or all that sympathy avail, unless some exertions are used towards effecting a redress?

Suppose no lady would suffer herself to be served, in the shops of these effeminate traders, by any of the short-clothed gentry, would it not be a means of compelling all those who chuse to carry

---

[6]Parish officers who kept order.

[7]As Radcliffe makes clear, not everyone qualified for this opportunity.

on the tragi-comic farce, to effect the business under the disguise of gown and petticoat?

But joking apart: believe me, ladies, it is past a joke, when poor, unfortunate females are compelled to go without clothing. . . .

Were a body of miserable women, be they really virtuous or not, to assemble with a petition to parliament, where is the person who would be persuaded to present it, particularly when they are all considered as worthless wretches.

But were a body of men artificers (be their conduct or morals as they may) to offer a representation of grievances, doubtless their case would be heard, and considered, in every sense of the word, both political and humane.

What statute is there, which grants that men alone shall live, and women scarcely exist?—Is it not an usurpation which every violator must blush at, when considered in the light it ought to be, as an act of the greatest injustice? Then, drive hence all such distress: let it not be said, that Britons can cherish a wish to oppress their sisters, wives, and mothers, but rather that they are merciful to the fatherless and the widow. . . .

The very poor, who are born in an abject state, are taught from their infancy to struggle through life in the same manner they see their needy connections: bread must be had, and all the instructions they can possibly get, is in what way to obtain it. Consequently, if by labour and industry, they can acquire a sufficiency to exist upon, they are perfectly at ease, without bestowing a single thought upon to-morrow.

But the poor, unfortunate woman, who has seen better days, and been reared and educated with tenderness and care, she it is that feels her broken slumbers can no longer give relief to her weary limbs. Her inability to wrestle with difficulties are great indeed; especially when she finds her whole endeavours fruitless: and, what is still as bad, by running to and fro, in pursuit of some means for bread, (which she is not able to obtain) the shrill voice of censure, or the destructive whisper of calumny, having breathed such a poisonous vapour over her character, she is despised by all. . . . O, cruel censure! what must be the sensations of oppressed innocence, . . . when they have tried every expedient to obtain employment, though to no effect?

from *Part Second. Which demonstrates that the Frailty of Female Virtue more frequently originates from embarrassed Circumstances, than from a depravity of Disposition.*

[Orphan Girls]

Pitiable object! thy fate seems hard indeed: yet so it but too frequently happens to hundreds. . . . Where wilt thou go, to secure thee from real want? A parish workhouse is but a poor consolation for so great a loss, at a period when neither reason nor religion is ripened into maturity, to moderate the grievance. But, if, perhaps, a friend step forward, the Asylum for the protection of Orphan Girls may receive the poor fugitive; in which blessed and happy institution, through time, the memory of her woeful loss, in parents and provision, may, in some degree, be wiped away in the benevolence of her new protectors, who not only provide for her temporal, but also for her spiritual concerns, in instructing her as a good Christian and a useful member. But, alas! small is the number which this institution can admit, when compared with the vast numbers left in similar situations. And for those, who are more advanced in age, to what standard can they repair? It is true, necessity will teach people to exert themselves, who have nothing but their own industry to depend upon, and consequently they seek for a female occupation. But how great their surprise, and inexpressible their grief, to find, like the rest, that they are repulsed in every pursuit of industry, whereby they might expect a maintenance! . . . Were there a capacious establishment for industry, built upon such a basis as would form a discrimination between the well-bred female, who is reduced by the unseen hand of fate, and the very poor and abject, whose birth has deprived them of the knowledge of refinement or delicacy; what crouds of unprovided women would flock to the standard! . . .

Where do we see the father or mother of a family, with an independent fortune, be it ever so small, who would not be shocked at the bare idea of placing their daughter in the world in such situations as would enable them to rise, through their own industry and merit, or fit them for becoming wives to some honest and industrious tradesman?—No: that would be a degradation which must not take place. It is the etiquette of the times for the daughters to be bred fine ladies, although it be without a fortune, either dependent or independent, to support it.

As for trade, that is out of the question. The sons indeed are differently provided: the eldest, in course, inherits the paternal estate, and the younger ones are placed in the church, the army, the navy, or at the bar; and others, again are genteelly situated in the mercantile world: the whole of which are fit professions for a gentleman, and by which, if they have merit and success, they may acquire a competency.

But for the female part of the family, what appears in their favour? what prospects have they in life?—The parents die, and leave them, without a provision, a burden upon their connections; which forms the first step to deprive them of friends as well as subsistence. A miserable inheritance, to be their best and only portion! What can be said in behalf of such parents? can their easy compliance with the fashion of the times form any apology for such a mistaken conduct?—This surely cannot be called true paternal affection, to entail upon these helpless young creatures such a succession of misery as must eventually ensue. . . .

Have we not had sufficient proofs, that the happiness and welfare of mortals have at all times been thought worthy the attention of a Briton. Witness the poor slaves; what exertions have not been used by the humane friends of liberty in their behalf? Yet less, much less, are their sufferings to be lamented than the poor females I speak of, who have been bred up and educated in the school of Christianity, and fostered by the tender hand of Care.

The slave is little acquainted with the severe pangs a virtuous mind labours under, when driven to the extreme necessity of forfeiting their virtue for bread. The slave cannot feel the pain at the loss of reputation, a term of which they never heard, and much less know the meaning. What are the untutored, wild imaginations of a slave, when put in the balance with the distressing sensations of a British female, who has received a refined, if not a classical, education, and is capable of the finest feelings the human heart is susceptible of. A slave, through want of education, has little more refinement than cattle in the field; nor can they know the want of what they never enjoyed, or were taught to expect; but a poor female, who has received the best instruction, and is endowed with a good understanding, what must not she feel in mind, independent of her corporeal wants, after the adversity of fate has set her up as a mark, for the ridicule, the censure, and contempt of the world? Her feelings cannot be described, nor her sufferings sufficiently lamented.

I recollect some observations, made some years ago, by a late honourable, humane, learned, and truly worthy member of the House of Commons,[8] respecting the business of the slave-trade, which doubly confirms my opinion of the great necessity there is for an investigation into the grievances I have been speaking of, since it leads to a clear demonstration, that the most judicious and benevolent may still remain in the dark, as to the sufferings of our Christian slaves at home.

"There is," said the honourable gentleman, "no state in human nature but had its compensations. What was a slave? a happy slave was a degraded man; his happiness consisted in having no thought of the past, or the future, and this deficiency of mind it was which lessened the dignity of man, and conferred happiness on the African."

A very striking and just observation, with regard to the African, it must be granted; yet I cannot but differ in opinion, when it is said, that all mankind are capable of a compensation. For, admitting the same mode of reasoning to stand good, if the oppressions of one part of the creation are moderated through their ignorance, how much must the other be heightened by their sensibility and the refinements of education. Nor can I see the smallest trait of compensation remaining for these miserable females, since the very education they have received in youth, redounds to their misfortunes in maturity.

Then, if an investigation into the business of the slave-trade has been founded on such humane and generous principles, how much greater pleasure must it give the feeling heart, to patronize the poor, unfortunate women of our own nation, who labour under the very worst kind of slavery, and must continue to languish under the fetters of a painful bondage, till death, or the kindly hand of interference, has severed the chain?

Hannah More (1745–1833)

Hannah More came from a High Church–Tory family, and though she would turn Evangelical and become a vigorous abolitionist, her politics were solidly centrist. In Village Politics *(1792), she criticized the French*

[8]Mr. Burke [Wakefield's note]; i.e., Edmund Burke, who opposed slavery.

*Revolution and the "Rights of Man," hewing to the Evangelical line that the lot of the poor was to be improved by philanthropy, hard work, and faith in ultimate salvation. "Rights of women! We shall be hearing of the Rights of Children next!" she scoffed on hearing of Wollstonecraft's Vin-*dication of the Rights of Woman. *Yet she shared many of its principles: the value of female rationality, modesty, chastity, and "practical education" over trivial "accomplishments" like needlework, painting, dancing, and musical performance. As a child, she was educated at home by her father, a schoolmaster in a poorly endowed charity school at Stapleton, near Bristol. She was regarded as the "genius" of the family, notable for her ability to learn (her father refused to teach her any more mathematics when she outstripped all his male students) and to write. As a young woman, she came to London and entered a lively literary world, becoming friends with Samuel Johnson, actor David Garrick, and Horace Walpole, as well as the women of the Bluestocking Club, celebrated in her long poem* The Bas Bleu *(1786). She was a successful writer even before she gained an annuity of £200 in compensation for a reneged marriage engagement; with this income she was able to live independently, never marrying, and devoting herself to philanthropy and writing, the latter with considerable financial success. In 1795, she began the project that would bring her lasting fame. Wishing to reach the illiterate poor of England, she published between 1795 and 1799 a series of over 100 stories, ballads, and songs in the format of the popular broadsides of the day. Her purpose, as she wrote in the advertisement, was "to improve the habits, and raise the principles of the common people . . . not only to counteract vice and profligacy on the one hand, but error, discontent, and false religion on the other." These* Cheap Repository Tracts, *which sold for no more than a halfpenny, were enormously popular. Bought by churchmen and aristocrats for their parishioners and tenants, they reached every corner of England; missionaries carried them abroad to Africa and India. By March 1796, over two million copies had been sold.*

After 1799, More devoted herself to writing educational and Evangelical religious tracts. Strictures on the Modern System of Female Education; with a View of the Principles and Conduct Prevalent among Women of Rank and Fortune *appeared in 1799. This influential treatise on the education of women assumed that there was an innate difference between the sexes and the social roles they should perform, but nonetheless endorsed Wollstonecraft's view that women were rational and should be educated to develop their intellectual and moral capacities to the fullest.* Strictures *sets a didactic curriculum, arguing for rational education, Christian virtue, and the role of women in public life: "the care of the poor is her profession."*

from *Strictures on the Modern System of Female Education* (1799)

from "Introduction"

It is a singular injustice which is often exercised towards women, first to give them a very defective education, and then to expect from them the most undeviating purity of conduct;—to train them in such a manner as shall lay them open to the most dangerous faults, and then to censure them for not proving faultless. Is it not unreasonable and unjust, to express disappointment if our daughters should, in their subsequent lives, turn out precisely that very kind of character for which it would be evident to an unprejudiced by-stander that the whole scope and tenour of their instruction had been systematically preparing them?

Some reflections on the present erroneous system are here with great deference submitted to public consideration. The author is apprehensive that she shall be accused of betraying the interests of her sex by laying open their defects; but surely an earnest wish to turn their attention to objects calculated to promote their true dignity, is not the office of an enemy. So to expose the weakness of the land, as to suggest the necessity of internal improvement, and to point out the means of effectual defence, is not treachery, but patriotism. . . .

Let it not be suspected that the author arrogantly conceives *herself* to be exempt from that natural corruption of the heart which it is one chief object of this slight work to exhibit; that she superciliously erects herself into the impeccable censor of her sex and of the world; as if from the critic's chair she were coldly pointing out the faults and errors of another order of beings, in whose welfare she had not that lively interest which can only flow from the tender and intimate participation of fellow-feeling.

Bath, March 14, 1799

from *Chapter 8. On Female Study*

Will it not be ascribed to a captious singularity, if I venture to remark that real knowledge and real piety, though they may have gained in many instances, have suffered in others from that profusion of little, amusing, sentimental books with which the youthful library overflows? Abundance has its dangers as well as scarcity. In the first place, may not the multiplicity of these alluring little works increase the natural reluctance to those more dry and uninteresting studies, of which, after all, the rudiments of every part of learning *must* consist? And, secondly, is there not some danger (though there are many honourable exceptions) that some of those engaging narratives may serve to infuse into the youthful heart a sort of spurious goodness, a confidence of virtue, a parade of charity? And that the benevolent actions with the recital of which they abound, when they are not made to flow from any source but *feeling,* may tend to inspire a self-complacency, a self-gratulation, a "stand by, for I am holier than thou?" May not the success with which the good deeds of the little heroes are uniformly crowned; the invariable reward which is made the instant concomitant of well-doing, furnish the young reader with false views of the condition of life, and the nature of the divine dealings with men? May they not help to suggest a false standard of morals, to infuse a love of popularity and an anxiety for praise, in the place of that simple and unostentatious rule of doing whatever good we do, *because it is the will of God?* The universal substitution of this principle would tend to purify the worldly morality of many a popular little story. And there are few dangers which good parents will more carefully guard against than that of giving their children a mere political piety; that sort of religion which just goes to make people more respectable, and to stand well with the world; a religion which is to save appearances without inculcating realities; a religion which affects to "preach peace and good will to men," but which forgets to give "glory to God in the highest."[1]

There is a certain precocity of mind which is much helped on by these superficial modes of instruction; for frivolous reading will produce its correspondent effect, in much less time than books of solid instruction; the imagination being liable to be worked upon, and the feelings to be set a going, much faster than the understanding can be opened and the judgment enlightened. A talent for conversation should be the result of instruction, not its precursor: it is a golden fruit when suffered to ripen gradually on the tree of knowledge; but if forced in the hot-bed of a circulating library,[2] it will turn out worthless and vapid in proportion as it was artificial and premature.

---

[1] An ingenious (and in many respects useful) French Treatise on Education has too much encouraged this political piety [More's note; her quotations are from Luke 2:14].

[2] Lending libraries that flourished from the 1790s carried stores of popular fiction, much of it written by and for women.

Girls who have been accustomed to devour a multitude of frivolous books, will converse and write with a far greater appearance of skill, as to style and sentiment, at twelve or fourteen years old, than those of a more advanced age, who are under the discipline of severer studies; but the former having early attained to that low standard which had been held out to them, become stationary; while the latter, quietly progressive, are passing through just gradations to a higher strain of mind; and those who early begin with talking and writing like women, commonly end with thinking and acting like children.

I would not, however, prohibit such works of imagination as suit this early period. When moderately used, they serve to stretch the faculties and expand the mind; but I should prefer works of vigorous genius and pure unmixed fable to many of those tame and more affected moral stories, which are not grounded on Christian principle. I should suggest the use, on the one hand, of original and acknowledged fictions; and, on the other, of accurate and simple facts; so that truth and fable may ever be kept separate and distinct in the mind. . . .

This suggestion is, however, by no means intended to exclude works of taste and imagination, which must always make the ornamental part, and of course a very considerable part of female studies. It is only intimated, that they should not form them entirely and exclusively. For what is called dry tough reading, independent of the knowledge it conveys, is useful as a habit, and wholesome as an exercise. Serious study serves to harden the mind for more trying conflicts; it lifts the reader from sensation to intellect; it abstracts her from the world and its vanities; it fixes a wandering spirit and fortifies a weak one; it divorces her from matter; it corrects that spirit of trifling which she naturally contracts from the frivolous turn of female conversation and the petty nature of female employments. . . .

Far be it from me to desire to make scholastic ladies or female dialecticians; but there is little fear that the kind of books here recommended, if thoroughly studied, and not superficially skimmed, will make them pedants, or induce conceit; for by showing them the possible powers of the human mind, you will bring them to see the littleness of their own: and surely to get acquainted with the mind, to regulate, to inform it; to show it its own ignorance and its own weakness, does not seem the way to puff it up. But let her who is disposed to be elated with her literary acquisitions check the rising vanity by calling to mind the just remark of Swift, "that after all her boasted acquirements, a woman will, generally speaking, be found to possess less of what is called learning than a common school-boy."[3]

Neither is there any fear that this sort of reading will convert ladies into authors. The direct contrary effect will be likely to be produced by the perusal of writers who throw the generality of readers at such an unapproachable distance as to check presumption, instead of exciting it. Who are those ever-multiplying authors, that with unparalleled fecundity are overstocking the world with their quick-succeeding progeny? They are NOVEL-WRITERS: the easiness of whose productions is at once the cause of their own fruitfulness, and of the almost infinitely numerous race of imitators to whom they give birth. Such is the frightful facility of this species of composition, that every raw girl, while she reads, is tempted to fancy that she can also write. And as Alexander, on perusing the Iliad, found by congenial sympathy the image of Achilles stamped on his own ardent soul, and felt himself the hero he was studying; and as Corregio, on first beholding a picture which exhibited the perfection of the graphic art, prophetically felt all his own future greatness, and cried out in rapture, "And I, too, am a painter!" so a thorough-paced novel-reading Miss, at the close of every tissue of hackneyed adventures, feels within herself the stirring impulse of corresponding genius, and triumphantly exclaims, "And I, too, am an author!" The glutted imagination soon overflows with the redundance of cheap sentiment and plentiful incident, and by a sort of arithmetical proportion, is enabled by the perusal of any three novels, to produce a fourth; till every fresh production, like the prolific progeny of Banquo, is followed by "Another, and another, and another!"[4] Is a lady, however destitute of talents, education, or knowledge of the world, whose studies have been completed by a circulating library, in any distress of mind? the writing a novel suggests itself as the best soother of her sorrows! Does she labour under any depression of circumstances? writing a novel occurs as the readiest receipt for mending them! and she solaces her imagination with the conviction that the

---

[3]From *Letter to a Young Lady* (1727) by Jonathan Swift: "Those who are commonly called Learned Women have lost all manner of Credit by their impertinent Talkativeness and Conceit of themselves; but there is an easy remedy for this, if you once consider, that after all the pains you may be at, you can never arrive in point of learning to the perfection of a School-boy."

[4]References are to the famous anecdote of Alexander the Great's sympathy with the Greek hero Achilles in Homer's epic of the Trojan War; to the Italian Renaissance painter; and to the vision of Banquo's royal heirs that frustrates Macbeth (4.1).

subscription which has been extorted by her importunity, or given to her necessities, has been offered as a homage to her genius; and this confidence instantly levies a fresh contribution for a succeeding work. Capacity and cultivation are so little taken into the account, that writing a book seems to be now considered as the only sure resource which the idle and the illiterate have always in their power.

May the Author be indulged in a short digression, while she remarks, though rather out of its place, that the corruption occasioned by these books has spread so wide, and descended so low, as to have become one of the most universal, as well as most pernicious, sources of corruption among us. Not only among milliners, mantua-makers, and other trades where numbers work together, the labour of one girl is frequently sacrificed that she may be spared to read those mischievous books to the others; but she has been assured by clergymen who have witnessed the fact, that they are procured and greedily read in the wards of our hospitals! an awful hint, that those who teach the poor to read, should not only take care to furnish them with principles which will lead them to abhor corrupt books, but that they should also furnish them with such books as shall strengthen and confirm their principles.[5]

from Chapter 14. The Practical Use of Female Knowledge, with a Sketch of the Female Character, and a Comparative View of the Sexes

The chief end to be proposed, in cultivating the understandings of women is to qualify them for the practical purposes of life. Their knowledge is not often, like the learning of men, to be reproduced in some literary composition, and never in any learned profession; but it is to come out in conduct: it is to be exhibited in life and manners. A lady studies, not that she may qualify herself to become an orator or a pleader; not that she may learn to debate, but to act. She is to read the best books, not so much to enable her to talk to them, as to

---

[5]The above facts furnish no argument on the side of those who would keep the poor in ignorance. Those who cannot *read* can *hear,* and are likely to hear to worse purpose than those who have been better taught. And that ignorance furnishes no security for integrity either in morals or politics, the late revolts in more than one country, remarkable for the ignorance of the poor, fully illustrate. It is earnestly hoped that the above facts may tend to impress ladies with the importance of superintending the instruction of the poor, and of making it an indispensable part of their charity to give them moral and religious books [More's note].

bring the improvement which they furnish to the rectification of her principles and the formation of her habits. The great uses of study to a woman are to enable her to regulate her own mind, and to be instrumental to the good of others. . . .

But there is one *human* consideration which would perhaps more effectually tend to damp in an aspiring woman the ardours of literary vanity—I speak not of real genius, though there the remark often applies—than any which she will derive from motives of humility, or propriety, or religion; which is, that in the judgment passed on her performances, she will have to encounter the mortifying circumstance of having her sex always taken into account, and her highest exertions will probably be received with the qualified approbation *that it is really extraordinary for a woman.* Men of learning, who are naturally disposed to estimate works in proportion as they appear to be the result of art, study, and institution, are inclined to consider even the happier performances of the other sex as the spontaneous productions of a fruitful but shallow soil, and to give them the same kind of praise which we bestow on certain salads, which often draw from us a sort of wondering commendation, not, indeed, as being worth much in themselves, but because, by the lightness of the earth, and a happy knack of the gardener, these indifferent cresses spring up in a night, and therefore we are ready to wonder they are no worse.

As to men of sense, however, they need be the less hostile to the improvement of the other sex, as they themselves will be sure to be gainers by it; the enlargement of the female understanding being the most likely means to put an end to those petty and absurd contentions for equality which female smatterers so anxiously maintain. I say smatterers, for between the first class of both sexes the question is much more rarely and always more temperately agitated. Cooperation, and not competition, is, indeed, the clear principle we wish to see reciprocally adopted by those higher minds in each sex which really approximate the nearest to each other. The more a woman's understanding is improved, the more obviously she will discern that there can be no happiness in any society where there is a perpetual struggle for power; and the more her judgment is rectified, the more accurate views will she take of the station she was born to fill, and the more readily will she accommodate herself to it. . . .

There is this singular difference between a woman vain of her wit, and a woman vain of her beauty; . . . she who is vain of her genius, more liberal at least in her vanity, is jealous for the honour of her whole sex, and contends for the equality of their pretensions as a body, in which she feels that her own are involved as an individual. The beauty vindicates her own rights, the wit the rights of women; . . . and while the more selfish though more moderate beauty "would but be Queen for life," the public-spirited wit struggles to abrogate the Salique law of intellect, and to enthrone "a whole sex of Queens."[6]

At the revival of letters in the sixteenth and the following century, the controversy about this equality was agitated with more warmth than wisdom; and the process was instituted and carried on, on the part of the female complainant, with that sort of acrimony which always raises a suspicion of the justice of any cause; for violence commonly implies doubt, and invective indicates weakness rather than strength. . . . Among the innovations of this innovating period, the imposing term of *rights* has been produced to sanctify the claim of our female pretenders,[7] with a view not only to rekindle in the minds of women a presumptuous vanity, dishonourable to their sex, but produced with a view to excite in their hearts an impious discontent with the post which God has assigned them in this world.[8]

But *they* little understand the true interests of woman who would lift her from the important duties of her allotted station, to fill, with fantastic dignity, a loftier but less appropriate niche. Nor do they understand her true happiness, who seek to annihilate distinctions from which she derives advantages, and to attempt innovations which would depreciate her real value. Each sex has its proper excellences, which would be lost were they melted down into the common character by the fusion of the new philosophy. Why should we do away distinctions which increase the mutual benefits and enhance the satisfactions of life? Whence, but by carefully preserving the original marks of difference, stamped by the hand of the Creator, would be derived the superior advantage of mixed society? Is either sex so

[6]Pope's *Epistle II,* "of the Characters of Women," assumes that "ev'ry Lady would be Queen for life" and shudders at the thought of "a whole Sex of Queens! / Pow'r all their end" (218–20). Salique (Salic) law, deriving from old French law, excludes females from the line of succession to a throne.

[7]False claimants, especially to a throne; More is also suggesting "fantasizers" and dissemblers.

[8]This was written soon after the publication of a work intitled "The Rights of Woman" [More's note, referring to Wollstonecraft's *Vindication of the Rights of Woman*].

abounding in perfection, as to be independent on the other for improvement? Have men no need to have their rough angles filed off, and their harshnesses and asperities smoothed and polished by assimilating with beings of more softness and refinement? Are the ideas of women naturally so *very* judicious, are their principles so *invincibly* firm, are their views so *perfectly* correct, are their judgments so *completely* exact, that there is occasion for no additional weight, no superadded strength, no increased clearness, none of that enlargement of mind, none of that additional invigoration, which may be derived from the aids of the stronger sex? What identity could advantageously supersede such an enlivening opposition, such an interesting variety of character? . . .

Natural propensities best mark the designations of Providence as to their application. The fin was not more clearly bestowed on the fish that he should swim, nor the wing given to the bird that he should fly, than superior strength of body and a firmer texture of mind were given to man, that he might preside in the deep and daring scenes of action and of council; in the complicated arts of government, in the contention of arms, in the intricacies and depths of science, in the bustle of commerce, and in those professions which demand a higher reach and a wider range of powers. The true value of woman is not diminished by the imputation of inferiority in those talents which do not belong to her, of those qualities in which her claim to excellence does not consist. She has other requisites, better adapted to answer the end and purposes of her being, from "Him who does all things well;" who suits the agent to the action; who accommodates the instrument to the work.

Let not, then, aspiring, because ill-judging, woman view with pining envy the keen satirist, hunting vice through all the doublings and windings of the heart; the sagacious politician, leading senates, and directing the fate of empires; the acute lawyer, detecting the obliquities of fraud; and the skilful dramatist, exposing the pretensions of folly; but let her ambition be consoled by reflecting, that those who thus excel, to all that Nature bestows and books can teach, must add besides that consummate knowledge of the world to which a delicate woman has no fair avenues, and which, even if she could attain, she would never be supposed to have come honestly by.

In almost all that comes under the description of polite letters, in all that captivates by vivid imagery or warms by just and affecting sentiment, women are excellent. They possess in a high degree that delicacy and quickness of perception, and that nice discernment between the beautiful and defective which comes under the denomination of taste. Both in composition and in action they excel in details; but they do not so much generalise their ideas as men, nor do their minds seize a great subject with so large a grasp. They are acute observers, and accurate judges of life and manners, as far as their own sphere of observation extends, but they describe a smaller circle. A woman sees the world, as it were, from a little elevation in her own garden, whence she makes an exact survey of home scenes, but takes not in that wider range of distant prospects which he who stands on a loftier eminence commands.

William Thompson (1775–1833) and Anna Wheeler (1785–post 1848)

Karl Marx's Manifesto of the Communist Party, *published in 1848, assured proletarians that they "have nothing to lose but their chains" and closed with the call, "Working Men of All Countries, Unite!" In these ringing phrases, English socialists heard a striking echo of the "Address to Women" that concluded William Thompson and Anna Wheeler's Appeal: "Women of England! women, in whatever country ye breathe—wherever ye breathe, degraded—awake! . . . O wretched slaves of such wretched masters! Awake, arise, shake off these fetters!" The work of two leading socialists of the 1820s,* Appeal of One Half the Human Race, Women, Against the Pretensions of the Other Half, Men, to Retain Them in Political, and Thence in Civil and Domestic Slavery *is the most important English feminist document between Wollstonecraft's* Vindication *(1792) and John Stuart Mill's* Subjection of Women *(1869).*

Born into Protestant Irish gentry, Thompson came of age during the tumultuous era of the French Revolution. At his father's death in 1814, he inherited a thousand-acre estate and prosperous businesses, including a fleet of trading vessels. He did not fall into step with Protestant capitalism, however, but agitated for Catholic Emancipation, denounced the division between laborers and "idle classes," and experimented with socialist alternatives, including organizing the seven hundred vagrants on the family estate into a highly successful community. He then went to London, where he befriended leading social theorists John Stuart Mill, Jeremy Bentham, and Robert Owen. He published books on labor and wealth, including An

Inquiry into the Principles of the Distribution of Wealth Most Conducive to Human Happiness, Applied to the Newly Proposed System of Voluntary Equality of Wealth *(1824)*. *Another London friend was Wheeler, whose family, like his, was Irish gentry. A "reigning beauty" in her youth, at fifteen she married a pampered Irish nobleman, bore six children (only two surviving infancy), and still found time to read widely, especially in philosophy and social theory. Increasingly disaffected from her idle, heavily drinking husband, she left him in 1812, eventually heading for London and France, where she met leading socialists and feminists. A dynamic figure in the movement for women's rights, she struck Benjamin Disraeli as "very clever, but awfully revolutionary."*

Thompson and Wheeler were dismayed over the indifference of some of their socialist friends to women's rights. Some were even opposed—for instance, Bentham's disciple, James Mill, whose Article on Government for the 1824 Encyclopaedia Britannica, *published as a separate pamphlet in 1825, argued against political representation for women, contending that their interests were "involved" and "included" with their fathers' or their husbands' and had no separate claim. Thompson and Wheeler's refutations appeared the same year. Only Thompson's name was on the title page, but his introduction credited Wheeler as coauthor: He was the scribe of their "feelings, sentiments, and reasonings" and the work was their "joint property." Patently allied with Wollstonecraft,* Appeal *expands its social analysis into a critique of the underlying economic system. As the full title suggests, it also expands Wollstonecraft's discourse of female slavery. Blunt comparisons of English women to Turkish harem slaves and New World plantation slaves ally the polemic with the moral consensus fueling the expanding movement for the abolition of colonial slavery.*

from *Appeal of One Half the Human Race, Women, Against the Pretensions of the Other Half, Men, to Retain Them in Political, and Thence in Civil and Domestic Slavery* (1825)

> "'Tis all stern duty on the female side;
> On man's, mere sensual gust and surly pride."[1]

---

[1] A slight misquotation of Dryden's *Palamon and Arcite; or, The Knight's Tale, From Chaucer* (3.230–31) in *Fables Ancient and Modern; Translated into Verse* (1700); the virgin Emily begs the goddess Cynthia to accept her as a votress, pleading, "Like Death, thou know'st, I loath the Nuptial state, / And Man, the Tyrant of our Sex, I hate, / A lowly Servant, but a lofty Mate. / Where Love is Duty, on the Female side; / On theirs meer sensual Gust, and sought with surly Pride" (227–32); "Gust" is appetite. In *Rights of Woman*, ch. VI, Wollstonecraft quotes 230–31 correctly, using these lines to gloss the lack of "satisfaction" that any woman of delicate affections would confront "in a union with such a man."

from "Introductory Letter to Mrs. Wheeler"

The days of dedication and patronage are gone by. It is *not* with the view of obtaining the support of your name or your influence to the cause of truth and humanity that these lines are addressed to you. . . . I address you then simply to perform towards you a debt of justice. . . . Anxious that you should take up the cause of your proscribed sex, and state to the world in writing, in your own name, what you have so often and so well stated in conversation, and under feigned names in such of the periodical publications of the day as would tolerate such a theme, I long hesitated to arrange our common ideas, even upon a branch of the subject like the present. Anxious that the hand of a woman should have the honor of raising from the dust that neglected banner which a woman's hand nearly thirty years ago unfolded boldly, in face of the prejudices of thousands of years, and for which a woman's heart bled, and her life was all but the sacrifice—I hesitated to write. Were courage the quality wanting, you would have shown, what every day's experience proves, that women have more fortitude in endurance than men. Were comprehensiveness of mind, above the narrow views which too often marred Mary Wolstonecroft's [*sic*] pages and narrowed their usefulness, the quality wanting,—above the timidity and impotence of conclusion accompanying the gentle eloquence of Mary Hays, addressed, about the same time that Mary Wolstonecroft wrote, in the shape of an *"Appeal"* to the then closed ears of unreasoning men[2]; yours was the eye which no prejudice obscured, open to the rays of truth from whatever quarter they might emanate. But leisure and resolution to undertake the drudgery of the task were wanting. A few only therefore of the following pages are the exclusive produce of your mind and pen, and written with your own hand. The remainder are our joint property, I being your interpreter and the scribe of your sentiments. . . .

You look forward, as I do, to a state of society very different from that which now exists, in which the effort of all is to out wit, supplant, and snatch from each other; where interest is systematical-

[2]Mary Hays, disciple and friend of Wollstonecraft, published her feminist polemic, *Appeal to the Men of Great Britain in Behalf of Women* anonymously in 1798, by which time Wollstonecraft was a scandal and the English political climate increasingly conservative as it confronted growing social unrest at home and the emergence of Napoleon abroad. Despite her numerous defenses of Wollstonecraft, Hays felt it unwise to include her in her *Female Biography, or Memoirs of Illustrious and Celebrated Women of All Ages and Countries* (1803).

ly opposed to duty; where the so-called system of morals is little more than a mass of hypocrisy preached by knaves, unpractised by them, to keep their slaves, male as well as female, in blind uninquiring obedience; and where the whole motley fabric is kept together by fear and blood. You look forward to a better aspect of society, where the principle of benevolence shall supersede that of fear; where restless and anxious individual competition shall give place to mutual co-operation and joint possession; where individuals in large numbers, male and female, forming voluntary associations, shall become a mutual guarantee to each other for the supply of all useful wants, and form an unsalaried and uninsolvent insurance company against all insurable casualties; where perfect freedom of opinion and perfect equality will reign amongst the co-operators; and where the children of all will be equally educated and provided for by the whole, even these children longer the slaves of individual caprice.

In truth, under the present arrangements of society, the principle of individual competition remaining, as it is, the master-key and moving principle of the whole social organization, *individual* wealth the great object sought after by all, and the quantum of happiness of each individual (other things being equal) depending on the quantum of wealth, the means of happiness, possessed by each; it seems impossible—even were all unequal legal and unequal moral restraints removed, and were no secret current of force or influence exerted to baffle new regulations of equal justice—that women should attain to equal happiness with men. Two circumstances—permanent inferiority of strength, and occasional loss of time in gestation and rearing infants—must eternally render the average exertions of women in the race of the competition for wealth less successful than those of men. The pleasant compensation that men now affect to give for these two natural sources of inferior accumulation of wealth on the part of women (aggravated a thousand degrees by their exclusions from knowledge and almost all means of useful exertions, (the very lowest only excepted)), is the existing system of marriage; under which, for the mere faculty of eating, breathing and living, in whatever degree of comfort husbands may think fit, women are reduced to domestic slavery, without will of their own, or power of locomotion, otherwise than as permitted by their respective masters. . . .

With you I would equally elevate both sexes. Really enlightened women, disdaining equally the submissive tricks of the slave and the caprices of the despot, breathing freely only in the air of the esteem of equals, and of mutual, *unbought, uncommanded,* affection, would find it difficult to meet with associates worthy of them in men as now formed, full of ignorance and vanity, priding themselves on a *sexual* superiority, entirely independent of any merit, any superior qualities, or pretensions to them, claiming respect from the strength of their arm and the lordly faculty of producing beards attached by nature to their chins! No: unworthy of, as incapable of appreciating, the delight of the society of such women, are the great majority of the existing race of men. The pleasures of mere animal appetite, the pleasures of commanding (the prettier and more helpless the slave, the greater these pleasures of the brute), are the only pleasures which the majority of men seek for from women, are the only pleasures which their education and the hypocritical system of morals with which they have been necessarily imbued, permit them to expect. . . .

Even under the present arrangements of society, founded as they all are on the basis of individual competition, nothing could be more easy than to put the *rights* of women, political and civil, on a perfect equality with those of men. It is only to abolish all prohibitory and exclusive laws,—statute or what are called "common,"—the remnants of the barbarous customs of our ignorant ancestors; particularly the horrible and odious inequality and indissolubility of that disgrace of civilization, the present marriage code. Women then might exert in a free career with men their faculties of mind and body, to whatever degree developed, in pursuit of happiness by means of exertion, as men do. But this would not raise women to an equality of happiness with men: their rights might be equal, but not their happiness, because unequal powers under free competition must produce unequal effects.

In truth, the system of the most enlightened of the school of those reformers called political economists, is still founded on exclusions. Its basis is too narrow for human happiness. A more comprehensive system, founded on equal benevolence, on the true development of the principle of Utility, is wanting.[3] Let the *competitive* political economists be satisfied with the praise of causing the removal of some of the rubbish of ignorant restrictions, under the name of laws,

[3]The philosophy of utilitarianism, formulated by contemporaries Jeremy Bentham and James Mill, that there is no inherent right and wrong; the only issue is consequence, whether an action contributes to "the happiness of man."

impeding the development of human exertion in the production of wealth. To build up a new fabric of social happiness, comprehending equally the interests of all existing human beings, has never been contemplated by them, and is altogether beyond the scope of their little theories; aiming at the utmost at increasing the number of what they style the happy middling orders, but leaving the great bulk of human beings to eternal ignorance and toil, requited by the mere means of prolonging from day to day an unhealthy and precarious existence. To a new science, the *social science,* or the science of promoting human happiness, that of political economy, or the mere science of producing wealth by individual competition, must give way.

from *Part 2*
[On Daughters]

Business, professions, political concerns, local affairs, the whole field of sciences and arts, are open to the united and mutually sympathizing efforts of the males. To their mutual judgments and speculations, the disposal of the family income and capital are intrusted. From all these commanding sources of intellectual and muscular activity, the daughters, like the little children, are excluded, previous care having been taken, by shutting them out from all means of intellectual culture, and from the view of and participation in the real incidents of active life, to render them as unfit for, as unambitious of, such high occupations. Confined, like other domestic animals, to the house and its little details, their "sober wishes" are never permitted "to stray" into the enlarged plains of general speculation and action. The dull routine of domestic incidents is the world to them. . . .

So much more completely is the interest of the sons involved than that of the daughters in the interest of fathers, that as soon as the daughters become adult, they, necessarily operated upon by the system under which they live, look out of their artificial cages of restraint and imbecility, to catch glances at the world with the hope of freedom from parental control, by leaving behind them the very name of their fathers, and vainly hoping for happiness without independence, in the gratification of one passion, love, round which their absurd training for blind male sensuality, has caused all their little anxieties to centre. The adult sons go in and out of the father's house when they choose: they are frequently treated with liberality as visitors or equals. But the adult daughters are, for the most part, under as much restraint as little children: they must ask leave to open the door or take a walk: not one of their actions that does not depend on the will of another: they are never permitted, like the sons, to regulate their conduct by their own notions of propriety and prudence and to restrain them where necessary, like rational beings, from a regard to their consequences: every thing is prescribed to them: their reason and foresight are not cultivated like those of the sons; and the despotism which creates their imbecility, adduces its own work as a justification of its unrelenting pressure and of its eternal duration. To marriage therefore, as the only means allowed them of emerging from paternal control; as the only means of gratifying one passion, to which all their thoughts have been exclusively directed, but which they are at the same time told it is highly improper they should wish to enjoy; as the only means of obtaining, through cunning and blandishment, that direction of their own voluntary actions, which all rational beings ought to possess, and which is the sure and only basis of intelligence and morals; to marriage, as the fancied haven of pleasure and freedom—the freedom of the slave to-be-sure, to be acquired not by right but by coaxing, by the influence of passions inapplicable to the cold despotism of the fathers—daughters look forward. No sooner adult, than their home and their name are daughters anxious to get rid of, because the retaining of them is made incompatible with the only views of happiness presented to them.

[On Wives]

By way of distinguishing and honoring this class of the proscribed half of the human race, man condescends to enter into what he calls a *contract* with certain women, for certain purposes, the most important of which is, the producing and rearing of children to maturity. Each man yokes a woman to his establishment, and calls it a *contract*. Audacious falsehood! A contract! where are any of the attributes of contracts, of equal and just contracts, to be found in this transaction? A contract implies the voluntary assent of both the contracting parties. Can even both the parties, man and woman, by agreement alter the terms, as to *indissolubility* and *inequality*, of this pretended contract? No. Can any individual man divest himself, were he even so inclined, of his power of despotic control? He cannot.

Have women been consulted as to the terms of this pretended contract? A contract, all of whose enjoyments—wherever nature has not imposed a physical bar on the depravity of selfishness—are on one side, while all of its pains and privations are on the other! A contract, giving all power, arbitrary will and unbridled enjoyment to the one side; to the other, unqualified obedience, and enjoyments meted out or withheld at the caprice of the ruling and enjoying party. Such a contract, as the owners of *slaves* in the West Indies and every other slave-polluted soil, enter into with their slaves—the law of the stronger imposed on the weaker, *in contempt* of the interests and wishes of the weaker. . . .

As soon as adult daughters become wives, their civil rights disappear; they fall back again, and remain all their lives—should their owners and directors live so long—into the state of children or idiots, the passive property of their owners; protected by the law in some few respects only, like other slaves, from the excessive abuse of despotic power.

Woman is then compelled, in marriage, by the possession of superior strength on the part of men, by the want of knowledge, skill and wealth, by the positive, cruel, partial, and cowardly enactments of law, by the terrors of superstition, by the mockery of a pretended vow of obedience, and to crown all, and as the result of all, by the force of an unrelenting, unreasoning, unfeeling, public opinion, to be the literal unequivocal *slave* of the man who may be styled her husband. I say emphatically the slave; for a slave is a person whose actions and earnings, instead of being, under his own control, liable only to equal laws, to public opinion, and to his own calculations, under these, of his own interest, are under the arbitrary control of any other human being, by whatever name called. This is the essence of slavery, and what distinguishes it from freedom. A domestic, a civil, a political slave, in the plain unsophisticated sense of the word—in no metaphorical sense—is every married woman. No matter with what wealth she may be surrounded, with what dainties she may be fed, with what splendor of trappings adorned, with what voluptuousness her corporeal, mental, or moral sweets may be gathered; that high prerogative of human nature, the faculty of self-government, the basis of intellectual development, without which no moral conduct can exist, is to her wanting. . . . Till laws afford married women the same protection against the restraints and violence of the men to whom they are married, that they affect to afford them against all other individuals; till they afford them the same protection against the restraints and violence of their husbands, that their husbands enjoy against their caprices and violence, the social condition of the civilized wife will remain more completely slavish than that of the female slave of the West Indies.

[Exhortation to Men]

Be consistent, men! Ye stronger half of the race, be at length rational! Three or four thousand years have worn threadbare your vile cloak of hypocrisy. Even women, your poor, weak, contented slaves, at whose impotence of penetration, the result of your vile exclusions, you have been accustomed to laugh, begin to see through it and to shudder at the loathsomeness beneath. Cast aside this tattered cloak before it leaves you naked and exposed. Clothe yourselves with the new garments of sincerity. Be rational human beings, not mere male sexual creatures. Cast aside the ferocious brute of your nature: give up the pleasures of the brute, those of mere lust and command, for the pleasures of the rational being. So shall you enjoy the love of your *equals*, enlightened, benevolent, graceful, like yourselves, founded on an appreciation of your real merits: so shall you be happy. For the intercourse of the *bought* prostitute, or of the *commanded* household slave, you shall have full and equal participation in the compounded and associated pleasures of sense, intellect and benevolence. To the highest enjoyments of which your nature is susceptible, there is no shorter road than the simple road of equal justice.

[What Do Women Want?]

The simple and modest request is, that they may be permitted equal enjoyments with men, *provided they can by the free and equal development and exercise of their faculties procure for themselves such enjoyments.* They ask the same means that men possess of acquiring every species of knowledge, of unfolding every one of their faculties of mind and body that can be made tributary to their happiness. They ask every facility of access to every art, occupation, profession, from the highest to the lowest, without one exception, to which their inclination and talents may direct and may fit them to occupy. They ask the removal of *all* restraints and exclusions not applicable to men of equal capacities. They ask for perfectly equal political, civil and domestic rights. They ask for equal obligations and equal punishments from the law with men in case of infraction of the same law by either party. They ask for an equal system of morals, founded on utility instead of caprice and unreasoning despotism, in which the same action attended with the same consequences, whether done by man or woman, should be attended with the same portion of approbation or disapprobation; in which every pleasure, accompanied or followed by no preponderant evil, should be equally permitted to women and to men; in which every pleasure accompanied or followed by preponderant evil should be equally censured in women and in men.

* * *

Women of England! women, in whatever country ye breathe—wherever ye breathe, degraded—awake! Awake to the contemplation of the happiness that awaits you when all your faculties of mind and body shall be fully cultivated and developed; when every path in which ye can exercise those improved faculties shall be laid open and rendered delightful to you, even as to them who now ignorantly enslave and degrade you. If degradation from long habitude have lost its sting, if the iron have penetrated so deeply into your frame that it has been gradually taken up into the system and mingles unperceived amidst the fluids of your life; if the prostration of reason and the eradication of feeling have kept pace within you, so that you are insensible alike to what you suffer and to what you might enjoy,—your case were all but hopeless. Nothing less, then, than the sight presented before your eyes, of the superior happiness enjoyed by other women, under arrangements of perfect equality with men, could arouse you. Such a sight, even under such circumstances, would excite your envy and kindle up all your extinct desires. But you are not so degraded. The unvaried despotism of so many thousand years, has not so entirely degraded you, has not been able to extinguish within you the feelings of nature, the love of happiness and of equal justice. The united exertions of law, superstition, and pretended morals of past ages of ignorance, have not entirely succeeded. . . .

Nor will your fellow-creatures, men, long resist the change. They are too deeply concerned to continue long to oppose what palpably tends to their happiness: they are too deeply concerned not to be compelled to re-consider the barbarous systems of law and morals under which they have been brought up. In justice, in pity to them, submit no longer; no longer *willingly* submit to their caprices. Though your bodies may be a little longer kept in servitude, degrade not yourselves by the repetition of superfluous vows of obedience: cease to kiss the rod: let your *minds* be henceforth free. The morn of loosening your physical chains will not be far distant.

O woman, from your auspicious hands may the new destiny of your species proceed! The collective voices of your sex raised against oppression will ultimately make men themselves your advocates and debtors. Reflect then seriously on your miserable and degraded position—your youth, your beauty, your feelings, your opinions, your actions, your time, your few years' fever of meritricious life—all made tributary to the appetites and passions of men. Whatever pleasures you enjoy, are permitted you for man's sake. Nothing is your own; protection of person and of property are alike withheld from you. Nothing is yours, but secret pangs, the bitter burning tears of regret, the stifled sobs of outraged nature thrown back upon your own hearts, where the vital principle itself stands checked, or is agitated with malignant passions, until body and mind become the frequent prey to overwhelming disease; now finding vent in sudden phrensy, now plunged in pining melancholy, or bursting the weak tenement of reason, seeking relief in self-destruction.

How many thousand of your sex *daily* perish thus unpitied and unknown; often victims of pressing want, always of privation and the arbitrary laws of heartless custom; condemned to cheerless solitude, or an idiot round of idle fashionable pursuits; your morning of life perhaps passed by, and with it the lingering darling hope of sympathy expired—puppets once of doting ignorant parents, whose tenderness for you outlived not your first youth; who, careless of your future fate, "launched you into life without an oar," indigent and ignorant, to eat the tear-steeped bread of dependence as wives, sisters, hired mistresses or unpitied prostitutes! This is the fate of the many, nay, of all your sex, subject only to those shades of difference arising from very peculiar circumstances or the accident of independent fortune; though even here the general want of knowledge, withheld from your sex, keeps even those individuals who are favored by fortune bowed to the relentless yoke which man's laws, his superstitions, and hypocritical morality, have prepared for you.

For once then instruct man in what is good, wash out the foul stain, equally disgraceful to both sexes—that your sex has unbounded influence in making men to do evil, but cannot induce them to do good.

How many Thaises are there, who, vain of the empire they hold over the passions of men, exercise at all risks this contemptible and pernicious influence—the only influence permitted them—in stimulating these masters of the world to destroy cities; and, regardless of the whispers of conscience and humanity, often shake men's tardy resolutions to repair the evils they have caused![4]—Shall none be found with sufficient knowledge and elevation of mind to persuade men to do good, to make the most certain step towards the regeneration of degraded humanity, by opening a free course for justice and benevolence, for intellectual and social enjoyments, by no colour, by no sex to be restrained? As your bondage has chained down man to the ignorance and vices of despotism, so will your liberation reward him with knowledge, with freedom and with happiness.[5]

---

[4]Probably the 4th-c. BCE Athenian courtesan, patronized by Alexander the Great and then by the King of Egypt; she was said to have accompanied Alexander on his conquests. Another Thais was a 1st-c. Alexandrian, famous for her beauty, wealth, and sexual indulgences, who repented and converted to Christianity and a life of piety.

[5]The last paragraph of *Appeal*.

Literary Sources for The Wrongs of Woman, or Maria

Jean-Jacques Rousseau (1712–1778)

Jean-Jacques Rousseau, one of the leading Enlightenment thinkers and proponents of the Revolution in France, aroused deeply ambivalent feelings in Wollstonecraft. She admired his argument in The Social Contract *(1762) that man was everywhere born free, but everywhere in chains. But she despised the chapter on "Sophy" in his novel of education,* Émile *(1762), which insists that females should be trained to obey and care for men, however unjust and irrational the men might be. His most famous and widely read epistolary novel,* Julie, ou la Nouvelle Héloïse *(1761), is a modernized retelling of the passionate but unconsummated love between the medieval monk Father Abelard and the nun Eloise. Through a series of letters, Rousseau's novel chronicles the love between a tutor, St. Preux, and his young pupil, Julie. Because of their disparity in class, the lovers attempt to conceal the relationship from Julie's family. When their secret is discovered, Julie follows her father's orders by renouncing her love for St. Preux and marrying the Baron Wolmar. For several years she fulfills the part of a model wife and loving mother. Then, after saving her youngest child from drowning, she falls ill and dies. Her final letter to St. Preux contains the acknowledgment that she has always loved him. Reading this novel, Wollstonecraft's Maria immediately identifies Darnford with St. Preux. The passages excerpted here begin after St. Preux has declared his love for Julie. In Letter IV—the heroine's first epistle— Julie writes to St. Preux, admitting her passion, and despairing that such a pronouncement has caused her to forsake her honor. Letter V is*

St. Preux's ecstatic response, and Letter XIV is his account of their kiss (see the illustration on p. 271).

from *Julie, ou la Nouvelle Héloïse* (1761)[1]

Letter IV

from Eloisa (to St. Preux)

Must I then, at last, confess the fatal, the ill-disguised secret! How often have I sworn that it should never burst from my heart but with my life! Thy danger wrests it from me. It is gone, and my honour is lost for ever. Alas! I have but too religiously performed my vow: can there be a death more cruel than to survive one's honour?

What shall I say? how shall I break the painful silence? or rather, have I not said all, and am I not already too well understood? Alas! thou hast seen too much not to divine the rest. Imperceptibly deluded into the snare of the seducer, I see, without being able to avoid it, the horrid precipice before me. Artful man! It is not thy passion, but mine, which excites thy presumption. Thou observest the distraction of my soul; thou availest thyself of it to accomplish my ruin; and, now thou hast rendered me despicable, my greatest misfortune is, that I am forced to behold thee also in a despicable light. Ungrateful wretch! In return for my esteem, thou hast ruined me. Had I supposed thy heart capable of exulting, believe me, thou hadst never enjoyed this triumph.

Well dost thou know, and it will increase thy remorse, that there was not in my soul one vicious inclination. My virtue and innocence were inexpressibly dear to me; and I pleased myself with the hopes of cherishing them in a life of industrious simplicity. But to what purpose my endeavour, since Heaven rejects my offering? The very first day we met, I imbibed the poison which now infects my senses and my reason; I felt it instantly, and thine eyes, thy sentiments, thy discourse, thy guilty pen, daily increase its malignity.

I have neglected nothing to stop the progress of this fatal passion. Sensible of my own weakness, how gladly would I have evaded the attack; but the eagerness of thy pursuit hath baffled my precaution. A thousand times I have resolved to cast myself at the feet of those who gave me being; a thousand times I have determined to open to them

[1]Trans. William Kenrick, *Eloisa, or a Series of Original Letters* (1764).

my guilty heart: but they can form no judgment of its condition; they would apply but common remedies to a desperate disease; my mother is weak and without authority; I know the inflexible severity of my father; and I should bring down ruin and dishonour upon myself, my family, and thee. My friend is absent; my brother is no more.

I have not a protector in the world to save me from the persecution of my enemy. In vain I implore the assistance of Heaven; Heaven is deaf to the prayers of irresolution. Every thing conspires to increase my anxiety—every circumstance combines to abandon me to myself, or rather cruelly to deliver me up to thee—all nature seems thy accomplice—my efforts are vain; I adore thee in spite of myself. And shall that heart which, in its full vigour, was unable to resist, shall it only half surrender? Shall a heart which knows no dissimulation attempt to conceal the poor remains of its weakness? No; the first step was the most difficult, and the only one which I ought never to have taken. Shall I now pretend to stop at the rest? No; that first false step plunged me into the abyss, and now my degree of misery is entirely in thy power.

Such is my horrid situation, that I am forced to turn to the author of my misfortunes, and implore his protection against himself. I might—I know I might—have deferred this confession of my despair; I might, for some time longer, have disguised my shameful weakness, and by yielding gradually, have imposed upon myself. Vain dissimulation! which could only have flattered my pride, but could not save my virtue. I see but too plainly whither my first error tends, and shall not endeavour to prepare for, but to escape, perdition.

Nevertheless, if thou art not the very lowest of mankind—if the least spark of virtue lives within thy soul—if it retain any vestige of those sentiments of honour which seemed to penetrate thy heart, thou canst not possibly be so vile as to take any unjust advantage of a confession forced from me by a fatal distraction of my senses. No; I know thee well: thou wilt support my weakness; thou wilt become my safeguard; thou wilt defend my person against my own heart. Thy virtue is the last refuge of my innocence; my honour dares confide in thine, for thou canst not preserve one without the other. Ah! let thy generous soul preserve them both, and, at least for thy own sake, be merciful.

Good God! am I thus sufficiently humbled? I write to thee on my knees; I bathe my paper with my tears; I pay to thee my timorous homage: and yet thou art not to believe me ignorant that it was in my power to have reversed the scene; and that, with a little art, which would have rendered me despicable in my own eyes, I might have been obeyed and worshipped. Take the frivolous empire, I relinquish it to my friend; but leave me, ah! leave me my innocence. I had rather live thy slave, and preserve my virtue, than purchase thy obedience at the price of my honour. . . .

Letter V

St. Preux to Eloisa

Celestial powers! I possessed a soul capable of affliction, O inspire me with one that can bear felicity! Divine love! spirit of my existence, O support me! for I sink down oppressed with ecstasy. How inexpressible are the charms of virtue! How invincible the power of a beloved object! Fortune, pleasure, transport, how poignant your impression! O, how shall I withstand the rapid torrent of bliss which overflows my heart, and how dispel the apprehensions of a timorous maid? Eloisa—no! my Eloisa on her knees! my Eloisa weep!—Shall she to whom the universe should bend, supplicate the man who adores her, to be careful of her honour, and to preserve his own? Were it possible for me to be out of humour with you, I should be a little angry at your fears; they are disgraceful to us both. Learn, thou chaste and heavenly beauty, to know better the nature of thy empire. If I adore thy charming person, is it not for the purity of that soul by which it is animated, and which bears such eneffable marks of its divine origin? You tremble with apprehension: Good God! what hath she to fear, who stamps with reverence and honour every sentiment she inspires? Is there a man upon earth who could be vile enough to offer the least insult to such virtue? Permit, O permit me, to enjoy the unexpected happiness of being beloved—beloved by such—Ye princes of the world, I now look down upon your grandeur. Let me read a thousand and a thousand times that enchanting epistle, where thy tender sentiments are painted in such strong and glowing colours; where I observe with transport, notwithstanding the violent agitation of thy soul, that even the most lively passions of a noble heart never lose sight of virtue. What monster, after having read that affecting letter, could take advantage of your generous confession, and attempt a crime which must infallibly make him wretched and despicable even to himself?

No, my dearest Eloisa, there can be nothing to fear from a friend, a lover, who must ever be incapable of deceiving you. Though I should entirely have lost my reason, though the discomposure of my senses should hourly increase, your person will always appear to me, not only the most beautiful, but the most sacred deposit with which mortal was ever intrusted. My passion, like its object, is unalterably pure. The horrid idea of incest does not shock me more than the thought of polluting your heavenly charms with a sacrilegious touch: you are not more inviolably safe with your own parent than with your lover. If ever that happy lover should in your presence forget himself but for a moment—O! it is impossible. When I am no longer in love with virtue, my love for Eloisa must expire; on my first offence, withdraw your affection, and cast me off for ever. . . .

Letter XIV

St. Preux to Eloisa

Ah! Eloisa, Eloisa! what have you done? You meant to reward me, and you are the cause of my ruin;—I am intoxicated or, rather, I am mad—My brains are turned—all my senses are disordered by this fatal kiss. You designed to alleviate my pain; but you have cruelly increased my torment. The poison I have imbibed from your lips will destroy me—my blood boils within my veins; I shall die, and your pity will but hasten my death.

O immortal remembrance of that illusive, frantic, and enchanting moment! Never, never to be effaced so long as Eloisa lives within my soul. Till my heart is deprived of all sensation, thou wilt continue to be the happiness and torment of my life! . . . we arrived at Clarens; my heart beat quick at the sight of my beloved Eloisa; her sweet voice caused a strange emotion; I became almost transported, and it was lucky for me that your cousin was present to engage your mother's attention. We rambled in the garden, dined comfortably, you found an opportunity, unperceived, to give me your charming letter, which I durst not open before this formidable witness: the sun began to decline, and we hastened to the woods for the benefit of the shade. Alas! I was quite happy, and I did not even conceive a state of greater bliss.

As we approached the bower, I perceived, not without a secret emotion, your significant winks, your mutual smiles, and the increasing glow in thy charming cheeks. Soon as we entered, I was surprised to see your cousin approach me, and, with an affected air of humility, ask me for a kiss. Without comprehending the mystery, I complied with her request; and, charming as she is, I never could have had a more convincing proof of the insipidity of those sensations which proceed not from the heart. But what became of me a moment after, when I felt—my hands shook—a gentle tremor—thy balmy lips—my Eloisa's lips—touch, pressed to mine, and myself within her arms? quicker than lightning a sudden fire darted through my soul; I seemed all over sensible of the ravishing condescension, and my heart sunk down oppressed with unsupportable delight;—when all at once, I perceived your colour change, your eyes close; you leant upon your cousin, and fainted away. Fear extinguished all my joy, and my happiness vanished like a shadow.

I scarce know any thing that has passed since that fatal moment. The impression it has made on my heart will never be effaced. A favour!—it is an extreme torment—No, keep thy kisses, I cannot bear them—they are too penetrating, too painful—they distract me. I am no more myself, and you appear to me no more the same object. You seem not, as formerly, chiding and severe; but, methinks I see and feel you lovely and tender, as at that happy instant when I pressed you to my bosom. O, Eloisa! whatever may be the consequence of my ungovernable passion, use me as severely as you please, I cannot exist in my present condition, and I perceive I must at last expire at your feet—or in your arms.

Hannah More (1745–1833)

In this poem, Hannah More promotes her culture's association of the female body as having a greater capacity for sensibility than the male body. In her day, sensibility—defined as an acute sensitivity to the feelings and needs of others, leading to compassion and sympathy for the downtrodden—was grounded on the human nervous system, which in the case of females was considered to be more delicate and high-strung. More takes this premise to argue that only those with such capacity can truly care for others. She argues that genuine sensibility produces a life of moral action, the direct movement from private pain to social philan-

thropy. Sensibility is not the cultivation of feeling for its own sake, but compassion channeled by "reason" to moral "principle" and charitable work. Women, thus, become the embodiment of active virtue, the moral conscience of the nation as a whole.

from *Sensibility: A Poetical Epistle to the Hon. Mrs. Boscawen* (1782)

Accept, BOSCAWEN! these unpolish'd lays,   1
Nor blame too much the verse you cannot praise.
For you, far other bards have wak'd the string,
Far other bards for you were wont to sing;
Yet on the gale their parting music steals,   5
Yet your charm'd ear the lov'd impression feels

*   *   *

Forgive, BOSCAWEN, if my sorrowing heart,   122
Intent on grief, forget the rules of art;
Forgive, if wounded recollection melt—
You best can pardon who have oft'nest felt.
You, who for many a friend and hero[1] mourn,
Who bend in anguish o'er the frequent urn;
You who have found how much the feeling heart
Shapes its own wound, and points itself the dart;
You, who from tender sad experience feel   130
The wounds such minds receive can never heal;
That grief a thousand entrances can find,
Where parts superior dignify the mind;
Wou'd you renounce the pangs those feelings give,
Secure in joyless apathy to live?   135

For tho' in souls, where taste and sense abound,
Pain thro' a thousand avenues can wound;
Yet the same avenues are open still,
To casual blessings as to casual ill.
Nor is the trembling temper more awake   140

---

[1]Admiral Boscawen [More's note]. Admiral Edward Boscawen (1711–61), known as "Old Dreadnaught," defeated the French Navy off Finistere (1747), at Newfoundland (1755), at Cape Breton (1758), and in Lagos Bay (1759). The poem is addressed to his wife.

To every wound which misery can make,
Than is the finely-fashion'd nerve alive
To every transport pleasure has to give.
For if, when home-felt joys the mind elate,
It mourns in secret for another's fate;   145
Yet when its own sad griefs invade the breast,
Abroad, in others blessings, see it blest!
Ev'n the soft sorrow of remember'd woe
A not unpleasing sadness may bestow,

    Let not the vulgar read this pensive strain,   150
Their jests the tender anguish wou'd profane:
Yet these some deem the happiest of their kind,
Whose low enjoyments never reach'd the mind;
Who ne'er a pain but for themselves have known,
Nor ever felt a sorrow but their own;   155
Who call romantic every finer thought,
Conceiv'd by pity, or by friendship wrought.
Ah! wherefore happy? where's the kindred mind?
Where, the large soul that takes in human kind?
Where, the best passions of the mortal breast?   160
Where, the warm blessing when another's blest?
Where, the soft lenitives of others' pain,
The social sympathy, the sense humane?
The sigh of rapture, and the tear of joy,
Anguish that charms, and transports that destroy?   165
For tender Sorrow has her pleasures too;
Pleasures, which prosp'rous Dulness never knew.
She never knew, in all her coarser bliss,
The sacred rapture of a pain like this!
Nor think, the cautious only are the just;   170
Who never was deceiv'd I wou'd not trust.
Then take, ye happy vulgar! take your part
Of sordid joy, which never touch'd the heart.
Benevolence, which seldom stays to chuse,
Lest pausing Prudence teach her to refuse;   175
Friendship, which once determin'd, never swerves,
Weighs ere it trusts, but weighs not ere it serves;
And soft-ey'd Pity, and Forgiveness bland,
And melting Charity with open hand;

And artless Love, believing and believ'd,   180
and gen'rous Confidence which ne'er deceiv'd;
And Mercy stretching out, ere Want can speak,
To wipe the tear from pale Afflication's cheek;
These ye have never known!—then take your part
Of sordid joy, which never touch'd the heart.   185

    Ye, who have melted in bright Glory's flame,
Or felt the spirit-stirring breath of fame!
Ye noble few! in whom her promis'd meed
Wakes the great thought, and makes the wish the deed!
Ye, who have tasted the delight to give,   190
And, God's own agents, bid the wretched live;
Who the chill haunts of Desolation seek,
Raise the sunk heart, and flush the fading cheek!
Ye, who with pensive Petrarch love to mourn,
Or weave fresh chaplets for Tibullus' urn;   195
Who cherish both in Hammond's plaintive lay,[2]
The Provence myrtle, and the Roman bay!
Ye, who divide the joys, and share the pains
Which merit feels, or Heav'n-born Fancy Feigns;
Wou'd you renounce such joys, such pains as these,   200
For vulgar pleasures, or for selfish ease?
Wou'd you, to 'scape the pain the joy forego;
And miss the transport, to avoid the woe?
Wou'd you the sense of real sorrow lose,
Or cease to wooe the melancholy Muse?   205
No, Greville![3] no!—Thy song tho' steep'd in tears,
Tho' all thy soul in all thy strain appears;
Yet wou'dst thou all thy well-sung anguish chuse,
And all th' inglorious peace thou begg'st, refuse.

❋ ❋ ❋

---

[2]**Petrarch:** Francesco Petrarca (1304–74), Italian humanist and poet, most famous for his love sonnets (*Canzoniere*) to Laura, the wife of Count Hughes de Sade, who died in 1348 after bearing eleven children. **Tibullus:** Albius Tibullus (54?–18? BCE), Roman poet famed for his elegies. **Hammond:** James Hammond (1710–42), author of *Love Elegies* (1732).

[3]See the beautiful "Ode to Indifference." [More's note]. Frances Greville's "Prayer for Indifference" was probably written after the death of her son in 1756.

Yet, while I hail the Sympathy Divine,   232
Which makes, O man! the wants of others thine:
I mourn heroic JUSTICE, scarcely own'd,
And PRINCIPLE for SENTIMENT dethron'd.
While FEELING boasts her ever-tearful eye,
Stern VIRTUE, firm FAITH, and manly VIRTUE fly.

Sweet SENSIBILITY! thou soothing pow'r,
Who shedd'st thy blessings on the natal hour,
Like fairy favours! Art can never seize,   240
Nor Affectation catch thy pow'r to please:
Thy subtile essence still eludes the chains
Of Definition, and defeats her pains.
Sweet Sensibility! thou keen delight!
Thou hasty moral! sudden sense of right!   245
Thou untaught goodness! Virtue's precious seed!
Thou sweet precursor of the gen'rous deed!
Beauty's quick relish! Reason's radiant morn,
Which dawns soft light before Reflexion's born!
To those who know thee not, no words can paint!   250
And those who know thee, know all words are faint!
'Tis not to mourn because a sparrow dies;
To rave in artificial extasies:
'Tis not to melt in tender *Otway's* fires;
'Tis not to faint, when injur'd *Shore* expires: 255
'Tis not because the ready eye o'erflows
At *Clementina's* or *Clarissa's* woes.

Forgive, O RICHARDSON![4] nor think I mean,
With cold contempt, to blast thy peerless scene:
If some faint love of virtue glow in me,   260
Pure spirit! I first caught that flame from thee.

[4]**Otway:** Thomas Otway (1652–85), author of several great tragedies, *Don Carlos* (1676), *The Orphan* (1680), and *Venice Preserv'd* (1682). **Shore:** Jane Shore (d. 1527), mistress of King Edward IV, accused by Richard III of sorcery and forced to do public penance in 1483, died in poverty. Her tribulations were the subject of many 18th-c. works, most notably Nicholas Rowe's drama *Jane Shore* (1714). **Richardson:** Samuel Richardson (1689–1761), novelist, author of *Clarissa* (1747–48), the story of a virtuous heroine who, once raped, prefers to die rather than to marry her seducer Lovelace, and of *Sir Charles Grandison* (1753–54), which includes the tale of the long-suffering Clementina.

While soft Compassion silently relieves,
Loquacious *Feeling* hints how much she gives;
Laments how oft her wounded heart has bled,
And boasts of many a tear she never shed. 265

As words are but th' external marks, to tell
The fair ideas in the mind that dwell;
And only are of things the outward sign,
And not the things themselves, they but define;
So exclamations, tender tones, fond tears, 270
And all the graceful drapery Pity wears;
These are not Pity's self, they but express
Her inward sufferings by their pictur'd dress;
And these fair marks, reluctant I relate,
These lovely symbols may be counterfeit. 275
Celestial Pity! why must I deplore,
Thy sacred image stamp'd on basest ore?
There are, who fill with brilliant plaints the page
If a poor linnet meet the gunner's rage:
There are, who for a dying fawn display 280
The tend'rest anguish in the sweetest lay;
Who for a wounded animal deplore,
As if friend, parent, country were no more;
Who boast quick rapture trembling in their eye,
If from the spider's snare they save a fly; 285
Whose well-sung sorrows every breast inflame,
And break all hearts but his from whom they came:
Yet, scorning life's *dull* duties to attend,
Will persecute a wife, or wrong a friend;
Alive to every woe by *fiction* dress'd; 290
The innocent he wrong'd, the wretch distress'd,
May plead in vain; their suff'rings come not near,
Or he relieves them cheaply, with a tear.
Not so the tender moralist of Tweed;[5]
His *Man of Feeling* is a man indeed. 295

---

[5]**Tweed:** Scottish novelist and editor Henry Mackenzie (1745–1831), author of the famed novel of male sensibility, *The Man of Feeling* (1771).

Oh, bless'd Compassion! Angel Charity!
More dear one genuine deed perform'd for thee,
Than all the periods Feeling e'er can turn,
Than all thy soothing pages, polish'd STERNE![6]

Not that by deeds alone this love's exprest,   300
If so, the affluent only were the blest.
One silent wish, one pray'r, one soothing word,
The precious page of Mercy shall record;
One soul-felt sigh by pow'rless Pity giv'n,
Accepted incense! shall ascend to Heav'n.   305

Since trifles make the sum of human things,
And half our mis'ry from our foibles springs;
Since life's best joys consist in peace and ease,
And few can save or serve, but all may please:
Oh! let th' ungentle spirit learn from hence,   310
A small unkindness is a great offence.
Large bounties to bestow we wish in vain;
But all may shun the guilt of giving pain.
To bless mankind with tides of flowing wealth;
With pow'r to grace them, or to crown with health,   315
Our little lot denies; but Heav'n decrees
To all, the gift of minist'ring to ease.
The gentle offices of patient love,
Beyond all flatt'ry, and all price above;
The mild forbearance at another's fault,   320
The taunting word, suppress'd as soon as thought;
On these Heav'n bade the bliss of life depend,
And crush'd ill-fortune when he made a FRIEND. . . .

Ann Radcliffe (1764–1823)

*Known as "the Great Enchantress," Ann Radcliffe was one of the most
celebrated writers of the 1790s, establishing herself as the foremost practitioner of the gothic novel with* The Romance of the Forest *(1791), The*

---

[6]**Sterne:** Novelist Laurence Sterne (1713–68), author of *Tristram Shandy* (1760–67)
and *Sentimental Journey* (1768).

Mysteries of Udolpho *(1794), and* The Italian *(1797). In* A Sicilian Romance, *the Marquis of Mazzini has three children from his marriage to Louisa Bernini: Ferdinand, Emilia, and Julia. After losing Louisa, he remarries and departs for Naples with his second wife, Maria de Vellorno. Emilia and Julia are left behind at castle Mazzini, on the Northern shores of Sicily, under the care of Madame de Menon, a friend of their departed mother's. Throughout the novel, the inhabitants of the castle experience a series of supernatural events—mysterious lights and strange noises emerge and then fade away without explanation. In this selection, after escaping from the clutches of an unwelcome suitor, Julia seeks shelter in a secluded forest cavern. Upon opening a hidden door, she uncovers a shocking scene: Her mother, still very much alive, has been imprisoned in this recess by her father. With this dramatic discovery, Radcliffe rationalizes her supernatural machinery and restores the departed Louisa to her loving children. Radcliffe's gothic narrative of a mother's incarceration bears strong resemblance to the predicament of Maria in Wollstonecraft's* The Wrongs of Woman. *Yet while Radcliffe often displaced the wrongs committed against women onto a romanticized, continental past (here, sixteenth-century Italy), Wollstonecraft focused on the atrocities in present-day England.*

from *A Sicilian Romance*, Volume II (1790)

from Chapter XIV

She[1] groped along the winding walls for some time, when she perceived the way was obstructed. She now discovered that a door interrupted her progress, and sought for the bolts which might fasten it. These she found; and strengthened by desperation forced them back. The door opened, and she beheld in a small room, which received its feeble light from a window above, the pale and emaciated figure of a woman, seated, with half closed eyes, in a kind of elbow chair. On perceiving Julia, she started from her seat, and her countenance expressed a wild surprize. Her features, which were worn by sorrow, still retained the traces of beauty, and in her air was a mild dignity that excited in Julia an involuntary veneration.

She seemed as if about to speak, when fixing her eyes earnestly and steadily upon Julia, she stood for a moment in eager gaze, and suddenly exclaiming, "My daughter!" fainted away.

[1]Julia.

The astonishment of Julia would scarcely suffer her to assist the lady, who lay senseless on the floor. A multitude of strange imperfect ideas rushed upon her mind, and she was lost in confusion and perplexity; but as she examined the features of the stranger, which were now re-kindling into life, she thought she discovered the resemblance of Emilia!

The lady breathing a deep sigh, unclosed her eyes; she raised them to Julia, who hung over her in speechless astonishment, and fixing them upon her with a tender earnest expression—-they filled with tears. She pressed Julia to her heart, and a few moments of exquisite, unutterable emotion followed. When the lady grew more composed, "Thank heaven!" said she, "my prayer is granted. I am permitted to embrace one of my children before I die. Tell me what brought you hither. Has the marquis at last relented, and allowed me once more to behold you, or has his death dissolved my wretched bondage?"

Truth now glimmered upon the mind of Julia, but so faintly, that instead of enlightening, it served only to encrease her perplexity.

"Is the marquis Mazzini living?" continued the lady. These words were not to be doubted; Julia threw herself at the feet of her mother, and embracing her knees in an energy of joy, answered only in sobs.

The marchioness eagerly enquired after her children. "Emilia is living," answered Julia, "but my dear brother—" "Tell me," cried the marchioness, with quickness. An explanation ensued. When she was informed concerning Ferdinand, she sighed deeply, and raising her eyes to heaven, endeavoured to assume a look of pious resignation; but the struggle of maternal feeling was visible in her countenance, and almost overcame her powers of resistance.

Julia gave a short account of the preceding adventures, and of her entrance into the cavern; and found to her inexpressible suprize, that she was now in a subterranean abode belonging to the southern buildings of the castle of Mazzini! The marchioness was beginning her narrative, when a door was heard to unlock above, and the sound of a footstep followed.

"Fly!" cried the marchioness, "secrete yourself if possible, for the marquis is coming." Julia's heart sunk at these words; she paused not a moment, but retired through the door by which she had entered. This she had scarcely done, when another door of the cell was unlocked, and she heard the voice of her father. Its sounds thrilled her with universal tremour; the dread of discovery so strongly operated upon her mind, that she stood in momentary expectation of seeing the door of the passage unclosed by the marquis; and she was deprived of all power of seeking refuge in the cavern.

At length the marquis, who came with food, quitted the cell, and re-locked the door, when Julia stole forth from her hiding place. The marchioness again embraced, and wept over her daughter. The narrative of her sufferings upon which she now entered, entirely dissipated the mystery which had so long enveloped the southern buildings of the castle.

"Oh! why," said the marchioness, "is it my task to discover to my daughter the vices of her father? In relating my sufferings, I reveal his crimes! It is now about fifteen years, as near as I can guess from the small means I have of judging, since I entered this horrible abode. My sorrows, alas! began not here; they commenced at an earlier period. But it is sufficient to observe, that the passion whence originated all my misfortunes, was discovered by me long before I experienced the more baleful effect of its influence."

"Seven years had elapsed since my marriage, when the charms of Maria de Vellorno, a young lady singularly beautiful, inspired the marquis with a passion as violent as it was irregular. I observed with deep and silent anguish, the cruel indifference of my lord towards me, and the rapid progress of his passion for another. I severely examined my past conduct, which I am thankful to say presented a retrospect of only blameless actions; and I endeavoured by meek submission, and tender assiduities, to recall that affection which was, alas! gone for ever. My meek submission was considered as marks of a servile and insensible mind; and my tender assiduities, to which his heart no longer responded, created only disgust, and exalted the proud spirit it was meant to conciliate."

"The secret grief which this change occasioned, consumed my spirits, and preyed upon my constitution, till at length a severe illness threatened my life. I beheld the approach of death with a steady eye, and even welcomed it as the pass-port to tranquillity; but it was destined that I should linger through new scenes of misery."

"One day, which it appears was the paroxysm of my disorder, I sunk into a state of total torpidity, in which I lay for several hours. It is impossible to describe my feelings, when, on recovering, I found myself in this hideous abode. For some time I doubted my senses, and afterwards believed that I had quitted this world for another; but I was not long suffered to continue in my error, the appearance of the marquis bringing me to a perfect sense of my situation."

"I now understood that I had been conveyed by his direction to this recess of horror, where it was his will I should remain. My prayers, my supplications were ineffectual; the hardness of his heart repelled my sorrows back upon myself; and as no entreaties could prevail upon him to inform me where I was, or of his reason for placing me here, I remained for many years ignorant of my vicinity to the castle, and of the motive for my confinement."

"From that fatal day, until very lately, I saw the marquis no more—but was attended by a person who had been for some years dependant upon his bounty, and whom necessity, united to an insensible heart, had doubtless induced to accept this office. He generally brought me a week's provisions, at stated intervals, and I remarked that his visits were always in the night."

"Contrary to my expectation, or my wish, nature did that for me which medicine had refused, and I recovered as if to punish with disappointment and anxiety my cruel tyrant. I afterwards learned, that in obedience to the marquis's order, I had been carried to this spot by Vincent during the night, and that I had been buried in effigy at a neighbouring church, with all the pomp of funeral honour due to my rank."

At the name of Vincent, Julia started; the doubtful words he had uttered on his death bed were now explained—the cloud of mystery which had so long involved the southern buildings broke at once away; and each particular circumstance that had excited her former terror, arose to her view entirely unveiled by the words of the marchioness.—The long and total desertion of this part of the fabric—the light that had appeared through the casement—the figure she had seen issue from the tower—the midnight noises she had heard—were circumstances evidently dependant on the imprisonment of the marchioness; the latter of which incidents were produced either by Vincent, or the marquis, in their attendance upon her.

When she considered the long and dreadful sufferings of her mother, and that she had for many years lived so near her ignorant

of her misery, and even of her existence—she was lost in astonishment and pity. . . .

William Godwin (1756–1836)

William Godwin's first novel, Things As They Are; or, The Adventures of
Caleb Williams, *was one of the most popular novels of the 1790s. It is
essentially a fictionalized version of his revolutionary tract* Political Justice *(1793), a critique of corrupt institutions that advocated, instead,
rational anarchism. The novel's amalgamation of genres—romance,
gothic story, pursuit narrative, sensational criminal history, didactic tale,
detective fiction—features Caleb's account of his battles against his former friend and master, Mr. Falkland, sparked by a discovery of Falkland's
mysterious secret. To ensure his silence, Falkland has Caleb incarcerated
and continues to pursue him ruthlessly after his escape. In the following
excerpts, Caleb speaks with a political consciousness and fortitude that
resonate with Wollstonecraft's descriptions of Maria in the madhouse.*

from *Caleb Williams*, Volume II (1794)

from Chapter XI

For my own part I had never seen a prison, and like the majority of
my brethren had given myself little concern to enquire what was the
condition of those who committed offence against, or became obnoxious to suspicion from the community. Oh, how enviable is the most
tottering shed under which the labourer retires to rest, compared with
the residence of these walls!

To me every thing was new, the massy doors, the resounding
locks, the gloomy passages, the grated windows, and the characteristic looks of the keepers, accustomed to reject every petition, and to
steel their hearts against feeling and pity. Curiosity, and a sense of my
situation; induced me to fix my eyes on the faces of these men, but in a
few minutes I drew them away with unconquerable loathing. It is
impossible to describe the sort of squalidness and filth with which
these mansions are distinguished. I have seen dirty faces in dirty
apartments, which have nevertheless borne the impression of health,
and spoke carelessness and levity rather than distress. But the dirt of a

prison speaks sadness to the heart, and appears to be already in a state of putridity and infection.

I was detained for more than an hour in the apartment of the keeper, one turnkey after another coming in, that they might make themselves familiar with my person. As I was already considered as guilty of felony to a considerable amount, I underwent a rigorous search, and they took from me a penknife, a pair of scissars, and that part of my money which was in gold. It was debated whether or not these should be sealed up, to be returned to me, as they said, as soon as I should be acquitted; and had I not displayed an unexpected firmness of manner and vigour of expostulation, such was the conduct that would have been pursued. Having undergone these ceremonies, I was thrust into a day room in which all the persons then under confinement for felony were assembled, to the number of eleven. Each of them was too much engaged in his own reflections to take notice of me. Of these two were imprisoned for horse-stealing, and three for having stolen a sheep, one for shop lifting, one for coining, two for highway robbery, and two for burglary. . . .

The whole day I was obliged to spend in the company of these men, some of them having really committed the actions laid to their charge, others whom their ill fortune had rendered the victims of suspicion. The whole was a scene of misery such as nothing short of actual observation can suggest to the mind. Some were noisy and obstreperous, endeavouring by a false bravery to keep at bay the remembrance of their condition; while others, incapable even of this effort, had the torment of their thoughts aggravated by the perpetual noise and confusion that prevailed around them. In the faces of those who assumed the most courage you might trace the furrows of anxious care, and in the midst of their laboured hilarity dreadful ideas would ever and anon intrude, convulsing their features and working every line into an expression of the keenest agony. To these men the sun brought no return of joy. Day after day rolled on, but their state was immutable. Existence was to them a theatre of invariable melancholy; every moment was a moment of anguish, yet did they wish to prolong that moment, fearful that the coming period would bring a severer fate. They thought of the past with insupportable repentance, each man contented to give his right hand to have again the choice of that peace and liberty which he had unthinkingly bartered away. We talk of instruments of torture; Englishmen take credit to themselves for having banished the use of them from their happy shore! Alas, he that has observed the secrets of a prison, well knows that there is infinitely more torture in the lingering existence of a criminal, in the silent, intolerable minutes that he spends, than in the tangible misery of whips and racks!

Such were our days. At sun set our jailors appeared, and ordered each man to come away, and be locked into his dungeon. It was a bitter aggravation of our fate to be under the arbitrary control of these fellows. They felt no man's sorrow; they were of all men least capable of any sort of feeling. They had a barbarous and sullen pleasure in issuing their detested mandates, and observing the mournful reluctance with which they were obeyed. Whatever they directed, it was in vain to expostulate; fetters and bread and water were the sure consequences of resistance. Their tyranny had no other limit than their own caprice; to whom shall the unfortunate felon appeal? To what purpose complain, when his complaints are sure to be received with incredulity? A tale of mutiny and necessary precaution is the unfailing refuge of the keeper, and this tale is an everlasting bar against redress.

Our dungeons were cells, 7½ feet by 6½, below the surface of the ground, damp, without window, light or air, except from a few holes worked for that purpose in the door. In some of these miserable receptacles three persons were put to sleep together.[1] I was fortunate enough to have one to myself. It was now the approach of winter. We were not allowed to have candles; and, as I have already said, were thrust in here at sun set and not liberated till the returning day. This was our situation for fourteen or fifteen hours out of the four and twenty. I had never been accustomed to sleep more than six or seven hours, and my inclination to sleep was now less than ever. Thus was I reduced to spend half my day in this dreary abode and in complete darkness. This was no trifling aggravation of my lot.

Among my melancholy reflections I tasked my memory, and counted over the doors, the locks, the bolts, the chains, the massy walls and grated windows that were between me and liberty. These, said I, are the engines that tyranny sits down in cold and serious

---

[1] See Howard on Prisons [Godwin's note]. John Howard (1726–90), *The State of the Prisons in England and Wales* (1777), the first attempt to describe the conditions of the British prisons using systematic evidence and statistical data.

meditation to invent. This is the empire that man exercises over man. Thus is a being, formed to expatiate, to act, to smile and enjoy, restricted and benumbed. How great must be his depravity or heedlessness who vindicates this scheme for changing health and gaiety and serenity, into the wanness of a dungeon and the deep furrows of agony and despair!

Thank God, exclaims the Englishman, we have no Bastille![2] Thank God, with us no man can be punished without a crime! Unthinking wretch! Is that a country of liberty where thousands languish in dungeons and fetters? Go, go, ignorant fool! and visit the scenes of our prisons! witness their unwholesomeness, their filth, the tyranny of their governors, the misery of their inmates! After that show me the man shameless enough to triumph, and say, England has no Bastille! Is there any charge so frivolous upon which men are not consigned to those detested abodes? Is there any villainy that is not practised by justices and prosecutors? But against all this, perhaps you have been told, there is redress. Yes, a redress, that it is the consummation of insult so much as to name! Where shall the poor wretch, reduced to the last despair, and to whom acquittal perhaps comes just time enough to save him from perishing,—where shall this man find leisure, and much less money, to fee counsel and officers, and purchase the tedious dear-bought remedy of the law? No, he is too happy to leave his dungeon and the memory of his dungeon behind him; and the same tyranny and wanton oppression become the inheritance of his successor.

For myself I looked round upon my walls, and forward upon the premature death I had too much reason to expect; I consulted my own heart that whispered nothing but innocence; and I said, This is society. This is the object, the distribution of justice, which is the end of human reason. For this sages have toiled, and the midnight oil has been wasted. This!

The reader will forgive this digression from the immediate subject of my story. If it should be said, these are general remarks; let it be remembered that they are the dear bought result of experience. It is from the fulness of a bursting heart that invective thus flows to my pen. These are not the declamations of a man desirous to be eloquent. I have felt the iron of slavery grating upon my soul.

[2]See Maria's reference to the Bastille (p. 316).

I believed that misery, more pure than that which I now endured, had never fallen to the lot of a human being. I recollected with astonishment my puerile eagerness to be brought to the test and have my innocence examined. I execrated it as the vilest and most insufferable pedantry. I exclaimed in the bitterness of my heart, Of what value is a fair fame? It is the jewel of men formed to be amused with baubles. Without it I might have had serenity of heart and cheerfulness of occupation, peace and liberty; why should I consign my happiness to other men's arbitration? But, if a fair fame were of the most inexpressible value, is this the method which common sense would prescribe to retrieve it? The language which these institutions hold out to the unfortunate is, Come, and be shut out from the light of day, be the associate of those whom society has marked out for her abhorrence, be the slave of jailers, be loaded with fetters; thus shall you be cleared from every unworthy aspersion, and restored to reputation and honour! This is the consolation she affords to those whom malignity or folly, private pique or unfounded positiveness have without the smallest foundation loaded with calumny. For myself I felt my own innocence, and I soon found upon enquiry that three fourths of those who are regularly subjected to a similar treatment, are persons, whom even with all the superciliousness and precipitation of our courts of justice no evidence can be found sufficient to convict. How slender then must be that man's portion of information and discernment, who is willing to commit his character and welfare to such guardianship!

But my case was even worse than this. I intimately felt that a trial, such as our institution is able to make it, is only the worthy sequel of such a beginning. What chance had I after the purgation I was now suffering, that I should come out acquitted at last? What probability was there that the trial I had just endured in the house of Mr. Falkland was not just as fair as any that might be expected to follow? No, I already anticipated my own condemnation.

Thus was I cut off, for ever from all that existence has to bestow, from all the high hopes I had so often conceived, from all the future excellence my soul so much delighted to imagine, to spend a few weeks in a miserable prison, and then to perish by the hand of the public executioner. No language can do justice to the indignant and soul-sickening loathing that these ideas excited. My resentment was not restricted to my prosecutor, but extended itself to the whole machine of human society. I could never believe that all this was the fair result of institutions inseparable from the general good. I regarded the whole human species as so many hangmen and torturers, I considered them as confederated to tear me to pieces; and this wide scene of inexorable persecution inflicted upon me inexpressible agony. I looked on this side and on that; I was innocent; I had a right to expect assistance; but every heart was steeled against me; every hand was ready to lend its force to make my ruin secure. No man that has not felt in his own most momentous concerns justice, eternal truth, unalterable equity engaged in his behalf, and on the other side brute force, impenetrable obstinacy and unfeeling insolence, can imagine the sensations that then passed through my mind. I saw treachery triumphant and enthroned; I saw the sinews of innocence crumbled into dust by the gripe of almighty guilt.

What relief had I from these sensations? Was it relief that I spent the day in the midst of profligacy and execrations, that I saw reflected from every countenance agonies only inferior to my own? He that would form a lively idea of the regions of the damned, needed only to witness for six hours a scene to which I was confined for many months. Not for one hour could I withdraw myself from this complexity of horrors, or take refuge in the calmness of meditation. Air, exercise, series, contrast, those grand enliveners of the human frame, I was for ever debarred, by the inexorable tyranny under which I was fallen. Nor did I find the solitude of my nightly dungeon less insupportable. Its only furniture was the straw that served me for my repose. It was narrow, damp and unwholesome. The slumbers of a mind, wearied, like mine with the most detestable uniformity, to whom neither amusement nor occupation ever offered themselves to beguile the painful hours, were short, disturbed and unrefreshing. My sleeping, still more than my waking thoughts, were full of perplexity, deformity and disorder. To these slumbers succeeded the hours which by the regulations of our prison I was obliged though awake to spend in solitary and cheerless darkness. Here I had neither books, nor pens, nor any thing upon which to engage my attention; all was a sightless blank. How was a mind, active and indefatigable like mine, to endure this misery? I could not sink it in lethargy; I could nor forget my woes; they haunted me with unintermitted and demoniac malice. Cruel, inexorable policy of human affairs, that condemns a man to torture like this; that sanctions it and knows not what is done under its sanction; that is too supine and unfeeling to enquire into these petty details; that calls this the ordeal of innocence and the protector of freedom! A thousand times I could have dashed my brains against the walls of my dungeon; a thousand times I longed for death, and wished with inexpressible ardour for an end to what I suffered; a thousand times I meditated suicide, and ruminated in the bitterness of my soul upon the different means of escaping from the load of existence. What had I to do with life? I had seen enough to make me regard it with detestation. Why should I wait the lingering process of legal despotism, and not dare so much as to die but when and how its instruments decreed? Still some inexplicable suggestion withheld my hand. I clung with desperate fondness to this shadow of existence, its mysterious attractions and its hopeless prospects.

from Chapter XII

Such were the reflections that haunted the first days of my imprisonment, in consequence of which they were spent in perpetual anguish. But after a time nature, wearied with distress, would no longer stoop to the burthen; thought, which is incessantly varying, introduced a series of reflections totally different.

My fortitude revived. I had always been accustomed to cheerfulness, good-humour and serenity, and this habit now returned to visit me at the bottom of my dungeon. No sooner did my contemplations take this turn, than I saw the reasonableness and possibility of tranquillity and peace, and my mind whispered to me the propriety of showing in this forlorn condition that I was superior to all my persecutors. Blessed state of innocence and self approbation! The sunshine of conscious integrity pierced through all the barriers of my cell, and spoke ten thousand times more joy to my heart than the accumulated splendours of nature and art can communicate to the slaves of vice.

I found out the secret of employing my mind. I said, I am shut up for half the day in total darkness without any external source of amusement; the other half I spend in the midst of noise, turbulence and confusion. What then? Can I not draw amusement from the stores of my own mind? Is it not freighted with various knowledge? Have I not been employed from my infancy in gratifying an insatiable curiosity? When should I derive benefit from these superior advantages, if not at present?" Accordingly I tasked the stores of my memory and my powers of invention. I amused myself with recollecting the history of my life. By degrees I called to mind a number of minute circumstances which but for this exercise would have been for ever forgotten. I repassed in my thoughts whole conversations, I recollected their subjects, their arrangement, their incidents and frequently their very words. I mused upon these ideas till I was totally absorbed in thought. I repeated them till my mind glowed with enthusiasm. I had my different employments fitted for the solitude of the night in which I could give full scope to the impulses of my mind, and the uproar of the day in which my chief object was to be insensible to the disorder with which I was surrounded.

By degrees I quitted my own story, and amused myself in imaginary adventures. I figured to myself every situation in which I could be placed, and conceived the conduct to be observed in each. Thus scenes of insult and danger, of tenderness and oppression became familiar to me. In fancy I often passed the awful hour of dissolving nature. In some of my reveries I boiled with impetuous indignation, and in others patiently collected the whole force of my mind for some fearful encounter. I cultivated the powers of oratory suited to these different states, and improved more in eloquence in the solitude of my dungeon, than perhaps I should have done in the busiest and most crowded scenes. At length I proceeded to as regular a disposition of my time, as the man in his study who passes from mathematics to poetry, and from poetry to the law of nations in the different parts of each single day; and I as seldom infringed upon my plan. Nor were my subjects of disquisition less numerous than his. I went over, by the assistance of memory only, a considerable part of Euclid during my confinement, and revived day after day the series of facts and incidents in some of the most celebrated historians.

While I was thus employed I reflected with exultation upon the degree in which man is independent of the smiles and frowns of fortune. I was beyond her reach, for I could fall no lower. To an ordinary eye I might seem destitute and miserable, but in reality I wanted for nothing. My fare was coarse; but I was in health. My dungeon was noisome; but I felt no inconvenience. I was shut up from the usual means of exercise and air; but I found the method of exercising myself even to perspiration in my dungeon.

I had no power of withdrawing my person from a disgustful society in the most cheerful and valuable part of the day; but I soon brought to perfection the art of withdrawing my thoughts, and saw and heard the people about me for just as short a time and as seldom as I pleased. . . .

Frances Burney (1752–1840)

The publication of Evelina *(1778) made Frances Burney one of the most critically acclaimed women novelists in the late eighteenth century. In her third novel* Camilla, or A Picture of Youth, *Camilla's younger sister Eugenia is scarred and maimed as a child through the carelessness of an affectionate uncle, Sir Hugh Tyrold. Sheltered in girlhood, Eugenia emerges as a kind-hearted, naïve young woman—shielded by her family from the social disadvantages of her deformity. For his part, Sir Hugh provides Eugenia with a classical education and makes her heir to his estate, yet these gifts prove a dubious boon: Schooling feeds her naïveté, convincing her that the stories of virtue she has dutifully studied are accurate depictions of society, while her wealth renders her vulnerable to fortune-hunters. Reckless scoundrel Bellamy woos her, kidnaps her, then threatens to commit suicide if she will not marry him. The following excerpts are from the final volume of the novel. Here Eugenia gives an account of the events that led to her husband Bellamy's death and then announces plans to record her history in a didactic memoir. Burney's situation of violent episodes within a domestic framework makes her an important model for Wollstonecraft, who praised* Camilla *in the* Analytical Review.

from *Camilla*, Volume V, Book X (1796)

from Chapter XII: "Means to obtain a Boon"

In the evening, while, with apprehensions surpassing all description, she[1] was waiting some news, a chaise drove up to the door. She flew out, but saw in it . . . alone, cold, trembling, and scarce in her senses, Eugenia. Instantly imagining she came with tidings of fatal tendency

---

[1]Mrs. Tyrold, mother of Lavinia, Camilla, and Eugenia. In this section, Mrs. Tyrold is relating Eugenia's recent history to Camilla.

concerning Camilla,[2] she started back, exclaiming, "All then, is over?" The chaise-door had been opened; but Eugenia, shaking too violently to get out; only, and faintly, answered, "Yes! my Mother . . . all is over!—" The mistake was almost instantaneous death to her—though the next words of Eugenia cleared it up, and led to her own dreadful narrative.

Bellamy, as soon as Camilla had left Belfont, had made a peremptory demand that his wife should claim, as if for some purpose of her own, a large sum of Sir Hugh. Her steady resistance sent him from the house in a rage; and she saw no more of him till that day at noon, when he returned in deeper, blacker wrath than she had ever yet seen; and vowed that nothing less than her going in person to her uncle with his request, should induce him ever to forgive her. When he found her resolute in refusal, he ordered a chaise, and made her get into it, without saying for what purpose. She saw they were travelling towards Cleves, but he did not once speak, except where they changed horses, till they came upon the cross-road, leading to the half-way-house. Suddenly then, bidding the postillion stop at the end of a lane, he told him he was going to look at a little farm, and, ordering him to wait, made her alight and walk down it till they were out of sight of the man and the carriage. Fiercely, then stopping short, "Will you give me," he cried, "your promise, upon oath, that you will ask your Uncle for the money?" "Indeed, Mr. Bellamy, I cannot!" she answered. "Enough!" he cried, and took from his pocket a pistol. "Good Heaven," she said, "you will not murder me?"—"I cannot live without the money myself," he answered, "and why should I let you?" He then felt in his waiscoat pocket, whence he took two bullets, telling her, she should have the pleasure of seeing him load the pistol; and that when one bullet had dispatched her, the other should disappoint the executioner. Horrour now conquered her, and she solemnly promised to ask whatever he dictated. "I must hold the pistol to your ear," cried he, "while you take your oath. See! 'tis loaded—This is no child's play." He then lifted it up; but, at the same moment, a distant voice exclaimed, "Hold villain! or you are a dead man!" Starting, and meaning to hide it within his waistcoat, his hand shook—the pistol went off—it shot him through the body, and he

---

[2]During this period, Camilla has been missing, and the Tyrold family has feared for her safety.

dropt down dead. Without sense or motion, she fell by his side; and, upon recovering, found herself again in the chaise. The postillion, who knew her, had carried her thither, and brought her on to Etherington. She then conjured that proper persons might go back with the driver, and that her Father would have the benevolence to superintend all that could be done that would be most respectfully decent.

The postillion acknowledged that it was himself who had cried, Hold, villain! A suspicion of some mischief had occurred to him, from seeing the end of a pistol jerk from the pocket of the gentleman, as he got out of the chaise; and begging a man, who accidentally passed while he waited, to watch his horses, he ran down a field by the side of the lane, whence he heard the words: "The pistol is loaded, and for no child's play!" upon which, seeing it raised, and the young Lady shrink, he called out. Yet Eugenia protested herself convinced that Bellamy had no real design against either his own life or her's, though terrour, at the moment, had conquered her: he had meant but to affright her into consent, knowing well her word once given, with whatever violence torn from her, would be held sacred. The rest was dreadful accident, or Providence in that form playing upon himself his own toils. The pious young Widow was so miserable at this shocking exit, and the shocking manner in which the remains were left exposed, that her Mother had set out herself to give orders in person, from the half-way-house, for bringing thither the body, till Mr. Tyrold could give his own directions. She found, however, that business already done. The man called by the postillion had been joined by a party of labourers, just leaving off work; those had gathered others; they had procured some broad planks which served for a bier, and had humanely conveyed the body to the inn, where the landlord was assured the postillion would come back with some account of him, though little Peggy had only learnt in general that he had been found murdered near a wood.

"Eugenia is just now," said Mrs. Tyrold, in conclusion, "plunged into an abyss of ideas, frightful to her humanity, and oppressive to the tenderness of her heart. Her nature is too noble to rejoice in a release to herself, worked by means so horrible, and big with notions of retribution for the wretched culprit, at which even vengeance the most implacable might shudder. Nevertheless, all will imperceptibly pass away, save the pity inherent in all good minds for vice and its penalties. To know his abrupt punishment, and not to be shocked, would

be inhuman; but to grieve with any regard for a man of such principles and conduct, would be an outrage to all that they have injured
and offended."

This view of the transaction, by better reconciling Camilla to the
ultimate lot of her sister, brought her back to reflect upon her own. . . .

from Chapter XIV: "The last Touches of the Picture"

Eugenia wept with joy at tidings so precious of her beloved sister,[3]
through whom, and her other dear friends, she was alone, she said,
susceptible of joy, though to all sorrow she henceforth bid adieu, "For
henceforth," she cried, "I mean to regard myself as if already I had
passed the busy period of youth and of life, and were only a specta-
tress of others. For this purpose, I have begun writing my memoirs,
which will amuse my solitude, and confirm my—I hope, philosophical idea."

She then produced the opening of her intended book.

Section I.

"No blooming coquette, elated with adulation and triumphant with conquest, here counts the glories of her eyes, or
enumerates the train of her adorers: no beauteous prude,
repines at the fatigue of admiration, nor bewails the necessity
of tyranny: O gentle reader! you have the story of one from
whom fate has withheld all the delicacy of vanity, all the
regale of cruelty—!"

"Here," interrupted the young biographer, "will follow my portrait, and then this further address to my readers."

"O ye, who, young and fair, revel in the attractions of
beauty, and exult in the pride of admiration, say, where is
your envy of the heiress to whom fortune comes with such
alloys? And which, however distressed or impoverished,
would accept my income with my personal defects?

"Ye, too, O lords of the creation, mighty men! impute not
to native vanity the repining spirit with which I lament the loss

---

[3]Camilla has just told Eugenia that she plans to marry Edgar Mandlebert, the hero of
the novel.

of beauty; attribute not to the innate weakness of my sex, the
concern I confess for my deformity; nor to feminine littleness
of soul, a regret of which the true source is to be traced to your
own bosoms, and springs from your own tastes: for the value
you yourselves set upon external attractions, your own neglect
has taught me to know; and the indifferency with which you
consider all else, your own duplicity has instructed me to feel."

Camilla sought to dissuade her from reflexions so afflictive, and
retrospections so poignant; but they aided her, she said, in her task of
acquiring composure for the regulation of her future life.

Contemporary Reviews

In the politically partisan press of the day, Wollstonecraft's *Vindication of the Rights of Woman* was widely reviewed after its publication in 1792. *The Analytical Review*, edited by Joseph Johnson, was the most radical journal in England and regularly defended the principles of democracy and the rights of man espoused by the French revolutionary philosophers. Wollstonecraft herself was a regular reviewer. At the opposite end of the spectrum, the *Anti-Jacobin Review and Magazine* consistently denounced the French Revolution and any attack on England's monarchy, established church, or class hierarchy. "Anti-Jacobin" signals opposition to "Jacobin" or revolutionary French ideas. The more politically moderate *Monthly Review* and *Critical Review* catered to the upwardly mobile and professional middle classes.

Reviews of A Vindication of the Rights of Woman

from *The Analytical Review*, 12 (1792): 241–49

It might have been supposed that Mrs. W. had taken advantage of the popular topic of the 'Rights of Man' in calling her work 'A Vindication of the Rights of Woman,' had she not already published a work, one of the first answers that appeared to Mr. Burke, under the title of, 'A Vindication of the Rights of Man.' But in reality the present work is an elaborate *treatise* of *female education*. The lesser wits will probably affect to make themselves merry at the title and apparent object of this publication; but we have no doubt if even her contemporaries should fail to do her justice, posterity will compensate the defect; and have no hesitation in declaring, that if the bulk of the great truths which this publication contains were reduced to practice, the nation would be better, wiser and happier, than it is upon the wretched, trifling, useless and absurd system of education which is now prevalent.

from the *Monthly Review*, ns 8 (1792): 198–209

From the copious extracts which we have made from this truly original work, a better judgment may be formed of its merit, than from any summary of its leading sentiments which we could have given. It will be easily perceived that the author is possessed of great energy of intellect, vigour of fancy, and command of language; and that the performance suggests many reflections, which well deserve the attention of the public, and which, pursued under the direction of good sense and sage experience, may greatly contribute to the improvement of the condition and character of the female world. We do not, however, so zealously adopt Miss W.'s plan for a REVOLUTION in female education and manners, as not to perceive that several of her opinions are fanciful, and some of her projects romantic. We do not see, that the condition or the character of women would be improved, by assuming an active part in civil government. It does not appear to us to be necessary, in order to enlighten the understandings of women, that we should prohibit the employment of their fingers in those useful and elegant labours of the needle, for which, from the days of Penelope,[1] they have obtained so much deserved applause. Certain associations, now too firmly established to be easily broken, forbid us to think that women are degraded by the trivial attention which the men are inclined to pay them; or that it would be any increase of the pleasures of society, if, 'except where love animates, the behaviour, the distinction of sex were to be confounded.' This distinction, we apprehend, will never be overlooked,

---

[1]Penelope is the wife of Odysseus in Homer's *Odyssey*. She faithfully awaits her husband's return, despite the eager suits of several local nobles. Asserting that she cannot remarry until she has finished weaving a shroud for Laertes, Odysseus's father, she holds these men at bay by secretly unraveling her work every night. (*Oxford Classical Dictionary*)

till the time arives, "when we shall neither marry nor be given in marriage, but be as the angels of God in heaven."[2] Notwithstanding all this, however, we entirely agree with the fair writer, that both the condition and the character of women are capable of great improvement; and that, by means of a more rational plan of female education, in which a judicious attention should be paid to the cultivation of their understanding and taste, as well as of their dispositions and manners, women might be rendered at once more agreeable, more respectable, and more happy in every station of life. Both men and women should certainly, in the first place, regard themselves, and should be treated by each other, as human beings. It might, perhaps, in some measure, contribute to this end, if, beside the sexual appellations of man and woman, we had some general term to denote the species, like [*Anthropos*] and *Homo*[3] in the Greek and Roman languages. The want of such a general term is a material defect in our language.

What practical measures may be reasonably adopted, in order to produce the improvement so strongly recommended in this work, we expect to be more distinctly informed in the second part; in which we are promised a more minute consideration of the laws relative to women, and of their particular duties.

from the *Critical Review*, ns 4 (1792): 389–98; ns 5 (1792): 187–91

One of the strictest proofs in mathematical demonstrations, is the reducing the question to an absurdity; by allowing, for instance, that the proposition is not true, and then showing that this would lead to the most obvious inconsistencies. Miss Wollstonecraft has converted this method of proceeding with the same success: reasoning on the boasted principles of the Rights of Man, she finds they lead very clearly to the object of her work, a Vindication of the Rights of

---

[2]Mark 12:25: "For when they shall rise from the dead, they neither marry, nor are given in marriage; but are as the angels which are in heaven."

[3]The nouns in Greek and Latin, respectively, for humanity in general, or humankind. Both, however, are frequently translated "man."

Woman; and, by the absurdity of many of her conclusions, shows, while we admit the reasoning, that the premises must be, in some respects, fallacious.

> 'Dismissing then those pretty femenine phrases, which the men condescendingly use to soften our slavish dependence, and despising that weak elegancy of mind, exquisite sensibility, and sweet docility of manners, supposed to be the sexual characteristics of the weaker vessel, I wish to shew that elegance is inferior to virtue, that the first object of laudable ambition is to obtain a character as a human being, regardless of the distinction of sex; and that secondary views should be brought to this simple touchstone.'[1]

This is the outline of her plan; but before she proceeds to show that this change would be suitable, useful, advantageous, it will be first necessary to prove that there is no sexual distinction of character, that the female mind is equally fitted for the more arduous mental operations; that women are equally able to pursue the toilsome road of minute, laborious, investigation; that their judgments are equally sound, their resolution equally strong. After this is done, the benefit derived must be considered; and, when all are strong, to whom must the weaker operations belong? The female Plato will find it unsuitable to 'the dignity of her virtue' to dress the child, and descend to the disgusting offices of a nurse: the new Archimedes will measure the shirts by means of the altitude taken by a quadrant; and the young lady, instead of studying the softer and more amiable arts of pleasing, must contend with her lover for superiority of mind, for greater dignity of virtue; and before she condescends to become his wife, must prove herself his equal or superior.—It may be fancy, prejudice, or obstinacy, we contend not for a name, but we are infinitely better pleased with the present system; and, in truth, dear young lady, for by the appellation sometimes prefixed to your name we must suppose you to be young, endeavour to attain 'the weak elegancy of mind,' the 'sweet docility of manners,' 'the exquisite sensibility,' the former ornaments of your sex; we are certain you will be more pleasing, and we dare pronounce that you will be infinitely happier. Mental superiority is not an object worth contending

---

[1]From the Introduction to *Vindication*. See pp. 25–26.

for, if happiness be the aim. But, as this is the first female combatant in the new field of the Rights of Woman, if we smile only, we shall be accused of wishing to decline the contest; if we content ourselves with paying a compliment to her talents, it will be styled inconsistent with 'true dignity,' and as showing that we want to continue the 'slavish dependence.'—We must contend then with this new Atalanta[2]; and who knows whether, in this modern instance, we may not gain two victories by the contest? There is more than one batchelor in our corps; and, if we should *succeed*, miss Wollstonecraft may take her choice. [. . .]

On the whole, we cannot praise this work, or look for the continuation with eagerness. It is, in our opinion, weak, desultory and trifling. Some parts of its subject have given it a splendor in the eyes of individuals; before whom prejudice has interposed a fallacious medium, or whose views party has limited or distorted. If miss Wollstonecraft means it as a trial of skill with the stronger sex, she has wholly failed: she has betrayed her own cause by defending it, and has lost that credit which female authors have sometimes claimed. What shall we say of her language? It is flowing and flowery; but weak, diffuse, and confused: of the indelicacy of her ideas and expressions? Here we must draw the veil, though it was our attention to have collected a bouquet from the parterre. We have desisted, from a respect to *our* readers, which the lady has not paid to her's; and we have blushed to copy in the closet, what she has openly published. We call on men therefore to speak, if they would wish the women to be pupils of this new school? we call on the women to declare, whether they will sacrifice their pleasing qualities for the severity of reason, the bold unabashed dignity of speaking what they feel, of rising superior to the vulgar prejudices of decency and propriety.—We may easily anticipate the answer; and shall leave miss Wollstonecraft at least to oblivion: her best friends can never wish that her work should be remembered.

---

[2]Atalanta is a mythical Greek heroine. When her father wished to give her in marriage, she agreed to marry the man who could beat her in a foot race. Hippomenes succeeded by dropping some golden apples into her path, which she stopped to pick up. (*Oxford Classical Dictionary*)

Reviews of The Wrongs of Woman, or Maria

from the *Anti-Jacobin Review and Magazine*, 1 (July 1798): 94–102

To this work there are prefixed two prefaces; one by Godwin, editor of the author's posthumous works—the other by herself.

Maria is in the form of a novel. Its object is to shew the miseries to which women are exposed, owing *to the inferior state which they occupy in society.* It is a tale intended to illustrate the doctrines which Mrs. W. had attempted to establish in her "Rights of Woman." Besides illustration of her own opinions, the principles supported and the practices recommended have a very great coincidence with those inculcated by the philosopher himself, in that part of his "Political Justice"[1] in which he describes the promiscuous intercourse of the sexes, as one of the highest improvements to result from *political justice!* The editor regrets that this work is only a fragment of a plan which "if it had been filled up in a manner adequate to the writer's conception, would perhaps have given a new impulse to the manners of the world."—The *purity* of the lady's *conception of female excellence*, and the usefulness to society of the conduct to the adoption of which she exhorts her sex, our readers may, from the following sketch, be able to comprehend.

Maria had been captivated by the figure and manners of George Venables, a young merchant, and had bestowed on him her heart and hand. Venables turned out to be a very different character from that which the impassioned Maria had supposed. She had fancied him a miracle of goodness; but on better acquaintance, found him a shallow, foolish, dissipated, and unprincipled man. He squanders all that part of her fortune which was not settled on herself exclusively, and, when he cannot prevail on her to part with the remainder, contrives to have her kidnapped and sent to a private mad-house. This misfortune, arising from her own injudicious choice of a husband, she imputes to

[1] In his treatise *Political Justice* (1793), Godwin argues for a society without government whose members are led by reason, rather than fear of law and authority. Godwin viewed marriage as a kind of restrictive property law, in which possession of a woman was based on prejudice and jealousy, rather than merit and the free pursuit of reason.

the unequal state of women in society. In the mad-house, she gains the confidence and affections of her attendant, Jemima. This person had been a prostitute and a thief: these occupations, according to Maria, had sharpened and invigorated her understanding, in such a degree, indeed, as to make her a political philosopher, without the advantage of any other education. As a proof of the able reasoning which this mode of tuition produces, she agrees with Maria that *their* distresses in particular, and, THEREFORE, *those of women in general*, arise from the arbitrary usurpations of men.

The pleasure of political discussion is not the only comfort which Maria derives from the kindness of Jemima. There happened to be confined in the same house, in his full senses, a Mr. Darnford, in whom, on seeing him from her window, Maria recognizes a very great favourite. He had been kidnapped also, so that, according to her own story, women are not the only persons placed unjustly in madhouses; and *her argument* concerning the WRONGS OF WOMAN, founded on that species of imprisonment, *is destroyed by herself*. A principle often inculcated by the author, both in Maria's character and her own, is, that there can *exist no duty unless prompted by feeling*; that, therefore, if a woman feel herself disinclined to her husband, the feeling constitutes a dissolution of every obligation to fidelity: and also, that when she feels herself inclined towards another man, she has a *natural* right to follow that inclination; that the prohibition in the present state of society to unrestrained compliance with the dictates of the passions, constitutes one of the greatest WRONGS OF WOMAN. Jemima, attentive to the *rights* of the sex, affords Maria an opportunity of reducing her theories to *practice* by permitting Darnford to spend his nights in her apartment. To assist the reader's imagination, *the virtuous Maria*, whose writings and example were to give so *beneficial an impulse to the manners* of the world, informs us that she was a very *voluptuous* figure, that Darnford was a handsome man, but peculiarly remarkable for *muscular strength*.—Maria, by no means of the same opinion with Square the philosopher,[2] that "things are fitting to be done which are not fitting to be boasted of," having with her paramour escaped from confinement, openly and boldly manifests

---

[2]*Tom Jones*, Book V, Chapter v. Square is one of Tom's tutors, described as a man of great learning and little natural ability. Tom has discovered his mistress and Square in bed together.

her conduct.—The husband prosecutes her gallant for criminal con-versation. The lady appears in court herself, and pleads her feelings, not as her apology, but as her justification. This was indeed a conduct, according to Godwin's own heart.[3] It avowed a disregard for the insti-tution of marriage, an institution so strongly reprobated in the new system of political justice, it banished concealment, the only evil, according to the philosopher, that can detract from the political and moral blessings of a promiscuous intercourse of the sexes, guided by the feelings of the parties. On the trial, the judge (England being the scene) retains the old system of morals, and does not admit Maria's plea of her feelings as a vindication of her adultery, however con-formable it may be to the new philosophy. *The restrictions upon adul-tery* constitute, in Maria's opinion, A MOST FLAGRANT WRONG TO WOMEN. Such is the moral tendency of this work, such are the lessons which may be learned from the writings of Mrs. Wollstonecroft; such the advantages which the public may derive from this perfor-mance given to the world by Godwin, celebrated by him, and per-fectly consonant to the principles of *his* Political Justice.—But as there have been writers, who have in theory promulgated opinions subversive of morality, yet in their conduct have not been immoral, Godwin has laboured to inform the world, that the theory of Mrs. Wollstonecroft was reduced to practice; that she lived and acted, as she wrote and taught.

from the *Monthly Review*, 27 (Nov. 1798): 325–27

Mr. Godwin, the editor, with a partiality which all readers of feeling will be tempted to excuse, supposes that, had his wife lived to fill up the sketch exhibited in the fragment intitled "The Wrongs of Woman," (which, in its present state, occupies the first and second volumes,) it would have given 'a new impulse to the manners of the world.' Novels, however, though generally read, and though it is now the practice to make them the vehicles of new opinions, do not make

---

[3]*Political Justice*: For Godwin, marriage was the worst kind of law because its con-straints were determined by romantic delusions rather than by a reasonable concern for the greater good.

so permanant an impression on the mind as their authors may imagine. That writer must be vain indeed who fancies that, by a fictitious tale, however well told, and interspersed with fine sentiments, he can give a new impulse to the manners of the world. Had Mrs. Wollstonecraft Godwin lived to finish her "Maria," the story might have been more satisfactory to her readers: but its moral effect or utility would not, we apprehend, have been at all increased. It is a proof of her genius; and the incidents are designed to justify an opinion respecting marriage, which circumstances of her own history, together with her husband's system, might have impressed deeply on her mind, viz., that it is the source of the greatest evil in society, and that women particularly suffer by it: but we ought to recollect that a particular recital, whether real or feigned, of matrimonial vice and misery, is no argument against the institution of marriage; which, on the whole, as Dr. Johnson says, "is no otherwise unhappy than human life is unhappy."[1] Though the laws concerning it be far from being perfect, and might be much improved, we should beware of lessening the respect that is due to this legitimate bond of love; and of so blackening the picture of married life, as to leave an impression on the public mind favourable to love unrecognized by the law.

Mrs. Godwin says, in her preface, that 'she should despise or rather call her an ordinary woman, who could endure such an husband as she has sketched:' but we would observe that the atrocious conduct of the husband does not justify *all* the subsequent conduct of the injured wife; and it is better to persuade the sex to submit to some inconveniencies, than to encourage them to break down all the barriers of social virtue, and to prompt them to exclaim with Eloisa

"Curse on all laws but those which love has made."[2]

We offer these remarks not because we wish to abet tyranny in husbands, and to persuade wives, under the most cruel treatment, to think of nothing but tame unconditional submission, but because we think it a pernicious doctrine that a woman, when she deems herself ill-used by her husband, has a right to leave him, and to select

---

[1] See *Rasselas*, Chapter XXVI: "Marriage has many pains, but celibacy has no pleasures." *Rambler* 18 also includes a discussion of unhappy marriages.

[2] Alexander Pope, "Eloisa to Abelard," 74.

another man to supply the husband's place. In all connections, evils or disagreeable circumstances may arise: but society is at an end if every individual be permitted to redress his own grievances;—and we add that religion is at an end if every female, who is *crossed in love,* or disappointed in her husband, is to be encouraged to commit an act of *suicide.*[3]

While, therefore, we would do ample justice to the abilities manifested in this fragment, we cannot admire its moral tendency. Mrs. Godwin might tell us, perhaps, were she now alive, as she said of us in one of her letters to Mr. Johnson, that we have a "*cant*[4] of virtue:" but we hope that we *love* it, and are sincerely anxious to promote its interests; especially among the fair sex, who, by reading novels, may possibly be turned out of its paths. Indeed, we are almost ashamed to *argue* on these topics against the opinions of Mrs. Godwin; for we think that no great portion of experience, of common sense, and of consideration, can be requisite to enable every reader to controvert her doctrines.

[3]A possible allusion to Romeo and Juliet, Shakespeare's "star-crossed lovers," both of whom commit suicide after a series of "misadventur'd piteous overthrows" (Prologue, lines 6–7).

[4]"Language used as a kind of phraseology; phraseology taken up and used for fashion's sake without being a genuine expression of sentiment" (*Oxford English Dictionary,* n.3, 6a).

Further Reading

Barker-Benfield, J. B. *The Culture of Sensibility—Sex and Society in Eighteenth-Century Britain*. Chicago: University of Chicago Press, 1992.

Franklin, Caroline. *Mary Wollstonecraft, A Literary Life*. New York: Palgrave Macmillan, 2004.

Johnson, Claudia. *Equivocal Beings: Politics, Gender and Sentimentality in the 1790s, Wollstonecraft, Radcliffe, Burney, Austen*. Chicago: Chicago University Press, 1995.

———, ed. *The Cambridge Companion to Mary Wollstonecraft*. Cambridge: Cambridge University Press, 2002.

Jones, Chris. *Radical Sensibility: Literature and Ideas in the 1790s*. Cambridge: Cambridge University Press, 1993.

Kelly, Gary. *Revolutionary Feminism—The Mind and Career of Mary Wollstonecraft*. New York: St. Martin's Press, 1992. Superb analysis of Wollstonecraft's rhetorical style.

Mellor, Anne K. *Romanticism and Gender*. New York: Routledge, 1993. See esp. Chapter 2.

———. "Righting the Wrongs of Woman: Mary Wollstonecraft's Maria," *Nineteenth-Century Contexts* 19 (1996): 413–24.

Mellor, Anne K., and Richard Matlak, eds. *British Literature: 1780–1830*. Fort Worth: Harcourt Brace, 1996.

Pateman, Carol. *The Sexual Contract*. Cambridge: Polity Press, 1988.

Poovey, Mary. *The Proper Lady and the Woman Writer*. Chicago: University of Chicago Press, 1984. See esp. Chapters 2 and 3.

Sapiro, Virginia. *A Vindication of Political Virtue—The Political Theory of Mary Wollstonecraft*. Chicago: University of Chicago Press, 1992.

Taylor, Barbara. *Mary Wollstonecraft and the Feminist Imagination*. Cambridge: Cambridge University Press, 2003.

Tomalin, Claire. *The Life and Death of Mary Wollstonecraft*. New York: Harcourt Brace Jovanovich, 1974.

Van Sant, Ann Jessie. *Eighteenth-Century Sensibility and the Novel*. Cambridge: Cambridge University Press, 1993.

Wolfson, Susan, and Peter J. Manning, eds. *The Romantics and Their Contemporaries*, 2d edition (volume 2a), from *The Longman Anthology of British Literature*, gen. ed. David Damrosch. New York: Longman, 2003.

Wollstonecraft, Mary. *The Complete Works of Mary Wollstonecraft*, 7 volumes, eds. Janet Todd and Marilyn Butler. New York: New York University Press, 1989.